NINTH EDITION

Theory and Practice *of* Counseling and Psychotherapy

GERALD COREY

California State University, Fullerton
Diplomate in Counseling Psychology
American Board of Professional Psychology

CENGAGE
Learning·

Andover • Melbourne • Mexico City • Stamford, CT • Toronto • Hong Kong • New Delhi • Seoul • Singapore • Tokyo

About the Author

GERALD COREY is a Professor Emeritus of Human Services at California State University at Fullerton and a licensed psychologist. He received his doctorate in counseling from the University of Southern California. He is a Diplomate in Counseling Psychology, American Board of Professional Psychology; a National Certified Counselor; a Fellow of the American Psychological Association (Counseling Psychology); a Fellow of the American Counseling Association; and a Fellow of the Association for Specialists in Group Work. He also holds memberships in the American Group Psychotherapy Association; the American Mental Health Counselors Association; the Association for Spiritual, Ethical, and Religious Values in Counseling; the Association for Counselor Education and Supervision; and the Western Association for Counselor Education and Supervision.

Along with Marianne Schneider Corey, Jerry received the Lifetime Achievement Award from the American Mental Health Counselors Association in 2011 and the Eminent Career Award from the Association for Specialists in Group Work in 2001. Jerry was the recipient of the Outstanding Professor of the Year Award from California State University at Fullerton in 1991. He teaches both undergraduate and graduate courses in group counseling, as well as courses in experiential groups, the theory and practice of counseling, theories of counseling, and professional ethics. He is the author or coauthor of 16 textbooks in counseling currently in print, 5 student videos/DVDs with workbooks, and more than 60 articles in professional publications. *Theory and Practice of Counseling and Psychotherapy* has been translated into the Arabic, Indonesian, Portuguese, Korean, Chinese, and Turkish languages. *Theory and Practice of Group Counseling* has been translated into Chinese, Korean, Russian, and Spanish. *Issues and Ethics in the Helping Professions* has been translated into Korean, Japanese, and Chinese.

Jerry and Marianne Corey often presents workshop in group counseling. In the past 35 years the Coreys have conducted group counseling training workshops for mental health professionals at many universities in the United States as well as in Korea, Ireland, Germany, Belgium, Scotland, Mexico, China, Hong Kong, and Canada. The Coreys also frequently give presentations and workshops at state and national professional conferences. In his leisure time, Jerry likes to travel, hike and bicycle in the mountains, and drive his 1931 Model A Ford.

Recent publications by Jerry Corey, all with Brooks/Cole, Cengage Learning, include:

- *Case Approach to Counseling and Psychotherapy*, Eighth Edition (2013)
- *The Art of Integrative Counseling*, Third Edition (2013)
- *Theory and Practice of Group Counseling* (and *Student Manual*, Eighth Edition, 2012)
- *Becoming a Helper*, Sixth Edition (2011, with Marianne Schneider Corey)
- *Issues in Ethics in the Helping Professions*, Eighth Edition (2011, with Marianne Schneider Corey and Patrick Callanan)
- *Groups: Process and Practice*, Eighth Edition (2010, with Marianne Schneider Corey and Cindy Corey)
- *I Never Knew I Had a Choice*, Ninth Edition (2010, with Marianne Schneider Corey)
- *Group Techniques*, Third Edition (2004, with Marianne Schneider Corey, Patrick Callanan, and J. Michael Russell)

Jerry is coauthor (with Barbara Herlihy) of *Boundary Issues in Counseling: Multiple Roles and Responsibilities*, Second Edition (2006) and *ACA Ethical Standards Casebook*, Sixth Edition (2006); he is coauthor (with Robert Haynes, Patrice Moulton, and Michelle Muratori) of *Clinical Supervision in the Helping Professions: A Practical Guide*, Second Edition (2010); he is the author of *Creating Your Professional Path: Lessons From My Journey* (2010). All four of these books are published by the American Counseling Association.

He also has made several educational DVD and video programs on various aspects of counseling practice: *DVD for Theory and Practice of Counseling and Psychotherapy: The Case of Stan and Lecturettes* (2013); *DVD for Integrative Counseling: The Case of Ruth and Lecturettes* (2013, with Robert Haynes); *DVD—Theory and Practice of Group Counseling* (2012); *Groups in Action: Evolution and Challenges—DVD and Workbook* (2006, with Marianne Schneider Corey and Robert Haynes); and *Ethics in Action: CD-ROM* (2003, with Marianne Schneider Corey and Robert Haynes). All of these programs are available through Brooks/Cole, Cengage Learning.

Theory and Practice of Counseling and Psychotherapy, 9e
Gerald Corey

ISBN-13: 978-81-315-1898-4
ISBN-10: 81-315-1898-1

Cengage Learning India Private Limited
418, F.I.E., Patparganj
Delhi 110092
India

Tel: 91-11-43641111
Fax: 91-11-43641100
Email: asia.infoindia@cengage.com

Cengage Learning is a leading provider of customized learning solutions with office locations around the globe, including Andover, Melbourne, Mexico City, Stamford (CT), Toronto, Hong Kong, New Delhi, Seoul, Singapore, and Tokyo. Locate your local office at: www.cengage.com/global

Cengage Learning Products are represented in Canada by Nelson Education, Ltd.

For product information, visit our website at **www.cengage.co.in**

Printed in India
Second Indian reprint 2013

To Terry Hendrix and in memory of Claire Verduin,
our first editors at Brooks/Cole; they had faith
in the potential of this book and encouraged us to
write early in our careers.

Contents

PART 2

Theories and Techniques of Counseling   55

Preface

This book is intended for counseling courses for undergraduate and graduate students in psychology, counselor education, human services, and the mental health professions. It surveys the major concepts and practices of the contemporary therapeutic systems and addresses some ethical and professional issues in counseling practice. The book aims to teach students to select wisely from various theories and techniques and to begin to develop a personal style of counseling.

I have found that students appreciate an overview of the divergent contemporary approaches to counseling and psychotherapy. They also consistently say that the first course in counseling means more to them when it deals with them personally. Therefore, I stress the practical application of the material and encourage reflection. Using this book can be both a personal and an academic learning experience.

In this ninth edition, every effort has been made to retain the major qualities that students and professors have found helpful in the previous editions: the succinct overview of the key concepts of each theory and their implications for practice, the straightforward and personal style, and the book's comprehensive scope. Care has been taken to present the theories in an accurate and fair way. I have attempted to be simple, clear, and concise. Because many students want suggestions for supplementary reading as they study each therapy approach, I have included an updated reading list at the end of each chapter.

This edition updates the material and refines existing discussions. Part 1 deals with issues that are basic to the practice of counseling and psychotherapy. Chapter 1 puts the book into perspective, then students are introduced to the counselor— as a person and a professional—in Chapter 2. This chapter addresses a number of topics pertaining to the role of the counselor as a person and the therapeutic relationship. Chapter 3 introduces students to some key ethical issues in counseling practice, and several of the topics in this chapter have been updated and expanded.

Part 2 is devoted to a consideration of 11 theories of counseling. Each of the theory chapters follows a common organizational pattern, and students can easily compare and contrast the various models. This pattern includes core topics such as key concepts, the therapeutic process, therapeutic techniques and procedures, multicultural perspectives, theory applied to the case of Stan, and summary and evaluation. In this ninth edition, all of the chapters in Part 2 have been revised, updated, and expanded to reflect recent trends. Revisions were based on the recommendations of experts in each theory, all of whom are listed in the Acknowledgments section. Both expert and general reviewers provided suggestions for adding, replacing, and expanding material for this edition. Attention was given to current trends and recent developments in the practice of each theoretical approach. For each chapter in Part 2, the citations have been updated.

Each of the 11 theory chapters summarizes key points and evaluates the contributions, strengths, limitations, and applications of these theories. Special attention is given to evaluating each theory from a multicultural perspective as well, with a commentary on the strengths and shortcomings of the theory in working with diverse client populations. The consistent organization of the summary and evaluation sections makes comparing theories easier. Students are given recommendations regarding where to look for further training for all of the approaches. Updated annotated lists of reading suggestions and extensive references at the end of these chapters are offered to stimulate students to expand on the material and broaden their learning through further reading. In addition, a list of DVD resources has been added to the ninth edition for each of the theory chapters.

WHAT'S NEW IN THIS EDITION

Significant changes for the ninth edition for each of the theory chapters are outlined below:

CHAPTER 4   Psychoanalytic Therapy
- Increased emphasis on the role of the relationship in analytic therapy
- Increased coverage on contemporary psychodynamic therapy
- Broadened discussion of relational psychoanalysis
- A new perspective on therapist neutrality and anonymity
- More emphasis on the role of termination in analytic therapy
- New material on countertransference, its role in psychoanalytic therapy, and guidelines for effectively dealing with countertransference
- Expanded discussion of resistance and how to work with it effectively
- Revised and expanded section on brief psychodynamic therapy

CHAPTER 5   Adlerian Therapy
- Revised material on the concept of lifestyle
- Expanded discussion of social interest
- New material on early recollections
- Streamlined discussion of some key concepts

CHAPTER 6   Existential Therapy
- Revised material on existential themes
- New and expanded coverage of the contributions of Irvin Yalom and James Bugental to existential therapy
- More attention on international developments of existential therapy
- New material on main aims of existential therapy
- Revised section on the client–therapist relationship
- Revised discussion of strengths of the approach from a diversity perspective
- New discussion of integration of existential concepts in other therapies

CHAPTER 7   Person-Centered Therapy

- Expanded coverage on the contributions and influence of Carl Rogers on the counseling profession
- New section on the Abraham Maslow's contributions to humanistic philosophy and psychology
- New material on Maslow's concept of self-actualization and relation to person-centered philosophy
- Broadened discussion of clients as active self-healers
- Updated coverage of the core conditions of congruence, unconditional positive regard, and empathy
- Recent research on contextual factors as the main predictors of effective therapy
- New material on the limitations and criticisms of the approach
- New material on the diversity of styles of practicing person-centered therapy
- More emphasis on how the basic philosophy of the person-centered approach can be applied to other therapeutic modalities
- Inclusion of emotion-focused therapy, stressing the role of emotions as a route to change
- Revised coverage on person-centered expressive arts
- New section on motivational interviewing (person-centered approach with a twist)
- Additional coverage of the stages of change as applied to motivational interviewing

CHAPTER 8   Gestalt Therapy

- Revised discussion of the role of experiments in Gestalt therapy
- More emphasis on therapist presence
- Added description of emotion-focused therapy and its relationship to Gestalt therapy
- More attention to the relational approach to Gestalt practice

CHAPTER 9   Behavior Therapy

- Increased attention to the trends in contemporary behavior therapy
- Broadened discussion of the role of the therapeutic relationship in behavior therapy
- Expanded and updated discussion of social skills training
- Revision of multimodal therapy section
- Revised discussion of systematic desensitization and exposure procedures
- Revision of section on EMDR
- More attention to the role of mindfulness and acceptance strategies in contemporary behavior therapy
- New material on mindfulness-based cognitive therapy and stress reduction
- Expanded and revised treatment of dialectical behavior therapy

CHAPTER 10   Cognitive Behavior Therapy

- Revised and expanded coverage of Aaron Beck's cognitive therapy
- Increased coverage of Judith Beck's role in the development of cognitive therapy

- Increased attention on Donald Meichenbaum's influence in the development of CBT
- New material on Meichenbaum's stress inoculation training
- Revised section on Meichenbaum's constructivist approach to CBT
- Increased coverage of relapse prevention
- Increased discussion of CBT from a multicultural perspective
- New material on the potential limitations of the multicultural applications of CBT

CHAPTER 11 Reality Therapy

- Revised discussion of the relationship of choice theory to reality therapy
- Expanded discussion of the role of questions in reality therapy
- Revision of section on the role of planning in reality therapy
- More emphasis on the value of reality therapy with reluctant clients
- Additional material on reality therapy from a diversity perspective

CHAPTER 12 Feminist Therapy

- Updated treatment of the principles of feminist therapy
- Updated discussion of the role of assessment and diagnosis in feminist therapy
- Increased attention given to empowerment
- New example of applying feminist therapy interventions with the case of Alma
- Revised and expanded discussion on therapeutic techniques and strategies

CHAPTER 13 Postmodern Approaches

- Additional material on parallels between solution-focused brief therapy and positive psychology
- Broadened discussion of the key concepts of solution-focused brief therapy (SFBT)
- More emphasis on the client-as-expert in the therapy relationship in postmodern approaches
- Revision of material on techniques in the postmodern approaches
- New material on listening with an open mind in narrative therapy
- More emphasis on the collaborative nature of narrative therapy and SFBT

CHAPTER 14 Family Systems Therapy

- A reconceptualization and streamlining of the chapter
- New section describing the multilayered process of family therapy
- More emphasis on the personal development of the family therapist
- Addition of reflection questions to assist in the personal application of family theory
- New material on genogram work for understanding the self of the therapist and clients
- Expanded section on recent developments in family therapy
- New material on the postmodern perspective on family therapy
- More attention given to feminism, multiculturalism, and postmodern constructionism as applied to family therapy

In Part 3 readers are helped to put the concepts together in a meaningful way through a discussion of the integrative perspective and consideration of a case study. Chapter 15 ("An Integrative Perspective") pulls together themes from all 11 theoretical orientations. This chapter has been revised to expand discussion of the psychotherapy integration movement; revise treatment of the various integrative approaches; update and expand the section on integration of multicultural issues in counseling; revise the section on integration of spirituality in counseling; add material on research demonstrating the importance of the therapeutic relationship; more discussion on the central role of the client in determining therapy outcomes; and update coverage of the conclusions from the research literature on the effectiveness of psychotherapy. Chapter 15 develops the notion that an integrative approach to counseling practice is in keeping with meeting the needs of diverse client populations in many different settings. Numerous tables and other integrating material help students compare and contrast the 11 approaches.

The "Case of Stan" has been retained in Chapter 16 to help readers see the application of a variety of techniques at various stages in the counseling process with the same client. This chapter illustrates an integrative approach that draws from all the therapies and applies a thinking, feeling, and behaving model in counseling Stan. Applying the various theories to a single case example allows for a comparison among the approaches. The video program (*DVD for Theory and Practice of Counseling and Psychotherapy: The Case of Stan and Lecturettes*) can be used as an ideal supplement to this chapter. For each of the 13 sessions in the DVD program in my counseling with Stan, I apply just a few selected techniques designed to illustrate each theory in action. New to accompany this ninth edition is a series of lecturettes that I present for each chapter in this textbook. This expanded DVD program now includes both demonstrations of my counseling with Stan and brief lectures that highlight my perspective on the practical applications of each theory.

This text can be used in a flexible way. Some instructors will follow my sequencing of chapters. Others will prefer to begin with the theory chapters (Part 2) and then deal later with the student's personal characteristics and ethical issues. The topics can be covered in whatever order makes the most sense. Readers are offered some suggestions for using this book in Chapter 1.

In this edition I have made every effort to incorporate those aspects that have worked best in the courses on counseling theory and practice that I regularly teach. To help readers apply theory to practice, I have also revised the *Student Manual*, which is designed for experiential work. The *Student Manual for Theory and Practice of Counseling and Psychotherapy* still contains open-ended questions, many new cases for exploration and discussion, structured exercises, self-inventories, and a variety of activities that can be done both in class and out of class. The ninth edition features a structured overview, as well as a glossary, for each of the theories, and chapter quizzes for assessing the level of student mastery of basic concepts.

CourseMate, a new online resource, is available to accompany this textbook. It contains the video program for *Theory and Practice of Counseling and Psychotherapy:*

The Case of Stan and Lecturettes, as well as a glossary of key terms, interviews with experts (questions and answers by experts in the various theories), and case examples for each of the theories illustrating ways of applying these concepts and techniques to a counseling case.

The newly revised and enlarged *Case Approach to Counseling and Psychotherapy* (Eighth Edition) features experts working with the case of Ruth from the various therapeutic approaches. The casebook can either supplement this book or stand alone. An additional chapter covering transactional analysis is available on WebTutor.® This material is provided in the same format as the 11 theory chapters in this book and includes experiential exercises that can be completed individually or in small groups.

Accompanying this ninth edition of the text and *Student Manual* is a *DVD for Integrative Counseling: The Case of Ruth and Lecturettes*, in which I demonstrate an integrative approach in counseling Ruth (the central character in the casebook). It contains lecturettes on how I draw from key concepts and techniques from the various theories presented in the book. This DVD program has been developed for student purchase and use as a self-study program, and it makes an ideal learning package that can be used in conjunction with this text and the *Student Manual*. *The Art of Integrative Counseling* (Third Edition), which expands on the material in Chapter 15 of the textbook, also complements this book.

Some professors have found the textbook and the *Student Manual* or the online program (CourseMate) to be ideal companions and realistic resources for a single course. Others like to use the textbook and the casebook as companions. With this revision it is now possible to have a unique learning package of several books, along with the *DVD for Integrative Counseling: The Case of Ruth and Lecturettes*. The *Case Approach to Counseling and Psychotherapy* and the *Art of Integrative Counseling* can also be used in a various classes, a few of which include case-management practicum, fieldwork courses, or counseling techniques courses.

Also available is a revised and updated *Instructor's Resource Manual,* which includes suggestions for teaching the course, class activities to stimulate interest, PowerPoint presentations for all chapters, and a variety of test questions and final examinations. This instructor's manual is now geared for the following learning package: *Theory and Practice of Counseling and Psychotherapy, Student Manual for Theory and Practice of Counseling and Psychotherapy, Case Approach to Counseling and Psychotherapy, The Art of Integrative Counseling,* and two video programs: *DVD for Integrative Counseling: The Case of Ruth and Lecturettes,* and *DVD for Theory and Practice of Counseling and Psychotherapy: The Case of Stan and Lecturettes.*

Acknowledgments

The suggestions I received from the many readers of prior editions who took the time to complete the survey at the end of the book have been most helpful. Many other people have contributed ideas that have found their way into this ninth edition. I especially appreciate the time and efforts of the manuscript reviewers, who offered constructive criticism and supportive commentaries, as well as those professors who have used this book and provided me with feedback that has been most useful in these revisions. Those who reviewed the complete manuscript of the ninth edition are:

Sylinda Banks, Norfolk State University
Jayne Barnes, Nashua Community College
Eric Bruns, Campbellsville University
Joya Crear, George Mason University
Samantha Daniel, Fayetteville State University
Melodie Frick, West Texas A&M University
Amanda Healey, Sam Houston State University
Paula Nelson, Saint Leo University
Terence Patterson, University of San Francisco
Holly Seirup, Hofstra University

Special thanks are extended to the chapter reviewers, who provided consultation and detailed critiques. Their insightful and valuable comments have generally been incorporated into this edition:

- Chapter 4 (Psychoanalytic Therapy): William Blau, Copper Mountain College, Joshua Tree, California; and J. Michael Russell of California State University, Fullerton

- Chapter 5 (Adlerian Therapy): James Robert Bitter, East Tennessee State University, and I coauthored Chapter 5

- Chapter 6 (Existential Therapy): Emmy van Deurzen, New School of Psychotherapy and Counselling, London, England, and University of Sheffield; J. Michael Russell of California State University, Fullerton; David N. Elkins, Graduate School of Education and Psychology, Pepperdine University; Bryan Farha, Oklahoma City College; Jamie Bludworth, private practice, Phoeniz, Arizona; Kirk Schneider, the Existential-Humanistic Institute; and Victor Yalom, president, Psychotherapy.Net

- Chapter 7 (Person-Centered Therapy): Natalie Rogers, Person-Centered Expressive Arts Associates, Cotati, California; David N. Elkins, Graduate School of Education and Psychology, Pepperdine University; and David Cain, California School of Professional Psychology at Alliant International University, San Diego

- Chapter 8 (Gestalt Therapy): Jon Frew, Private Practice, Vancouver, Washington, and Pacific University, Oregon; Ansel Woldt, Kent State University

- Chapter 9 (Behavior Therapy): Sherry Cormier, West Virginia University; Frank M. Dattilio, Harvard Medical School, and the University of Pennsylvania School of Medicine; and Arnold A. Lazarus, Rutgers University, and the Lazarus Institute

- Chapter 10 (Cognitive Behavior Therapy): Sherry Cormier, West Virginia University; Frank M. Dattilio, Harvard Medical School, and the University of Pennsylvania School of Medicine; Windy Dryden, Professor of Psychotherapeutic Studies at Goldsmiths College, London; and Donald Meichenbaum, Research Director of the Melissa Institute for Violence Prevention

- Chapter 11 (Reality Therapy): Robert Wubbolding, Center for Reality Therapy, Cincinnati, Ohio
- Chapter 12 (Feminist Therapy): Carolyn Zerbe Enns, Cornell College; Barbara Herlihy, University of New Orleans, and I coauthored Chapter 12
- Chapter 13 (Postmodern Approaches): John Winslade, California State University, San Bernardino; Linda Metcalf, Texas Women's University, and the Solution Focused Institute for Education and Training; and John Murphy, University of Central Arkansas
- Chapter 14 (Family Systems Therapy): Jon Carlson, Governors State University; James Robert Bitter, East Tennessee State University, and I coauthored Chapter 14

I want to acknowledge those on the Brooks/Cole, Cengage Learning team who are involved with our projects. These people include Seth Dobrin, editor of counseling, social work, and human services; Julie Martinez, consulting editor, who monitored the review process; Caryl Gorska, for her work on the interior design and cover of this book; Elizabeth Momb, media editor; Naomi Dreyers, supplemental materials for the book; Michelle Muratori, Johns Hopkins University, for her work on updating the *Instructor's Resource Manual* and assisting in developing the other supplements; and Rita Jaramillo, project manager. We thank Ben Kolstad of Cenveo Publisher Services, who coordinated the production of this book. Special recognition goes to Kay Mikel, the manuscript editor of this edition, whose exceptional editorial talents continue to keep this book reader friendly. We appreciate Susan Cunningham's work in preparing the index. The efforts and dedication of all of these people certainly contribute to the high quality of this edition.

– Gerald Corey

PART 1

Basic Issues in Counseling Practice

Introduction and Overview

INTRODUCTION

Counseling students can begin to acquire a counseling style tailored to their own personality by familiarizing themselves with the major approaches to therapeutic practice. This book surveys 11 approaches to counseling and psychotherapy, presenting the key concepts of each approach and discussing features such as the therapeutic process (including goals), the client–therapist relationship, and specific procedures used in the practice of counseling. This information will help you develop a balanced view of the major ideas of each of the theories and acquaint you with the practical techniques commonly employed by counselors who adhere to each approach. I encourage you to keep an open mind and to seriously consider both the unique contributions and the particular limitations of each therapeutic system presented in Part 2.

You do not gain the knowledge and experience needed to synthesize various approaches by merely completing an introductory course in counseling theory. This process will take many years of study, training, and practical counseling experience. Nevertheless, I recommend a personal integration as a framework for the professional education of counselors. The danger in presenting one model to which all students are expected to subscribe is that it can limit their effectiveness in working with a diverse range of future clients.

An undisciplined mixture of approaches, however, can be an excuse for failing to develop a sound rationale for systematically adhering to certain concepts and to the techniques that are extensions of them. It is easy to pick and choose fragments from the various therapies because they support our biases and preconceptions. By studying the models presented in this book, you will have a better sense of how to integrate concepts and techniques from different approaches when defining your own personal synthesis and framework for counseling.

Each therapeutic approach has useful dimensions. It is not a matter of a theory being "right" or "wrong," as every theory offers a unique contribution to understanding human behavior and has unique implications for counseling practice. Accepting the validity of one model does not necessarily imply rejecting other models. There is a clear place for theoretical pluralism, especially in a society that is becoming increasingly diverse.

Although I suggest that you remain open to incorporating diverse approaches into your own personal synthesis—or integrative approach to counseling—let me caution that you can become overwhelmed and confused if you attempt to learn everything at once, especially if this is your introductory course in counseling theories. A case can be made for initially getting an overview of the major theoretical orientations, and then learning a particular approach by becoming steeped in that approach for some time, rather than superficially grasping many theoretical approaches. An integrative perspective is not developed in a random fashion; rather, it is an ongoing process that is well thought out. Successfully integrating concepts and techniques from diverse models requires years of reflective practice and a great deal of reading about the various theories. In Chapter 15

I discuss in more depth some ways to begin designing your integrative approach to counseling practice.

 See the video program for Chapter 1, *DVD for Theory and Practice of Counseling and Psychotherapy: The Case of Stan and Lecturettes*. I suggest that you view the brief lecturette for each chapter in this book prior to reading the chapter.

WHERE I STAND

My philosophical orientation is strongly influenced by the existential approach. Because this approach does not prescribe a set of techniques and procedures, I draw techniques from the other models of therapy that are presented in this book. I particularly like to use role-playing techniques. When people reenact scenes from their lives, they tend to become more psychologically engaged than when they merely report anecdotes about themselves. I also incorporate many techniques derived from cognitive behavior therapy.

The psychoanalytic emphasis on early psychosexual and psychosocial development is useful. Our past plays a crucial role in shaping our current personality and behavior. I challenge the deterministic notion that humans are the product of their early conditioning and, thus, are victims of their past. But I believe that an exploration of the past is often useful, particularly to the degree that the past continues to influence present-day emotional or behavioral difficulties.

I value the cognitive behavioral focus on how our thinking affects the way we feel and behave. These therapies also emphasize current behavior. Thinking and feeling are important dimensions, but it can be a mistake to overemphasize them and not explore how clients are behaving. What people are doing often gives us a good clue to what they really want. I also like the emphasis on specific goals and on encouraging clients to formulate concrete aims for their own therapy sessions and in life. *Contracts* between clients and therapists can be very useful. I frequently suggest either specific *homework assignments* or ask my clients to devise their own assignments, or together we develop goals and tasks that guide the therapy process.

More approaches have been developing methods that involve collaboration between therapist and client, making the therapeutic venture a shared responsibility. This collaborative relationship, coupled with teaching clients ways to use what they learn in therapy in their everyday lives, empowers clients to take an active stance in their world. It is imperative that clients be active, not only in their counseling sessions but in daily life as well. Homework can be a vehicle for assisting clients in putting into action what they are learning in therapy.

A related assumption of mine is that we can exercise increasing freedom to create our future. The acceptance of personal responsibility does not imply that we can be anything that we want. Social, environmental, cultural, and biological realities oftentimes limit our freedom of choice. Being able to choose must be considered in the sociopolitical contexts that exert pressure or create constraints; oppression is a reality that can restrict our ability to choose our future. We are also influenced by our social environment, and much of our behavior is a product of learning and conditioning. That being said, I believe an increased awareness of these contextual forces enables us to address these realities. It is crucial to learn how to cope with the external and internal forces that limit our decisions and behavior.

Feminist therapy has contributed an awareness of how environmental and social conditions contribute to the problems of women and men and how gender-role socialization leads to a lack of gender equality. Family therapy teaches us that it is not possible to understand the individual apart from the context of the system. Both family therapy and feminist therapy are based on the premise that to understand the individual it is essential to take into consideration the interpersonal dimensions and the sociocultural context rather than focusing primarily on the intrapsychic domain. Thus a comprehensive approach to counseling goes beyond focusing on our internal dynamics and addresses those environmental and systemic realities that influence us.

My philosophy of counseling does not include the assumption that therapy is exclusively for the "sick" and is aimed at "curing" psychological "ailments." Such a focus on the medical model restricts therapeutic practice because it stresses deficits rather than strengths. Instead, I agree with the postmodern approaches (see Chapter 13), which are grounded on the assumption that people have both internal and external resources to draw upon when constructing solutions to their problems. Therapists will view these individuals quite differently if they acknowledge that their clients possess competencies rather than pathologies. I view each individual as having resources and competencies that can be discovered and built upon in therapy.

Psychotherapy is a process of engagement between two people, both of whom are bound to change through the therapeutic venture. At its best, this is a collaborative process that involves both the therapist and the client in co-constructing solutions to concerns. Most of the theories described in this book emphasize the collaborative nature of the practice of psychotherapy.

Therapists are not in business to change clients, to give them quick advice, or to solve their problems for them. Instead, counselors facilitate healing through a process of genuine dialogue with their clients. The kind of person a therapist is remains the most critical factor affecting the client and promoting change. If practitioners possess wide knowledge, both theoretical and practical, yet lack human qualities of compassion, caring, good faith, honesty, presence, realness, and sensitivity, they are more like technicians. In my judgment those who function exclusively as technicians do not make a significant difference in the lives of their clients. It is essential that counselors explore their own values, attitudes, and beliefs in depth and work to increase their own awareness. Throughout the book, I encourage you to find ways to personally relate to each of the therapies. Applying this material to yourself personally takes you beyond a mere academic understanding of theories.

With respect to mastering the techniques of counseling and applying them appropriately and effectively, it is my belief that you are your own very best technique. Your reactions to your clients, including sharing how you are affected in the relationship with them, are useful in moving the therapeutic process along.

It is impossible to separate the techniques you use from your personality and the relationship you have with your clients.

Administering techniques to clients without regard for the relationship variables is ineffective. Techniques cannot substitute for the hard work it takes to develop a constructive client–therapist relationship. Although you can learn attitudes and skills and acquire certain knowledge about personality dynamics and the therapeutic process, much of effective therapy is the product of artistry. Counseling entails far more than becoming a skilled technician. It implies that you are able to establish and maintain a good working relationship with your clients, that you can draw on your own experiences and reactions, and that you can identify techniques suited to the needs of your clients.

As a counselor, you need to remain open to your own personal development and to address your personal problems. The most powerful ways for you to teach your clients is by the behavior you model and by the ways you connect with them. I suggest you experience a wide variety of techniques yourself *as a client*. Reading about a technique in a book is one thing; actually experiencing it from the vantage point of a client is quite another. If you have practiced mindfulness exercises, for example, you will have a much better sense for guiding clients in the practice of becoming increasingly mindful in daily life. If you have carried out real-life homework assignments as part of your own self-change program, you can increase your empathy for clients and their potential problems. Your own anxiety over self-disclosing and addressing personal concerns can be a most useful anchoring point as you work with the anxieties of your clients. The courage you display in your therapy will help you appreciate how essential courage is for your clients.

Your personal characteristics are of primary importance in becoming a counselor, but it is not sufficient to be merely a good person with good intentions. To be effective, you also must have supervised experiences in counseling and sound knowledge of counseling theory and techniques. Further, it is essential to be well grounded in the various *theories of personality* and to learn how they are related to *theories of counseling*. Your conception of the person and the individual characteristics of your client affect the interventions you will make. Differences between you and your client may require modification of certain aspects of the theories. Some practitioners make the mistake of relying on one type of intervention (supportive, confrontational, information giving) for most clients with whom they work. In reality, different clients may respond better to one type of intervention than to another. Even during the course of an individual's therapy, different interventions may be needed at different times. Practitioners should acquire a broad base of counseling techniques that are suitable for individual clients rather than forcing clients to fit one approach to counseling.

SUGGESTIONS FOR USING THE BOOK

Here are some specific recommendations on how to get the fullest value from this book. The personal tone of the book invites you to relate what you are reading to your own experiences. As you read Chapter 2, "The Counselor: Person and Professional," begin the process of reflecting on your needs, motivations, values, and life experiences. Consider how you are likely to bring the person you are becoming into your professional work. You will assimilate much more knowledge about the various therapies if you make a conscious attempt to apply their key concepts and techniques to your own personal life. Chapter 2 helps you think about how to use yourself as your single most important therapeutic instrument, and it addresses a number of significant ethical issues in counseling practice.

Before you study each therapy in depth in Part 2, I suggest that you at least briefly read Chapter 15, which provides a comprehensive review of the key concepts from all 11 theories presented in this textbook. I try to show how an integration of these perspectives can form the basis for creating your own personal synthesis to counseling. In developing an integrative perspective, it is essential to think holistically. To understand human functioning, it is imperative to account for the physical, emotional, mental, social, cultural, political, and spiritual dimensions. If any of these facets of human experience is neglected, a theory is limited in explaining how we think, feel, and act.

To provide you with a consistent framework for comparing and contrasting the various therapies, the 11 theory chapters share a common format. This format includes a few notes on the personal history of the founder or another key figure; a brief historical sketch showing how and why each theory developed at the time it did; a discussion of the approach's key concepts; an overview of the therapeutic process, including the therapist's role and client's work; therapeutic techniques and procedures; applications of the theory from a multicultural perspective; application of the theory to the case of Stan; a summary and evaluation; suggestions of how to continue your learning about each approach; and suggestions for further reading.

Refer to the preface for a complete description of other resources that fit as a package and complement this textbook, including *Student Manual for Theory and Practice of Counseling and Psychotherapy* and *DVD for Integrative Counseling: The Case of Ruth and Lecturettes*. In addition, in *DVD for Theory and Practice of Counseling and Psychotherapy: The Case of Stan and Lecturettes*, I demonstrate my way of counseling Stan from the various theoretical approaches in 13 sessions and present my perspective on the key concepts of each theory in a brief lecture, with emphasis on the practical application of the theory.

OVERVIEW OF THE THEORY CHAPTERS

I have selected 11 therapeutic approaches for this book. Table 1.1 presents an overview of these approaches, which are explored in depth in Chapters 4 through 14. I have grouped these approaches into four general categories.

First are the *psychodynamic approaches. Psychoanalytic therapy* is based largely on insight, unconscious motivation, and reconstruction of the personality. The psychoanalytic model appears first because it has had a major influence on all of the other formal systems of psychotherapy. Some of the therapeutic models are basically extensions of psychoanalysis, others are modifications of analytic concepts and procedures, and still others are positions that emerged as a reaction against

TABLE 1.1 Overview of Contemporary Counseling Models

Psychodynamic Approaches

Psychoanalytic therapy

Founder: Sigmund Freud. A theory of personality development, a philosophy of human nature, and a method of psychotherapy that focuses on unconscious factors that motivate behavior. Attention is given to the events of the first 6 years of life as determinants of the later development of personality.

Adlerian therapy

Founder: Alfred Adler. Key Figure: Following Adler, Rudolf Dreikurs is credited with popularizing this approach in the United States. This is a growth model that stresses assuming responsibility, creating one's own destiny, and finding meaning and goals to create a purposeful life. Key concepts are used in most other current therapies.

Experiential and Relationship-Oriented Therapies

Existential therapy

Key figures: Viktor Frankl, Rollo May, and Irvin Yalom. Reacting against the tendency to view therapy as a system of well-defined techniques, this model stresses building therapy on the basic conditions of human existence, such as choice, the freedom and responsibility to shape one's life, and self-determination. It focuses on the quality of the person-to-person therapeutic relationship.

Person-centered therapy

Founder: Carl Rogers. Key figure: Natalie Rogers. This approach was developed during the 1940s as a nondirective reaction against psychoanalysis. Based on a subjective view of human experiencing, it places faith in and gives responsibility to the client in dealing with problems and concerns.

Gestalt therapy

Founders: Fritz and Laura Perls. Key figures: Miriam and Erving Polster. An experiential therapy stressing awareness and integration; it grew as a reaction against analytic therapy. It integrates the functioning of body and mind.

Cognitive Behavioral Approaches

Behavior therapy

Key figures: B. F. Skinner, Arnold Lazarus, and Albert Bandura. This approach applies the principles of learning to the resolution of specific behavioral problems. Results are subject to continual experimentation. The methods of this approach are always in the process of refinement.

Cognitive behavior therapy

Key figure: A. T. Beck founded cognitive therapy, which gives a primary role to thinking as it influences behavior; Judith Beck continues to develop CBT. Donald Meichenbaum is a prominent contributor to the development of cognitive behavior therapy.

Rational emotive behavior therapy	Key figure: Albert Ellis founded rational emotive behavior therapy, a highly didactic, cognitive, action-oriented model of therapy that stresses the role of thinking and belief systems as the root of personal problems.
Reality therapy	Founder: William Glasser. Key figure: Robert Wubbolding. This short-term approach is based on choice theory and focuses on the client assuming responsibility in the present. Through the therapeutic process, the client is able to learn more effective ways of meeting her or his needs.

Systems and Postmodern Approaches

Feminist therapy	This approach grew out of the efforts of many women, a few of whom are Jean Baker Miller, Carolyn Zerbe Enns, Oliva Espin, and Laura Brown. A central concept is the concern for the psychological oppression of women. Focusing on the constraints imposed by the sociopolitical status to which women have been relegated, this approach explores women's identity development, self-concept, goals and aspirations, and emotional well-being.
Postmodern approaches	A number of key figures are associated with the development of these various approaches to therapy. Steve de Shazer and Insoo Kim Berg are the co-founders of solution-focused brief therapy. Michael White and David Epston are the major figures associated with narrative therapy. Social constructionism, solution-focused brief therapy, and narrative therapy all assume that there is no single truth; rather, it is believed that reality is socially constructed through human interaction. These approaches maintain that the client is an expert in his or her own life.
Family systems therapy	A number of significant figures have been pioneers of the family systems approach, including Alfred Adler, Murray Bowen, Virginia Satir, Carl Whitaker, Salvador Minuchin, Jay Haley, and Cloé Madanes. This systemic approach is based on the assumption that the key to changing the individual is understanding and working with the family.

psychoanalysis. Many theories of counseling and psychotherapy have borrowed and integrated principles and techniques from psychoanalytic approaches.

Adlerian therapy differs from psychoanalytic theory in many respects, but it can broadly be considered an analytic perspective. Adlerians focus on meaning, goals, purposeful behavior, conscious action, belonging, and social interest. Although Adlerian theory accounts for present behavior by studying childhood experiences, it does not focus on unconscious dynamics.

The second category comprises the *experiential and relationship-oriented therapies*: the existential approach, the person-centered approach, and Gestalt therapy. The *existential approach* stresses a concern for what it means to be fully human.

It suggests certain themes that are part of the human condition, such as freedom and responsibility, anxiety, guilt, awareness of being finite, creating meaning in the world, and shaping one's future by making active choices. This approach is not a unified school of therapy with a clear theory and a systematic set of techniques. Rather, it is a philosophy of counseling that stresses the divergent methods of understanding the subjective world of the person. The *person-centered approach,* which is rooted in a humanistic philosophy, places emphasis on the basic attitudes of the therapist. It maintains that the quality of the client–therapist relationship is the prime determinant of the outcomes of the therapeutic process. Philosophically, this approach assumes that clients have the capacity for self-direction without active intervention and direction on the therapist's part. Another experiential approach is *Gestalt therapy,* which offers a range of experiments to help clients gain awareness of what they are experiencing in the here and now—that is, the present. In contrast to person-centered therapists, Gestalt therapists tend to take an active role, yet they follow the leads provided by their clients. These approaches tend to emphasize emotion as a route to bringing about change, and in a sense, they can be considered emotion-focused therapies.

Third are the *cognitive behavioral approaches,* sometimes known as the action-oriented therapies, because they all emphasize translating insights into behavioral action. These approaches include reality therapy, behavior therapy, rational emotive behavior therapy, and cognitive therapy. *Reality therapy* focuses on clients' current behavior and stresses developing clear plans for new behaviors. Like reality therapy, *behavior therapy* puts a premium on doing and on taking steps to make concrete changes. A current trend in behavior therapy is toward paying increased attention to cognitive factors as an important determinant of behavior. *Rational emotive behavior therapy* and *cognitive therapy* highlight the necessity of learning how to challenge inaccurate beliefs and automatic thoughts that lead to behavioral problems. These cognitive behavioral approaches are used to help people modify their inaccurate and self-defeating assumptions and to develop new patterns of acting.

The fourth general approach encompasses the *systems and postmodern perspectives.* Feminist therapy and family therapy are systems approaches, but they also share postmodern notions. The systems orientation stresses the importance of understanding individuals in the context of the surroundings that influence their development. To bring about individual change, it is essential to pay attention to how the individual's personality has been affected by his or her gender-role socialization, culture, family, and other systems.

The *postmodern approaches* include social constructionism, solution-focused brief therapy, and narrative therapy. These newer approaches challenge the basic assumptions of most of the traditional approaches by assuming that there is no single truth and that reality is socially constructed through human interaction. Both the postmodern and the systemic theories focus on how people produce their own lives in the context of systems, interactions, social conditioning, and discourse.

In my view, practitioners need to pay attention to what their clients are *thinking, feeling,* and *doing,* and a complete therapy system must address all three of these facets. Some of the therapies included here highlight the role that cognitive factors play in counseling. Others place emphasis on the experiential aspects of counseling and the role of feelings. Still others emphasize putting plans into action and learning by doing. Combining all of these dimensions provides the basis for a comprehensive therapy. If any of these dimensions is excluded, the therapy approach is incomplete.

INTRODUCTION TO THE CASE OF STAN

You will learn a great deal by seeing a theory in action, preferably in a live demonstration or as part of experiential activities in which you function in the alternating roles of client and counselor. An online program (available in DVD format as well) demonstrates one or two techniques from each of the theories. As Stan's counselor, I show how I would apply some of the principles of each of the theories you are studying to Stan. Many of my students find this case history of the hypothetical client (Stan) helpful in understanding how various techniques are applied to the same person. Stan's case, which describes his life and struggles, is presented here to give you significant background material to draw from as you study the applications of the theories. Each of the 11 theory chapters in Part 2 includes a discussion of how a therapist with the orientation under discussion is likely to proceed with Stan. We examine the answers to questions such as these:

- What themes in Stan's life merit special attention in therapy?
- What concepts would be useful to you in working with Stan on his problems?
- What are the general goals of Stan's therapy?
- What possible techniques and methods would best meet these goals?
- What are some characteristics of the relationship between Stan and his therapist?
- How might the therapist proceed?
- How might the therapist evaluate the process and treatment outcomes of therapy?

In Chapter 16 (which I recommend you read early) I present how I would work with Stan, suggesting concepts and techniques I would draw on from many of the models (forming an integrative approach).

A single case illustrates both contrasts and parallels among the approaches. It also will help you understand the practical applications of the 11 models and provide a basis for integrating them. A summary of the intake interview with Stan, his autobiography, and some key themes in his life are presented next to provide a context for making sense of the way therapists with various theoretical orientations might work with Stan. Try to find attributes of each approach that you can incorporate into a personalized style of counseling.

Intake Interview and Stan's Autobiography

The setting is a community mental health agency where both individual and group counseling are available. Stan comes to counseling because of his drinking. He was convicted of driving under the influence, and the judge determined that he needed professional help. Stan recognizes that he does have problems, but he is not convinced that he is addicted to alcohol. Stan arrives for an intake interview and provides the counselor with this information:

> At the present time I work in construction. I like building houses, but probably won't stay in construction for the rest of my life. When it comes to my personal life, I've always had difficulty in getting along with people. I could be called a "loner." I like people in my life, but I don't seem to know how to stay close to people. It probably has a lot to do with why I drink. I'm not very good at making friends or getting close to people. Probably the reason I sometimes drink a bit too much is because I'm so scared when it comes to socializing. Even though I hate to admit it, when I drink, things are not quite so overwhelming. When I look at others, they seem to know the right things to say. Next to them I feel dumb. I'm afraid that people don't find me very interesting. I'd like to turn my life around, but I just don't know where to begin. That's why I went back to school. I'm a part-time college student majoring in psychology. I want to better myself. In one of my classes, Psychology of Personal Adjustment, we talked about ourselves and how people change. We also had to write an autobiographical paper.

That is the essence of Stan's introduction. The counselor says that she would like to read his autobiography. Stan hopes it will give her a better understanding of where he has been and where he would like to go. He brings her the autobiography, which reads as follows:

> Where am I currently in my life? At 35 I feel that I've wasted most of my life. I should be finished with college and into a career by now, but instead I'm only a junior. I can't afford to really commit myself to pursuing college full time because I need to work to support myself. Even though construction work is hard, I like the satisfaction I get when I look at what I have done.

> I want to get into a profession where I could work with people. Someday, I'm hoping to get a master's degree in counseling or in social work and eventually work as a counselor with kids who are in trouble. I know I was helped by someone who cared about me, and I would like to do the same for someone else.

> I have few friends and feel scared around most people. I feel good with kids. But I wonder if I'm smart enough to get through all the classes I'll need to become a counselor. One of my problems is that I frequently get drunk. This happens when I feel alone and when I'm scared of the intensity of my feelings. At first drinking seemed to help, but later on I felt awful. I have abused drugs in the past also.

> I feel overwhelmed and intimidated when I'm around attractive women. I feel cold, sweaty, and terribly nervous. I think they may be judging me and see me as not much of a man. I'm afraid I just don't measure up to being a real *man*. When I am sexually intimate with a woman, I am anxious and preoccupied with what she is thinking about me.

> I feel anxiety much of the time. I often feel as if I'm dying inside. I think about committing suicide, and I wonder who would care. I can see my family coming to my funeral feeling sorry for me. I feel guilty that I haven't worked up to my potential, that I've been a failure, that I've wasted much of my time, and that I let people down a lot. I get down on myself and wallow in guilt and feel *very depressed*. At times like this I feel hopeless and that I'd be better off dead. For all these reasons, I find it difficult to get close to anyone.

> There are a few bright spots. I did put a lot of my shady past behind me, and did get into college. I like this determination in me—I *want* to change. I'm tired of feeling the way I do. I know that nobody is going to change my life for me. It's up to me to get what I want. Even though I feel scared at times, I like that I'm willing to take risks.

> What was my past like? A major turning point for me was the confidence my supervisor had in me at the youth camp where I worked the past few summers. He helped me get my

job, and he also encouraged me to go to college. He said he saw a lot of potential in me for being able to work well with young people. That was hard for me to believe, but his faith inspired me to begin to believe in myself. Another turning point was my marriage and divorce. This marriage didn't last long. It made me wonder about what kind of man I was! Joyce was a strong and dominant woman who kept repeating how worthless I was and how she did not want to be around me. We had sex only a few times, and most of the time I was not very good at it. That was hard to take. It made me afraid to get close to a woman. My parents should have divorced. They fought most of the time. My mother (Angie) constantly criticized my father (Frank Sr.). I saw him as weak and passive. He would *never* stand up to her. There were four of us kids. My parents compared me unfavorably with my older sister (Judy) and older brother (Frank Jr.). They were "perfect" children, successful honors students. My younger brother (Karl) and I fought a lot. They spoiled him. It was all very hard for me.

In high school I started using drugs. I was thrown into a youth rehabilitation facility for stealing. Later I was expelled from regular school for fighting, and I landed in a continuation high school, where I went to school in the mornings and had afternoons for on-the-job training. I got into auto mechanics, was fairly successful, and even managed to keep myself employed for 3 years as a mechanic.

I can still remember my father asking me: "Why can't you be like your sister and brother? Why can't you do anything right?" And my mother treated me much the way she treated my father. She would say: "Why do you do so many things to hurt me? Why can't you grow up and be a man? Things are so much better around here when you're gone." I recall crying myself to sleep many nights, feeling terribly alone. There was no talk of religion in my house, nor was there any talk of sex. In fact, I find it hard to imagine my folks ever having sex.

Where would I like to be 5 years from now? What kind of person do I want to become? Most of all, I would like to start feeling better about myself. I would like to be able to stop drinking altogether and still feel good. I want to like myself much more than I do now. I hope I can learn to love at least a few other people, most of all, a woman. I want to lose my fear of women. I would like to feel equal with others and not always have to feel apologetic for my existence. I want to let go of my anxiety and guilt. I want to become a good counselor for kids. I'm not certain how I'll change or even what all the changes are I hope for. I do know that I want to be free of my self-destructive tendencies and learn how to trust people more. Perhaps when I begin to like myself more, I'll be able to trust that others will find something about me to like.

Effective therapists, regardless of their theoretical orientation, would pay attention to suicidal thoughts. In his autobiography Stan says, "I think about committing suicide." At times he doubts that he will ever change and wonders if he'd be "better off dead." Before embarking on the therapeutic journey, the therapist would need to make an assessment of Stan's current *ego strength* (or his ability to manage life realistically), which would include a discussion of his suicidal thoughts.

Overview of Some Key Themes in Stan's Life

A number of themes appear to represent core struggles in Stan's life. Here are some of the statements we can assume that he may make at various points in his therapy and themes that will be addressed from the theoretical perspectives in Chapters 4 through 14:

- Although I'd like to have people in my life, I just don't seem to know how to go about making friends or getting close to people.
- I'd like to turn my life around, but I have no sense of direction.

- I want to make a difference.
- I am afraid of failure.
- I know that when I feel alone, scared, and overwhelmed, I drink heavily to feel better.
- I am afraid of women.
- Sometimes at night I feel a terrible anxiety and feel as if I'm dying.
- I often feel guilty that I've wasted my life, that I've failed, and that I've let people down. At times like this, I get depressed.
- I like it that I have determination and that I really want to change.
- I've never really felt loved or wanted by my parents.
- I'd like to get rid of my self-destructive tendencies and learn to trust people more.
- I put myself down a lot, but I'd like to feel better about myself.

In Chapters 4 through 14, I write about how I would apply selected concepts and techniques of the particular theory in counseling Stan. In addition, in these chapters you are asked to think about how you would continue counseling Stan from each of these different perspectives. In doing so, refer to the introductory material given here and to Stan's autobiography as well. To make the case of Stan come alive for each theory, I highly recommend that you view and study the video program, *DVD for Theory and Practice of Counseling and Psychotherapy: The Case of Stan and Lecturettes*. In this video program I counsel Stan from each of the various theories and provide brief lectures that highlight each theory.

The Counselor: Person and Professional

INTRODUCTION

One of the most important instruments you have to work with as a counselor is yourself as a person. In preparing for counseling, you will acquire knowledge about the theories of personality and psychotherapy, learn assessment and intervention techniques, and discover the dynamics of human behavior. Such knowledge and skills are essential, but by themselves they are not sufficient for establishing and maintaining effective therapeutic relationships. To every therapy session we bring our human qualities and the experiences that have influenced us. In my judgment, this human dimension is one of the most powerful influences on the therapeutic process.

A good way to begin your study of contemporary counseling theories is by reflecting on the personal issues raised in this chapter. By remaining open to self-evaluation, you not only expand your awareness of self but also build the foundation for developing your abilities and skills as a professional. The theme of this chapter is that the *person* and the *professional* are intertwined facets that cannot be separated in reality. We know, clinically and scientifically, that the person of the therapist and the therapeutic relationship contribute to therapy outcome at least as much as the particular treatment method used (Duncan, Miller, Wampold, & Hubble, 2010; Norcross, 2011; Norcross & Guy, 2007).

 See the DVD program for Chapter 2, *DVD for Theory and Practice of Counseling and Psychotherapy: The Case of Stan and Lecturettes.* I suggest that you view the brief lecture for each chapter prior to reading the chapter.

THE COUNSELOR AS A THERAPEUTIC PERSON

Because counseling is an intimate form of learning, it demands a practitioner who is willing to be an authentic person in the therapeutic relationship. It is within the context of such a person-to-person connection that the client experiences growth. If we hide behind the safety of our professional role, our clients will likely keep themselves hidden from us. If we strive for technical expertise alone, and leave our own reactions and self out of our work, the result is likely to be ineffective counseling. Our own genuineness can have a significant effect on our relationship with our clients. If we are willing to look at our lives and make the changes we want, we can model that process by the way we reveal ourselves and respond to our clients. If we are inauthentic, our clients will probably pick that up and be discouraged by it. Our clients can be encouraged by our way of being with them. If we model authenticity by engaging in appropriate self-disclosure, our clients will tend to be honest with us as well.

I believe that who the psychotherapist is directly relates to his or her ability to establish and maintain effective therapy relationships with clients. But what does the research reveal about the role of the counselor as a person and the therapeutic relationship on psychotherapy outcome? Abundant research indicates the centrality of the person of the therapist as a primary factor in successful therapy

(Norcross & Lambert, 2011; Norcross & Wampold, 2011). Clients place more value on the personality of the therapist than on the specific techniques used (Lambert, 2011). Norcross and Lambert (2011) cite considerable evidence indicating that the *person* of the psychotherapist is inextricably intertwined with the outcome of psychotherapy. Indeed, evidence-based psychotherapy relationships are critical to the psychotherapy endeavor.

Techniques themselves have limited importance in the therapeutic process. Wampold (2001) conducted a meta-analysis of many research studies on therapeutic effectiveness and found that the personal and interpersonal components are essential to effective psychotherapy, whereas techniques have relatively little effect on therapeutic outcome. The *contextual factors*—the alliance, the relationship, the personal and interpersonal skills of the therapist, client agency, and extra-therapeutic factors—are the primary determinants of therapeutic outcome. This research supports what humanistic psychologists have maintained for years: "It is not theories and techniques that heal the suffering client but the human dimension of therapy and the 'meetings' that occur between therapist and client as they work together" (Elkins, 2009, p. 82). In short, both the *therapy relationship* and the *therapy methods* used influence the outcomes of treatment, but it is essential that the methods used support the therapeutic relationship being formed with the client.

Personal Characteristics of Effective Counselors

Particular personal qualities and characteristics of counselors are significant in creating a therapeutic alliance with clients. My views regarding these personal characteristics are supported by research on this topic (Norcross, 2011; Skovholt & Jennings, 2004). I do not expect any therapist to fully exemplify all the traits described in the list that follows. Rather, the willingness to struggle to become a more therapeutic person is the crucial variable. This list is intended to stimulate you to examine your own ideas about what kind of person can make a significant difference in the lives of others.

- *Effective therapists have an identity.* They know who they are, what they are capable of becoming, what they want out of life, and what is essential.
- *Effective therapists respect and appreciate themselves.* They can give and receive help and love out of their own sense of self-worth and strength. They feel adequate with others and allow others to feel powerful with them.
- *Effective therapists are open to change.* They exhibit a willingness and courage to leave the security of the known if they are not satisfied with the way they are. They make decisions about how they would like to change, and they work toward becoming the person they want to become.
- *Effective therapists make choices that are life oriented.* They are aware of early decisions they made about themselves, others, and the world. They are not the victims of these early decisions, and they are willing to revise them if necessary. They are committed to living fully rather than settling for mere existence.
- *Effective therapists are authentic, sincere, and honest.* They do not hide behind rigid roles or facades. Who they are in their personal life and in their professional work is congruent.

- *Effective therapists have a sense of humor.* They are able to put the events of life in perspective. They have not forgotten how to laugh, especially at their own foibles and contradictions.
- *Effective therapists make mistakes and are willing to admit them.* They do not dismiss their errors lightly, yet they do not choose to dwell on them, either.
- *Effective therapists generally live in the present.* They are not riveted to the past, nor are they fixated on the future. They are able to experience and be present with others in the "now."
- *Effective therapists appreciate the influence of culture.* They are aware of the ways in which their own culture affects them, and they respect the diversity of values espoused by other cultures. They are sensitive to the unique differences arising out of social class, race, sexual orientation, and gender.
- *Effective therapists have a sincere interest in the welfare of others.* This concern is based on respect, care, trust, and a real valuing of others.
- *Effective therapists possess effective interpersonal skills.* They are capable of entering the world of others without getting lost in this world, and they strive to create collaborative relationships with others. They readily entertain another person's perspective and can work together toward consensual goals.
- *Effective therapists become deeply involved in their work and derive meaning from it.* They can accept the rewards flowing from their work, yet they are not slaves to their work.
- *Effective therapists are passionate.* They have the courage to pursue their dreams and passions, and they radiate a sense of energy.
- *Effective therapists are able to maintain healthy boundaries.* Although they strive to be fully present for their clients, they don't carry the problems of their clients around with them during leisure hours. They know how to say no, which enables them to maintain balance in their lives.

This picture of the characteristics of effective therapists might appear unrealistic. Who could be all those things? Certainly I do not fit this bill! Do not think of these personal characteristics from an all-or-nothing perspective; rather, consider them on a continuum. A given trait may be highly characteristic of you, at one extreme, or it may be very uncharacteristic of you, at the other extreme. I have presented this picture of the therapeutic person with the hope that you will examine it and develop your own concept of what personality traits you think are essential to strive for to promote your own personal growth. For a more detailed discussion of the person of the counselor and the role of the therapeutic relationship in outcomes of treatments, see *Psychotherapy Relationships That Work* (Norcross, 2011) and *Master Therapists: Exploring Expertise in Therapy and Counseling* (Skovholt & Jennings, 2004).

PERSONAL THERAPY FOR THE COUNSELOR

Discussion of the counselor as a therapeutic person raises another issue debated in counselor education: Should people be required to participate in counseling or therapy before they become practitioners? My view is that counselors can benefit greatly from the experience of being clients at some time, a view that is supported by research. Some type of self-exploration can increase your level of self-awareness. This experience can be obtained before your training, during it, or both, but I strongly support some form of personal exploration as vital preparation in learning to counsel others.

The vast majority of mental health professionals have experienced personal therapy, typically on several occasions (Geller, Norcross, & Orlinsky, 2005b). A review of research studies on the outcomes and impacts of the psychotherapist's own psychotherapy revealed that more than 90% of mental health professionals report satisfaction and positive outcomes from their own counseling experiences (Orlinsky, Norcross, Ronnestad, & Wiseman, 2005). Orlinsky and colleagues suggest that personal therapy contributes to the therapist's professional work in the following three ways: (1) as part of the therapist's training, personal therapy offers a model of therapeutic practice in which the trainee experiences the work of a more experienced therapist and learns experientially what is helpful or not helpful; (2) a beneficial experience in personal therapy can further enhance a therapist's interpersonal skills that are essential to skillfully practicing therapy; and (3) successful personal therapy can contribute to a therapist's ability to deal with the ongoing stresses associated with clinical work.

In his research on personal therapy for mental health professionals, Norcross (2005) states that lasting lessons practitioners learn from their personal therapy experiences pertain to interpersonal relationships and the dynamics of psychotherapy. Some of these lessons learned are the centrality of warmth, empathy, and the personal relationship; having a sense of what it is like to be a therapy client; valuing patience and tolerance; and appreciating the importance of learning how to deal with transference and countertransference. By participating in personal therapy, counselors can prevent their potential future countertransference from harming clients.

Through our work as therapists, we can expect to confront our own unexplored personal blocks such as loneliness, power, death, and intimate relationships. This does not mean that we need to be free of conflicts before we can counsel others, but we should be aware of what these conflicts are and how they are likely to affect us as persons and as counselors. For example, if we have great difficulty dealing with anger or conflict, we may not be able to assist clients who are dealing with anger or with relationships in conflict.

When I began counseling others, old wounds were opened, and feelings I had not explored in depth came to the surface. It was difficult for me to encounter a client's depression because I had failed to come to terms with the way I had escaped from my own depression. I did my best to cheer up depressed clients by talking them out of what they were feeling, mainly because of my own inability to deal with such feelings. In the years I worked as a counselor in a university counseling center, I frequently wondered what I could do for my clients. I often had no idea what, if anything, my clients were getting from our sessions. I couldn't tell if they were getting better, staying the same, or getting worse. It was very important to me to note progress and see change in my clients. Because I did not see immediate results, I had many doubts about whether I could become an effective counselor. What I did not understand at the time was that my clients needed to struggle to find their own answers. To see my clients feel better quickly was *my need,* not theirs, for then I would know that I was helping them. It never occurred to me that clients often feel worse for a time as they give up their defenses and open themselves to their pain. My early experiences as a counselor showed me that I could benefit by participating in further personal therapy to better understand how my personal issues were affecting my professional work. I realized that periodic therapy, especially early in one's career, can be most useful.

Personal therapy can be instrumental in healing the healer. If student counselors are not actively involved in the pursuit of healing their psychological wounds, they will probably have considerable difficulty entering the world of a client. As counselors, can we take our clients any further than we have gone ourselves? If we are not committed personally to the value of examining our own life, how can we inspire clients to examine their lives? By becoming clients ourselves, we gain an experiential frame of reference with which to view ourselves. This provides a basis for understanding and compassion for our clients, for we can draw on our own memories of reaching impasses in our therapy, of both wanting to go farther and at the same time resisting change. Our own therapy can help us develop patience with our patients! We learn what it feels like to deal with anxieties that are aroused by self-disclosure and self-exploration and how to creatively facilitate deeper levels of self-exploration in clients. Through our own therapy, we can gain increased appreciation for the courage our clients display in their therapeutic journey. Being willing to participate in a process of self-exploration can reduce the chances of assuming an attitude of arrogance or of being convinced that we are totally healed. Our own therapy helps us avoid assuming a stance of superiority over others and makes it less likely that we would treat people as objects to be pitied or disrespected. Indeed, experiencing counseling as a client is very different from merely reading about the counseling process.

For a comprehensive discussion of personal therapy for counselors, see *The Psychotherapist's Own Psychotherapy: Patient and Clinician Perspectives* (Geller, Norcross, & Orlinsky, 2005a).

THE COUNSELOR'S VALUES AND THE THERAPEUTIC PROCESS

As alluded to in the previous section, the importance of self-exploration for counselors carries over to the values and beliefs they hold. My experience in teaching and supervising students of counseling shows me how crucial it is that students be aware of their values, of where and how they acquired them, and of how their values can influence their interventions with clients.

The Role of Values in Counseling

Our values are core beliefs that influence how we act, both in our personal and our professional lives. Personal values influence how we view counseling and the manner in which we interact with clients, including the way we conduct client assessments, our views of the goals of counseling, the interventions we choose, the topics we select for discussion in a counseling session, how we evaluate progress, and how we interpret clients' life situations.

Although total objectivity cannot be achieved, we can strive to avoid being encapsulated by our own worldview. As counselors we need to guard against the tendency to use our power to influence the client to accept our values because it is not our function to persuade clients to accept or adopt our value system From my perspective, the counselor's role is to create a climate in which clients can examine their thoughts, feelings, and actions and to empower them to arrive at their own solutions to problems they face. The counseling task is to assist individuals in finding answers that are most congruent with their own values. It is not beneficial to provide advice or to give clients your answers to their questions.

You may not agree with certain of your clients' values, but you need to respect their right to hold divergent values from yours. This is especially true when counseling clients who have a different cultural background and perhaps do not share your own core cultural values. Your role is to provide a safe and inviting context in which clients can explore the congruence between their values and their behavior. If clients acknowledge that what they are doing is not getting them what they want, it is appropriate to assist them in developing new ways of thinking and behaving to help them move closer to their goals. This is done with full respect for their right to decide which values they will use as a framework for living. Individuals seeking counseling need to clarify their own values and goals, make informed decisions, choose a course of action, and assume responsibility and accountability for the decisions they make.

There is a difference between exposing our values and imposing our values on clients. **Value imposition** refers to counselors directly attempting to define a client's values, attitudes, beliefs, and behaviors. It is possible for counselors to impose their values either actively or passively. Counselors are cautioned about not imposing their values on their clients. On this topic, the American Counseling Association's *Code of Ethics* (ACA, 2005) has this standard:

> Personal Values. Counselors are aware of their own values, attitudes, beliefs, and behaviors and avoid imposing values that are inconsistent with counseling goals and respect for the diversity of clients, trainees, and research participants. (A.4.b.)

Even though therapists should not directly teach the client or impose specific values, therapists do implement a philosophy of counseling, which is, in effect, a philosophy of life. Counselors communicate their values by the therapeutic goals to which they subscribe and by the procedures they employ to reach these goals.

The Role of Values in Developing Therapeutic Goals

Who should establish the goals of counseling? Almost all theories are in agreement that it is largely the client's responsibility to decide upon goals, collaborating with the therapist as therapy proceeds. Counselors have general goals, which are reflected in their behavior during the therapy session, in their observations of the client's behavior, and in the interventions they make. The general goals of counselors must be congruent with the personal goals of the client.

24

Setting goals is inextricably related to values. The client and the counselor need to explore what they hope to obtain from the counseling relationship, whether they can work with each other, and whether their goals are compatible. Even more important, it is essential that the counselor be able to understand, respect, and work within the framework of the client's world rather than forcing the client to fit into the therapist's scheme of values.

In my view, therapy ought to begin with an exploration of the client's expectations and goals. Clients initially tend to have vague ideas of what they expect from therapy. They may be seeking solutions to problems, they may want to stop hurting, they may want to change others so they can live with less anxiety, or they may seek to be different so that some significant persons in their lives will be more accepting of them. In some cases clients have no goals; they are in the therapist's office simply because they were sent for counseling by their parents, probation officer, or teacher.

So where can a counselor begin? The initial interview can be used most productively to focus on the client's goals or lack of them. The therapist may begin by asking any of these questions: "What do you expect from counseling? Why are you here? What do you want? What do you hope to leave with? How is what you are currently doing working for you? What aspects of yourself or your life situation would you most like to change?"

When a person seeks a counseling relationship with you, it is important to cooperatively discover what this person is expecting from the relationship. If you try to figure out in advance how to proceed with a client, you may be depriving the client of the opportunity to become an active partner in her or his own therapy. Why is this person coming in for counseling? It is the client's place to decide on the goals of therapy. It is important to keep this focus in mind so that the client's agenda is addressed rather than an agenda of your own.

BECOMING AN EFFECTIVE MULTICULTURAL COUNSELOR

Part of the process of becoming an effective counselor involves learning how to recognize diversity issues and shaping one's counseling practice to fit the client's worldview. It is an *ethical obligation* for counselors to develop sensitivity to cultural differences if they hope to make interventions that are consistent with the values of their clients. The therapist's role is to assist clients in making decisions that are congruent with their worldview, not to live by the therapist's values.

Diversity in the therapeutic relationship is a two-way street. As a counselor, you bring your own heritage with you to your work, so you need to recognize the ways in which cultural conditioning has influenced the directions you take with your clients. Unless the social and cultural context of clients and counselors are taken into consideration, it is difficult to appreciate the nature of clients' struggles. Counseling students often hold values—such as making their own choices, expressing what they are feeling, being open and self-revealing, and striving for independence—that differ from the values of clients from different cultural backgrounds. Some clients may be very slow to disclose and have different expectations about counseling than the therapist has. Counselors need to become aware of how clients from diverse cultures may perceive them as therapists, as well as how clients may perceive the value of formal helping. It is the task of counselors to determine whether the assumptions they have made about the nature and functioning of therapy are appropriate for culturally diverse clients.

Clearly, effective counseling must take into account the impact of culture on the client's functioning, including the client's degree of acculturation. Culture is, quite simply, the values and behaviors shared by a group of individuals. It is important to realize that culture refers to more than ethnic or racial heritage; culture also includes factors such as age, gender, religion, sexual orientation, physical and mental ability, and socioeconomic status.

Acquiring Competencies in Multicultural Counseling

Effective counselors understand their own cultural conditioning, the conditioning of their clients, and the sociopolitical system of which they are a part. Acquiring this understanding begins with counselors' awareness of the cultural origins of any values, biases, and attitudes they may hold. Counselors from all cultural groups must examine their expectations, attitudes, biases, and assumptions about the counseling process and about persons from diverse groups. Recognizing our biases and prejudices takes courage because most of us do not want to acknowledge that we have cultural biases. Everyone has biases, but being unaware of the biased attitudes we hold is an obstacle to client care. It takes a concerted effort and vigilance to monitor our biases, attitudes, and values so that they do not interfere with establishing and maintaining successful counseling relationships.

A major part of becoming a diversity-competent counselor involves challenging the idea that the values we hold are automatically true for others. We also need to understand how our values are likely to influence our practice with diverse clients who embrace different values. Furthermore, becoming a diversity-competent practitioner is not something that we arrive at once and for all; rather, it is an ongoing process.

Sue, Arredondo, and McDavis (1992) and Arredondo and her colleagues (1996) have developed a conceptual framework for competencies and standards in multicultural counseling. Their dimensions of competency involve three areas: (1) beliefs and attitudes, (2) knowledge, and (3) skills. For an in-depth treatment of multicultural counseling and therapy competence, refer to *Counseling the Culturally Diverse: Theory and Practice* (D. W. Sue & Sue, 2008).

BELIEFS AND ATTITUDES First, effective counselors have moved from being culturally unaware to ensuring that their personal biases, values, or problems will not interfere with their ability to work with clients who are culturally different from them. They believe cultural self-awareness and sensitivity to one's own cultural heritage are essential for any form of helping. Counselors are aware of their positive and negative emotional reactions toward persons from other racial and ethnic groups that may prove detrimental to establishing collaborative helping relationships.

They seek to examine and understand the world from the vantage point of their clients. They respect clients' religious and spiritual beliefs and values. They are comfortable with differences between themselves and others in terms of race, ethnicity, culture, and beliefs. Rather than maintaining that their cultural heritage is superior, they are able to accept and value cultural diversity. They realize that traditional theories and techniques may not be appropriate for all clients or for all problems. Culturally skilled counselors monitor their functioning through consultation, supervision, and further training or education.

KNOWLEDGE Second, culturally effective practitioners possess certain knowledge. They know specifically about their own racial and cultural heritage and how it affects them personally and professionally. Because they understand the dynamics of oppression, racism, discrimination, and stereotyping, they are in a position to detect their own racist attitudes, beliefs, and feelings. They understand the worldview of their clients, and they learn about their clients' cultural backgrounds. They do not impose their values and expectations on their clients from differing cultural backgrounds and avoid stereotyping clients. Culturally skilled counselors understand that external sociopolitical forces influence all groups, and they know how these forces operate with respect to the treatment of minorities. These practitioners are aware of the institutional barriers that prevent minorities from utilizing the mental health services available in their communities. They possess knowledge about the historical background, traditions, and values of the client populations with whom they work. They know about minority family structures, hierarchies, values, and beliefs. Furthermore, they are knowledgeable about community characteristics and resources. Those who are culturally skilled know how to help clients make use of indigenous support systems. In areas where they are lacking in knowledge, they seek resources to assist them. The greater their depth and breadth of knowledge of culturally diverse groups, the more likely they are to be effective practitioners.

SKILLS AND INTERVENTION STRATEGIES Third, effective counselors have acquired certain skills in working with culturally diverse populations. Counselors take responsibility for educating their clients about the therapeutic process, including matters such as setting goals, appropriate expectations, legal rights, and the counselor's orientation. Multicultural counseling is enhanced when practitioners use methods and strategies and define goals consistent with the life experiences and cultural values of their clients. Such practitioners modify and adapt their interventions to accommodate cultural differences. They do not force their clients to fit within one counseling approach, and they recognize that counseling techniques may be culture-bound. They are able to send and receive both verbal and nonverbal messages accurately and appropriately. They become actively involved with minority individuals outside the office (community events, celebrations, and neighborhood groups). They are willing to seek out educational, consultative, and training experiences to enhance their ability to work with culturally diverse client populations. They consult regularly with other multiculturally sensitive professionals regarding issues of culture to determine whether referral may be necessary.

Incorporating Culture in Counseling Practice

It is unrealistic to expect a counselor to know everything about the cultural background of a client, but some understanding of the client's cultural and ethnic background is essential. There is much to be said for letting clients teach counselors about relevant aspects of their culture. It is a good idea for counselors to ask clients to provide them with the information they will need to work effectively. Incorporating culture into the therapeutic process is not limited to working with clients from a certain ethnic or cultural background. It is critical that therapists take into account the worldview and background of *every* client. Failing to do this seriously restricts the potential impact of the therapeutic endeavor.

In the case of individuals who have lived in more than one culture, it is useful to assess the degree of acculturation and identity development that has taken place. Clients often have allegiance to their culture of origin, and yet they may find certain characteristics of their new culture attractive. They may experience conflicts in integrating the two cultures in which they live. Different rates of acculturation among family members is a common complaint of clients who are experiencing family problems. These core struggles can be explored productively in the therapeutic context if the counselor understands and respects this cultural conflict.

WELCOMING DIVERSITY Counseling is by its very nature diverse in a multicultural society, so it is easy to see that there are no ideal therapeutic approaches. Instead, different theories have distinct features that have appeal for different cultural groups. Some theoretical approaches have limitations when applied to certain populations. Effective multicultural practice demands an open stance on the part of the practitioner, flexibility, and a willingness to modify strategies to fit the needs and the situation of the individual client. Practitioners who truly respect their clients will be aware of clients' hesitations and will not be too quick to misinterpret this behavior. Instead, they will patiently attempt to enter the world of their clients as much as they can. Although practitioners may not have had the same experiences as their clients, the empathy shown by counselors for the feelings and struggles of their clients is essential to good therapeutic outcomes. We are more often challenged by our differences than by our similarities to look at what we are doing.

PRACTICAL GUIDELINES IN ADDRESSING CULTURE If the counseling process is to be effective, it is essential that cultural concerns be addressed with all clients. Here are some guidelines that may increase your effectiveness when working with clients from diverse backgrounds:

- Learn more about how your own cultural background has influenced your thinking and behaving. Take steps to increase your understanding of other cultures.
- Identify your basic assumptions, especially as they apply to diversity in culture, ethnicity, race, gender, class, spirituality, religion, and sexual orientation. Think about how your assumptions are likely to affect your professional practice.
- Examine where you obtained your knowledge about culture.
- Remain open to ongoing learning of how the various dimensions of culture may affect therapeutic work. Realize that this skill does not develop quickly or without effort.

- Be willing to identify and examine your own personal worldview and any prejudices you may hold about other racial/ethnic groups.
- Learn to pay attention to the common ground that exists among people of diverse backgrounds.
- Be flexible in applying the methods you use with clients. Don't be wedded to a specific technique if it is not appropriate for a given client.
- Remember that practicing from a multicultural perspective can make your job easier and can be rewarding for both you and your clients.

It takes time, study, and experience to become an effective multicultural counselor. Multicultural competence cannot be reduced simply to cultural awareness and sensitivity, to a body of knowledge, or to a specific set of skills. Instead, it requires a combination of all of these factors.

ISSUES FACED BY BEGINNING THERAPISTS

In this section I identify some of the major issues that most of us typically face, particularly during the beginning stages of learning how to be therapists. When you complete formal course work and begin facing clients, you will be challenged to integrate and to apply what you have learned. At that point some real concerns are likely to arise about your adequacy as a person and as a professional. Here are some useful guidelines for your reflection on becoming an effective counselor.

Dealing With Your Anxieties

Most beginning counselors have ambivalent feelings when meeting their first clients. A certain level of anxiety demonstrates that you are aware of the uncertainties of the future with your clients and of your abilities to really be there for them. A willingness to recognize and deal with these anxieties, as opposed to denying them, is a positive sign. That we have self-doubts is normal; it is how we deal with them that matters. One way is to openly discuss our self-doubts with a supervisor and peers. The possibilities are rich for meaningful exchanges and for gaining support from fellow interns who probably have many of the same concerns and anxieties.

Being Yourself and Self-Disclosure

Because you may be self-conscious and anxious when you begin counseling, you may have a tendency to be overly concerned with what the books say and with the mechanics of how to proceed. Inexperienced therapists too often fail to appreciate the values inherent in simply being themselves. If we are able to be ourselves in our therapeutic work and appropriately disclose our reactions in counseling sessions, we increase the chances of being authentic. It is this level of genuineness and presence that enables us to connect with our clients and to establish an effective therapeutic relationship with them.

It is possible to err by going to extremes in two different directions. At one end are counselors who lose themselves in their fixed role and hide behind a professional facade. These counselors are so caught up in maintaining stereotyped role expectations that little of their personal selves shows through. Counselors who adopt this behavior will likely remain anonymous to clients, and clients may perceive them as hiding behind a professional role.

At the other end of the spectrum is engaging in too much self-disclosure. Some counselors make the mistake of inappropriately burdening their clients with their spontaneous impressions about their clients. Judging the appropriate amount of self-disclosure can be a problem even for seasoned counselors, and it is often especially worrisome for new counselors. In determining the appropriateness of self-disclosure, consider *what* to reveal, *when* to reveal, and *how much* to reveal. It may be useful to mention something about ourselves from time to time, but we must be aware of our motivations for making ourselves known in this way. Assess the readiness of a client to hear these disclosures as well as the impact doing so might have on the client. Remain observant during any self-disclosure to get a sense of how the client is being affected by it.

The most productive form of self-disclosure is related to what is going on between the counselor and the client within the counseling session. The skill of immediacy involves revealing what we are thinking or feeling in the here and now with the client, but be careful to avoid pronouncing judgments about the client. When done in a timely way, sharing persistent reactions can facilitate therapeutic progress and improve the quality of our relationship with the client. Even when we are talking about reactions based on the therapeutic relationship, caution is necessary, and discretion and sensitivity are required in deciding what reactions we might share.

Avoiding Perfectionism

Perhaps one of the most common self-defeating beliefs with which we burden ourselves is that we must never make a mistake. Although we may well know *intellectually* that humans are not perfect, *emotionally* we often feel that there is little room for error. To be sure, you *will* make mistakes, whether you are a beginning or a seasoned therapist. If our energies are tied up presenting an image of perfection, this will affect our ability to be present for our clients. I tell students to question the notion that they should know everything and be perfectly skilled. I encourage them to share their mistakes or what they perceive as errors during their supervision meetings. Students willing to risk making mistakes in supervised learning situations and willing to reveal their self-doubts will find a direction that leads to growth.

Being Honest About Your Limitations

You cannot realistically expect to succeed with every client. It takes honesty to admit that you cannot work successfully with every client. It is important to learn *when* and *how* to make a referral for clients when your limitations prevent you from helping them. However, there is a delicate balance between learning your realistic limits and challenging what you sometimes think of as being "limits." Before deciding that you do not have the life experiences or the personal qualities to work with a given population, try working in a setting with a population you do not intend to specialize in. This can be done through diversified field placements or visits to agencies.

Understanding Silence

Silent moments during a therapeutic session may seem like silent hours to a beginning therapist, yet this silence can have many meanings. The client may be quietly thinking about some things that were discussed earlier or evaluating some insight just acquired. The client may be waiting for the therapist to take the lead and decide what to say next, or the therapist may be waiting for the client to do this. Either the client or the therapist may be distracted or preoccupied, or neither may have anything to say for the moment. The client and the therapist may be communicating without words. The silence may be refreshing, or the silence may be overwhelming. Perhaps the interaction has been on a surface level, and both persons have some fear or hesitancy about getting to a deeper level. When silence occurs, acknowledge and explore with your client the meaning of the silence.

Dealing With Demands From Clients

A major issue that puzzles many beginning counselors is how to deal with clients who seem to make constant demands. Because therapists feel they should extend themselves in being helpful, they often burden themselves with the unrealistic idea that they should give unselfishly, regardless of how great clients' demands may be. These demands may manifest themselves in a variety of ways. Clients may want to see you more often or for a longer period than you can provide. They may want to see you socially. Some clients may expect you to continually demonstrate how much you care or demand that you tell them what to do and how to solve a problem. One way of heading off these demands is to make your expectations and boundaries clear during the initial counseling sessions or in the disclosure statement.

Dealing With Clients Who Lack Commitment

Involuntary clients may be required by a court order to obtain therapy, and you may be challenged in your attempt to establish a working relationship with them. It is possible to do effective work with mandated clients, but practitioners must begin by openly discussing the nature of the relationship. Counselors who omit preparation and do not address clients' thoughts and feelings about coming to counseling are likely to encounter resistance. It is critical that therapists not promise what they cannot or will not deliver. It is good practice to make clear the limits of confidentiality as well as any other factors that may affect the course of therapy. In working with involuntary clients, it is especially important to prepare them for the process; doing so can go a long way toward lessening resistance.

Tolerating Ambiguity

Many beginning therapists experience the anxiety of not seeing immediate results. They ask themselves: "Am I really doing my client any good? Is the client perhaps getting worse?" I hope you will learn to tolerate the ambiguity of not knowing for sure whether your client is improving, at least during the initial sessions. Realize that oftentimes clients may seemingly "get worse" before they show therapeutic gains. Also, realize that the fruitful effects of the joint efforts of the therapist and the client may manifest themselves after the conclusion of therapy.

Becoming Aware of Your Countertransference

Working with clients can affect you in personal ways, and your own vulnerabilities and countertransference are bound to surface. If you are unaware of your personal dynamics, you are in danger of being overwhelmed by a client's emotional experiences. Beginning counselors need to learn how to "let clients go" and not carry around their problems until we see them again. The most therapeutic thing is to be as fully present as we are able to be during the therapy hour, but to let clients assume the responsibility of their living and choosing outside of the session. If we become lost in clients' struggles and confusion, we cease being effective agents in helping them find solutions to their problems. If we accept responsibility for our clients' decisions, we are blocking rather than fostering their growth.

Countertransference, defined broadly, includes any of our projections that influence the way we perceive and react to a client. This phenomenon occurs when we are triggered into emotional reactivity, when we respond defensively, or when we lose our ability to be present in a relationship because our own issues become involved. Recognizing the manifestations of our countertransference reactions is an essential step in becoming competent counselors. Unless we are aware of our own conflicts, needs, assets, and liabilities, we can use the therapy hour more for our own purposes than for being available for our clients. Because it is not appropriate for us to use clients' time to work through our reactions to them, it is all the more important that we be willing to work on ourselves in our own sessions with another therapist, supervisor, or colleague. If we do not engage in this kind of self-exploration, we increase the danger of losing ourselves in our clients and using them to meet our unfulfilled needs.

The emotionally intense relationships we develop with clients can be expected to tap into our own unresolved problem areas. Our clients' stories and pain are bound to affect us; we will be touched by their stories and can express compassion and empathy. However, we have to realize that it is their pain and not carry it *for* them lest we become overwhelmed by their life stories and thus render ourselves ineffective in working with them. Although we cannot completely free ourselves from any traces of countertransference or ever fully resolve all personal conflicts from the past, we can become aware of ways these realities influence our professional work. Our personal therapy can be instrumental in enabling us to recognize and manage our countertransference reactions.

Developing a Sense of Humor

Therapy is a responsible endeavor, but it need not be deadly serious. Both clients and counselors can enrich a relationship through humor. What a welcome relief when we can admit that pain is not our exclusive domain. It is important to recognize that laughter or humor does not mean that clients are not respected or work is not being accomplished. There are times, of course, when laughter is used to cover up anxiety or to escape from the experience of facing threatening material. The therapist needs to distinguish between humor that distracts and humor that enhances the situation.

Sharing Responsibility With the Client

You might struggle with finding the optimum balance in sharing responsibility with your clients. One mistake is to assume full responsibility for the direction and outcomes of therapy. This will lead to taking from your clients their rightful responsibility of making their own decisions. It could also increase the likelihood of your early burnout. Another mistake is for you to refuse to accept the responsibility for making accurate assessments and designing appropriate treatment plans for your clients. How responsibility will be shared should be addressed early in the course of counseling. It is your responsibility to discuss specific matters such as length and overall duration of the sessions, confidentiality, general goals, and methods used to achieve goals. (Informed consent is discussed in Chapter 3.)

It is important to be alert to your clients' efforts to get you to assume responsibility for directing their lives. Many clients seek a "magic answer" as a way of escaping the anxiety of making their own decisions. It is not your role to assume responsibility for directing your clients' lives. Collaboratively designing contracts and homework assignments with your clients can be instrumental in your clients' increasingly finding direction within themselves. Perhaps the best measure of our effectiveness as counselors is the degree to which clients are able to say to us, "I appreciate what you have been to me, and because of your faith in me, and what you have taught me, I am confident that I can go it alone." Eventually, if we are effective, we will be out of business!

Declining to Give Advice

Quite often clients who are suffering come to a therapy session seeking and even demanding advice. They want more than direction; they want a wise counselor to make a decision or resolve a problem for them. However, counseling should not be confused with dispensing information. Therapists help clients discover their own solutions and recognize their own freedom to act. Even if we, as therapists, were able to resolve clients' struggles for them, we would be fostering their dependence on us. They would continually need to seek our counsel for every new twist in their difficulties. Our task is to help clients make independent choices and accept the consequences of their choices. The habitual practice of giving advice does not work toward this end.

Defining Your Role as a Counselor

One of your challenges as a counselor will be to define and clarify your professional role. As you read about the various theoretical orientations in Part 2, you will discover the many different roles of counselors that are related to these diverse theories. As a counselor, you will likely be expected to function with a diverse range of roles.

From my perspective, the central function of counseling is to help clients recognize their own strengths, discover what is preventing them from using their resources, and clarify what kind of life they want to live. Counseling is a process by which clients are invited to look honestly at their behavior and make certain decisions about how they want to modify the quality of their life. In this framework counselors provide support and warmth yet care enough to challenge clients so that they will be able to take the actions necessary to bring about significant change.

Keep in mind that the professional roles you assume are likely to be dependent on factors such as the client populations with whom you are working, the specific therapeutic services you are providing, the particular stage of counseling, and the setting in which you work. Your role will not be defined once and for all. You will have to reassess the nature of your professional commitments and redefine your role at various times.

Learning to Use Techniques Appropriately

When you are at an impasse with a client, you may have a tendency to look for a technique to get the sessions moving. As discussed in Chapter 1, relying on techniques too much can lead to mechanical counseling. Ideally, therapeutic techniques should evolve from the therapeutic relationship and the material presented, and they should enhance the client's awareness or suggest possibilities for experimenting with new behavior. Know the theoretical rationale for each technique you use, and be sure the techniques are appropriate for the goals of therapy. This does not mean that you need to restrict yourself to drawing on procedures within a single model; quite the contrary. However, it is important to avoid using techniques in a hit-or-miss fashion, to fill time, to meet your own needs, or to get things moving. Your methods need to be thoughtfully chosen as a way to help clients make therapeutic progress.

Developing Your Own Counseling Style

Be aware of the tendency to copy the style of a supervisor, therapist, or some other model. There is no one way to conduct therapy, and wide variations in approach can be effective. You will inhibit your potential effectiveness in reaching others if you attempt to imitate another therapist's style or if you fit most of your behavior during the session into the procrustean bed of some expert's theory. Your counseling style will be influenced by your teachers, therapists, and supervisors, but don't blur your potential uniqueness by trying to imitate them. I advocate borrowing from others, yet at the same time, doing it in a way that is distinctive to you.

Maintaining Your Vitality as a Person and as a Professional

Ultimately, your single most important instrument is the person you are, and your most powerful technique is your ability to model aliveness and realness. It is of paramount importance that we take care of ourselves, for how can we take care of others if we are not taking care of ourselves? We need to work at dealing with those factors that threaten to drain life from us and render us helpless. I encourage you to consider how you can apply the theories you will be studying to enhance your life from both a personal and a professional standpoint.

Learn to look within yourself to determine what choices you are making (and not making) to keep yourself vital. If you are aware of the factors that sap your vitality as a person, you are in a better position to prevent the condition known as *professional burnout*. You have considerable control over whether you become burned out or not. You cannot always control stressful events, but you do have a great deal of control over how you interpret and react to these events. It is important to realize that you cannot continue to give and give while getting little in return. There is a price to pay for always being available and for assuming responsibility over the lives and destinies of others. Become attuned to the subtle signs of burnout rather than waiting for a full-blown condition of emotional and physical exhaustion to set in. You would be wise to develop your own strategy for keeping yourself alive personally and professionally.

Self-monitoring is a crucial first step in self-care. If you make an honest inventory of how well you are taking care of yourself in specific domains, you will have a framework for deciding what you may want to change. By making periodic assessments of the direction of your own life, you can determine whether you are living the way you want to live. If not, decide what you are willing to actually *do* to *make* changes occur. By being in tune with yourself, by having the experience of centeredness and solidness, and by feeling a sense of personal power, you have the foundation for integrating your life experiences with your professional experiences. Such an awareness can provide the basis for retaining your physical and psychological vitality and for being an effective professional.

Counseling professionals tend to be caring people who are good at taking care of others, but often we do not treat ourselves with the same level of care. Self-care is not a luxury but an ethical mandate. If we neglect to care for ourselves, our clients will not be getting the best of us. If we are physically drained and psychologically depleted, we will not have much to give to those with whom we work. It is not possible to provide nourishment to our clients if we are not nourishing ourselves.

Mental health professionals often comment that they do not have time to take care of themselves. My question to them is, "Can you afford *not* to take care of yourself?" To successfully meet the demands of our professional work, we must take care of ourselves physically, psychologically, intellectually, socially, and spiritually. Ideally, our self-care should mirror the care we provide for others. If we hope to have the vitality and stamina required to stay focused on our professional goals, we need to incorporate a wellness perspective into our daily living. Wellness is the result of our conscious commitment to a way of life that leads to zest, peace, vitality, and happiness.

Wellness and self-care are being given increased attention in professional journals (see *Counseling Today*, January 2011) and at professional conferences. When reading about self-care and wellness, reflect on what you can do to put what you know into action. If you are interested in learning more about therapist self-care, I highly recommend *Leaving It at the Office: A Guide to Psychotherapist Self-Care* (Norcross & Guy, 2007) and *Empathy Fatigue: Healing the Mind, Body, and Spirit of Professional Counselors* (Stebnicki, 2008). For more on the topic of the counselor as a person and as a professional, see *Creating Your Professional Path: Lessons From My Journey* (Corey, 2010).

SUMMARY

One of the basic issues in the counseling profession concerns the significance of the counselor as a person in the therapeutic relationship. In your professional work, you are asking people to take an honest look at their lives and to make choices concerning how they want to change, so it is critical that you do this in your own life. Ask yourself questions such as "What do I personally have to offer others who are struggling to find their way?" and "Am I doing in my own life what I may be urging others to do?"

You can acquire an extensive theoretical and practical knowledge and can make that knowledge available to your clients. But to every therapeutic session you also bring yourself as a person. If you are to promote change in your clients, you need to be open to change in your own life. This willingness to attempt to live in accordance with what you teach and thus to be a positive model for your clients is what makes you a "therapeutic person."

Ethical Issues in Counseling Practice

INTRODUCTION

This chapter introduces some of the ethical principles and issues that will be a basic part of your professional practice. Its purpose is to stimulate you to think about ethical practice so that you can form a sound basis for making **ethical decisions**. To help you make these decisions, you can consult with colleagues, keep yourself informed about laws affecting your practice, keep up to date in your specialty field, stay abreast of developments in ethical practice, reflect on the impact your values have on your practice, and be willing to engage in honest self-examination. Topics addressed include balancing clients' needs against your own needs, ways of making good ethical decisions, educating clients about their rights, parameters of confidentiality, ethical concerns in counseling diverse client populations, ethical issues involving diagnosis, evidence-based practice, and dealing with multiple relationships.

At times students think of ethics in a negative way, merely as a list of rules and prohibitions that result in sanctions and malpractice actions if practitioners do not follow them. **Mandatory ethics** is the view of ethical practice that deals with the minimum level of professional practice, whereas **aspirational ethics** is a higher level of ethical practice that addresses doing what is in the best interests of clients. Ethics is more than a list of things to avoid for fear of punishment. Ethics is a way of thinking about becoming the best practitioner possible. **Positive ethics** is an approach taken by practitioners who want to do their best for clients rather than simply meet minimum standards to stay out of trouble (Knapp & VandeCreek, 2006).

 See the video program for Chapter 3, *DVD for Theory and Practice of Counseling and Psychotherapy: The Case of Stan and Lecturettes*. I suggest that you view the brief lecture for each chapter prior to reading the chapter.

PUTTING CLIENTS' NEEDS BEFORE YOUR OWN

As counselors we cannot always keep our personal needs completely separate from our relationships with clients. Ethically, it is essential that we become aware of our own needs, areas of unfinished business, potential personal problems, and especially our sources of countertransference. We need to realize how such factors could interfere with effectively and ethically serving our clients.

Our professional relationships with our clients exist for their benefit. A useful question to frequently ask yourself is this: "Whose needs are being met in this relationship, my client's or my own?" It takes considerable professional maturity to make an honest appraisal of how your behavior affects your clients. It is not unethical for us to meet our personal needs through our professional work, but it is essential that these needs be kept in perspective. An ethical problem exists when we meet our needs, in either obvious or subtle ways, at the expense of our clients' needs. It is crucial that we avoid exploiting or harming clients.

We all have certain blind spots and distortions of reality. As helping professionals, we have responsibilities to work actively toward expanding our own self-awareness and to learn to recognize areas of prejudice and vulnerability. If we are aware of our personal problems and are willing to work through them, there is less chance that we will project them onto clients. If certain problem areas surface and old conflicts become reactivated, we have an ethical obligation to do whatever it takes to avoid harming our clients.

We must also examine other, less obviously harmful personal needs that can get in the way of creating growth-producing relationships, such as the need for control and power; the need to be nurturing and helpful; the need to change others in the direction of our own values; the need for feeling adequate, particularly when it becomes overly important that the client confirm our competence; and the need to be respected and appreciated. It is crucial that we do not meet our needs at the expense of our clients. For an expanded discussion of this topic, see M. Corey and Corey (2011, chap. 1).

ETHICAL DECISION MAKING

The ready-made answers to ethical dilemmas provided by professional organizations typically contain only broad guidelines for responsible practice. As a practitioner, ultimately you will have to apply the ethics codes of your profession to the many practical problems you face. Professionals are expected to exercise prudent judgment when it comes to interpreting and applying ethical principles to specific situations. Although you are responsible for making ethical decisions, you do not have to do so alone. Part of the process of making ethical decisions involves learning about the resources from which you can draw when you are dealing with an ethical question. You should also be aware of the consequences of practicing in ways that are not sanctioned by organizations of which you are a member or the state in which you are licensed to practice.

The Role of Ethics Codes as a Catalyst for Improving Practice

Professional codes of ethics serve a number of purposes. They educate counseling practitioners and the general public about the responsibilities of the profession. They provide a basis for accountability, and through their enforcement, clients are protected from unethical practices. Perhaps most important, ethics codes can provide a basis for reflecting on and improving your professional practice. Self-monitoring is a better route for professionals to take than being policed by an outside agency (Herlihy & Corey, 2006a).

From my perspective, one of the unfortunate trends is for ethics codes to increasingly take on legalistic dimensions. Many practitioners are so anxious to avoid becoming embroiled in a lawsuit that they gear their practices mainly toward fulfilling legal minimums rather than thinking of what is right for their clients. If we are too concerned with being sued, it is unlikely that we will be very creative or effective in our work. In this era of litigation, it makes sense to be aware of the legal aspects of practice and to do what is possible to reduce a malpractice suit, but it is a mistake to equate behaving legally with being ethical. Although following the law is part of ethical behavior, being an ethical practitioner involves far more. One of the best ways to prevent being sued for malpractice rests in demonstrating respect for clients, having their welfare as a central concern, and practicing within the framework of professional codes.

No code of ethics can delineate what would be the appropriate or best course of action in each problematic situation a professional will face. In my view, ethics codes are best used as guidelines to formulate sound reasoning and serve practitioners in making the best judgments possible. A number of professional organizations and their websites are listed at the end of this chapter; each has its own code of ethics, which you can access through its website. Compare your professional organization's code of ethics to several others to understand their similarities and differences.

Some Steps in Making Ethical Decisions

There are a number of different models for ethical decision making; most tend to focus on the application of principles to ethical dilemmas. After reviewing a few of these models, my colleagues and I have identified a series of procedural steps to help you think through ethical problems (see Corey, Corey, & Callanan, 2011):

- Identify the problem or dilemma. Gather information that will shed light on the nature of the problem. This will help you decide whether the problem is mainly ethical, legal, professional, clinical, or moral.
- Identify the potential issues. Evaluate the rights, responsibilities, and welfare of all those who are involved in the situation.
- Look at the relevant ethics codes for general guidance on the matter. Consider whether your own values and ethics are consistent with or in conflict with the relevant guidelines.
- Consider the applicable laws and regulations, and determine how they may have a bearing on an ethical dilemma.
- Seek consultation from more than one source to obtain various perspectives on the dilemma, and document in the client's record what suggestions you received from this consultation.
- Brainstorm various possible courses of action. Continue discussing options with other professionals. Include the client in this process of considering options for action. Again, document the nature of this discussion with your client.
- Enumerate the consequences of various decisions, and reflect on the implications of each course of action for your client.
- Decide on what appears to be the best possible course of action. Once the course of action has been implemented, follow up to evaluate the outcomes and to determine whether further action is necessary. Document the reasons for the actions you took as well as your evaluation measures.

In reasoning through any ethical dilemma, there is rarely just one course of action to follow, and practitioners may make different decisions. The more subtle the ethical dilemma, the more complex and demanding the decision-making process.

Professional maturity implies that you are open to questioning and discussing your quandaries with colleagues. In seeking consultation, it is generally possible to protect the identity of your client and still get useful input that is critical to making sound ethical decisions. Because ethics codes do not make decisions for you, it is a good practice to demonstrate a willingness to explore various aspects of a problem, raise questions, discuss ethical concerns with others, and continually clarify your values and examine your motivations. To the degree that it is possible, include the client in all phases of the ethical decision-making process. Again, it is essential to document how you included your client as well as the steps you took to ensure ethical practice.

THE RIGHT OF INFORMED CONSENT

Regardless of your theoretical framework, informed consent is an ethical and legal requirement that is an integral part of the therapeutic process. It also establishes a basic foundation for creating a working alliance and a collaborative partnership between the client and the therapist. **Informed consent** involves the right of clients to be informed about their therapy and to make autonomous decisions pertaining to it. Providing clients with information they need to make informed choices tends to promote the active cooperation of clients in their counseling plan. By educating your clients about their rights and responsibilities, you are both empowering them and building a trusting relationship with them. Seen in this light, informed consent is something far broader than simply making sure clients sign the appropriate forms. It is a positive approach that helps clients become active partners and true collaborators in their therapy. Some aspects of the informed consent process include the general goals of counseling, the responsibilities of the counselor toward the client, the responsibilities of clients, limitations of and exceptions to confidentiality, legal and ethical parameters that could define the relationship, the qualifications and background of the practitioner, the fees involved, the services the client can expect, and the approximate length of the therapeutic process. Further areas might include the benefits of counseling, the risks involved, and the possibility that the client's case will be discussed with the therapist's colleagues or supervisors. This process of educating the client begins with the initial counseling session and continues for the duration of counseling.

The challenge of fulfilling the spirit of informed consent is to strike a balance between giving clients too much information and giving them too little. For example, it is too late to tell minors that you intend to consult with their parents *after* they have disclosed that they are considering an abortion. In such a case the young people involved have a right to know about the limitations of confidentiality before they make such highly personal disclosures. Clients can be overwhelmed, however, if counselors go into too much detail initially about the interventions they are likely to make. It takes both intuition and skill for practitioners to strike a balance.

Informed consent in counseling can be provided in written form, orally, or some combination of both. If it is done orally, therapists must make an entry in the client's clinical record documenting the nature and extent of informed consent

(Nagy, 2011). I think it is a good idea to have basic information about the therapy process in writing, as well as to discuss with clients topics that will enable them to get the maximum benefit from their counseling experience. Written information protects both clients and therapists and enables clients to think about the information and bring up questions at the following session. For a more complete discussion of informed consent and client rights, see *Issues and Ethics in the Helping Professions* (Corey, Corey, & Callanan, 2011, chap. 5), *Ethical, Legal, and Professional Issues in Counseling* (Remley & Herlihy, 2010), and *Essential Ethics for Psychologists* (Nagy, 2011, chap. 5).

DIMENSIONS OF CONFIDENTIALITY

Confidentiality and privileged communication are two related but somewhat different concepts. Both of these concepts are rooted in a client's right to privacy. **Confidentiality** is an ethical concept, and in most states it is the legal duty of therapists not to disclose information about a client. **Privileged communication** is a legal concept that generally bars the disclosure of confidential communications in a legal proceeding (Committee on Professional Practice and Standards, 2003). All states have enacted into law some form of psychotherapist–client privilege, but the specifics of this privilege vary from state to state. These laws ensure that disclosures clients make in therapy will be protected from exposure by therapists in legal proceedings. Generally speaking, the legal concept of privileged communication does *not* apply to group counseling, couples counseling, family therapy, or child and adolescent therapy. However, the therapist is still bound by confidentiality with respect to circumstances not involving a court proceeding.

Confidentiality is central to developing a trusting and productive client–therapist relationship. Because no genuine therapy can occur unless clients trust in the privacy of their revelations to their therapists, professionals have the responsibility to define the degree of confidentiality that can be promised. Counselors have an ethical and legal responsibility to discuss the nature and purpose of confidentiality with their clients early in the counseling process. In addition, clients have a right to know that their therapist may be discussing certain details of the relationship with a supervisor or a colleague.

Although most counselors agree on the essential value of confidentiality, they realize that it cannot be considered an absolute. There are times when confidential information must be divulged, and there are many instances in which keeping or breaking confidentiality becomes a cloudy issue. In determining when to breach confidentiality, therapists must consider the requirements of the law, the institution in which they work, and the clientele they serve. Because these circumstances are frequently not clearly defined by accepted ethics codes, counselors must exercise professional judgment.

There is a legal requirement to break confidentiality in cases involving child abuse, abuse of the elderly, abuse of dependent adults, and danger to self or others. All mental health practitioners and interns need to be aware of their duty to report in these situations and to know the limitations of confidentiality. Here are some other circumstances in which information must legally be reported by counselors:

- When the therapist believes a client under the age of 16 is the victim of incest, rape, child abuse, or some other crime
- When the therapist determines that the client needs hospitalization
- When information is made an issue in a court action
- When clients request that their records be released to them or to a third party

In general, the counselor's primary obligation is to protect client disclosures as a vital part of the therapeutic relationship. Informing clients about the limits of confidentiality does not necessarily inhibit successful counseling.

For a more complete discussion of confidentiality, see *Issues and Ethics in the Helping Professions* (Corey, Corey, & Callanan, 2011, chap. 6), *The Ethical and Professional Practice of Counseling and Psychotherapy* (Sperry, 2007, chap. 6), and *Essential Ethics for Psychologists* (Nagy, 2011, chap. 6).

ETHICAL ISSUES IN A MULTICULTURAL PERSPECTIVE

Ethical practice requires that we take the client's cultural context into account in counseling practice. In this section we look at how it is possible for practitioners to practice unethically if they do not address cultural differences in counseling practice.

Are Current Theories Adequate in Working With Culturally Diverse Populations?

I believe current theories need to be, and can be, expanded to include a multicultural perspective. With respect to many of the traditional theories, assumptions made about mental health, optimum human development, the nature of psychopathology, and the nature of effective treatment may have little relevance for some clients. For traditional theories to be relevant in a multicultural and diverse society, they must incorporate an interactive person-in-the-environment focus. That is, individuals are best understood by taking into consideration salient cultural and environmental variables. It is essential for therapists to create therapeutic strategies that are congruent with the range of values and behaviors that are characteristic of a pluralistic society.

Is Counseling Culture Bound?

Historically, therapists have relied on Western therapeutic models to guide their practice and to conceptualize problems that clients present in mental health settings. Value assumptions made by culturally different counselors and clients have resulted in culturally biased counseling and have led to underuse of mental health services by diverse populations (Pedersen, 2000; D. W. Sue & Sue, 2008). Multicultural specialists have asserted that theories of counseling and psychotherapy represent different worldviews, each with its own values, biases, and assumptions about human behavior. Some of these approaches may not be applicable to clients from different racial, ethnic, and cultural backgrounds. Western models of counseling have some limitations when applied to special populations and cultural groups such as Asian and Pacific Islanders, Latinos, Native Americans, and African Americans. A therapist's methods often need to be modified when working with clients from diverse cultural backgrounds.

Contemporary therapy approaches are grounded on a core set of values, which are neither value-neutral nor applicable to all cultures. For example, the values implicit in most traditional counseling theories include an emphasis on individualism, the separate existence of the self, individuation as the foundation for maturity, and decision making and responsibility resting with the individual rather than the group. These values of individual choice and autonomy do not have universal applicability. In some cultures the key values are collectivist, and primary consideration is given to what is good for the group. Regardless of the therapist's orientation, it is crucial to listen to clients and determine why they are seeking help and how best to deliver the help that is appropriate for them. Unskilled clinicians may inappropriately apply certain techniques that are not relevant to particular clients. Competent therapists understand themselves as social and cultural beings and possess at least a minimum level of knowledge and skill that they can bring to bear on any counseling situation. These practitioners understand what their clients need and avoid forcing clients into a preconceived mold.

The attitudes, values, and behaviors counselors and clients bring to the therapy relationship can vary widely. Denying the importance of these cultural variables or overemphasizing cultural differences both can result in counselors losing their spontaneity and failing to be present for their clients. Counselors need to understand and accept clients who have a different set of assumptions about life, and they need to be alert to the possibility of imposing their own worldview. In working with clients from different cultural backgrounds and life experiences, it is important that counselors resist making value judgments for them.

Focusing on Both Individual and Environmental Factors

A theoretical orientation provides practitioners with a map to guide them in a productive direction with their clients. It is hoped that the theory orients them but does not control what they attend to in the therapeutic venture. Counselors who operate from a multicultural framework also have certain assumptions and a focus that guides their practice. They view individuals in the context of the family and the culture, and their aim is to facilitate social action that will lead to change within the client's community rather than merely increasing the individual's insight. Both multicultural practitioners and feminist therapists maintain that therapeutic practice will be effective only to the extent that interventions are tailored toward social action aimed at changing those factors that are creating the client's problem rather than blaming the client for his or her condition. These topics are developed in more detail in later chapters.

An adequate theory of counseling *does* deal with the social and cultural factors of an individual's problems. However, there is something to be said for helping clients deal with their response to environmental realities. Counselors may well be at a loss in trying to bring about social change when they are sitting with a client who is in pain because of social injustice. By using techniques from many of the traditional therapies, counselors can help clients increase their awareness of their options in dealing with barriers and struggles. However, it is essential to focus on both individual and social factors if change is to occur, as the feminist, postmodern, and family systems approaches to therapy teach us. Indeed, the person-in-the-environment perspective acknowledges this interactive reality. For a more detailed treatment of the ethical issues in multicultural counseling, see Corey, Corey, and Callanan (2011, chap. 4).

ETHICAL ISSUES IN THE ASSESSMENT PROCESS

Both clinical and ethical issues are associated with the use of assessment and diagnostic procedures. As you will see when you study the various theories of counseling, some approaches place heavy emphasis on the role of assessment as a prelude to the treatment process; other approaches find assessment less useful in this regard.

The Role of Assessment and Diagnosis in Counseling

Assessment and diagnosis are integrally related to the practice of counseling and psychotherapy, and both are often viewed as essential for planning treatment. For some approaches, a comprehensive assessment of the client is the initial step in the therapeutic process. The rationale is that specific counseling goals cannot be formulated and appropriate treatment strategies cannot be designed until a client's past and present functioning is understood. Regardless of their theoretical orientation, therapists need to engage in assessment, which is generally an ongoing part of the therapeutic process. This assessment may be subject to revision as the clinician gathers further data during therapy sessions. Some practitioners consider *assessment* as a part of the process that leads to a *formal diagnosis*.

Assessment consists of evaluating the relevant factors in a client's life to identify themes for further exploration in the counseling process. **Diagnosis**, which is sometimes part of the assessment process, consists of identifying a specific mental disorder based on a pattern of symptoms. Both assessment and diagnosis can be understood as providing direction for the treatment process.

Diagnosis may include an explanation of the causes of the client's difficulties, an account of how these problems developed over time, a classification of any disorders, a specification of preferred treatment procedure, and an estimate of the chances for a successful resolution. The purpose of diagnosis in counseling and psychotherapy is to identify disruptions in a client's present behavior and lifestyle. Once problem areas are clearly identified, the counselor and client are able to establish the goals of the therapy process, and then a treatment plan can be tailored to the unique needs of the client. A diagnosis provides a working hypothesis that guides the practitioner in understanding the client. The therapy sessions provide useful clues about the nature of the client's problems. Thus diagnosis begins with the intake interview and continues throughout the duration of therapy.

The classic book for guiding practitioners in making diagnostic assessments is the fourth edition of the American Psychiatric Association's (2000) *Diagnostic and Statistical Manual of Mental Disorders, Text Revision* (also known as the *DSM-IV-TR*), which is presently being revised. The DSM-5 is scheduled to be published in 2013. Clinicians who work in community mental health agencies, private practice, and other human service settings are generally expected to assess client problems within this framework. This manual advises practitioners that it represents only an initial step in a comprehensive evaluation and that it is necessary to gain information about the person being evaluated beyond that required for a *DSM-IV-TR* diagnosis.

Although some clinicians view diagnosis as central to the counseling process, others view it as unnecessary, as a detriment, or as discriminatory against ethnic minorities and women. As you will see when you study the therapeutic models in this book, some approaches do not use diagnosis as a precursor to treatment.

CONSIDERING ETHNIC AND CULTURAL FACTORS IN ASSESSMENT AND DIAGNOSIS A danger of the diagnostic approach is the possible failure of counselors to consider ethnic and cultural factors in certain patterns of behavior. The *DSM-IV-TR* emphasizes the importance of being aware of unintentional bias and keeping an open mind to the presence of distinctive ethnic and cultural patterns that could influence the diagnostic process. Unless cultural variables are considered, some clients may be subjected to erroneous diagnoses. Certain behaviors and personality styles may be labeled neurotic or deviant simply because they are not characteristic of the dominant culture. Counselors who work with diverse client populations may erroneously conclude that a client is repressed, inhibited, passive, and unmotivated, all of which are seen as undesirable by Western standards.

ASSESSMENT AND DIAGNOSIS FROM VARIOUS THEORETICAL PERSPECTIVES The theory from which you operate influences your thinking about the use of a diagnostic framework in your therapeutic practice. Many practitioners who use the cognitive behavioral approaches and the medical model place heavy emphasis on the role of assessment as a prelude to the treatment process. The rationale is that specific therapy goals cannot be designed until a clear picture emerges of the client's past and present functioning. Counselors who base their practices on the relationship-oriented approaches tend to view the process of assessment and diagnosis as external to the immediacy of the client–counselor relationship, impeding their understanding of the subjective world of the client. As you will see in Chapter 12, feminist therapists contend that traditional diagnostic practices are often oppressive and that such practices are based on a White, male-centered, Western notion of mental health and mental illness. Both the feminist perspective and the postmodern approaches (Chapter 13) charge that these diagnoses ignore societal contexts. Therapists with a feminist, social constructionist, solution-focused, or narrative therapy orientation challenge many *DSM-IV-TR* diagnoses. However, these practitioners do make assessments and draw conclusions about client problems and strengths. Regardless of the particular theory espoused by a therapist, both clinical and ethical issues are associated with the use of assessment procedures and possibly a diagnosis as part of a treatment plan.

A COMMENTARY ON ASSESSMENT AND DIAGNOSIS Most practitioners and many writers in the field consider assessment and diagnosis to be a continuing process that focuses on understanding the client. The collaborative perspective that involves the client as an active participant in the therapy process implies that both the therapist and the client are engaged in a search-and-discovery process from the first session to the last. Even though some practitioners may avoid formal diagnostic procedures and terminology, making tentative hypotheses and sharing them with clients throughout the process is a form of ongoing diagnosis. This perspective on assessment and diagnosis is consistent with the principles of feminist therapy, an approach that is critical of traditional diagnostic procedures.

Ethical dilemmas may be created when diagnosis is done strictly for insurance purposes, which often entails arbitrarily assigning a client to a diagnostic classification. However, it is a clinical, legal, and ethical obligation of therapists to screen clients for life-threatening problems such as organic disorders, schizophrenia, bipolar disorder, and suicidal types of depression. Students need to learn the clinical skills necessary to do this type of screening, which is a form of diagnostic thinking.

It is essential to assess the whole person, which includes assessing dimensions of mind, body, and spirit. Therapists need to take into account the biological processes as possible underlying factors of psychological symptoms and work closely with physicians. Clients' values can be instrumental resources in the search for solutions to their problems, and spiritual and religious values often illuminate client concerns.

For a more detailed discussion of assessment and diagnosis in counseling practice as it is applied to a single case, consult *Case Approach to Counseling and Psychotherapy* (Corey, 2013b), in which theorists from 12 different theoretical orientations share their diagnostic perspectives on the case of Ruth.

ETHICAL ASPECTS OF EVIDENCE-BASED PRACTICE

Mental health practitioners are faced with the task of choosing the best interventions with a particular client. For many practitioners this choice is based on their theoretical orientation. In recent years, however, a shift has occurred toward promoting the use of specific interventions for specific problems or diagnoses based on empirically supported treatments (APA Presidential Task Force on Evidence-based Practice, 2006; Cukrowicz et al., 2005; Deegear & Lawson, 2003; Edwards, Dattilio, & Bromley, 2004).

This trend toward specific, empirically supported treatment is referred to as **evidence-based practice (EBP):** "the integration of the best available research with clinical expertise in the context of patient characteristics, culture, and preferences" (APA Presidential Task Force on Evidence-based Practice, 2006, p. 273).

Increasingly, those practitioners who work in a behavioral health care system must cope with the challenges associated with evidence-based practice. Norcross, Hogan, and Koocher (2008) advocate for inclusive evidence-based practices that incorporate the three pillars of EBP: looking for the best available research, relying on clinical expertise, and taking into consideration the client's characteristics, culture, and preferences. The central aim of evidence-based practice is to require psychotherapists to base their practice on techniques that have empirical evidence to support their efficacy. Research studies empirically analyze the most effective and efficient treatments, which then can be widely implemented in clinical practice (Norcross, Beutler, & Levant, 2006).

Evidence-based practice is a potent force in psychotherapeutic practice today, and it may mandate the types of treatments therapists can offer in the future (Wampold & Bhati, 2004). In many mental health settings, clinicians are pressured to use interventions that are both brief and standardized. In such settings, treatments are operationalized by reliance on a treatment manual that identifies what is to be done in each therapy session and how many sessions will be required (Edwards et al., 2004). Edwards and his colleagues point out that psychological assessment and treatment is a business involving financial gain and reputation. In seeking to specify the treatment for a specific diagnosis as precisely as possible, health insurance companies are concerned with determining the minimum amount of treatment that can be expected to be effective. This raises ethical questions about whether the insurance company's need to save money is being placed above the needs of clients.

Many practitioners believe this approach is mechanistic and does not take into full consideration the relational dimensions of the psychotherapy process and individual variability. Indeed, relying exclusively on standardized treatments for specific problems may raise another set of ethical concerns because the reliability and validity of these empirically based techniques is questionable. Human change is complex and difficult to measure beyond such a simplistic level that the change may be meaningless. Furthermore, not all clients come to therapy with clearly defined psychological disorders. Many clients have existential concerns that do not fit with any diagnostic category and do not lend themselves to clearly specified symptom-based outcomes. EBP may have something to offer mental health professionals who work with individuals with specific emotional, cognitive, and behavioral disorders, but it does not have a great deal to offer practitioners working with individuals who want to pursue more meaning and fulfillment in their lives.

Counseling is not merely a technique that needs to be empirically validated. Many aspects of treatment—the therapy relationship, the therapist's personality and therapeutic style, the client, and environmental factors—are vital contributors to the success of psychotherapy. Evidence-based practices tend to emphasize only one of these aspects—interventions based on the best available research. Norcross and his colleagues (2006) argue for the centrality of the therapeutic relationship as a determinant of therapy outcomes. They add, however, that the *client* actually accounts for more of the treatment outcome than either the relationship or the method employed.

Norcross and his colleagues (2006) believe the call for accountability in mental health care is here to stay and that all mental health professionals are challenged by the mandate to demonstrate the efficiency, efficacy, and safety of the services they provide. They emphasize that the overarching goal of EBP is to enhance the effectiveness of client services and to improve public health and warn that mental health professionals need to take a proactive stance to make sure this goal is kept in focus. They realize there is potential for misuse and abuse by third-party payers who could selectively use research findings as cost-containment measures rather than ways of improving the quality of services delivered.

Miller, Duncan, and Hubble (2004) are critical of the EBP movement and argue that "significant improvements in client retention and outcome have been shown where therapists have feedback on the client's experience of the alliance and progress in treatment. Rather than evidence-based practice, therapists tailor their work through practice-based evidence" (p. 2). *Practice-based evidence* involves using data generated during treatment to inform the process and outcome of treatment. This topic is discussed in more detail in Chapter 15.

For further reading on the topic of evidence-based practice, I recommend *Clinician's Guide to Evidence-based Practice* (Norcross, Hogan, & Koocher, 2008).

MANAGING MULTIPLE RELATIONSHIPS IN COUNSELING PRACTICE

Dual or multiple relationships, either sexual or nonsexual, occur when counselors assume two (or more) roles simultaneously or sequentially with a client. This may involve assuming more than one professional role or combining professional and nonprofessional roles. The term *multiple relationship* is more often used than the term *dual relationship* because of the complexities involved in these relationships. The terms *dual relationships* and *multiple relationships* are used interchangeably in various professional codes of ethics, and the ACA (2005) uses the term *nonprofessional relationships*. In this section I use the broader term of *multiple relationships* to encompass both dual relationships and nonprofessional relationships.

When clinicians blend their professional relationship with another kind of relationship with a client, ethical concerns must be considered. Many forms of nonprofessional interactions or nonsexual multiple relationships pose a challenge to practitioners. Some examples of *nonsexual* dual or multiple relationships are combining the roles of teacher and therapist or of supervisor and therapist; bartering for goods or therapeutic services; borrowing money from a client; providing therapy to a friend, an employee, or a relative; engaging in a social relationship with a client; accepting an expensive gift from a client; or going into a business venture with a client. Some multiple relationships are clearly exploitative and do serious harm both to the client and to the professional. For example, becoming emotionally or sexually involved with a *current* client is clearly unethical, unprofessional, and illegal. Sexual involvement with a *former* client is unwise, can be exploitative, and is generally considered unethical.

Because nonsexual multiple relationships are necessarily complex and multi-dimensional, there are few simple and absolute answers to resolve them. It is not always possible to play a single role in your work as a counselor, nor is it always desirable. You may have to deal with managing multiple roles, regardless of the setting in which you work or the client population you serve. It is a wise practice to give careful thought to the complexities of multiple roles and relationships before embroiling yourself in ethically questionable situations.

Ethical reasoning and judgment come into play when ethics codes are applied to specific situations. The *ACA Code of Ethics* (ACA, 2005) stresses that counseling professionals must learn how to *manage* multiple roles and responsibilities in an ethical way. This entails dealing effectively with the power differential that is inherent in counseling relationships and training relationships, balancing boundary issues, addressing nonprofessional relationships, and striving to avoid using power in ways that might cause harm to clients, students, or supervisees (Herlihy & Corey, 2006b).

Although multiple relationships do carry inherent risks, it is a mistake to conclude that these relationships are always unethical and necessarily lead to harm and exploitation. Some of these relationships can be beneficial to clients if they are implemented thoughtfully and with integrity (Zur, 2007). An excellent resource on the ethical and clinical dimensions of multiple relationships is *Boundaries in Psychotherapy: Ethical and Clinical Explorations* (Zur, 2007).

Perspectives on Multiple Relationships

What makes multiple relationships so problematic? Herlihy and Corey (2006b) contend that some of the problematic aspects of engaging in multiple relationships are that they are pervasive; they can be difficult to recognize; they are unavoidable at times; they are potentially harmful, but not necessarily always harmful; they can be beneficial; and they are the subject of conflicting advice from various experts. A review of the literature reveals that dual and multiple relationships are hotly debated. Except for sexual intimacy with current clients, which is unequivocally unethical, there is not much consensus regarding the appropriate way to deal with multiple relationships.

Some of the codes of the professional organizations advise against forming multiple relationships, mainly because of the potential for misusing power, exploiting the client, and impairing objectivity. When multiple relationships exploit clients, or have significant potential to harm clients, they are unethical. The ethics codes do not mandate avoidance of all such relationships, however; nor do the codes imply that nonsexual multiple relationships are unethical. The current focus of ethics codes is to remain alert to the possibilities of harm to clients and to develop safeguard to protect clients. Although codes can provide some general guidelines, good judgment, the willingness to reflect on one's practices, and being aware of one's motivations are critical dimensions of an ethical practitioner. It bears repeating that multiple relationship issues cannot be resolved with ethics codes alone; counselors must think through all of the ethical and clinical dimensions involved in a wide range of boundary concerns.

A consensus of many writers is that multiple relationships are inevitable and unavoidable in some situations and that a global prohibition is not a realistic answer. Because interpersonal boundaries are not static but undergo redefinition over time, the challenge for practitioners is to learn how to manage boundary fluctuations and to deal effectively with overlapping roles (Herlihy & Corey, 2006b). One key to learning how to manage multiple relationships is to think of ways to minimize the risks involved.

WAYS OF MINIMIZING RISK In determining whether to proceed with a multiple relationship, it is critical to consider whether the potential benefit to the client of such a relationship outweighs its potential harm. Some relationships may have more potential benefits to clients than potential risks. It is your responsibility to develop safeguards aimed at reducing the potential for negative consequences. Herlihy and Corey (2006b) identify the following guidelines:

- Set healthy boundaries early in the therapeutic relationship. Informed consent is essential from the beginning and throughout the therapy process.
- Involve clients in ongoing discussions and in the decision-making process, and document your discussions. Discuss with your clients what you expect of them and what they can expect of you.
- Consult with fellow professionals as a way to maintain objectivity and identify unanticipated difficulties. Realize that you don't need to make a decision alone.
- When multiple relationships are potentially problematic, or when the risk for harm is high, it is always wise to work under supervision. Document the nature of this supervision and any actions you take in your records.
- Self-monitoring is critical throughout the process. Ask yourself whose needs are being met and examine your motivations for considering becoming involved in a dual or multiple relationship.

In working through a multiple relationship concern, it is best to begin by ascertaining whether such a relationship can be avoided. Nagy (2011) points out that multiple relationships cannot always be avoided, especially in small towns. Nor should every multiple relationship be considered unethical. However, when a therapist's objectivity and competence are compromised, the therapist may find that personal needs surface and diminish the quality of the therapist's professional work. Sometimes nonprofessional interactions are avoidable and your involvement would put the client needlessly at risk. In other cases multiple relationships are unavoidable. One way of dealing with any potential problems is to adopt a policy of completely avoiding any kind of nonprofessional interaction. As a general guideline, Nagy (2011) recommends avoiding multiple relationships to the extent this is possible. Therapists should document precautions taken to protect clients when such relationships are unavoidable. Another alternative is to deal with each dilemma as it develops, making full use of informed consent and at the same time seeking consultation and supervision in dealing with the situation. This second alternative includes a professional requirement for self-monitoring. It is one of the hallmarks of professionalism to be willing to grapple with these ethical complexities of day-to-day practice.

ESTABLISHING PERSONAL AND PROFESSIONAL BOUNDARIES Establishing and maintaining consistent yet flexible boundaries is necessary if you are to effectively counsel clients. If you have difficulty establishing and maintaining boundaries in your personal life, you are likely to find that you will have difficulty when it comes to managing boundaries in your professional life. Developing appropriate and effective boundaries in your counseling practice is the first step to learning how to manage multiple relationships. There is a relationship between developing appropriate boundaries in the personal and professional realms. If you are successful in establishing boundaries in various aspects of your personal life, you have a good foundation for creating sound boundaries with clients.

One important aspect of maintaining appropriate professional boundaries is to recognize boundary crossings and prevent them from becoming boundary violations. A **boundary crossing** is a departure from a commonly accepted practice that could *potentially* benefit a client. For example, attending the wedding of a client may be extending a boundary, but it could be beneficial for the client. In contrast, a **boundary violation** is a serious breach that harms the client and is therefore unethical. A boundary violation is a boundary crossing that takes the practitioner out of the professional role, which generally involves exploitation and results in harm to a client (Gutheil & Brodsky, 2008). Flexible boundaries can be useful in the counseling process when applied ethically. Some boundary crossings pose no ethical problems and may enhance the counseling relationship. Other boundary crossings may lead to a pattern of blurred professional roles and become problematic.

BECOMING AN ETHICAL COUNSELOR

Knowing and following your profession's code of ethics is part of being an ethical practitioner, but these codes do not make decisions for you. As you become involved in counseling, you will find that interpreting the ethical guidelines of your professional organization and applying them to particular situations demand the utmost ethical sensitivity. Even responsible practitioners differ over how to apply established ethical principles to specific situations. In your professional work you will deal with questions that do not always have obvious answers. You will have to assume responsibility for deciding how to act in ways that will further the best interests of your clients.

Throughout your professional life you will need to reexamine the ethical questions raised in this chapter. You can benefit from both formal and informal opportunities to discuss ethical dilemmas during your training program. Even if you resolve some ethical matters while completing a graduate program, there is no guarantee that these matters have been settled once and for all. These topics are bound to take on new dimensions as you gain more experience. Oftentimes students burden themselves unnecessarily with the expectation that they should resolve all potential ethical problem areas before they begin to practice. Throughout your professional life, seek consultation from trusted colleagues and supervisors whenever you face an ethical dilemma. Ethical decision-making is an evolutionary process that requires you to be continually open and self-reflective. Becoming an ethical practitioner is not a final destination but a journey that will continue throughout your career.

SUMMARY

It is essential that you learn a process for thinking about and dealing with ethical dilemmas, keeping in mind that most ethical issues are complex and defy simple solutions. A sign of good faith is your willingness to share your struggles with colleagues. Such consultation can be helpful in clarifying issues by giving you another perspective on a situation. The task of developing a sense of professional and ethical responsibility is never really finished, and new issues are constantly surfacing. Positive ethics demands periodic reflection and an openness to change.

If there is one fundamental question that can serve to tie together all the issues discussed in this chapter, it is this: "Who has the right to counsel another person?" This question can be the focal point of your reflection on ethical and professional issues. It also can be the basis of your self-examination each day that you meet with clients. Continue to ask yourself: "What makes me think I have a right to counsel others?" "What do I have to offer the people I'm counseling?" "Am I doing in my own life what I'm encouraging my clients to do?" At times you may feel that you have no ethical right to counsel others, perhaps because your own life isn't always the model you would like it to be for your clients. More important than resolving all of life's issues is knowing what kinds of questions to ask and remaining open to reflection.

This chapter has introduced you to a number of ethical issues that you are bound to face at some point in your counseling practice. I hope your interest has been piqued and that you will want to learn more. For further reading on this important topic, choose some of the books listed in the Recommended Supplementary Readings section for further study.

WHERE TO GO FROM HERE

The following professional organizations provide helpful information about what each group has to offer, including the code of ethics for the organization.

American Association for Marriage and Family Therapy (AAMFT)	www.aamft.org
American Counseling Association (ACA)	www.counseling.org
American Mental Health Counselors Association (AMHCA)	www.amhca.org
American Music Therapy Association	www.musictherapy.org
American Psychological Association (APA)	www.apa.org
American School Counselor Association (ASCA)	www.schoolcounselor.org
Commission on Rehabilitation Counselor Certification (CRCC)	www.crccertification.com
National Association of Alcohol and Drug Abuse Counselors (NAADAC)	www.naadac.org
National Association of Social Workers (NASW)	www.socialworkers.org
National Organization for Human Services (NOHS)	www.nationalhumanservices.org

Free Podcasts for ACA Members

You can download ACA Podcasts (prerecorded interviews) relevant to topics discussed in Chapter 3 by going to www.counseling.org, clicking on the Resource button, and selecting the Podcast Series:

Multicultural and Diversity (Dr. Courtland Lee)

The Counselor and the Law: A Guide to Legal and Ethical Practice (Drs. Nancy Wheeler and Burt Bertram)

The Ethics of Confidentiality, Who Needs to Know What? (Larry Freeman)

The Death of Dual Relationships, or Relationships with Clients, Beneficial Versus Harmful (Dr. Rocco Cottone)

Clinical Supervision in the Helping Professions (Drs. Gerald Corey, Robert Haynes, Patrice Moulton, and Michelle Muratori)

For interviews on topics introduced in subsequent chapters, see the following podcasts:

Chapter 5: Adlerian Theory and Practice (Dr. Jon Carlson)

Chapter 6: Existential Therapy (Dr. Gerald Corey)

Chapter 7: Carl Rogers and the Person-Centered Approach (Dr. Howard Kirschenbaum)

Chapter 11: Reality Therapy, Choice Theory: What's the Difference? (Dr. Robert Wubbolding)

Chapter 13: Solution-Focused Counseling in Schools (Dr. John Murphy)

Chapter 13: Narrative Therapy: Remembering Lives, Conversations With the Dying and Bereaved (Lorraine Hedtke, MSW, LCSW, and Dr. John Winslade)

PART 2

Theories and Techniques of Counseling

Psychoanalytic Therapy

SIGMUND FREUD

Index Stock Imagery/PhotoLibrary

SIGMUND FREUD (1856–1939) was the firstborn in a Viennese family of three boys and five girls. His father, like many others of his time and place, was very authoritarian. Freud's family background is a factor to consider in understanding the development of his theory.

Even though Freud's family had limited finances and was forced to live in a crowded apartment, his parents made every effort to foster his obvious intellectual capacities. Freud had many interests, but his career choices were restricted because of his Jewish heritage. He finally settled on medicine. Only 4 years after earning his medical degree from the University of Vienna at the age of 26, he attained a prestigious position there as a lecturer.

Freud devoted most of his life to formulating and extending his theory of psychoanalysis. Interestingly, the most creative phase of his life corresponded to a period when he was experiencing severe emotional problems of his own. During his early 40s, Freud had numerous psychosomatic disorders, as well as exaggerated fears of dying and other phobias, and was involved in the difficult task of self-analysis. By exploring the meaning of his own dreams, he gained insights into the dynamics of personality development. He first examined his childhood memories and came to realize the intense hostility he had felt for his father. He also recalled his childhood sexual feelings for his mother, who was attractive, loving, and protective. He then clinically formulated his theory as he observed his patients work through their own problems in analysis.

Freud had very little tolerance for colleagues who diverged from his psychoanalytic doctrines. He attempted to keep control over the movement by expelling those who dared to disagree. Carl Jung and Alfred Adler, for example, worked closely with Freud, but each founded his own therapeutic school after repeated disagreements with Freud on theoretical and clinical issues.

Freud was highly creative and productive, frequently putting in 18-hour days. His collected works fill 24 volumes. Freud's productivity remained at this prolific level until late in his life when he contracted cancer of the jaw. During his last two decades, he underwent 33 operations and was in almost constant pain. He died in London in 1939.

As the originator of psychoanalysis, Freud distinguished himself as an intellectual giant. He pioneered new techniques for understanding human behavior, and his efforts resulted in the most comprehensive theory of personality and psychotherapy ever developed.

INTRODUCTION

Freud's views continue to influence contemporary practice. Many of his basic concepts are still part of the foundation on which other theorists build and develop. Indeed, most of the theories of counseling and psychotherapy discussed in this book have been influenced by psychoanalytic principles and techniques. Some of these therapeutic approaches extended the psychoanalytic model, others modified its concepts and procedures, and others emerged as a reaction against it.

Freud's psychoanalytic system is a model of personality development and an approach to psychotherapy. He gave psychotherapy a new look and new horizons, calling attention to psychodynamic factors that motivate behavior, focusing on the role of the unconscious, and developing the first therapeutic procedures for understanding and modifying the structure of one's basic character. Freud's theory is a benchmark against which many other theories are measured.

I begin with a discussion of the basic psychoanalytic concepts and practices that originated with Freud, then provide a glimpse of a few of the diverse approaches that fall well within his legacy. We are in an era of theoretical pluralism in psychoanalytic theory today and can no longer speak of *the* psychoanalytic theory of treatment (Wolitzky, 2011b). Both psychoanalysis and its more flexible variant, psychoanalytically oriented psychotherapy, are discussed. In addition, I summarize Erik Erikson's theory of psychosocial development, which extends Freudian theory in several ways, and give brief attention to Carl Jung's approach. Finally, we look at contemporary self-psychology, object relations theory, and the relational model of psychoanalysis, which are variations on psychoanalytic theory that entail modification or abandonment of Freud's drive theory but take Freud's theories as their point of departure (Wolitzky, 2011b). Although deviating significantly from traditional Freudian psychoanalysis, these approaches retain the emphasis on the unconscious, the role of transference and countertransference, and the importance of early life experiences.

 See the DVD program for Chapter 4, *DVD for Theory and Practice of Counseling and Psychotherapy: The Case of Stan and Lecturettes*. I suggest that you view the brief lecture for each chapter prior to reading the chapter.

KEY CONCEPTS

View of Human Nature

The Freudian view of human nature is basically deterministic. According to Freud, our behavior is determined by irrational forces, unconscious motivations, and biological and instinctual drives as these evolve through key psychosexual stages in the first years of life.

Instincts are central to the Freudian approach. Although he originally used the term **libido** to refer to sexual energy, he later broadened it to include the energy of all the **life instincts**. These instincts serve the purpose of the survival of the individual and the human race; they are oriented toward growth, development, and creativity. Libido, then, should be understood as a source of motivation that encompasses sexual energy but goes beyond it. Freud includes all pleasurable acts in his concept of the life instincts; he sees the goal of much of life as gaining pleasure and avoiding pain.

Freud also postulates **death instincts**, which account for the aggressive drive. At times, people manifest through their behavior an unconscious wish to die or to hurt themselves or others. Managing this aggressive drive is a major challenge to the human race. In Freud's view, both sexual and aggressive drives are powerful determinants of why people act as they do.

Structure of Personality

According to the Freudian psychoanalytic view, the personality consists of three systems: the id, the ego, and the superego. These are names for psychological structures and should not be thought of as manikins that separately operate the personality; one's personality functions as a whole rather than as three discrete segments. The **id** is roughly all the untamed drives or impulses that might be likened to the biological component. The **ego** attempts to organize and mediate between the id and the reality of dangers posed by the id's impulses. One way to protect ourselves from the dangers of our own drives is to establish a **superego**, which is the internalized social component, largely rooted in what the person imagines to be the expectations of parental figures. Because the point of taking in these imagined expectations is to protect ourselves from our own impulses, the superego may be more punitive and demanding than the person's parents really were. Actions of the ego may or may not be conscious. For example, defenses typically are not conscious. Because ego and consciousness are not the same, the slogan for psychoanalysis has shifted from "making the unconscious conscious" to "where there was id, let there be ego."

From the orthodox Freudian perspective, humans are viewed as energy systems. The dynamics of personality consist of the ways in which psychic energy is distributed to the id, ego, and superego. Because the amount of energy is limited, one system gains control over the available energy at the expense of the other two systems. Behavior is determined by this psychic energy.

THE ID The **id** is the original system of personality; at birth a person is all id. The id is the primary source of psychic energy and the seat of the instincts. It lacks organization and is blind, demanding, and insistent. A cauldron of seething excitement, the id cannot tolerate tension, and it functions to discharge tension immediately. Ruled by the **pleasure principle**, which is aimed at reducing tension, avoiding pain, and gaining pleasure, the id is illogical, amoral, and driven to satisfy instinctual needs. The id never matures, remaining the spoiled brat of personality. It does not think, but only wishes or acts. The id is largely unconscious, or out of awareness.

THE EGO The **ego** has contact with the external world of reality. It is the "executive" that governs, controls, and regulates the personality. As a "traffic cop," it mediates between the instincts and the surrounding environment. The ego controls consciousness and exercises censorship. Ruled by the **reality principle**, the ego does realistic and logical thinking and formulates plans of action for satisfying needs. The ego, as the seat of intelligence and rationality, checks and controls the blind impulses of the id. Whereas the id knows only subjective reality, the ego distinguishes between mental images and things in the external world.

THE SUPEREGO The **superego** is the judicial branch of personality. It includes a person's moral code, the main concern being whether an action is good or bad, right or wrong. It represents the ideal rather than the real and strives not for pleasure but for perfection. The superego represents the traditional values and ideals of society as they are handed down from parents to children. It functions to inhibit the id impulses, to persuade the ego to substitute moralistic goals for realistic ones, and to strive for perfection. The superego, then, as the internalization of the standards of parents and society, is related to psychological rewards and punishments. The rewards are feelings of pride and self-love; the punishments are feelings of guilt and inferiority.

Consciousness and the Unconscious

Perhaps Freud's greatest contributions are his concepts of the unconscious and of the levels of consciousness, which are the keys to understanding behavior and the problems of personality. The unconscious cannot be studied directly but is inferred from behavior. Clinical evidence for postulating the unconscious includes the following: (1) dreams, which are symbolic representations of unconscious needs, wishes, and conflicts; (2) slips of the tongue and forgetting, for example, a familiar name; (3) posthypnotic suggestions; (4) material derived from free-association techniques; (5) material derived from projective techniques; and (6) the symbolic content of psychotic symptoms.

For Freud, consciousness is a thin slice of the total mind. Like the greater part of the iceberg that lies below the surface of the water, the larger part of the mind exists below the surface of awareness. The **unconscious** stores all experiences, memories, and repressed material. Needs and motivations that are inaccessible—that is, out of awareness—are also outside the sphere of conscious control. Most psychological functioning exists in the out-of-awareness realm. The aim of psychoanalytic therapy, therefore, is to make the unconscious motives conscious, for only then can an individual exercise choice. Understanding the role of the unconscious is central to grasping the essence of the psychoanalytic model of behavior.

Unconscious processes are at the root of all forms of neurotic symptoms and behaviors. From this perspective, a "cure" is based on uncovering the meaning of symptoms, the causes of behavior, and the repressed materials that interfere with healthy functioning. It is to be noted, however, that intellectual insight alone does not resolve the symptom. The client's need to cling to old patterns (repetition) must be confronted by working through transference distortions, a process discussed later in this chapter.

Anxiety

Also essential to the psychoanalytic approach is its concept of anxiety. **Anxiety** is a feeling of dread that results from repressed feelings, memories, desires, and experience that emerge to the surface of awareness. It can be considered as a state of tension that motivates us to do something. It develops out of a conflict among the id, ego, and superego over control of the available psychic energy. The function of anxiety is to warn of impending danger.

There are three kinds of anxiety: reality, neurotic, and moral. **Reality anxiety** is the fear of danger from the external world, and the level of such anxiety is proportionate to the degree of real threat. Neurotic and moral anxieties are evoked by threats to the "balance of power" within the person. They signal to the ego that unless appropriate measures are taken the danger may increase until the ego is overthrown. **Neurotic anxiety** is the fear that the instincts will get out of hand and cause one to do something for which one will be punished. **Moral anxiety** is the fear of one's own conscience. People with a well-developed conscience tend to feel guilty when they do something contrary to their moral code. When the ego cannot control anxiety by rational and direct methods, it relies on indirect ones—namely, ego-defense behavior.

Ego-Defense Mechanisms

Ego-defense mechanisms help the individual cope with anxiety and prevent the ego from being overwhelmed. Rather than being pathological, ego defenses are normal behaviors that can have adaptive value provided they do not become a style of life that enables the individual to avoid facing reality. The defenses employed depend on the individual's level of development and degree of anxiety. Defense mechanisms have two characteristics in common: (1) they either deny or distort reality, and (2) they operate on an unconscious level. Table 4.1 provides brief descriptions of some common ego defenses.

TABLE 4.1 Ego-Defense Mechanisms

	DEFENSE	USES FOR BEHAVIOR
Repression	Threatening or painful thoughts and feelings are excluded from awareness.	One of the most important Freudian processes, it is the basis of many other ego defenses and of neurotic disorders. Freud explained repression as an involuntary removal of something from consciousness. It is assumed that most of the painful events of the first 5 or 6 years of life are buried, yet these events do influence later behavior.
Denial	"Closing one's eyes" to the existence of a threatening aspect of reality.	Denial of reality is perhaps the simplest of all self-defense mechanisms. It is a way of distorting what the individual thinks, feels, or perceives in a traumatic situation. This mechanism is similar to repression, yet it generally operates at preconscious and conscious levels.
Reaction formation	Actively expressing the opposite impulse when confronted with a threatening impulse.	By developing conscious attitudes and behaviors that are diametrically opposed to disturbing desires, people do not have to face the anxiety that would result if they were to recognize these dimensions of themselves. Individuals may conceal hate with a facade of love, be extremely nice when they harbor negative reactions, or mask cruelty with excessive kindness.
Projection	Attributing to others one's own unacceptable desires and impulses.	This is a mechanism of self-deception. Lustful, aggressive, or other impulses are seen as being possessed by "those people out there, but not by me."
Displacement	Directing energy toward another object or person when the original object or person is inaccessible.	Displacement is a way of coping with anxiety that involves discharging impulses by shifting from a threatening object to a "safer target." For example, the meek man who feels intimidated by his boss comes home and unloads inappropriate hostility onto his children.
Rationalization	Manufacturing "good" reasons to explain away a bruised ego.	Rationalization helps justify specific behaviors, and it aids in softening the blow connected with disappointments. When people do not get positions they have applied for in their work, they think of logical reasons they did not succeed, and they sometimes attempt to convince themselves that they really did not want the position anyway.

(continues)

TABLE 4.1 Ego-Defense Mechanisms *(continued)*

	DEFENSE	USES FOR BEHAVIOR
Sublimation	Diverting sexual or aggressive energy into other channels.	Energy is usually diverted into socially acceptable and sometimes even admirable channels. For example, aggressive impulses can be channeled into athletic activities, so that the person finds a way of expressing aggressive feelings and, as an added bonus, is often praised.
Regression	Going back to an earlier phase of development when there were fewer demands.	In the face of severe stress or extreme challenge, individuals may attempt to cope with their anxiety by clinging to immature and inappropriate behaviors. For example, children who are frightened in school may indulge in infantile behavior such as weeping, excessive dependence, thumbsucking, hiding, or clinging to the teacher.
Introjection	Taking in and "swallowing" the values and standards of others.	Positive forms of introjection include incorporation of parental values or the attributes and values of the therapist (assuming that these are not merely uncritically accepted). One negative example is that in concentration camps some of the prisoners dealt with overwhelming anxiety by accepting the values of the enemy through identification with the aggressor.
Identification	Identifying with successful causes, organizations, or people in the hope that you will be perceived as worthwhile.	Identification can enhance self-worth and protect one from a sense of being a failure. This is part of the developmental process by which children learn gender-role behaviors, but it can also be a defensive reaction when used by people who feel basically inferior.
Compensation	Masking perceived weaknesses or developing certain positive traits to make up for limitations.	This mechanism can have direct adjustive value, and it can also be an attempt by the person to say "Don't see the ways in which I am inferior, but see me in my accomplishments."

Development of Personality

IMPORTANCE OF EARLY DEVELOPMENT A significant contribution of the psychoanalytic model is delineation of the stages of psychosexual and psychosocial stages of development from birth through adulthood. The **psychosexual stages** refer to the Freudian chronological phases of development, beginning in infancy.

Freud postulated three early stages of development that often bring people to counseling when not appropriately resolved. First is the **oral stage,** which deals with the inability to trust oneself and others, resulting in the fear of loving and forming close relationships and low self-esteem. Next is the **anal stage,** which deals with the inability to recognize and express anger, leading to the denial of one's own power as a person and the lack of a sense of autonomy. Third is the **phallic stage,** which deals with the inability to fully accept one's sexuality and sexual feelings, and also to difficulty in accepting oneself as a man or woman. According to the Freudian psychoanalytic view, these three areas of personal and social development—love and trust, dealing with negative feelings, and developing a positive acceptance of sexuality—are all grounded in the first 6 years of life. This period is the foundation on which later personality development is built. When a child's needs are not adequately met during these stages of development, an individual may become fixated at that stage and behave in psychologically immature ways later on in life.

ERIKSON'S PSYCHOSOCIAL PERSPECTIVE The developmental stages postulated by Freud have been expanded by other theorists. Erik Erikson's (1963) psychosocial perspective on personality development is especially significant. Erikson built on Freud's ideas and extended his theory by stressing the psychosocial aspects of development beyond early childhood. The **psychosocial stages** refer to Erikson's basic psychological and social tasks, which individuals need to master at intervals from infancy through old age. This stage perspective provides the counselor with the conceptual tools for understanding key developmental tasks characteristic of the various stages of life. Erikson's theory of development holds that psychosexual growth and psychosocial growth take place together, and that at each stage of life we face the task of establishing equilibrium between ourselves and our social world. He describes development in terms of the entire life span, divided by specific crises to be resolved. According to Erikson, a **crisis** is equivalent to a turning point in life when we have the potential to move forward or to regress. At these turning points, we can either resolve our conflicts or fail to master the developmental task. To a large extent, our life is the result of the choices we make at each of these stages.

Erikson is often credited with bringing an emphasis on social factors to contemporary psychoanalysis. **Classical psychoanalysis** is grounded on **id psychology,** and it holds that instincts and intrapsychic conflicts are the basic factors shaping personality development (both normal and abnormal). **Contemporary psychoanalysis** tends to be based on **ego psychology,** which does not deny the role of intrapsychic conflicts but emphasizes the striving of the ego for mastery and competence throughout the human life span. Ego psychology deals with both the early and the later developmental stages, for the assumption is that current problems cannot simply be reduced to repetitions of unconscious conflicts from early childhood. The stages of adolescence, mid-adulthood, and later adulthood all involve particular crises that must be addressed. As one's past has meaning in terms of the future, there is continuity in development, reflected by stages of growth; each stage is related to the other stages.

Viewing an individual's development from a combined perspective that includes both psychosexual and psychosocial factors is useful. Erikson believed Freud did not go far enough in explaining the ego's place in development and did not give enough attention to social influences throughout the life span. A comparison of Freud's psychosexual view and Erikson's psychosocial view of the stages of development is presented in Table 4.2.

TABLE 4.2 Comparison of Freud's Psychosexual Stages and Erikson's Psychosocial Stages		
PERIOD OF LIFE	**FREUD**	**ERIKSON**
First year of life	*Oral stage* Sucking at mother's breasts satisfies need for food and pleasure. Infant needs to get basic nurturing, or later feelings of greediness and acquisitiveness may develop. Oral fixations result from deprivation of oral gratification in infancy. Later personality problems can include mistrust of others, rejecting others; love, and fear of or inability to form intimate relationships.	*Infancy: Trust versus mistrust* If significant others provide for basic physical and emotional needs, infant develops a sense of trust. If basic needs are not met, an attitude of mistrust toward the world, especially toward interpersonal relationships, is the result.
Ages 1–3	*Anal stage* Anal zone becomes of major significance in formation of personality. Main developmental tasks include learning independence, accepting personal power, and learning to express negative feelings such as rage and aggression. Parental discipline patterns and attitudes have significant consequences for child's later personality development.	*Early childhood: Autonomy versus shame and doubt* A time for developing autonomy. Basic struggle is between a sense of self-reliance and a sense of self-doubt. Child needs to explore and experiment, to make mistakes, and to test limits. If parents promote dependency, child's autonomy is inhibited and capacity to deal with world successfully is hampered.
Ages 3–6	*Phallic stage* Basic conflict centers on unconscious incestuous desires that child develops for parent of opposite sex and that, because of their threatening nature, are repressed. Male phallic stage, known as *Oedipus complex,* involves mother as love object for boy. Female phallic stage, known as *Electra complex,* involves girl's striving for father's love and approval. How parents respond, verbally and nonverbally, to child's emerging sexuality has an impact on sexual attitudes and feelings that child develops.	*Preschool age: Initiative versus guilt* Basic task is to achieve a sense of competence and initiative. If children are given freedom to select personally meaningful activities, they tend to develop a positive view of self and follow through with their projects. If they are not allowed to make their own decisions, they tend to develop guilt over taking initiative. They then refrain from taking an active stance and allow others to choose for them

Ages 6–12	Latency stage After the torment of sexual impulses of preceding years, this period is relatively quiescent. Sexual interests are replaced by interests in school, playmates, sports, and a range of new activities. This is a time of socialization as child turns outward and forms relationships with others.	School age: Industry versus inferiority Child needs to expand understanding of world, continue to develop appropriate gender-role identity, and learn the basic skills required for school success. Basic task is to achieve a sense of industry, which refers to setting and attaining personal goals. Failure to do so results in a sense of inadequacy.
Ages 12–18	Genital stage Old themes of phallic stage are revived. This stage begins with puberty and lasts until senility sets in. Even though there are societal restrictions and taboos, adolescents can deal with sexual energy by investing it in various socially acceptable activities such as forming friendships, engaging in art or in sports, and preparing for a career.	Adolescence: Identity versus role confusion A time of transition between childhood and adulthood. A time for testing limits, for breaking dependent ties, and for establishing a new identity. Major conflicts center on clarification of self-identity, life goals, and life's meaning. Failure to achieve a sense of identity results in role confusion.
Ages 18–35	Genital stage continues Core characteristic of mature adult is the freedom "to love and to work." This move toward adulthood involves freedom from parental influence and capacity to care for others.	Young adulthood: Intimacy versus isolation. Developmental task at this time is to form intimate relationships. Failure to achieve intimacy can lead to alienation and isolation.
Ages 35–60	Genital stage continues	Middle age: Generativity versus stagnation. There is a need to go beyond self and family and be involved in helping the next generation. This is a time of adjusting to the discrepancy between one's dream and one's actual accomplishments. Failure to achieve a sense of productivity often leads to psychological stagnation.
Ages 60+	Genital stage continues	Later life: Integrity versus despair If one looks back on life with few regrets and feels personally worthwhile, ego integrity results. Failure to achieve ego integrity can lead to feelings of despair, hopelessness, guilt, resentment, and self-rejection.

COUNSELING IMPLICATIONS By taking a combined psychosexual and psychosocial perspective, counselors have a helpful conceptual framework for understanding developmental issues as they appear in therapy. The key needs and developmental tasks, along with the challenges inherent at each stage of life, provide a model for understanding some of the core conflicts clients explore in their therapy sessions. Questions such as these can give direction to the therapeutic process:

- What are some major developmental tasks at each stage in life, and how are these tasks related to counseling?
- What themes give continuity to this individual's life?
- What are some universal concerns of people at various points in life? How can people be challenged to make life-affirming choices at these points?
- What is the relationship between an individual's current problems and significant events from earlier years?
- What choices were made at critical periods, and how did the person deal with these various crises?
- What are the sociocultural factors influencing development that need to be understood if therapy is to be comprehensive?

Psychosocial theory gives special weight to childhood and adolescent factors that are significant in later stages of development while recognizing that the later stages also have their significant crises. Themes and threads can be found running throughout clients' lives.

THE THERAPEUTIC PROCESS

Therapeutic Goals

The ultimate goal of psychoanalytic treatment is to increase adaptive functioning, which involves the reduction of symptoms and the resolution of conflicts (Wolitzky, 2011a). Two goals of Freudian psychoanalytic therapy are to make the unconscious conscious and to strengthen the ego so that behavior is based more on reality and less on instinctual cravings or irrational guilt. Successful analysis is believed to result in significant modification of the individual's personality and character structure. Therapeutic methods are used to bring out unconscious material. Then childhood experiences are reconstructed, discussed, interpreted, and analyzed. It is clear that the process is not limited to solving problems and learning new behaviors. Rather, there is a deeper probing into the past to develop the level of self-understanding that is assumed to be necessary for a change in character. Psychoanalytic therapy is oriented toward achieving insight, but not just an intellectual understanding; it is essential that the feelings and memories associated with this self-understanding be experienced.

Therapist's Function and Role

In classical psychoanalysis, analysts typically assume an anonymous stance, which is sometimes called the **"blank-screen" approach**. They engage in very little self-disclosure and maintain a sense of neutrality to foster a **transference relationship**, in which their clients will make *projections* onto them. This transference relationship, which is a cornerstone of psychoanalysis, "refers to the transfer of feelings originally experienced in an early relationship to other important people in a person's present environment" (Luborsky, O'Reilly-Landry, & Arlow, 2011, p. 18). If therapists say little about themselves and rarely share their personal reactions, the assumption is that whatever the client feels toward them will largely be the product of feelings associated with other significant figures from the past. These projections, which have their origins in unfinished and repressed situations, are considered "grist for the mill," and their analysis is the very essence of therapeutic work.

One of the central functions of analysis is to help clients acquire the freedom to love, work, and play. Other functions include assisting clients in achieving self-awareness, honesty, and more effective personal relationships; in dealing with anxiety in a realistic way; and in gaining control over impulsive and irrational behavior. The analyst must first establish a working relationship with the client and then do a great deal of listening and interpreting. The empathic attunement to the client facilitates the analyst's apprehension and appreciation of the client's intrapsychic world (Wolitzky, 2011b). Particular attention is given to the client's resistances. The analyst listens, learns, and decides when to make appropriate interpretations. A major function of interpretation is to accelerate the process of uncovering unconscious material. The analyst listens for gaps and inconsistencies in the client's story, infers the meaning of reported dreams and free associations, and remains sensitive to clues concerning the client's feelings toward the analyst.

Organizing these therapeutic processes within the context of understanding personality structure and psychodynamics enables the analyst to formulate the nature of the client's problems. One of the central functions of the analyst is to teach clients the meaning of these processes (through interpretation) so that they are able to achieve insight into their problems, increase their awareness of ways to change, and thus gain more control over their lives.

The process of psychoanalytic therapy is somewhat like putting the pieces of a puzzle together. Whether clients change depends considerably more on their readiness to change than on the accuracy of the therapist's interpretations. If the therapist pushes the client too rapidly or offers ill-timed interpretations, therapy will not be effective. Change occurs through the process of reworking old patterns so that clients might become freer to act in new ways (Luborsky et al., 2011).

Client's Experience in Therapy

Clients interested in traditional (or classical) psychoanalysis must be willing to commit themselves to an intensive and long-term therapy process. After some face-to-face sessions with the analyst, clients lie on a couch and engage in **free association**; that is, they try to say whatever comes to mind without self-censorship. This process of free association is known as the "fundamental rule." Clients report their feelings, experiences, associations, memories, and fantasies to the analyst. Lying on the couch encourages deep, uncensored reflections and reduces the stimuli that might interfere with getting in touch with internal conflicts and productions. It also reduces clients' ability to "read" their analyst's face for reactions and, hence, fosters the projections characteristic of a transference. At the same time, the analyst is freed from having to carefully monitor facial clues.

The client in psychoanalysis experiences a unique relationship with the analyst. The client is free to express any idea or feeling, no matter how irresponsible, scandalous, politically incorrect, selfish, or infantile. The analyst remains nonjudgmental, listening carefully and asking questions and making interpretations as the analysis progresses. This structure encourages the client to loosen defense mechanisms and "regress," experiencing a less rigid level of adjustment that allows for positive therapeutic growth but also involves some vulnerability. It is a responsibility of the analyst to keep the analytic situation safe for the client, so the analyst is *not* free to engage in spontaneous self-expression. Every intervention by the therapist is made to further the client's progress. Therapeutic neutrality and anonymity are valued by the analytic therapist, and holding a consistent setting or "frame" plays a large part in this analytic technique. Therapeutic change requires an extended period of "working through" old patterns in the safety of the therapeutic relationship.

What has just been described is **classical psychoanalysis**. Psychodynamic therapy emerged as a way of shortening and simplifying the lengthy process of classical psychoanalysis (Luborsky et al., 2011). Many psychoanalytically oriented practitioners, or psychodynamic therapists (as distinct from analysts), do not use all the techniques associated with classical analysis. However, psychodynamic therapists do remain alert to transference manifestations, explore the meaning of clients' dreams, explore both the past and the present, and are concerned with unconscious material. Traditional analytic therapists make more frequent interpretations of transferences and engage in fewer supportive interventions than is the case with psychodynamic therapists (Wolitzky, 2011a).

Clients in psychoanalytic therapy make a commitment with the therapist to stick with the procedures of an intensive therapeutic process. They agree to talk because their verbal productions are the heart of psychoanalytic therapy. They are typically asked not to make any radical changes in their lifestyle during the period of analysis, such as getting a divorce or quitting their job. The reason for avoiding making such changes pertains to the therapeutic process that oftentimes is unsettling and also associated with loosening of defenses. These restrictions are less relevant to psychoanalytic psychotherapy than to classical psychoanalysis. Psychoanalytic psychotherapy typically involves fewer sessions per week, the sessions are usually face to face, and the therapist is supportive; hence, there is less therapeutic "regression."

Psychoanalytic clients are ready to terminate their sessions when they and their analyst mutually agree that they have resolved those symptoms and core conflicts that were amenable to resolution, have clarified and accepted their remaining emotional problems, have understood the historical roots of their difficulties, have mastery of core themes, have insight into how their environment affects them and how they affect the environment, have achieved reduced defensiveness, and can integrate their awareness of past problems with their present relationships. Wolitzky (2011a) lists other optimal criteria for termination, including the reduction of transference, accomplishing the main goals of therapy, an acceptance of the futility of certain strivings and childhood fantasies, an increased capacity for love and work, achieving more stable coping patterns, and a self-analytic capacity. Successful analysis answers a client's "why" questions regarding his or her life. Curtis and Hirsch (2011) suggest that termination tends to bring up intense feelings of attachment, separation, and loss. Thus a termination date is set well enough in advance to talk about these feelings and about what the client learned in psychotherapy. Therapists assist clients in clarifying what they have done to bring about changes.

Relationship Between Therapist and Client

There are some differences between how the therapeutic relationship is conceptualized by classical analysis and current relational analysis. The classical analyst stands outside the relationship, comments on it, and offers insight-producing interpretations. In contemporary relational psychoanalysis, the therapist does not strive for a nonparticipating, detached, and objective stance, but is attuned to the nature of the therapeutic relationship, which is viewed as a key factor in bringing about change (Ainslie, 2007; Curtis & Hirsch, 2011; Wolitzky, 2011b). Contemporary analysts focus as much on here-and-now transference as on earlier reenactment. By bringing the past into the present relationship, a new understanding of the past can unfold (Wolitzky, 2011a). Contemporary psychodynamic therapists view their emotional communication with clients as a useful way to gain information and create connection (Luborsky et al., 2011; Wolitzky, 2011a, 2011b).

A significant aspect of the therapeutic relationship is manifested through transference reactions. **Transference** is the client's unconscious shifting to the analyst of feelings and fantasies that are reactions to significant others in the client's past. Transference involves the unconscious repetition of the past in the present. "It reflects the deep patterning of old experiences in relationships as they emerge in current life" (Luborsky et al., 2011, p. 47). A client often has a variety of feelings and reactions to a therapist, including a mixture of positive and negative feelings. When these feelings become conscious, clients can understand and resolve "unfinished business" from these past relationships. As therapy progresses, childhood feelings and conflicts begin to surface from the depths of the unconscious. Clients regress emotionally. Some of their feelings arise from conflicts such as trust versus mistrust, love versus hate, dependence versus independence, and autonomy versus shame and guilt. Transference takes place when clients resurrect from their early years intense conflicts relating to love, sexuality, hostility, anxiety, and resentment; bring them into the present; reexperience them; and attach them to the therapist. For example, clients may transfer unresolved feelings toward a stern and unloving father to the therapist, who, in their eyes, becomes stern and unloving. Angry feelings are the product of negative transference, but clients also may develop a positive transference and, for example, fall in love with the therapist, wish to be adopted, or in many other ways seek the love, acceptance, and approval of an all-powerful therapist. In short, the therapist becomes a current substitute for significant others.

If therapy is to produce change, the transference relationship must be worked through. The **working-through** process consists of repetitive and elaborate explorations of unconscious material and defenses, most of which originated in early childhood. Working through is achieved by repeating interpretations and by exploring forms of resistance. It results in a resolution of old patterns and allows clients to make new choices. Effective therapy requires that the client develop a relationship with the therapist in the present that is a corrective and integrative experience. By experiencing a therapist who is engaged, caring, and reliable, clients can be changed in profound ways, which can lead to new experiences of human relationships (Ainslie, 2007).

Clients have many opportunities to see the variety of ways in which their core conflicts and core defenses are manifested in their daily life. It is assumed that for clients to become psychologically independent they must not only become aware of this unconscious material but also achieve some level of freedom from behavior motivated by infantile strivings, such as the need for total love and acceptance from parental figures. If this demanding phase of the therapeutic relationship is not properly worked through, clients simply transfer their infantile wishes for universal love and acceptance to other figures. It is precisely in the client–therapist relationship that the manifestation of these childhood motivations becomes apparent.

Regardless of the length of psychoanalytic therapy, traces of our childhood needs and traumas will never be completely erased. Infantile conflicts may not be fully resolved, even though many aspects of transference are worked through with a therapist. We may need to struggle at times throughout our life with feelings that we project onto others as well as with unrealistic demands that we expect others to fulfill. In this sense we experience transference with many people, and our past is always a vital part of the person we are presently becoming.

It is a mistake to assume that all feelings clients have toward their therapists are manifestations of transference. Many of these reactions may have a reality base, and clients' feelings may well be directed to the here-and-now style the therapist exhibits. Not every positive response (such as liking the therapist) should be labeled "positive transference." Conversely, a client's anger toward the therapist may be a function of the therapist's behavior; it is a mistake to label all negative reactions as signs of "negative transference." According to Wolitzky (2011b), the contemporary psychoanalytic therapist does not view transference as a distortion but as a plausible perspective taken by the client based on perceptions of the therapist's personality and behavior. When there are differences in inferences between client and therapist, these differences are negotiated to reach a consensus.

The notion of never becoming completely free of past experiences has significant implications for therapists who become intimately involved in the unresolved conflicts of their clients. Even if the conflicts of therapists have surfaced to awareness, and even if therapists have dealt with these personal issues in their own intensive therapy, they may still project distortions onto clients. The intense therapeutic relationship is bound to ignite some of the conscious and unconscious conflicts within therapists. From a traditional psychoanalytic perspective, **countertransference** is viewed as a phenomenon that occurs when there is inappropriate affect, when therapists respond in irrational ways, or when they lose their objectivity in a relationship because their own conflicts are triggered. Wolitzky (2011b) states that over the years this traditional view of countertransference has broadened to include all of the therapist's reactions, not only to the client's transference but to all aspects of the client's personality and behavior. In this broader perspective, countertransference involves the therapist's total emotional response to a client. In today's psychoanalytic practice, countertransference is manifested in the form of subtle nonverbal, tonal, and attitudinal actions that inevitably affect clients, either consciously or unconsciously (Curtis & Hirsch, 2011).

It is critical that therapists become aware of their countertransference so that their reactions toward clients do not interfere with their objectivity. For example, a male client may become excessively dependent on his female therapist. The client may look to her to direct him and tell him how to live, and he may look to her for the love and acceptance that he felt he was unable to secure from his mother. The therapist herself may have unresolved needs to nurture, to foster a dependent relationship, and to be told that she is significant, and she may be meeting her own needs by in some way keeping her client dependent. Unless she is aware of her own needs as well as her own dynamics, it is very likely that her dynamics will interfere with the progress of therapy.

Not all countertransference reactions are detrimental to therapeutic progress. Indeed, countertransference reactions are often the strongest source of data for understanding the world of the client and for self-understanding on the therapist's part. The therapist's countertransference reactions are inevitable because all therapists have unresolved conflicts, personal vulnerabilities, and unconscious "soft spots" that are activated through their professional work (Curtis & Hirsch, 2011; Hayes, Gelso, & Hummel, 2011; Wolitkzy, 2011a). Hayes (2004) reports that most research on countertransference has dealt with its deleterious effects and how to manage these reactions. Hayes adds that it would be useful to undertake systematic study of the potential therapeutic benefits of countertransference.

Although countertransference can greatly benefit the therapeutic work, this is true only if therapists study their internal reactions and use them to understand their clients (Ainslie, 2007; Gelso & Hayes, 2002; Wolitzky, 2011a, 2011b). It is critical that therapists monitor their own feelings during therapy sessions and use their responses as a source for increased self-awareness and understanding of their clients.

A therapist who pays attention to his or her countertransference reactions and observations to a particular client may use this as a part of the therapy. The therapist who notes a countertransference mood of irritability, for instance, may learn something about a client's pattern of being demanding, which can be explored in therapy. Viewed in this more positive way, countertransference can become a key avenue for helping the client gain self-understanding.

Psychoanalytic therapists vary in the manner in which they use their observations of countertransference. In some instances the feelings may be shared with the client, but traditional analytic therapists strive to minimize their expression of countertransference while silently learning from its inevitable occurrence. Hayes,

Gelso, and Hummel (2011) present the following guidelines for working effectively with countertransference:

- Effective therapists prevent acting out and are aware of and manage their countertransference in a way that benefits the therapeutic work.
- The ability of therapists to gain self-understanding and to establish appropriate boundaries with clients are fundamental to managing and effectively using their countertransference reactions.
- Personal therapy and clinical supervision for therapists can be most helpful in better understanding how their internal reactions influence the therapy process and how to use these countertransference reactions to benefit the work of therapy.

It is of paramount importance that therapists develop some level of objectivity and not react defensively and subjectively in the face of anger, love, adulation, criticism, and other intense feelings expressed by their clients. Most psychoanalytic training programs require that trainees undergo their own extensive analysis as a client. If psychotherapists become aware of a strong aversion to certain types of clients, a strong attraction to other types of clients, psychosomatic reactions that occur at definite times in therapeutic relationships, and the like, it is imperative for them to seek professional consultation, clinical supervision, or enter their own therapy for a time to work out these personal issues that stand in the way of their being effective therapists.

As a result of the client–therapist relationship, particularly in working through the transference situation, clients acquire insights into the workings of their unconscious process. Awareness of and insights into repressed material are the bases of the analytic growth process. Clients come to understand the association between their past experiences and their current behavior. The psychoanalytic approach assumes that without this dynamic self-understanding there can be no substantial personality change or resolution of present conflicts.

APPLICATION: THERAPEUTIC TECHNIQUES AND PROCEDURES

This section deals with the techniques most commonly used by psychoanalytically oriented therapists. It also includes a section on the applications of the psychoanalytic approach to group counseling. Psychoanalytic therapy, or psychodynamic therapy (as opposed to traditional psychoanalysis), includes these features:

- The therapy is geared more to limited objectives than to restructuring one's personality.
- The therapist is less likely to use the couch.
- There are fewer sessions each week.
- There is more frequent use of supportive interventions such as reassurance, expressions of empathy and support, and suggestions.
- There is more emphasis on the here-and-now relationship between therapist and client.
- There is more latitude for therapist self-disclosure without "polluting the transference."

- Less emphasis is given to the therapist's neutrality.
- There is a focus on mutual transference and countertransference enactments.
- The focus is more on pressing practical concerns than on working with fantasy material.

The techniques of psychoanalytic therapy are aimed at increasing awareness, fostering insights into the client's behavior, and understanding the meanings of symptoms. The therapy proceeds from the client's talk to catharsis (or expression of emotion), to insight, to working through unconscious material. This work is done to attain the goals of intellectual and emotional understanding and reeducation, which, it is hoped, will lead to personality change. The six basic techniques of psychoanalytic therapy are (1) maintaining the analytic framework, (2) free association, (3) interpretation, (4) dream analysis, (5) analysis of resistance, and (6) analysis of transference. See *Case Approach to Counseling and Psychotherapy* (Corey, 2013, chap. 2), where Dr. William Blau, a psychoanalytically oriented therapist, illustrates some treatment techniques in the case of Ruth.

Maintaining the Analytic Framework

The psychoanalytic process stresses maintaining a particular framework aimed at accomplishing the goals of this type of therapy. **Maintaining the analytic framework** refers to a whole range of procedural and stylistic factors, such as the analyst's relative anonymity, maintaining neutrality and objectivity, the regularity and consistency of meetings, starting and ending the sessions on time, clarity on fees, and basic boundary issues such as the avoidance of advice giving or imposition of the therapist's values (Curtis & Hirsch, 2011). One of the most powerful features of psychoanalytically oriented therapy is that the consistent framework is itself a therapeutic factor, comparable on an emotional level to the regular feeding of an infant. Analysts attempt to minimize departures from this consistent pattern (such as vacations, changes in fees, or changes in the meeting environment). Where departures are unavoidable, these will often be the focus of interpretations.

Free Association

Free association is a central technique in psychoanalytic therapy, and it plays a key role in the process of maintaining the analytic framework. In **free association,** clients are encouraged to say whatever comes to mind, regardless of how painful, silly, trivial, illogical, or irrelevant it may seem. In essence, clients try to flow with any feelings or thoughts by reporting them immediately without censorship. As the analytic work progresses, most clients will occasionally depart from this basic rule, and these resistances will be interpreted by the therapist when it is timely to do so.

Free association is one of the basic tools used to open the doors to unconscious wishes, fantasies, conflicts, and motivations. This technique often leads to some recollection of past experiences and, at times, a catharsis or release of intense feelings that have been blocked. This release is not seen as crucial in itself, however. During the free-association process, the therapist's task is to identify the repressed material that is locked in the unconscious. The sequence of associations guides the therapist in understanding the connections clients make among events. Blockings or disruptions in associations serve as cues to anxiety-arousing material. The therapist interprets the material to clients, guiding them toward increased insight into the underlying dynamics.

As analytic therapists listen to their clients' free associations, they hear not only the surface content but also the hidden meaning. Nothing the client says is taken at face value. For example, a slip of the tongue can suggest that an expressed emotion is accompanied by a conflicting affect. Areas that clients do not talk about are as significant as the areas they do discuss.

Interpretation

Interpretation consists of the analyst's pointing out, explaining, and even teaching the client the meanings of behavior that is manifested in dreams, free association, resistances, and the therapeutic relationship itself. The functions of interpretations are to enable the ego to assimilate new material and to speed up the process of uncovering further unconscious material. Interpretation is grounded in the therapist's assessment of the client's personality and of the factors in the client's past that contributed to his or her difficulties. Under contemporary definitions, interpretation includes identifying, clarifying, and translating the client's material. Relational psychoanalytic therapists present possible meanings associated with a client's thoughts, feelings, or events as an hypothesis rather than a truth about a client's inner world (Curtis & Hirsch, 2011). Interpretations are provided in a collaborative manner to help clients make sense of their lives and to expand their consciousness.

The therapist uses the client's reactions as a gauge in determining a client's readiness to make an interpretation. It is important that interpretations be appropriately timed because the client will reject therapist interpretations that are poorly timed. A general rule is that interpretation should be presented when the phenomenon to be interpreted is close to conscious awareness. In other words, the therapist should interpret material that the client has not yet seen but is capable of tolerating and incorporating. Another general rule is that interpretation should start from the surface and go only as deep as the client is able to go.

Dream Analysis

Dream analysis is an important procedure for uncovering unconscious material and giving the client insight into some areas of unresolved problems. During sleep, defenses are lowered and repressed feelings surface. Freud sees dreams as the "royal road to the unconscious," for in them one's unconscious wishes, needs, and fears are expressed. Some motivations are so unacceptable to the person that they are expressed in disguised or symbolic form rather than being revealed directly.

Dreams have two levels of content: latent content and manifest content. **Latent content** consists of hidden, symbolic, and unconscious motives, wishes, and fears. Because they are so painful and threatening, the unconscious sexual and aggressive impulses that make up latent content are transformed into the more acceptable **manifest content**, which is the dream as it appears to the dreamer. The process by which the latent content of a dream is transformed into the less threatening manifest content is called **dream work**. The therapist's task is to uncover disguised meanings by studying the symbols in the manifest content of the dream.

During the session, therapists may ask clients to free associate to some aspect of the manifest content of a dream for the purpose of uncovering the latent meanings. Therapists participate in the process by exploring clients' associations with them. Interpreting the meanings of the dream elements helps clients unlock the repression that has kept the material from consciousness and relate the new insight to their present struggles. Dreams may serve as a pathway to repressed material, but they also provide an understanding of clients' current functioning. Relational psychoanalytic therapists are particularly interested in the connection of dreams to clients' lives. The dream is viewed as a significant message to clients to examine something that could be problematic if left unexamined (Curtis & Hirsch, 2011).

Analysis and Interpretation of Resistance

Resistance, a concept fundamental to the practice of psychoanalysis, is anything that works against the progress of therapy and prevents the client from producing previously unconscious material. Specifically, resistance is the client's reluctance to bring to the surface of awareness unconscious material that has been repressed. Resistance refers to any idea, attitude, feeling, or action (conscious or unconscious) that fosters the status quo and gets in the way of change. During free association or association to dreams, the client may evidence an unwillingness to relate certain thoughts, feelings, and experiences. Freud viewed resistance as an unconscious dynamic that people use to defend against the intolerable anxiety and pain that would arise if they were to become aware of their repressed impulses and feelings.

As a defense against anxiety, resistance operates specifically in psychoanalytic therapy to prevent clients and therapists from succeeding in their joint effort to gain insights into the dynamics of the unconscious. Resistances are designed to protect individuals against anxiety and fear of change. Clients tend to cling to their familiar patterns, regardless of how painful they may be. An assumption of analytic treatment is that clients wish both to change and to remain embedded in their old world. Thus resistance needs to be recognized and dealt with in therapy (Curtis & Hirsch, 2011; Wolitzky, 2011a). Therapists need to create a safe climate that allows clients to explore their defenses and resistances. Because resistance blocks threatening material from entering awareness, analytic therapists point it out, and clients need to address their fears if they hope to deal with conflicts realistically. The therapists' interpretation is aimed at helping clients become aware of the reasons for the resistance so that they can deal with them. As a general rule, therapists point out and interpret the most obvious resistances to lessen the possibility of clients' rejecting the interpretation and to increase the chance that they will begin to look at their resistive behavior.

Resistances are not just something to be overcome. Because they are representative of usual defensive approaches in daily life, they need to be recognized as devices that defend against anxiety but that interfere with the ability to accept change that could lead to experiencing a more gratifying life. It is crucial that therapists respect the resistances of clients and assist them in working therapeuti-cally with their defenses. When handled properly, exploring resistance can be an extremely valuable tool in understanding the client.

Analysis and Interpretation of Transference

As was mentioned earlier, transference manifests itself in the therapeutic process when clients' earlier relationships contribute to their distorting the present with the therapist. The transference situation is considered valuable because its mani-festations provide clients with the opportunity to reexperience a variety of feelings that would otherwise be inaccessible. Through the relationship with the therapist, clients express feelings, beliefs, and desires that they have buried in their uncon-scious. Interpreting transference is a route to elucidating the client's intrapsychic life (Wolitzky, 2011b). Through this interpretation, clients can recognize how they are repeating the same dynamic patterns in their relationships with the therapist, with significant figures from the past, and in present relationships with significant others. Through appropriate interpretations and working through of these current expressions of early feelings, clients are able to become aware of and to gradu-ally change some of their long-standing patterns of behavior. Analytically oriented therapists consider the process of exploring and interpreting transference feelings as the core of the therapeutic process because it is aimed at achieving increased awareness and personality change.

The analysis of transference is a central technique in psychoanalysis and psychoanalytically oriented therapy, for it allows clients to achieve here-and-now insight into the influence of the past on their present functioning. Interpretation of the transference relationship enables clients to work through old conflicts that are keeping them fixated and retarding their emotional growth. In essence, the effects of early relationships are counteracted by working through a similar emotional conflict in the current therapeutic relationship. An example of utilizing transfer-ence is given in a later section on the case of Stan.

Application to Group Counseling

I find that the psychodynamic model offers a conceptual framework for understand-ing the history of the members of a group and a way of thinking about how their past is affecting them now in the group and in their everyday lives. Group leaders can *think* psychoanalytically, even if they do not use many psychoanalytical tech-niques. Regardless of their theoretical orientation, it is well for group therapists to understand such psychoanalytic phenomena as transference, countertransference, resistance, and the use of ego-defense mechanisms as reactions to anxiety.

Transference and countertransference have significant implications for the practice of group counseling and therapy. Group work may re-create early life sit-uations that continue to affect the client. In most groups, individuals elicit a range of feelings such as attraction, anger, competition, and avoidance. These transfer-ence feelings may resemble those that members experienced toward significant people in their past. Members will most likely find symbolic mothers, fathers, siblings, and lovers in their group. Group participants frequently compete for the attention of the leader—a situation reminiscent of earlier times when they had to vie for their parents' attention with their brothers and sisters. This rivalry can be explored in group as a way of gaining increased awareness of how the participants dealt with competition as children and how their past success or lack of it affects their present interactions with others. A basic tenet of psychodynamic therapy groups is the notion that group participants, through their interactions within the group, re-create their social situation, implying that the group becomes a microcosm of their everyday lives (Rutan, Stone, & Shay, 2007). Groups can provide a dynamic understanding of how people function in out-of-group situations. Projections onto the leader and onto other members are valuable clues to unresolved conflicts within the person that can be identified, explored, and worked through in the group.

The group leader also has reactions to members and is affected by members' reactions. Countertransference can be a useful tool for the group therapist to understand the dynamics that might be operating in a group. However, group leaders need to be alert to signs of unresolved internal conflicts that could interfere with effective group functioning and create a situation in which members are used to satisfy the leaders' own unfulfilled needs. If, for example, a group leader has an extreme need to be liked and approved of, the leader might behave in ways to get members' approval and confirmation, resulting in behaviors primarily designed to please the group members and ensure their continued support. It is important to differentiate between appropriate emotional reactions and countertransference.

Group counselors need to exercise vigilance lest they misuse their power by turning the group into a forum for pushing clients to adjust by conforming to the dominant cultural values at the expense of losing their own worldviews and cultural identities. Group practitioners also need to be aware of their own potential biases. The concept of countertransference can be expanded to include unacknowledged bias and prejudices that may be conveyed unintentionally through the techniques used by group therapists. For a more extensive discussion on the psychoanalytic approach to group counseling, refer to *Theory and Practice of Group Counseling* (Corey, 2012, chap. 6). For an entire volume on this subject, refer to *Psychodynamic Group Psychotherapy* (Rutan, Stone, & Shay, 2007).

JUNG'S PERSPECTIVE ON THE DEVELOPMENT OF PERSONALITY

At one time Freud referred to Carl Jung as his spiritual heir, but Jung eventually developed a theory of personality that was markedly different from Freudian psychoanalysis. Jung's **analytical psychology** is an elaborate explanation of human nature that combines ideas from history, mythology, anthropology, and religion (Schultz & Schultz, 2009). Jung made monumental contributions to our deep understanding of the human personality and personal development, particularly during middle age.

Jung's pioneering work places central importance on the psychological changes that are associated with midlife. He maintained that at midlife we need to let go of many of the values and behaviors that guided the first half of our life and confront our unconscious. We can best do this by paying attention to the messages of our dreams and by engaging in creative activities such as writing or painting. The task facing us during the midlife period is to be less influenced by rational thought and to instead give expression to these unconscious forces and integrate them into our conscious life (Schultz & Schultz, 2009).

Jung learned a great deal from his own midlife crisis. At age 81 he wrote about his recollections in his autobiography, *Memories, Dreams, Reflections* (1961), in which he also identified some of his major contributions. Jung made a choice to focus on the unconscious realm in his personal life, which also influenced the development of his theory of personality. However, he had a very different conception of the unconscious than did Freud. Jung was a colleague of Freud's and valued many of his contributions, but Jung eventually came to the point of not being able to support some of Freud's basic concepts, especially his theory of sexuality. Jung (1961) recalled Freud's words to him: "My dear Jung, promise me never to abandon the sexual theory. This is the most essential thing of all. You see, we must make a dogma of it, an unshakable bulwark" (p. 150). Jung became convinced that he could no longer collaborate with Freud because he believed Freud placed his own authority over truth. Freud had little tolerance for other theoreticians, such as Jung and Adler, who dared to challenge his theories. Although Jung had a lot to lose professionally by withdrawing from Freud, he saw no other choice. He subsequently developed a spiritual approach that places great emphasis on being impelled to find meaning in life in contrast to being driven by the psychological and biological forces described by Freud.

Jung maintained that we are not merely shaped by past events (Freudian determinism), but that we are influenced by our future as well as our past. Part of the nature of humans is to be constantly developing, growing, and moving toward a balanced and complete level of development. For Jung, our present personality is shaped both by who and what we have been and also by what we aspire to be in the future. His theory is based on the assumption that humans tend to move toward the fulfillment or realization of all of their capabilities. Achieving **individuation**—the harmonious integration of the conscious and unconscious aspects of personality—is an innate and primary goal. For Jung, we have both constructive and destructive forces, and to become integrated, it is essential to accept our dark side, or shadow, with its primitive impulses such as selfishness and greed. Acceptance of our shadow does not imply being dominated by this dimension of our being, but simply recognizing that this is a part of our nature.

Jung taught that many dreams contain messages from the deepest layer of the unconscious, which he described as the source of creativity. Jung referred to the **collective unconscious** as "the deepest level of the psyche containing the accumulation of inherited experiences of human and prehuman species" (as cited in Schultz & Schultz, 2009, p. 109). Jung saw a connection between each person's personality and the past, not only childhood events but also the history of the species. This means that some dreams may deal with an individual's relationship to a larger whole such as the family, universal humanity, or generations over time. The images of universal experiences contained in the collective unconscious are called **archetypes**. Among the most important archetypes are the persona, the anima and animus, and the shadow. The **persona** is a mask, or public face, that we wear to protect ourselves. The **animus** and the **anima** represent both the biological and psychological aspects of masculinity and femininity, which are thought to coexist in both sexes. The **shadow** has the deepest roots and is the most dangerous and powerful of the archetypes. It represents our dark side, the thoughts, feelings, and actions that we tend to disown by projecting them outward. In a dream all of these parts can be considered manifestations of who and what we are.

Jung agreed with Freud that dreams provide a pathway into the unconscious, but he differed from Freud on their functions. Jung wrote that dreams have two purposes. They are prospective; that is, they help people prepare themselves for the experiences and events they anticipate in the near future. They also serve a compensatory function, working to bring about a balance between opposites within the person. They compensate for the overdevelopment of one facet of the individual's personality (Schultz & Schultz, 2009).

Jung viewed dreams more as an attempt to express than as an attempt to repress and disguise. Dreams are a creative effort of the dreamer in struggling with contradiction, complexity, and confusion. The aim of the dream is resolution and integration. According to Jung, each part of the dream can be understood as some projected quality of the dreamer. His method of interpretation draws on a series of dreams obtained from a person, during the course of which the meaning gradually unfolds. If you are interested in further reading, I suggest *Memories, Dreams, Reflections* (Jung, 1961) and *Living With Paradox: An Introduction to Jungian Psychology* (Harris, 1996).

CONTEMPORARY TRENDS: OBJECT-RELATIONS THEORY, SELF PSYCHOLOGY, AND RELATIONAL PSYCHOANALYSIS

Psychoanalytic theory continues to evolve. Freud emphasized intrapsychic conflicts pertaining to the gratification of basic needs. Writers in the neo-Freudian school moved away from this orthodox position and contributed to the growth and expansion of the psychoanalytic movement by incorporating the cultural and social influences on personality. **Ego psychology** is part of classical psychoanalysis with the emphasis placed on the vocabulary of id, ego, and superego, and on Anna Freud's identification of defense mechanisms. She spent most of her professional life adapting psychoanalysis to children and adolescents. Erikson expanded this perspective by emphasizing psychosocial development throughout the life span.

Ainslie (2007) notes that, "psychoanalytic theory has undergone a variety of reformulations in the years since its inception and today it is actually comprised of a variety of schools, including the classical perspective, object relations theory, self psychology, and the interpersonal and relational schools" (pp. 19–20). All of these psychoanalytic approaches share certain basic assumptions, one of which is that "as human beings we are profoundly affected by experiences with others that take place over the course of development, and the assumption that emotional conflicts and psychological symptoms often have a great deal to do with these experiences" (p. 20).

Object-relations theory encompasses the work of a number of rather different psychoanalytic theorists. Their emphasize is how our relationships with other people are affected by the way we have internalized our experiences of others and set up representations of others within ourselves. Object relations are interpersonal relationships as these are represented intrapsychically, and as they influence our interactions with the people around us. The term *object* was used by Freud to refer to that which satisfies a need, or to the significant person or thing that is the object, or target, of one's feelings or drives. It is used interchangeably with the term *other* to refer to an important person to whom the child, and later the adult, becomes attached. Rather than being individuals with separate identities, others are perceived by an infant as objects for gratifying needs. Object-relations theories have diverged from orthodox psychoanalysis. However, some theorists, most notably Otto Kernberg, attempt to integrate the increasingly varied ideas that characterize this school of thought within a classical psychoanalytic framework (St. Clair, 2004).

Traditional psychoanalysis assumes that the analyst can discover and name the intrapersonal "truth" about individual clients. As psychoanalytic theory has evolved, the approach has more fully considered the unconscious influence of other people. **Self-psychology**, which grew out of the work of Heinz Kohut (1971), emphasizes how we use interpersonal relationships (self objects) to develop our own sense of self.

The **relational model** is based on the assumption that therapy is an interactive process between client and therapist. Whether called intersubjective, interpersonal, or relational, a number of contemporary approaches to analysis are based on the exploration of the complex conscious and unconscious dynamics at play with respect to both therapist and client.

Mitchell (1988, 2000) has written extensively about these new conceptualizations of the analytic relationship. He integrates developmental theory, attachment theory, systems theory, and interpersonal theory to demonstrate the profound ways in which we seek attachments with others, especially early caregivers. Interpersonal analysts believe that countertransference provides an important source of information about the client's character and dynamics. Mitchell adds to this object-relations position a cultural dimension, noting that the caregiver's qualities reflect the particular culture in which the person lives. We are all deeply embedded within our cultures. Different cultures maintain different values, so there can be no objective psychic truths. Our internal (unconscious) structures are all relational and relative. This is in stark contrast to the Freudian notion of universal biological drives that could be said to function in every human.

Contemporary relational theorists have challenged what they consider to be the authoritarian nature of the traditional psychoanalytic relationship and replaced it with a more egalitarian model. From the time of Freud to the late 20th century, the power between analyst and patient was unequal. The traditional analytic therapist could help the client only if the client attempted to abide by the therapeutic contract and had faith in the therapist's expertise to make the analytic session a safe environment for self-exploration. Relational analysts assume a more equal power relationship. Theoretically, this shift is seen not so much as a political statement about equality as it is a recognition that analysis consists of two individuals encountering each other in a complex interplay of emotions. The analyst is no longer cast in a detached and anonymous role but is able to be responsive and emotionally present. The task of analysis is to explore each client's life in a creative way, customized to the therapist and client working together in a particular culture at a particular moment in time.

SUMMARY OF STAGES OF DEVELOPMENT Most contemporary psychoanalytic theories center on predictable developmental sequences in which the early experiences of the self shift in relation to an expanding awareness of others. Once self–other patterns are established, it is assumed they influence later interpersonal relationships. Specifically, people search for relationships that match the patterns established by their earlier experiences. People who are either overly dependent or overly detached, for example, can be repeating patterns of relating they established with their mother when they were toddlers (Hedges, 1983). These newer theories provide insight into how an individual's inner world can cause difficulties in living in the everyday world of people and relationships (St. Clair, 2004).

A central influence on contemporary object-relations theory is Margaret Mahler (1968), a pediatrician who emphasized the observation of children. In her view, the resolution of the Oedipus complex during Freud's proposed phallic stage is less critical than the child's progression from a symbiotic relationship with a maternal figure toward separation and individuation. Her studies focus on the interactions between the child and the mother in the first 3 years of life. Mahler conceptualizes the development of the self somewhat differently from the traditional Freudian psychosexual stages. Her belief is that the individual begins in a state of psychological fusion with the mother and progresses gradually to separation. The unfinished crises and residues of the earlier state of fusion, as well as the process of separating and individuating, have a profound influence on later relationships. Object relations of later life build on the child's search for a reconnection with the mother (St. Clair, 2004). Psychological development can be thought of as the evolution of the way in which individuals separate and differentiate themselves from others.

Mahler calls the first 3 or 4 weeks of life *normal infantile autism*. Here the infant is presumed to be responding more to states of physiological tension than to psychological processes. Mahler believes the infant is unable to differentiate itself from its mother in many respects at this age. According to Melanie Klein (1975), another major contributor to the object-relations perspective, the infant perceives parts—breasts, face, hands, and mouth—rather than a unified self. In this undifferentiated state there is no whole self, and there are no whole objects. When adults show the most extreme lack of psychological organization and sense of self, they may be thought of as returning to this most primitive infantile stage. Subsequent infant research by Daniel Stern (1985) has challenged this aspect of Mahler's theory, maintaining that infants are interested in others practically from birth.

Mahler's next phase, called *symbiosis,* is recognizable by the 3rd month and extends roughly through the 8th month. At this age the infant has a pronounced dependency on the mother. She (or the primary caregiver) is clearly a partner and not just an interchangeable part. The infant seems to expect a very high degree of emotional attunement with its mother.

The *separation–individuation* process begins in the 4th or 5th month. During this time the child moves away from symbiotic forms of relating. The child experiences separation from significant others yet still turns to them for a sense of confirmation and comfort. The child may demonstrate ambivalence, torn between enjoying separate states of independence and dependence. The toddler who proudly steps away from the parents and then runs back to be swept up in approving arms illustrates some of the main issues of this period (Hedges, 1983, p. 109). Others are looked to as approving mirrors for the child's developing sense of self; optimally, these relationships can provide a healthy self-esteem.

Children who do not experience the opportunity to differentiate, and those who lack the opportunity to idealize others while also taking pride in themselves, may later suffer from *narcissistic* character disorders and problems of self-esteem. The **narcissistic personality** is characterized by a grandiose and exaggerated sense of self-importance and an exploitive attitude toward others, which serve the function of masking a frail self-concept. Such individuals seek attention and admiration from others. They unrealistically exaggerate their accomplishments, and they have a tendency toward extreme self-absorption. Kernberg (1975) characterizes narcissistic people as focusing on themselves in their interactions with others, having a great need to be admired, possessing shallow affect, and being exploitive and, at times, parasitic in their relationships with others. Kohut (1971) characterizes such people as perceiving threats to their self-esteem and as having feelings of emptiness and deadness.

"Borderline" conditions are also rooted in the period of separation–individuation. People with a **borderline personality disorder** have moved into the separation process but have been thwarted by parental rejection of their individuation. In other words, a crisis ensues when the child does develop beyond the stage of symbiosis but the parents are unable to tolerate this beginning individuation and withdraw emotional support. Borderline people are characterized by instability, irritability, self-destructive acts, impulsive anger, and extreme mood shifts. They typically experience extended periods of disillusionment, punctuated by occasional euphoria. Kernberg (1975) describes the syndrome as including a lack of clear identity, a lack of deep understanding of other people, poor impulse control, and the inability to tolerate anxiety.

Mahler's final subphase in the *separation–individuation* process involves a move toward constancy of self and object. This development is typically pronounced by the 36th month (Hedges, 1983). By now others are more fully seen as separate from the self. Ideally, children can begin to relate without being overwhelmed with fears of losing their sense of individuality, and they may enter into the later psychosexual and psychosocial stages with a firm foundation of selfhood. Borderline and narcissistic disorders seem to be rooted in traumas and developmental disturbances during the separation–individuation phase. However, the full manifestations of the personality and behavioral symptoms tend to develop in early adulthood.

This chapter permits only a glimpse of the newer formulations in psychoanalytic theory. If you would like to pursue this emerging approach, good overviews can be found in Mitchell (1988, 2000), Mitchell and Black (1995), and Wolitzky (2011b).

TREATING BORDERLINE AND NARCISSISTIC DISORDERS Some of the most powerful tools for understanding borderline and narcissistic personality disorders have emerged from the psychoanalytic models. Among the most significant theorists in this area are Kernberg (1975, 1976, 1997), Kohut (1971, 1977, 1984), and Masterson (1976). A great deal of recent psychoanalytic writing deals with the nature and treatment of borderline and narcissistic personality disorders and sheds new light on the understanding of these disorders. Kohut (1984) maintains that people are their healthiest and best when they can feel both independence and attachment, taking joy in themselves and also being able to idealize others. Mature adults feel a basic security grounded in a sense of freedom, self-sufficiency, and self-esteem; they are not compulsively dependent on others but also do not have to fear closeness. If you are interested in learning more about treating individuals with borderline personality disorders from an object-relations perspective, see *Psychotherapy for Borderline Personality* (Clarkin, Yeomans, & Kernberg, 2006).

SOME DIRECTIONS OF CONTEMPORARY PSYCHODYNAMIC THERAPY Strupp (1992) maintains that the various contemporary modifications of psychoanalysis have infused psychodynamic psychotherapy with renewed vitality and vigor. Some of the directions in psychodynamic theory and practice that Strupp identifies are summarized here:

- Increased attention is being given to disturbances during childhood and adolescence.
- The emphasis on treatment has shifted from the "classical" interest in curing neurotic disorders to the problems of dealing therapeutically with chronic personality disorders, borderline conditions, and narcissistic personality disorders. There is also a movement toward devising specific treatments for specific disorders.
- Increased attention is being paid to establishing a good therapeutic alliance early in therapy. A collaborative working relationship is now viewed as a key factor in a positive therapeutic outcome.
- There is a renewed interest in the development of briefer forms of psychodynamic therapy, largely due to societal pressures for accountability and cost-effectiveness. The indications are that time-limited dynamic therapy will be used more in the future.

It appears that Strupp's assessment of the current scene and his predictions of what was to come were quite accurate.

THE TREND TOWARD BRIEF, TIME-LIMITED PSYCHODYNAMIC THERAPY Many psychoanalytically oriented therapists are adapting their work to a time-limited framework while retaining their original focus on depth and the inner life, which are characteristic of the psychoanalytic model. These therapists support the move to the use of briefer therapy when this is indicated by the client's needs rather than by arbitrary limits set by a managed care system. Although there are different approaches to brief psychodynamic therapy, Prochaska and Norcross (2010) believe they all share these common characteristics:

- Work within the framework of time-limited therapy.
- Target a specific interpersonal problem during the initial session.
- Assume a less neutral therapeutic stance than is true of traditional analytic approaches.
- Establish a strong working alliance.
- Use interpretation relatively early in the therapy relationship.

In keeping with the context of brief, time-limited therapy, Messer and Warren (2001) describe **brief psychodynamic therapy (BPT)** as a promising approach. This adaptation applies the principles of psychodynamic theory and therapy to treating selective disorders within a preestablished time limit of, generally, 10 to 25 sessions. BPT uses key psychodynamic concepts such as the enduring impact of psychosexual, psychosocial, and object-relational stages of development; the existence of unconscious processes and resistance; the usefulness of interpretation; the importance of the working alliance; and reenactment of the client's past emotional issues in relation to the therapist. Most forms of this time-limited approach call upon the therapist to assume an active and directive role in quickly formulating a therapeutic focus, such as a central theme or problem area that guides the work (Levenson, 2010). Some possible goals of this approach might include conflict resolution, greater access to feelings, increasing choice possibilities, improving interpersonal relationships, and symptom remission. Levenson emphasizes that the aim of time-limited dynamic therapy is not to bring about a cure but to foster changes in behavior, thinking, and feeling. This is accomplished by using the client–therapist relationship as a way to understand how the person interacts in the world. It is assumed that clients interact with the therapist in the same dysfunctional ways they interact with significant others.

The goals, therapeutic focus, and active role of the therapist have implications for the practice of individual therapy. Levenson (2010) acknowledges that brief psychodynamic therapy is not suited for all clients and all therapists. For example, this approach is generally not suited for individuals with severe characterological disorders or for those with severe depression. Some therapists are not well suited to the interactive, directive, and self-disclosing strategies of brief psychodynamic therapy. Although BPT is not suitable for all clients, it meets a variety of clients' needs.

Brief dynamic therapy tends to emphasize a client's strengths and resources in dealing with real-life issues. Levenson (2010) notes that a major modification of the psychoanalytic technique is the emphasis on the here and now of the client's life rather than exploring the there and then of childhood. Also, the brief dynamic therapist tends to think psychodynamically and at the same time is open to using a variety of intervention strategies. BPT is an opportunity to begin the process of change, which continues long after therapy is terminated. By the end of brief therapy, clients tend to have acquired a richer range of interactions with others, and they continue to have opportunities to practice functional behaviors in daily life. At some future time, clients may have a need for additional therapy sessions to address different concerns. Instead of thinking of time-limited dynamic psychotherapy as a definitive intervention, it is best to view this approach as offering multiple, brief therapy experiences over an individual's life span.

If you want to learn more about time-limited dynamic therapy, I recommend *Brief Dynamic Therapy* (Levenson, 2010)

PSYCHOANALYTIC THERAPY FROM A MULTICULTURAL PERSPECTIVE

Strengths From a Diversity Perspective

Psychoanalytically oriented therapy can be made appropriate for culturally diverse populations if techniques are modified to fit the settings in which a therapist practices. All of us have a background of childhood experiences and have addressed developmental crises throughout our lives. Erikson's psychosocial approach, with its emphasis on critical issues in stages of development, has particular application to people of color. Therapists can help their clients review environmental situations at the various critical turning points in their lives to determine how certain events have affected them either positively or negatively.

Psychotherapists need to recognize and confront their own potential sources of bias and how countertransference could be conveyed unintentionally through their interventions. To the credit of the psychoanalytic approach, it stresses the value of intensive psychotherapy as part of the training of therapists. This helps therapists become aware of their own sources of countertransference, including their biases, prejudices, and racial or ethnic stereotypes.

Shortcomings From a Diversity Perspective

Traditional psychoanalytic approaches are costly, and psychoanalytic therapy is generally perceived as being based on upper- and middle-class values. All clients do not share these values, and for many the cost of treatment is prohibitive. Another shortcoming pertains to the ambiguity inherent in most psychoanalytic approaches. This can be problematic for clients from cultures who expect direction from a professional. For example, many Asian American clients may prefer a more structured, directive, problem-oriented approach to counseling and may not continue therapy if a nondirective or unstructured approach is employed. Furthermore, intrapsychic analysis may be in direct conflict with some clients' social framework and environmental perspective. Psychoanalytic therapy is generally more concerned with long-term personality reconstruction than with short-term problem solving.

Atkinson, Thompson, and Grant (1993) underscore the need for therapists to consider possible external sources of clients' problems, especially if clients have experienced an oppressive environment. The psychoanalytic approach can be criticized for failing to adequately address the social, cultural, and political factors that result in an individual's problems. If there is not a balance between the external and internal perspectives, clients may be held responsible for their condition. However, the nonjudgmental stance that is a cornerstone of the psychoanalytic tradition may ameliorate any tendency to blame the client.

There are likely to be some difficulties in applying a psychoanalytic approach with low-income clients. If these clients seek professional help, they are generally concerned with dealing with a crisis situation and with finding solutions to concrete problems, or at least some direction in addressing survival needs pertaining to housing, employment, and child care. This does not imply that low-income clients are unable to profit from analytic therapy; rather, this particular orientation could be more beneficial *after* more pressing issues and concerns have been resolved. On this topic, Smith (2005) contends that psychotherapists' willingness and ability to work with low-income clients is compromised by unexamined classist attitudes and that these attitudes constitute a significant obstacle for practitioners' success in working with the poor. Smith makes a case for considering alternative therapeutic models such as psychoeducation, counseling, preventive psychology, or community psychology rather than traditional analytic psychotherapy for people who are in a low socioeconomic situation. Another alternative is for therapists to do pro-bono work for some clients.

Psychoanalytic Therapy Applied to the Case of Stan

In each of the chapters in Part 2, the case of Stan is used to demonstrate the practical applications of the theory in question. To give you a focus on Stan's central concerns, refer to the end of Chapter 1, where his biography is given. I also recommend that you at least skim Chapter 16, which deals with an integrative approach as applied to Stan.

The psychoanalytic approach focuses on the unconscious psychodynamics of Stan's behavior. Considerable attention is given to material that he has repressed. At the extreme Stan demonstrated a self-destructive tendency, which is a way of inflicting punishment on himself. Instead of directing his hostility toward his parents and siblings, he turned it inward toward himself. Stan's preoccupation with drinking could be hypothesized as evidence of an oral fixation. Because he never received love and acceptance during his early childhood, he is still suffering from this deprivation and continues to desperately search for approval and acceptance from others. Stan's gender-role identification was fraught with difficulties. He learned the basis of female–male relationships through his early experiences with his parents. What he saw was fighting, bickering, and discounting. His father was the weak one who always lost, and his

mother was the strong, domineering force who could and did hurt men. Stan generalized his fear of his mother to all women. It could be further hypothesized that the woman he married was similar to his mother, both of whom reinforced his feelings of impotence.

The opportunity to develop a transference relationship and work through it is the core of the therapy process. Stan will eventually relate to me, as his therapist, as he did to his father, and this process will be a valuable means of gaining insight into the origin of Stan's difficulties in relating to others. The analytic process stresses an intensive exploration of Stan's past. Stan devotes much therapy time to reliving and exploring his early past. As he talks, he gains increased understanding of the dynamics of his behavior. He begins to see connections between his present problems and early experiences in his childhood. Stan explores memories of relationships with his siblings and with his mother and father and also explores how he has generalized his view of women and men from his view of these family members. It is expected that he will reexperience old feelings and uncover buried feelings related to traumatic events. From another perspective, apart from whatever conscious insight Stan may acquire, the goal is for him to have a more integrated self, where feelings split off as foreign (the id) become more a part of what he is comfortable with (the ego). In Stan's relationship with me, his old feelings can have different outcomes from his past experiences with significant others and can result in deep personality growth.

I am likely to explore some of these questions with Stan: "What did you do when you felt unloved?" "As a child, what did you do with your negative feelings?" "As a child, could you express your anger, hurt, and fears?" "What effects did your relationship with your mother and father have on you?" "What did this teach you about women and about men?" Brought into the here and now of the transference relationship, I might ask, "When have you felt anything like you felt with your parents?"

The analytic process focuses on key influences in Stan's developmental years, sometimes explicitly, sometimes in terms of how those earlier events are being relived in the present analytic relationship. As he comes to understand how he has been shaped by these past experiences, he is increasingly able to exert control over his present functioning. Many of Stan's fears become conscious, and then his energy does not have to remain fixed on defending himself from unconscious feelings. Instead, he can make new decisions about his current life. He can do this only if he works through the transference relationship, however, for the depth of his endeavors in therapy largely determine the depth and extent of his personality changes.

If I am operating from a contemporary object-relations psychoanalytic orientation, my focus may well be on Stan's developmental sequences. Particular attention is paid to understanding his current behavior in the world as largely a repetition of one of his earlier developmental phases. Because of his dependency, it is useful in understanding his behavior to see that he is now repeating patterns that he formed with his mother during his infancy. Viewed from this perspective, Stan has not accomplished the task of separation and individuation. He is still "stuck" in the symbiotic phase on some levels. He is unable to obtain his confirmation of worth from himself, and he has not resolved the dependence–independence struggle. Looking at his behavior from the viewpoint of self

psychology can shed light on his difficulties in forming intimate relationships.

Follow-Up: You Continue as Stan's Psychoanalytic Therapist

With each of the 11 theoretical orientations, you will be encouraged to try your hand at applying the principles and techniques you have just studied in the chapter to working with Stan from that particular perspective. The information presented about Stan from each of these theory chapters will provide you with some ideas of how you might continue working with him if he were referred to you. Do your best to stay within the general spirit of each theory by identifying specific concepts you would draw from and techniques that you might use in helping him explore the struggles he identifies. Here are a series of questions to provide some structure in your thinking about his case:

- How much interest would you have in Stan's early childhood? What are some ways you'd help him see patterns between his childhood issues and his current problems?

- Consider the transference relationship that is likely to be established between you and Stan. How might you react to his making you into a significant person in his life?

- In working with Stan, what countertransference issues might arise for you?

- What resistances and defenses might you predict in your work with Stan? From a psychoanalytic perspective, how would you interpret and work with this resistance?

- Which of the various forms of psychoanalytic therapy—classical, relational, or object relations— would you be most inclined to apply in working with Stan?

See *DVD for Theory and Practice of Counseling and Psychotherapy: The Case of Stan and Lecturettes* (Session 1, an initial session with Stan, and Session 2, on psychoanalytic therapy) for a demonstration of my approach to counseling Stan from this perspective. The first session consists of the intake and assessment process. The second session focuses on Stan's resistance and dealing with transference.

SUMMARY AND EVALUATION

Summary

Some major concepts of psychoanalytic theory include the dynamics of the unconscious and its influence on behavior, the role of anxiety, an understanding of transference and countertransference, and the development of personality at various stages in the life cycle.

Erikson broadened Freud's developmental perspective by including psychosocial trends. In his model, each of the eight stages of human development is characterized by a crisis, or turning point. We can either master the developmental task or fail to resolve the core struggle (Table 4.2 compares Freud's and Erikson's views on the developmental stages).

Psychoanalytic therapy consists largely of using methods to bring out unconscious material that can be worked through. It focuses primarily on childhood experiences, which are discussed, reconstructed, interpreted, and analyzed. The assumption is that this exploration of the past, which is typically accomplished by working through the transference relationship with the therapist, is necessary for character change. The most important techniques typically employed in psychoanalytic practice are maintaining the analytic framework, free association, interpretation, dream analysis, analysis of resistance, and analysis of transference.

Unlike Freudian theory, Jungian theory is not reductionist. Jung viewed humans positively and focused on individuation, the capacity of humans to move toward wholeness and self-realization. To become what they are capable of becoming, individuals must explore the unconscious aspects of their personality, both the personal unconscious and the collective unconscious. In Jungian analytical therapy, the therapist assists the client in tapping his or her inner wisdom. The goal of therapy is not merely the resolution of immediate problems but the transformation of personality.

The contemporary trends in psychoanalytic theory are reflected in these general areas: ego psychology, object-relations approaches, self psychology, and relational approaches. Ego psychology does not deny the role of intrapsychic conflicts but emphasizes the striving of the ego for mastery and competence throughout the human life span. The object-relations approaches are based on the notion that at birth there is no differentiation between others and self and that others represent objects of need gratification for infants. Separation–individuation is achieved over time. When this process is successful, others are perceived as both separate and related. Self psychology focuses on the nature of the therapeutic relationship, using empathy as a main tool. The relational approaches emphasize what evolves through the client–therapist relationship.

Contributions of the Psychoanalytic Approach

I believe therapists can broaden their understanding of clients' struggles by appreciating Freud's many significant contributions. It must be emphasized that competent use of psychoanalytic techniques requires training beyond what most therapists are afforded in their training program. The psychoanalytic approach provides practitioners with a conceptual framework for looking at behavior and for understanding the origins and functions of symptoms. Applying the psychoanalytic point of view to therapy practice is particularly useful in (1) understanding resistances that take the form of canceling appointments, fleeing from therapy prematurely, and refusing to look at oneself; (2) understanding that unfinished business can be worked through, so that clients can provide a new ending to some of the events that have restricted them emotionally; (3) understanding the value and role of transference; and (4) understanding how the overuse of ego defenses, both in the counseling relationship and in daily life, can keep clients from functioning effectively.

Although there is little to be gained from blaming the past for the way a person is now or from dwelling on the past, considering the early history of a client is often useful in understanding and working with a client's current situation. The client can use this awareness in making significant changes in the present and in future directions. Even though you may not agree with all of the premises of the classical psychoanalytic position, you can still draw on many of the psychoanalytic concepts as a framework for understanding your clients and for helping them achieve a deeper understanding of the roots of their conflicts.

If the psychoanalytic (or psychodynamic) approach is considered in a broader context than is true of classical psychoanalysis, it becomes a more powerful and useful model for understanding human behavior. Although I find Freud's psychosexual concepts of value, adding Erikson's emphasis on psychosocial factors gives a more complete picture of the critical turning points at each stage of development. Integrating these two perspectives is, in my view, most useful for understanding key themes in the development of personality. Erikson's developmental schema does not avoid the psychosexual issues and stages postulated by Freud; rather, Erikson extends the stages of psychosexual development throughout life. His perspective integrates psychosexual and psychosocial concepts without diminishing the importance of either.

Therapists who work from a developmental perspective are able to see continuity in life and to see certain directions their clients have taken. This perspective gives a broader picture of an individual's struggle, and clients are able to discover some significant connections among the various life stages.

Contributions of Modern Psychoanalytic Approaches

The contemporary trends in psychoanalytic thinking contribute to the understanding of how our current behavior in the world is largely a repetition of patterns set during one of the early phases of development. Object-relations theory helps us see the ways in which clients interacted with significant others in the past and how they are superimposing these early experiences on present relationships. For the many clients in therapy who are struggling with issues such as separation and individuation, intimacy, dependence versus independence, and identity, these newer formulations can provide a framework for understanding how and where aspects of development have been fixated. They have significant implications for many areas of human interaction such as intimate relationships, the family and child rearing, and the therapeutic relationship.

In my opinion, it is possible to use a psychodynamic framework to provide structure and direction to a counseling practice and at the same time to draw on other therapeutic techniques. I find value in the contributions of those writers who have built on the basic ideas of Freud and have added an emphasis on the social and cultural dimensions affecting personality development. In contemporary psychoanalytic practice more latitude is given to the therapist in using techniques and in developing the therapeutic relationship. The newer psychoanalytic theorists have enhanced, extended, and refocused classical analytic techniques. They are concentrating on the development of the ego, are paying attention to the social and cultural factors that influence the differentiation of an individual from others, and are giving new meaning to the relational dimensions of therapy.

Although contemporary psychodynamic approaches diverge considerably in many respects from the original Freudian emphasis on drives, the basic Freudian concepts of unconscious motivation, the influence of early development, transference, countertransference, and resistance are still central to the newer approaches. These concepts are of major importance in therapy and can be incorporated into therapeutic practices based on various theoretical approaches.

Limitations and Criticisms of the Psychoanalytic Approach

Some criticize psychoanalytic practitioners for ignoring empirical research. In the eyes of psychoanalytic practitioners, the systematic, controlled observations that are required for empirical studies sacrifice the complexity of what occurs in the therapeutic process. "Thus, most analysts are not consumers of research, let alone contributors to it, because such research is also generally felt to be an unacceptable intrusion into the sanctity of the analytic relationship" (Wolitzky, 2011, p. 68).

There are a number of practical limitations of psychoanalytic therapy. Considering factors such as time, expense, and availability of trained psychoanalytic therapists, the practical applications of many psychoanalytic techniques are limited. This is especially true of methods such as free association on the couch, dream analysis, and extensive analysis of the transference relationship. A factor limiting the practical application of classical psychoanalysis is that many severely disturbed clients lack the level of ego strength needed for this treatment.

A major limitation of traditional psychoanalytic therapy is the relatively long time commitment required to accomplish analytic goals. Contemporary psychoanalytically oriented therapists are interested in their clients' past, but they intertwine that understanding with the present and with future goals. The emergence of brief, time-limited psychodynamic therapy is a partial response to the criticism of lengthy therapy. Psychodynamic psychotherapy evolved from traditional analysis to address the need for treatment that was not so lengthy and involved (Luborsky et al., 2011). In a critique of long-term psychodynamic therapy, Strupp (1992) assumes that psychoanalytic therapy will remain a luxury for most people in our society. Strupp notes a decline in practices based on the classical analytic model due to reasons such as time commitment, expense, limited applications to diverse client populations, and questionable benefits. He believes there will be an increasing emphasis on short-term treatments for specific disorders, limited goals, and containment of costs.

A potential limitation of the psychoanalytic approach is the anonymous role assumed by some therapists. This stance can be justified on theoretical grounds, but in therapy situations other than classical psychoanalysis this stance is unduly restrictive. The newer formulations of psychoanalytic practice place considerable emphasis on the interaction between therapist and client in the here and now, and therapists can decide when and what to disclose to clients. Yalom (2003) contends that therapist anonymity is not a good model for effective therapy. He suggests that appropriate therapist self-disclosure tends to enhance therapy outcomes. Rather than adopting a blank screen, he believes it is far better to strive to understand the past as a way of shedding light on the dynamics of the present therapist–client relationship. This is in keeping with the spirit of the relational analytic approach, which emphasizes the here-and-now interaction between therapist and client.

From a feminist perspective there are distinct limitations to a number of Freudian concepts, especially the Oedipus and Electra complexes. In her review of feminist counseling and therapy, Enns (1993) also notes that the object-relations approach has been criticized for its emphasis on the role of the mother–child relationship in determining later interpersonal functioning. The approach gives great responsibility to mothers for deficiencies and distortions in development. Fathers are conspicuously absent from the hypothesis about patterns of early development; only mothers are blamed for inadequate parenting. Linehan's (1993a, 1993b) dialectical behavior therapy (DBT), addressed in some detail in Chapter 9, is an eclectic approach that avoids mother bashing while accepting the notion that the borderline client experienced a childhood environment that was "invalidating" (Linehan, 1993a, pp. 49–52).

Luborsky, O'Reilly-Landry, and Arlow (2011) note that psychoanalytic therapies have been criticized for being irrelevant to contemporary culture and being appropriate only to an elite, highly educated clientele. To this criticism, they counter with the following statement: "Psychoanalysis is a continually evolving field that has been revised and altered by psychoanalytic theorists and clinicians ever since its origin. This evolution began with Freud himself, who often rethought and substantially revised his own ideas" (p. 27).

WHERE TO GO FROM HERE

If this chapter has provided the impetus for you to learn more about the psychoanalytic approach or the contemporary offshoots of psychoanalysis, you might consider selecting a few books from the Recommended Supplementary Readings and References and Suggested Readings listed at the end of the chapter.

If you are using the *DVD for Integrative Counseling: The Case of Ruth and Lecturettes,* refer to Session 10 ("Transference and Countertransference") and compare what I've written here with how I deal with transference and countertransference.

A number of DVDs from the American Psychological Association's Systems of Psychotherapy Video Series address the psychoanalytic approaches discussed in this chapter. They include *Psychoanalytic Therapy* (N. McWilliams, 2007), *Relational Psychotherapy* (J. Safran, 2008), *Psychoanalytic Therapy Over Time* (J. Safran, 2010), *Integrative Relational Psychotherapy* (P. Wachtel, 2008), and *Brief Dynamic Therapy Over Time* (H. Levenson, 2009).

Psychotherapy.net (www.Psychotherapy.net) is a comprehensive resource for students and professionals, offering videos and interviews with renowned psychoanalysts such as Otto Kernberg and Nancy McWilliams. New articles, interviews, blogs, and videos are published monthly. Two from 2011 by Otto Kernberg are *Otto Kernberg: Live Case Consultation* and *Psychoanalytic Psychotherapy for Personality Disorders: An Interview with Otto Kernberg, MD.*

Various colleges and universities offer special workshops or short courses through continuing education on topics such as therapeutic considerations in working with borderline and narcissistic personalities. These workshops could give you a new perspective on the range of applications of contemporary psychoanalytic therapy. For further information about training programs, workshops, and graduate programs in various states, contact:

American Psychoanalytic Association
309 East 49th Street, New York, NY 10017-1601
Telephone: (212) 752-0450
Fax: (212) 593-0571
Website: www.apsa.org

Adlerian Therapy

Coauthored by Gerald Corey and James Robert Bitter

Hulton Archive/Getty Images

ALFRED ADLER (1870–1937) grew up in a Vienna family of six boys and two girls. His younger brother died at a very young age in the bed next to Alfred. Adler's early childhood was not a happy time. He was sickly and very much aware of death. At age 4 he almost died of pneumonia. He heard the doctor tell his father that "Alfred is lost." Adler associated this time with his decision to become a physician. Because he was ill so much during the first few years of his life, Adler was pampered by his mother. He developed a trusting relationship with his father, but did not feel very close to his mother. He was extremely jealous of his older brother, Sigmund, which led to a strained relationship between the two during childhood and adolescence. When we consider Adler's strained relationship with Sigmund Freud, one cannot help but suspect that patterns from his early family constellation were repeated in this relationship with Freud.

Adler's early childhood experiences had an impact on the formation of his theory. Adler is an example of a person who shaped his own life as opposed to having it determined by fate. Adler was a poor student. His teacher advised his father to prepare Adler to be a shoemaker, but not much else. With determined effort Adler eventually rose to the top of his class. He went on to study medicine at the University of Vienna, entering private practice as an ophthalmologist, and then shifting to general medicine. He eventually specialized in neu-

rology and psychiatry, and he had a keen interest in incurable childhood diseases.

Adler had a passionate concern for the common person and was outspoken about child-rearing practices, school reforms, and prejudices that resulted in conflict. He spoke and wrote in simple, nontechnical language so that the general population could understand and apply the principles of his approach in a practical way, which helped people meet the challenges of daily life. Adler's (1927/1959) *Understanding Human Nature* was the first major psychology book to sell hundreds of thousands of copies in the United States. After serving in World War I as a medical officer, Adler created 32 child guidance clinics in the Vienna public schools and began training teachers, social workers, physicians, and other professionals. He pioneered the practice of teaching professionals through live demonstrations with parents and children before large audiences, now called "open-forum" family counseling. The clinics he founded grew in number and in popularity, and he was indefatigable in lecturing and demonstrating his work.

Although Adler had an overcrowded work schedule most of his professional life, he still took some time to sing, enjoy music, and be with friends. In the mid-1920s he began lecturing in the United States, and he later made frequent visits and tours. He ignored the warning of his friends to slow down, and on May 28, 1937, while taking a walk before a scheduled lecture in Aberdeen, Scotland, Adler collapsed and died of heart failure.

If you have an interest in learning more about Adler's life, see Edward Hoffman's (1996) excellent biography, *The Drive for Self*.

INTRODUCTION

Along with Freud and Jung, Alfred Adler was a major contributor to the initial development of the psychodynamic approach to therapy. After 8 to 10 years of collaboration, Freud and Adler parted company, with Freud taking the position that Adler was a heretic who had deserted him. Adler resigned as president of the Vienna Psychoanalytic Society in 1911 and founded the Society for Individual Psychology in 1912. Freud then asserted that it was not possible to support Adlerian concepts and still remain in good standing as a psychoanalyst.

Later, a number of other psychoanalysts deviated from Freud's orthodox position (see Chapter 4). These Freudian revisionists—including Karen Horney, Erich Fromm, and Harry Stack Sullivan—agreed that relational, social, and cultural factors were of great significance in shaping personality. Even though these three therapists are typically called neo-Freudians, it would be more appropriate, as Heinz Ansbacher (1979) has suggested, to refer to them as neo-Adlerians because they moved away from Freud's biological and deterministic point of view and toward Adler's social-psychological and teleological (or goal-oriented) view of human nature.

Adler stresses the unity of personality, contending that people can only be understood as integrated and complete beings. This view also espouses the purposeful nature of behavior, emphasizing that where we have come from is not as important as where we are striving to go. Adler saw humans as both the creators and the creations of their own lives; that is, people develop a unique style of living that is both a movement toward and an expression of their selected goals. In this sense, we create ourselves rather than merely being shaped by our childhood experiences.

After Adler's death in 1937, Rudolf Dreikurs was the most significant figure in bringing Adlerian psychology to the United States, especially as its principles applied to education, individual and group therapy, and family counseling. Dreikurs is credited with giving impetus to the idea of child guidance centers and to training professionals to work with a wide range of clients.

 See the DVD program for Chapter 5, *DVD for Theory and Practice of Counseling and Psychotherapy: The Case of Stan and Lecturettes*. I suggest that you view the brief lecture for each chapter prior to reading the chapter.

KEY CONCEPTS

View of Human Nature

Adler abandoned Freud's basic theories because he believed Freud was excessively narrow in his emphasis on biological and instinctual determination. Adler believed that the individual begins to form an approach to life somewhere in the first 6 years of living. He focused on the person's past as perceived in the present and how an individual's interpretation of early events continued to influence that person's present behavior. According to Adler, humans are motivated primarily by social relatedness rather than by sexual urges; behavior is purposeful and goal-directed; and consciousness, more than unconsciousness, is the focus of therapy. Adler stressed choice and responsibility, meaning in life, and the striving for success, completion, and perfection. Adler and Freud created very different theories, even though both men grew up in the same city in the same era and were educated as physicians at the same university. Their individual and distinct childhood experiences, their personal struggles, and the populations with whom they worked were key factors in the development of their particular views of human nature (Schultz & Schultz, 2009).

Adler's theory starts with a consideration of inferiority feelings, which he saw as a normal condition of all people and as a source of all human striving. Rather than being considered a sign of weakness or abnormality, **inferiority feelings** can be the wellspring of creativity. They motivate us to strive for mastery, success (superiority), and completion. We are driven to overcome our sense of inferiority and to strive for increasingly higher levels of development (Ansbacher & Ansbacher, 1956/1964). Indeed, at around 6 years of age our fictional vision of ourselves as perfect or complete begins to form into a life goal. The life goal unifies the personality and becomes the source of human motivation; every striving and every effort to overcome inferiority is now in line with this goal.

From the Adlerian perspective, human behavior is not determined solely by heredity and environment. Instead, we have the capacity to interpret, influence, and create events. Adler asserted that genetics and heredity are not as important as what we choose to do with the abilities and limitations we possess. Although Adlerians reject a deterministic stance, they do not go to the other extreme and maintain that individuals can become whatever they want to be. Adlerians recognize that biological and environmental conditions limit our capacity to choose and to create.

Adlerians put the focus on reeducating individuals and reshaping society. Adler was the forerunner of a subjective approach to psychology that focuses on internal determinants of behavior such as values, beliefs, attitudes, goals, interests, and the individual perception of reality. He was a pioneer of an approach that is holistic, social, goal oriented, systemic, and humanistic. Adler also was the first systemic therapist: he maintained that it is essential to understand people within the systems in which they live.

Subjective Perception of Reality

Adlerians attempt to view the world from the client's subjective frame of reference, an orientation described as **phenomenological**. Paying attention to the individual way in which people perceive their world, referred to as "subjective reality," includes the individual's perceptions, thoughts, feelings, values, beliefs, convictions, and conclusions. Behavior is understood from the vantage point of this subjective perspective. From the Adlerian perspective, objective reality is less important than how we interpret reality and the meanings we attach to what we experience.

As you will see in subsequent chapters, many contemporary theories have incorporated this notion of the client's subjective worldview as a basic factor explaining behavior, including existential therapy, person-centered therapy, Gestalt therapy, the cognitive behavioral therapies, reality therapy, feminist therapy, and the postmodern approaches.

Unity and Patterns of Human Personality

Adler chose the name **Individual Psychology** (from the Latin *individuum*, meaning indivisible) for his theoretical approach because he wanted to avoid reductionism. Adler emphasized the unity and indivisibility of the person and stressed understanding the whole person in the context of his or her life—how all dimensions of a person are interconnected components, and how all of these components are unified by the individual's movement toward a life goal. This **holistic concept** implies that we cannot be understood in parts; rather, all aspects of ourselves must be understood in relationship (Carlson & Englar-Carlson, 2008). The focus is on understanding whole persons within their socially embedded contexts of family, culture, school, and work. We are social, creative, decision-making beings who act with purpose and cannot be fully known outside the contexts that have meaning in our lives (Sherman & Dinkmeyer, 1987).

The human personality becomes unified through development of a life goal. An individual's thoughts, feelings, beliefs, convictions, attitudes, character, and actions are expressions of his or her uniqueness, and all reflect a plan of life that allows for movement toward a self-selected life goal. An implication of this *holistic view of personality* is that the client is an integral part of a social system. There is more emphasis on interpersonal relationships than on the individual's internal psychodynamics.

BEHAVIOR AS PURPOSEFUL AND GOAL ORIENTED Individual Psychology assumes that all human behavior has a purpose. The concept of the purposeful nature of behavior is perhaps the cornerstone of Adler's theory. Adler replaced deterministic explanations with teleological (purposive, goal-oriented) ones. A basic assumption of Individual Psychology is that we can only think, feel, and act in relation to our goal; we can be fully understood only in light of knowing the purposes and goals toward which we are striving. Although Adlerians are interested in the future, they do not minimize the importance of past influences. They assume that most decisions are based on the person's experiences, on the present situation, and on the direction in which the person is moving—with the latter being the most important. They look for continuity by paying attention to themes running through a person's life.

Adler was influenced by the philosopher Hans Vaihinger (1965), who noted that people often live by fictions (or views of how the world should be). Many Adlerians use the term **fictional finalism** to refer to an imagined life goal that guides a person's behavior. It should be noted, however, that Adler ceased using this term and replaced it with "guiding self-ideal" and "goal of perfection" to account for our striving toward superiority or perfection (Watts & Holden, 1994). Very early in life, we begin to envision what we might be like if we were successful, complete, whole, or perfect. Applied to human motivation, a guiding self-ideal might be expressed in this way: "Only when I am perfect can I be secure" or "Only when I am important can I be accepted." The guiding self-ideal represents an individual's image of a goal of perfection, for which he or she strives in any given situation. Because of our subjective final goal, we have the creative power to choose what we will accept as truth, how we will behave, and how we will interpret events.

STRIVING FOR SIGNIFICANCE AND SUPERIORITY Adler stressed that the recognition of inferiority feelings and the consequent striving for perfection or mastery are innate (Ansbacher & Ansbacher, 1979)—they are two sides of the same coin. To understand human behavior, it is essential to grasp the ideas of basic inferiority and compensation. From our earliest years, we recognize that we are helpless in many ways, which is characterized by feelings of inferiority.

This inferiority is not a negative factor in life. According to Adler, the moment we experience inferiority we are pulled by the striving for superiority. He maintained that the goal of success pulls people forward toward mastery and enables them to overcome obstacles. The goal of superiority contributes to the development of human community. However, it is important to note that "superiority," as used by Adler, does not necessarily mean superiority over others. Rather, it means moving from a perceived lower (or minus) position to a perceived better (or plus) position. People cope with feelings of helplessness by striving for competence, mastery, and perfection. They can seek to change a weakness into a strength, for example, or strive to excel in one area to compensate for defects in other areas. The unique ways in which people develop a style of striving for competence is what constitutes individuality or lifestyle. The manner in which Adler reacted to his childhood and adolescent experiences is a living example of this aspect of his theory.

LIFESTYLE The movement from a felt minus to a desired plus results in the development of a life goal, which in turn unifies the personality and the individual's core beliefs and assumptions. These core beliefs and assumptions guide each person's movement through life and organize his or her reality, giving meaning to life events. Adler called this life movement the individual's "lifestyle." Synonyms for this term include "plan of life," "style of life," "strategy for living," and "road map of life." **Lifestyle** includes the connecting themes and rules of interaction that give meaning to our actions. Lifestyle is often described as our perceptions regarding self, others, and the world. It includes an individual's characteristic way of thinking, acting, feeling, living, and striving toward long-term goals (Mosak & Maniacci, 2011).

Adler saw us as actors, creators, and artists. Understanding one's lifestyle is somewhat like understanding the style of a composer: "We can begin wherever we choose: every expression will lead us in the same direction—toward the one motive, the one melody, around which the personality is built" (Adler, as cited in Ansbacher & Ansbacher, 1956/1964, p. 332).

People are viewed as adopting a proactive, rather than a reactive, approach to their social environment. Although events in the environment influence the development of personality, such events are not the causes of what people become; rather, it is our interpretation of these events that shape personality. Faulty interpretations may lead to mistaken notions in our private logic, which will significantly influence present behavior. Once we become aware of the patterns and continuity of our lives, we are in a position to modify those faulty assumptions and make basic changes. We can reframe childhood experiences and *consciously* create a new style of living.

Social Interest and Community Feeling

Social interest and community feeling (*Gemeinschaftsgefühl*) are probably Adler's most significant and distinctive concepts (Ansbacher, 1992). These terms refer to individuals' awareness of being part of the human community and to individuals' attitudes in dealing with the social world.

Social interest is the action line of one's community feeling, and it involves being as concerned about others as one is about onself. This concept involves the capacity to cooperate and contribute (Milliren & Clemmer, 2006). Social interest requires that we have enough contact with the present to make a move toward a meaningful future, that we are willing to give and to take, and that we develop our capacity for contributing to the welfare of others and striving for the betterment of humanity. The socialization process associated with social interest begins in childhood and involves helping children to find a place in society and acquire a sense of belonging, as well as the ability to make a contribution (Kefir, 1981). While Adler considered social interest to be innate, he also believed that it must be learned, developed, and used.

Adler equated social interest with a sense of identification and empathy with others: "to see with the eyes of another, to hear with the ears of another, to feel with the heart of another" (as cited in Ansbacher & Ansbacher, 1979, p. 42). Social interest is the central indicator of mental health. Those with social interest tend to direct the striving toward the healthy and socially useful side of life. From the Adlerian perspective, as social interest develops, feelings of inferiority and alienation diminish. People express social interest through shared activity and mutual respect.

Individual Psychology rests on a central belief that our happiness and success are largely related to this social connectedness. Because we are embedded in a society, and indeed in the whole of humanity, we cannot be understood in isolation from that social context. We are primarily motivated by a desire to belong. **Community feeling** embodies the feeling of being connected to all of humanity—past, present, and future—and to being involved in making the world a better place. Those who lack this community feeling become discouraged and end up on the useless side of life. We seek a place in the family and in society to fulfill basic needs for security, acceptance, and worthiness. Many of the problems we experience are related to the fear of not being accepted by the groups we value. If our sense of belonging is not fulfilled, anxiety is the result. Only when we feel united with others are we able to act with courage in facing and dealing with our problems (Adler, 1938/1964).

Adler taught that we must successfully master three universal life tasks: building friendships (social task), establishing intimacy (love–marriage task), and contributing to society (occupational task). All people need to address these tasks, regardless of age, gender, time in history, culture, or nationality. Each of these tasks requires the development of psychological capacities for *friendship* and *belonging*, for *contribution* and *self-worth*, and for *cooperation* (Bitter, 2006). These basic life tasks are so fundamental to human living that impairment in any one of them is often an indicator of a psychological disorder (American Psychiatric Association, 2000). More often than not, when people seek therapy, it is because they are struggling unsuccessfully to meet one or more of these life tasks. The aim of therapy is to assist clients in modifying their lifestyle so they can more effectively navigate each of these tasks (Carlson & Englar-Carlson, 2008).

Birth Order and Sibling Relationships

The Adlerian approach is unique in giving special attention to the relationships between siblings and the psychological birth position in one's family. Adler identified five psychological positions, or vantage points, from which children tend to view life: oldest, second of only two, middle, youngest, and only. **Birth order** is not a deterministic concept but does increase an individual's probability of having a certain set of experiences. Actual birth order is less important than the individual's interpretation of his or her place in the family. Because Adlerians view most human problems as social in nature, they emphasize relationships within the family as our earliest and, perhaps, our most influential social system.

Adler (1931/1958) observed that many people wonder why children in the same family often differ so widely, and he pointed out that it is a fallacy to assume that children of the same family are formed in the same environment. Although siblings share aspects in common in the family constellation, the psychological situation of each child is different from that of the others due to birth order. The following description of the influence of birth order is based on Ansbacher and Ansbacher (1964), Dreikurs (1953), and Adler (1931/1958).

1. The *oldest child* generally receives a good deal of attention, and during the time she is the only child, she is typically somewhat spoiled as the center of attention. She tends to be dependable and hard working and strives to keep ahead. When a new brother or sister arrives on the scene, however, she finds herself ousted from her favored position. She is no longer unique or special. She may readily believe that the newcomer (or intruder) will rob her of the love to which she is accustomed. Most often, she reasserts her position by becoming a model child, bossing younger children, and exhibiting a high achievement drive.

2. The *second child* of only two is in a different position. From the time she is born, she shares the attention with another child. The typical second child behaves as if she were in a race and is generally under full steam at all times. It is as though this second child were in training to surpass the older brother or sister. This competitive struggle between the first two children influences the later course of their lives. The younger child develops a knack for finding out the elder child's weak spots and proceeds to win praise from both parents and teachers by achieving successes where the older sibling has failed. If one is talented in a given area, the other strives for recognition by developing other abilities. The second-born is often opposite to the firstborn.

3. The *middle child* often feels squeezed out. This child may become convinced of the unfairness of life and feel cheated. This person may assume a "poor me" attitude and can become a problem child. However, especially in families characterized by conflict, the middle child may become the switchboard and the peacemaker, the person who holds things together. If there are four children in a family, the second child will often feel like a middle child and the third will be more easygoing, more social, and may align with the firstborn.

4. The *youngest child* is always the baby of the family and tends to be the most pampered one. Because of being pampered or spoiled, he may develop helplessness into an art form and become expert at putting others in his service. Youngest children tend to go their own way, often developing in ways no others in the family have attempted and may outshine everyone.

5. The *only child* has a problem of her own. Although she shares some of the characteristics of the oldest child (for example, a high achievement drive), she may not learn to share or cooperate with other children. She will learn to deal with adults well, as they make up her original familial world. Often, the only child is pampered by her parents and may become dependently tied to one or both of them. She may want to have center stage all of the time, and if her position is challenged, she will feel it is unfair.

Birth order and the interpretation of one's position in the family have a great deal to do with how adults interact in the world. Individuals acquire a certain style of relating to others in childhood and form a definite picture of themselves that they carry into their adult interactions. In Adlerian therapy, working with family dynamics, especially relationships among siblings, assumes a key role. Although it is important to avoid stereotyping individuals, it does help to see how certain personality trends that began in childhood as a result of sibling rivalry influence individuals throughout life.

THE THERAPEUTIC PROCESS
Therapeutic Goals
Adlerian counseling rests on a collaborative arrangement between the client and the counselor. In general, the therapeutic process includes forming a relationship based on mutual respect; a holistic *psychological investigation* or lifestyle assessment; and disclosing *mistaken goals* and *faulty assumptions* within the person's style of living. This is followed by a reeducation or reorientation of the client toward the useful side of life. The main aim of therapy is to develop the client's sense of belonging and to assist in the adoption of behaviors and processes characterized by community feeling and social interest. This is accomplished by increasing the client's self-awareness and challenging and modifying his or her fundamental premises, life goals, and basic concepts (Dreikurs, 1967, 1997). Milliren, Evans, and Newbauer (2007), identify this goal of Adlerian therapy: "to assist clients to understand their unique lifestyles . . . and to act in such a way as to meet the tasks of life with courage and social interest" (p. 145).

Adlerians do not view clients as being "sick" and in need of being "cured." They favor the growth model of personality rather than the medical model. As Mosak and Maniacci (2011) put it: "The Adlerian is interested not in curing sick individuals or a sick society but in reeducating individuals and in reshaping society" (p. 78). Rather than being stuck in some kind of pathology, Adlerians contend that clients are often discouraged. The counseling process focuses on providing information, teaching, guiding, and offering encouragement to discouraged clients. Encouragement is the most powerful method available for changing a person's beliefs, for it helps clients build self-confidence and stimulates courage. Courage is the willingness to act *even when fearful* in ways that are consistent with social interest. Fear and courage go hand in hand; without fear, there would be no need for courage. The loss of courage, or discouragement, results in mistaken and dysfunctional behavior. Discouraged people do not act in line with social interest.

Adlerian counselors provide clients with an opportunity to view things from a different perspective, yet it is up to the clients to decide whether to accept an alternative perspective. Adlerians work collaboratively with clients to help them reach their self-defined goals. Adlerians educate clients in new ways of looking at themselves, others, and life. Through the process of providing clients with a new "cognitive map," a fundamental understanding of the purpose of their behavior, counselors assist them in changing their perceptions. Mosak and Maniacci (2011) lists these goals for the educational process of therapy:

- Fostering social interest
- Helping clients overcome feelings of discouragement and inferiority
- Modifying clients' views and goals—that is, changing their lifestyle
- Changing faulty motivation
- Encouraging the individual to recognize equality among people
- Helping people to become contributing members of society

Therapist's Function and Role

Adlerian counselors realize that clients can become discouraged and function ineffectively because of mistaken beliefs, faulty values, and useless or self-absorbed goals. These therapists operate on the assumption that clients will feel and behave better once they discover and correct their basic mistakes. Therapists tend to look for major mistakes in thinking and valuing such as mistrust, selfishness, unrealistic ambitions, and lack of confidence.

Adlerians assume a nonpathological perspective and thus do not label clients with pathological diagnoses. One way of looking at the role of Adlerian therapists is that they assist clients in better understanding, challenging, and changing their life story. "When individuals develop a life story that they find limiting and problem saturated, the goal is to free them from that story in favor of a preferred and equally viable alternative story" (Disque & Bitter, 1998, p. 434).

A major function of the therapist is to make a comprehensive assessment of the client's functioning. Therapists often gather information about the individual's style of living by means of a questionnaire on the client's **family constellation**, which includes parents, siblings, and others living in the home, life tasks, and early recollections. When summarized and interpreted, this questionnaire gives a picture of the individual's early social world. From this information on the family constellation, the therapist is able to get a perspective on the client's major areas of success and failure and on the critical influences that have had a bearing on the role the client has assumed in the world.

The counselor also uses early recollections as an assessment procedure. **Early recollections** (ERs) are defined as "stories of events that a person *says* occurred [one time] before he or she was 10 years of age" (Mosak & Di Pietro, 2006, p. 1). ERs are *specific* incidents that clients recall, along with the feelings and thoughts that accompanied these childhood incidents. These recollections are quite useful in getting a better understanding of the client (Clark, 2002). After these early recollections are summarized and interpreted, the therapist identifies some of the major successes and mistakes in the client's life. The aim is to provide a point of departure for the therapeutic venture. ERs are particularly useful as a functional assessment device because they indicate what clients do and how they think in both adaptive and maladaptive ways (Mosak & Di Pietro, 2006). The process of gathering early memories is part of what is called a **lifestyle assessment**, which involves learning to understand the goals and motivations of the client. When this process is completed, the therapist and the client have targets for therapy.

Mosak and Maniacci (2011) consider dreams to be a useful part of the assessment process. Freud assumed that dreams were wish fulfillment, or, in some instances, an attempt at solving an old problem; Adler, on the other hand, viewed dreams as a rehearsal for possible future actions. Just as early recollections reflect a client's long-range goals, dreams suggest possible answers to a client's present problems. In interpreting dreams, the therapist considers their purposive function. Mosak and Maniacci (2011) assert that "dreams serve as weather vanes for treatment, bringing problems to the surface and pointing to the patient's movement" (p. 88).

Client's Experience in Therapy

How do clients maintain their lifestyle, and why do they resist changing it? A person's style of living serves the individual by staying stable and constant. In other words, it is predictable. It is, however, also resistant to change throughout most of one's life. Generally, people fail to change because they do not recognize the errors in their thinking or the purposes of their behaviors, do not know what to do differently, and are fearful of leaving old patterns for new and unpredictable outcomes. Thus, even though their ways of thinking and behaving are not successful, they tend to cling to familiar patterns (Sweeney, 2009). Clients in Adlerian counseling focus their work on desired outcomes and a resilient lifestyle that can provide a new blueprint for their actions.

In therapy, clients explore what Adlerians call **private logic**, the concepts about self, others, and life that constitute the philosophy on which an individual's lifestyle is based. Private logic involves our convictions and beliefs that get in the way of social interest and that do not facilitate useful, constructive belonging (Carlson, Watts, & Maniacci, 2006). Clients' problems arise because the conclusions based on their private logic often do not conform to the requirements of social living. The heart of therapy is helping clients to discover the purposes of behaviors or symptoms and the basic mistakes associated with their personal coping. Learning how to correct faulty assumptions and conclusions is central to therapy.

To provide a concrete example, think of a chronically depressed middle-aged man who begins therapy. After a lifestyle assessment is completed, these basic mistakes are identified:

- He has convinced himself that nobody could really care about him.
- He rejects people before they have a chance to reject him.
- He is harshly critical of himself, expecting perfection.
- He has expectations that things will rarely work out well.
- He burdens himself with guilt because he is convinced he is letting everyone down.

Even though this man may have developed these mistaken ideas about himself and life when he was young, he is still clinging to them as rules for living. His expectations, most of which are pessimistic, tend to be fulfilled because on some level he is seeking to validate his beliefs. Indeed, his depression will eventually serve the purpose of helping him avoid contact with others, a life task at which he expects to fail. In therapy, this man will learn how to challenge the structure of his private logic. In his case the syllogism goes as follows:

- "I am basically unlovable."
- "The world is filled with people who are likely to be rejecting."
- "Therefore, I must keep to myself so I won't be hurt."

This person holds onto several basic mistakes, and his private logic offers a psychological focus for treatment. A central theme or convictions in this client's life might be: "I must control everything in my life." "I must be perfect in everything I do."

It is easy to see how depression might follow from this thinking, but Adlerians also know that the depression serves as an excuse for this man's retreat from life. It is important for the therapist to listen for the underlying purposes of this client's behavior. Adlerians see feelings as being aligned with thinking and as the fuel for behaving. First we think, then we feel, and then we act. Because emotions and cognitions serve a purpose, a good deal of therapy time is spent in discovering and understanding this purpose and in reorienting the client toward effective ways of being. Because the client is not perceived by the therapist to be mentally ill or emotionally disturbed, but as mainly discouraged, the therapist will offer the client encouragement so that change is possible. Through the therapeutic process, the client will discover that he or she has resources and options to draw on in dealing with significant life issues and life tasks.

Relationship Between Therapist and Client

Adlerians consider a good client–therapist relationship to be one between equals that is based on cooperation, mutual trust, respect, confidence, collaboration, and alignment of goals. They place special value on the counselor's modeling of communication and acting in good faith. From the beginning of therapy, the relationship is a collaborative one, characterized by two persons working equally toward specific, agreed-upon goals. Adlerian therapists strive to establish and maintain an egalitarian therapeutic alliance and a person-to-person relationship with their clients. Developing a strong therapeutic relationship is essential to successful outcomes (Carlson et al., 2006). Dinkmeyer and Sperry (2000) maintain that at the outset of counseling clients should begin to formulate a plan, or contract, detailing what they want, how they plan to get where they are heading, what is preventing them from successfully attaining their goals, how they can change nonproductive behavior into constructive behavior, and how they can make full use of their assets in achieving their purposes. This therapeutic contract sets forth the goals of the counseling process and specifies the responsibilities of both therapist and client. Developing a contract is not a requirement of Adlerian therapy, but a contract can bring a tight focus to therapy.

APPLICATION: THERAPEUTIC TECHNIQUES AND PROCEDURES

Adlerian counseling is structured around four central objectives that correspond to the four phases of the therapeutic process (Dreikurs, 1967). These phases are not linear and do not progress in rigid steps; rather, they can best be understood as a weaving that leads to a tapestry. These phases are as follows:

1. Establish the proper therapeutic relationship.
2. Explore the psychological dynamics operating in the client (an assessment).
3. Encourage the development of self-understanding (insight into purpose).
4. Help the client make new choices (reorientation and reeducation).

Dreikurs (1997) incorporated these phases into what he called *minor psychotherapy* in the context and service of holistic medicine. His approach to therapy has been elaborated in what is now called **Adlerian brief therapy**, or ABT (Bitter, Christensen, Hawes, & Nicoll, 1998). This way of working is discussed in the following sections.

Phase 1: Establish the Relationship

The Adlerian practitioner works in a collaborative way with clients, and this relationship is based on a sense of interest that grows into caring, involvement, and friendship. Therapeutic progress is possible only when there is an alignment of clearly defined goals between therapist and client. The counseling process, to be effective, must deal with the personal issues the client recognizes as significant and is willing to explore and change. The therapeutic efficacy in the later phases of Adlerian therapy is predicated upon the development and continuation of a solid therapeutic relationship during this first phase of therapy (Watts, 2000; Watts & Pietrzak, 2000).

Adlerian therapists focus on making person-to-person contact with clients rather than starting with "the problem." Clients' concerns surface rather quickly in therapy, but the initial focus should be on the person, not the problem. One way to create effective contact is for counselors to help clients become aware of their assets and strengths rather than dealing continually with their deficits and liabilities. During the initial phase, a positive relationship is created by listening; responding; demonstrating respect for clients' capacity to understand purpose and seek change; and exhibiting faith, hope, and caring. When clients enter therapy, they typically have a diminished sense of self-worth and self-respect. They lack faith in their ability to cope with the tasks of life. Therapists provide support, which is an antidote to despair and discouragement. For some people, therapy may be one of the few times in which they have truly experienced a caring human relationship.

Adlerians pay more attention to the subjective experiences of the client than they do to using techniques. They fit their techniques to the needs of each client. During the initial phase of counseling, the main techniques are attending and listening with empathy, following the subjective experience of the client as closely as possible, identifying and clarifying goals, and suggesting initial hunches about purpose in client's symptoms, actions, and interactions. Adlerian counselors are generally active, especially during the initial sessions. They provide structure and assist clients to define personal goals, they conduct psychological assessments, and they offer interpretations (Carlson et al., 2006). Adlerians attempt to grasp both the verbal and nonverbal messages of the client; they want to access the core patterns in the client's life. If the client feels deeply understood and accepted, the client is likely to focus on what he or she wants from therapy and thus establish goals. At this stage the counselor's function is to provide a wide-angle perspective that will eventually help the client view his or her world differently.

Phase 2: Explore the Individual's Psychological Dynamics

The aim of the second phase of Adlerian counseling is to get a deeper understanding of an individual's lifestyle. During this assessment phase, the focus is on the individual's social and cultural context. Rather than attempting to fit clients into a preconceived model, Adlerian practitioners allow salient cultural identity concepts to emerge in the therapy process, and these issues are then addressed (Carlson & Englar-Carlson, 2008). This assessment phase proceeds from two interview forms: the *subjective interview* and the *objective interview* (Dreikurs, 1997). In the **subjective interview,** the counselor helps the client to tell his or her life story as completely as possible. This process is facilitated by a generous use of empathic listening and responding. Active listening, however, is not enough. The subjective interview must follow from a sense of wonder, fascination, and interest. What the client says will spark an interest in the counselor and lead, naturally, to the next most significant question or inquiry about the client and his or her life story. Indeed, the best subjective interviews treat clients as experts in their own lives, allowing clients to feel completely heard. Throughout the subjective interview, the Adlerian counselor is listening for clues to the purposive aspects of the client's coping and approaches to life. "The subjective interview should extract patterns in the person's life, develop hypotheses about what works for the person, and determine what accounts for the various concerns in the client's life" (Bitter et al., 1998, p. 98). Toward the end of this part of the interview, Adlerian brief therapists ask, "Is there anything else you think I should know to understand you and your concerns?"

An initial assessment of the purpose that symptoms, actions, or difficulties serve in a person's life can be gained from what Dreikurs (1997) calls "The Question." Adlerians often end a subjective interview with this question: "How would your life be different, and what would you be *doing* differently, if you did not have this symptom or problem?" Adlerians use this question to help with differential diagnosis. More often, the symptoms or problems experienced by the client help the client avoid something that is perceived as necessary but from which the person wishes to retreat, usually a life task: "If it weren't for my depression, I would get out more and see my friends." Such a statement betrays the client's concern about the possibility of being a good friend or being welcomed by his or her friends. "I need to get married, but how can I with these panic attacks?" indicates the person's worry about being a partner in a marriage. Depression can serve as the client's solution when faced with problems in relationships. If a client reports that nothing would be different, especially with physical symptoms, Adlerians suspect that the problem may be organic and require medical intervention.

The **objective interview** seeks to discover information about (a) how problems in the client's life began; (b) any precipitating events; (c) a medical history, including current and past medications; (d) a social history; (e) the reasons the client chose therapy at this time; (f) the person's coping with life tasks; and (g) a lifestyle assessment. Mozdzierz and his colleagues (1986) describe the counselor as a "lifestyle investigator" during this phase of therapy. Based on interview approaches developed by Adler and Dreikurs, the lifestyle assessment starts with an investigation of the person's family constellation and early childhood history (Powers & Griffith, 1987; Shulman & Mosak, 1988). Counselors also interpret the person's early memories, seeking to understand the meaning that she or he has attached to life experiences. They operate on the assumption that it is the interpretations people develop about themselves, others, the world, and life that govern what they do. Lifestyle assessment seeks to develop a holistic narrative of the person's life, to make sense of the way the person copes with life tasks, and to uncover the private interpretations and logic involved in that coping. For example, if Jenny has lived most of her life in a critical environment, and now she believes she must be perfect to avoid even the appearance of failure, the assessment process will highlight the restricted living that flows from this perspective.

THE FAMILY CONSTELLATION Adler considered the family of origin as having a central impact on an individual's personality. Adler suggested that it was through the family constellation that each person forms his or her unique view of self, others, and life. Factors such as cultural and familial values, gender-role expectations, and the nature of interpersonal relationships are all influenced by a child's observation of the interactional patterns within the family. Adlerian assessment relies heavily on an exploration of the client's **family constellation**, including the client's evaluation of conditions that prevailed in the family when the person was a young child (family atmosphere), birth order, parental relationship and family values, and extended family and culture. Some of these questions are almost always explored:

- Who was the favorite child?
- What was your father's relationship with the children? Your mother's?
- Which child was most like your father? Your mother? In what respects?
- Who among the siblings was most different from you? In what ways?
- Who among the siblings was most like you? In what ways?
- What were you like as a child?
- How did your parents get along? In what did they both agree? How did they handle disagreements? How did they discipline the children?

An investigation of family constellation is far more comprehensive than these few questions, but these questions give an idea of the type of information the counselor is seeking. The questions are always tailored to the individual client with the goal of eliciting the client's perceptions of self and others, of development, and of the experiences that have affected that development.

EARLY RECOLLECTIONS As you will recall, another assessment procedure used by Adlerians is to ask the client to provide his or her earliest memories, including the age of the person at the time of the remembered events and the feelings or reactions associated with the recollections. Early recollections are one-time occurrences, usually before the age of 9, pictured by the client in clear detail. Adler reasoned that out of the millions of early memories we might have we select those special memories that project the essential convictions and even the basic mistakes of our lives. Early recollections are a series of small mysteries that can be woven together into a tapestry that leads to an understanding of how we view ourselves, how we see the world, what our life goals are, what motivates us, what we value and believe in, and what we anticipate for our future (Clark, 2002; Mosak & Di Pietro, 2006).

Early memories cast light on the "story of our life" because they represent metaphors for our current views. From the thousands of experiences we have before the age of 9, we tend to remember only 6 to 12 memories. By understanding why we retain these memories and what they tell us about how we see ourselves, others, and life in the present, it is possible to get a clear sense of our mistaken notions, present attitudes, social interests, and possible future behavior. Early recollections are specific instances that clients tell therapists, and they are very useful in understanding those who are sharing a story (Mosak & Di Pietro, 2006). Exploring early recollections involves discovering how mistaken notions based on faulty goals and values continue to create problems in a client's life.

To tap such recollections, the counselor might proceed as follows: "I would like to hear about your early memories. Think back to when you were very young, as early as you can remember (before the age of 10), and *tell me something that happened one time.*" After receiving each memory, the counselor might also ask: "What part stands out to you? What was the most vivid part of your early memory? If you played the whole memory like a movie and stopped it at one frame, what would be happening? Putting yourself in that moment, what are you feeling? What's your reaction?" Three memories are usually considered a minimum to assess a pattern, and some counselors ask for as many as a dozen memories.

Adlerian therapists use early recollections as a projective technique (Clark, 2002; Hood & Johnson, 2007) and to (a) assess the client's convictions about self, others, life, and ethics; (b) assess the client's stance in relation to the counseling session and the counseling relationship; (c) verify the client's coping patterns; and (d) assess individual strengths, assets, and interfering ideas (Bitter et al., 1998, p. 99).

In interpreting these early recollections, Adlerians may consider questions such as these:

- What part does the client take in the memory? Is the client an observer or a participant?
- Who else is in the memory? What position do others take in relation to the client?
- What are the dominant themes and overall patterns of the memories?
- What feelings are expressed in the memories?
- Why does the client choose to remember this event? What is the client trying to convey?

INTEGRATION AND SUMMARY Once material has been gathered from both subjective and objective interviews with the client, integrated summaries of the data are developed. Different summaries are prepared for different clients, but common ones are a narrative summary of the person's subjective experience and life story; a summary of family constellation and developmental data; a summary of early recollections, personal strengths or assets, and interfering ideas; and a summary of coping strategies. The summaries are presented to the client and discussed in the session, with the client and the counselor together refining specific points. This information provides the client with the chance to discuss specific topics and to raise questions.

Mosak and Maniacci (2011) believe lifestyle can be conceived of as a personal mythology. People behave *as if* the myths were true because, for them, they *are true*. Mosak and Maniacci list five *basic mistakes* in what is essentially an integration of Adlerian psychology and cognitive behavioral theory: overgeneralizations, false or impossible goals of security, misperceptions of life and life's demands, minimization or denial of one's basic worth, and faulty values.

In addition to the concept of basic mistakes, Adlerian theory is useful in assisting clients to identify and examine some of their common fears. These fears include being imperfect, being vulnerable, being disapproved of, and suffering from past regrets (Carlson & Englar-Carlson, 2008).

The Student Manual that accompanies this textbook includes a concrete example of the lifestyle assessment as it is applied to the case of Stan. In *Case Approach to Counseling and Psychotherapy* (Corey, 2013, chap. 3), Drs. Jim Bitter and Bill Nicoll present a lifestyle assessment of another hypothetical client, Ruth.

Phase 3: Encourage Self-Understanding and Insight

During this third phase, Adlerian therapists interpret the findings of the assessment as an avenue for promoting self-understanding and insight. Mosak and Maniacci (2011) define **insight** as "understanding translated into constructive action" (p. 89). When Adlerians speak of insight, they are referring to an understanding of the motivations that operate in a client's life. Self-understanding is only possible when hidden purposes and goals of behavior are made conscious. Adlerians consider insight as a special form of awareness that facilitates a meaningful understanding within the therapeutic relationship and acts as a foundation for change. Insight is a means to an end, and not an end in itself. People can make rapid and significant changes without much insight.

Disclosure and well-timed interpretations are techniques that facilitate the process of gaining insight. **Interpretation** deals with clients' underlying motives for behaving the way they do in the here and now. Adlerian disclosures and interpretations are concerned with creating awareness of one's direction in life, one's goals and purposes, one's private logic and how it works, and one's current behavior.

Adlerian interpretations are suggestions presented tentatively in the form of open-ended questions that can be explored in the sessions. They are hunches or guesses, and they often begin with phrases such as "I could be wrong, but I am wondering if . . . ," "Could it be that . . . ," or "Is it possible that . . ." Because interpretations are presented in this manner, clients are not led to defend themselves, and they feel free to discuss and even argue with the counselor's hunches and impressions. Through this process, both counselor and client eventually come to understand the client's motivations, the ways in which these motivations are now contributing to the maintenance of the problem, and what the client can do to correct the situation. During this phase of therapy, the counselor helps the client understand the limitations of the style of life the client has chosen.

Phase 4: Reorientation and Reeducation

The final stage of the therapeutic process is the action-oriented phase known as reorientation and reeducation: putting insights into practice. This phase focuses on helping clients discover a new and more functional perspective. Clients are both encouraged and challenged to develop the courage to take risks and make changes in their life. During this phase, clients can choose to adopt a new style of life based on the insights they gained in the earlier phases of therapy.

Adlerians are interested in more than changes in behavior. **Reorientation** involves shifting rules of interaction, process, and motivation. These shifts are facilitated through changes in awareness, which often occur during the therapy session and which are transformed into action outside of the therapy office (Bitter & Nicoll, 2004). In addition, especially at this phase of therapy, Adlerians focus on reeducation (see the section on therapeutic goals).

In some cases, significant changes are needed if clients are to overcome discouragement and find a place for themselves in this life. More often, however, clients merely need to be reoriented toward the useful side of life. The useful side involves a sense of belonging and being valued, having an interest in others and their welfare, courage, the acceptance of imperfection, confidence, a sense of humor, a willingness to contribute, and an outgoing friendliness. The useless side of life is characterized by self-absorption, withdrawal from life tasks, self-protection, or acts against one's fellow human beings. People acting on the useless side of life become less functional and are more susceptible to psychopathology. Adlerian therapy stands in opposition to self-depreciation, isolation, and retreat, and it seeks to help clients gain courage and to connect to strengths within themselves, to others, and to life. Throughout this phase, no intervention is more important than encouragement.

THE ENCOURAGEMENT PROCESS Encouragement is the most distinctive Adlerian procedure, and it is central to all phases of counseling and therapy. It is especially important as people consider change in their lives. Encouragement literally means "to build courage." Courage develops when people become aware of their strengths, when they feel they belong and are not alone, and when they have a sense of hope and can see new possibilities for themselves and their daily living. **Encouragement** entails showing faith in people, expecting them to assume responsibility for their lives, and valuing them for who they are (Carlson et al., 2006). Carlson and Englar-Carlson (2008) note that encouragement involves acknowledging that life can be difficult, yet it is critical to instill a sense of faith in clients that they can make changes in life. Milliren, Evans, and Newbauer (2007) consider encouragement key in promoting and activating social interest. They add that encouragement is the universal therapeutic intervention for Adlerian counselors, that it is a fundamental attitude rather than a technique. Because clients often do not recognize or accept their positive qualities, strengths, or internal resources, one of the counselor's main tasks is to help them do so.

Adlerians believe discouragement is the basic condition that prevents people from functioning, and they see encouragement as the antidote. As a part of the encouragement process, Adlerians use a variety of relational, cognitive, behavioral, emotional, and experiential techniques to help clients identify and challenge self-defeating cognitions, generate perceptional alternatives, and make use of assets, strengths, and resources (Ansbacher & Ansbacher, 1964; Dinkmeyer & Sperry, 2000; Watts & Pietrzak, 2000; Watts & Shulman, 2003).

Encouragement takes many forms, depending on the phase of the counseling process. In the relationship phase, encouragement results from the mutual respect the counselor seeks to engender. In the assessment phase, which is partially designed to illuminate personal strengths, clients are encouraged to recognize that they are in charge of their own lives and can make different choices based on new understandings. During reorientation, encouragement comes when new possibilities are generated and when clients are acknowledged and affirmed for taking positive steps to change their lives for the better.

CHANGE AND THE SEARCH FOR NEW POSSIBILITIES During the reorientation phase of counseling, clients make decisions and modify their goals. They are encouraged to act *as if* they were the people they want to be, which can serve to challenge self-limiting assumptions. Clients are asked to *catch themselves* in the process of repeating old patterns that have led to ineffective behavior. Commitment is an essential part of reorientation. If clients hope to change, they must be willing to set tasks for themselves in everyday life and do something specific about their problems. In this way, clients translate their new insights into concrete actions. Bitter and Nicoll (2004) emphasize that real change happens between sessions, and not in therapy itself. They state that arriving at a strategy for change is an important first step, and stress that it takes courage and encouragement for clients to apply what they have learned in therapy to daily living.

This action-oriented phase is a time for solving problems and making decisions. The counselor and the client consider possible alternatives and their consequences, evaluate how these alternatives will meet the client's goals, and decide on a specific course of action. The best alternatives and new possibilities are those generated by the client, and the counselor must offer the client a great deal of support and encouragement during this stage of the process.

MAKING A DIFFERENCE Adlerian counselors seek to make a difference in the lives of their clients. That difference may be manifested by a change in behavior or attitude or perception. Adlerians use many different techniques to promote change, some of which have become common interventions in other therapeutic models. Techniques that go by the names of immediacy, advice, humor, silence, paradoxical intention, acting as if, spitting in the client's soup, catching oneself, the push-button technique, externalization, reauthoring, avoiding the traps, confrontation, use of stories and fables, early recollection analysis, lifestyle assessment, encouraging, task setting and commitment, giving homework, and terminating and summarizing have all been used (Carlson & Slavik, 1997; Carlson et al., 2006; Dinkmeyer & Sperry, 2000; Disque & Bitter, 1998; Mosak & Maniacci, 2011; Mozdzierz, Peluso, & Lisiecki, 2009). Adlerian practitioners can creatively employ a wide range of other techniques, as long as these methods are philosophically consistent with the basic theoretical premises of Adlerian psychology (Milliren et al., 2007). Adlerians are pragmatic when it comes to using techniques that are appropriate for a given client. In general, however, Adlerian practitioners focus on motivation modification more than behavior change and encourage clients to make holistic changes on the useful side of living. All counseling is a cooperative effort, and making a difference depends on the counselor's ability to win the client's cooperation.

Areas of Application

Adler anticipated the future direction of the helping professions by calling upon therapists to become social activists and by addressing the prevention and remediation of social conditions that were contrary to social interest and resulted in human problems. Adler's pioneering efforts on prevention services in mental health led him to increasingly advocate for the role of Individual Psychology in schools and families. Because Individual Psychology is based on a growth model, not a medical model, it is applicable to such varied spheres of life as child guidance; parent–child counseling; couples counseling; family counseling and therapy; group counseling and therapy; individual counseling with children, adolescents, and adults; cultural conflicts; correctional and rehabilitation counseling; and mental health institutions. Adler's basic ideas have been incorporated into the practices of school psychology, school counseling, the community mental health movement, and parent education. Adlerian principles have been widely applied to substance abuse programs, social problems to combat poverty and crime, problems of the aged, school systems, religion, and business.

APPLICATION TO EDUCATION Adler (1930/1978) advocated training both teachers and parents in effective practices that foster the child's social interests and result in a sense of competence and self-worth. Adler had a keen interest in applying his ideas to education, especially in finding ways to remedy faulty lifestyles of schoolchildren. He initiated a process to work with students in groups and to educate parents and teachers. By providing teachers with ways to prevent and correct basic mistakes of children, he sought to promote social interest and mental health. Adler was ahead of his time in advocating for schools to take an active role in developing social skills and character education as well as teaching the basics. Many of the major teacher education models are based on principles of Adlerian psychology (see Albert, 1996). Besides Adler, the main proponent of Individual Psychology as a foundation for the teaching–learning process was Dreikurs (1968, 1971).

APPLICATION TO PARENT EDUCATION Parent education seeks to improve the relationship between parent and child by promoting greater understanding and acceptance. Parents are taught how to recognize the mistaken goals of children and to use logical and natural consequences to guide children toward more productive behavior. Adlerian parent education also stresses listening to children, helping children accept the consequences of their behavior, applying emotion coaching, holding family meetings, and using encouragement. Two of the leading parent education programs in the United States—STEP (Dinkmeyer & McKay, 1997) and Active Parenting (Popkin, 1993)—are based on Adlerian principles.

APPLICATION TO COUPLES COUNSELING Adlerian therapy with couples is designed to assess a couple's beliefs and behaviors while educating them in more effective ways of meeting their relational goals. Clair Hawes has developed an approach to couples counseling within the Adlerian brief therapy model. In addition to addressing the compatibility of lifestyles, Hawes looks at the early recollections of the marriage and each partner's relationship to a broad set of life tasks, including occupation, social relationships, intimate relationships, spirituality, self-care, and self-worth (Bitter et al., 1998; Hawes, 1993; Hawes & Blanchard, 1993). Carlson, Watts, and Maniacci (2006) describe how Adlerians achieve the goals of brief couples therapy: they foster social interest, assist couples in decreasing feelings of inferiority and overcoming discouragement, help couples modify their views and goals, help couples to feel a sense of quality in their relationships, and provide skill-building opportunities. Therapists aim to create solutions for problems, increase choices of couples, and help clients discover and use their individual and collective resources.

The full range of techniques applicable to other forms of counseling can be used when working with couples. In couples counseling, couples are taught specific techniques that enhance communication and cooperation. Some of these techniques are listening, paraphrasing, giving feedback, having marriage conferences, listing expectations, doing homework, and enacting problem solving. Adlerians use psychoeducational methods and skills training in counseling couples. For useful books on this topic, see Carlson and Dinkmeyer (2003) and Sperry, Carlson, and Peluso (2006).

Adlerians will sometimes see clients as a couple, sometimes individually, and then alternately as a couple and as individuals. Rather than looking for who is at fault in the relationship, the therapist considers the lifestyles of the partners and the interaction of the two lifestyles. Emphasis is given to helping them decide if they want to maintain their relationship, and, if so, what changes they are willing to make.

APPLICATION TO FAMILY COUNSELING With its emphasis on the family constellation, holism, and the freedom of the therapist to improvise, Adler's approach contributed to the foundation of the family therapy perspective. Adlerians working with families focus on the family atmosphere, the family constellation, and the interactive goals of each member (Bitter, 2009). The family atmosphere is the climate characterizing the relationship between the parents and their attitudes toward life, gender roles, decision making, competition, cooperation, dealing with conflict, responsibility, and so forth. This atmosphere, including the role models the parents provide, influences the children as they grow up. The therapeutic process seeks to increase awareness of the interaction of the individuals within the family system. Those who practice Adlerian family therapy strive to understand the goals, beliefs, and behaviors of each family member and the family as an entity in its own right. Adler's and Dreikurs's influence on family therapy is covered in more depth in Chapter 14.

APPLICATION TO GROUP COUNSELING Adler and his coworkers used a group approach in their child guidance centers in Vienna as early as 1921 (Dreikurs, 1969). Dreikurs extended and popularized Adler's work with groups and used group psychotherapy in his private practice for more than 40 years. Although Dreikurs introduced group therapy into his psychiatric practice as a way to save time, he quickly discovered some unique characteristics of groups that made them an effective way of helping people change. Inferiority feelings can be challenged and counteracted effectively in groups, and the mistaken concepts and values that are at the root of social and emotional problems can be deeply influenced because the group is a value-forming agent (Sonstegard & Bitter, 2004).

The rationale for Adlerian group counseling is based on the premise that our problems are mainly of a social nature. The group provides the social context in which members can develop a sense of belonging, social connectedness, and community. Sonstegard and Bitter (2004) write that group participants come to see that many of their problems are interpersonal in nature, that their behavior has social meaning, and that their goals can best be understood in the framework of social purposes.

The use of early recollections is a unique feature of Adlerian group counseling. As mentioned earlier, from a series of early memories, individuals can get a clear sense of their mistaken notions, current attitudes, social interests, and possible future behavior. Through the mutual sharing of these early recollections, members develop a sense of connection with one another, and group cohesion is increased. The group becomes an agent of change because of the improved interpersonal relationships among members and the emergence of hope.

We particularly value the way Adlerian group counselors implement action strategies at each of the group sessions and especially during the reorientation stage when new decisions are made and goals are modified. To challenge self-limiting assumptions, members are encouraged to act *as if* they were the persons they want to be. They are asked to "catch themselves" in the process of repeating old patterns that have led to ineffective or self-defeating behavior. The members come to appreciate that if they hope to change, they need to set tasks for themselves, apply group lessons to daily life, and take steps in finding solutions to their problems. This final stage is characterized by group leaders and members working together to challenge erroneous beliefs about self, life, and others. During this stage, members are considering alternative beliefs, behaviors, and attitudes.

Adlerian group counseling can be considered a brief approach to treatment. The core characteristics associated with brief group therapy include rapid establishment of a strong therapeutic alliance, clear problem focus and goal alignment, rapid assessment, emphasis on active and directive therapeutic interventions, a focus on strengths and abilities of clients, an optimistic view of change, a focus on both the present and the future, and an emphasis on tailoring treatment to the unique needs of clients in the most time-efficient manner possible (Carlson et al., 2006).

Adlerian brief group therapy is addressed by Sonstegard, Bitter, Pelonis-Peneros, and Nicoll (2001). For more on the Adlerian approach to group counseling, refer to *Theory and Practice of Group Counseling* (Corey, 2012, chap. 7) and Sonstegard and Bitter (2004).

ADLERIAN THERAPY FROM A MULTICULTURAL PERSPECTIVE

Strengths From a Diversity Perspective

Adlerian theory addressed social equality issues and social embeddedness of humans long before multiculturalism assumed central importance in the profession (Watts & Pietrzak, 2000). Adler introduced notions with implications toward multiculturalism that have as much or more relevance today as they did during Adler's time (Pedersen, as cited in Nystul, 1999b). Some of these ideas include (1) the importance of the cultural context, (2) the emphasis on health as opposed to pathology, (3) a holistic perspective on life, (4) the value of understanding individuals in terms of their core goals and purposes, (5) the ability to exercise freedom within the context of societal constraints, and (6) the focus on prevention and the development of a proactive approach in dealing with problems. Adler's holistic perspective is an articulate expression of what Pedersen calls a "culture-centered" or multicultural approach to counseling. Carlson and Englar-Carlson (2008) maintain that Adlerian theory is well suited to counseling diverse populations and doing social justice work. They assert: "Perhaps Adler's greatest contribution is that he developed a theory that recognizes and stresses the effects of social class, racism, sex, and gender on the behavior of individuals. His ideas, therefore, are well received by those living in today's global society" (p. 134).

Although the Adlerian approach is called Individual Psychology, its focus is on the person in a social context. Thus clients are encouraged to define themselves within their social environments. Adlerians allow broad concepts of age, ethnicity, lifestyle, sexual/affectional orientations, and gender differences to emerge in therapy. The therapeutic process is grounded within a client's culture and worldview rather than attempting to fit clients into preconceived models.

In their analysis of the various theoretical approaches to counseling, Arciniega and Newlon (2003) state that Adlerian theory holds a great deal of promise for addressing diversity issues. They note a number of characteristics of Adlerian theory that are congruent with the values of many racial, cultural, and ethnic groups, including the emphasis on understanding the individual in a familial and sociocultural context; the role of social interest and contributing to others; and the focus on belonging and the collective spirit. Cultures that stress the welfare of the social group and emphasize the role of the family will find the basic assumptions of Adlerian psychology to be consistent with their values.

Adlerian therapists tend to focus on cooperation and socially oriented values as opposed to competitive and individualistic values (Carlson & Carlson, 2000). Native American clients, for example, tend to value cooperation over competition. One such client told a story about a group of boys who were in a race. When one boy got ahead of the others, he would slow down and allow the others to catch up, and they all made it to the finish line at the same time. Although the coach tried to explain that the point of the race was for an individual to finish first, these boys were socialized to work together cooperatively as a group. Adlerian therapy is easily adaptable to cultural values that emphasize community.

Not only is Adlerian theory congruent with the values of people from diverse cultural groups, but the approach offers flexibility in applying a range of cognitive and action-oriented techniques to helping clients explore their practical problems in a cultural context. Adlerian practitioners are not wedded to any particular set of procedures. Instead, they are conscious of the value of fitting their techniques to each client's situation. Although they utilize a diverse range of methods, most of them do conduct a lifestyle assessment. This assessment is heavily focused on the structure and dynamics within the client's family. Because of their cultural background, many clients have been conditioned to respect their family heritage and to appreciate the impact of their family on their own personal development. It is essential that counselors be sensitive to the conflicting feelings and struggles of their clients. If counselors demonstrate an understanding of these cultural values, it is likely that these clients will be receptive to an exploration of their lifestyle. Such an exploration will involve a detailed discussion of their own place within their family.

It should be noted that Adlerians investigate culture in much the same way that they approach birth order and family atmosphere. Culture is a vantage point from which life is experienced and interpreted; it is also a background of values, history, convictions, beliefs, customs, and expectations that must be addressed by the individual. Culture provides a way of grasping the subjective and experiential perspective of an individual. Although culture influences each person, it is expressed within each individual differently, according to the perception, evaluation, and interpretation of culture that the person holds. Contemporary Adlerians appreciate the role of spirituality and religion in the lives of clients because these factors are manifestations of social interest and responsibility to others (Carlson & Englar-Carlson, 2008).

Adler was one of the first psychologists at the turn of the century to advocate equality for women. He recognized that men and women were different in many ways, but he felt that the two genders were deserving of equal value and respect. This respect and appreciation for difference extends to culture as well as gender. Adlerians find in different cultures opportunities for viewing the self, others, and the world in multidimensional ways.

Shortcomings From a Diversity Perspective

As is true of most Western models, the Adlerian approach tends to focus on the self as the locus of change and responsibility. Because other cultures have different conceptions, this primary emphasis on changing the autonomous self may be problematic for many clients. Assumptions about the Western nuclear family are built into the Adlerian concepts of birth order and family constellation. For people brought up in extended family contexts, some of these ideas may be less relevant or at least may need to be reconfigured.

Adlerian theory has some potential drawbacks for clients from those cultures who are not interested in exploring past childhood experiences, early memories, family experiences, and dreams. This approach also has limited effectiveness with clients who do not understand the purpose of exploring the details of a lifestyle analysis when dealing with life's current problems (Arciniega & Newlon, 2003).

In addition, the culture of some clients may contribute to their viewing the counselor as the "expert" and expecting that the counselor will provide them with solutions to their problems. For these clients, the role of the Adlerian therapist may pose problems because Adlerian therapists are not experts in solving other people's problems. Instead, they view it as their function to collaboratively teach people alternative methods of coping with life concerns.

Many clients who have pressing problems are likely to be hesitant to discuss areas of their lives that they may not see as connected to the struggles that bring them into therapy. Individuals may believe that it is inappropriate to reveal family information. On this point Carlson and Carlson (2000) suggest that a therapist's sensitivity and understanding of a client's culturally constructed beliefs about disclosing family information are critical. If the therapist is able to demonstrate an understanding of a client's cultural values, it is likely that this person will be more open to the assessment and treatment process.

Adlerian Therapy Applied to the Case of Stan

 The basic aims of an Adlerian therapist working with Stan are fourfold and correspond to the four stages of counseling: (1) establishing and maintaining a good working relationship with Stan, (2) exploring Stan's dynamics, (3) encouraging Stan to develop insight and understanding, and (4) helping Stan see new alternatives and make new choices.

To develop mutual trust and respect, I pay close attention to Stan's subjective experience and attempt to get a sense of how he has reacted to the turning points in his life. During the initial session, Stan reacts to me as the expert who has the answers. He is convinced that when he makes decisions he generally ends up regretting the results. Stan approaches me out of desperation. Because I view counseling as a relationship between equals, I initially focus on his feeling of being unequal to most other people. A good place to begin is exploring his feelings of inferiority, which he says he feels in most situations. The goals of counseling are developed mutually, and I avoid deciding for Stan what his goals should be. I also resist giving Stan the simple formula he is requesting.

I prepare a lifestyle assessment based on a questionnaire that taps information about Stan's early years, especially his experiences in his family. (See the *Student Manual for Theory and Practice of Counseling and Psychotherapy* for a complete description of this lifestyle assessment form as it is applied to Stan.) This assessment includes a determination of whether he poses a danger to himself because Stan did mention suicidal ideation. During the assessment phase, which might take a few sessions, I explore with Stan his social relationships, his relationships with members of his family, his work responsibilities, his role as a man, and his feelings about himself. I place considerable emphasis on Stan's goals in life and his priorities. I do not pay a great deal of attention to his past, except to show him the consistency between his past and present as he moves toward the future.

As an Adlerian counselor, I place value on exploring early recollections as a source of understanding his goals, motivations, and values. I ask Stan to report his earliest memories. He replies as follows:

I was about 6. I went to school, and I was scared of the other kids and the teacher. When I came home, I cried and told my mother I didn't want to go back to school. She yelled at me and called me a baby. After that I felt horrible and even more scared.

Another of Stan's early recollections was at age 8:

> My family was visiting my grandparents. I was playing outside, and some neighborhood kid hit me for no reason. We started fighting, and my mother came out and scolded me for being such a rough kid. She wouldn't believe me when I told her he started the fight. I felt angry and hurt that she didn't believe me.

Based on these early recollections, I suggest that Stan sees life as frightening and unpredictably hostile and that he feels he cannot count on women; they are likely to be harsh, unbelieving, and uncaring.

Having gathered the data based on the lifestyle assessment about his family constellation and his early recollections, I assist Stan in the process of summarizing and interpreting this information. I give particular attention to identifying basic mistakes, which are faulty conclusions about life and self-defeating perceptions. Here are some of the mistaken conclusions Stan has reached:

- "I must not get close to people, because they will surely hurt me."
- "Because my own parents didn't want me and didn't love me, I'll never be desired or loved by anybody."
- "If only I could become perfect, maybe people would acknowledge and accept me."
- "Being a man means not showing emotions."

The information I summarize and interpret leads to insight and increased self-understanding on Stan's part. He gains increased awareness of his need to control his world so that he can keep painful feelings in check. He sees more clearly some of the ways he tries to gain control over his pain: through the use of alcohol, avoiding interpersonal situations that are threatening, and being unwilling to count on others for psychological support. Through continued emphasis on his beliefs, goals, and intentions, Stan comes to see how his private logic is inaccurate. In his case, a syllogism for his style of life can be explained in this way: (1) "I am unloved, insignificant, and do not count"; (2) "The world is a threatening place to be, and life is unfair"; (3) "Therefore, I must find ways to protect myself and be safe." During this phase of the process, I make interpretations centering on his lifestyle, his current direction, his goals and purposes, and how his private logic works. Of course, Stan is expected to carry out homework assignments that assist him in translating his insights into new behavior. In this way he is an active participant in his therapy.

In the reorientation phase of therapy, Stan and I work together to consider alternative attitudes, beliefs, and actions. By now Stan sees that he does not have to be locked into past patterns, feels encouraged, and realizes that he has the power to change his life. He accepts that he will not change merely by gaining insights and knows that he will have to make use of these insights by carrying out an action-oriented plan. Stan begins to feel that he can create a new life for himself and not remain the victim of circumstances.

Follow-Up: You Continue as Stan's Adlerian Therapist

Use these questions to help you think about how you would counsel Stan using an Adlerian approach:

- What are some ways you would attempt to establish a relationship with Stan based on trust and mutual respect? Can you imagine any difficulties in developing this relationship with him?
- What aspects of Stan's lifestyle particularly interest you? In counseling him, how would these be explored?
- The Adlerian therapist identified four of Stan's mistaken conclusions. Can you identify with any of these basic mistakes? If so, do you think this would help or hinder your therapeutic effectiveness with him?
- How might you assist Stan in discovering his social interest and going beyond a preoccupation with his own problems?
- What strengths and resources in Stan might you draw on to support his determination and commitment to change?

See the *DVD for Theory and Practice of Counseling and Psychotherapy: The Case of Stan and Lecturettes* (Session 3 on Adlerian therapy) for a demonstration of my approach to counseling Stan by focusing on his early recollections.

SUMMARY AND EVALUATION

Summary

Adler was far ahead of his time, and most contemporary therapies have incorporated at least some of his ideas. Individual Psychology assumes that people are motivated by social factors; are responsible for their own thoughts, feelings, and actions; are the creators of their own lives, as opposed to being helpless victims; and are impelled by purposes and goals, looking more toward the future than back to the past.

The basic goal of the Adlerian approach is to help clients identify and change their mistaken beliefs about, self, others, and life and thus to participate more fully in a social world. Clients are not viewed as psychologically sick but as discouraged. The therapeutic process helps individuals become aware of their patterns and make some basic changes in their style of living, which lead to changes in the way they feel and behave. The role of the family in the development of the individual is emphasized. Therapy is a cooperative venture that challenges clients to translate their insights into action in the real world. Contemporary Adlerian theory is an integrative approach, combining cognitive, constructivist, existential, psychodynamic, and systems perspectives. Some of these common characteristics include an emphasis on establishing a respectful client–therapist relationship, an emphasis on clients' strengths and resources, and an optimistic and future orientation.

The Adlerian approach gives practitioners a great deal of freedom in working with clients. Major Adlerian contributions have been made in the following areas: elementary education, consultation groups with teachers, parent education groups, couples and family therapy, and group counseling.

Contributions of the Adlerian Approach

A strength of the Adlerian approach is its flexibility and its integrative nature. Adlerian therapists can be both theoretically integrative and technically eclectic (Watts & Shulman, 2003). This therapeutic approach allows for the use of a variety of relational, cognitive, behavioral, emotive, and experiential techniques. Adlerian therapists are resourceful and flexible in drawing on many methods, which can be applied to a diverse range of clients in a variety of settings and formats. Therapists are mainly concerned with doing what is in the best interests of clients rather than squeezing clients into one theoretical framework (Watts, 1999, 2000; Watts & Pietrzak, 2000; Watts & Shulman, 2003).

Another contribution of the Adlerian approach is that it is suited to brief, time-limited therapy. Adler was a proponent of time-limited therapy, and the techniques used by many contemporary brief therapeutic approaches are very similar to interventions created by or commonly used by Adlerian practitioners (Carlson et al., 2006). Adlerian therapy and contemporary brief therapy have in common a number of characteristics, including quickly establishing a strong therapeutic alliance, a clear problem focus and goal alignment, rapid assessment and application to treatment, an emphasis on active and directive intervention, a psychoeducational focus, a present and future orientation, a focus on clients' strengths and abilities and an optimistic expectation of change, and a time sensitivity that tailors treatment to the unique needs of the client (Carlson et al., 2006). According to Mosak and Di Pietro (2006), early recollections are a significant assessment intervention in brief therapy. They claim that early recollections are often useful in minimizing the number of therapy sessions. This procedure takes little time to administer and interpret and provides a direction for therapists to pursue.

Bitter and Nicoll (2000) identify five characteristics that form the basis for an integrative framework in brief therapy: time limitation, focus, counselor directiveness, symptoms as solutions, and the assignment of behavioral tasks. Bringing a time-limitation process to therapy conveys to clients the expectation that change will occur in a short period of time. When the number of sessions is specified, both client and therapist are motivated to stay focused on desired outcomes and to work as efficiently as possible. Because there is no assurance that a future session will occur, brief therapists tend to ask themselves this question: "If I had only one session to be useful in this person's life, what would I want to accomplish?" (p. 38).

The Adlerian concepts I (Jerry Corey) draw on most in my professional work are (1) the importance of looking to one's life goals, including assessing how these goals influence an individual; (2) the focus on the individual's interpretation of early experiences in the family, with special emphasis on their current impact; (3) the clinical use of early recollections in both assessment and treatment; (4) the use of dreams as rehearsals for future action; (5) the need to understand and confront basic mistakes; (6) the cognitive emphasis, which holds that emotions and behaviors are largely influenced by one's beliefs and thinking processes; (7) the idea of working out an action plan designed to help clients make changes; (8) the collaborative relationship, whereby the client and therapist work toward mutually agreed-upon goals; and (9) the emphasis given to encouragement during the entire counseling process. Several Adlerian concepts have implications for personal development. One of these notions that has helped me to understand the direction of my life is the assumption that feelings of inferiority are linked to a striving for superiority (Corey, 2010).

It is difficult to overestimate the contributions of Adler to contemporary therapeutic practice. Many of his ideas were revolutionary and far ahead of his time. His influence went beyond counseling individuals, extending into the community mental health movement (Ansbacher, 1974). Abraham Maslow, Viktor Frankl, Rollo May, Paul Watzlawick, Karen Horney, Erich Fromm, Aaron T. Beck, and Albert Ellis have all acknowledged their debt to Adler. Both Frankl and May see him as a forerunner of the existential movement because of his position that human beings are free to choose and are entirely responsible for what they make of themselves. This view also makes him a forerunner of the subjective approach to psychology, which focuses on the internal determinants of behavior: values, beliefs, attitudes, goals, interests, personal meanings, subjective perceptions of reality, and strivings toward self-realization. Bitter (2008) and his colleagues (Bitter, Robertson, Healey, & Cole, 2009) have drawn attention to the link between Adlerian thinking and feminist therapy approaches.

One of Adler's most important contributions was his influence on other therapy systems. Many of his basic ideas have found their way into most of the other psychological schools, a few of which include existential therapy, cognitive behavior therapy, rational emotive behavior therapy, reality therapy, solution-focused therapy, and family therapy. In many respects, Adler seems to have paved the way for current developments in both the cognitive and constructivist therapies (Watts, 2003). Adlerians' basic premise is that if clients can change their thinking then they can change their feelings and behavior. A study of contemporary counseling theories reveals that many of Adler's notions have reappeared in these modern approaches with different nomenclature, and often without giving Adler the credit that is due to him (Watts, 1999; Watts & Pietrzak, 2000; Watts & Shulman, 2003). It is clear that there are significant linkages between Adlerian theory and most of the present-day theories, especially those that view the person as purposive, self-determining, and striving for growth. Carlson and Englar-Carlson (2008) assert that Adlerians face the challenge of continuing to develop their approach so that it meets the needs of contemporary global society: "Whereas Adlerian ideas are alive in other theoretical approaches, there is a question about whether Adlerian theory as a stand-alone approach is viable in the long term" (p. 133). These authors believe that for the Adlerian model to survive and thrive it will be necessary to find ways to strive for significance.

Limitations and Criticisms of the Adlerian Approach

Adler had to choose between devoting his time to formalizing his theory and teaching others the basic concepts of Individual Psychology. He placed practicing and teaching before organizing and presenting a well-defined and systematic theory. As a result, his written presentations are often difficult to follow, and many of them are transcripts of lectures he gave. Initially, many people considered his ideas somewhat loose and too simplistic.

Research supporting the effectiveness of Adlerian theory is limited but has improved over the last 25 years (Watts & Shulman, 2003). However, a large part of the theory still requires empirical testing and comparative analysis. This is especially true in the conceptual areas that Adlerians accept as axiomatic: for example, the development of lifestyle; the unity of the personality and an acceptance of a singular view of self; the rejection of the prominence of heredity in determining behavior, especially pathological behavior; and the usefulness of the multiple interventions used by various Adlerians.

WHERE TO GO FROM HERE

Refer to the *DVD for Integrative Counseling: The Case of Ruth and Lecturettes,* Session 6 ("Cognitive Focus in Counseling"), which illustrates Ruth's striving to live up to expectations and measure up to perfectionist standards. In this particular therapy session with Ruth, you will see how I draw upon cognitive concepts and apply them in practice.

Free Podcasts for ACA Members

You can download ACA Podcasts (prerecorded interviews) by going to www. counseling.org and then clicking on the Resource button, and then the Podcast Series. For Chapter 5, look for Podcast 11, Adlerian Therapy, by Dr. Jon Carlson.

Other Resources

Videos from Psychotherapy.net demonstrate Adlerian therapy with adults, families, and children, and are available to students and professionals at their website, www.Psychotherapy.net. New articles, interviews, blogs, therapy cartoons, and videos are published monthly. For this chapter, see the following:

Carlson, J. (1997). *Adlerian Therapy* (Psychotherapy with the Experts Series)

Carlson, J. (2001). *Adlerian Parent Consultation* (Child Therapy with the Experts Series)

Kottman, T. (2001). *Adlerian Play Therapy* (Child Therapy with the Experts Series)

If your thinking is allied with the Adlerian approach, you might consider seeking training in Individual Psychology or becoming a member of the North American Society of Adlerian Psychology (NASAP). To obtain information on NASAP and a list of Adlerian organizations and institutes, contact:

North American Society of Adlerian Psychology (NASAP)
614 Old West Chocolate Avenue
Hershey, PA 17033
Telephone: (717) 579-8795
Fax: (717) 533-8616
E-mail: nasap@msn.com
Website: www.alfredadler.org

The society publishes a newsletter and a quarterly journal and maintains a list of institutes, training programs, and workshops in Adlerian psychology. *The Journal of Individual Psychology* presents current scholarly and professional research. Columns on counseling, education, and parent and family education are regular features. Information about subscriptions is available by contacting the society.

If you are interested in pursuing training, postgraduate study, continuing education, or a degree, contact NASAP for a list of Adlerian organizations and institutes. A few training institutes are listed here:

Adler School of Professional Psychology
65 East Wacker Place, Suite 2100
Chicago, IL 60601-7298
Telephone: (312) 201-5900
Fax: (312) 201-5917
E-mail: admissions@adler.edu
Website: www.adler.edu

Adler Graduate School
1550 East 78th Street
Richfield, MN 55423
Telephone: 612-861-7554
Fax: 612-861-7559
E-mail:info@alfredadler.edu

Adler School of Professional Psychology, Vancouver Campus

595 Burrard Street, Suite 753
P.O. Box 49104
Vancouver, BC, Canada V7X 1G4
Telephone: (604) 482-5510
Fax: (604) 874-4634

Adlerian Training Institute, Inc.

Dr. Bill Nicoll, Coordinator
P.O. Box 881581
Port St. Lucie, FL 34988
Telephone/Fax: (772) 807-4141
Cell Phone: (954) 650-0637
E-mail: adleriantraining@aol.com
Website: www.adleriantraining.com

The Alfred Adler Institute of Northwestern Washington

2565 Mayflower Lane
Bellingham, WA 98226
Telephone: (360) 647-5670
E-mail: HTStein@att.net
Website: http://ourworld.compuserv.com/homepages/hstein/

Alfred Adler Institute of San Francisco

266 Bemis Street
San Francisco, CA 94131
Telephone: (415) 584-3833
E-mail: DPienkow@msn.com

The International Committee of Adlerian Summer Schools and Institutes

Michael Balla, ICASSI Administrator
257 Billings Avenue
Ottawa, Ontario, Canada K1H 5L1
Fax: (613) 733-0289
E-mail: mjballa@sympatico.ca
Website: www.icassi.net

Existential Therapy

VIKTOR FRANKL (1905-1997) was born and educated in Vienna. He founded the Youth Advisement Centers there in 1928 and directed them until 1938. From 1942 to 1945 Frankl was a prisoner in the Nazi concentration camps at Auschwitz and Dachau, where his parents, brother, wife, and children died. He vividly remembered his horrible experiences in these camps, yet he was able to use them in a constructive way and did not allow them to dampen his love and enthusiasm for life. He traveled all around the world, giving lectures in Europe, Latin America, Southeast Asia, and the United States.

Frankl received his MD in 1930 and his PhD in philosophy in 1949, both from the University of Vienna. He became an associate professor at the University of Vienna and later was a distinguished speaker at the United States International University in San Diego. He was a visiting professor at Harvard, Stanford, and Southern Methodist universities. Frankl's works have been translated into more than 20 languages, and his ideas continue to have a major impact on the development of existential therapy. His compelling book *Man's Search for Meaning* (1963) has been a best-seller around the world.

Although Frankl had begun to develop an existential approach to clinical practice before his grim years in the Nazi death camps, his experiences there confirmed his views. Frankl (1963) observed and personally experienced the truths expressed by existential philosophers and writers who hold that we have choices in every situation. Even in terrible circumstances, he believed, we could preserve a vestige of spiritual freedom and independence of mind. He learned experientially that everything could be taken from a person except one thing: "the last of human freedoms—to choose one's attitude in any given set of circumstances, to choose one's own way" (p. 104).). Frankl believed that the essence of being human lies in searching for meaning and purpose. He believed that love is the highest goal to which humans can aspire and that our salvation is through love. We can discover this meaning through our actions and deeds, by experiencing a value (such as love or achievements through work), and by suffering.

Frankl knew and read Freud and attended some of the meetings of Freud's psychoanalytic group. Frankl acknowledged his indebtedness to Freud, although he disagreed with the rigidity of Freud's psychoanalytic system. Frankl often remarked that Freud was a *depth* psychologist and that he is a *height* psychologist who built on Freud's foundations. Reacting against most of Freud's deterministic notions, Frankl developed his own theory and practice of psychotherapy, which emphasized the concepts of freedom, responsibility, meaning, and the search for values. He established his international reputation as the founder of what has been called "The Third School of Viennese Psychoanalysis," the other two being Sigmund Freud's psychoanalysis and Alfred Adler's Individual Psychology.

I have selected Frankl as one of the key figures of the existential approach because of the dramatic way in which his theories were tested by the tragedies of his life. His life was an illustration of his theory, for he lived what his theory espouses.

ROLLO MAY (1909-1994) first lived in Ohio and then moved to Michigan as a young child along with his five brothers and a sister. He remembered his home life as being unhappy, a situation that contributed to his interest in psychology and counseling. In his personal life May struggled with his own existential concerns and the failure of two marriages.

Despite his unhappy life experiences, he graduated from Oberlin College in 1930 and then went to Greece as a teacher. During his summers in Greece he traveled to Vienna to study with Alfred Adler. After receiving a degree in theology from Union Theological Seminary, May decided that the best way to reach out and help people was through psychology instead of theology. He completed his doctorate in clinical psychology at Columbia University and started a private practice in New York; he also became a supervisory training analyst for the William Alanson Institute.

While May was pursuing his doctoral program, he came down with tuberculosis, which resulted in a 2-year stay in a sanitarium. During his recovery period, May spent much time learning firsthand about the nature of anxiety. He also spent time reading, and he studied the works of Søren Kierkegaard, which was the catalyst for his recognizing the existential dimensions of anxiety. This study resulted in his book *The Meaning of Anxiety* (1950). His popular book *Love and Will* (1969) reflects his own personal struggles with love and intimate relationships and mirrors Western society's questioning of its values pertaining to sex and marriage.

The greatest personal influence on Rollo May was the existential theologian Paul Tillich (author of *The Courage to Be,* 1952), who became his mentor and a personal friend. The two spent much time together discussing philosophical, religious, and psychological topics. Most of May's writings reflect a concern with the nature of human experience, such as recognizing and dealing with power, accepting freedom and responsibility, and discovering one's identity. He draws from his rich knowledge based on the classics and his existential perspective.

Rollo May was one of the main proponents of humanistic approaches to psychotherapy, and he was the principal American spokesperson of European existential thinking as it is applied to psychotherapy. He believed psychotherapy should be aimed at helping people discover the meaning of their lives and should be concerned with the problems of *being* rather than with problem solving. Questions of being include learning to deal with issues such as sex and intimacy, growing old, facing death, and taking action in the world. According to May, the real challenge is for people to be able to live in a world where they are alone and where they will eventually have to face death. He contends that our individualism should be balanced by what Adler refers to as social interest. It is the task of therapists to help individuals find ways to contribute to the betterment of the society in which they live.

Photo courtesy of Joseph Siroker.

IRVIN YALOM (b. 1931-) was born of parents who immigrated from Russia shortly after World War I. During his early childhood, Yalom lived in the inner city of Washington, D.C., in a poor neighborhood. Life on the streets was perilous, and Yalom took refuge indoors reading novels and other works. Twice a week he made the hazardous bicycle trek to the library to stock up on reading supplies. He found an alternative and satisfying world in reading fiction, which was a source of inspiration and wisdom to him. Early in his life he decided that writing a novel was the very finest thing a person could do, and subsequently he has written several teaching novels.

Irvin Yalom is professor emeritus of psychiatry at the Stanford University School of Medicine. A psychiatrist and author, Yalom has been a major figure in the field of group psychotherapy since publication in 1970 of his influential book *The Theory and Practice of Group Psychotherapy* (1970/2005), which has been translated into 12 languages and is currently in its fifth edition. His pioneering work, *Existential Psychotherapy,* written in 1980, is a classic and authoritative textbook on existential therapy. Drawing on his clinical experience and on empirical research, philosophy, and literature, Yalom developed an existential approach to psychotherapy that addresses four "givens of existence" or ultimate human concerns: freedom and responsibility, existential isolation, meaninglessness, and death. These existential themes deal with the client's existence, or being-in-the-world. Yalom urges all therapists, regardless of theoretical orientation, to develop a sensibility to existential issues because generally these issues emerge in all courses of therapy.

Psychotherapy has been endlessly intriguing for Yalom, who has approached all of his patients with a sense of wonderment at the stories they reveal. He believes that a different therapy must be designed for each client because each has a unique story. He advocates using the here and now of the therapeutic relationship to explore the client's interpersonal world, and he believes the therapist must be transparent, especially regarding his or her experience of the client. His basic philosophy is existential and interpersonal, which he applies to both individual and group therapy.

Irvin Yalom has authored many stories and novels related to psychotherapy, including *Love's Executioner* (1987), *When Nietzsche Wept* (1992), *Lying on the Couch* (1997), *Momma and the Meaning of Life* (2000), and *The Schopenhauer Cure* (2005a). His 2008 nonfiction book, *Staring at the Sun:*

Overcoming the Terror of Death, is a treatise on the role of death anxiety in psychotherapy, illustrating how death and the meaning of life are foundational themes associated with in-depth therapeutic work. Yalom's works, translated into more than 20 languages, have been widely read by therapists and laypeople alike.

Yalom's wife, Marilyn, has a PhD in comparative literature and has had a successful career as a university professor and writer. His four children have chosen a variety of careers—medicine, photography, creative writing, theater directing, and clinical psychology. He has five grandchildren and is still counting.

INTRODUCTION

Existential therapy is more a way of thinking, or an attitude about psychotherapy, than a particular style of practicing psychotherapy. It is neither an independent nor separate school of therapy, nor is it a clearly defined model with specific techniques. Existential therapy can best be described as a *philosophical approach* that influences a counselor's therapeutic practice. Yalom and Josselson (2011) capture the essence of this approach:

> Existential psychotherapy is an attitude toward human suffering [that] has no manual. It asks deep questions about the nature of the human being and the nature of anxiety, despair, grief, loneliness, isolation, and anomie. It also deals centrally with the questions of meaning, creativity, and love. (p. 310)

Existential therapy focuses on exploring themes such as mortality, meaning, freedom, responsibility, anxiety, and aloneness as these relate to a person's current struggle. The goal of existential therapy is to assist clients in their exploration of the existential "givens of life," how these are sometimes ignored or denied, and how addressing them can ultimately lead to a deeper, more reflective and meaningful existence. Clients are invited to reflect on life, to recognize their range of alternatives, and to decide among them.

The existential approach rejects the deterministic view of human nature espoused by traditional psychoanalysis and radical behaviorism. Psychoanalysis sees the individual as primarily determined by unconscious forces, irrational drives, and past events; behaviorists see the individual as primarily determined by sociocultural conditioning. Although deterministic forces affect us and we sometimes cannot control external events thrust upon us, existential therapists believe we retain the freedom to choose how we respond to such events. Existential therapy is grounded on the assumption that we are free and therefore responsible for our choices and actions. We are the authors of our lives, and we design the pathways we follow. This chapter addresses some of the existential concepts and themes that have significant implications for the existentially oriented practitioner.

A basic existential premise is that we are not victims of circumstance because, to a large extent, we are what we choose to be. Once clients begin the process of recognizing the ways in which they have passively accepted circumstances and surrendered control, they can start down a path of consciously shaping their own lives. The first step in the therapeutic journey is for clients to accept responsibility. As Yalom (2003) puts it, "Once individuals recognize their role in creating their own life predicament, they also realize that they, and only they, have the power to change that situation" (p. 141). One of the aims of existential therapy is to challenge people to stop deceiving themselves regarding their lack of responsibility for what is happening to them and their excessive demands on life (van Deurzen, 2002b).

Emmy van Deurzen (2002a), a key contributor to British existential psychology, writes that existential counseling is not designed to "cure" people of illness in the tradition of the medical model. She does not view clients as being sick, but as "sick of life or clumsy at living" (p. 18) and unable to live a productive life.

 See the DVD program for Chapter 6, *DVD for Theory and Practice of Counseling and Psychotherapy: The Case of Stan and Lecturettes.* I suggest that you view the brief lecture for each chapter prior to reading the chapter.

Historical Background in Philosophy and Existentialism

The existential therapy movement was not founded by any particular person or group; many streams of thought contributed to it. Drawing from a major orientation in philosophy, existential therapy arose spontaneously in different parts of Europe and among different schools of psychology and psychiatry in the 1940s and 1950s. Many Europeans found that their lives had been devastated by World War II, and they struggled with existential issues including feelings of isolation, alienation, and meaninglessness. Early writers focused on the individual's experience of being alone in the world and facing the anxiety of this situation. The European existential perspective focused on human limitations and the tragic dimensions of life (Sharp & Bugental, 2001).

The thinking of existential psychologists and psychiatrists was influenced by a number of philosophers and writers during the 19th century. To understand the philosophical underpinnings of modern existential psychotherapy, one must have some awareness of such figures as Søren Kierkegaard, Friedrich Nietzsche, Martin Heidegger, Jean-Paul Sartre, and Martin Buber. These major figures of existentialism and existential phenomenology and their cultural, philosophical, and religious writings provided the basis for the formation of existential therapy. Ludwig Binswanger and Medard Boss are also included in this section because both were early existential psychoanalysts who contributed key ideas to existential psychotherapy.

SØREN KIERKEGAARD (1813–1855) A Danish philosopher and Christian theologian, Kierkegaard was particularly concerned with *angst*—a Danish and German word whose meaning lies between the English words *dread* and *anxiety*—and he addressed the role of anxiety and uncertainty in life. Existential anxiety is associated with making basic decisions about how we want to live, and it is not pathological. Kierkegaard believed that anxiety is the school in which we are educated to be a self. Without the experience of angst, we may go through life as sleepwalkers. But many of us, especially in adolescence, are awakened into real life by a terrible uneasiness. Life is one contingency after another, with no guarantees beyond the certainty of death. This is by no means a comfortable state, but it is necessary to our becoming human. Kierkegaard believed that "the sickness unto death" arises when we are not true to ourselves. What is needed is the willingness to risk a leap of faith in making choices. Becoming human is a *project,* and our task is not so much to discover who we are as to *create* ourselves.

FRIEDRICH NIETZSCHE (1844–1900) The German philosopher Nietzsche is the iconoclastic counterpart to Kierkegaard, expressing a revolutionary approach to the self, to ethics, and to society. Like Kierkegaard, he emphasized the importance of subjectivity. Nietzsche set out to prove that the ancient definition of humans as *rational* was entirely misleading. We are far more creatures of will than we are impersonal intellects. But where Kierkegaard emphasized the "subjective truth" of an intense concern with God, Nietzsche located values within the individual's "will to power." We give up an honest acknowledgment of this source of value when society invites us to rationalize powerlessness by advocating other worldly concerns. If, like sheep, we acquiesce in "herd morality," we will be nothing but mediocrities. But if we release ourselves by giving free rein to our will to power, we will tap our potentiality for creativity and originality. Kierkegaard and Nietzsche, with their pioneering analyses of anxiety, depression, subjectivity, and the authentic self, together are generally considered to be the originators of the existential perspective (Sharp & Bugental, 2001).

MARTIN HEIDEGGER (1889–1976) Heidegger's phenomenological existentialism reminds us that we exist "in the world" and should not try to think of ourselves as beings apart from the world into which we are thrown. The way we fill our everyday life with superficial conversation and routine shows that we often assume we are going to live forever and can afford to waste day after day. Our moods and feelings (including anxiety about death) are a way of understanding whether we are living authentically or whether we are inauthentically constructing our lives around the expectations of others. When we translate this wisdom from vague feeling to explicit awareness, we may develop a more positive resolve about how we want to be. Phenomenological existentialism, as presented by Heidegger, provides a view of human history that does not focus on past events but motivates individuals to look forward to "authentic experiences" that are yet to come.

MARTIN BUBER (1878–1965) Leaving Germany to live in the new state of Israel, Buber took a less individualistic stand than most of the other existentialists. He said that we humans live in a kind of *betweenness;* that is, there is never just an *I,* but always an *other.* The *I,* the person who is the agent, changes depending on whether the other is an *it* or a *Thou.* But sometimes we make the serious mistake of reducing another person to the status of a mere object, in which case the relationship becomes *I/it.* Although Buber recognizes that of necessity we must have many *I/it* interactions (in everyday life), we are seriously limited if we live only in the world of the *I/it.* Buber stresses the importance of *presence,* which has three functions: (1) it enables true I/Thou relationships; (2) it allows for meaning to exist in a situation; and (3) it enables an individual to be responsible in the here and now (Gould, 1993). In a famous dialogue with Carl Rogers, Buber argued that the therapist and client could never be on the same footing because the latter comes to the former for help. When the relationship is fully mutual, we have become "dialogic," a fully human condition.

LUDWIG BINSWANGER (1881–1966) An existential analyst, Binswanger proposed a holistic model of self that addresses the relationship between the person and his or her environment. He used a phenomenological approach to explore significant features of the self, including choice, freedom, and caring. He based his existential approach largely on the ideas of Heidegger and accepted Heidegger's notion that we are "thrown into the world." However, this "thrown-ness" does not release us from the responsibility of our choices and for planning for the future (Gould, 1993). **Existential analysis** (*dasein analyse*) emphasizes the subjective and spiritual dimensions of human existence. Binswanger (1975) contended that crises in therapy were typically major choice points for the client. Although he originally looked to psychoanalytic theory to shed light on psychosis, he moved toward an existential view of his patients. This perspective enabled him to understand the worldview and immediate experience of his patients, as well as the meaning of their behavior, as opposed to superimposing his view as a therapist on their experience and behavior.

MEDARD BOSS (1903–1991) Both Binswanger and Boss were early existential psychoanalysts and significant figures in the development of existential psychotherapy. They made reference to *dasein* or *being-in-the-world*, which pertains to our ability to reflect on life events and attribute meaning to these events. They believed that the therapist must enter the client's subjective world without presuppositions that would get in the way of this experiential understanding. Both Binswanger and Boss were significantly influenced by Heidegger's seminal work, *Being and Time* (1962), which provided a broad basis for understanding the individual (May, 1958). Boss was deeply influenced by Freudian psychoanalysis, but even more so by Heidegger. Boss's major professional interest was applying Heidegger's philosophical notions to therapeutic practice, and he was especially concerned with integrating Freud's methods with Heidegger's concepts, as described in his book *Daseinanalysis and Psychoanalysis* (1963).

JEAN-PAUL SARTRE (1905–1980) A philosopher and novelist, Sartre was convinced, in part by his years in the French Resistance in World War II, that humans are even more free than earlier existentialists had believed. The existence of a space—nothingness—between the whole of our past and the *now* frees us to choose what we will. Our values are what we choose. The failure to acknowledge our freedom and choices results in emotional problems. This freedom is hard to face, so we tend to invent an excuse by saying, "I can't change now because of my past conditioning." Sartre called excuses "bad faith." No matter what we have been, we can make choices now and become something quite different. We are condemned to be free. To choose is to become committed; this is the responsibility that is the other side of freedom. Sartre's view was that at every moment, by our actions, we are choosing who we are being. Our existence is never fixed or finished.

Every one of our actions represents a fresh choice. When we attempt to pin down who we are, we engage in self-deception (Russell, 2007).

Key Figures in Contemporary Existential Psychotherapy

Viktor Frankl, Rollo May, Irvin Yalom, and James Bugental all developed their existential approaches to psychotherapy from strong backgrounds in both existential and humanistic psychology. Some of their contributions to psychotherapy are illustrated in the brief sketches that follow.

VIKTOR FRANKL (1905–1997) Viktor Frankl was a central figure in developing existential therapy in Europe and also in bringing it to the United States. As a youth, Frankl was deeply influenced by Freud, but he became a student of Adler. Later, he was influenced by the writings of existential philosophers, and he began developing his own existential philosophy and psychotherapy. He was fond of quoting Nietzsche: "He who has a *why* to live for can bear with almost any *how*" (as cited in Frankl, 1963, pp. 121, 164). Frankl contended that those words could be the motto for all psychotherapeutic practice. Another quotation from Nietzsche seems to capture the essence of his own experience and his writings: "That which does not kill me, makes me stronger" (as cited in Frankl, 1963, p. 130).

Frankl developed **logotherapy**, which means "therapy through meaning." Frankl's philosophical model sheds light on what it means to be fully alive. The central themes running through his works are *life has meaning*, under all circumstances; the central motivation for living is the *will to meaning*; we have the *freedom to find meaning* in all that we think; and we must *integrate body, mind, and spirit* to be fully alive. Frankl said that Freud viewed humans as motivated by the "will to pleasure" and that Adler focused on the "will to power." For Frankl, the most powerful motivation for humans is the "will to meaning." Frankl's writings reflect the theme that the modern person has the means to live, but often has no meaning to live for. The therapeutic process is aimed at challenging individuals to find meaning and purpose through, among other things, suffering, work, and love (Frankl, 1965). (For more background information on Viktor Frankl, see his biography at the beginning of this chapter).

ROLLO MAY (1909–1994) Along with Frankl, psychologist Rollo May was deeply influenced by the existential philosophers, by the concepts of Freudian psychology, and by many aspects of Alfred Adler's Individual Psychology. May was one of the key figures responsible for bringing existentialism from Europe to the United States and for translating key concepts into psychotherapeutic practice. His writings have had a significant impact on existentially oriented practitioners. Of primary importance in introducing existential therapy to the United States was the book *Existence: A New Dimension in Psychiatry and Psychology* (May, Angel, & Ellenberger, 1958). According to May, it takes courage to "be," and our choices determine the kind of person we become. There is a constant struggle within us. Although we want to grow toward maturity and independence, we realize that expansion is often a painful process. Hence, the struggle is between the security of dependence and the joys and pains of growth. (For more background information on Rollo May, see his biography at the beginning of this chapter).

IRVIN YALOM (1931-) Irvin Yalom is a significant contemporary existential therapist in the United States. He acknowledges the contributions of both European and American psychologists and psychiatrists who have influenced the development of existential thinking and practice (Yalom, 1980). Yalom has developed his approach to individual and group psychotherapy based on the notion that existentialism deals with basic "givens of existence": isolation and relationship with others; death and living fully; and meaninglessness and meaning. Yalom believes the vast majority of experienced therapists, regardless of their theoretical orientation, employ many of the core existential themes. He also contends that how we address these existential themes has a good deal to do with the design and quality of our lives. Yalom recognizes Frankl as an eminently pragmatic thinker who has had an impact on his writing and practice. He also acknowledges the influence on his writings of several novelists and philosophers. More specifically, he draws on the following themes from those philosophers discussed earlier:

- From Kierkegaard: creative anxiety, despair, fear and dread, guilt, and nothingness
- From Nietzsche: death, suicide, and will
- From Heidegger: authentic being, caring, death, guilt, individual responsibility, and isolation
- From Sartre: meaninglessness, responsibility, and choice
- From Buber: interpersonal relationships, I/Thou perspective in therapy, and self-transcendence

(For more background information on Irvin Yalom, see his biography at the beginning of this chapter.)

JAMES BUGENTAL (1915-2008) James Bugental coined the term "existential-humanistic" psychotherapy, and he was a leading spokesman for this approach. His philosophical and therapeutic approach included a curiosity and focus that moved him away from the traditional therapeutic milieu of labeling and diagnosing clients. His work emphasized the cultivation of both client and therapist *presence*. He developed techniques to assist the client in deepening inner exploration, or *searching*. The therapist's primary task involved helping clients to make new discoveries about themselves in the living moment, as opposed to merely *talking about* themselves.

Central to Bugental's approach is his view of *resistance*, which from an existential-humanistic perspective is not resistance to therapy per se but rather to being fully present both during the therapy hour and in life. Resistance is seen as part of the *self-and-world construct*—how a person understands his or her being and relationship to the world at large. Forms of resistance include intellectualizing, being argumentative, always seeking to please, and any other life-limiting pattern. As resistance emerges in the therapy sessions, the therapist repeatedly notes, or "tags," the resistance so the client increases his or her awareness and ultimately has an increased range of choices.

Bugental's theory and practice emphasized the distinction between therapeutic process and content. He became known for being a masterful teacher and psychotherapist, primarily because he lived his work. He was an existentialist at heart, which made him a great model and mentor, not only for clients but also for students and professionals. In his workshops, he developed many exercises to help therapists refine and practice their skills. He frequently brought his techniques to life with live demonstrations, which emphasized therapeutic work taking place in the moment, impromptu *here-and-now* dialogue, and exploring in the context of self as client or therapist. Bugental's (1987) classic text, *The Art of the Psychotherapist*, is widely recognized for deconstructing the therapy process and moving beyond theory and generalizations to show what actually occurs moment-to-moment in the therapeutic encounter. *Psychotherapy Isn't What You Think* (Bugental, 1999) is the last book he wrote before he died in 2008, at the age of 93.

OTHER CONTRIBUTORS TO EXISTENTIAL THERAPY A more recent influential figure in contemporary existential psychology is Kirk Schneider, who with colleagues Orah Krug, David Elkins, and Ken Bradford are helping to extend existential principles to a new generation of practitioners. Schneider and his colleagues developed an existential-integrative therapy (see Schneider, 2008, 2011; Schneider & Krug, 2010) mainly because of the need to address today's ethnically and diagnostically diverse clinical populations. The existential-integrative approach emphasizes such areas as personal and interpersonal presence, the working through of resistance, the rediscovery of meaning and awe, and contemplative practices. These themes are increasingly being incorporated into the therapeutic mainstream.

Significant developments in the existential approach are also occurring in Britain, largely due to the efforts of Emmy van Deurzen, who is developing academic and training programs at the New School of Psychotherapy and Counselling (see Other Resources at the end of the chapter for details). In the past decades the existential approach has spread rapidly in Britain and is now an alternative to traditional methods (van Deurzen, 2002b). For a description of the historical context and development of existential therapy in Britain, see van Deurzen (2002b) and Cooper (2003); for an excellent overview of the theory and practice of existential therapy, see van Deurzen (2002a) and Schneider and Krug (2010).

KEY CONCEPTS

View of Human Nature

The crucial significance of the existential movement is that it reacts against the tendency to identify therapy with a set of techniques. Instead, it bases therapeutic practice on an understanding of what it means to be human. The existential movement stands for respect for the person, for exploring new aspects of human behavior, and for divergent methods of understanding people. It uses numerous approaches to therapy based on its assumptions about human nature.

The **existential tradition** seeks a balance between recognizing the limits and tragic dimensions of human existence on one hand and the possibilities and opportunities of human life on the other hand. It grew out of a desire to help people engage the dilemmas of contemporary life, such as isolation, alienation, and meaninglessness. The current focus of the existential approach is on the individual's experience of being in the world alone and facing the anxiety of this isolation.

"No relationship can eliminate existential isolation, but aloneness can be shared in such a way that love compensates for its pain" (Yalom & Josselson, 2011, p. 326).

The existential view of human nature is captured, in part, by the notion that the significance of our existence is never fixed once and for all; rather, we continually recreate ourselves through our projects. Humans are in a constant state of transition, emerging, evolving, and becoming in response to the tensions, contradictions, and conflicts in our lives. Being a person implies that we are discovering and making sense of our existence. We continually question ourselves, others, and the world. Although the specific questions we raise vary in accordance with our developmental stage in life, the fundamental themes do not vary. We pose the same questions philosophers have pondered throughout Western history: "Who am I?" "What can I know?" "What ought I to do?" "What can I hope for?" "Where am I going?"

The basic dimensions of the human condition, according to the existential approach, include (1) the capacity for self-awareness; (2) freedom and responsibility; (3) creating one's identity and establishing meaningful relationships with others; (4) the search for meaning, purpose, values, and goals; (5) anxiety as a condition of living; and (6) awareness of death and nonbeing. I develop these propositions in the following sections by summarizing themes that emerge in the writings of existential philosophers and psychotherapists, and I also discuss the implications for counseling practice of each of these propositions.

Proposition 1: The Capacity for Self-Awareness

Freedom, choice, and responsibility constitute the foundation of self-awareness. The greater our awareness, the greater our possibilities for freedom (see Proposition 2). Schneider (2008) explains that the core existential position is that we are both *free* (willful, creative, and expressive) and *limited* (by environmental and social constraints). We increase our capacity to live fully as we expand our awareness in the following areas:

- We are finite and do not have unlimited time to do what we want in life.
- We have the potential to take action or not to act; inaction is a decision.
- We choose our actions, and therefore we can partially create our own destiny.
- Meaning is the product of discovering how we are "thrown" or situated in the world and then, through commitment, living creatively.
- As we increase our awareness of the choices available to us, we also increase our sense of responsibility for the consequences of these choices.
- We are subject to loneliness, meaninglessness, emptiness, guilt, and isolation.
- We are basically alone, yet we have an opportunity to relate to other beings.

We can choose either to expand or to restrict our consciousness. Because self-awareness is at the root of most other human capacities, the decision to expand it is fundamental to human growth. Here are some areas of emerging awareness that individuals may experience in the counseling process:

- They see how they are trading the security of dependence for the anxieties that accompany choosing for themselves.
- They begin to see that their identity is anchored in someone else's definition of them; that is, they are seeking approval and confirmation of their being in others instead of looking to themselves for affirmation.

- They learn that in many ways they are keeping themselves prisoner by some of their past decisions, and they realize that they can make new decisions.
- They learn that although they cannot change certain events in their lives they can change the way they view and react to these events.
- They learn that they are not condemned to a future similar to the past, for they can learn from their past and thereby reshape their future.
- They realize that they are so preoccupied with suffering, death, and dying that they are not appreciating living.
- They are able to accept their limitations yet still feel worthwhile, for they understand that they do not need to be perfect to feel worthy.
- They come to realize that they are failing to live in the present moment because of preoccupation with the past, planning for the future, or trying to do too many things at once.

Increasing self-awareness—which includes awareness of alternatives, motivations, factors influencing the person, and personal goals—is an aim of all counseling. Clients need to learn that a price must be paid for increased awareness. As we become more aware, it is more difficult to "go home again." Ignorance of our condition may have brought contentment along with a feeling of partial deadness, but as we open the doors in our world, we can expect more turmoil as well as the potential for more fulfillment.

Proposition 2: Freedom and Responsibility

A characteristic existential theme is that people are free to choose among alternatives and therefore play a large role in shaping their own destiny. Schneider and Krug (2010) write that existential therapy embraces three values: (1) the *freedom to become* within the context of natural and self-imposed limitations; (2) the capacity to *reflect* on the meaning of our choices; and (3) the capacity to *act* on the choices we make. A central existential concept is that although we long for freedom, we often try to escape from our freedom by defining ourselves as a fixed or static entity (Russell, 2007). We have no choice about being thrust into the world, yet the manner in which we live and what we become are the result of our choices. Because of the reality of this freedom, our task is to accept responsibility for directing our lives. However, it is possible to avoid this reality by making excuses. In speaking about "bad faith," the existential philosopher Jean-Paul Sartre (1971) refers to the **inauthenticity** of not accepting personal responsibility. Here are two statements that reveal bad faith: "Since that's the way I'm made, I couldn't help what I did" or "Naturally I'm this way, because I grew up in a dysfunctional family." An inauthentic mode of existence consists of lacking awareness of personal responsibility for our lives and passively assuming that our existence is largely controlled by external forces. Sartre claims we are constantly confronted with the choice of what kind of person we are becoming, and to exist is never to be finished with this kind of choosing.

Freedom implies that we are responsible for our lives, for our actions, and for our failures to take action. From Sartre's perspective people are condemned to freedom. He calls for a *commitment* to choosing for ourselves. **Existential guilt** is being aware of having evaded a commitment, or having chosen not to choose.

guilt is a condition that grows out of a sense of incompleteness, or a realization that we are not what we might have become. Guilt may be a sign that we have
failed to rise to the challenge of our anxiety and that we have tried to evade it by
not doing what we know is possible for us to do (van Deurzen, 2002a). This condition is not viewed as neurotic, nor is it seen as a symptom that needs to be cured.
Instead, the existential therapist explores it to see what clients can learn about the
ways in which they are living their life. This guilt also results from allowing others
to define us or to make our choices for us. Sartre said, "We are our choices."
Authenticity implies that we are living by being true to our own evaluation of what
is a valuable existence for ourselves; it is the courage to be who we are.

For existentialists, then, being free and being human are identical. Freedom
and responsibility go hand in hand. We are the authors of our lives in the sense
that we create our destiny, our life situation, and our problems (Russell, 1978).
Assuming responsibility is a basic condition for change. Clients who refuse to
accept responsibility by persistently blaming others for their problems are not
likely to profit from therapy.

Frankl (1978) also links freedom with responsibility. He suggested that the
Statue of Liberty on the East Coast should be balanced with a Statue of Responsibility on the West Coast. His basic premise is that freedom is bound by certain
limitations. We are not free from conditions, but we are free to take a stand against
these restrictions. Ultimately, these conditions are subject to our decisions, which
means we are responsible.

The therapist assists clients in discovering how they are avoiding freedom
and encourages them to learn to risk using it. Not to do so is to cripple clients
and make them dependent on the therapist. Therapists have the task of teaching
clients that they can explicitly accept that they have choices, even though they may
have devoted most of their life to evading them. Those who are in therapy often
have mixed feelings when it comes to choice. As Russell (2007) puts it: "We resent
it when we don't have choices, but we get anxious when we do! Existentialism is all
about broadening the vision of our choices" (p. 111).

People often seek psychotherapy because they feel that they have lost control
of how they are living. They may look to the counselor to direct them, give them
advice, or produce magical cures. They may also need to be heard and understood.
Two central tasks of the therapist are inviting clients to recognize how they have
allowed others to decide for them and encouraging them to take steps toward
choosing for themselves. In inviting clients to explore other ways of being that are
more fulfilling than their present restricted existence, some existential counselors
ask, "Although you have lived in a certain pattern, now that you recognize the price
of some of your ways, are you willing to consider creating new patterns?" Others
may have a vested interest in keeping the client in an old pattern, so the initiative
for changing it will have to come from the client.

Cultural factors need to be taken into account in assisting clients in the process
of examining their choices. A person who is struggling with feeling limited by her
family situation can be invited to look at her part in this process and values that
are a part of her culture. For example, Meta, a Norwegian American, is working to

attain a professional identity as a social worker, but her family thinks she is being selfish and neglecting her primary duties. The family is likely to exert pressure on her to give up her personal interests in favor of what they feel is best for the welfare of the entire family. Meta may feel trapped in the situation and see no way out unless she rejects what her family wants. In cases such as this, it is useful to explore the client's underlying values and to help her determine whether her values are working for her and for her family. Clients such as Meta have the challenge of weighing values and balancing behaviors between two cultures. Ultimately, Meta must decide in what ways she might change her situation, and she needs to assess values based on her culture. The existential therapist will invite Meta to begin to explore what she *can* do and to realize that she can be authentic in spite of pressures on her by her situation. According to Vontress (2008), we can be authentic in any society, whether we are a part of an individualistic or collectivistic society.

It is essential to respect the purpose that people have in mind when they initiate therapy. If we pay careful attention to what our clients tell us about what they want, we can operate within an existential framework. We can encourage individuals to weigh the alternatives and to explore the consequences of what they are doing with their lives. Although oppressive forces may be severely limiting the quality of their lives, we can help people see that they are not solely the victims of circumstances beyond their control. Even though we sometimes cannot control things that happen to us, we have complete control over how we choose to perceive and handle them. Although our freedom *to act* is limited by external reality, our freedom *to be* relates to our internal reality. At the same time that people are learning how to change their external environment, they can be challenged to look within themselves to recognize their own contributions to their problems. Through the therapy experience, clients may be able to discover new courses of action that will lead to a change in their situation.

Proposition 3: Striving for Identity and Relationship to Others

People are concerned about preserving their uniqueness and centeredness, yet at the same time they have an interest in going outside of themselves to relate to other beings and to nature. Each of us would like to discover a self or, to put it more authentically, to create our personal identity. This is not an automatic process, and creating an identity takes courage. As relational beings, we also strive for connectedness with others. Many existential writers discuss loneliness, uprootedness, and alienation, which can be seen as the failure to develop ties with others and with nature.

The trouble with so many of us is that we have sought directions, answers, values, and beliefs from the important people in our world. Rather than trusting ourselves to search within and find our own answers to the conflicts in our life, we sell out by becoming what others expect of us. Our being becomes rooted in their expectations, and we become strangers to ourselves.

THE COURAGE TO BE Paul Tillich (1886–1965), a leading Protestant theologian of the 20th century, believes awareness of our finite nature gives us an appreciation of ultimate concerns. It takes courage to discover the true "ground of our being" and to use its power to transcend those aspects of nonbeing that would destroy us (Tillich, 1952). Courage entails the will to move forward in spite of anxiety-producing situations, such as facing our death (May, 1975). We struggle to discover, to create, and to maintain the core deep within our being. One of the greatest fears of clients is that they will discover that there is no core, no self, no substance, and that they are merely reflections of everyone's expectations of them. A client may say, "My fear is that I'll discover I'm nobody, that there really is nothing to me. I'll find out that I'm an empty shell, hollow inside, and nothing will exist if I shed my masks." If clients demonstrate the courage to confront these fears, they might well leave therapy with an increased tolerance for the uncertainty of life. By assisting clients in facing the fear that their lives or selves are empty and meaningless, therapists can help clients to *create* a self that has meaning and substance that *they have chosen.*

Existential therapists may begin by asking their clients to allow themselves to intensify the feeling that they are nothing more than the sum of others' expectations and that they are merely the introjects of parents and parent substitutes. How do they feel now? Are they condemned to stay this way forever? Is there a way out? Can they create a self if they find that they are without one? Where can they begin? Once clients have demonstrated the courage to recognize this fear, to put it into words and share it, it does not seem so overwhelming. I find that it is best to begin work by inviting clients to accept the ways in which they have lived outside themselves and to explore ways in which they are out of contact with themselves.

THE EXPERIENCE OF ALONENESS The existentialists postulate that part of the human condition is the experience of aloneness. But they add that we can derive strength from the experience of looking to ourselves and sensing our separation. The sense of isolation comes when we recognize that we cannot depend on anyone else for our own confirmation; that is, we alone must give a sense of meaning to life, and we alone must decide how we will live. If we are unable to tolerate ourselves when we are alone, how can we expect anyone else to be enriched by our company? Before we can have any solid relationship with another, we must have a relationship with ourselves. We are challenged to learn to listen to ourselves. We have to be able to stand alone before we can truly stand beside another.

There is a paradox in the proposition that humans are existentially both alone and related, but this very paradox describes the human condition. To think that we can cure the condition, or that it should be cured, is erroneous. Ultimately we are alone, yet our aloneness is set in the context of our inevitable relatedness to other people.

THE EXPERIENCE OF RELATEDNESS We humans depend on relationships with others. We want to be significant in another's world, and we want to feel that another's presence is important in our world. When we are able to stand alone and tap into our own strength, our relationships with others are based on our fulfillment, not our deprivation. If we feel personally deprived, however, we can expect little but a clinging and symbiotic relationship with someone else.

Perhaps one of the functions of therapy is to help clients distinguish between a neurotically dependent attachment to another and a life-affirming relationship in which both persons are enhanced. The therapist can challenge clients to examine what they get from their relationships, how they avoid intimate contact, how they prevent themselves from having equal relationships, and how they might create therapeutic, healthy, and mature human relationships. Existential therapists speak of intersubjectivity, which is the fact of our interrelatedness with others and the need for us to struggle with this in a creative way.

STRUGGLING WITH OUR IDENTITY Because of our fear of dealing with our aloneness, Farha (1994) points out that some of us get caught up in ritualistic behavior patterns that cement us to an image or identity we acquired in early childhood. He writes that some of us become trapped in a *doing mode* to avoid the experience of being.

Part of the therapeutic journey consists of the therapist challenging clients to begin to examine the ways in which they have lost touch with their identity, especially by letting others design their life for them. The therapy process itself is often frightening for clients when they realize that they have surrendered their freedom to others and that in the therapy relationship they will have to assume their freedom again. By refusing to give easy solutions or answers, existential therapists confront clients with the reality that they alone must find their own answers.

Proposition 4: The Search for Meaning

A distinctly human characteristic is the struggle for a sense of significance and purpose in life. In my experience the underlying conflicts that bring people into counseling and therapy are centered in these existential questions: "Why am I here?" "What do I want from life?" "What gives my life purpose?" "Where is the source of meaning for me in life?"

Existential therapy can provide the conceptual framework for helping clients challenge the meaning in their lives. Questions that the therapist might ask are, "Do you like the direction of your life?" "Are you pleased with what you now are and what you are becoming?" "If you are confused about who you are and what you want for yourself, what are you doing to get some clarity?"

THE PROBLEM OF DISCARDING OLD VALUES One of the problems in therapy is that clients may discard traditional (and imposed) values without creating other, suitable ones to replace them. What does the therapist do when clients no longer cling to values that they never really challenged or internalized and now experience a vacuum? Clients may report that they feel like a boat without a rudder. They seek new guidelines and values that are appropriate for the newly discovered facets of themselves, and yet for a time they are without them. One of the tasks of the therapeutic process is to help clients create a value system based on a way of living that is consistent with their way of being.

The therapist's job is to trust in the capacity of clients to eventually create an internally derived value system that provides the foundation for a meaningful life. They will no doubt flounder for a time and experience anxiety as a result of the absence of clear-cut values. The therapist's trust is important in helping clients trust their own capacity to create a new source of values.

MEANINGLESSNESS When the world they live in seems meaningless, clients may wonder whether it is worth it to continue struggling or even living. Faced with the prospect of our mortality, we might ask, "Is there any point to what I do now, since I will eventually die? Will what I do be forgotten when I am gone? Given the fact of mortality, why should I busy myself with anything?" A man in one of my groups captured precisely the idea of personal significance when he said, "I feel like another page in a book that has been turned quickly, and nobody bothered to read the page." For Frankl (1978) such a feeling of meaninglessness is the major existential neurosis of modern life.

Meaninglessness in life can lead to emptiness and hollowness, or a condition that Frankl calls the **existential vacuum.** This condition is often experienced when people do not busy themselves with routine or with work. Because there is no preordained design for living, people are faced with the task of creating their own meaning. At times people who feel trapped by the emptiness of life withdraw from the struggle of creating a life with purpose. Experiencing meaninglessness and establishing values that are part of a meaningful life are issues that become the heart of counseling.

CREATING NEW MEANING Logotherapy is designed to help clients find meaning in life. The therapist's function is not to tell clients what their particular meaning in life should be but to point out that they can create meaning even in suffering (Frankl, 1978). This view holds that human suffering (the tragic and negative aspects of life) can be turned into human achievement by the stand an individual takes when faced with it. Frankl also contends that people who confront pain, guilt, despair, and death can effectively deal with their despair and thus triumph.

Yet meaning is not something that we can directly search for and obtain. Paradoxically, the more rationally we seek it, the more likely we are to miss it. Frankl (1978) and Yalom and Josselson (2011) are in basic agreement that, like pleasure, meaning must be pursued obliquely. Finding satisfaction and meaning in life is a by-product of engagement, which is a commitment to creating, loving, working, and building. Meaning is created out of an individual's engagement with what is valued, and this commitment provides the purpose that makes life worthwhile (van Deurzen, 2002a). I like the way Vontress (2008) captures the idea that meaning in life is an ongoing process we struggle with throughout our lives: "What provides meaning one day may not provide meaning the next, and what has been meaningful to a person throughout life may be meaningless when a person is on his or her deathbed" (p. 158).

Proposition 5: Anxiety as a Condition of Living

Anxiety arises from one's personal strivings to survive and to maintain and assert one's being, and the feelings anxiety generates are an inevitable aspect of the human condition. **Existential anxiety** is the unavoidable result of being confronted with the "givens of existence"—death, freedom, choice, isolation, and meaninglessness (Vontress, 2008; Yalom, 1980; Yalom & Josselson, 2011). Existential anxiety arises as we recognize the realities of our mortality, our confrontation with pain and suffering, our need to struggle for survival, and our basic fallibility. We experience this anxiety as we become increasingly aware of our freedom and the consequences of accepting or rejecting that freedom. In fact, when we make a decision that involves reconstruction of our life, the accompanying anxiety can be a signal that we are ready for personal change and can be a stimulus for growth. If we learn to listen to the subtle messages of anxiety, we can dare to take the steps necessary to change the direction of our lives.

Existential therapists differentiate between normal and neurotic anxiety, and they see anxiety as a potential source of growth. **Normal anxiety** is an appropriate response to an event being faced. Further, this kind of anxiety does not have to be repressed, and it can be used as a motivation to change. Because we could not survive without some anxiety, it is not a therapeutic goal to eliminate normal anxiety. Existential philosophers have argued that at the root of our normal (or *ontic*) anxiety, which is an appropriate anxiety that relates to concrete things in the world, is a more fundamental existential (or *ontological*) anxiety, which is based on our awareness of our own temporality and is present even when we do not have to face particularly difficult situations. **Neurotic anxiety**, in contrast, is anxiety about concrete things that is out of proportion to the situation. Neurotic anxiety is typically out of awareness, and it tends to immobilize the person. Being psychologically healthy entails living with as little neurotic anxiety as possible, while accepting and struggling with the unavoidable existential anxiety that is a part of living.

Many people who seek counseling want solutions that will enable them to eliminate anxiety. Attempts to avoid anxiety by creating the illusion that there is security in life may help us cope with the unknown, yet we really know on some level that we are deceiving ourselves when we think we have found fixed security. Facing existential anxiety involves viewing life as an adventure rather than hiding behind imagined securities that seem to offer protection. Opening up to new life means opening up to anxiety. We pay a steep price when we short-circuit anxiety.

People who have the courage to face themselves are, nonetheless, frightened. I am convinced that those who are willing to live with their anxiety for a time profit from personal therapy. Those who flee too quickly into comfortable patterns might experience temporary relief but in the long run seem to experience the frustration of being stuck in old ways.

The existential therapist can help clients recognize that learning how to tolerate ambiguity and uncertainty and how to live without props can be a necessary phase in the journey from dependence to autonomy. The therapist and client can explore the possibility that although breaking away from crippling patterns and building new ways of living will be fraught with anxiety for a while, anxiety will diminish as the client experiences more satisfaction with newer ways of being. When a client becomes more self-confident, the anxiety that results from an expectation of catastrophe is likely to decrease.

Proposition 6: Awareness of Death and Nonbeing

The existentialist does not view death negatively but holds that awareness of death as a basic human condition gives significance to living. A distinguishing human characteristic is the ability to grasp the reality of the future and the inevitability of death. It is necessary to think about death if we are to think significantly about life.

Death should not be considered a threat; death provides the motivation for us to take advantage of appreciating the present moment. Instead of being frozen by the fear of death, death can be viewed as a positive force that enables us to live as fully as possible. Although the notion of death is a wake-up call, it is also something that we strive to avoid (Russell, 2007). If we defend ourselves against the reality of our eventual death, life becomes insipid and meaningless. But if we realize that we are mortal, we know that we do not have an eternity to complete our projects and that the present is crucial. Our awareness of death is the source of zest for life and creativity. Death and life are interdependent, and though physical death destroys us, the idea of death saves us (Yalom, 1980, 2003).

Yalom (2008) recommends that therapists talk directly to clients about the reality of death. He believes the fear of death percolates beneath the surface and haunts us throughout life. Death is a visitor in the therapeutic process, and Yalom believes that ignoring its presence sends the message that death is too overwhelming to explore. Confronting this fear can be the factor that helps us transform an inauthentic mode of living into a more authentic one. Accepting the reality of our personal death can result in a massive shift in the way we live in the world (Yalom & Josselson, 2011). We can turn our fear of death into a positive force when we accept the reality of our mortality. In *Staring at the Sun: Overcoming the Terror of Death*, Yalom (2008) develops the idea that confronting death enables us to live in a more compassionate way.

One focus in existential therapy is on exploring the degree to which clients are doing the things they value. Without being morbidly preoccupied by the ever-present threat of nonbeing, clients can develop a healthy awareness of death as a way to evaluate how well they are living and what changes they want to make in their lives. Those who fear death also fear life. When we emotionally accept the reality of our eventual death, we realize more clearly that our actions do count, that we do have choices, and that we must accept the ultimate responsibility for how well we are living (Corey & Corey, 2010).

THE THERAPEUTIC PROCESS
Therapeutic Goals

Existential therapy is best considered as an invitation to clients to recognize the ways in which they are not living fully authentic lives and to make choices that will lead to their becoming what they are capable of being. An aim of therapy is to assist clients in moving toward authenticity and learning to recognize when they are deceiving themselves (van Deurzen, 2002a). The existential orientation holds that there is no escape from freedom as we will always be held responsible. We can relinquish our freedom, however, which is the ultimate inauthenticity. Existential therapy aims at helping clients face anxiety and engage in action that is based on the authentic purpose of creating a worthy existence.

May (1981) contends that people come to therapy with the self-serving illusion that they are inwardly enslaved and that someone else (the therapist) can free them. Existential therapists are mainly concerned about helping people to reclaim and reown their lives. The task of existential therapy is to teach clients to listen to what they already know about themselves, even though they may not be attending to what they know. Schneider and Krug (2010) identify four essential aims of existential-humanistic therapy: (1) to help clients become more present to both themselves and others; (2) to assist clients in identifying ways they block themselves from fuller presence; (3) to challenge clients to assume responsibility for designing their present lives; and (4) to encourage clients to choose more expanded ways of being in their daily lives.

Increased awareness is the central goal of existential therapy, which allows clients to discover that alternative possibilities exist where none were recognized before. Clients come to realize that they are able to make changes in their way of being in the world.

Therapist's Function and Role

Existential therapists are primarily concerned with understanding the subjective world of clients to help them come to new understandings and options. Existential therapists are especially concerned about clients avoiding responsibility; they consistently invite clients to accept personal responsibility. When clients complain about the predicaments they are in and blame others, the therapist is likely to ask them how they contributed to their situation.

Therapists with an existential orientation usually deal with people who have what could be called a **restricted existence.** These clients have a limited awareness of themselves and are often vague about the nature of their problems. They may see few, if any, options for dealing with life situations, and they tend to feel trapped, helpless, and stuck. For Bugental (1997), a therapist's function is to assist clients in seeing the ways in which they constrict their awareness and the cost of such constrictions. The therapist may hold up a mirror, so to speak, so that clients can gradually engage in self-confrontation. In this way clients can see how they became the way they are and how they might enlarge the way they live. Once clients are aware of factors in their past and of stifling modes of their present existence, they can begin to accept responsibility for changing their future.

Existential practitioners may make use of techniques that originate from diverse theoretical orientations, yet no set of techniques is considered essential. The therapeutic journey is creative and uncertain and different for each client. Russell (2007) captures this notion well when he writes: "There is no one right way to do therapy, and certainly no rigid doctrine for existentially rooted techniques. What is crucial is that you create your own authentic way of being attuned to your clients" (p. 123). Existential therapists encourage experimentation not only within the therapy office but also outside of the therapy setting, based on the belief that life outside therapy is what counts. Practitioners often ask clients to reflect on or write about problematic events they encounter in daily life (Schneider, 2011).

Client's Experience in Therapy

Clients in existential therapy are clearly encouraged to assume responsibility for how they are currently choosing to be in their world. Effective therapy does not stop with this awareness itself, for the therapist encourages clients to take action on the basis of the insights they develop through the therapeutic process. Experimentation with new ways of behaving in the outside world is necessary if clients are to change. Further, clients must be active in the therapeutic process, for during the sessions they must decide what fears, guilt feelings, and anxieties they will explore.

Merely deciding to enter psychotherapy is itself a frightening prospect for most people. The experience of opening the doors to oneself can be frightening, exciting, joyful, depressing, or a combination of all of these. As clients wedge open the closed doors, they also begin to loosen the deterministic shackles that have kept them psychologically bound. Gradually, they become aware of what they have been and who they are now, and they are better able to decide what kind of future they want. Through the process of their therapy, individuals can explore alternatives for making their visions real.

When clients plead helplessness and attempt to convince themselves that they are powerless, May (1981) reminds them that their journey toward freedom began by putting one foot in front of the other to get to his office. As narrow as their range of freedom may be, individuals can begin building and augmenting that range by taking small steps. The therapeutic journey that opens up new horizons is poetically described by van Deurzen (2010):

> Embarking on our existential journey requires us to be prepared to be touched and shaken by what we find on the way and to not be afraid to discover our own limitations and weaknesses, uncertainties and doubts. It is only with such an attitude of openness and wonder that we can encounter the impenetrable everyday mysteries, which take us beyond our own preoccupations and sorrows and which by confronting us with death, make us rediscover life. (p. 5)

Another aspect of the experience of being a client in existential therapy is confronting ultimate concerns rather than coping with immediate problems. Rather than being solution-oriented, existential therapy is aimed toward removing roadblocks to meaningful living and helping clients assume responsibility for their actions (Yalom & Josselson, 2011). Existential therapists assist people in facing life with courage, hope, and a willingness to find meaning in life.

Relationship Between Therapist and Client

Existential therapists give central prominence to their relationship with the client. The relationship is important in itself because the quality of this person-to-person encounter in the therapeutic situation is the stimulus for positive change. Attention is given to the client's immediate, ongoing experience, especially what is going on in the interaction between the therapist and the client. Therapy is viewed as a social microcosm in the sense that the interpersonal and existential problems of the client will become apparent in the here and now of the therapy relationship (Yalom & Josselson, 2011).

Therapists with an existential orientation believe their basic attitudes toward the client and their own personal characteristics of honesty, integrity, and courage are what they have to offer. Therapy is a journey taken by therapist and client that delves deeply into the world as perceived and experienced by the client. But this type of quest demands that therapists also be in contact with their own phenomenological world. Existential therapy is a voyage into self-discovery and a journey of life-discovery for both client and therapist (van Deurzen, 2010; Yalom & Josselson, 2011).

Buber's (1970) conception of the I/Thou relationship has significant implications here. His understanding of the self is based on two fundamental relationships: the "I/it" and the "I/Thou." The I/it is the relation to time and space, which is a necessary starting place for the self. The I/Thou is the relationship essential for connecting the self to the spirit and, in so doing, to achieve true dialogue. This form of relationship is the paradigm of the fully human self, the achievement of which is the goal of Buber's existential philosophy. Relating in an I/Thou fashion means that there is direct, mutual, and present interaction. Rather than prizing therapeutic objectivity and professional distance, existential therapists strive to create caring and intimate relationships with clients.

The core of the therapeutic relationship is respect, which implies faith in clients' potential to cope authentically with their troubles and in their ability to discover alternative ways of being. Existential therapists share their reactions to clients with genuine concern and empathy as one way of deepening the therapeutic relationship. Therapists invite clients to grow by modeling authentic behavior. If therapists keep themselves hidden during the therapeutic session or if they engage in inauthentic behavior, clients will also remain guarded and persist in their inauthentic ways.

Bugental (1987) emphasizes the crucial role the *presence* of the therapist plays in the therapeutic relationship. In his view many therapists and therapeutic systems overlook its fundamental importance. He contends that therapists are too often so concerned with the content of what is being said that they are not aware of the distance between themselves and their clients:

> The therapeutic alliance is the powerful joining of forces which energizes and supports the long, difficult, and frequently painful work of life-changing psychotherapy. The conception of the therapist here is not of a disinterested observer-technician but of a fully alive human companion for the client. (p. 49)

Schneider (2011) believes that the therapist's *presence* is both a condition and a goal of therapeutic change. Presence serves the dual functions of reconnecting people to their pain and to attuning them to the opportunities to transform their pain.

APPLICATION: THERAPEUTIC TECHNIQUES AND PROCEDURES

The existential approach is unlike most other therapies in that it is not technique-oriented. Although existentially oriented therapists may incorporate many techniques from other models, these interventions are made within the context of striving to understand the subjective world of the client. The interventions existential practitioners employ are based on philosophical views about the nature of human existence. These practitioners prefer description, understanding, and exploration of the client's subjective reality, as opposed to diagnosis, treatment, and prognosis (van Deurzen, 2002b). As Vontress (2008) puts it: "Existential therapists prefer to be thought of as philosophical companions, not as people who repair psyches" (p. 161). Yalom and Josselson (2011) assert that existential therapists are "fellow travelers" (p. 332), willing to make themselves known through appropriate self-disclosure. As mentioned earlier, existential therapists are free to draw from techniques that flow from many other orientations. However, they do not employ an array of unintegrated techniques; they have a set of assumptions and attitudes that guide their interventions with clients. See *Case Approach to Counseling and Psycho-therapy* (Corey, 2013, chap. 4) for an illustration of how Dr. J. Michael Russell works in an existential way with some key themes in the case of Ruth.

Van Deurzen (2010) identifies as a primary ground rule of existential work the openness to the individual creativity of the therapist and the client. She maintains that existential therapists need to adapt their interventions to their own person-ality and style, as well as being sensitive to what each client requires. The main guideline is that the existential practitioner's interventions are responsive to the uniqueness of each client.

Van Deurzen (2002a, 2002b) believes that the starting point for existential work is for practitioners to clarify their views on life and living. She stresses the importance of therapists reaching sufficient depth and openness in their own lives to venture into clients' murky waters without getting lost. The nature of existential work is assisting people in the process of living with greater expertise and ease. Van Deurzen (2010) identifies how therapists make a difference with clients: "We help them to get better at reflecting on their situation, deal with their dilemma, face their predicament and think for themselves" (p. 236). Van Deurzen reminds us that existential therapy is a collaborative adventure in which both client and therapist will be transformed if they allow themselves to be touched by life. When the deepest self of the therapist meets the deepest part of the client, the counseling process is at its best. Therapy is a creative, evolving process of discovery that can be conceptualized in three general phases.

Phases of Existential Counseling

During the initial phase of counseling, therapists assist clients in identifying and clarifying their assumptions about the world. Clients are invited to define and question the ways in which they perceive and make sense of their existence. They examine their values, beliefs, and assumptions to determine their validity. This is a difficult task for many clients because they may initially present their problems as resulting almost entirely from external causes. They may focus on what other people "make them feel" or on how others are largely responsible for their actions or inaction. The counselor teaches them how to reflect on their own existence and to examine their role in creating their problems in living.

During the middle phase of existential counseling, clients are assisted in more fully examining the source and authority of their present value system. This proc-ess of self-exploration typically leads to new insights and some restructuring of values and attitudes. Individuals get a better idea of what kind of life they consider worthy to live and develop a clearer sense of their internal valuing process.

The final phase of existential counseling focuses on helping people take what they are learning about themselves and put it into action. Transformation is not limited to what takes place during the therapy hour. The therapeutic hour is a small contribution to a person's renewed engagement with life, or a rehearsal for life (van Deurzen, 2002b). The aim of therapy is to enable clients to discover ways of implementing their examined and internalized values in a concrete way between sessions and after therapy has terminated. Clients typically discover their strengths and find ways to put them to the service of living a purposeful existence.

Clients Appropriate for Existential Counseling

Existential practice has been applied in a variety of settings and with a diverse population of clients, including those with substance abuse issues, ethnic and racial minorities, gay and lesbian clients, and psychiatric inpatients (Schneider, 2011). A strength of the perspective is its focus on available choices and pathways toward personal growth. For people who are coping with developmental crises, experiencing grief and loss, confronting death, or facing a major life decision, existential therapy is especially appropriate. Some examples of these critical turning points that mark passages from one stage of life into another are the struggle for identity in adolescence, coping with possible disappointments in middle age, adjusting to children leaving home, coping with failures in marriage and work, and dealing with increased physical limitations as one ages. These developmental challenges involve both dangers and opportunities. Uncertainty, anxiety, and struggling with decisions are all part of this process.

Van Deurzen (2002b) suggests that this form of therapy is most appropriate for clients who are committed to dealing with their problems about living, for people who feel alienated from the current expectations of society, or for those who are searching for meaning in their lives. It tends to work well with people who are at a crossroads and who question the state of affairs in the world and are willing to challenge the status quo. It can be useful for people who are on the edge of existence, such as those who are dying or contemplating suicide, who are working through a developmental or situational crisis, who feel that they no longer belong in their surroundings, or who are starting a new phase of life.

Application to Brief Therapy

The existential approach can focus clients on significant areas such as assuming personal responsibility, making a commitment to deciding and acting, and expanding their awareness of their current situation. It is possible for a time-limited approach to serve as a catalyst for clients to become actively and fully involved in each of their therapy sessions. Strasser and Strasser (1997), who are connected to the British school of existential analysis, maintain that there are clear benefits to time-limited therapy, which mirrors the time-limited reality of human existence. Sharp and Bugental (2001) maintain that short-term applications of the existential approach require more structuring and clearly defined and less ambitious goals. At the termination of short-term therapy, it is important for individuals to evaluate what they have accomplished and what issues may need to be addressed later. It is essential that both therapist and client determine that short-term work is appropriate, and that beneficial outcomes are likely.

Application to Group Counseling

An existential group can be described as people making a commitment to a lifelong journey of self-exploration with these goals: (1) enabling members to become honest with themselves, (2) widening their perspectives on themselves and the world around them, and (3) clarifying what gives meaning to their present and future life (van Deurzen, 2002b). An open attitude toward life is essential, as is the willingness to explore unknown territory. Recurring universal themes evolve in many groups and challenge members to seriously explore existential concerns such as choice, freedom and anxiety, awareness of death, meaning in life, and living fully.

Yalom (1980) contends that the group provides the optimal conditions for therapeutic work on responsibility. The members are responsible for the way they behave in the group, and this provides a mirror for how they are likely to act in the world. A group represents a microcosm of the world in which participants live and function. Over time the interpersonal and existential problems of the participants become evident in the here-and-now interactions within the group (Yalom & Josselson, 2011). Through feedback, members learn to view themselves through others' eyes, and they learn the ways in which their behavior affects others. Building on what members learn about their interpersonal functioning in the group, they can take increased responsibility for making changes in everyday life. The group experience provides the opportunity to participants to relate to others in meaningful ways, to learn to be themselves in the company of other people, and to establish rewarding, nourishing relationships.

In existential group counseling, members come to terms with the paradoxes of existence: that life can be undone by death, that success is precarious, that we are determined to be free, that we are responsible for a world we did not choose, that we must make choices in the face of doubt and uncertainty. Members experience anxiety when they recognize the realities of the human condition, including pain and suffering, the need to struggle for survival, and their basic fallibility. Clients learn that there are no ultimate answers for ultimate concerns. Through the support that is within a group, participants are able to tap the strength needed to create an internally derived value system that is consistent with their way of being.

A group provides a powerful context to look at oneself, and to consider what choices might be more authentically one's own. Members can openly share their fears related to living in unfulfilling ways and come to recognize how they have compromised their integrity. Members can gradually discover ways in which they have lost their direction and can begin to be more true to themselves. Members learn that it is not in others that they find the answers to questions about significance and purpose in life. Existential group leaders help members live in authentic ways and refrain from prescribing simple solutions. For a more detailed discussion of the existential approach to group counseling, see Corey (2012, chap. 9).

EXISTENTIAL THERAPY FROM A MULTICULTURAL PERSPECTIVE

Strengths From a Diversity Perspective

Because the existential approach does not dictate a particular way of viewing or relating to reality, and because of its broad perspective, this approach is highly relevant in working in a multicultural context (van Deurzen, 2002a). Vontress and colleagues (1999) write about the existential foundation of cross-cultural counseling: "Existential counseling is probably the most useful approach to helping clients of all cultures find meaning and harmony in their lives, because it focuses on the sober issues each of us must inevitably face: love, anxiety, suffering, and death" (p. 32). These are the human experiences that transcend the boundaries that separate cultures.

Existential therapy is useful in working with culturally diverse clients because of its focus on universality, or the common ground that we all share. This approach emphasizes presence, the I/Thou relationship, and courage. As such, it can be effectively applied with diverse client populations with a range of specific problems and in a wide array of settings (Schneider, 2008, 2011; Schneider & Krug, 2010). Schneider's (2008) "existential-integrative" model of practice coordinates a variety of therapeutic modes within an overarching existential or experiential framework. Vontress (1996) points out that all people are multicultural in the sense that they are all products of many cultures. He encourages counselors-in-training to focus on the universal commonalities of clients first and secondarily on areas of differences. In working with cultural diversity, it is essential to recognize simultaneously the commonalities and differences of human beings: "Cross-cultural counseling, in short, does not intend to teach specific interventions for each culture, but to infuse the counselor with a cultural sensitivity and tolerant philosophical outlook that will befit all cultures" (p. 164).

The focus on subjective experience, or phenomenology, is a strength from a multicultural perspective. Another strength of the existential approach is that it enables clients to examine the degree to which their behavior is being influenced by social and cultural conditioning. Clients can be challenged to look at the price they are paying for the decisions they have made. Although it is true that some clients may not feel a sense of freedom, their freedom can be increased if they recognize the social limits they are facing. Their freedom can be hindered by institutions and limited by their family. In fact, it may be difficult to separate individual freedom from the context of their family structure.

There is wide-ranging international interest in the existential approach. Several Scandinavian societies, an East European society (encompassing Estonia, Latvia, Lithuania, Russia, Ukraine, and Belarus), and Mexican and South American societies are thriving. In addition, an Internet course, SEPTIMUS, is taught in Ireland, Iceland, Sweden, Poland, Czech Republic, Romania, Italy, Portugal, France, Belgium, the United Kingdom, Israel, and Australia. Most recently, the First International East-West Existential Psychology conference was held in Nanjing, China, with representatives from the United States, Korea, and Japan. These international developments, as well as the creation of the International Collaborative of Existential Counselors and Psychotherapists, which has members from all over the world, reveal that existential therapy has wide appeal to diverse populations in many parts of the world.

Shortcomings From a Diversity Perspective

For those who hold a systemic perspective, the existentialists can be criticized on the grounds that they are excessively individualistic and that they ignore the social factors that cause human problems. However, with the advent of the "existential-integrative" model of practice (Schneider, 2008), this situation is beginning to change. According to Schneider (2011), existential practitioners are not only concerned with facilitating individual change but with promoting an in-depth inquiry that has implications for social change: "One cannot simply heal individuals to the neglect of the social context within which they are thrust. To be a responsible practitioner, one must develop a vision of responsible social change alongside and in coordination with one's vision of individual transformation" (p. 281).

Some individuals who seek counseling may operate on the assumption that they have very little choice because environmental circumstances severely restrict their ability to influence the direction of their lives. Even if they change internally, they see little hope that the external realities of racism, discrimination, and oppression will change. They are likely to experience a deep sense of frustration and feelings of powerlessness when it comes to making changes outside of themselves. As you will see in Chapter 12, feminist therapists maintain that therapeutic practice will be effective only to the extent that therapists intervene with some form of social action to change those factors that are creating clients' problems. In working with people of color who come from the barrio or ghetto, for example, it is important to engage their survival issues. If a counselor too quickly puts across the message to these clients that they have a choice in making their lives better, they may feel patronized and misunderstood. These real-life concerns can provide a good focus for counseling, assuming the therapist is willing to deal with them.

A potential problem within existential theory is that it is highly focused on the philosophical assumption of self-determination, which may not take into account the complex factors that many people who have been oppressed must deal with. In many cultures it is not possible to talk about the self and self-determination apart from the context of the social network and environmental conditions. However, a case can be made for the existential approach being instrumental in enabling clients to make conscious choices when it comes to the values they live by. Existential therapists do not push autonomy apart from a client's culture. They do assist clients in critically evaluating the source of their values and making a choice rather than uncritically accepting the values of their culture and family.

Many clients expect a structured and problem-oriented approach to counseling that is not found in the conventional existential approach. Although clients may feel better if they have an opportunity to talk and to be understood, they are likely to expect the counselor to do something to bring about a change in their life situation. A major task for the counselor who practices from an existential perspective is to provide enough concrete direction for these clients without taking the responsibility away from them.

Existential Therapy Applied to the Case of Stan

 As an existentially oriented therapist, I counsel Stan with the assumption that he has the capacity to increase his self-awareness and decide for himself the future direction of his life. I want him to realize more than anything else that he does not have to be the victim of his past conditioning but can be the architect in redesigning his future. He can free himself of his deterministic shackles and accept the responsibility that comes with directing his own life. This approach emphasizes the importance of my understanding of Stan's world, primarily by establishing an authentic relationship as a means to a fuller degree of self-understanding.

Stan is demonstrating what Sartre would call "bad faith" by not accepting personal responsibility. I confront Stan with the ways in which he is attempting to escape from his freedom through alcohol and drugs. Eventually, I challenge Stan's passivity. I reaffirm that he is now entirely responsible for his life, for his actions, and for his failure to take action. I do this in a supportive yet firm manner.

I do not see Stan's anxiety as something negative, but as a vital part of living with uncertainty and freedom. Because there are no guarantees and because the individual is ultimately alone, Stan can expect to experience some degree of healthy anxiety, aloneness, guilt, and even despair. These conditions are not neurotic in themselves, but the way in which Stan orients himself and copes with these conditions is critical.

Stan sometimes talks about his suicidal feelings. Certainly, I investigate further to determine if he poses an immediate threat to himself. In addition to this assessment to determine lethality, I view his thoughts of "being better off dead" as symbolic. Could it be that Stan feels he is dying as a person? Is Stan using his human potential? Is he choosing a way of merely existing instead of affirming life? Is Stan mainly trying to elicit sympathy from his family? I invite Stan to explore the meaning and purpose in his life. Is there any reason for him to want to continue living? What are some of the projects that enrich his life? What can he do to find a sense of purpose that will make him feel more significant and alive?

Stan needs to accept the reality that he may at times feel alone. Choosing for oneself and living from one's own center accentuates the experience of aloneness. He is not, however, condemned to a life of isolation, alienation from others, and loneliness. I hope to help Stan discover his own centeredness and live by the values he chooses and creates for himself. By doing so, Stan can become a more substantial person and come to appreciate himself more. When he does, the chances are lessened that he will have a need to secure approval from others, particularly his parents and parental substitutes. Instead of forming a dependent relationship, Stan could choose to relate to others out of his strength. Only then would there be the possibility of overcoming his feelings of separateness and isolation.

Follow-Up: You Continue as Stan's Existential Therapist

Use these questions to help you think about how you would counsel Stan using an existential approach:

- If Stan resisted your attempts to help him see that he is responsible for the direction of his life, how might you intervene?
- Stan experiences a great deal of anxiety. From an existential perspective, how do you view his anxiety? How might you work with his anxiety in helpful ways?
- If Stan talks with you about suicide as a response to despair and a life without meaning, how would you respond?

See the *DVD for Theory and Practice of Counseling and Psychotherapy: The Case of Stan and Lecturettes* (Session 4 on existential therapy) for a demonstration of my approach to counseling Stan from this perspective. This session focuses on the themes of death and the meaning of life.

SUMMARY AND EVALUATION

Summary

As humans, according to the existentialist view, we are capable of self-awareness, which is the distinctive capacity that allows us to reflect and to decide. With this awareness we become free beings who are responsible for choosing the way we live, and we influence our own destiny. This awareness of freedom and responsibility gives rise to existential anxiety, which is another basic human characteristic. Whether we like it or not, we are free, even though we may seek to avoid reflecting on this freedom. The knowledge that we must choose, even though the outcome is not certain, leads to anxiety. This anxiety is heightened when we reflect on the reality that we are mortal. Facing the inevitable prospect of eventual death gives the present moment significance, for we become aware that we do not have forever to accomplish our projects. Our task is to create a life that has meaning and purpose. As humans we are unique in that we strive toward fashioning purposes and values that give meaning to living. Whatever meaning our life has is developed through freedom and a commitment to make choices in the face of uncertainty.

Existential therapy places central prominence on the person-to-person relationship. It assumes that client growth occurs through this genuine encounter. It is not the techniques a therapist uses that make a therapeutic difference; rather, it is the quality of the client–therapist relationship that heals. It is essential that therapists reach sufficient depth and openness in their own lives to allow them to venture into their clients' subjective world without losing their own sense of identity. Presence is both a condition for therapy to occur and a goal of therapy. Existential therapists are fellow travelers, and as such they strive to be authentic and self-disclosing in their therapy work. Because this approach focuses on the goals of therapy, basic conditions of being human, and therapy as a shared journey, practitioners are not bound by specific techniques. Although existential therapists may apply techniques from other orientations, their interventions are guided by a philosophical framework about what it means to be human.

Contributions of the Existential Approach

The existential approach has helped bring the person back into central focus. It concentrates on the central facts of human existence: self-consciousness and our consequent freedom. To the existentialist goes the credit for providing a new view of death as a positive force, not a morbid prospect to fear, for death gives life meaning. Existentialists have contributed a new dimension to the understanding of anxiety, guilt, frustration, loneliness, and alienation.

I particularly appreciate the way van Deurzen (2002a) views the existential practitioner as a mentor and fellow traveler who encourages people to reflect upon the problems they encounter in living. What clients need is "some assistance in surveying the terrain and in deciding on the right route so that they can again find their way" (p. 18). According to van Deurzen, the existential approach encourages people to live life by their own standards and values: "The aim of existential work is to assist people in developing their talents in their own personal way, helping them in being true to what they value" (p. 21).

One of the major contributions of the existential approach is its emphasis on the human quality of the therapeutic relationship. This aspect lessens the chances of dehumanizing psychotherapy by making it a mechanical process. Existential counselors reject the notions of therapeutic objectivity and professional distance, viewing them as being unhelpful.

I very much value the existential emphasis on freedom and responsibility and the person's capacity to redesign his or her life by choosing with awareness.

This perspective provides a sound philosophical base on which to build a personal and unique therapeutic style because it addresses itself to the core struggles of the contemporary person.

CONTRIBUTIONS TO THE INTEGRATION OF PSYCHOTHERAPIES

From my perspective, the key concepts of the existential approach can be integrated into most therapeutic schools. Regardless of a therapist's orientation, the foundation for practice can be based on existential themes. Existential psychotherapy continues to have an enduring impact on a variety of psychological practices. "Indeed, existential psychotherapy is in the ironic position of being one of the most widely influential yet least officially embraced orientations on the professional scene" (Schneider, 2008, p. 1). Bruce Wampold (2008), a leading researcher in the psychotherapy field, agrees "that an understanding of the principles of existential therapy is needed by all therapists, as it adds a perspective that might . . . form the basis for all effective treatments" (p. 6).

A key contribution is the possibility of a creative integration of the conceptual propositions of existential therapy with many other therapeutic orientations (Bugental & Bracke, 1992; Schneider, 2008, 2011; Schneider & Krug, 2010). One example of such a creative integration is provided by Dattilio (2002), who integrates cognitive behavioral techniques with the themes of an existential approach. As a cognitive behavior therapist and author, Dattilio maintains that he directs much of his efforts to "helping clients make a deep existential shift—to a new understanding of the world" (p. 75). He uses techniques such as restructuring of belief systems, relaxation methods, and a variety of cognitive and behavioral strategies, but he does so within an existential framework that can begin the process of real-life transformation. Many of his clients suffer from panic attacks or depression. Dattilio often explores with these people existential themes of meaning, guilt, hopelessness, anxiety—and at the same time he provides them with cognitive behavioral tools to cope with the problems of daily living. In short, he grounds symptomatic treatment in an existential approach.

Some people have argued that the new trend toward positive psychology is similar to the existential approach, but this rests on a superficial comparison of these two approaches. Existential therapists favor intensity and passionate experience, including that of happiness, but they equally value the darker side of human nature and would encourage clients to learn to value both sides of their experience (van Deurzen, 2009).

Limitations and Criticisms of the Existential Approach

A major criticism often aimed at this approach is that it lacks a systematic statement of the principles and practices of psychotherapy. Some practitioners have trouble with what they perceive as its mystical language and concepts. Some therapists who claim adherence to an existential orientation describe their therapeutic style in vague and global terms such as *self-actualization, dialogic encounter, authenticity,* and *being in the world.* This particular use of language causes confusion at times and makes it difficult to conduct research on the process or outcomes of existential therapy.

Both beginning and advanced practitioners who are not of a philosophical turn of mind tend to find many of the existential concepts lofty and elusive. As we have seen, this approach places primary emphasis on a subjective understanding of the world of clients. It is assumed that techniques follow understanding. The fact that few techniques are generated by this approach makes it essential for practitioners to develop their own innovative procedures or to borrow from other schools of therapy. For counselors who believe they need a specific set of techniques to counsel effectively, this approach has limitations (Vontress, 2008).

Practitioners who prefer a counseling practice based on research contend that the concepts should be empirically sound, that definitions should be operational, that the hypotheses should be testable, and that therapeutic practice should be based on the results of research into both the process and outcomes of counseling. Certainly, the notions of manualized therapy and evidence-based practice are not part of the existential perspective because every psychotherapy experience is unique (Walsh & McElwain, 2002). According to Cooper (2003), existential practitioners generally reject the idea that the therapeutic process can be measured and evaluated in quantitative and empirical ways. Although existential practices are generally upheld by recent research on therapeutic effectiveness (see Elkins, 2009), few studies directly evaluate and examine the existential approach. To a large extent, existential therapy makes use of techniques from other theories, which makes it difficult to apply research to this approach to study its effectiveness (Sharf, 2012).

According to van Deurzen (2002b), the main limitation of this approach is that of the level of maturity, life experience, and intensive training required of practitioners. Existential therapists need to be wise and capable of profound and wide-ranging understanding of what it means to be human. Authenticity is a cardinal characteristic of a competent existential practitioner, which is certainly more involved than mastering a body of knowledge and acquiring technical skills. Russell (2007) puts this notion nicely: "Authenticity means being able to sign your own name on your work and your life. It means you will want to take responsibility for creating your own way of being a therapist" (p.123).

WHERE TO GO FROM HERE

Refer to the *DVD for Integrative Counseling: The Case of Ruth and Lecturettes*, Session 11 ("Understanding How the Past Influences the Present and the Future"), for a demonstration of ways I utilize existential notions in counseling Ruth. We engage in a role play where Ruth becomes the voice of her church and I take on a new role as Ruth—one in which I have been willing to challenge certain beliefs from church. This segment illustrates how I assist Ruth in finding new values. In Session 12 ("Working Toward Decisions and Behavioral Changes") I challenge Ruth to make new decisions, which is also an existential concept.

Free Podcasts for ACA Members

You can download ACA Podcasts (prerecorded interviews) at www.counseling.org; click on the Resource button and then the Podcast Series. For Chapter 6, Existential Therapy, look for Podcast 14 by Dr. Gerald Corey.

Other Resources

The American Psychological Association offers a DVD by K. J. Schneider (2009) titled *Existential-Humanistic Therapy* in their Systems of Psychotherapy Video Series.

Psychotherapy.net is a comprehensive resource for students and professionals that offers videos and interviews on existential therapy featuring Irvin Yalom, James Bugental, and Rollo May. New video and editorial content is made available monthly. DVDs relevant to this chapter are available at www.psychotherapy.net and include the following:

Bugental, J.F.T. (1995). *Existential-Humanistic Psychotherapy in Action*

Bugental, J. (1997). *Existential-Humanistic Psychotherapy* (Psychotherapy with the Experts Series)

Bugental, J. (2008). *James Bugental: Live Case Consultation*

May, R. (2007). *Rollo May on Existential Psychotherapy*

Yalom, I. (2002) *The Gift of Therapy: A Conversation with Irvin Yalom, M.D.*

Yalom, I. (2006). *Irvin Yalom: Live Case Consultation*

Yalom, I. (2011) *Confronting Death and Other Existential Issues in Psychotherapy*

If you are interesting in further information on Irvin Yalom, check out his website at www.yalom.com.

The Existential-Humanistic Institute, Dr. Kirk Schneider, Orah Krug, and Nader Shabahangi

Website:www.ehinstitute.org

The Existential-Humanistic Institute's (EHI) primary focus is training; offering courses, and in conjunction with Saybrook University, a new certificate program in existential-humanistic therapy and theory. A secondary focus is community building. EHI was formed as a nonprofit organization under the auspices of the Pacific Institute in 1997 and provides a home for those mental health professionals, scholars, and students who seek in-depth training in existential-humanistic theory and practice. EHI's year-long certificate program offers graduate and postgraduate students an opportunity to gain a basic foundation in the theory and practice of existential-humanistic therapy. EHI offers courses on the principles of existential-humanistic practice and case seminars in existential-humanistic theory and practice. Most of EHI's instructors have studied extensively with such masters as James Bugental, Irvin Yalom, and Rollo May, and are, like Kirk Schneider and Orah Krug, acknowledged leaders of the existential-humanistic movement today.

Society for Existential Analysis

Website: www.existentialanalysis.co.uk/

Additional Information: www.dilemmas.org

The Society for Existential Analysis is a professional organization devoted to exploring issues pertaining to an existential/phenomenological approach to counseling and therapy. Membership is open to anyone interested in this approach and includes students, trainees, psychotherapists, philosophers, psychiatrists, counselors, and psychologists. Members receive a regular newsletter and an annual copy of the *Journal of the Society for Existential Analysis*. The society provides a list of existentially oriented psychotherapists for referral purposes. The School of Psychotherapy and Counselling at Regent's College in London offers an advanced diploma in existential psychotherapy as well as short courses in the field.

International Society for Existential Psychotherapy and Counselling
Website: www.existentialpsychotherapy.net

The International Society for Existential Psychotherapy and Counselling was created in London in July 2006 and was renamed International Collaborative of Existential Counselors and Psychotherapists soon after (www.icecap.org.uk). It brings together the existing national societies as well as providing a forum for the development and accreditation of the approach.

Psychotherapy Training on the Net: SEPTIMUS
Website: www.septimus.info
Additional Information: www.psychotherapytraining.net

SEPTIMUS is an Internet-based course taught in Ireland, Iceland, Sweden, Poland, Czech Republic, Romania, Italy, Portugal, Austria, Belgium, France, Israel, Australia, and the United Kingdom.

New School of Psychotherapy and Counselling
Royal Waterloo House
51-55 Waterloo Road
London, England SE1 8TX
Telephone: +44 (0) 20 7928 43 44
E-mail: Admin@nspc.org.uk
Website: www.nspc.org.uk

The New School of Psychotherapy and Counselling (NSPC) is set up especially for training existential therapists. It offers an MA and doctoral program in Existential Psychotherapy and Counseling together with Middlesex University, as well as an MSC and professional doctorate in Existential Counseling Psychology and Psychotherapy also jointly with Middlesex University. NSPC offers intensive courses for distance learners (worldwide student body), including e-learning.

Person-Centered Therapy

Person-Centered Therapy

© Roger Ressmeyer/Corbis

CARL ROGERS (1902–1987), a major spokesperson for humanistic psychology, led a life that reflected the ideas he developed for half a century. He showed a questioning stance, a deep openness to change, and the courage to forge into unknown territory both as a person and as a professional. In writing about his early years, Rogers (1961) recalled his family atmosphere as characterized by close and warm relationships but also by strict religious standards. Play was discouraged, and the virtues of the Protestant ethic were extolled. His boyhood was somewhat lonely, and he pursued scholarly interests instead of social ones. Rogers was an introverted person, and he spent a lot of time reading and engaging in imaginative activity and reflection. During his college years his interests and academic major changed from agriculture to history, then to religion, and finally to clinical psychology.

Rogers held academic positions in various fields, including education, social work, counseling, psychotherapy, group therapy, peace, and interpersonal relations, and he earned recognition around the world for originating and developing the humanistic movement in psychotherapy. His foundational ideas, especially the central role of the client–therapist relationship as a means to growth and change, have been incorporated by many other theoretical approaches. Rogers was a pioneer whose groundbreaking discoveries continue to have far-reaching effects on the field of psychotherapy (Cain, 2010).

It is difficult to overestimate the significance of Rogers's contributions to clinical and counseling psychology. He was a courageous pioneer who "was about 50 years ahead of his time and has been waiting for us to catch up" (Elkins, 2009, p. 20). Often called the "father of psychotherapy research," Rogers was the first to study the counseling process in depth by analyzing the transcripts of actual therapy sessions; he was the first clinician to conduct major studies on psychotherapy using quantitative methods; he was the first to formulate a comprehensive theory of personality and psychotherapy grounded in empirical research; and he contributed to developing a theory of psychotherapy that de-emphasized pathology and focused on the strengths and resources of individuals. He was not afraid to take a strong position and challenged the status quo throughout his professional career.

During the last 15 years of his life, Rogers applied the person-centered approach to world peace by training policymakers, leaders, and groups in conflict. Perhaps his greatest passion was directed toward the reduction of interracial tensions and the effort to achieve world peace, for which he was nominated for the Nobel Peace Prize.

For a detailed video presentation of the life and works of Carl Rogers, see *Carl Rogers: A Daughter's Tribute* (CD ROM, 2002), which is described at the end of this chapter. See also *Carl Rogers: The Quiet Revolutionary* (Rogers & Russell, 2002) and *The Life and Work of Carl Rogers* (Kirschenbaum, 2009).

159

PERSON-CENTERED THERAPY

INTRODUCTION

Of all the pioneers who have founded a therapeutic approach, for me Carl Rogers stands out as one of the most influential figures in revolutionizing the direction of counseling theory and practice. Rogers has become known as a "quiet revolutionary" who both contributed to theory development and whose influence continues to shape counseling practice today (see Cain, 2010; Kirschenbaum, 2009; Rogers & Russell, 2002).

The person-centered approach shares many concepts and values with the existential perspective presented in Chapter 6. Rogers's basic assumptions are that people are essentially trustworthy, that they have a vast potential for understanding themselves and resolving their own problems without direct intervention on the therapist's part, and that they are capable of self-directed growth if they are involved in a specific kind of therapeutic relationship. From the beginning, Rogers emphasized the attitudes and personal characteristics of the therapist and the quality of the client–therapist relationship as the prime determinants of the outcome of the therapeutic process. He consistently relegated to a secondary position matters such as the therapist's knowledge of theory and techniques. This belief in the client's capacity for self-healing is in contrast with many theories that view the therapist's techniques as the most powerful agents that lead to change (Bohart & Tallman, 2010). Clearly, Rogers revolutionized the field of psychotherapy by proposing a theory that centered on the client as the primary agent for constructive self-change (Bohart & Tallman, 2010; Bozarth, Zimring, & Tausch, 2002).

Contemporary person-centered therapy is the result of an evolutionary process that continues to remain open to change and refinement (see Cain, 2010; Cain & Seeman, 2002). Rogers did not present the person-centered theory as a fixed and completed approach to therapy. He hoped that others would view his theory as a set of tentative principles relating to how the therapy process develops, not as dogma. Rogers expected his model to evolve and was open and receptive to change.

 See the video program for Chapter 7, *DVD for Theory and Practice of Counseling and Psychotherapy: The Case of Stan and Lecturettes.* I suggest that you view the brief lecture for each chapter prior to reading the chapter.

Four Periods of Development of the Approach

In tracing the major turning points in Rogers's approach, Zimring and Raskin (1992) and Bozarth, Zimring, and Tausch (2002) have identified four periods of development. In the first period, during the 1940s, Rogers developed what was known as *nondirective counseling,* which provided a powerful and revolutionary alternative to the directive and interpretive approaches to therapy then being practiced. While he was a professor at Ohio State University, Rogers (1942) published *Counseling and Psychotherapy: Newer Concepts in Practice,* which described the philosophy and practice of nondirective counseling. Rogers's theory emphasized the counselor's creation of a permissive and nondirective climate. His theory took power away from the therapist and honored the inherent power of the client. When he challenged the basic assumption that "the counselor knows best," he realized this radical idea would affect the power dynamics and politics of the counseling profession, and indeed it caused a great furor (Elkins, 2009).

Rogers also challenged the validity of commonly accepted therapeutic procedures such as advice, suggestion, direction, persuasion, teaching, diagnosis, and interpretation. Based on his conviction that diagnostic concepts and procedures were inadequate, prejudicial, and often misused, Rogers omitted them from his approach. Nondirective counselors avoided sharing a great deal about themselves with clients and instead focused mainly on reflecting and clarifying the clients' verbal and nonverbal communications.

In the second period, during the 1950s, Rogers (1951) wrote *Client-Centered Therapy* and renamed his approach *client-centered therapy,* to reflect its emphasis on the *client* rather than on nondirective methods. In addition, he started the Counseling Center at the University of Chicago. This period was characterized by a shift from clarification of feelings to a focus on the phenomenological world of the client. Rogers assumed that the best vantage point for understanding how people behave was from their own internal frame of reference. He focused more explicitly on the actualizing tendency as the basic motivational force that leads to client change.

The third period, which began in the late 1950s and extended into the 1970s, addressed the necessary and sufficient conditions of therapy. Rogers (1957) set forth a hypothesis that resulted in three decades of research. A significant publication was *On Becoming a Person* (Rogers, 1961), which addressed the nature of "becoming the self that one truly is," an idea he borrowed from Kierkegaard. Rogers published this work during the time that he held joint appointments in the departments of psychology and psychiatry at the University of Wisconsin. In this book he described the process of "becoming one's experience," which is characterized by an openness to experience, a trust in one's experience, an internal locus of evaluation, and the willingness to be in process. During the 1950s and 1960s, Rogers and his associates continued to test the underlying hypotheses of the client-centered approach by conducting extensive research on both the process and the outcomes of psychotherapy. He was interested in how people best progress in psychotherapy, and he studied the qualities of the client–therapist relationship as a catalyst leading to personality change. On the basis of this research the approach was further refined and expanded (Rogers, 1961). For example, client-centered philosophy was applied to education and was called *student-centered teaching* (Rogers & Freiberg, 1994). The approach was also applied to encounter groups (Rogers, 1970).

The fourth phase, during the 1980s and the 1990s, was marked by considerable expansion to education, couples and families, industry, groups, conflict resolution, politics, and the search for world peace. Because of Rogers's ever-widening scope of influence, including his interest in how people obtain, possess, share, or surrender power and control over others and themselves, his theory became known as the *person-centered approach*. This shift in terms reflected the broadening application of the approach. Although the person-centered approach has been applied mainly to individual and group counseling, important areas of further application include education, family life, leadership and administration, organizational development, health care, cross-cultural and interracial activity, and international relations. It was during the 1980s that Rogers directed his efforts toward applying the person-centered approach to politics, especially to efforts related to the achievement of world peace.

In a comprehensive review of the research on person-centered therapy over a period of 60 years, Bozarth, Zimring, and Tausch (2002) concluded the following:

- In the earliest years of the approach, the client rather than the therapist determined the direction and goals of therapy and the therapist's role was to help the client clarify feelings. This style of nondirective therapy was associated with increased understanding, greater self-exploration, and improved self-concepts.

- Later a shift from clarification of feelings to a focus on the client's lived experiences took place. Many of Rogers's hypotheses were confirmed, and there was strong evidence for the value of the therapeutic relationship and the client's resources as the crux of successful therapy.

- As person-centered therapy developed further, research centered on the core conditions assumed to be both necessary and sufficient for successful therapy. The attitude of the therapist—an empathic understanding of the client's world and the ability to communicate a nonjudgmental stance to the client—along with the therapist's genuineness were found to be basic to a successful therapy outcome.

- The main source of successful psychotherapy is the client. The therapist's attention to the client's frame of reference fosters the client's utilization of inner and outer resources.

Existentialism and Humanism

In the 1960s and 1970s there was a growing interest among counselors in a "third force" in therapy as an alternative to the psychoanalytic and behavioral approaches. Under this heading fall existential therapy (Chapter 6), person-centered therapy (Chapter 7), Gestalt therapy (Chapter 8), and certain other experiential and relationship-oriented approaches.

Partly because of this historical connection and partly because representatives of existentialist thinking and humanistic thinking have not always clearly sorted out their views, the connections between the terms *existentialism* and *humanism* have tended to be confusing for students and theorists alike. The two viewpoints have much in common, yet there also are significant philosophical differences between them. They share a respect for the client's subjective experience, the uniqueness and individuality of each client, and a trust in the capacity of the client to make positive and constructive conscious choices. They have in common an emphasis on concepts such as freedom, choice, values, personal responsibility, autonomy, purpose, and meaning. Both approaches place little value on the role of techniques in the therapeutic process and emphasize instead the importance of genuine encounter. They differ in that existentialists take the position that we are faced with the anxiety of choosing to create an identity in a world that lacks intrinsic meaning. Existentialists tend to acknowledge the stark realities of human experience, and their writings often focus on death, anxiety, depression, and isolation. The humanists, in contrast, take the somewhat less anxiety-evoking position and more optimistic view that each of us has a natural potential that we can actualize and through which we can find meaning. Many contemporary existential therapists refer to themselves as *existential-humanistic* practitioners, indicating that their roots are in existential philosophy but that they have incorporated many aspects of North American humanistic psychotherapies (Cain, 2002a; Schneider & Krug, 2010).

As will become evident in this chapter, the existential and person-centered approaches have parallel concepts with regard to the client–therapist relationship at the core of therapy. The phenomenological emphasis that is basic to the existentialist approach is also fundamental to person-centered theory. Both approaches focus on the client's perceptions and call for the therapist to be fully present with the client so that it is possible to understand the client's subjective world, and they both emphasize the client's capacity for self-awareness and self-healing. The therapist aims to provide the client with a safe, responsive, and caring relationship to facilitate self-exploration, growth, and healing (Watson, Goldman, & Greenberg, 2011).

Abraham Maslow's Contributions to Humanistic Psychology

Abraham Maslow (1970) was a pioneer in the development of humanistic psychology and was influential in furthering the understanding of self-actualizing individuals. Many of Carl Rogers's ideas, especially on the positive aspects of being human and the fully functioning person, are built on Maslow's basic philosophy. Maslow criticized Freudian psychology for what he saw as its preoccupation with the sick and negative side of human nature. Maslow believed too much research was being conducted on anxiety, hostility, and neuroses and too little into joy, creativity, and self-fulfillment. Self-actualization was the central theme of the work of Abraham Maslow (1968, 1970, 1971). The *positive psychology* movement that recently has come into prominence shares many concepts on the healthy side of human existence with the humanistic approach.

Maslow studied what he called "self-actualizing people" and found that they differed in important ways from so-called normal individuals. The core characteristics of self-actualizing people are self-awareness, freedom, basic honesty and caring, and trust and autonomy. Other characteristics of self-actualizing individuals include a capacity to welcome uncertainty in their lives, acceptance of themselves and others, spontaneity and creativity, a need for privacy and solitude, autonomy, a capacity for deep and intense interpersonal relationships, a genuine caring for others, an inner-directedness (as opposed to the tendency to live by others' expectations), the absence of artificial dichotomies within themselves (such as work/play, love/hate, and weak/strong), and a sense of humor (Maslow, 1970). All of these personal characteristics have been identified by Rogers as being central to the person-centered philosophy.

Maslow postulated a *hierarchy of needs* as a source of motivation, with the most basic needs being physiological needs. If we are hungry and thirsty, our attention is riveted on meeting these basic needs. Next are the safety needs, which include a sense of security and stability. Once our physical and safety needs are fulfilled, we become concerned with meeting our needs for belonging and love, followed by working on our need for esteem, both from self and others. We are able to strive toward self-actualization only after these four basic needs are met. The key factor determining which need is dominant at a given time is the degree to which those below it are satisfied. We cannot strive toward self-actualization, for example, if our self-esteem is low.

THE VISION OF HUMANISTIC PHILOSOPHY The underlying vision of humanistic philosophy is captured by the metaphor of how an acorn, if provided with the appropriate conditions, will "automatically" grow in positive ways, pushed naturally toward its actualization as an oak. In contrast, for many existentialists there is nothing that we "are," no internal "nature" we can count on. We are faced at every moment with a choice about what to make of this condition. Maslow's emphasis on the healthy side of being human and the emphasis on joy, creativity, and self-fulfillment are part of the person-centered philosophy. The humanistic philosophy on which the person-centered approach rests is expressed in attitudes and behaviors that create a growth-producing climate. According to Rogers (1986b), when this philosophy is lived, it helps people develop their capacities and stimulates constructive change in others. Individuals are empowered, and they are able to use this power for personal and social transformation.

View of Human Nature

A common theme originating in Rogers's early writing and continuing to permeate all of his works is a basic sense of trust in the client's ability to move forward in a constructive manner if conditions fostering growth are present. His professional experience taught him that if one is able to get to the core of an individual, one finds a trustworthy, positive center (Rogers, 1987a). In keeping with the philosophy of humanistic psychology, Rogers firmly maintained that people are trustworthy, resourceful, capable of self-understanding and self-direction, able to make constructive changes, and able to live effective and productive lives. When therapists are able to experience and communicate their realness, support, caring, and nonjudgmental understanding, significant changes in the client are most likely to occur.

Rogers maintained that three therapist attributes create a growth-promoting climate in which individuals can move forward and become what they are capable of becoming: (1) *congruence* (genuineness, or realness), (2) *unconditional positive regard* (acceptance and caring), and (3) *accurate empathic understanding* (an ability to deeply grasp the subjective world of another person). According to Rogers, if therapists communicate these attitudes, those being helped will become less defensive and more open to themselves and their world, and they will behave in prosocial and constructive ways.

Brodley (1999) writes about the **actualizing tendency**, a directional process of striving toward realization, fulfillment, autonomy, and self-determination. This natural inclination of humans is based on Maslow's (1970) studies of self-actualizing people. This growth force within us provides an internal source of healing, but it does not imply a movement away from relationships, interdependence, connection, or socialization. This humanistic view of human nature has significant implications for the practice of therapy. Because of the belief that the individual has an inherent capacity to move away from maladjustment and toward psychological health and growth, the therapist places the primary responsibility on the client. The person-centered approach rejects the role of the therapist as the authority who knows best and of the passive client who merely follows the beliefs of the therapist. Therapy is rooted in the client's capacity for awareness and self-directed change in attitudes and behavior.

In the person-centered approach the emphasis is on how clients act in their world with others, how they can move forward in constructive directions, and how they can successfully deal with obstacles (both from within themselves and outside of themselves) that are blocking their growth. By promoting self-awareness and self-reflection, clients learn to exercise choice. Humanistic therapists emphasize a discovery-oriented approach in which clients are the experts on their own inner experience (Watson, Goldman, & Greenberg, 2011), and they encourage clients to make changes that will lead to living fully and authentically, with the realization that this kind of existence demands a continuing struggle. Maslow taught us that becoming self-actualizing individuals is an ongoing process rather than a final destination.

THE THERAPEUTIC PROCESS

Therapeutic Goals

The person-centered approach aims toward the client achieving a greater degree of independence and integration. Its focus is on the person, not on the person's presenting problem. Rogers did not believe the goal of therapy was merely to solve problems. Rather, the goal is to assist clients in their growth process so clients can better cope with problems as they identify them.

Rogers (1961) wrote that people who enter psychotherapy often ask: "How can I discover my real self? How can I become what I deeply wish to become? How can I get behind my facades and become myself?" The underlying aim of therapy is to provide a climate conducive to helping the individual strive toward self-actualization. Before clients are able to work toward that goal, they must first get behind the masks they wear, which they develop through the process of socialization. Clients come to recognize that they have lost contact with themselves by using facades. In a climate of safety in the therapeutic session, they also come to realize that there are more authentic ways of being.

When the facades are put aside during the therapeutic process, what kind of person emerges from behind the pretenses? Rogers (1961) described people who are becoming increasingly actualized as having (1) an openness to experience, (2) a trust in themselves, (3) an internal source of evaluation, and (4) a willingness to continue growing. Encouraging these characteristics is the basic goal of person-centered therapy.

These four characteristics provide a general framework for understanding the direction of therapeutic movement. The therapist does not choose specific goals for the client. The cornerstone of person-centered theory is the view that clients in a relationship with a facilitating therapist have the capacity to define and clarify their own goals. Person-centered therapists are in agreement on the matter of not setting goals for *what* clients need to change, yet they differ on the matter of *how* to best help clients achieve their own goals and to find their own answers (Bohart & Watson, 2011).

Therapist's Function and Role

The role of person-centered therapists is rooted in their ways of being and attitudes, not in techniques designed to get the client to "do something." Research on person-centered therapy seems to indicate that the attitude of therapists, rather than their knowledge, theories, or techniques, facilitate personality change in the client (Rogers, 1961). Basically, therapists use themselves as an instrument of change. When they encounter the client on a person-to-person level, their "role" is to be without roles. They do not get lost in a professional role. It is the therapist's attitude and belief in the inner resources of the client that creates the therapeutic climate for growth (Bozarth et al., 2002).

Thorne (2002a) reinforces the importance of therapists encountering clients in a person-to-person way, as opposed to being overly reliant on a professional contract. He cautions about retreating into a stance of pseudo-professionalism characterized by presenting a detailed contract to clients, rigid observation of boundaries, and the commitment to empirically validated methods. He suggests that this overemphasis on professionalism is aimed at protecting therapists from overinvolvement with clients, which often results in underinvolvement with them.

Person-centered theory holds that the therapist's function is to be present and accessible to clients and to focus on their immediate experience. First and foremost, the therapist must be willing to be real in the relationship with clients. By being congruent, accepting, and empathic, the therapist is a catalyst for change. Instead of viewing clients in preconceived diagnostic categories, the therapist meets them on a moment-to-moment experiential basis and enters their world. Through the therapist's attitude of genuine caring, respect, acceptance, support, and understanding, clients are able to loosen their defenses and rigid perceptions and move to a higher level of personal functioning. When these therapist attitudes are present, clients then have the necessary freedom to explore areas of their life that were either denied to awareness or distorted.

Client's Experience in Therapy

Therapeutic change depends on clients' perceptions both of their own experience in therapy and of the counselor's basic attitudes. If the counselor creates a climate conducive to self-exploration, clients have the opportunity to explore the full range of their experience, which includes their feelings, beliefs, behavior, and worldview. What follows is a general sketch of clients' experiences in therapy.

Clients come to the counselor in a state of incongruence; that is, a discrepancy exists between their self-perception and their experience in reality. For example, Leon, a college student, may see himself as a future physician, yet his below-average grades could exclude him from medical school. The discrepancy between how Leon sees himself (self-concept) or how he would *like* to view himself (ideal self-concept) and the reality of his poor academic performance may result in anxiety and personal vulnerability, which can provide the necessary motivation to enter therapy. Leon must perceive that a problem exists or, at least, that he is uncomfortable enough with his present psychological adjustment to want to explore possibilities for change.

One reason clients seek therapy is a feeling of basic helplessness, powerlessness, and an inability to make decisions or effectively direct their own lives. They may hope to find "the way" through the guidance of the therapist. Within the person-centered framework, however, clients soon learn that they can be responsible for themselves in the relationship and that they can learn to be more free by using the relationship to gain greater self-understanding.

As counseling progresses, clients are able to explore a wider range of beliefs and feelings. They can express their fears, anxiety, guilt, shame, hatred, anger, and other emotions that they had deemed too negative to accept and incorporate into their self-structure. With therapy, people distort less and move to a greater acceptance and integration of conflicting and confusing feelings. They increasingly discover aspects within themselves that had been kept hidden. As clients feel understood and accepted, they become less defensive and become more open to their experience. Because they feel safer and are less vulnerable, they become more realistic, perceive others with greater accuracy, and become better able to understand and accept others. Individuals in therapy come to appreciate themselves more as they are, and their behavior shows more flexibility and creativity. They become less concerned about meeting others' expectations, and thus begin to behave in ways that are truer to themselves. These individuals direct their own lives instead of looking outside of themselves for answers. They move in the direction of being more in contact with what they are experiencing at the present moment, less bound by the past, less determined, freer to make decisions, and increasingly trusting in themselves to manage their own lives. In short, their experience in therapy is like throwing off the self-imposed shackles that had kept them in a psychological prison. With increased freedom they tend to become more mature psychologically and move toward increased self-actualization.

Person-centered therapy is grounded on the assumption that it is clients who heal themselves, who create their own self-growth, and who are active self-healers (Bohart & Tallman, 1999, 2010; Bohart & Watson, 2011). The therapy relationship provides a supportive structure within which clients' self-healing capacities are activated. What clients value most is being understood and accepted, which results in creating a safe place to explore feelings, thoughts, behaviors, and experiences; clients also value support for trying out new behaviors (Bohart & Tallman, 2010).

Relationship Between Therapist and Client

Rogers (1957) based his hypothesis of the "necessary and sufficient conditions for therapeutic personality change" on the quality of the relationship: "If I can provide a certain type of relationship, the other person will discover within himself or herself the capacity to use that relationship for growth and change, and personal development will occur" (Rogers, 1961, p. 33). Rogers (1967) hypothesized further that "significant positive personality change does not occur except in a relationship" (p. 73). Rogers's hypothesis was formulated on the basis of many years of his professional experience, and it remains basically unchanged to this day. This hypothesis (cited in Cain 2002a, p. 20) is stated thusly:

1. Two persons are in psychological contact.
2. The first, whom we shall term the client, is in a state of incongruence, being vulnerable or anxious.
3. The second person, whom we term the therapist, is congruent (real or genuine) in the relationship.
4. The therapist experiences unconditional positive regard for the client.

5. The therapist experiences an empathic understanding of the client's internal frame of reference and endeavors to communicate this experience to the client.
6. The communication to the client of the therapist's empathic understanding and unconditional positive regard is to a minimal degree achieved.

Rogers hypothesized that no other conditions were necessary. If the **therapeutic core conditions** exist over some period of time, constructive personality change will occur. The core conditions do not vary according to client type. Further, they are both necessary *and* sufficient for therapeutic change to occur.

From Rogers's perspective the client–therapist relationship is characterized by equality. Therapists do not keep their knowledge a secret or attempt to mystify the therapeutic process. The process of change in the client depends to a large degree on the quality of this equal relationship. As clients experience the therapist listening in an accepting way to them, they gradually learn how to listen acceptingly to themselves. As they find the therapist caring for and valuing them (even the aspects that have been hidden and regarded as negative), clients begin to see worth and value in themselves. As they experience the realness of the therapist, clients drop many of their pretenses and are real with both themselves and the therapist.

This humanistic approach is perhaps best characterized as a *way of being* and as a *shared journey* in which therapist and client reveal their humanness and participate in a growth experience. The therapist can be a relational guide on this journey because he or she is usually more experienced and more psychologically experienced in this role than the client. Thorne (2002b) delivered this message: "Therapists cannot confidently invite their clients to travel further than they have journeyed themselves, but for person-centred therapists the quality, depth and continuity of their own experiencing becomes the very cornerstone of the competence they bring to their professional activity" (p. 144). Therapists are invested in broadening their own life experiences and are willing to do what it takes to deepen their self-knowledge.

Rogers admitted that his theory was striking provocative and radical. His formulation has generated considerable controversy, for he maintained that many conditions other therapists commonly regard as necessary for effective psychotherapy were nonessential. The core therapist conditions of congruence, unconditional positive regard, and accurate empathic understanding subsequently have been embraced by many therapeutic schools as essential in facilitating therapeutic change. These core qualities of therapists, along with the therapist's presence, work holistically to create a safe environment for learning (Cain, 2010). Regardless of theoretical orientation, most therapists strive to listen fully and empathically to clients, especially during the initial stages of therapy. We now turn to a detailed discussion of how these core conditions are an integral part of the therapeutic relationship.

CONGRUENCE, OR GENUINENESS implies that therapists are real; that is, they are genuine, integrated, and authentic during the therapy hour. They are without a false front, their inner experience and outer expression of that experience match, and they can openly express feelings, thoughts, reactions, and attitudes that are present in the relationship with the client. This communication is done with careful reflection and considered judgment on the therapist's part (Kolden, Klein, Wang, & Austin, 2011).

Through authenticity the therapist serves as a model of a human being struggling toward greater realness. Being congruent might necessitate expressing a range of feelings including anger, frustration, liking, concern, and annoyance. This does not mean that therapists should impulsively share all their reactions, for self-disclosure must be appropriate, well timed, and have a constructive therapeutic intent. Counselors can try too hard to be genuine; sharing because one thinks it will be good for the client, without being genuinely moved to express something regarded as personal, can be incongruent. Person-centered therapy stresses that counseling will be inhibited if the counselor feels one way about the client but acts in a different way. For example, if the practitioner dislikes or disapproves of the client but feigns acceptance, therapy will be impaired. Cain (2010) stresses that therapists need to be attuned to the emerging needs of the client and to respond in ways that are in the best interests of the individual. If therapists keep this in mind, they are likely to make sound clinical decisions most of the time.

Rogers's concept of congruence does not imply that only a fully self-actualized therapist can be effective in counseling. Because therapists are human, they cannot be expected to be fully authentic. Congruence exists on a continuum from highly congruent to very incongruent. This is true of all three characteristics.

UNCONDITIONAL POSITIVE REGARD AND ACCEPTANCE The second attitude therapists need to communicate is deep and genuine caring for the client as a person, or a condition of **unconditional positive regard**, which can best be achieved through empathic identification with the client (Farber & Doolin, 2011). The caring is nonpossessive and is not contaminated by evaluation or judgment of the client's feelings, thoughts, and behavior as good or bad. Therapists value and warmly accept clients without placing stipulations on their acceptance. It is not an attitude of "I'll accept you when . . ."; rather, it is one of "I'll accept you as you are." Therapists communicate through their behavior that they value their clients as they are and that clients are free to have feelings and experiences. Acceptance is the recognition of clients' rights to have their own beliefs and feelings; it is not the approval of all behavior. All overt behavior need not be approved of or accepted.

According to Rogers's (1977) research, the greater the degree of caring, prizing, accepting, and valuing of the client in a nonpossessive way, the greater the chance that therapy will be successful. He also makes it clear that it is not possible for therapists to genuinely feel acceptance and unconditional caring at all times. However, if therapists have little respect for their clients, or an active dislike or disgust, it is not likely that the therapeutic work will be fruitful. If therapists' caring stems from their own need to be liked and appreciated, constructive change in the client is inhibited. This notion of positive regard has implications for all therapists, regardless of their theoretical orientation (Farber & Doolin, 2011).

ACCURATE EMPATHIC UNDERSTANDING One of the main tasks of the therapist is to understand clients' experience and feelings sensitively and accurately as they are revealed in the moment-to-moment interaction during the therapy session. The therapist strives to sense clients' subjective experience, particularly in the here and now. The aim is to encourage clients to get closer to themselves, to feel more deeply and intensely, and to recognize and resolve the incongruity that exists within them.

Empathy is a deep and subjective understanding of the client *with* the client. Empathy is not sympathy, or feeling sorry for a client. Therapists are able to share the client's subjective world by drawing from their own experiences that may be similar to the client's feelings. Yet therapists must not lose their own separateness. Rogers asserts that when therapists can grasp the client's private world as the client sees and feels it—without losing the separateness of their own identity—constructive change is likely to occur. Empathy, particularly emotionally focused empathy, helps clients (1) pay attention to and value their experiencing, (2) process their experience both cognitively and bodily, (3) view prior experiences in new ways, and (4) increase their confidence in making choices and in pursuing a course of action (Cain, 2010).

Clark (2010) describes an integral model of empathy in the counseling process that is based on three ways of knowing: (1) *subjective empathy* enables practitioners to experience what it is like to be the client; (2) *interpersonal empathy* pertains to understanding a client's internal frame of reference and conveying a sense of the private meanings to the person; and (3) *objective empathy* relies on knowledge sources outside of a client's frame of reference. By using a multiple-perspective model of empathy, counselors have a broader way to understand clients.

Accurate empathy is the cornerstone of the person-centered approach, and it is a necessary ingredient of any effective therapy (Cain, 2010). **Accurate empathic understanding** implies that the therapist will sense clients' feelings *as if* they were his or her own without becoming lost in those feelings. It is a way for therapists to hear the meanings expressed by their clients that often lie at the edge of their awareness. A primary means of determining whether an individual experiences a therapist's empathy is to secure feedback from the client (Norcross, 2010). According to Watson (2002), full empathy entails understanding the meaning and feeling of a client's experiencing. Therapists need to understand clients on both emotional and cognitive levels. Empathy is an active ingredient of change that facilitates clients' cognitive processes and emotional self-regulation. Watson (2002) states that 60 years of research has consistently demonstrated that empathy is the most powerful determinant of client progress in therapy.

Clients' perceptions of feeling understood by their therapists relate favorably to outcome. Empathic therapists strive to discover the meaning of the client's experience, understand the overall goals of the client, and tailor their responses to the particular client. Effective empathy is grounded in authentic caring for the client (Elliott, Bohart, Watson, & Greenberg, 2011).

APPLICATION: THERAPEUTIC TECHNIQUES AND PROCEDURES

Early Emphasis on Reflection of Feelings

Rogers's original emphasis was on grasping the world of the client and reflecting this understanding. As his view of psychotherapy developed, however, his focus shifted away from a nondirective stance and emphasized the therapist's relationship with the client. Many followers of Rogers simply imitated his reflective style, and client-centered therapy has often been identified primarily with the technique of reflection despite Rogers's contention that the therapist's relational attitudes and fundamental ways of being with the client constitute the heart of the change process. Rogers and other contributors to the development of the person-centered approach have been critical of the stereotypic view that this approach is basically a simple restatement of what the client just said.

Evolution of Person-Centered Methods

Contemporary person-centered therapy is the result of an evolutionary process of more than 70 years, and it continues to remain open to change and refinement. One of Rogers's main contributions to the counseling field is the notion that the quality of the therapeutic relationship, as opposed to administering techniques, is the primary agent of growth in the client. The therapist's ability to establish a strong connection with clients is *the* critical factor determining successful counseling outcomes.

No techniques are basic to the practice of person-centered therapy; "being with" clients and entering imaginatively into their world of perceptions and feelings is sufficient for facilitating a process of change. Person-centered therapists are not prohibited from suggesting techniques, but *how* these suggestions are presented is crucial. Techniques may be suggested when doing so fosters the process of client and therapist being together in an empathic way. Techniques are not attempts at "doing anything" to a client (Bohart & Watson, 2011).

The person-centered philosophy is based on the assumption that clients have the resourcefulness for positive movement without the counselor assuming an active, directive, or problem-solving role. Traditional person-centered therapists would not tend to suggest a technique (Bohart & Watson, 2011). What is essential for clients' progress is the therapist's **presence**, being completely attentive to and immersed in the client as well as in the client's expressed concerns (Cain, 2010). This way of being is far more powerful than any technique a therapist might use to bring about change. Qualities and skills such as listening, accepting, respecting, understanding, and responding must be honest expressions by the therapist. As discussed in Chapter 2, counselors need to evolve as persons, not just acquire a repertoire of therapeutic strategies. Therapists mainly stay within the client's frame of reference and strive to understand and reflect the client's communication and experience.

Rogers expected person-centered therapy to continue to evolve and supported others in breaking new ground. One of the main ways in which person-centered therapy has evolved is the diversity, innovation, and individualization in practice. There is no longer one way of practicing person-centered therapy (Cain, 2010), and there has been increased latitude for therapists to share their reactions, to confront clients in a caring way, and to participate more actively and fully in the therapeutic process (Bozarth et al., 2002). **Immediacy**, or addressing what is going on between the client and therapist, is highly valued in this approach. This development encourages the use of a wider variety of methods and allows for considerable diversity in personal style among person-centered therapists. The shift toward genuineness enables person-centered therapists both to practice in more flexible and integrative ways that suit their personalities and to have greater flexibility in tailoring the counseling relationship to suit different clients (Bohart & Watson, 2011).

Cain (2008, 2010) believes it is essential for therapists to adapt their therapeutic style to accommodate the unique needs of each client. Person-centered therapists have the freedom to use a variety of responses and methods to assist their clients; a guiding question therapists need to ask is, "Does it fit?" Cain contends that, ideally, therapists will continually monitor whether what they are doing fits, especially whether their therapeutic style is compatible with their clients' way of viewing and understanding their problems. For an illustration of how Dr. David Cain works with the case of Ruth in a person-centered style, see *Case Approach to Counseling and Psychotherapy* (Corey, 2013, chap. 5).

Today, those who practice a person-centered approach work in diverse ways that reflect both advances in theory and practice and a plethora of personal styles. This is appropriate and fortunate, for none of us can emulate the style of Carl Rogers and still be true to ourselves. If we strive to model our style after Rogers, and if that style does not fit for us, we are not being ourselves and we are not being fully congruent.

The Role of Assessment

Assessment is frequently viewed as a prerequisite to the treatment process. Many mental health agencies use a variety of assessment procedures, including diagnostic screening, identification of clients' strengths and liabilities, and various tests. Person-centered therapists generally do not find traditional assessment and diagnosis to be useful because these procedures encourage an external and expert perspective on the client (Bohart & Watson, 2011). What matters is not how the counselor assesses the client but the client's self-assessment. From a person-centered perspective, the best source of knowledge about the client is the individual client.

In the early development of nondirective therapy, Rogers (1942) recommended caution in using psychometric measures or in taking a complete case history at the outset of counseling. If a counseling relationship began with a battery of psychological tests and a detailed case history, he believed clients could get the impression that the counselor would be providing the solutions to their problems. Assessment seems to be gaining in importance in short-term treatments in most counseling agencies, and it is imperative that clients be involved in a collaborative process in making decisions that are central to their therapy. Today it may not be a question of whether to incorporate assessment into therapeutic practice but of *how* to involve clients as fully as possible in their assessment and treatment process.

Application of the Philosophy of the Person-Centered Approach

The person-centered approach has been applied to working with individuals, groups, and families. Bozrath, Zimring, and Tausch (2002) cite studies done through the 1990s that revealed the effectiveness of person-centered therapy with a wide range of client problems including anxiety disorders, alcoholism, psychosomatic problems, agoraphobia, interpersonal difficulties, depression, cancer, and personality disorders.

Person-centered therapy has been shown to be as viable as the more goal-oriented therapies. Furthermore, outcome research conducted in the 1990s revealed that effective therapy is based on the client–therapist relationship in combination with the inner and external resources of the client (Duncan, Miller, Wampold, & Hubble, 2010).

The person-centered approach has been applied extensively in training both professionals and paraprofessionals who work with people in a variety of settings. This approach emphasizes staying with clients as opposed to getting ahead of them with interpretations. People without advanced psychological education are able to benefit by translating the therapeutic conditions of genuineness, empathic understanding, and unconditional positive regard into both their personal and professional lives. Learning to listen with acceptance to oneself is a valuable life skill that enables individuals to be their own therapists. The basic concepts are straightforward and easy to comprehend, and they encourage locating power in the person rather than fostering an authoritarian structure in which control and power are denied to the person. These core skills also provide an essential foundation for virtually all of the other therapy systems covered in this book. If counselors are lacking in these relationship and communication skills, they will not be effective in carrying out a treatment program for their clients.

The person-centered approach demands a great deal of the therapist. An effective person-centered therapist must be grounded, centered, genuine, respectful, caring, present, a focused and astute listener, patient, and accepting in a way that involves maturity. Without a person-centered *way of being*, mere application of skills is likely to be hollow. Natalie Rogers (2011) points out that the person-centered approach is a way of being that is easy to understand intellectually but is very difficult to put into practice. She continues to find the core conditions of genuineness, positive regard, and empathy most important in developing trust, safety, and growth in a group.

Application to Crisis Intervention

The person-centered approach is especially applicable in crisis intervention such as an unwanted pregnancy, an illness, a disastrous event, or the loss of a loved one. People in the helping professions (nursing, medicine, education, the ministry) are often first on the scene in a variety of crises, and they can do much if the basic attitudes described in this chapter are present. When people are in crisis, one of the first steps is to give them an opportunity to fully express themselves. Sensitive listening, hearing, and understanding are essential at this point. Being heard and understood helps ground people in crises, helps to calm them in the midst of turmoil, and enables them to think more clearly and make better decisions. Although a person's crisis is not likely to be resolved by one or two contacts with a helper, such contacts can pave the way for being open to receiving help later. If the person in crisis does not feel understood and accepted, he or she may lose hope of "returning to normal" and may not seek help in the future. Genuine support, caring, and nonpossessive warmth can go a long way in building bridges that can motivate people to *do* something to work through and resolve a crisis. Communicating a deep sense of understanding should always precede other more problem-solving interventions.

In crisis situations person-centered therapists may need to provide more structure and direction than would be the case for clients who are not experiencing a crisis. Suggestions, guidance, and even direction may be called for if clients are not able to function effectively. For example, in certain cases it may be necessary to take action to hospitalize a suicidal client to protect this person from self-harm.

Application to Group Counseling

The person-centered approach emphasizes the unique role of the group counselor as a facilitator rather than a leader. The primary function of the facilitator is to create a safe and healing climate—a place where the group members can interact in honest and meaningful ways. In this climate members become more appreciative and trusting of themselves as they are and are able to move toward self-direction and empowerment. Ultimately, group members make their own choices and bring about change for themselves. Yet with the presence of the facilitator and the support of other members, participants realize that they do not have to experience the struggles of change alone and that groups as collective entities have their own source of transformation. The facilitator's way of being can create a productive climate within a group:

> Facilitators cannot make participants trust the group process. Facilitators earn trust by being respectful, caring, and even loving. Being an effective group facilitator has much to do with one's "way of being." No method or technique can evoke trust unless the facilitator herself has a capacity to be fully present, considerate, caring, authentic, and responsive. This includes the ability to challenge people constructively (N. Rogers, 2011, p. 57)

Rogers (1970) clearly believed that groups tend to move forward if the facilitator exhibits a deep sense of trust in the members and refrains from using techniques or exercises to get a group moving. The core conditions of person-centered therapy apply to the process of a group. The role of the facilitator is to empathically understand what an individual is communicating within the group. Instead of leading the members toward specific goals, the group facilitator assists members in developing attitudes and behaviors of genuineness, acceptance, and empathy, which enables the members to interact with each other in therapeutic ways to find their own sense of direction as a group.

From Rogers's perspective, facilitators should avoid making interpretive comments or group process observations because such comments are apt to make the group self-conscious and slow the process down. Group process observations should come from members, a view that is consistent with Rogers's philosophy of placing the responsibility for the direction of the group on the members. According to Raskin, Rogers, and Witty (2008), groups are fully capable of articulating and pursuing their own goals. They assert, "when the therapeutic conditions are present in a group and when the group is trusted to find its own way of being, group members tend to develop processes that are right for them and to resolve conflicts within time constraints in the situation" (p. 143).

Regardless of a group leader's theoretical orientation, the core conditions that have been described here are highly applicable to any leader's style of group facilitation. Only when the leader is able to create a person-centered climate will movement take place within a group. All of the theories discussed in this book depend on the quality of the therapeutic relationship as a foundation. As you will see, the cognitive behavioral approaches to group work place emphasis on creating a working alliance and collaborative relationships. In this way, most effective approaches to group work share key elements of a person-centered philosophy. For a more detailed treatment of person-centered group counseling, see Corey (2012, chap. 10). Also see Natalie Rogers's (2011), *The Creative Connection for Groups: Person-Centered Expressive Arts for Healing and Social Change.*

PERSON-CENTERED EXPRESSIVE ARTS THERAPY*

Natalie Rogers (1993, 2011) expanded on her father, Carl Rogers's (1961), theory of creativity using the expressive arts to enhance personal growth for individuals and groups. Rogers's approach, known as **expressive arts therapy,** extends the person-centered approach to spontaneous creative expression, which symbolizes deep and sometimes inaccessible feelings and emotional states. Counselors trained in person-centered expressive arts offer their clients the opportunity to create movement, visual art, journal writing, sound, and music to express their feelings and gain insight from these activities.

Principles of Expressive Arts Therapy

Expressive arts therapy uses various artistic forms—movement, drawing, painting, sculpting, music, writing, and improvisation—toward the end of growth, healing, and self-discovery. This is a multimodal approach integrating mind, body, emotions, and inner spiritual resources. Methods of expressive arts therapy are based on humanistic principles but giving fuller form to Carl Rogers's notions of creativity. These principles include the following (N. Rogers, 1993):

- All people have an innate ability to be creative.
- The creative process is transformative and healing. The healing aspects involve activities such as meditation, movement, art, music, and journal writing.
- Personal growth and higher states of consciousness are achieved through self-awareness, self-understanding, and insight.
- Self-awareness, understanding, and insight are achieved by delving into our feelings of grief, anger, pain, fear, joy, and ecstasy.
- Our feelings and emotions are an energy source that can be channeled into the expressive arts to be released and transformed.
- The expressive arts lead us into the unconscious, thereby enabling us to express previously unknown facets of ourselves and bring to light new information and awareness.
- One art form stimulates and nurtures the other, bringing us to an inner core or essence that is our life energy.

---

*Much of the material in this section is based on key ideas that are more fully developed in two of Natalie Rogers's books, *The Creative Connection: Expressive Arts as Healing* (Rogers, 1993) and *The Creative Connection for Groups: Person-Centered Expressive Arts for Healing and Social Change* (Rogers, 2011). This section was written in close collaboration with Natalie Rogers.

- A connection exists between our life force—our inner core, or soul—and the essence of all beings.
- As we journey inward to discover our essence or wholeness, we discover our relatedness to the outer world, and the inner and outer become one.

The various art modes interrelate in what Natalie Rogers calls the "creative connection." When we move, it affects how we write or paint. When we write or paint, it affects how we feel and think.

Natalie Rogers's approach is based on a person-centered theory of individual and group process. The same conditions that Carl Rogers and his colleagues found basic to fostering a facilitative client–counselor relationship also help support creativity. Personal growth takes place in a safe, supportive environment created by counselors or facilitators who are genuine, warm, empathic, open, honest, congruent, and caring—qualities that are best learned by first being experienced. Taking time to reflect on and evaluate these experiences allows for personal integration at many levels—intellectual, emotional, physical, and spiritual.

Creativity and Offering Stimulating Experiences

According to Natalie Rogers, this deep faith in the individual's innate drive to become fully oneself is basic to the work in person-centered expressive arts. Individuals have a tremendous capacity for self-healing through creativity if given the proper environment. When one feels appreciated, trusted, and given support to use individuality to develop a plan, create a project, write a paper, or to be authentic, the challenge is exciting, stimulating, and gives a sense of personal expansion. N. Rogers believes the tendency to actualize and become one's full potential, including innate creativity, is undervalued, discounted, and frequently squashed in our society. Traditional educational institutions tend to promote conformity rather than original thinking and the creative process.

Person-centered expressive arts therapy utilizes the arts for spontaneous creative expression that symbolizes deep and sometimes inaccessible feelings and emotional states. The conditions that foster creativity require acceptance of the individual, a nonjudgmental setting, empathy, psychological freedom, and availability of stimulating and challenging experiences. With this type of environment in place, the facilitative internal conditions of the client are encouraged and inspired: a nondefensive openness to experience and an internal locus of evaluation that receives but is not overly concerned with the reactions of others. N. Rogers (1993) believes that we cheat ourselves out of a fulfilling and joyous source of creativity if we cling to the idea that an artist is the only one who can enter the realm of creativity. Art is not only for the few who develop a talent or master a medium. We all can use various art forms to facilitate self-expression and personal growth.

Contributions of Natalie Rogers

As is clear from this brief section, Natalie Rogers has built upon a person-centered philosophy and incorporated expressive and creative arts as a basis for personal growth. Cain (2010) believes "Natalie Rogers's expressive arts therapy represents a major innovation in practice and helped open the way for other person-centered therapists to expand the variety and range of practice" (p. 60). Sommers-Flanagan

(2007) notes that person-centered expressive arts therapy may be a solution for clients who are stuck in linear and rigid ways of being. He concludes: "Using her own love of creativity and art in combination with her father's renowned therapeutic approach, Natalie Rogers developed a form of therapy that extends person-centered counseling into a new and exciting domain" (p. 124). Rogers continues her active professional life, conducting workshops in the United States, Europe, Japan, Hong Kong, Latin America, and Russia. At the end of this chapter are some resources for those interested in training in the person-centered approach to expressive arts therapy.

MOTIVATIONAL INTERVIEWING

Motivational Interviewing (MI) is a humanistic, client-centered, psychosocial, directive counseling approach that was developed by William R. Miller and Stephen Rollnick in the early 1980s. The clinical and research applications of motivational interviewing have received increased attention in recent years, and MI has been shown to be effective as a relatively brief intervention (Levensky, Kersh, Cavasos, & Brooks, 2008). MI has been defined as "a directive, client centered counseling style for eliciting behavior change by helping clients to explore and resolve ambivalence" (Rollnick & Miller, 1995, p. 326). Motivational interviewing is based on humanistic principles, has some basic similarities with person-centered therapy, and expands the traditional person-centered approach.

Motivational interviewing was initially designed as a brief intervention for problem drinking, but more recently this approach has been applied to a wide range of clinical problems including substance abuse, compulsive gambling, eating disorders, anxiety disorders, depression, suicidality, chronic disease management, and health behavior change practices (Arkowitz & Miller, 2008; Arkowitz & Westra, 2009). MI stresses client self-responsibility and promotes an invitational style for working cooperatively with clients to generate alternative solutions to behavioral problems. MI therapists avoid arguing with clients, avoid assuming a confrontational stance, reframe resistance as a healthy response, express empathy, and listen reflectively. MI therapists do not view clients as opponents to be defeated but as allies who play a major role in their present and future success. Both MI and person-centered practitioners believe in the client's abilities, strengths, resources, and competencies. The underlying assumption is that clients want to be healthy and desire positive change.

The MI Spirit

MI is rooted in the philosophy of person-centered therapy, but with a "twist." Unlike the nondirective and unstructured person-centered approach, MI is deliberately directive and is aimed at reducing client ambivalence about change and increasing intrinsic motivation (Arkowitz & Miller, 2008). It is essential that therapists function within the spirit of MI, rather than simply applying the strategies of the approach (Levensky et al., 2008). The attitudes and skills in MI are based on a person-centered philosophy and include using open-ended questions, employing reflective listening, affirming and supporting the client, responding to resistance in a nonconfrontational manner, guiding a discussion of ambivalence, summarizing and linking at the end of sessions, and eliciting and reinforcing *change talk*. MI works by activating clients' own motivation for change and adherence to treatment. Practitioners assist clients in becoming their own advocates for change and the primary agents of change in their lives.

In both person-centered therapy and MI, the counselor provides the conditions for growth and change by communicating attitudes of accurate empathy and unconditional positive regard. In MI, the therapeutic relationship is as important in achieving successful outcomes as the specific theoretical model or school of psychotherapy from which the therapist operates (Miller & Rollnick, 2002). Both MI and person-centered therapy are based on the premise that individuals have within themselves the capacity to generate intrinsic motivation to change. Responsibility for change rests with clients, not with the counselor, and therapist and client share a sense of hope and optimism that change is possible. Once clients believe that they have the capacity to change and heal, new possibilities open up for them.

The Basic Principles of Motivational Interviewing

Miller and Rollnick (2002) formulated five basic principles of MI, which are summarized below:

1. Therapists practicing motivational interviewing strive to experience the world from the client's perspective without judgment or criticism. MI emphasizes reflective listening, which is a way for practitioners to better understand the subjective world of clients. Expressing empathy is foundational in creating a safe climate for clients to explore their ambivalence for change. When clients are slow to change, it may be assumed that they have compelling reasons to remain as they are as well as having reasons to change.

2. MI is designed to evoke and explore both discrepancies and ambivalence. Counselors using MI reflect discrepancies between the behaviors and values of clients to increase the motivation to change. Counselors pay particular attention to clients' arguments for changing compared to their arguments for not changing. Therapists elicit and reinforce *change talk* by employing specific strategies to strengthen discussion about change. MI therapists assume a directive stance by steering the conversation in the direction of considering change without persuading clients to change. Clinicians encourage clients to determine whether change will occur, and if so, what kinds of changes will occur and when.

3. Reluctance to change is viewed as a normal and expected part of the therapeutic process. Although individuals may see advantages to making life changes, they also may have many concerns and fears about changing. People who seek therapy are often ambivalent about change, and their motivation may ebb and flow during the course of therapy. A central goal of MI is to increase internal motivation to change based on the personal goals and values of clients (Arkowitz & Miller, 2008). MI therapists assume a respectful view of resistance and work therapeutically with any reluctance or caution on the part of clients.

4. Practitioners operating from an MI orientation support clients' self-efficacy, mainly by encouraging them to use their own resources to take necessary actions that can lead to success in changing. MI clinicians strive to enhance client agency about change and emphasize the right and inherent ability of clients to formulate their own personal goals and to make their own decisions. MI focuses on present and future conditions and empowers clients to find ways to achieve their goals.

5. When clients show signs of readiness to change through decreased resistance to change and increased talk about change, a critical phase of MI begins. In this stage, clients may express a desire and ability to change, show an interest in questions about change, experiment with making changes between sessions, and envision a future picture of how their life will be different once the desired changes have been made. At this time therapists shift their focus toward strengthening clients' commitments to change and helping them implement a change plan.

The Stages of Change

The stages of change model assumes that people progress through a series of five identifiable stages in the counseling process. In the *precontemplation stage*, there is no intention of changing a behavior pattern in the near future. In the *contemplation stage*, people are aware of a problem and are considering overcoming it, but they have not yet made a commitment to take action to bring about the change. In the *preparation stage*, individuals intend to take action immediately and report some small behavioral changes. In the *action stage*, individuals are taking steps to modify their behavior to solve their problems. During the *maintenance stage*, people work to consolidate their gains and prevent relapse.

People do not pass neatly through these five stages in linear fashion, and a client's readiness can fluctuate throughout the change process. If change is initially unsuccessful, individuals may return to an earlier stage (Prochaska & Norcross, 2010). MI therapists strive to match specific interventions with whatever stage of change clients are experiencing. If there is a mismatch between process and stage, movement through the stage will be impeded and is likely to be manifested in reluctant behavior. When clients demonstrate any form of reluctance or resistance, this could be due to a therapist's misjudgment of a client's readiness to change. Certain behaviors on a therapist's part may lead to a client feeling invalidated or misunderstood, which is likely to result in what appears to be a client's resistive behavior (Levensky et al., 2008).

Working within the framework of the stages of change model has implications for the therapist's role at the different stages. Norcross, Krebs, and Prochaska (2011) describe the relational stances and roles taken by therapists during the course of therapy. With clients in the precontemplation stage, the role assumed is that of a *nurturing parent*. With clients in contemplation, therapists function as a *Socratic teacher* who encourages them to achieve their own insights. For clients who are in the preparation stage, therapists take the stance of an *experienced coach*. With clients who are progressing into action and maintenance, therapists function in the role of a *consultant*. As termination approaches, therapists are consulted less often as a way to foster client autonomy.

Motivational interviewing is but one example of how therapeutic strategies have been developed based on the foundational principles and philosophy of the person-centered approach. Indeed, most of the therapeutic models illustrate how the core therapeutic conditions are necessary aspects leading to client change. Where many therapeutic approaches, including motivational interviewing, diverge from traditional person-centered therapy is the assumption that the therapeutic factors are both *necessary and sufficient* in bringing about change. Many other models employ specific intervention strategies to address specific concerns clients bring to therapy.

PERSON-CENTERED THERAPY FROM A MULTICULTURAL PERSPECTIVE

Strengths From a Diversity Perspective

One of the strengths of the person-centered approach is its impact on the field of human relations with diverse cultural groups. Person-centered philosophy and practice can now be studied in several European countries, South America, and Japan. Here are some examples of ways in which this approach has been incorporated in various countries and cultures:

- In several European countries person-centered concepts have had a significant impact on the practice of counseling as well as on education, cross-cultural communication, and reduction of racial and political tensions. In the 1980s Rogers (1987b) elaborated on a theory of reducing tension among antagonistic groups that he began developing in 1948.
- In the 1970s Rogers and his associates began conducting workshops promoting cross-cultural communication. Well into the 1980s he led large workshops in many parts of the world. International encounter groups have provided participants with multicultural experiences.
- Japan, Australia, South America, Mexico, and the United Kingdom have all been receptive to person-centered concepts and have adapted these practices to fit their cultures.
- Shortly before his death, Rogers conducted intensive workshops with professionals in the former Soviet Union.

Cain (1987c) sums up the reach of the person-centered approach to cultural diversity: "Our international family consists of millions of persons worldwide whose lives have been affected by Carl Rogers's writings and personal efforts as well as his many colleagues who have brought his and their own innovative thinking and programs to many corners of the earth" (p. 149).

There is no doubt that Carl Rogers has had a global impact. His work has reached more than 30 countries, and his writings have been translated into 12 languages. In addition to this global impact, the emphasis on the core conditions makes the person-centered approach useful in understanding diverse worldviews. The underlying philosophy of person-centered therapy is grounded on the importance of hearing the deeper messages of a client. Empathy, being present, and respecting the values of clients are essential attitudes and skills in counseling culturally diverse clients. Cain (2008, 2010) contends that although person-centered therapists are aware of diversity factors, they do not make initial assumptions about individuals. They realize that each client's journey is unique and take steps to tailor their methods to fit each individual.

Several writers consider person-centered therapy as being ideally suited to clients in a diverse world. Cain (2008, 2010) views this approach as being a potent way of working with individuals representing a wide range of cultural backgrounds because the core therapeutic conditions are qualities that are universal. Bohart and Watson (2011) claim that the person-centered philosophy is particularly appropriate for working with diverse client populations because the counselor does not assume the role of expert who is going to impose a "right way of being" on the client. Instead, the therapist is a "fellow explorer" who attempts to understand the client's phenomenological world in an interested, accepting, and open way and checks with the client to confirm that the therapist's perceptions are accurate. Motivational interviewing, which is based on the philosophy of person-centered therapy, is a culturally sensitive approach that can be effective across population domains, including gender, age, ethnicity, and sexual orientation (Levensky et al., 2008).

Shortcomings From a Diversity Perspective

Although the person-centered approach has made significant contributions to counseling people from diverse social, political, and cultural backgrounds, there are some shortcomings to practicing exclusively within this framework. Many clients who come to community mental health clinics or who are involved in outpatient treatment want more structure than this approach provides. Some clients seek professional help to deal with a crisis, to alleviate emotional problems, or to learn coping skills in dealing with everyday problems. Because of certain cultural messages, when these clients do seek professional help, it may be as a last resort. They often expect a directive counselor and can be put off by a professional who does not provide sufficient structure.

A second shortcoming of the person-centered approach is that it is difficult to translate the core therapeutic conditions into actual practice in certain cultures. Communication of these core conditions must be consistent with the client's cultural framework. Consider, for example, the expression of therapist congruence and empathy. Clients accustomed to indirect communication may not be comfortable with direct expressions of empathy or self-disclosure on the therapist's part. For some clients the most appropriate way to express empathy is for the therapist to demonstrate it indirectly through respecting their need for distance or through suggesting task-focused interventions (Bohart & Greenberg, 1997).

A third shortcoming in applying the person-centered approach with clients from diverse cultures pertains to the fact that this approach extols the value of an *internal* locus of evaluation. The humanistic foundation of person-centered therapy emphasizes dimensions such as self-awareness, freedom, autonomy, self-acceptance, inner-directedness, and self-actualization. In collectivist cultures, clients are likely to be highly influenced by societal expectations and not simply motivated by their own personal preferences. The focus on development of individual autonomy and personal growth may be viewed as being selfish in a culture that stresses the common good. Cain (2010) contends that "persons from collectivistic cultures are oriented less toward self-actualization and more toward intimacy, connection, and harmony with others and toward what is best for the community and the common good" (p. 143).

Consider Lupe, a Latina client who values the interests of her family over her self-interests. From a person-centered perspective she could be viewed as being in danger of "losing her own identity" by being primarily concerned with her role in taking care of others in the family. Rather than pushing her to make her personal wants a priority, the counselor will explore Lupe's cultural values and her level of commitment to these values in working with her. It would be inappropriate for the counselor to impose a vision of the kind of woman she should be. (This topic is discussed more extensively in Chapter 12.)

Although there may be particular shortcomings in practicing exclusively within a person-centered perspective, it should not be concluded that this approach is unsuitable for working with clients from diverse cultures. There is great diversity among any group of people, and therefore, there is room for a variety of therapeutic styles. According to Cain (2010), rigid insistence on a nondirective style of counseling for all clients, regardless of their cultural background or personal preference, may be perceived as an imposition that does not fit the client's interpersonal and therapeutic needs. Counseling a culturally different client may require more activity and structuring than is usually the case in a person-centered framework, but the potential positive impact of a counselor who responds empathically to a culturally different client cannot be overestimated.

Person-Centered Therapy Applied to the Case of Stan

Stan's autobiography indicates that he has a sense of what he wants for his life. As a person-centered therapist, I rely on his self-report of the way he views himself rather than on a formal assessment and diagnosis. My concern is with understanding him from his internal frame of reference. Stan has stated goals that are meaningful for him. He is motivated to change and seems to have sufficient anxiety to work toward these desired changes. I have faith in Stan's ability to find his own way, and I trust that he has the necessary resources for reaching his therapy goals. I encourage Stan to speak freely about the discrepancy between the person he sees himself as being and the person he would like to become; about his feelings of being a failure, being inadequate; about his fears and uncertainties; and about his hopelessness at times. I attempt to create an atmosphere of freedom and security that will encourage Stan to explore the threatening aspects of his self-concept.

Stan has a low evaluation of his self-worth. Although he finds it difficult to believe that others really like him, he wants to feel loved. He says, "I hope I can learn to love at least a few people, most of all, women." He wants to feel equal to others and not have to apologize for his existence, yet most of the time he feels inferior. By creating a supportive, trusting, and encouraging atmosphere, I can help Stan learn to be more accepting of himself, with both his strengths and limitations. He has the opportunity to openly express his fears of women, of not being able to work with people, and of feeling inadequate and stupid. He can explore how he feels judged by his parents and by authorities. He has an opportunity to express his guilt—that is, his feelings that he has not lived up to his parents' expectations and that he has let them and himself down. He can also relate his feelings of hurt over not having ever felt loved and wanted. He can express the loneliness and isolation that he so often feels, as well as the need to numb these feelings with alcohol or drugs.

Stan is no longer totally alone, for he is taking the risk of letting me into his private world of feelings. Stan gradually gets a sharper focus on his experiencing and is able to clarify his own feelings and attitudes. He sees that he has the capacity to make his own decisions. In short, our therapeutic relationship frees him from his self-defeating ways. Because of the caring and faith he experiences from me in our relationship, Stan is able to increase his own faith and confidence in himself.

My empathy assists Stan in hearing himself and accessing himself at a deeper level. Stan gradually becomes more sensitive to his own internal messages and less dependent on confirmation from others around him. As a result of the therapeutic venture, Stan discovers that there is someone in his life whom he can depend on—himself.

Follow-Up: You Continue as Stan's Person-Centered Therapist

Use these questions to help you think about how you would counsel Stan using a person-centered approach:

- How would you respond to Stan's deep feelings of self-doubt? Could you enter his frame of reference and respond in an empathic manner that lets Stan know you hear his pain and struggle without needing to give advice or suggestions?
- How would you describe Stan's deeper struggles? What sense do you have of his world?
- To what extent do you think that the relationship you would develop with Stan would help him move forward in a positive direction? What, if anything, might get in your way—either with him or in yourself—in establishing a therapeutic relationship?

See DVD for Theory and Practice of Counseling and Psychotherapy: The Case of Stan and Lecturettes (Session 5 on person-centered therapy) for a demonstration of my approach to counseling Stan from this perspective. This session focuses on exploring the immediacy of our relationship and assisting Stan in finding his own way.

SUMMARY AND EVALUATION
Summary
Person-centered therapy is based on a philosophy of human nature that postulates an innate striving for self-actualization. Further, Rogers's view of human nature is phenomenological; that is, we structure ourselves according to our perceptions of reality. We are motivated to actualize ourselves in the reality that we perceive.

Rogers's theory rests on the assumption that clients can understand the factors in their lives that are causing them to be unhappy. They also have the capacity for self-direction and constructive personal change. Change will occur if a congruent therapist makes psychological contact with a client in a state of anxiety or incongruence. It is essential for the therapist to establish a relationship the client perceives as genuine, accepting, and understanding. Therapeutic counseling is based on an I/Thou, or person-to-person, relationship in the safety and acceptance of which clients drop their defenses and come to accept and integrate aspects that they have denied or distorted. The person-centered approach emphasizes this personal relationship between client and therapist; the therapist's attitudes are more critical than are knowledge, theory, or techniques employed. In the context of this relationship, clients unleash their growth potential and become more of the person they are capable of becoming.

This approach places primary responsibility for the direction of therapy on the client. In the therapeutic context, individuals have the opportunity to decide for themselves and come to terms with their own personal power. The underlying assumption is that no one knows the client better than the client; in short, the client is viewed as an expert on his or her own life (Cain, 2010). The general goals of therapy are becoming more open to experience, achieving self-trust, developing an internal source of evaluation, and being willing to continue growing. Specific goals are not suggested for clients; rather, clients choose their own values and goals. Current applications of the theory emphasize more active participation by the therapist than was the case earlier. Counselors are now encouraged to be fully involved as persons in the therapeutic relationship. More latitude is allowed for therapists to express their reactions and feelings as they are appropriate to what is occurring in therapy. Person-centered practitioners are willing to be transparent about persistent feelings that exist in their relationships with clients (Watson et al., 2011). It is the therapist's job to adapt and accommodate in a manner that works best for each client, which means being flexible in the application of methods in the counseling process (Cain, 2010).

Contributions of the Person-Centered Approach

When Rogers founded nondirective counseling more than 70 years ago, there were very few other therapeutic models. The longevity of this approach is certainly a factor to consider in assessing its influence. Cain (2008) states: "An extensive body of research has been generated and provides support for the effectiveness of person-centered therapy with a wide range of clients and problems of all age groups" (p. 214).

Rogers had, and his theory continues to have, a major impact on the field of counseling and psychotherapy. When he introduced his revolutionary ideas in the 1940s, he provided a powerful and radical alternative to psychoanalysis and to the directive approaches then practiced. Rogers was a pioneer in shifting the therapeutic focus from an emphasis on technique and reliance on therapist authority to that of the power of the therapeutic relationship.

Kirschenbaum (2009) contends that the scope and influence of Rogers's work has continued well beyond his death; the person-centered approach is alive, well, and expanding. Today there is not one version of person-centered therapy, but a number of continuously evolving person-centered psychotherapies (Cain, 2010). Although few psychotherapists claim to have an exclusive person-centered theoretical orientation, the philosophy and principles of this approach permeate the practice of most therapists. Other schools of therapy are increasingly recognizing the centrality of the therapeutic relationship as a route to therapeutic change (Kirschenbaum, 2009).

Person-centered therapy is strongly represented in Europe, and there is continuing interest in this approach in both South America and the Far East. The person-centered approach has established a firm foothold in British universities. According to Natalie Rogers (2011), some of the most in-depth training of person-centered counselors is in the United Kingdom. In addition, British scholars including Fairhurst (1999), Keys (2003), Lago and Smith (2003), Mearns and Cooper (2005), Mearns and Thorne (2000, 2007), Merry (1999), Natiello (2001), Thorne (2002a, 2002b), and Watson (2003) continue to expand and refine this approach.

As we have seen, Natalie Rogers has made a significant contribution to the application of the person-centered approach by incorporating the expressive arts as a medium to facilitate healing and social change, primarily in a group setting. She has been instrumental in the evolution of the person-centered approach by using nonverbal methods to enable individuals to heal and to develop. Many individuals who have difficulty expressing themselves verbally can find new possibilities for self-expression through nonverbal channels and through the expressive arts (N. Rogers, 2011).

EMPHASIS ON RESEARCH One of Rogers's contributions to the field of psychotherapy was his willingness to state his concepts as testable hypotheses and to submit them to research. He literally opened the field to research. He was truly a pioneer in his insistence on subjecting the transcripts of therapy sessions to critical examination and applying research technology to counselor–client dialogues (Combs, 1988). Rogers's basic hypothesis gave rise to a great deal of research and debate in the field of psychotherapy, perhaps more than any other school of therapy (Cain, 2002a). According to Cain (2010), an enormous body of research, conducted over a period of 70 years, supports the effectiveness of the person-centered approach. This research is ongoing in many parts of the world and continues to expand and refine our understanding of what constitutes effective psychotherapy. Cain (2010) concludes, "person centered therapy is as vital and effective as it has ever been and continues to develop in ways that will make it increasingly so in the years to come" (p. 169).

Even his critics give Rogers credit for having conducted and inspired others to conduct extensive studies of counseling process and outcome. Rogers presented a challenge to psychology to design new models of scientific investigation capable of dealing with the inner, subjective experiences of the person. His theories of therapy and personality change have had a tremendous heuristic effect, and though much controversy surrounds this approach, his work has challenged practitioners and theoreticians to examine their own therapeutic styles and beliefs.

THE IMPORTANCE OF EMPATHY Among the major contributions of person-centered therapy are the implications of empathy for the practice of counseling. More than any other approach, person-centered therapy has demonstrated that therapist empathy plays a vital role in facilitating constructive change in the client. Watson's (2002) comprehensive review of the research literature on therapeutic empathy has consistently demonstrated that therapist empathy is the most potent predictor of client progress in therapy. Indeed, empathy is an essential component of successful therapy in every therapeutic modality.

Person-centered research has been conducted predominantly on the hypothesized necessary and sufficient conditions of therapeutic personality change (Cain,

1986, 1987b). Most of the other counseling approaches covered in this book have incorporated the importance of the therapist's attitude and behavior in creating a therapeutic relationship that is conducive to the use of their techniques. For instance, the cognitive behavioral approaches have developed a wide range of strategies designed to help clients deal with specific problems, and they recognize that a trusting and accepting client–therapist relationship is necessary for successful application of these procedures. In contrast to the person-centered approach, however, cognitive behavioral practitioners contend that the working relationship is not sufficient to produce change. They contend that active procedures, in combination with a collaborative relationship, are needed to bring about change.

INNOVATIONS IN PERSON-CENTERED THERAPY One of the strengths of the person-centered approach is "the development of innovative and sophisticated methods to work with an increasingly difficult, diverse, and complex range of individuals, couples, families, and groups" (Cain, 2002b, p. xxii). A number of people have made significant advancements that are compatible with the essential values and concepts of person-centered therapy. Table 7.1 describes some of the innovators who have played a role in the evolution of person-centered therapy.

Rogers consistently opposed the institutionalization of a client-centered "school." Likewise, he reacted negatively to the idea of founding institutes, granting certificates, and setting standards for membership. He feared this institutionalization would lead to an increasingly narrow, rigid, and dogmatic perspective. If Rogers (1987a) were to give students-in-training advice it would be: "There is one *best* school of therapy. It is the school of therapy you develop for yourself based on a continuing critical examination of the effects of your way of being in the relationship" (p. 185).

EMOTION-FOCUSED THERAPY One of the developments associated with the person-centered approach is the emergence of emotion-focused therapy (EFT). Leslie Greenberg (2011) is a prominent figure in the development of this integrative approach. Emotion-focused therapy is rooted in a person-centered philosophy, but it is integrative in that it synthesizes aspects of Gestalt therapy and existential therapy. EFT is a therapeutic practice informed by an understanding of the role of emotion in psychotherapeutic change. A number of strategies in EFT are aimed at the goal of strengthening the self, regulating affect, and creating new meaning. Many traditional therapies emphasize conscious understanding and cognitive and behavioral change, yet they often neglect the foundational role of emotional change. EFT emphasizes the importance of awareness, acceptance, and understanding of emotion and the visceral experience of emotion. In EFT, clients are assisted to identify, experience, accept, explore, transform, and manage their emotions. A premise of EFT is that we can change only when we accept ourselves as we are. This approach has a good deal to offer with respect to teaching us about the role of emotion in personal change and how emotional change can be a primary pathway to cognitive and behavioral change.

Other therapeutic approaches are increasingly focusing on emotions. For example, both psychoanalytic and cognitive behavioral approaches are giving more attention to the role of emotions and are rapidly assimilating many aspects of EFT.

TABLE 7.1 Therapists Who Contributed to the Evolution of Person-Centered Theory

INNOVATOR	CONTRIBUTION
Natalie Rogers (1993, 1995, 2011)	Expanded the theory by developing person-centered expressive arts therapy in groups.
Virginia Axline (1964, 1969)	Made significant contributions to client-centered therapy with children and play therapy.
Eugene Gendlin (1996)	Developed experiential techniques, such as focusing, as a way to enhance client experiencing.
Laura Rice (Rice & Greenberg, 1984)	Taught therapists to be more evocative in re-creating crucial experiences that continue to trouble the client.
Peggy Natiello (2001)	Works on collaborative power and gender issues.
Art Combs (1988, 1989, 1999)	Developed perceptual psychology.
Leslie Greenberg (2011); Greenberg and colleagues (Greenberg, Korman, & Paivio, 2002; Greenberg, Rice, & Elliott, 1993)	Contributed to the development of emotion-focused therapy. Focused on the importance of facilitating emotional change in therapy and advanced person-centered theory and methods. Demonstrated that the emotional route can be a key to changing cognitions and behavior.
David Rennie (1998)	Provided a glimpse at the inner workings of the therapeutic process.
Art Bohart (Bohart & Greenberg, 1997; Bohart & Tallman, 1999; 2010; Bohart & Watson, 2011)	Contributed to a deeper understanding of empathy in therapeutic practice and the active role of the client.
Jeanne Watson (2002)	Demonstrated that when empathy is operating on the cognitive, affective, and interpersonal levels it is one of the therapist's most powerful tools.
Dave Mearns and Brian Thorne (2000, 2007)	Contributed to understanding new frontiers in the theory and practice of the person-centered approach and have been significant figures in teaching and supervising in the United Kingdom.
C. H. Patterson (1995)	Showed that client-centered therapy is a universal system of psychotherapy.
Barry Duncan, Scott Miller, Bruce Wampold, & Mark Hubble (2010)	Demonstrated that the client-centered relationship and the core conditions are essential to all therapeutic approaches.

A strength of EFT is that it is an evidence-based approach, an idea that is increasingly being emphasized in graduate programs (Greenberg, 2011).

Limitations and Criticisms of the Person-Centered Approach

Although I applaud person-centered therapists for their willingness to subject their hypotheses and procedures to empirical scrutiny, some researchers have been critical of the methodological errors contained in some of these studies. Accusations of scientific shortcomings involve using control subjects who are not candidates for therapy, failing to use an untreated control group, failing to account for placebo effects, relying on self-reports as a major way to assess the outcomes of therapy, and using inappropriate statistical procedures.

There is a similar limitation shared by both the person-centered and existential (experiential) approaches. Neither of these therapeutic modalities emphasizes the role of techniques aimed at bringing about change in clients' behavior. Proponents of psychotherapy manuals, or manualized treatment methods for specific disorders, find serious limitations in the experiential approaches due to their lack of attention to proven techniques and strategies. Those who call for accountability as defined by evidence-based practices within the field of mental health also are quite critical of the experiential approaches.

I do not believe manualized treatment methods can be considered the gold standard in psychotherapy, however. There is good research demonstrating that techniques account for only 15% of client outcome (see Duncan et al., 2010), whereas contextual factors have powerful effects on what happens in therapy (Elkins, 2009). Research points to relational and client factors as the main predictors of effective therapy. Furthermore, the evaluation of evidence-based practices should be broadened to include best available research, the expertise of the clinician, and client characteristics, culture, and preferences (see Norcross, Hogan, & Koocher, 2008).

A potential limitation of the person-centered approach is that some students-in-training and practitioners with this orientation may have a tendency to be very supportive of clients without being challenging. Out of their misunderstanding of the basic concepts of the approach, some have limited the range of their responses and counseling styles mainly to reflections and empathic listening. Although there is value in really hearing a client and in reflecting and communicating understanding, counseling entails more than this. I believe that the therapeutic core conditions are *necessary* for therapy to succeed, yet I do not see them as being *sufficient* conditions for change for all clients at all times. From my perspective, these basic attitudes are the foundation on which counselors must then build the *skills* of therapeutic intervention. Motivational interviewing rests on the therapeutic core conditions, for example, but MI employs a range of strategies that enable clients to develop action plans leading to change.

A related challenge for counselors using this approach is to truly support clients in finding their own way. Counselors sometimes experience difficulty in allowing clients to decide their own specific goals in therapy. It is easy to give lip service to the concept of clients' finding their own way, but it takes considerable respect for clients and faith on the therapist's part to encourage clients to listen to themselves and follow their own directions, particularly when they make choices that are not what the therapist hoped for.

More than any other quality, the therapist's genuineness determines the power of the therapeutic relationship. If therapists submerge their unique identity and style in a passive and nondirective manner, they are not likely to affect clients in powerful ways. Therapist authenticity and congruence are so vital to this approach that those who practice within this framework must feel natural in doing so and must find a way to express their own reactions to clients. If not, a real possibility is that person-centered therapy will be reduced to a bland, safe, and ineffectual approach.

WHERE TO GO FROM HERE

In the *DVD for Integrative Counseling: The Case of Ruth and Lecturettes,* you will see a concrete illustration of how I view the therapeutic relationship as the foundation for our work together. Refer especially to Session 1 ("Beginning of Counseling"), Session 2 ("The Therapeutic Relationship"), and Session 3 ("Establishing Therapeutic Goals") for a demonstration of how I apply principles from the person-centered approach to my work with Ruth.

Free Podcasts for ACA Members

You can download ACA Podcasts (prerecorded interviews) by going to www.counseling.org; click on the Resource button and then select the Podcast Series. For Chapter 7, Carl Rogers and the Person-Centered Approach, look for Podcast 7 by by Dr. Howard Kirschenbaum.

Other Resources

The American Psychological Association offers the following DVDs in their Psychotherapy Video Series:

> Greenberg, L. S. (2010). *Emotion-Focused Therapy Over Time*
> Cain, D. J. (2010). *Person-Centered Therapy Over Time*

Psychotherapy.net is a comprehensive resource for students and professionals that offers videos and interviews featuring Natalie Rogers, Rollo May, and more. New articles, interviews, blogs, therapy cartoons, and videos are published monthly. DVDs relevant to this chapter are available at www.psychotherapy.net and include the following:

> Rogers, N. (1997). *Person-Centered Expressive Arts Therapy*
> May, R. (2007). *Rollo May on Existential Psychotherapy*

Association for the Development of the Person-Centered Approach, Inc. (ADPCA)

P. O. Box 3876
Chicago, IL 60690-3876
E-mail: enquiries@adpca.org
Website: www.adpca.org
Journal Editor: jonmrose@aol.com

The Association for the Development of the Person-Centered Approach (ADPCA) is an interdisciplinary and international organization that consists of a network of individuals who support the development and application of the person-centered approach. Membership includes a subscription to the *Person-Centered Journal,* the association's newsletter, a membership directory, and information about the annual meeting. ADPCA also provides information about continuing education and supervision and training in the person-centered approach. For information about the *Person-Centered Journal,* contact the editor (Jon Rose).

Association for Humanistic Psychology

1516 Oak Street #320A
Alameda, CA 94501-2947
Telephone: (510) 769-6495
Fax: (510) 769-6433
E-mail: AHPOffice@aol.com
Website: www.ahpweb.org
Journal website: http://jhp.sagepub.com

The Association for Humanistic Psychology (AHP) is devoted to promoting personal integrity, creative learning, and active responsibility in embracing the challenges of being human in these times. Information about the *Journal of Humanistic Psychology* is available from the Association for Humanistic Psychology or at publisher's website.

Society for Humanistic Psychology

Website: http://www.societyforhumanisticpsychology.com/

Division 32 of APA, Society for Humanistic Psychology, represents a constellation of "humanistic psychologies" that includes the earlier Rogerian, transpersonal, and existential orientations as well as the more recently developing perspectives. Division 32 seeks to contribute to psychotherapy, education, theory, research, epistemological diversity, cultural diversity, organization, management, social responsibility, and change. The division has been at the forefront in the development of qualitative research methodologies. The Society for Humanistic Psychology offers journal access to *The Humanistic Psychologist.* Information about membership, conferences, and journals is available from the website of Division 32.

Carl Rogers: A Daughter's Tribute

Website: www.nrogers.com

The Carl Rogers CD-ROM is a visually beautiful and lasting archive of the life and works of the founder of humanistic psychology. It includes excerpts from his 16 books, over 120 photographs spanning his lifetime, and award-winning video footage of two encounter groups and Carl's early counseling sessions. It is an essential resource for students, teachers, libraries, and universities. It is a profound tribute to one of the most important thinkers, influential psychologists, and peace activists of the 20th century. Developed for Natalie Rogers, PhD, by Mindgarden Media, Inc.

Center for Studies of the Person

1150 Silverado, Suite #112
La Jolla, CA 92037
Telephone: (858) 459-3861
E-mail: centerfortheperson@yahoo.com
Website: www.centerfortheperson.org

The Center for Studies of the Person (CSP) offers workshops, training seminars, experiential small groups, residential workshops, and sharing of learning in community meetings. The Distance Learning Project and the Carl Rogers Institute for Psychotherapy Training and Supervision provide experiential and didactic training and supervision for professionals interested in developing their own person-centered orientation.

Saybrook Graduate School
E-mail: admissions@saybrook.edu
Website: www.nrogers.com

For training in expressive art therapy, you could join Natalie Rogers, PhD, and Shellee Davis, MA, faculty of the certificate program at Saybrook Graduate School in their course, "Expressive Arts for Healing and Social Change: A Person-Centered Approach." A 16-unit certificate program includes 6 separate weeks spread over 2 years at a retreat center north of San Francisco. Rogers and Davis offer expressive arts within a person-centered counseling framework. They use counseling demonstrations, practice counseling sessions, readings, discussions, papers, and a creative project to teach experiential and theoretical methods.

Gestalt Therapy

FREDERICK S. ("FRITZ") PERLS, MD, PhD
(1893–1970), was the main originator and developer of Gestalt therapy. Born in Berlin, Germany, into a lower-middle-class Jewish family, he later identified himself as a source of much trouble for his parents. Although he failed the seventh grade twice and was expelled from school because of difficulties with the authorities, his brilliance was never quashed, and he returned—not only to complete high school but to earn his medical degree (MD) with a specialization in psychiatry. In 1916 he joined the German Army and served as a medic in World War I. His experiences with soldiers who were gassed on the front lines led to his interest in mental functioning, which led him to Gestalt psychology.

After the war Perls worked with Kurt Goldstein at the Goldstein Institute for Brain-Damaged Soldiers in Frankfurt. It was through this association that he came to see the importance of viewing humans as a whole rather than as a sum of discretely functioning parts. It was also through this association that he met his wife, Laura, who was earning her PhD with Goldstein. Later he moved to Vienna and began his psychoanalytic training. Perls was in analysis with Wilhelm Reich, a psychoanalyst who pioneered methods of self-understanding and personality change by working with the body.

Perls and several of his colleagues established the New York Institute for Gestalt Therapy in 1952. Eventually Fritz left New York and settled in Big Sur, California, where he conducted workshops and seminars at the Esalen Institute, carving out his reputation as an innovator in psychotherapy. Here he had a great impact on people, partly through his professional writings, but mainly through personal contact in his workshops.

Personally, Perls was both vital and perplexing. People typically either responded to him in awe or found him harshly confrontational and saw him as meeting his own needs through showmanship. Having a predilection for the theater since childhood, he loved being on stage and putting on a show. He was viewed variously as insightful, witty, bright, provocative, manipulative, hostile, demanding, and inspirational. Unfortunately, some of the people who attended his workshops went on to mimic the less attractive side of Perls's personality. Even though Perls was not happy with this, he did little to discourage it.

For a firsthand account of the life of Fritz Perls, I recommend his autobiography, *In and Out of the Garbage Pail* (1969b). For a well-researched chapter on the history of Gestalt therapy, see Bowman (2005).

LAURA POSNER PERLS, PhD (1905–1990), was born in Pforzheim, Germany, the daughter of well-to-do parents. She began playing the piano at the age of 5 and played with professional skill by the time she was 18. From the age of 8 she was involved in modern dance, and both music and modern dance remained vital parts of her adult life and were incorporated into her therapy with some clients. By the time Laura began her practice as a psychoanalyst she had prepared for a career as a concert pianist, had attended law school, achieved a doctoral degree in Gestalt psychology, and made an intensive study of existential philosophy with Paul Tillich and Martin Buber. Clearly, Laura

already had a rich background when she met Fritz in 1926 and they began their collaboration, which resulted in the theoretical foundations of Gestalt therapy. Laura and Fritz were married in 1930 and had two children while living and practicing in South Africa. Laura continued to be the mainstay for the New York Institute for Gestalt Therapy after Fritz abandoned his family to become internationally famous as the traveling minstrel for Gestalt therapy. Laura also made significant contributions to the development and maintenance of the Gestalt therapy movement in the United States and throughout the world (although in very different ways) from the late 1940s until her death in 1990. Laura's own words make it clear that Fritz was a generator, not a developer or organizer. At the 25th anniversary of the New York Institute for Gestalt Therapy, Laura Perls (1990) stated, "Without the constant support from his friends, and from me, without the constant encouragement and collaboration, Fritz would never have written a line, nor founded anything" (p. 18).

Laura paid a great deal of attention to contact and support, which differed from Fritz's attention to intrapsychic phenomena and his focus on awareness. Her emphasis on contact underscored the role of the interpersonal and of being responsive at a time when the popular notion of Gestalt therapy was that it fostered responsibility only to oneself. She corrected some of the excesses committed in the name of Gestalt therapy and adhered to the basic principles of Gestalt therapy theory as written in *Gestalt Therapy: Excitement and Growth in the Human Personality* (Perls, Hefferline, & Goodman, 1951). She taught that every Gestalt therapist needs to develop his or her own therapeutic style. From her perspective, whatever is integrated in our personality becomes support for what we use technically (Humphrey, 1986).

INTRODUCTION

Gestalt therapy is an existential, phenomenological, and process-based approach created on the premise that individuals must be understood in the context of their ongoing relationship with the environment. Awareness, choice, and responsibility are cornerstones of practice. The initial goal is for clients to expand their *awareness* of what they are experiencing in the present moment. Through this awareness, change automatically occurs. The approach is phenomenological because it focuses on the client's perceptions of reality and existential because it is grounded in the notion that people are always in the process of becoming, remaking, and rediscovering themselves. As an existential approach, Gestalt therapy gives special attention to existence as individuals experience it and affirms the human capacity for growth and healing through interpersonal contact and insight (Yontef, 1995). In a nutshell, this approach focuses on the here and now, the what and how, and the I/Thou of relating (Brown, 2007; Yontef & Jacobs, 2011).

Contemporary Gestalt therapy, sometimes called **relational Gestalt therapy**, stresses dialogue and relationship between client and therapist. Following the lead of Laura Perls and the "Cleveland school," when Erving and Miriam Polster and Joseph Zinker were on the faculty in the 1960s and 1970s, this model includes more support and increased sensitivity and compassion in therapy as compared to the confrontational and dramatic style of Fritz Perls (Yontef, 1999). The majority of today's Gestalt therapists employ a style that is supportive, accepting, empathic, respectful, dialogical, as well as challenging. The emphasis is on the quality of the therapist–client relationship and empathic attunement while tapping the client's wisdom and resources (Cain, 2002).

Although Fritz Perls was influenced by psychoanalytic concepts, he took issue with Freud's theory on a number of grounds. Whereas Freud's view of human beings is basically mechanistic, Perls stressed a holistic approach to personality. Freud focused on repressed intrapsychic conflicts from early childhood, whereas Perls valued examining the present situation. The Gestalt approach focuses much more on process than on content. Therapists devise experiments designed to increase clients' awareness of *what* they are doing and *how* they are doing it. Perls asserted that how individuals behave in the present moment is far more crucial to self-understanding than why they behave as they do. Awareness usually involves insight and sometimes introspection, but Gestalt therapists consider it to be much more than either.

Self-acceptance, knowledge of the environment, responsibility for choices, and the ability to make contact with their **field** (a dynamic system of interrelationships) and the people in it are important awareness processes and goals, all of which are based on a here-and-now experiencing that is always changing. Clients are expected to do their own seeing, feeling, sensing, and interpreting, as opposed to waiting passively for the therapist to provide them with insights and answers.

Gestalt therapy is lively and promotes direct experiencing rather than the abstractness of talking about situations. The approach is experiential in that clients come to grips with what and how they are thinking, feeling, and doing as they interact with the therapist. Gestalt practitioners value being fully present during the therapeutic encounter with the belief that growth occurs out of genuine contact between client and therapist.

The experiential therapies focus on emotion as a route to both cognitive and behavioral change, and these therapies encourage clients to stay with their moment-by-moment experiencing. **Emotion-focused therapy** (EFT), developed by Leslie Greenberg (2011), is related to Gestalt therapy. EFT entails the practice of therapy being informed by understanding the role of emotion in psychotherapeutic change. Emotion-focused therapy blends the relational aspects of the person-centered approach with the active phenomenological awareness experiments of Gestalt therapy. EFT is an integrative model, drawing from the relationship-oriented approaches of existential therapy, person-centered therapy, and Gestalt therapy. EFT methodology is similar to Gestalt therapy but emphasizes empirically supported treatments. In-depth presentations of emotion-focused therapy can be found in *Learning Emotion-Focused Therapy: The Process-Experiential Approach to Change* (Elliott, Watson, Goldman, & Greenberg, 2004) and *Emotion-Focused Therapy* (Greenberg, 2011).

 See the video program for Chapter 8, *DVD for Theory and Practice of Counseling and Psychotherapy: The Case of Stan and Lecturettes.* I suggest that you view the brief lecture for each chapter prior to reading the chapter.

KEY CONCEPTS

View of Human Nature

Fritz Perls (1969a) practiced Gestalt therapy paternalistically. Clients have to grow up, stand on their own two feet, and "deal with their life problems themselves" (p. 225). Perls's style of doing therapy involved two personal agendas: moving the client from environmental support to self-support and reintegrating the disowned parts of one's personality. His conception of human nature and these two agendas set the stage for a variety of techniques and for his confrontational style of conducting therapy. He was a master at intentionally frustrating clients to enhance their awareness.

The Gestalt view of human nature is rooted in existential philosophy, phenomenology, and field theory. Genuine knowledge is the product of what is immediately evident in the experience of the perceiver. Therapy aims at awareness and contact with the environment, which consists of both the external and internal worlds. The quality of contact with aspects of the external world (for example, other people) and the internal world (for example, parts of the self that are disowned) are monitored. The process of "reowning" parts of oneself that have been disowned and the unification process proceed step by step until clients can carry on with their own personal growth. By becoming aware, clients become able to make informed choices and thus to live a more meaningful existence.

A basic assumption of Gestalt therapy is that individuals have the capacity to self-regulate when they are aware of what is happening in and around them. Therapy provides the setting and opportunity for that awareness to be supported and restored. The therapist is attentive to the client's present experience and trusts in the process, thereby assisting the client in moving toward increased awareness, contact, and integration (Brown, 2007).

The Gestalt theory of change posits that the more we work at becoming who or what we are not, the more we remain the same. Fritz's good friend and psychiatrist colleague Arnie Beisser (1970) suggested that authentic change occurs more from being who we are than from trying to be who we are not. Beisser called this simple tenet the **paradoxical theory of change.** It is important for clients to "be" as fully as possible in their current condition, rather than striving to become what they "should be." Gestalt therapists focus on creating the conditions that promote client growth rather than relying on therapist-directed change (Yontef, 2005).

Some Principles of Gestalt Therapy Theory

Several basic principles underlying the theory of Gestalt therapy are briefly described in this section: holism, field theory, the figure-formation process, and organismic self-regulation. Other key concepts of Gestalt therapy are developed in more detail in the sections that follow.

HOLISM Gestalt is a German word meaning a whole or completion, or a form that cannot be separated into parts without losing its essence. All of nature is seen as a unified and coherent whole, and the whole is different from the sum of its parts. Because Gestalt therapists are interested in the whole person, they place no superior value on a particular aspect of the individual. Gestalt practice attends to a client's thoughts, feelings, behaviors, body, memories, and dreams. Emphasis may be on a **figure** (those aspects of the individual's experience that are most salient at any moment) or the **ground** (those aspects of the client's presentation that are often out of his or her awareness). Cues to this background can be found on the surface through physical gestures, tone of voice, demeanor, and other nonverbal content. This is often referred to by Gestalt therapists as "attending to the obvious," while paying attention to how the parts fit together, how the individual makes contact with the environment, and integration.

FIELD THEORY Gestalt therapy is based on **field theory**, which, simply put, asserts that the organism must be seen in its environment, or in its context, as part of the constantly changing field. Gestalt therapy rests on the principle that everything is relational, in flux, interrelated, and in process. Gestalt therapists pay attention to and explore what is occurring at the boundary between the person and the environment.

THE FIGURE-FORMATION PROCESS Derived from the study of visual perception by a group of Gestalt psychologists, the figure-formation process describes how the individual organizes experience from moment to moment. In Gestalt therapy the field differentiates into a foreground (figure) and a background (ground). The **figure-formation process** tracks how some aspect of the environmental field emerges from the background and becomes the focal point of the individual's attention and interest. The dominant needs of an individual at a given moment influence this process (Frew, 1997).

ORGANISMIC SELF-REGULATION The figure-formation process is intertwined with the principle of **organismic self-regulation,** a process by which equilibrium is "disturbed" by the emergence of a need, a sensation, or an interest. Organisms will do their best to regulate themselves, given their own capabilities and the resources of their environment (Latner, 1986). Individuals can take actions and make contacts that will restore equilibrium or contribute to growth and change. What emerges in therapeutic work is associated with what is of interest or what the client needs to pursue a sense of equilibrium or change. Gestalt therapists direct the client's awareness to the figures that emerge from the background during a therapy session and use the figure-formation process as a guide for the focus of therapeutic work.

The Now

One of the main contributions of the Gestalt approach is its emphasis on learning to appreciate and fully experience the present moment. Focusing on the past and the future can be a way to avoid coming to terms with the present. Polster and Polster (1973) developed the thesis that "power is in the present." It is a common tendency for clients to invest their energies in bemoaning their past mistakes and ruminating about how life could and should have been different or engaging in endless resolutions and plans for the future. As clients direct their energy toward what was or what might have been or live in fantasy about the future, the power of the present diminishes.

Phenomenological inquiry involves paying attention to what is occurring now. To help the client make contact with the present moment, Gestalt therapists ask "what" and "how" questions, but rarely ask "why" questions. To promote "now" awareness, the therapist encourages a dialogue in the present tense by asking questions like these: "What is happening now?" "What is going on now?" "What are you experiencing as you sit there and attempt to talk?" "What is your awareness at this moment?" "How are you experiencing your fear?" "How are you attempting to withdraw at this moment?" Phenomenological inquiry also involves suspending any preconceived ideas, assumptions, or interpretations concerning the meaning of a client's experience.

Most people can stay in the present for only a short time and are inclined to find ways of interrupting the flow of the present. Instead of experiencing their feelings in the here and now, clients often *talk about* their feelings, almost as if their feelings were detached from their present experiencing. One of the aims of Gestalt therapy is to help clients become aware of their present experience. For example, if Josephine begins to talk about sadness, pain, or confusion, the Gestalt therapist invites her to experience her sadness, pain, or confusion *now*. As she attends to the present experience, the therapist gauges how much anxiety or discomfort is present and chooses further interventions accordingly. The therapist might choose not to comment as Josephine moves away from the present moment, only to extend another invitation several minutes later. If a feeling emerges, the therapist might suggest an experiment that would help Josephine to increase her awareness of the feeling, such as exploring where and how she experiences it. Likewise, if a thought or idea emerges, introducing an experiment can help her delve into the thought, explore it more fully, and consider its effects and possible ramifications.

Gestalt therapists recognize that the past will make regular appearances in the present moment, usually because of some lack of completion of that past experience. When the past seems to have a significant bearing on clients' present attitudes or behavior, it is dealt with by bringing it into the present as much as possible. When clients speak about their past, the therapist may ask them to reenact it as though they were living it now. The therapist directs clients to "bring the fantasy here" or "tell me the dream as though you were having it now," striving to help them relive what they experienced earlier. For example, rather than talking about a past childhood trauma with her father, a client becomes the hurt child and talks directly to her father in fantasy, or by imagining him being present in the room in an empty chair.

Unfinished Business

When figures emerge from the background but are not completed and resolved, individuals are left with **unfinished business**, which can be manifested in unexpressed feelings such as resentment, rage, hatred, pain, anxiety, grief, guilt, and abandonment. Unacknowledged feelings create unnecessary emotional debris that clutters present-centered awareness. Because the feelings are not fully experienced in awareness, they linger in the background and are carried into present life in ways that interfere with effective contact with oneself and others: "These incomplete directions *do seek* completion and when they get powerful enough, the individual is beset with preoccupation, compulsive behavior, wariness, oppressive energy and much self-defeating behavior" (Polster & Polster, 1973, p. 36). Unfinished business persists until the individual faces and deals with the unexpressed feelings. The effects of unfinished business often show up in some blockage within the body. Gestalt therapists emphasize paying attention to the bodily experience on the assumption that if feelings are unexpressed they tend to result in some physical sensations or problems.

The **impasse**, or stuck point, is the time when external support is not available or the customary way of being does not work. The therapist's task is to accompany clients in experiencing the impasse without rescuing or frustrating them.

The counselor assists clients by providing situations that encourage them to fully experience their condition of being stuck. By completely experiencing the impasse, they are able to get into contact with their frustrations and accept whatever is, rather than wishing they were different. Gestalt therapy is based on the notion that individuals have a striving toward actualization and growth and that if they accept all aspects of themselves without judging these dimensions they can begin to think, feel, and act differently.

Contact and Resistances to Contact

In Gestalt therapy, contact is necessary if change and growth are to occur. **Contact** is made by seeing, hearing, smelling, touching, and moving. Effective contact means interacting with nature and with other people without losing one's sense of individuality. Prerequisites for good contact are clear awareness, full energy, and the ability to express oneself (Zinker, 1978). Miriam Polster (1987) claimed that contact is the lifeblood of growth. It is the continually renewed creative adjustment of individuals to their environment. It entails zest, imagination, and creativity. There are only moments of this type of contact, so it is most accurate to think of levels of contact rather than a final state to achieve. After a contact experience, there is typically a withdrawal to integrate what has been learned. Gestalt therapists talk about the two functions of boundaries: to connect and to separate. Both contact and withdrawal are necessary and important to healthy functioning.

Gestalt therapists also focus on interruptions, disturbances, and resistances to contact, which were developed as coping processes but often end up preventing us from experiencing the present in a full and real way. Resistances are typically adopted out of our awareness, and, when they function in a chronic way, can contribute to dysfunctional behavior. Because resistances are developed as a means of coping with life situations, they possess positive qualities as well as problematic ones, and many contemporary Gestalt therapists refer to them as "contact boundary phenomena." Polster and Polster (1973) describe five different kinds of contact boundary disturbances: introjection, projection, retroflection, deflection, and confluence.

Introjection is the tendency to uncritically accept others' beliefs and standards without assimilating them to make them congruent with who we are. These introjects remain alien to us because we have not analyzed and restructured them. When we introject, we passively incorporate what the environment provides rather than clearly identifying what we want or need. If we remain in this stage, our energy is bound up in taking things as we find them and believing that authorities know what is best for us rather than working for things ourselves.

Projection is the reverse of introjection. In projection we disown certain aspects of ourselves by assigning them to the environment. Those attributes of our personality that are inconsistent with our self-image are disowned and put onto, assigned to, and seen in other people; thus, blaming others for lots of our problems. By seeing in others the very qualities that we refuse to acknowledge in ourselves, we avoid taking responsibility for our own feelings and the person who we are, and this keeps us powerless to initiate change. People who use projection as a pattern tend to feel that they are victims of circumstances, and they believe that people have hidden meanings behind what they say.

Retroflection consists of turning back onto ourselves what we would like to do to someone else or doing to ourselves what we would like someone else to do to or for us. This process is principally an interruption of the action phase in the cycle of experience and typically involves a fair amount of anxiety. People who rely on retroflection tend to inhibit themselves from taking action out of fear of embarrassment, guilt, and resentment. People who self-mutilate or who injure themselves, for example, are often directing aggression inward out of fear of directing it toward others. Depression and psychosomatic complaints are often created by retroflecting. Typically, these maladaptive styles of functioning are adopted outside of our awareness; part of the process of Gestalt therapy is to help us discover a self-regulatory system so that we can deal realistically with the world.

Deflection is the process of distraction or veering off, so that it is difficult to maintain a sustained sense of contact. We attempt to diffuse or defuse contact through the overuse of humor, abstract generalizations, and questions rather than statements (Frew, 1986). When we deflect, we speak through and for others, beating around the bush rather than being direct and engaging the environment in an inconsistent and inconsequential basis, which results in emotional depletion.

Confluence involves blurring the differentiation between the self and the environment. As we strive to blend in and get along with everyone, there is no clear demarcation between internal experience and outer reality. Confluence in relationships involves the absence of conflicts, slowness to anger, and a belief that all parties experience the same feelings and thoughts we do. This style of contact is characteristic of clients who have a high need to be accepted and liked, thus finding enmeshment comfortable. This condition makes genuine contact extremely difficult. A therapist might assist clients who use this channel of resistance by asking questions such as: "What are you doing now?" "What are you experiencing at this moment?" "What do you want right now?"

Terms such as *interruptions in contact* or *boundary disturbance* refer to the characteristic styles people employ in their attempts to control their environment through one of these channels of resistance. The premise in Gestalt therapy is that contact is both normal and healthy, and clients are encouraged to become increasingly aware of their dominant style of blocking contact and their use of resistance. Today's Gestalt therapists readily attend to how clients interrupt contact, approaching the interruptive styles with respect and taking each style seriously, knowing that it has served an important function in the past. It is important to explore what the resistance does for clients: what it protects them from, and what it keeps them from experiencing.

Energy and Blocks to Energy

In Gestalt therapy special attention is given to where energy is located, how it is used, and how it can be blocked. Blocked energy is another form of defensive behavior. It can be manifested by tension in some part of the body, by posture, by keeping one's body tight and closed, by not breathing deeply, by looking away from people when speaking to avoid contact, by choking off sensations, by numbing feelings, and by speaking with a restricted voice, to mention only a few.

Some of the therapeutic endeavor involves finding the focus of interrupted energy and bringing these sensations to the client's awareness. Clients may not be aware of their energy or where it is located, and they may experience it in a negative way. One of the tasks of the therapist is to help clients identify the ways in which they are blocking energy and transform this blocked energy into more adaptive behaviors. Clients can be encouraged to recognize how their resistance is being expressed in their body. Rather than trying to rid themselves of certain bodily symptoms, clients can be encouraged to delve fully into tension states. For example, by allowing themselves to exaggerate their tight mouth and shaking legs, they can discover for themselves how they are diverting energy and keeping themselves from a full expression of aliveness.

THE THERAPEUTIC PROCESS
Therapeutic Goals

Gestalt therapy does not ascribe to a "goal-oriented" methodology per se. However, as Melnick and Nevis (2005) aptly say, "Because of the complexity of therapeutic work, a well-grounded methodology is essential. . . . The six methodological components we consider vital or integral to Gestalt therapy are: (a) the continuum of experience, (b) the here and now, (c) the paradoxical theory of change, (d) the experiment, (e) the authentic encounter, and (f) process-oriented diagnosis" (pp. 102–103). Despite not being focused on predetermined goals for their clients, Gestalt therapists clearly attend to a basic goal—namely, assisting the client to attain greater awareness, and with it, greater choice. Awareness includes knowing the environment, knowing oneself, accepting oneself, and being able to make contact. Increased and enriched awareness, by itself, is seen as curative. Without awareness clients do not possess the tools for personality change. With awareness they have the capacity to face and accept denied parts as well as to fully experience their subjectivity. They can experience their unity and wholeness. When clients stay with their awareness, important unfinished business will emerge and can be dealt with in therapy. The Gestalt approach helps clients note their own awareness process so that they can be responsible and can selectively and discriminatingly make choices. Awareness emerges within the context of a genuine meeting between client and therapist.

The existential view (see Chapter 6) is that we are continually engaged in a process of remaking and discovering ourselves. We do not have a static identity, but discover new facets of our being as we face new challenges. Gestalt therapy is basically an existential encounter out of which clients tend to move in certain directions. Through a creative involvement in Gestalt process, Zinker (1978) expects clients will do the following:

- Move toward increased awareness of themselves
- Gradually assume ownership of their experience (as opposed to making others responsible for what they are thinking, feeling, and doing)
- Develop skills and acquire values that will allow them to satisfy their needs without violating the rights of others

- Become more aware of all of their senses
- Learn to accept responsibility for what they do, including accepting the consequences of their actions
- Be able to ask for and get help from others and be able to give to others

Therapist's Function and Role

According to Perls, Hefferline, and Goodman (1951), the therapist's job is to invite clients into an active partnership where they can learn about themselves by adopting an experimental attitude toward life in which they try out new behaviors and notice what happens. Gestalt therapists use active methods and personal engagement with clients to increase their awareness, freedom, and self-direction rather than directing them toward preset goals (Yontef & Jacob, 2011).

Contemporary Gestalt practitioners view clients as the experts on their own experience and encourage them to attend to their sensory awareness in the present moment. Gestalt therapists value self-discovery and assume that clients can discover for themselves the ways in which they block or interrupt their awareness and experience (Watson, Goldman, & Greenberg, 2011). Yontef (1993) stresses that although the therapist functions as a guide and a catalyst, presents experiments, and shares observations, the basic work of therapy is done by the client. Yontef maintains that the therapist's task is to create a climate in which clients are likely to try out new ways of being and behaving. Gestalt therapists do not force change on clients through confrontation. Instead, they work within a context of I/Thou dialogue in a here-and-now framework.

An important function of Gestalt therapists is paying attention to clients' body language. These nonverbal cues provide rich information as they often represent feelings of which the client is unaware. The therapist needs to be alert for gaps in attention and awareness and for incongruities between verbalizations and what clients are doing with their bodies. Therapists might direct clients to speak for and become their gestures or body parts by asking, "What do your eyes say?" "If your hands could speak at this moment, what would they say?" "Can you carry on a conversation between your right and left hands?" Clients may verbally express anger and at the same time smile. Or they may say they are in pain and at the same time laugh. Therapists can ask clients to become aware of how they are using their laughter to mask feelings of anger or pain.

In addition to calling attention to clients' nonverbal language, the Gestalt counselor places emphasis on the relationship between language patterns and personality. Clients' speech patterns are often an expression of their feelings, thoughts, and attitudes. The Gestalt approach focuses on overt speaking habits as a way to increase clients' awareness of themselves, especially by asking them to notice whether their words are congruent with what they are experiencing or instead are distancing them from their emotions.

Language can both describe and conceal. By focusing on language, clients are able to increase their awareness of what they are experiencing in the present moment and of how they are avoiding coming into contact with this here-and-now experience. Here are some examples of the aspects of language that Gestalt therapists might focus on:

- *"It" talk*. When clients say "it" instead of "I," they are using depersonalizing language. The counselor may ask them to substitute personal pronouns for impersonal ones so that they will assume an increased sense of responsibility. For example, if a client says, "It is difficult to make friends," he could be asked to restate this by making an "I" statement: "I have trouble making friends."

- *"You" talk*. Global and impersonal language tends to keep the person hidden. The therapist often points out generalized uses of "you" and asks the client to substitute "I" when this is what is meant.

- *Questions*. Questions have a tendency to keep the questioner hidden, safe, and unknown. Gestalt counselors often ask clients to change their questions into statements. In making personal statements, clients begin to assume responsibility for what they say. They may become aware of how they are keeping themselves mysterious through a barrage of questions and how this serves to prevent them from making declarations that express themselves.

- *Language that denies power*. Some clients have a tendency to deny their personal power by adding qualifiers or disclaimers to their statements. The therapist may also point out to clients how certain qualifiers subtract from their effectiveness. Experimenting with omitting qualifiers such as "maybe," "perhaps," "sort of," "I guess," "possibly," and "I suppose" can help clients change ambivalent messages into clear and direct statements. Likewise, when clients say "I can't," they are really implying "I won't." Asking clients to substitute "won't" for "can't" often assists them in owning and accepting their power by taking responsibility for their decisions. The counselor must be careful in intervening so that clients do not feel that everything they say is subject to scrutiny. Rather than fostering a morbid kind of introspection, the counselor hopes to foster awareness of what is really being expressed through words.

- *Listening to clients' metaphors*. In his workshops, Erv Polster (1995) emphasizes the importance of a therapist learning how to listen to the metaphors of clients. By tuning into metaphors, the therapist gets rich clues to clients' internal struggles. Examples of metaphors that can be amplified include client statements such as "It's hard for me to spill my guts in here." "At times I feel that I don't have a leg to stand on." "I feel like I have a hole in my soul." "I need to be prepared, in case someone blasts me." "I felt ripped to shreds after you confronted me last week." "After this session, I feel as though I've been put through a meat grinder." Beneath the metaphor may lie a suppressed internal dialogue that represents critical unfinished business or reactions to a present interaction. For example, to the client who says she feels that she has been put through a meat grinder, the therapist could ask: "What is your experience of being ground meat?" or "Who is doing the grinding?" It is essential to encourage this client to say more about what she is experiencing. The art of therapy consists of assisting clients in translating the meaning of their metaphors so that they can be dealt with in therapy.

- *Listening for language that uncovers a story*. Polster (1995) also teaches the value of what he calls "fleshing out a flash." He reports that clients often use language that is elusive yet gives significant clues to a story that illustrates their life struggles. Effective therapists learn to pick out a small part of what someone says and then to focus on and develop this element. Clients are likely to slide over pregnant phrases, but the alert therapist can ask questions that will help them flesh out their story line. It is essential for therapists to pay attention to what is fascinating about the person who is sitting before them and get that person to tell a story.

In a workshop I observed Erv Polster's magnificent style in challenging a person (Joe) who had volunteered for a demonstration of an individual session. Although Joe had a fascinating story to reveal about a particular facet of his life, he was presenting himself in a lifeless manner, and the energy was going flat. Eventually, Polster asked him, "Are you keeping my interest right now? Does it matter to you whether I am engaged with you?" Joe looked shocked, but he soon got the point. He accepted Polster's challenge to make sure that he not only kept the therapist interested but also presented himself in a way to keep those in the audience interested. It was clear that Polster was directing Joe's attention to a process of how he was expressing his feelings and life experiences rather than being concerned with what he was talking about.

Polster believes storytelling is not always a form of resistance. Instead, it can be the heart of the therapeutic process. He maintains that people are storytelling beings. The therapist's task is to assist clients in telling their story in a lively way. Polster (1987b) believes many people come to therapy to change the titles of their stories rather than to transform their life stories.

Client's Experience in Therapy

The general orientation of Gestalt therapy is toward dialogue. Whereas Fritz Perls would have said that clients must be confronted about how they avoid accepting responsibility, the dialogic attitude carried into Gestalt therapy originally by Laura Perls creates the ground for a meeting place between client and therapist. Other issues that can become the focal point of therapy include the client–therapist relationship and the similarities in the ways clients relate to the therapist and to others in their environment.

Gestalt therapists do not make interpretations that explain the dynamics of an individual's behavior or tell a client why he or she is acting in a certain way because they are not the experts on the client's experience. Clients in Gestalt therapy are active participants who make their own interpretations and meanings. It is they who increase awareness and decide what they will or will not do with their personal meaning.

Miriam Polster (1987) described a three-stage integration sequence that characterizes client growth in therapy. The first part of this sequence consists of *discovery*. Clients are likely to reach a new realization about themselves or to acquire a novel view of an old situation, or they may take a new look at some significant person in their lives. Such discoveries often come as a surprise to them.

The second stage of the integration sequence is *accommodation*, which involves clients' recognizing that they have a choice. Clients begin by trying out new behaviors in the supportive environment of the therapy office, and then they expand their awareness of the world. Making new choices is often done awkwardly, but with therapeutic support clients can gain skill in coping with difficult situations. Clients are likely to participate in out-of-office experiments, which can be discussed in the next therapy session.

The third stage of the integration sequence is *assimilation,* which involves clients' learning how to influence their environment. At this phase clients feel capable of dealing with the surprises they encounter in everyday living. They are now beginning to do more than passively accept the environment. Behavior at this stage may include taking a stand on a critical issue. Eventually, clients develop confidence in their ability to improve and improvise. Improvisation is the confidence that comes from knowledge and skills. Clients are able to make choices that will result in getting what they want. The therapist points out that something has been accomplished and acknowledges the changes that have taken place within the client. At this phase, clients have learned what they can do to maximize their chances of getting what is needed from their environment.

Relationship Between Therapist and Client

As an existential brand of therapy, Gestalt practice involves a person-to-person relationship between therapist and client. Therapists are responsible for the quality of their presence, for knowing themselves and the client, and for remaining open to the client. They are also responsible for establishing and maintaining a therapeutic atmosphere that will foster a spirit of work on the client's part. It is important that therapists allow themselves to be affected by their clients and that they actively share their own present perceptions and experiences as they encounter clients in the here and now.

Gestalt therapists not only allow their clients to be who they are but also remain themselves and do not get lost in a role. Therapists are expected to encounter clients with honest and immediate reactions, and therapists share their personal experience and stories in relevant and appropriate ways. Further, they give feedback that allows clients to develop an awareness of what they are actually doing. Brown (2007) suggests that therapists share their reactions with clients, yet she also stresses the importance of demonstrating an attitude of respect, acceptance, present-centeredness, and presence.

A number of writers have given central importance to the I/Thou relationship and the quality of the therapist's presence, as opposed to technical skills. They warn of the dangers of becoming technique-bound and losing sight of their own being as they engage the client. The therapist's attitudes and behavior and the relationship that is established are what really count (Brown, 2007; Frew, 2008; Lee, 2004; Melnick & Nevis, 2005; Parlett, 2005; E. Polster, 1987a, 1987b; M. Polster, 1987; Yontef & Jacobs, 2011). These writers point out that current Gestalt therapy has moved beyond earlier therapeutic practices.

Many contemporary Gestalt therapists place increasing emphasis on factors such as presence, authentic dialogue, gentleness, more direct self-expression by the therapist, decreased use of stereotypic exercises, and greater trust in the client's experiencing. Laura Perls (1976) stressed the notion that the person of the therapist is more important than using techniques. She says, "There are as many styles as there are therapists and clients who discover themselves and each other and together invent their relationship" (p. 223). Jacobs (1989) asserts that a current trend in Gestalt practice is toward greater emphasis on the client–therapist relationship rather than on techniques divorced from the context of this encounter. She believes therapists who operate from this orientation are able to establish a present-centered, nonjudgmental dialogue that allows clients to deepen their awareness and to make contact with another person.

Polster and Polster (1973) emphasized the importance of therapists knowing themselves and being therapeutic instruments. Like artists who need to be in touch with what they are painting, therapists are artistic participants in the creation of new life. The Polsters implore therapists to use their own experiences as essential ingredients in the therapy process. According to them, therapists are more than mere responders or catalysts. If they are to make effective contact with clients, therapists must be in tune with both their clients and themselves. Therapy is a two-way engagement that changes both the client and the therapist. If therapists are not sensitively tuned to their own qualities of tenderness, toughness, and compassion and to their reactions to the client, they become technicians. Experiments should be aimed at awareness, not at simple solutions to a client's problem.

APPLICATION: THERAPEUTIC TECHNIQUES AND PROCEDURES

The Experiment in Gestalt Therapy

Although the Gestalt approach is concerned with the obvious, its simplicity should not be taken to mean that the therapist's job is easy. Developing a variety of interventions is simple, but employing these methods in a mechanical fashion allows clients to continue inauthentic living. If clients are to become authentic, they need contact with an authentic therapist. Yontef and Jacobs (2011) point out that techniques in Gestalt therapy are considered experiments and clients hear the message, "Try this out and see what it is like for you." Gestalt therapy methodology is tailored to the needs of clients, and experiments are typically presented in an invitational manner. Dr. Jon Frew, a Gestalt therapist, demonstrates Gestalt interventions applied to the case of Ruth in *Case Approach to Counseling and Psychotherapy* (Corey, 2013, chap. 6).

Before discussing the variety of Gestalt methods you could include in your repertoire of counseling procedures, it is helpful to differentiate between exercises (or techniques) and experiments. **Exercises** are ready-made techniques that are sometimes used to make something happen in a therapy session or to achieve a goal. They can be catalysts for individual work or for promoting interaction among members of a therapy group. **Experiments**, in contrast, grow out of the interaction between client and therapist, and they emerge within this dialogic process. They can be considered the very cornerstone of experiential learning. Frew (2008) defines the experiment "as a method that shifts the focus of counseling from talking about a topic to an activity that will heighten the client's awareness and understanding through experience" (p. 253). According to Melnick and Nevis (2005), experiments have been confused with techniques: "A technique is a performed experiment with specific learning goals. . . . An experiment, on the other hand, flows directly from psychotherapy theory and is crafted to fit the individual as he or she exists in the here and now" (p. 108). The purpose of an experiment is to assist an individual in active self-exploration. Melnick and Nevis suggest using the Gestalt continuum of experience as a guide for custom designing experiments.

The experiment is fundamental to Gestalt therapy. Zinker (1978) sees therapy sessions as a series of experiments, which are the avenues for clients to learn experientially. What is learned from an experiment is a surprise to both the client and the therapist. Gestalt experiments are a creative adventure and a way in which clients can express themselves behaviorally. Experiments are spontaneous, one-of-a-kind, and relevant to a particular moment and a particular development of a figure-formation process. They are not designed to achieve a particular goal but occur in the context of a moment-to-moment contacting process between therapist and client. Polster (1995) indicates that experiments are designed by the therapist and evolve from the theme already developing through therapeutic engagement, such as the client's report of needs, dreams, fantasies, and body awareness. Gestalt therapists invite clients to engage in experiments that lead to fresh emotional experiencing and new insights (Strumpfel & Goldman, 2002). Experimentation is an attitude inherent in all Gestalt therapy; it is a collaborative process with full participation of the client. Clients test an experiment to determine what does and does not fit for them through their own awareness (Yontef, 1993, 1995).

Miriam Polster (1987) says that an experiment is a way to bring out some kind of internal conflict by making this struggle an actual process. It is aimed at facilitating a client's ability to work through the stuck points of his or her life. Experiments encourage spontaneity and inventiveness by bringing the possibilities for action directly into the therapy session. By dramatizing or playing out problem situations or relationships in the relative safety of the therapy context, clients increase their range of flexibility of behavior. According to M. Polster, Gestalt experiments can take many forms: imagining a threatening future encounter; setting up a dialogue between a client and some significant person in his or her life; dramatizing the memory of a painful event; reliving a particularly profound early experience in the present; assuming the identity of one's mother or father through role playing; focusing on gestures, posture, and other nonverbal signs of inner expression; or carrying on a dialogue between two conflicting aspects within the person. Through these experiments, clients may actually experience the feelings associated with their conflicts. Experiments bring struggles to life by inviting clients to enact them in the present. It is crucial that experiments be tailored to each individual and used in a timely and appropriate manner; they also need to be carried out in a context that offers a balance between support and risk. Sensitivity and careful attention on the therapist's part are essential so that clients are "neither blasted into experiences that are too threatening nor allowed to stay in safe but infertile territory" (Polster & Polster, 1990, p. 104).

Preparing Clients for Gestalt Experiments

If students-in-training limit their understanding of Gestalt therapy to simply reading about the approach, Gestalt methods are likely to seem abstract and the notion of experiments may seem strange. Asking clients to "become" an object in one of their dreams, for instance, may seem silly and pointless. It is important for counselors to *personally* experience the power of Gestalt experiments and to feel comfortable suggesting them to clients. In this regard, it can be most useful for trainees to personally experience Gestalt methods as a client.

It is also essential that counselors establish a relationship with their clients, so that the clients will feel trusting enough to participate in the learning that can result from Gestalt experiments. Clients will get more from Gestalt experiments if they are oriented and prepared for them. Through a trusting relationship with the therapist, clients are likely to recognize their resistance and allow themselves to participate in these experiments.

If clients are to cooperate, counselors must avoid directing them in a commanding fashion to carry out an experiment. Typically, I ask clients if they are willing to try out an experiment to see what they might learn from it. I also tell clients that they can stop when they choose to, so the power is with them. Clients at times say that they feel silly or self-conscious or that the task feels artificial or unreal. At such times I am likely to respond by asking, "Are you willing to give it a try and see what happens?"

I cannot overemphasize the power of the therapeutic relationship and the necessity for trust as the foundation for implementing any experiment. If I meet with hesitation, I tend to be interested in exploring the client's reluctance. It is helpful to know the reason the client is stopping. Hesitation in becoming emotionally involved often is a function of the client's cultural background. Some clients have been conditioned to work hard to maintain emotional control. They may have reservations about expressing intense feelings openly, even if they are in an emotional state. This can well be due to their socialization and to cultural norms they abide by. In some cultures it is considered rude to express emotions openly, and there are certain cultural injunctions against showing one's vulnerability or psychological pain. Gestalt experiments work best when the therapist is respectful of the client's cultural background and is in good contact with the person. Therapists need to understand that for clients with a long history of containing their feelings, they will most likely be reluctant to participate in experiments that are likely to bring their emotions to the surface. Of course, many men have been socialized not to express intense feelings. Their reluctance to allow themselves to be emotional should be dealt with in a respectful manner.

Other clients may resist becoming emotionally involved because of their fear, lack of trust, concern over losing control, or some other concern. The *way* in which clients resist doing an experiment reveals a great deal about their personality and their way of being in the world. Therefore, Gestalt therapists expect and respect the emergence of reluctance on a client's part. The therapist's aim is not to eliminate clients' defenses but to meet clients wherever they are.

The essence of current Gestalt therapy involves honoring and respecting reluctance or resistance and supporting clients to become more aware of their experience. If the therapist meets with hesitation, it is a good idea to explore its meaning for the client. Contemporary Gestalt therapy places much less emphasis on resistance than the early version of Gestalt therapy. Although it is possible to look at "resistance to awareness" and "resistance to contact," the idea of resistance is viewed as unnecessary by some Gestalt therapists. Frew (2008) argues that the notion of resistance is completely foreign to the theory and practice of Gestalt therapy and suggests that resistance is a term frequently used for clients who are not doing what the therapist wants them to do. Polster and Polster (1976) suggest that it is best for therapists to observe what is actually and presently happening rather than trying to make something happen. This gets away from the notion that clients are resisting and thus behaving wrongly. According to the Polsters, change occurs through contact and awareness—one does not have to try to change. Maurer (2005) writes about "appreciating resistance" as a creative adjustment to a situation rather than something to overcome. Maurer claims that we need to respect resistance, take it seriously, and view it as "the energy" and not "the enemy."

It is well to remember that Gestalt experiments are designed to expand clients' awareness and to help them try out new modes of behavior. Within the safety of the therapeutic situation, clients are given opportunities and encouraged to "try on" a new behavior. This heightens the awareness of a particular aspect of functioning, which leads to increased self-understanding (Breshgold, 1989; Yontef, 1995). Experiments are only means to the end of helping people become more aware and making changes they most desire.

The Role of Confrontation

Students are sometimes put off by their perception that a Gestalt counselor's style is direct and confrontational. I tell my students that it is a mistake to equate the practice of any theory with its founder. As has been mentioned, the contemporary practice of Gestalt therapy has progressed beyond the style exhibited by Fritz Perls. Yontef (1993) refers to the Perlsian style as a "boom-boom-boom therapy" characterized by theatrics, abrasive confrontation, and intense catharsis. He implies that the charismatic style of Perls probably met more of his own narcissistic needs than the needs of his clients. Yontef (1993, 1999) is critical of the anti-intellectual, individualistic, dramatic, and confrontational flavor that characterized Gestalt therapy in the "anything goes environment" of the 1960s and 1970s. According to Yontef (1999), the newer version of relational Gestalt therapy has evolved to include more support and increased kindness and compassion in therapy. This approach "combines sustained empathic inquiry with crisp, clear, and relevant awareness focusing" (p. 10). Perls practiced a highly confrontational approach as a way to deal with avoidance. However, this confrontational model is not representative of Gestalt therapy as it is currently being practiced (Bowman, 2005; Frew, 2008; Yontef & Jacobs, 2011).

Confrontation is used at times in the practice of Gestalt therapy, yet it does not have to be viewed as a harsh attack. **Confrontation** can be done in such a way that clients cooperate, especially when they are *invited* to examine their behaviors, attitudes, and thoughts. Therapists can encourage clients to look at certain incongruities, especially gaps between their verbal and nonverbal expression. Further, confrontation does not have to be aimed at weaknesses or negative traits; clients can be challenged to recognize how they are blocking their strengths.

Counselors who care enough to make demands on their clients are telling them, in effect, that they could be in fuller contact with themselves and others. Ultimately, however, clients must decide for themselves if they want to accept this invitation to learn more about themselves. This caveat needs to be kept in mind with all of the experiments that are to be described.

Gestalt Therapy Interventions

Experiments can be useful tools to help the client gain fuller awareness, experience internal conflicts, resolve inconsistencies and dichotomies, and work through an impasse that is preventing completion of unfinished business. Exercises can be used to elicit emotion, produce action, or achieve a specific goal. When used at their best, the interventions described here fit the therapeutic situation and highlight whatever the client is experiencing. The following material is based on Levitsky and Perls (1970), with my own suggestions added for implementing these methods.

THE INTERNAL DIALOGUE EXERCISE One goal of Gestalt therapy is to bring about integrated functioning and acceptance of aspects of one's personality that have been disowned and denied. Gestalt therapists pay close attention to splits in personality function. A main division is between the "top dog" and the "underdog," and therapy often focuses on the war between the two.

The top dog is righteous, authoritarian, moralistic, demanding, bossy, and manipulative. This is the "critical parent" that badgers with "shoulds" and "oughts" and manipulates with threats of catastrophe. The underdog manipulates by playing the role of victim: by being defensive, apologetic, helpless, and weak and by feigning powerlessness. This is the passive side, the one without responsibility, and the one that finds excuses.

The top dog and the underdog are engaged in a constant struggle for control. The struggle helps to explain why one's resolutions and promises often go unfulfilled and why one's procrastination persists. The tyrannical top dog demands that one be thus-and-so, whereas the underdog defiantly plays the role of disobedient child. As a result of this struggle for control, the individual becomes fragmented into controller and controlled. The civil war between the two sides continues, with both sides fighting for their existence.

The conflict between the two opposing poles in the personality is rooted in the mechanism of introjection, which involves incorporating aspects of others, usually parents, into one's personality. It is essential that clients become aware of their introjects, especially the toxic introjects that poison the person and prevent personality integration.

The **empty-chair technique** is one way of getting the client to externalize the introject, a technique Perls used a great deal. Using two chairs, the therapist asks the client to sit in one chair and be fully the top dog and then shift to the other chair and become the underdog. The dialogue can continue between both sides of the client. Essentially, this is a role-playing technique in which all the parts are played by the client. In this way the introjects can surface, and the client can experience the conflict more fully. The conflict can be resolved by the client's acceptance and integration of both sides. This exercise helps clients get in touch with a feeling or a side of themselves that they may be denying; rather than merely talking about a conflicted feeling, they intensify the feeling and experience it fully. Further, by helping clients realize that the feeling is a very real part of themselves, the intervention discourages clients from disassociating the feeling.

The goal of this exercise is to promote a higher level of integration between the polarities and conflicts that exist in everyone. The aim is not to rid oneself of certain traits but to learn to accept and live with the polarities.

MAKING THE ROUNDS Making the rounds is a Gestalt exercise that involves asking a person in a group to go up to others in the group and either speak to or do something with each person. The purpose is to confront, to risk, to disclose the self, to experiment with new behavior, and to grow and change. I have experimented with "making the rounds" when I sensed that a participant needed to face each person in the group with some theme. For example, a group member might say: "I've been sitting here for a long time wanting to participate but holding back because I'm afraid of trusting people in here. And besides, I don't think I'm worth the time of the group anyway." I might counter with "Are you willing to do something right now to get yourself more invested and to begin to work on gaining trust and self-confidence?" If the person answers affirmatively, my suggestion could well be, "Go around to each person and finish this sentence: 'I don't trust you because . . .'." Any number of exercises could be invented to help individuals involve themselves and choose to work on the things that keep them frozen in fear.

Some other related illustrations and examples that I find appropriate for the making-the-rounds intervention are reflected in clients' comments such as these: "I would like to reach out to people more often." "Nobody in here seems to care very much." "I'd like to make contact with you, but I'm afraid of being rejected [or accepted]." "It's hard for me to accept compliments; I always discount good things people say to me."

THE REVERSAL EXERCISE Certain symptoms and behaviors often represent reversals of underlying or latent impulses. Thus, the therapist could ask a person who claims to suffer from severe inhibitions and excessive timidity to play the role of an exhibitionist. I remember a client in one of our therapy groups who had difficulty being anything but sugary sweet. I asked her to reverse her typical style and be as negative as she could be. The reversal worked well; soon she was playing her part with real gusto, and later she was able to recognize and accept her "negative side" as well as her "positive side."

The theory underlying the reversal technique is that clients take the plunge into the very thing that is fraught with anxiety and make contact with those parts of themselves that have been submerged and denied. This technique can help clients begin to accept certain personal attributes that they have tried to deny.

THE REHEARSAL EXERCISE Oftentimes we get stuck rehearsing silently to ourselves so that we will gain acceptance. When it comes to the performance, we experience stage fright, or anxiety, because we fear that we will not play our role well. Internal rehearsal consumes much energy and frequently inhibits our spontaneity and willingness to experiment with new behavior. When clients share their rehearsals out loud with a therapist, they become more aware of the many preparatory means they use in bolstering their social roles. They also become increasingly aware of how they try to meet the expectations of others, of the degree to which they want to be approved, accepted, and liked, and of the extent to which they go to attain acceptance.

THE EXAGGERATION EXERCISE One aim of Gestalt therapy is for clients to become more aware of the subtle signals and cues they are sending through body language. Movements, postures, and gestures may communicate significant meanings, yet the cues may be incomplete. In this exercise the person is asked to exaggerate the movement or gesture repeatedly, which usually intensifies the feeling attached to the behavior and makes the inner meaning clearer. Some examples of behaviors that lend themselves to the exaggeration technique are trembling (shaking hands, legs), slouched posture and bent shoulders, clenched fists, tight frowning, facial grimacing, crossed arms, and so forth. If a client reports that his or her legs are shaking, the therapist may ask the client to stand up and exaggerate the shaking. Then the therapist may ask the client to put words to the shaking limbs.

STAYING WITH THE FEELING Most clients desire to escape from fearful stimuli and to avoid unpleasant feelings. At key moments when clients refer to a feeling or a mood that is unpleasant and from which they have a great desire to flee, the therapist may urge clients to stay with their feeling and encourage them to go deeper into the feeling or behavior they wish to avoid. Facing and experiencing feelings not only takes courage but also is a mark of a willingness to endure the pain necessary for unblocking and making way for newer levels of growth.

THE GESTALT APPROACH TO DREAM WORK In psychoanalysis dreams are interpreted, intellectual insight is stressed, and free association is used to explore the unconscious meanings of dreams. The Gestalt approach does not interpret and analyze dreams. Instead, the intent is to bring dreams back to life and relive them as though they were happening now. The dream is acted out in the present, and the dreamer becomes a part of his or her dream. The suggested format for working with dreams includes making a list of all the details of the dream, remembering each person, event, and mood in it, and then becoming each of these parts by transforming oneself, acting as fully as possible and inventing dialogue. Each part of the dream is assumed to be a projection of the self, and the client creates scripts for encounters between the various characters or parts. All of the different parts of a dream are expressions of the client's own contradictory and inconsistent sides, and, by engaging in a dialogue between these opposing sides, the client gradually becomes more aware of the range of his or her own feelings.

Perls's concept of projection is central in his theory of dream formation; every person and every object in the dream represents a projected aspect of the dreamer. Perls (1969a) suggested that "we start with the impossible assumption that whatever we believe we see in another person or in the world is nothing but a projection" (p. 67). Recognizing the senses and understanding projections go hand in hand. Clients do not think about or analyze the dream but use it as a script and experiment with the dialogue among the various parts of the dream. Because clients can act out a fight between opposing sides, eventually they can appreciate and accept their inner differences and integrate the opposing forces. Freud called the dream the royal road to the unconscious, but to Perls dreams are the "royal road to integration" (p. 66).

According to Perls, the dream is the most spontaneous expression of the existence of the human being. It represents an unfinished situation, but every dream also contains an existential message regarding oneself and one's current struggle. Everything can be found in dreams if all the parts are understood and assimilated; dreams serve as an excellent way to discover personality voids by revealing missing parts and clients' methods of avoidance. Perls asserts that if dreams are properly worked with, the existential message becomes clearer. If people do not remember dreams, they may be refusing to face what is wrong with their life. At the very least, the Gestalt counselor asks clients to talk to their missing dreams. For example, as directed by her therapist, a client reported the following dream in the present tense, as though she were still dreaming:

> I have three monkeys in a cage. One big monkey and two little ones! I feel very attached to these monkeys, although they are creating a lot of chaos in a cage that is divided into three separate spaces. They are fighting with one another—the big monkey is fighting with the little monkey. They are getting out of the cage, and they are clinging onto me. I feel like pushing them away from me. I feel totally overwhelmed by the chaos that they are creating around me. I turn to my mother and tell her that I need help, that I can no longer handle these monkeys because they are driving me crazy. I feel very sad and very tired, and I feel discouraged. I am walking away from the cage, thinking that I really love these monkeys, yet I have to get rid of them. I am telling myself that I am like everybody else. I get pets, and then when things get rough, I want to get rid of them. I am trying very hard to find a solution to keeping these monkeys and not allowing them to have such a terrible effect on me. Before I wake up from my dream, I am making the decision to put each monkey in a separate cage, and maybe that is the way to keep them.

The therapist then asked his client, Brenda, to "become" different parts of her dream. Thus, she became the cage, and she became and had a dialogue with each monkey, and then she became her mother, and so forth. One of the most powerful aspects of this technique was Brenda's reporting her dream as though it were still happening. She quickly perceived that her dream expressed a struggle she was having with her husband and her two children. From her dialogue work, Brenda discovered that she both appreciated and resented her family. She learned that she needed to let them know about her feelings and that together they might work on improving an intensely difficult lifestyle. She did not need an interpretation from her therapist to understand the clear message of her dream.

Application to Group Counseling

As a therapeutic orientation based on field theory, Gestalt therapy is well suited for a group context. Gestalt therapy encourages direct experience and actions as opposed to merely *talking about* conflicts, problems, and feelings. If members have anxieties pertaining to some future event, they can enact these future concerns in the present. This here-and-now focus enlivens the group and assists members in vividly exploring their concerns. Moving from *talking about* to action is often done by the use of experiments in a group. Gestalt therapy employs a rich variety of interventions designed to intensify what group members are experiencing in the present moment for the purpose of leading to increased awareness.

When one member is the focus of work, other members can be used to enhance an individual's work. Through the skill of linking, the group leader can bring a number of members into the exploration of a problem. I prefer an interactive style of Gestalt group work and find that bringing in an interpersonal dimension maximizes the therapeutic potency within the group. I do not like to introduce a technique to promote something happening within a group; rather, I tend to invite members to try out different behavioral styles as a way to heighten what a given member might be experiencing at the moment. A group format provides a context for a great deal of creativity in using interventions and designing experiments. These experiments need to be tailored to each group member and used in a timely manner; they also need to be carried out in a context that offers a balance between support and risk. Experiments, at their best, evolve from what is going on within individual members and what is happening in the group at the moment.

Although Gestalt group leaders encourage members to heighten their awareness and attend to their interpersonal style of relating, leaders tend to take an active role in creating experiments to help members tap their resources. Gestalt leaders are actively engaged with the members, and leaders frequently engage in self-disclosure as a way to enhance relationships and create a sense of mutuality within the group. Gestalt leaders focus on awareness, contact, and experimentation (Yontef & Jacobs, 2011).

If members experience the group as being a safe place, they will be inclined to move into the unknown and challenge themselves. To increase the chances that members will benefit from Gestalt methods, group leaders need to communicate the general purpose of these interventions and create an experimental climate. Leaders are not trying to push an agenda; rather, members are free to try something new and determine for themselves the outcomes of an experiment.

In training workshops in group counseling that Marianne Schneider Corey and I conducted in Korea, the Gestalt approach was well accepted. Group members were very open and willing to share themselves emotionally once a climate of safety was created. Adopting the stance of phenomenological inquiry, we strive to avoid making assumptions about the members of a group, and we are careful not to impose our worldviews or values on them. Instead, we approach clients with respect, interest, compassion, and presence. We work collaboratively with our clients to discover how to best help them resolve the difficulties they experience internally, interpersonally, and in the context of their social environment. Although it is unrealistic to think you need to know everything about different cultures, it is essential to bring an attitude of respect and appreciation for differences to your work in diverse cultural environments around the world. With these attitudes we found that we were able to use many Gestalt interventions with Korean people in a group training context. In some ways this is not surprising because in Korea there is an emphasis on collectivistic values, and group work fits well into the Korean culture.

For a more detailed account of Gestalt therapy in groups, see Feder and Frew (2008), Feder (2006), and Corey (2012, chap. 11).

GESTALT THERAPY FROM A MULTICULTURAL PERSPECTIVE

Strengths From a Diversity Perspective

There are opportunities to creatively use Gestalt methods with culturally diverse populations if interventions are timed appropriately and used flexibly. Frew (2008) has made the case that "contemporary Gestalt therapy has evolved as a culturally sensitive and diversity friendly orientation" (p. 267). He notes that Gestalt therapy can be a useful and effective approach with clients from diverse backgrounds because it takes the clients' context into account. One of the advantages of drawing on Gestalt experiments is that they can be tailored to fit the unique way in which an individual perceives and interprets his or her culture. Although most therapists have preconceptions, Gestalt therapists strive to approach each client in an open way. They do this by checking out their biases and views in dialogue with the client. This is particularly important in working with individuals from other cultures.

Fernbacher and Plummer (2005) stress the importance of assisting Gestalt therapy trainees in developing their own awareness: "To develop awareness of one's cultural identity, one must attend to its influence not only in training but also as part of ongoing development of a Gestalt practitioner" (p. 121). Fernbacher and Plummer contend that "to undertake work across cultures from a Gestalt perspective, it is essential that we explore our own cultural selves . . . to make contact and encourage contact in and with others, we need to know about ourselves" (p. 131).

Gestalt therapy is particularly effective in helping people integrate the polarities within themselves. Many bicultural clients experience an ongoing struggle to reconcile what appears to be diverse aspects of the two cultures in which they live. In one of my weeklong groups, a dynamic piece of work was done by a woman with European roots. Her struggle consisted of integrating her American side with her experiences in Germany as a child. I suggested that she "bring her family into this group" by talking to selected members in the group as though they were members of her family. I invited her to imagine that she was 8 years old and that she could now say to her parents and siblings things that she had never expressed. She was asked to speak in German (since this was her primary language as a child). The combined factors of her trust in the group, her willingness to re-create an early scene by reliving it in the present moment, and her symbolic work with fantasy helped her achieve a significant breakthrough. She was able to put a new ending to an old and unfinished situation through her participation in this Gestalt experiment.

There are many opportunities to apply Gestalt experiments in creative ways with diverse client populations. In cultures where indirect speech is the norm, nonverbal behaviors may emphasize the unspoken content of verbal communication. These clients may express themselves nonverbally more expressively than they do with words. Gestalt therapists typically ask clients to focus on their gestures, facial expressions, and what they are experiencing within their own bodies. They attempt to fully understand the background of their clients' culture. They are concerned about which aspects of this background become central or figural for their clients and what meaning clients place on these figures.

Shortcomings From a Diversity Perspective

To a greater extent than is true of most other approaches, there are some potential problems in too quickly utilizing some Gestalt experiments with some clients. Gestalt methods can lead to a high level of intense feelings. This focus on affect has some clear limitations with those clients who have been culturally conditioned to be emotionally reserved and to avoid openly expressing feelings. As mentioned earlier, some individuals believe expressing feelings openly is a sign of weakness and a display of one's vulnerability. Counselors who operate on the assumption that catharsis is necessary for any change to occur are likely to find certain clients becoming increasingly reluctant to participate in experiments, and such clients may prematurely terminate counseling. Other individuals have strong cultural injunctions prohibiting them from directly expressing their emotions to their parents (such as "Never show your parents that you are angry at them" or "Strive for peace and harmony, and avoid conflicts"). I recall a client from India who was asked by his counselor to "bring your father into the room." The client was very reluctant to even symbolically tell his father of his disappointment with their relationship. In his culture the accepted way to deal with his father was to use his uncle as a go-between, and it was considered highly inappropriate to express any negative feelings toward his father. The client later said that he would have felt very guilty if he had symbolically told his father what he sometimes thought and felt.

Gestalt therapists who have truly integrated their approach are sensitive enough to practice in a flexible way. They consider the client's cultural framework and are able to adapt methods that are likely to be well received. They strive to help clients experience themselves as fully as possible in the present, yet they are not rigidly bound by dictates, nor do they routinely intervene whenever clients stray from the present. Sensitively staying in contact with a client's flow of experiencing entails the ability to focus on the person and not on the mechanical use of techniques for a certain effect.

Gestalt Therapy Applied to the Case of Stan

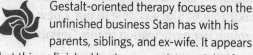 Gestalt-oriented therapy focuses on the unfinished business Stan has with his parents, siblings, and ex-wife. It appears that this unfinished business consists mainly of feelings of resentment, and Stan turns this resentment on himself. His present life situation is spotlighted, but he may also need to reexperience past feelings that could be interfering with his present attempts to develop intimacy with others.

Although the focus is on Stan's present behavior, I guide him toward becoming aware of how he is carrying old baggage around and how it interferes with his life today. My task is to assist him in re-creating the context in which he made *creative adjustments* during his childhood years that no longer serving him well. One of his cardinal introjections was, "I'm stupid, and it would be better if I did not exist."

Stan has been influenced by cultural messages that he has accepted. I am interested in exploring his cultural background, including his values and the values characteristic of his culture. With this focus, I assist Stan in identifying some of the following cultural introjections: "Don't talk about your family with strangers, and don't hang your dirty linen in public." "Don't confront your parents because they deserve respect." "Don't be too concerned about yourself." "Don't show your vulnerabilities; hide your feelings and weaknesses." I invite Stan to examine those introjections to assess their utility in his present circumstances. Although he can decide to retain those aspects of his culture that he prizes, he is in a position to modify or reject other cultural expectations. Of course, this will be done when these issues emerge in the foreground of his work.

I ask Stan to attend to what he becomes aware of as the session begins: "What are you experiencing as we are getting started today?" As I encourage Stan to tune in to his present experience and selectively make observations, a number of figures will emerge. The goal is to focus on a figure of interest, one that seems to hold the most energy or relevance for Stan. When a figure is identified, my task is to deepen Stan's awareness of this thought, feeling, body sensation, or insight through related experiments.

In typical Gestalt fashion, Stan deals with his present struggles within the context of our relationship and through experimentation. One possible experiment would involve Stan becoming some of those individuals who told him how to think, feel, and behave as a child. He can then become the child that he was and respond to them from the place where he feels the most confusion or pain. He experiences in new ways the feelings that accompany his beliefs about himself, and he comes to a deeper appreciation of how his feelings and thoughts influence what he is doing today.

Stan has learned to hide his emotions rather than to reveal them. Understanding this about him, we explore his objections and concerns about "getting into feelings." The figure of interest now is his hesitation to experience or express emotion.

Although I have no agenda to get Stan to experience his feelings at this point, it is important for him to increase his awareness of his reluctance and to explore the meaning it holds for him.

If Stan decides that he wants to experience his emotions rather than deny them, I ask: "What are you aware of now having said what you did?" Stan says that he can't get his ex-wife out of his mind. He tells me about the pain he feels over that relationship and how he is frightened of getting involved again lest he be hurt again. I continue to ask him to focus inward and get a sense of what stands out for him at this very moment. Stan replies: "I'm hurt and angry over all the pain that I've allowed her to inflict on me." I ask him to imagine himself in earlier scenes with his ex-wife, as though the painful situation were occurring in the here and now. He symbolically relives and reexperiences the situation by talking "directly" to his wife. By expressing his resentments and hurts directly, Stan can begin to complete some unfinished business that is interfering with his current functioning. By participating in this experiment, Stan is attaining more awareness of what he is now doing and how he keeps himself locked into his past.

Follow-Up: You Continue as Stan's Gestalt Therapist

Use these questions to help you think about how to work with Stan using the Gestalt approach:

- How might you begin a session with Stan? Would you suggest a direction he should pursue? Would you wait for him to initiate work? Would you ask him to continue from where he left off in the previous session? Would you attend to whatever theme or issue becomes figural to him?

- What unfinished business can you identify in Stan's case? Does any of his experience of being stuck remind you of yourself? How might you work with Stan if he did bring up your own unfinished business?

- What kind of an experiment might you propose to assist Stan in learning more about his hesitation and reluctance to access and express his feelings?

- Stan participated in an experiment to deal with pain, resentment, and hurt over situations with his ex-wife. How might you have worked with the material Stan brought up? What kind of experiment might you design? How would you decide what kind of experiment to create?
- How might you work with Stan's cultural messages? Would you be able to respect his cultural values and still encourage him to make

an assessment of some of the ways in which his culture is affecting him today?

 See *DVD* for *Theory and Practice of Counseling and Psychotherapy: The Case of Stan and Lecturettes* (Session 6 on Gestalt therapy) for a demonstration of my approach to counseling Stan from this perspective. This session consists of Stan exploring one of his dreams in Gestalt fashion.

SUMMARY AND EVALUATION

Summary

Gestalt therapy is an experiential approach that stresses present awareness and the quality of contact between the individual and the environment. The major focus is on assisting the client to become aware of how behaviors that were once part of creatively adjusting to past environments may be interfering with effective functioning and living in the present. The goal of the approach is, first and foremost, to gain awareness.

Another therapeutic aim is to assist clients in exploring how they make contact with elements of their environment. Change occurs through the heightened awareness of "what is." Because the Gestalt therapist has no agenda beyond assisting clients to increase their awareness, there is no need to label a client's behavior as "resistance." Instead, the therapist simply follows this new process as it emerges. The therapist has faith that self-regulation is a naturally unfolding process that does not have to be controlled (Breshgold, 1989). With expanded awareness, clients are able to reconcile polarities and dichotomies within themselves and proceed toward the reintegration of all aspects of themselves.

The therapist works with the client to identify the figures, or most salient aspects of the individual–environmental field, as they emerge from the background. The Gestalt therapist believes each client is capable of self-regulating if those figures are engaged and resolved so others can replace them. The role of the Gestalt therapist is to help clients identify the most pressing issues, needs, and interests and to design experiments that sharpen those figures or that explore resistances to contact and awareness. Gestalt therapists are encouraged to be appropriately self-disclosing, both about their here-and-now reactions in the therapy hour and about their personal experiences (Yontef & Jacobs, 2011; Zahm, 1998).

Contributions of Gestalt Therapy

One contribution of Gestalt therapy is the exciting way in which the past is dealt with in a lively manner by bringing relevant aspects into the present. Therapists challenge clients in creative ways to become aware of and work with issues that are obstructing current functioning. Further, paying attention to the obvious verbal and nonverbal leads provided by clients is a useful way to approach a counseling session. Through the skillful and sensitive use of Gestalt interventions, practitioners can assist clients in heightening their present-centered awareness of what they are thinking and feeling as well as what they are doing.

Gestalt methods bring conflicts and human struggles to life. Gestalt therapy is a creative approach that uses experiments to move clients from talk to action and experience. The creative and spontaneous use of active experiments is a pathway to experiential learning. The focus is on growth and enhancement rather than being a system of techniques to treat disorders, which reflects an early Gestalt motto, "You don't have to be sick to get better." Clients are provided with a wide range of tools—in the form of Gestalt experiments—for discovering new facets of themselves and making decisions about changing their course of living.

The Gestalt approach to working with dreams is a unique pathway for people to increase their awareness of key themes in their lives. By seeing each aspect of a dream as a projection of themselves, clients are able to bring the dream to life, to interpret its personal meaning, and to assume responsibility for it.

Gestalt therapy is a holistic approach that values each aspect of the individual's experience equally. Therapists allow the figure-formation process to guide them. They do not approach clients with a preconceived set of biases or a set agenda. Instead, they place emphasis on what occurs at the boundary between the individual and the environment. Therapists do not try to move the client anywhere. The main goal is to increase the client's awareness of "what is." Instead of trying to make something happen, the therapist's role is assisting the client to increase awareness that will allow reidentification with the part of the self from which he or she is alienated.

A key strength of Gestalt therapy is the attempt to integrate theory, practice, and research. Although Gestalt therapy was light on empirical research for several years, it has come more into vogue recently. Two books show potential for influencing future research: *Handbook for Theory, Research and Practice in Gestalt Therapy* (Brownell, 2008); and *Becoming a Practitioner Researcher: A Gestalt Approach to Holistic Inquiry* (Barber, 2006). Strumpfel and Goldman (2002) note that both process and outcome studies have advanced the theory and practice of Gestalt therapy, and they summarize a number of significant findings based on outcome research:

- Outcome studies have demonstrated Gestalt therapy to be equal to or greater than other therapies for various disorders.
- More recent studies have shown that Gestalt therapy has a beneficial impact with personality disturbances, psychosomatic problems, and substance addictions.
- The effects of Gestalt therapy tend to be stable in follow-up studies 1 to 3 years after the termination of treatment.
- Gestalt therapy has demonstrated effectiveness in treating a variety of psychological disorders.

Limitations and Criticisms of Gestalt Therapy

Most of my criticisms of Gestalt therapy pertain to the older version, or the style of Fritz Perls, which emphasized confrontation and de-emphasized the cognitive factors of personality. This style of Gestalt therapy placed more attention on using techniques to confront clients and getting them to experience their feelings. Contemporary Gestalt therapy has come a long way, and more attention is being given to theoretical instruction, theoretical exposition, and cognitive factors in general (Yontef, 1993, 1995).

In Gestalt therapy clients clarify their thinking, explore beliefs, and put meaning to experiences they are reliving in therapy. Clients assume an active role in participating in experiments, and they learn experientially. The emphasis is on *facilitating* the clients' own process of self-discovery and learning. This experiential and self-directed learning process is based on the fundamental belief in organismic self-regulation, which implies that clients arrive at their own truths through awareness and improved contact with the environment. It seems to me, however, that clients can engage in self-discovery and at the same time benefit from appropriate teaching by the therapist. In addition to the benefits of experiential learning, clients can profit from timely and useful information, and a psychoeducational focus can enhance the learning process.

Current Gestalt practice places a high value on the contact and dialogue between therapist and client. For Gestalt therapy to be effective, the therapist must have a high level of personal development. Being aware of one's own needs and seeing that they do not interfere with the client's process, being present in the moment, and being willing to be nondefensive and self-revealing all demand a lot of the therapist. There is a danger that therapists who are inadequately trained will be primarily concerned with impressing clients. Yontef and Jacobs (2011) maintain that the competent practice of Gestalt therapy requires a strong general clinical background and training, not only in the theory and practice of Gestalt theory but also in personality theory, psychopathology, and knowledge of psychodynamics. Competent practitioners need to have engaged in their own personal therapy and to have had advanced clinical training and supervised experience.

SOME CAUTIONS Typically, Gestalt therapists are highly active, and if they do not have the characteristics mentioned by Zinker (1978)—sensitivity, timing, inventiveness, empathy, and respect for the client—their experiments can easily boomerang. Some therapists who do not have a solid grounding in the theory and practice of Gestalt therapy have employed Fritz Perls's techniques, resulting in an abuse of power. Inept therapists may use powerful techniques to stir up feelings and open up problems clients have kept from full awareness, only to abandon the clients once they have managed to have a dramatic catharsis. Such a failure to stay with clients and help them work through what they have experienced and bring some closure to the experience can be detrimental and could be considered as unethical practice.

Ethical practice depends on adequate training and supervision of therapists, and the most immediate limitation of Gestalt or any other therapy is the skill, training, experience, and judgment of the therapist. Proper training in Gestalt therapy involves understanding the theory, hours of supervised practice, observing Gestalt therapists at work, and experiencing one's own personal therapy. Therapists who are trained in the theory and method of Gestalt therapy are likely to do effective work. Such therapists have learned to blend a phenomenological and dialogic approach, which is inherently respectful to the client, with well-timed experiments.

WHERE TO GO FROM HERE

In the *DVD for Integrative Counseling: The Case of Ruth and Lecturettes*, Session 7 ("Emotive Focus in Counseling"), I demonstrate how I create experiments to heighten Ruth's awareness. In my version of Gestalt work with Ruth, I watch for cues from Ruth about what she is experiencing in the here and now. By attending to what she is expressing both verbally and nonverbally, I am able to suggest experiments during our sessions. In this particular session I employ a Gestalt experiment, asking Ruth to talk to me as if I were her husband, John. During this experiment, Ruth becomes quite emotional. You will see ways of exploring emotional material and integrating this work into a cognitive framework as well.

Other Resources

Psychotherapy.net is a comprehensive resource for students and professionals that offers videos demonstrating Gestalt therapy with adults and children. New articles, interviews, blogs, therapy cartoons, and videos are published monthly. DVDs relevant to this chapter are available at www.psychotherapy.net and include the following:

> Oaklander, V. (2001). *Gestalt Therapy with Children* (Child Therapy with the Experts Series)
> Polster, I. (1997). *Psychotherapy With the Unmotivated Patient*

If you are interested in furthering your knowledge and skill in the area of Gestalt therapy, you might consider pursuing Gestalt training, which would include attending workshops, seeking out personal therapy from a Gestalt therapist, and enrolling in a Gestalt training program that would involve reading, practice, and supervision. In 2007 there were approximately 120 active Gestalt institutes in the United States and another 180 in other countries throughout the world. In addition, there are numerous professional associations, and other resources available in nearly every country and language (Woldt, personal communication, January 15, 2007). A comprehensive list of these resources, along with their Websites, is available in the Appendixes of Woldt and Toman's textbook (2005). Some of the most prominent training programs and associations are listed here.

Gestalt Institute of Cleveland. Inc.

1588 Hazel Drive
Cleveland, OH 44106-1791
Telephone: (216) 421-0468
Fax: (216) 421-1729
E-mail: registrar@gestaltcleveland.org
Website: www.gestaltcleveland.org

Pacific Gestalt Institute

1626 Westwood Blvd., Suite 104

Los Angeles, CA 90024
Telephone: (310) 446-9720
Fax: (310) 475-4704
E-mail: info@gestalttherapy.org
Website: www.gestalttherapy.org

Gestalt Center for Psychotherapy and Training

220 Fifth Avenue, Suite 802
New York, NY 10001
Telephone: (212) 387-9429
E-mail: info@gestaltnyc.org
Website: www.gestaltnyc.org

Gestalt International Study Center

1035 Cemetery Road
South Wellfleet, Cape Cod, MA 02667
Telephone: (508) 349-7900
E-mail: office@gisc.org
Website: www.GISC.org

Gestalt Therapy Training Center Northwest

757 SE 34th Avenue
Portland, OR 97214
Telephone: (503) 230-0900
E-mail: gttcnw@aol.com
Website: www.gttcnw.org

Gestalt Associates Training, Los Angeles

1460 Seventh Street, Suite 300
Santa Monica, CA 90401
Telephone/Fax: (310) 395-6844
E-mail: ritaresnick@gatla.org
Website: www.gatla.org

The most prominent professional associations for Gestalt therapy that hold international conferences follow.

Association for the Advancement of Gestalt Therapy (AAGT)
Website: www.AAGT.org

European Association for Gestalt Therapy (EAGT)
Website: www.EAGT.org

Gestalt Review
Website: www.gestaltreview.com

British Gestalt Journal
Website: www.britishgestaltjournal.com

Behavior Therapy

AP Photo

B. F. SKINNER (1904–1990) reported that he was brought up in a warm, stable family environment.* As he was growing up, Skinner was greatly interested in building all sorts of things, an interest that followed him throughout his professional life. He received his PhD in psychology from Harvard University in 1931 and eventually returned to Harvard after teaching in several universities. He had two daughters, one of whom is an educational psychologist and the other an artist.

Skinner was a prominent spokesperson for behaviorism and can be considered the father of the behavioral approach to psychology. Skinner championed radical behaviorism, which places primary emphasis on the effects of environment on behavior. Skinner was also a determinist; he did not believe that humans had free choice. He acknowledged that feelings and thoughts exist, but he denied that they *caused* our actions. Instead, he stressed the cause-and-effect links between objective, observable environmental conditions and behavior. Skinner maintained that too much attention had been given to internal states of mind and motives, which cannot be observed and changed directly, and that too little focus had been given to environmental factors that can be directly observed and changed. He was extremely interested in the concept of reinforcement, which he applied to his own life. For example, after working for many hours, he would go into his constructed cocoon (like a tent), put on headphones, and listen to classical music (Frank Dattilio, personal communication, September 24, 2010).

Most of Skinner's work was of an experimental nature in the laboratory, but others have applied his ideas to teaching, managing human problems, and social planning. *Science and Human Behavior* (Skinner, 1953) best illustrates how Skinner thought behavioral concepts could be applied to every domain of human behavior. In *Walden II* (1948) Skinner describes a utopian community in which his ideas, derived from the laboratory, are applied to social issues. His 1971 book, *Beyond Freedom and Dignity*, addressed the need for drastic changes if our society was to survive. Skinner believed that science and technology held the promise for a better future.

*This biography is based largely on Nye's (2000) discussion of B. F. Skinner's radical behaviorism.

Courtesy, Dr. Albert Bandura, Stanford University, Palo Alto, CA

ALBERT BANDURA (b. 1925) was born in a small town in northern Alberta, Canada; he was the youngest of six children in a family of Eastern European descent.* Bandura spent his elementary and high school years in the one school in town, which was short of teachers and resources. These meager educational resources proved to be an asset rather than a liability as Bandura early on learned the skills of self-directedness, which would later become one of his research themes. He earned his PhD in clinical psychology from the University of Iowa in 1952, and a year later he joined the faculty at Stanford University. Bandura and his colleagues did pioneering work in the area of social modeling and demonstrated that modeling is a powerful process that explains diverse forms of learning (see Bandura 1971a, 1971b; Bandura & Walters, 1963). In his research programs at Stanford University, Bandura and his colleagues explored social learning theory and the prominent role of observational learning and social modeling in human motivation, thought, and action. By the mid-1980s Bandura had renamed his theoretical approach *social cognitive theory*, which shed light on how we function as self-organizing, proactive, self-reflective, and self-regulating beings (see Bandura, 1986). This notion that we are not simply reactive organisms shaped by environmental forces or driven by inner impulses represented a dramatic shift in the development of behavior therapy. Bandura broadened the scope of behavior therapy by exploring the inner cognitive-affective forces that motivate human behavior.

There are some existential qualities inherent in Bandura's social cognitive theory. Bandura has produced a wealth of empirical evidence that demonstrates the life choices we have in all aspects of our lives. In *Self-Efficacy: The Exercise of Control* (Bandura, 1997), Bandura shows the comprehensive applications of his theory of self-efficacy to areas such as human development, psychology, psychiatry, education, medicine and health, athletics, business, social and political change, and international affairs.

Bandura has concentrated on four areas of research: (1) the power of psychological modeling in shaping thought, emotion, and action; (2) the mechanisms of human agency, or the ways people influence their own motivation and behavior through choice; (3) people's perceptions of their efficacy to exercise influence over the events that affect their lives; and (4) how stress reactions and depressions are caused. Bandura has created one of the few mega-theories that still thrive at the beginning of the 21st century. He has shown that people need a sense of self-efficacy and resilience to create a successful life and to meet the inevitable obstacles and adversities they encounter.

To date Bandura has written nine books, many of which have been translated into various languages. In 2004 he received the Outstanding Lifetime Contribution to Psychology Award from the American Psychological Association. In his early 80s, Bandura continues to teach and do research at Stanford University and to travel throughout the world. He still makes time for hiking, opera, being with his family, and wine tasting in the Napa and Sonoma valleys.

*This biography is based largely on Pajares's (2004) discussion of Bandura's life and work.

Courtesy of the Lazarus Institute

ARNOLD A. LAZARUS (b. 1932) was born and educated in Johannesburg, South Africa. The youngest of four children, he grew up in a neighborhood where there were very few children, and he remembers being lonely and frightened. He learned to play the piano at an early age and recalls, "When I was 7 I used to play like a talented 12-year-old, but when I turned 14 and still played like a 12-year-old, I decided to quit!" His interests then changed to bodybuilding, weight lifting, boxing, and wrestling. He adds, "I was a pathetically skinny kid, often beaten up and bullied, so I started training rather frantically" (personal communication, April 15, 2011). Through sheer determination he ended up winning boxing and weight-lifting competitions and planned to own and operate a gym or health center.

Although Lazarus grew up in South Africa, he strongly identified with the United States. At an early age he felt that racism and discrimination were totally unacceptable. He entered college intending to major in English with a view to journalism as a career but soon switched majors to psychology. He obtained his master's degree in experimental psychology in 1957 and a PhD in clinical psychology in 1960, and then went into full-time private practice in Johannesburg. In 1963 he was invited by Albert Bandura to teach at Stanford University. Later he held teaching positions at Temple University Medical School, Yale University, and Rutgers University.

He has received many honors and won numerous awards, including two Distinguished Professional Contributions Awards from the American Psychological Association and the prestigious Cummings PSYCHE AWARD. Lazarus has written 17 books and more than 300 professional articles. He is a pioneer in clinical behavior therapy and the developer of multimodal therapy, which is a comprehensive, systematic, holistic approach to behavior therapy. Although the assessment process is multimodal, the treatment is cognitive behavioral and draws on empirically supported methods. In terms of clinical practice, behavior therapy and multimodal therapy are very similar. He is recognized as an authority on brief, efficient, and effective psychotherapy.

In addition to his contribution to the development of behavior therapy, Lazarus has shown a keen interest in the subject of dual and multiple relationships in psychotherapy. Through his writing and lecturing on this topic, he has done a great deal to challenge the rigidity of a rule-based approach to practicing psychotherapy. One significant book is *Dual Relationships and Psychotherapy*, (Lazarus & Zur, 2002). Arnold Lazarus is currently the president of The Lazarus Institute in Skillman, New Jersey, where his son (Clifford N. Lazarus, PhD) is the executive director and his daughter-in-law (Donna Astor-Lazarus, MSW, LCSW) is the clinical director.

INTRODUCTION

Behavior therapy practitioners focus on directly observable behavior, current determinants of behavior, learning experiences that promote change, tailoring treatment strategies to individual clients, and rigorous assessment and evaluation. Behavior therapy has been used to treat a wide range of psychological disorders with different client populations. Anxiety disorders, depression, posttraumatic stress disorder, substance abuse, eating and weight disorders, sexual problems, pain management, and hypertension have all been successfully treated using this approach (Wilson, 2011). Behavioral procedures are used in the fields of developmental disabilities, mental illness, education and special education, community psychology, clinical psychology, rehabilitation, business, self-management, sports psychology, health-related behaviors, medicine, and gerontology (Miltenberger, 2012; Wilson, 2011).

Historical Background

The behavioral approach had its origin in the 1950s and early 1960s, and it was a radical departure from the dominant psychoanalytic perspective. The behavior therapy movement differed from other therapeutic approaches in its application of principles of classical and operant conditioning (which will be explained shortly) to the treatment of a variety of problem behaviors. Today, it is difficult to find a consensus on the definition of behavior therapy because the field has grown, become more complex, and is marked by a diversity of views. Contemporary behavior therapy is no longer limited to treatments based on traditional learning theory (Antony & Roemer, 2011b). Indeed, as behavior therapy has evolved and developed, it has increasingly overlapped in some ways with other psychotherapeutic approaches (Wilson, 2011). Behavior therapists now use a variety of evidence-based techniques in their practices, including cognitive therapy, social skills training, relaxation training, and mindfulness strategies—all of which are discussed in this chapter. The following historical sketch of behavior therapy is largely based on Spiegler and Guevremont (2010).

Traditional behavior therapy arose simultaneously in the United States, South Africa, and Great Britain in the 1950s. In spite of harsh criticism and resistance from psychoanalytic psychotherapists, the approach has survived. Its focus was on demonstrating that behavioral conditioning techniques were effective and were a viable alternative to psychoanalytic therapy.

In the 1960s Albert Bandura developed social learning theory, which combined classical and operant conditioning with observational learning. Bandura made cognition a legitimate focus for behavior therapy. During the 1960s a number of *cognitive behavioral approaches* sprang up, which focus on cognitive representations of the environment rather than on characteristics of the objective environment.

Contemporary behavior therapy emerged as a major force in psychology during the 1970s, and it had a significant impact on education, psychology, psychotherapy, psychiatry, and social work. Behavioral techniques were expanded to provide solutions for business, industry, and child-rearing problems as well. Behavior therapy techniques were viewed as the treatment of choice for many psychological problems.

The 1980s were characterized by a search for new horizons in concepts and methods that went beyond traditional learning theory. Behavior therapists continued to subject their methods to empirical scrutiny and to consider the impact of the practice of therapy on both their clients and the larger society. Increased attention was given to the role of emotions in therapeutic change, as well as to the role of biological factors in psychological disorders. Two of the most significant developments in the field were (1) the continued emergence of cognitive behavior therapy as a major force and (2) the application of behavioral techniques to the prevention and treatment of health-related disorders.

By the late 1990s the Association for Behavioral and Cognitive Therapies (ABCT) (formerly known as the Association for Advancement of Behavior Therapy) claimed a membership of about 4,500. Currently, ABCT includes approximately 6,000 mental health professionals and students who are interested in empirically based behavior therapy or cognitive behavior therapy. This name change and description reveals the current thinking of integrating behavioral and cognitive therapies.

By the early 2000s, the behavioral tradition had broadened considerably, which involved enlarging the scope of research and practice. This newest development, sometimes known as the "third wave" of behavior therapy, includes dialectical behavior therapy (DBT), mindfulness-based stress reduction (MBSR), mindfulness-based cognitive therapy (MBCT), and acceptance and commitment therapy (ACT).

See the video program for Chapter 9, *DVD for Theory and Practice of Counseling and Psychotherapy: The Case of Stan and Lecturettes*. I suggest that you view the brief lecture for each chapter prior to reading the chapter.

Four Areas of Development

Contemporary behavior therapy can be understood by considering four major areas of development: (1) classical conditioning, (2) operant conditioning, (3) social-cognitive theory, and (4) cognitive behavior therapy.

Classical conditioning (respondent conditioning) refers to what happens prior to learning that creates a response through pairing. A key figure in this area is Ivan Pavlov who illustrated classical conditioning through experiments with dogs. Placing food in a dog's mouth leads to salivation, which is respondent behavior. When food is repeatedly presented with some originally neutral stimulus (something that does not elicit a particular response), such as the sound of a bell, the dog will eventually salivate to the sound of the bell alone. However, if a bell is sounded repeatedly but not paired again with food, the salivation response will eventually diminish and become extinct. An example of a procedure that is based on the classical conditioning model is Joseph Wolpe's systematic desensitization, which is described later in this chapter. This technique illustrates how principles of learning derived from the experimental laboratory can be applied clinically. Desensitization can be applied to people who, through classical conditioning, developed an intense fear of flying after having a frightening experience while flying.

Technically one can develop an intense fear of flying without having a frightening experience personally. For example, someone may see visual images of a plane crashing off the coast of Brazil and develop a fear of flying even though that person has never flown anywhere. Some researchers hold a different view and believe that fear of flying may be due primarily to claustrophobia (Frank Dattilio, personal communication, September 24, 2010).

Most of the significant responses we make in everyday life are examples of operant behaviors, such as reading, writing, driving a car, and eating with utensils. **Operant conditioning** involves a type of learning in which behaviors are influenced mainly by the consequences that follow them. If the environmental changes brought about by the behavior are reinforcing—that is, if they provide some reward to the organism or eliminate aversive stimuli—the chances are increased that the behavior will occur again. If the environmental changes produce no reinforcement or produce aversive stimuli, the chances are lessened that the behavior will recur. Positive and negative reinforcement, punishment, and extinction techniques, described later in this chapter, illustrate how operant conditioning in applied settings can be instrumental in developing prosocial and adaptive behaviors. Operant techniques are used by behavioral practitioners in parent education programs and with weight management programs.

The behaviorists of both the classical and operant conditioning models excluded any reference to mediational concepts, such as the role of thinking processes, attitudes, and values. This focus is perhaps due to a reaction against the insight-oriented psychodynamic approaches. The **social learning approach** (or the *social-cognitive* approach) developed by Albert Bandura and Richard Walters (1963) is interactional, interdisciplinary, and multimodal (Bandura, 1977, 1982). *Social-cognitive theory* involves a triadic reciprocal interaction among the environment, personal factors (beliefs, preferences, expectations, self-perceptions, and interpretations), and individual behavior. In the social-cognitive approach the environmental events on behavior are mainly determined by cognitive processes governing how environmental influences are perceived by an individual and how these events are interpreted (Wilson, 2011). A basic assumption is that people are capable of self-directed behavior change and that the person is the agent of change. For Bandura (1982, 1997), *self-efficacy* is the individual's belief or expectation that he or she can master a situation and bring about desired change. An example of social learning is ways people can develop effective social skills after they are in contact with other people who effectively model interpersonal skills.

Cognitive behavior therapy (CBT) represents the mainstream of contemporary behavior therapy and is a popular theoretical orientation among psychologists. Cognitive behavioral therapy operates on the assumption that what people believe influences how they act and feel. Since the early 1970s, the behavioral movement has conceded a legitimate place to thinking, even to the extent of giving cognitive factors a central role in understanding and treating emotional and behavioral problems. By the mid-1970s *cognitive behavior therapy* had replaced *behavior therapy* as the accepted designation, and the field began emphasizing the interaction among affective, behavioral, and cognitive dimensions (Lazarus, 2008a; Wilson, 2011).

Today only the integrative therapies are more popular than CBT (Hollon & DiGiuseppe, 2011). A good example of this more integrative approach of cognitive and behavioral dimensions is multimodal therapy, which is discussed later in this chapter. Many techniques, particularly those developed within the last three decades, emphasize cognitive processes that involve private events such as the client's self-talk as mediators of behavior change (see Bandura, 1969, 1986; Beck, 1976; Beck & Weishaar, 2011).

Contemporary behavior therapy has much in common with cognitive behavior therapy in which the mechanism of change is both cognitive (modifying thoughts to change behaviors) and behavioral (altering external factors that lead to behavior change) (Follette & Callaghan, 2011). Considered broadly, the term "behavior therapy" refers to practices based primarily on social-cognitive theory and encompasses a range of cognitive principles and procedures (Wilson, 2011). This chapter goes beyond the traditional behavioral perspective and deals mainly with applied aspects of this model. Chapter 10 is devoted to the cognitive behavioral approaches, which focus on changing clients' cognitions (thoughts and beliefs) that maintain psychological problems.

KEY CONCEPTS

View of Human Nature

Modern behavior therapy is grounded on a scientific view of human behavior that accommodates a systematic and structured approach to counseling. This view does not rest on a deterministic assumption that humans are a mere product of their sociocultural conditioning. Rather, the current view is that the person is the producer *and* the product of his or her environment.

The current trend in behavior therapy is toward developing procedures that give control to clients and thus increase their range of freedom. Behavior therapy aims to increase people's skills so that they have more options for responding. By overcoming debilitating behaviors that restrict choices, people are freer to select from possibilities that were not available to them earlier, which increases individual freedom. People have the capacity to choose how they will respond to external events in their environment, which makes it possible for therapists to use behavioral methods to attain humanistic ends (Kazdin, 1978, 2001).

Basic Characteristics and Assumptions

Seven key characteristics of behavior therapy are described below.

1. Behavior therapy is based on the principles and procedures of the scientific method. Experimentally derived principles of learning are systematically applied to help people change their maladaptive behaviors. The distinguishing characteristic of behavioral practitioners is their systematic adherence to precision and to empirical evaluation. Behavior therapists state treatment goals in concrete objective terms to make replication of their interventions possible. Treatment goals are agreed upon by the client and the therapist. Throughout the course of therapy, the therapist assesses problem behaviors and the conditions that are maintaining them. Evaluation methods are used to discern the effectiveness of both assessment and treatment procedures. Therapeutic techniques employed must have demonstrated effectiveness. In short, behavioral concepts and procedures are stated explicitly, tested empirically within a conceptual framework, and revised continually.

2. Behavior is not limited to overt actions a person engages in that we can observe; behavior also includes internal processes such as cognitions, images, beliefs, and emotions. The key characteristic of a behavior is that it is something that can be *operationally defined.*

3. Behavior therapy deals with the client's current problems and the factors influencing them, as opposed to an analysis of possible historical determinants. Emphasis is on specific factors that influence present functioning and what factors can be used to modify performance. At times understanding of the past may offer useful information about environmental events related to present behavior. Behavior therapists look to the current environmental events that maintain problem behaviors and help clients produce behavior change by changing environmental events, through a process called *functional assessment,* or what Wolpe (1990) referred to as a "behavioral analysis." Behavior therapy recognizes the importance of the individual, the individual's environment, and the interaction between the person and the environment in facilitating change.

4. Clients involved in behavior therapy are expected to assume an active role by engaging in specific actions to deal with their problems. Rather than simply talking about their condition, clients are required to *do* something to bring about change. Clients monitor their behaviors both during and outside the therapy sessions, learn and practice coping skills, and role-play new behavior. Therapeutic tasks that clients carry out in daily life, or homework assignments, are a basic part of this approach. Behavior therapy is an action-oriented and an educational approach, and learning is viewed as being at the core of therapy. Clients learn new and adaptive behaviors to replace old and maladaptive behaviors.

5. This approach assumes that change can take place without insight into underlying dynamics and without understanding the origins of a psychological problem. Behavior therapists operate on the premise that changes in behavior can occur prior to or simultaneously with understanding of oneself, and that behavioral changes may well lead to an increased level of self-understanding. While it is true that insight and understanding about the contingencies that exacerbate one's problems can supply motivation to change, knowing that one has a problem and knowing *how* to change it are two different things (Martell, 2007).

6. Assessment is an ongoing process of observation and self-monitoring that focuses on the current determinants of behavior, including identifying the problem and evaluating the change; assessment informs the treatment process. Therapists also assess their clients' cultures as part of their social environments, including social support networks relating to target behaviors (Tanaka-Matsumi, Higginbotham, & Chang, 2002). Critical to behavioral approaches is the careful assessment and evaluation of the interventions used to determine whether the behavior change resulted from the procedure.

7. Behavioral treatment interventions are individually tailored to specific problems experienced by the client. Several therapy techniques may be used to treat an individual client's problems. An important question that serves as a guide for this choice is, *"What* treatment, by *whom,* is the most effective for *this* individual with *that* specific problem and under *which* set of circumstances?"* (Paul, 1967, p. 111).

THE THERAPEUTIC PROCESS
Therapeutic Goals

Goals occupy a place of central importance in behavior therapy. The general goals of behavior therapy are to increase personal choice and to create new conditions for learning. The client, with the help of the therapist, defines specific treatment goals at the outset of the therapeutic process. Although assessment and treatment occur together, a formal assessment takes place prior to treatment to determine behaviors that are targets of change. Continual assessment throughout therapy determines the degree to which identified goals are being met. It is important to devise a way to measure progress toward goals based on empirical validation.

Contemporary behavior therapy stresses clients' active role in deciding about their treatment. The therapist assists clients in formulating specific measurable goals. Goals must be clear, concrete, understood, and agreed on by the client and the counselor. The counselor and client discuss the behaviors associated with the goals, the circumstances required for change, the nature of subgoals, and a plan of action to work toward these goals. This process of determining therapeutic goals entails a negotiation between client and counselor that results in a contract that guides the course of therapy. Behavior therapists and clients alter goals throughout the therapeutic process as needed.

Therapist's Function and Role

Behavior therapists conduct a thorough **functional assessment** (or **behavioral analysis**) to identify the maintaining conditions by systematically gathering information about situational antecedents (A), the dimensions of the problem behavior (B), and the consequences (C) of the problem. This is known as the **ABC model**, and the goal of a functional assessment of a client's behavior is to understand the ABC sequence. This model of behavior suggests that *behavior* (B) is influenced by some particular events that precede it, called *antecedents* (A), and by certain events that follow it, called *consequences* (C). **Antecedent events** cue or elicit a certain behavior. For example, with a client who has trouble going to sleep, listening to a relaxation tape may serve as a cue for sleep induction. Turning off the lights and removing the television from the bedroom may elicit sleep behaviors as well. **Consequences** are events that maintain a behavior in some way, either by increasing or decreasing it. For example, a client may be more likely to return to counseling after the counselor offers verbal praise or encouragement for having come in or for having completed some homework. A client may be less likely to return if the counselor is consistently late to sessions. In doing a **behavioral assessment interview,** the therapist's task is to identify the particular antecedent and consequent events that influence, or are functionally related to, an individual's behavior (Cormier, Nurius, & Osborn, 2013).

Behaviorally oriented practitioners tend to be active and directive and to function as consultants and problem solvers. They rely heavily on empirical evidence about the efficacy of the techniques they apply to particular problems. Behavioral practitioners must possess intuitive skills and clinical judgment in selecting appropriate treatment methods and in determining when to implement specific techniques (Wilson, 2011). They pay close attention to the clues given by clients, and they are willing to follow their clinical hunches. They use some techniques common to other approaches, such as summarizing, reflection, clarification, and open-ended questioning. However, behavioral clinicians perform other functions as well (Miltenberger, 2012; Spiegler & Guevremont, 2010):

- The therapist strives to understand the function of client behaviors, including how certain behaviors originated and how they are sustained. With this understanding, the therapist formulates initial treatment goals and designs and implements a treatment plan to accomplish these goals.
- The behavioral clinician uses strategies that have research support for use with a particular kind of problem. These evidence-based strategies promote generalization and maintenance of behavior change. A number of these strategies are described later in this chapter.
- The clinician evaluates the success of the change plan by measuring progress toward the goals throughout the duration of treatment. Outcome measures are given to the client at the beginning of treatment (called a baseline) and collected again periodically during and after treatment to determine whether the strategy and treatment plan are working. If not, adjustments are made in the strategies being used.
- A key task of the therapist is to conduct follow-up assessments to see whether the changes are durable over time. Clients learn how to identify and cope with potential setbacks. The emphasis is on helping clients maintain changes over time and acquire behavioral and cognitive coping skills to prevent relapses.

Let's examine how a behavior therapist might perform these functions. A client comes to therapy to reduce her anxiety, which is preventing her from leaving the house. The therapist is likely to begin with a specific analysis of the nature of her anxiety. The therapist will ask how she experiences the anxiety of leaving her house, including what she actually *does* in these situations. Systematically, the therapist gathers information about this anxiety. When did the problem begin? In what situations does it arise? What does she do at these times? What are her feelings and thoughts in these situations? Who is present when she experiences anxiety? What does she do to reduce the anxiety? How do her present fears interfere with living effectively? After this assessment, specific behavioral goals are developed, and strategies such as relaxation training, systematic desensitization, and exposure therapy are designed to help the client reduce her anxiety to a manageable level. The therapist will get a commitment from the client to work toward the specified goals, and the two of them will evaluate the client's progress toward meeting these goals throughout the duration of therapy.

For a description of applying a behavioral approach to the assessment and treatment of an individual client, see Dr. Sherry Cormier's behavioral interventions with Ruth in *Case Approach to Counseling and Psychotherapy* (Corey, 2013a, chap. 7).

Client's Experience in Therapy

One of the unique contributions of behavior therapy is that it provides the therapist with a well-defined system of procedures to employ. Both therapist and client have clearly defined roles, and the importance of client awareness and participation in the therapeutic process is stressed. Behavior therapy is characterized by an active role for both therapist and client. A large part of the therapist's role is to teach concrete skills through the provision of instructions, modeling, and performance feedback. The client engages in behavioral rehearsal with feedback until skills are well learned and generally receives active homework assignments (such as self-monitoring of problem behaviors) to complete between therapy sessions. Behavior clinicians emphasize that changes clients make in therapy need to be translated into their daily lives. It is important for clients to be motivated to change, and they are expected to cooperate in carrying out therapeutic activities, both during therapy sessions and in everyday life. If clients are not involved in this way, the chances are slim that therapy will be successful. However, if clients are not motivated, another behavioral strategy that has considerable empirical support is motivational interviewing (Miller & Rollnick, 2002). This strategy involves honoring the client's resistance in such a way that his or her motivation to change is increased over time (Cormier et al., 2013).

Clients are encouraged to experiment for the purpose of enlarging their repertoire of adaptive behaviors. Counseling is not complete unless actions follow verbalizations. Behavioral practitioners make the assumption that it is only when the transfer of changes is made from the sessions to everyday life that the effects of therapy can be considered successful. Clients are as aware as the therapist is regarding when the goals have been accomplished and when it is appropriate to terminate treatment. It is clear that clients are expected to do more than merely gather insights; they need to be willing to make changes and to continue implementing new behavior once formal treatment has ended.

Relationship Between Therapist and Client

The charge is often made that the importance of the relationship between client and therapist is discounted in behavior therapy. Antony and Roemer (2011b) acknowledge that examining the efficacy of particular behavioral techniques has been given more emphasis than the quality of the therapeutic relationship in behavior therapy. However, behavioral practitioners have increasingly recognized the role of the therapeutic relationship and therapist behavior as critical factors related to the process and outcome of treatment. Today, most behavioral practitioners stress the value of establishing a collaborative working relationship with their clients. For example, Lazarus (1993) believes a flexible repertoire of relationship styles, plus a wide range of techniques, enhances treatment outcomes. He emphasizes the need for therapeutic flexibility and versatility above all else. Lazarus contends that the cadence of client–therapist interaction differs from individual to individual and even from session to session. The skilled behavior therapist conceptualizes problems behaviorally and makes use of the client–therapist relationship in facilitating change.

As you will recall, the experiential therapies (existential therapy, person-centered therapy, and Gestalt therapy) place primary emphasis on the nature of the engagement between counselor and client. In contrast, most behavioral practitioners contend that factors such as warmth, empathy, authenticity, permissiveness, and acceptance are necessary, but not sufficient, for behavior change to occur. The client–therapist relationship is a foundation on which therapeutic strategies are built to help clients change in the direction they wish.

APPLICATION: THERAPEUTIC TECHNIQUES AND PROCEDURES

A strength of the behavioral approaches is the development of specific therapeutic procedures that must be shown to be effective through objective means. The results of behavioral interventions become clear because therapists receive continual direct feedback from their clients. A hallmark of the behavioral approaches is that the therapeutic techniques are empirically supported and evidence-based practice is highly valued. To its credit, the effectiveness of behavior therapy has been researched with different populations and a wide array of disorders.

According to Lazarus (1989, 1992b, 1996b, 1997a, 2005, 2008a, 2008b), behavioral practitioners can incorporate into their treatment plans any technique that can be demonstrated to effectively change behavior. Lazarus advocates the use of diverse techniques, regardless of their theoretical origin. It is clear that behavior therapists do not have to restrict themselves only to methods derived from learning theory. Likewise, behavioral techniques can be incorporated into other approaches. This is illustrated later in this chapter in the sections on the incorporation of mindfulness and acceptance-based approaches into the practice of behavior therapy.

The therapeutic procedures used by behavior therapists are specifically designed for a particular client rather than being randomly selected from a "bag of techniques." Therapists are often quite creative in their interventions. In the following sections I describe a range of behavioral techniques available to the practitioner: applied behavioral analysis, relaxation training, systematic desensitization, exposure therapies, eye movement desensitization and reprocessing, social skills training, self-management programs and self-directed behavior, multimodal therapy, and mindfulness and acceptance-based approaches. These techniques do not encompass the full spectrum of behavioral procedures, but they do represent a sample of the approaches used in the practice of contemporary behavior therapy.

Applied Behavioral Analysis: Operant Conditioning Techniques

This section describes a few key principles of operant conditioning: positive reinforcement, negative reinforcement, extinction, positive punishment, and negative punishment. For a detailed treatment of the wide range of operant conditioning methods that are part of contemporary behavior modification, I recommend Miltenberger (2012).

In applied behavior analysis, operant conditioning techniques and methods of assessment and evaluation are applied to a wide range of problems in many different settings (Kazdin, 2001). The most important contribution of applied behavior analysis is that it offers a functional approach to understanding clients' problems and addresses these problems by changing antecedents and consequences (the ABC model).

Behaviorists believe we respond in predictable ways because of the gains we experience (positive reinforcement) or because of the need to escape or avoid unpleasant consequences (negative reinforcement). Once clients' goals have been assessed, specific behaviors are targeted. The goal of reinforcement, whether positive or negative, is to increase the target behavior. **Positive reinforcement** involves the *addition* of something of value to the individual (such as praise, attention, money, or food) as a consequence of certain behavior. The stimulus that follows the behavior is the positive reinforcer. For example, a child earns excellent grades and is praised for studying by her parents. If she values this praise, it is likely that she will have an investment in studying in the future. When the goal of a program is to decrease or eliminate undesirable behaviors, positive reinforcement is often used to increase the frequency of more desirable behaviors, which replace undesirable behaviors. In the above example, the parental praise functions as the positive reinforcer and makes it more likely that the child will maintain or even increase the frequency of studying and earning good grades. Note that if a child did *not* value parental praise, this would not serve as a reinforcer. The reinforcer is not defined by the form or substance that it takes but rather by the *function* it serves: namely, to maintain or increase the frequency of a desired behavior.

Negative reinforcement involves the *escape* from or the avoidance of aversive (unpleasant) stimuli. The individual is motivated to exhibit a desired behavior to avoid the unpleasant condition. For example, a friend of mine does not appreciate waking up to the shrill sound of an alarm clock. She has trained herself to wake up a few minutes before the alarm sounds to avoid the aversive stimulus of the alarm buzzer.

Another operant method of changing behavior is **extinction**, which refers to withholding reinforcement from a previously reinforced response. In applied settings, extinction can be used for behaviors that have been maintained by positive reinforcement or negative reinforcement. For example, in the case of children who display temper tantrums, parents often reinforce this behavior by the attention they give to it. An approach to dealing with problematic behavior is to eliminate the connection between a certain behavior (tantrums) and positive reinforcement (attention). In this example a parent uses extinction when during and after a child's temper tantrum, the parent ignores the child's tantrum-related behaviors. Doing so can decrease or eliminate such behaviors through the *extinction process*. It should be noted that extinction might well have negative side effects, such as anger and aggression. Also note that initially when using extinction that unwanted behaviors may increase temporarily. Extinction can reduce or eliminate certain behaviors, but extinction does not replace those responses that have been extinguished. For this reason, extinction is most often used in behavior modification programs in conjunction with various reinforcement strategies (Kazdin, 2001).

Another way behavior is controlled is through **punishment**, sometimes referred to as aversive control, in which the consequences of a certain behavior result in a decrease of that behavior. The goal of reinforcement is to *increase target behavior*, but the goal of punishment is to *decrease target behavior*. Miltenberger (2012) describes two kinds of punishment that may occur as a consequence of behavior: positive punishment and negative punishment. In **positive punishment** an aversive stimulus is *added* after the behavior to decrease the frequency of a behavior (such as a time-out procedure with a child who is displaying misbehavior).

In **negative punishment** a reinforcing stimulus is *removed* following the behavior to decrease the frequency of a target behavior (such as deducting money from a worker's salary for missing time at work, or taking television time away from a child for misbehavior). In both kinds of punishment, the behavior is less likely to occur in the future. These four operant procedures form the basis of behavior therapy programs for parent skills training and are also used in the self-management procedures that are discussed later in this chapter.

Some behavioral practitioners are opposed to using aversive control or punishment, and recommended substituting positive reinforcement. The key principle in the applied behavior analysis approach is to use the least aversive means possible to change behavior, and positive reinforcement is known to be the most powerful change agent. In everyday life, punishment often is used as a means of getting revenge or expressing frustration. However, as Kazdin (2001) has noted, "punishment in everyday life is not likely to teach lessons or suppress intolerable behavior because of the specific punishments that are used and how they are applied" (p. 231). Even in those cases when punishment suppresses undesirable responses, punishment does not result in teaching desirable behaviors. Punishment should be used only after nonaversive approaches have been implemented and found to be ineffective in changing problematic behavior (Kazdin, 2001; Miltenberger, 2012). It is essential that reinforcement be used as a way to develop appropriate behaviors that replace the behaviors that are suppressed.

Progressive Muscle Relaxation

Progressive muscle relaxation has become increasingly popular as a method of teaching people to cope with the stresses produced by daily living. It is aimed at achieving muscle and mental relaxation and is easily learned. After clients learn the basics of relaxation procedures, it is essential that they practice these exercises daily to obtain maximum results.

Jacobson (1938) is credited with initially developing the progressive muscle relaxation procedure. It has since been refined and modified, and relaxation procedures are frequently used in combination with a number of other behavioral techniques. These include systematic desensitization, assertion training, self-management programs, audiotape recordings of guided relaxation procedures, computer simulation programs, biofeedback-induced relaxation, hypnosis, meditation, and autogenic training (teaching control of bodily and imaginal functions through autosuggestion).

Progressive muscle relaxation involves several components. Clients are given a set of instructions that teaches them to relax. They assume a passive and relaxed position in a quiet environment while alternately contracting and relaxing muscles. This progressive muscle relaxation is explicitly taught to the client by the therapist. Deep and regular breathing also is associated with producing relaxation. At the same time clients learn to mentally "let go," perhaps by focusing on pleasant thoughts or images. Clients are instructed to actually feel and experience the tension building up, to notice their muscles getting tighter and study this tension, and to hold and fully experience the tension. It is useful for clients to experience the difference between a tense and a relaxed state. The client is then taught how to relax all the muscles while visualizing the various parts of the body, with emphasis on the facial muscles. The arm muscles are relaxed first, followed by the head, the neck and shoulders, the back, abdomen, and thorax, and then the lower limbs. Relaxation becomes a well-learned response, which can become a habitual pattern if practiced daily for about 25 minutes each day.

Relaxation procedures have been applied to a variety of clinical problems, either as a separate technique or in conjunction with related methods. The most common use has been with problems related to stress and anxiety, which are often manifested in psychosomatic symptoms. Relaxation training has benefits in areas such as preparing patients for surgery, teaching clients how to cope with chronic pain, and reducing the frequency of migraine attacks (Ferguson & Sgambati, 2008). Some other ailments for which progressive muscle relaxation is helpful include asthma, headache, hypertension, insomnia, irritable bowel syndrome, and panic disorder (Cormier et al., 2013).

For an exercise of the phases of the progressive muscle relaxation procedure that you can apply to yourself, see *Student Manual for Theory and Practice of Counseling and Psychotherapy* (Corey, 2013b). For an excellent audiotape demonstration of progressive muscle relaxation, see Dattilio (2006). For a more detailed discussion of progressive muscle relaxation, see Ferguson and Sgambati (2008).

Systematic Desensitization

Systematic desensitization, which is based on the principle of classical conditioning, is a basic behavioral procedure developed by Joseph Wolpe, one of the pioneers of behavior therapy. Clients imagine successively more anxiety-arousing situations at the same time that they engage in a behavior that competes with anxiety. Gradually, or systematically, clients become less sensitive (desensitized) to the anxiety-arousing situation. This procedure can be considered a form of exposure therapy because clients are required to expose themselves to anxiety-arousing images as a way to reduce anxiety.

Systematic desensitization is an empirically researched behavior therapy procedure that is time consuming, yet it is clearly effective and efficient in reducing maladaptive anxiety and treating anxiety-related disorders, particularly in the area of specific phobias (Cormier et al., 2013; Head & Gross, 2008; Spiegler & Guevremont, 2010). Before implementing the desensitization procedure, the therapist conducts an initial interview to identify specific information about the anxiety and to gather relevant background information about the client. This interview, which may last several sessions, gives the therapist a good understanding of who the client is. The therapist questions the client about the particular circumstances that elicit the conditioned fears. For instance, under what circumstances does the client feel anxious? If the client is anxious in social situations, does the anxiety vary with the number of people present? Is the client more anxious with women or men? The client is asked to begin a self-monitoring process consisting of observing and recording situations during the week that elicit anxiety responses. Some therapists also administer a questionnaire to gather additional data about situations leading to anxiety.

If the decision is made to use the desensitization procedure, the therapist gives the client a rationale for the procedure and briefly describes what is involved. Once it has been determined that systematic desensitization is an appropriate form of treatment, a three-step process unfolds: (1) relaxation training, (2) development of a graduated anxiety hierarchy, and (3) systematic desensitization proper that involves the presentation of hierarchy items while the client is in a deeply relaxed state (Head & Gross, 2008).

The steps in *progressive muscle relaxation,* which were described earlier, are presented to the client. The therapist uses a very quiet, soft, and pleasant voice to teach progressive muscular relaxation. The client is asked to create imagery of previously relaxing situations, such as sitting by a lake or wandering through a beautiful field. It is important that the client reach a state of calm and peacefulness. The client is instructed to practice relaxation both as a part of the desensitization procedure and also outside the session on a daily basis.

The therapist then works with the client to develop an *anxiety hierarchy* for each of the identified areas. Stimuli that elicit anxiety in a particular area, such as rejection, jealousy, criticism, disapproval, or any phobia, are analyzed. The therapist constructs a ranked list of situations that elicit increasing degrees of anxiety or avoidance. The hierarchy is arranged in order from the most anxiety-provoking situation the client can imagine down to the situation that evokes the least anxiety. If it has been determined that the client has anxiety related to fear of rejection, for example, the highest anxiety-producing situation might be rejection by the spouse, next, rejection by a close friend, and then rejection by a coworker. The least disturbing situation might be a stranger's indifference toward the client at a party.

Desensitization does not begin until several sessions after the initial interview has been completed. Enough time is allowed for clients to learn relaxation in therapy sessions, to practice it at home, and to construct their anxiety hierarchy. The desensitization process begins with the client reaching complete relaxation with eyes closed. A neutral scene is presented, and the client is asked to imagine it. If the client remains relaxed, he or she is asked to imagine the least anxiety-arousing scene on the hierarchy of situations that has been developed. The therapist moves progressively up the hierarchy until the client signals that he or she is experiencing anxiety, at which time the scene is terminated. Relaxation is then induced again, and the scene is reintroduced again until little anxiety is experienced to it. Treatment ends when the client is able to remain in a relaxed state while imagining the scene that was formerly the most disturbing and anxiety-producing. The core of systematic desensitization is repeated exposure in the imagination to anxiety-evoking situations without experiencing any negative consequences.

Homework and follow-up are essential components of successful desensitization. Clients are encouraged to practice selected relaxation procedures daily, at which time they visualize scenes completed in the previous session. Gradually, they can expose themselves to daily-life situations as a further way to manage their anxieties. Clients tend to benefit the most when they have a variety of ways to cope with anxiety-arousing situations that they can continue to use once therapy has ended (Head & Gross, 2008).

Systematic desensitization is among the most empirically supported therapy methods available, especially for the treatment of anxiety (Head & Gross, 2008). Not only does systematic desensitization have a good track record in dealing with fears, it also has been used to treat a variety of conditions including anger, asthmatic attacks, insomnia, motion sickness, nightmares, and sleepwalking (Spiegler, 2008). Systematic desensitization is often acceptable to clients because they are gradually and symbolically exposed to anxiety-evoking situations.

For a more detailed discussion of systematic desensitization, see Head and Gross (2008) and Cormier et al. (2013).

In Vivo Exposure and Flooding

Exposure therapies are designed to treat fears and other negative emotional responses by introducing clients, under carefully controlled conditions, to the situations that contributed to such problems. Exposure is a key process in treating a wide range of problems associated with fear and anxiety. Exposure therapy involves systematic confrontation with a feared stimulus, either through imagination or *in vivo* (live). Imaginal exposure can be used prior to implementing in vivo exposure when a client's fears are so severe that the client is unable to participate in live exposure (Hazlett-Stevens & Craske, 2008). Whatever route is used, exposure involves contact by clients with what they find fearful. Desensitization is one type of exposure therapy, but there are others. Two variations of traditional systematic desensitization are *in vivo exposure* and *flooding*.

IN VIVO EXPOSURE In vivo exposure involves client exposure to the actual anxiety-evoking events rather than simply imagining these situations. Live exposure has been a cornerstone of behavior therapy for decades. Hazlett-Stevens and Craske (2008) describe the key elements of the process of in vivo exposure. Typically, treatment begins with a functional analysis of objects or situations a person avoids or fears. Together, the therapist and the client generate a hierarchy of situations for the client to encounter in ascending order of difficulty. In vivo exposure involves repeated systematic exposure to fear items, beginning from the bottom of the hierarchy. Clients engage in a brief, graduated series of exposures to feared events. As is the case with systematic desensitization, clients learn responses incompatible with anxiety, such as responses involving muscle relaxation. Clients are encouraged eventually to experience their full fear response during exposure without engaging in avoidance. Between therapy sessions, clients carry out self-directed exposure exercises. Clients' progress with home practice is reviewed, and the therapist provides feedback on how the client could deal with any difficulties encountered.

In some cases the therapist may accompany clients as they encounter feared situations. For example, a therapist could go with clients in an elevator if they had phobias of using elevators. Of course, when this kind of out-of-office procedure is used, matters of safety and appropriate ethical boundaries are always considered. People who have extreme fears of certain animals could be exposed to these animals in real life in a safe setting with a therapist. Self-managed in vivo exposure—a procedure in which clients expose themselves to anxiety-evoking events on their own—is an alternative when it is not practical for a therapist to be with clients in real-life situations.

FLOODING Another form of exposure therapy is flooding, which refers to either in vivo or imaginal exposure to anxiety-evoking stimuli for a prolonged period of time. As is characteristic of all exposure therapies, even though the client experiences anxiety during the exposure, the feared consequences do not occur.

In vivo flooding consists of intense and prolonged exposure to the actual anxiety-producing stimuli. Remaining exposed to feared stimuli for a prolonged period without engaging in any anxiety-reducing behaviors allows the anxiety to decrease on its own. Generally, highly fearful clients tend to curb their anxiety through the use of maladaptive behaviors. In flooding, clients are prevented from engaging in their usual maladaptive responses to anxiety-arousing situations. In vivo flooding tends to reduce anxiety rapidly.

Imaginal flooding is based on similar principles and follows the same procedures except the exposure occurs in the client's imagination instead of in daily life. An advantage of using imaginal flooding over in vivo flooding is that there are no restrictions on the nature of the anxiety-arousing situations that can be treated. In vivo exposure to actual traumatic events (airplane crash, rape, fire, flood) is often not possible nor is it appropriate for both ethical and practical reasons. Imaginal flooding can re-create the circumstances of the trauma in a way that does not bring about adverse consequences to the client. Survivors of an airplane crash, for example, may suffer from a range of debilitating symptoms. They are likely to have nightmares and flashbacks to the disaster; they may avoid travel by air or have anxiety about travel by any means; and they probably have a variety of distressing symptoms such as guilt, anxiety, and depression. In vivo and imaginal exposure, as well as flooding, are frequently used in the behavioral treatment for anxiety-related disorders, specific phobia, social phobia, panic disorder, obsessive-compulsive disorder, posttraumatic stress disorder, and agoraphobia (Hazlett-Stevens & Craske, 2008).

Because of the discomfort associated with prolonged and intense exposure, some clients may not elect these exposure treatments. It is important for the behavior therapist to work with the client to create motivation and readiness for exposure. From an ethical perspective, clients should have adequate information about prolonged and intense exposure therapy before agreeing to participate. It is important that they understand that anxiety will be induced as a way to reduce it. Clients need to make informed decisions after considering the pros and cons of subjecting themselves to temporarily stressful aspects of treatment. Clients should be informed that they can terminate exposure if they experience a high level of anxiety.

The repeated success of exposure therapy in treating various disorders has resulted in exposure being used as a part of most behavioral treatments for anxiety disorders. Spiegler and Guevremont (2010) conclude that exposure therapies are the single most potent behavioral procedures available for anxiety-related disorders, and they can have long-lasting effects. However, they add, using exposure as a sole treatment procedure is not always sufficient. In cases involving severe and multifaceted disorders, more than one behavioral intervention is often required. Increasingly, imaginal and in vivo exposure are being used in combination, which fits with the trend in behavior therapy to use treatment packages as a way to enhance the effectiveness of therapy.

Eye Movement Desensitization and Reprocessing

Eye movement desensitization and reprocessing (EMDR) is a form of exposure therapy that entails assessment and preparation, imaginal flooding, and cognitive restructuring in the treatment of individuals with traumatic memories. The treatment involves the use of rapid, rhythmic eye movements and other bilateral stimulation to treat clients who have experienced traumatic stress. Developed by Francine Shapiro (2001), this therapeutic procedure draws from a wide range of behavioral interventions. Designed to assist clients in dealing with posttraumatic stress disorders, EMDR has been applied to a variety of populations including children, couples, sexual abuse victims, combat veterans, victims of crime, rape survivors, accident victims, and individuals dealing with anxiety, panic, depression, grief, addictions, and phobias. The treatment consists of three basic phases involving assessment and preparation, imaginal flooding, and cognitive restructuring.

Shapiro (2001) emphasizes the importance of the safety and welfare of the client when using this approach. EMDR may appear simple to some, but the ethical use of the procedure demands training and clinical supervision, as is true of using exposure therapies in general. Because of the powerful reactions from clients, it is essential that practitioners know how to safely and effectively manage these occurrences. Therapists should not use this procedure unless they receive proper training and supervision from an authorized EMDR instructor. A more complete discussion of this behavioral procedure can be found in Shapiro (2001, 2002a).

There is some controversy over whether the eye movements themselves create change or the application of cognitive techniques paired with eye movements act as change agents. The role of lateral eye movements has yet to be clearly demonstrated, and some evidence indicates that the eye movement component may not be integral to the treatment (Prochaska & Norcross, 2010; Spiegler & Guevremont, 2010). In a review of controlled studies of EMDR in the treatment of trauma, Shapiro (2002b) reports that EMDR clearly outperforms no treatment and achieves similar or superior results as other methods of treating trauma. When it comes to the overall effectiveness of EMDR, Prochaska and Norcross (2010) note that "in its 20-year history, EMDR has garnered more controlled research than any other method used to treat trauma" (p. 236). In writing about the future of EMDR, Prochaska and Norcross make several predictions: increasing numbers of practitioners will receive training in EMDR; outcome research will shed light on EMDR's effectiveness compared to other current therapies for trauma; and further research and practice will provide a sense of its effectiveness with disorders besides posttraumatic stress disorder.

Social Skills Training

Social skills training is a broad category that deals with an individual's ability to interact effectively with others in various social situations; it is used to help clients develop and achieve skills in interpersonal competence. *Social skills* involve being able to communicate with others in a way that is both appropriate and effective. Individuals who experience psychosocial problems that are partly caused by interpersonal difficulties are good candidates for social skills training. Typically, social skills training involves various behavioral techniques such as psychoeducation, modeling, behavior rehearsal, and feedback (Antony & Roemer, 2011b). Social skills training is effective in treating psychosocial problems by increasing clients' interpersonal skills (Segrin, 2008). Social skills involve the ability to relate to others in appropriate and effective ways. Some of the desirable aspects of this training are that it has a very broad base of applicability and that it can easily be tailored to suit the particular needs of individual clients.

Segrin (2008) identifies these key elements of social skills training, which entail a collection of techniques: assessment, direct instruction and coaching, modeling, role-playing, and homework assignments. Clients learn information that they can apply to various interpersonal situations, and skills are modeled for them so they can actually see how skills can be used. A key step involves the necessity of clients putting into action the information they are acquiring. It is through role-playing that individuals actively practice desired behaviors that are observed. Segrin notes that by monitoring clients' successes and failures therapists can fine-tune clients' performances. The feedback and reinforcement clients receive assists them in conceptualizing and using a new set of social skills that enables them to communicate more effectively. A follow-up phase is critical for clients in establishing a range of effective behaviors that can be applied to many social situations.

A few examples of evidence-based applications of social skills training include alcohol/substance abuse, attention-deficit/hyperactivity disorder, bullying, social anxiety, emotional and behavioral problems in children, behavioral treatment for couples, and depression (Antony & Roemer, 2011b; Segrin, 2008). A popular variation of social skills training is *anger management training,* which is designed for individuals who have trouble with aggressive behavior. *Assertion training,* which is described next, is useful for people who lack assertive skills.

ASSERTION TRAINING One specialized form of social skills training consists of teaching people how to be assertive in a variety of social situations. Many people have difficulty feeling that it is appropriate or right to assert themselves. People who lack social skills frequently experience interpersonal difficulties at home, at work, at school, and during leisure time. Assertion training can be useful for those (1) who have difficulty expressing anger or irritation, (2) who have difficulty saying no, (3) who are overly polite and allow others to take advantage of them, (4) who find it difficult to express affection and other positive responses, (5) who feel they do not have a right to express their thoughts, beliefs, and feelings, or (6) who have social phobias.

The basic assumption underlying **assertion training** is that people have the right (but not the obligation) to express themselves. One goal of assertion training is to increase people's behavioral repertoire so that they can make the *choice* of whether to behave assertively in certain situations. It is important that clients replace maladaptive social skills with new skills. Another goal is teaching people to express themselves in ways that reflect sensitivity to the feelings and rights of others. Assertion does not mean aggression; truly assertive people do not stand up for their rights at all costs, ignoring the feelings of others.

Generally, the therapist both teaches and models desired behaviors the client wants to acquire. These behaviors are practiced in the therapy office and then enacted in everyday life. Most assertion training programs focus on clients' negative self-statements, self-defeating beliefs, and faulty thinking. People often behave in unassertive ways because they don't think they have a right to state a viewpoint or ask for what they want or deserve. Thus their thinking leads to passive behavior. Effective assertion training programs do more than give people skills and techniques for dealing with difficult situations. These programs challenge people's beliefs that accompany their lack of assertiveness and teach them to make constructive self-statements and to adopt a new set of beliefs that will result in assertive behavior.

Assertion training is often conducted in groups. When a group format is used, the modeling and instructions are presented to the entire group, and members rehearse behavioral skills in role-playing situations. After the rehearsal, the member is given feedback that consists of reinforcing the correct aspects of the behavior and instructions on how to improve the behavior. Each member engages in further rehearsals of assertive behaviors until the skills are performed adequately in a variety of simulated situations (Miltenberger, 2012).

Because assertion training is based on Western notions of the value of assertiveness, it may not be suited for clients with a cultural background that places more emphasis on harmony than on being assertive. This approach is not a panacea, but it can be an effective treatment for clients who have skill deficits in assertive behavior or for individuals who experience difficulties in their interpersonal relationships. Although counselors can adapt this form of social skills training procedures to suit their own style, it is important to include behavioral rehearsal and continual assessment as basic aspects of the program. If you are interested in learning more assertion training, consult *Your Perfect Right: A Guide to Assertive Behavior* (Alberti & Emmons, 2008).

Self-Management Programs and Self-Directed Behavior

For some time there has been a trend toward "giving psychology away." This involves psychologists being willing to share their knowledge so that "consumers" can increasingly lead self-directed lives and not be dependent on experts to deal with their problems. Psychologists who share this perspective are primarily concerned with teaching people the skills they will need to manage their own lives effectively. An advantage of self-management techniques is that treatment can be extended to the public in ways that cannot be done with traditional approaches to therapy. Another advantage is that costs are minimal. Because clients have a direct role in their own treatment, techniques aimed at self-change tend to increase involvement and commitment to their treatment.

Self-management strategies include self-monitoring, self-reward, self-contracting, and stimulus control. The basic idea of self-management assessments and interventions is that change can be brought about by teaching people to use coping skills in problematic situations. Generalization and maintenance of the outcomes are enhanced by encouraging clients to accept the responsibility for carrying out these strategies in daily life.

In self-management programs people make decisions concerning specific behaviors they want to control or change. People frequently discover that a major reason they do not attain their goals is the lack of certain skills or unrealistic expectations of change. Hope can be a therapeutic factor that leads to change, but unrealistic hope can pave the way for a pattern of failures in a self-change program. A self-directed approach can provide the guidelines for change and a plan that will lead to change.

For people to succeed in such a program, a careful analysis of the context of the behavior pattern is essential, and people must be willing to follow some basic steps such as those provided by Watson and Tharp (2007):

1. *Selecting goals.* Goals should be established one at a time, and they should be measurable, attainable, positive, and significant for you. It is essential that expectations be realistic.

2. *Translating goals into target behaviors.* Identify behaviors targeted for change. Once targets for change are selected, anticipate obstacles and think of ways to negotiate them.

3. *Self-monitoring.* Deliberately and systematically observe your own behavior, and keep a *behavioral diary*, recording the behavior along with comments about the relevant antecedent cues and consequences.

4. *Working out a plan for change.* Devise an action program to bring about actual change. Various plans for the same goal can be designed, each of which can be effective. Some type of self-reinforcement system is necessary in this plan because reinforcement is the cornerstone of modern behavior therapy. Self-reinforcement is a temporary strategy used until the new behaviors have been implemented in everyday life. Take steps to ensure that the gains made will be maintained.

5. *Evaluating an action plan.* Evaluate the plan for change to determine whether goals are being achieved, and adjust and revise the plan as other ways to meet goals are learned. Evaluation is an ongoing process rather than a one-time occurrence, and self-change is a lifelong practice.

Self-management strategies have been successfully applied to many populations and problems, a few of which include coping with panic attacks, helping children to cope with fear of the dark, increasing creative productivity, managing anxiety in social situations, encouraging speaking in front of a class, increasing exercise, control of smoking, and dealing with depression (Watson & Tharp, 2007). Research on self-management has been conducted in a wide variety of health problems, a few of which include arthritis, asthma, cancer, cardiac disease, substance abuse, diabetes, headaches, vision loss, depression, nutrition, and self-health care (Cormier et al., 2013).

Multimodal Therapy: Clinical Behavior Therapy

Multimodal therapy is a comprehensive, systematic, holistic approach to behavior therapy developed by Arnold Lazarus (1989, 1997a, 2005, 2008a). Lazarus (2008a) claims that the term "multimodal behavior therapy" is somewhat of a misnomer. Although the assessment process is multimodal, the treatment is cognitive behavioral and draws upon empirically supported methods. In terms of clinical practice, behavior therapy and multimodal therapy are very similar (Wilson, 2011). Multimodal therapy is grounded in social-cognitive theory and applies diverse behavioral techniques to a wide range of problems. This approach serves as a major link between some behavioral principles and the cognitive behavioral approach that has largely replaced traditional behavioral therapy.

Multimodal therapy is an open system that encourages *technical eclecticism* in that it applies diverse behavioral techniques to a wide range of problems. Multimodal therapists borrow techniques from many other therapy systems (Lazarus, 2008b). New techniques are constantly being introduced and existing techniques refined, but they are never used in a shotgun manner. Multimodal therapists take great pains to determine precisely what relationship and what treatment strategies will work best with each client and under which particular circumstances. The underlying assumption of this approach is that because individuals are troubled by a variety of specific problems it is appropriate that a multitude of treatment strategies be used in bringing about change. Therapeutic flexibility and versatility, along with breadth over depth, are highly valued, and multimodal therapists are constantly adjusting their procedures to achieve the client's goals. Therapists need to decide when and how to be challenging or supportive and how to adapt their relationship style to the needs of the client (Lazarus, 1993, 1997a). Multimodal therapists tend to be very active during therapist sessions, functioning as trainers, educators, consultants, coaches, and role models. They provide information, instruction, and feedback as well as modeling assertive behaviors. They offer suggestions, positive reinforcements, and are appropriately self-disclosing.

THE BASIC I.D. The essence of Lazarus's multimodal approach is the premise that the complex personality of human beings can be divided into seven major areas of functioning: B = behavior; A = affective responses; S = sensations; I = images; C = cognitions; I = interpersonal relationships; and D = drugs, biological functions, nutrition, and exercise (Lazarus, 1989, 1992a, 1992b, 1997a, 1997b, 2000, 2006).

Multimodal therapy begins with a comprehensive assessment of the seven modalities of human functioning and the interaction among them. A complete assessment and treatment program must account for each modality of the BASIC I.D., which is the cognitive map linking each aspect of personality. Table 9.1 outlines this process using questions Lazarus typically asks.

TABLE 9.1 The BASIC I.D. Assessment Process

MODALITY	BEHAVIORS	QUESTIONS TO ASK
Behavior	Overt behaviors, including acts, habits, and reactions that are observable and measurable	What would you like to change? How active are you? What would you like to start doing? What would you like to stop doing? What are some of your main strengths? What specific behaviors keep you from getting what you want?
Affect	Emotions, moods, and strong feelings	What emotions do you experience most often? What makes you laugh? What makes you cry? What makes you sad, mad, glad, scared? What emotions are problematic for you?
Sensation	Basic senses of touch, taste, smell, sight, and hearing	Do you suffer from unpleasant sensations, such as pains, aches, dizziness, and so forth? What do you particularly like or dislike in the way of seeing, smelling, hearing, touching, and tasting?
Imagery	How we picture ourselves, including memories, dreams, and fantasies	What are some bothersome recurring dreams and vivid memories? Do you have a vivid imagination? How do you view your body? How do you see yourself now? How would you like to be able to see yourself in the future?
Cognition	Insights, philosophies, ideas, opinions, self-talk, and judgments that constitute one's fundamental values, attitudes, and beliefs	What are some ways in which you meet your intellectual needs? How do your thoughts affect your emotions? What are the values and beliefs you most cherish? What are some negative things you say to yourself? What are some of your central faulty beliefs? What are the main 'shoulds,' 'oughts,' and 'musts' in your life? How do they get in the way of effective living?

Interpersonal relationships	Interactions with other people	How much of a social being are you? To what degree do you desire intimacy with others? What do you expect from the significant people in your life? What do they expect from you? Are there any relationships with others that you would hope to change? If so, what kinds of changes do you want?
Drugs/biology	Drugs, nutritional habits, and exercise patterns	Are you healthy and health conscious? Do you have any concerns about your health? Do you take any prescribed drugs? What are your habits pertaining to diet, exercise, and physical fitness?

Source: Lazarus 1989, 1997a, 2000.

A major premise of multimodal therapy is that *breadth* is often more important than *depth*. The more coping responses a client learns in therapy, the less chance there is for a relapse. Therapists identify one specific issue from each aspect of the BASIC I.D. framework as a target for change and teach clients a range of techniques they can use to combat faulty thinking, to learn to relax in stressful situations, and to acquire effective interpersonal skills. Clients can then apply these skills to a broad range of problems in their everyday lives.

The preliminary investigation of the BASIC I.D. framework brings out some central and significant themes that can be productively explored using a detailed life-history questionnaire. (See Lazarus and Lazarus, 2005, for the Multimodal Life-History Inventory.) Once the main profile of a person's BASIC I.D. has been established, the next step consists of an examination of the interactions among the different modalities. It is essential that therapists start where the client is and then move into other productive areas for exploration. Failure to comprehend the client's situation can easily leave the client feeling alienated and misunderstood (Lazarus, 2000). For an illustration of how Dr. Lazarus applies the BASIC I.D. assessment model to the case of Ruth, along with examples of various techniques he uses, see *Case Approach to Counseling and Psychotherapy* (Corey, 2013a, chap. 7).

Mindfulness and Acceptance-Based Cognitive Behavior Therapy

Over the last decade behavior therapy has evolved, resulting in an expansion of the behavioral tradition. Newer facets of cognitive behavior therapy, labeled the "third wave" of behavior therapy, emphasize considerations that were considered off limits for behavior therapists until recently, including mindfulness, acceptance, the therapeutic relationship, spirituality, values, meditation, being in the present moment, and emotional expression (Hayes, Follette, & Linehan, 2004; Herbert & Forman, 2011). Third-generation behavior therapies have been developed that center around five interrelated core themes: (1) an expanded view of psychological health, (2) a broad view of acceptable outcomes in therapy, (3) acceptance, (4) mindfulness, and (5) creating a life worth living (Spiegler & Guevremont, 2010).

Mindfulness involves being aware of our experiencing in a receptive way and engaging in activity based on this nonjudgmental awareness (Robins & Rosenthal, 2011). In mindfulness practice, clients train themselves to intentionally focus on their present experience while at the same time achieving a distance from it. Mindfulness involves developing an attitude of curiosity and compassion to present experience. Clients learn to focus on one thing at a time and to bring their attention back to the present moment when distractions arise.

As a clinical intervention, mindfulness shows promise across a broad range of clinical problems, including for depression, generalized anxiety disorder, relationship problems, and borderline personality disorder (Dimidjian & Linehan, 2008) as well as being useful in the treatment of posttraumatic stress disorder among military veterans. Through mindfulness exercises, veterans may be better able to observe repetitive negative thinking and prevent extensive engagement with maladaptive ruminative processes (Vujanovic, Niles, Pietrefesa, Schmertz, & Potter, 2011). Many therapeutic approaches are incorporating mindfulness, meditation, and other Eastern practices in the counseling process, and this trend seems likely to continue (Worthington, 2011).

Acceptance is a process involving receiving one's present experience without judgment or preference, but with curiosity and kindness, and striving for full awareness of the present moment (Germer, 2005b). Acceptance is not resigning oneself to life's problems; rather, it is an active process of self-affirmation (Wilson, 2011). Acceptance is an alternative way of responding to our internal experience. By replacing judgment, criticism, and avoidance with acceptance, the likely result is increased adaptive functioning (Antony & Roemer, 2011b). The mindfulness and acceptance approaches are good avenues for the integration of spirituality in the counseling process.

The subjects of mindfulness and acceptance are only briefly described in this chapter. For a useful and extensive discussion of these topics, see Herbert and Forman (2011), *Acceptance and Mindfulness in Cognitive Behavior Therapy: Understanding and Applying the New Therapies.*

The four major approaches in the recent development of the behavioral tradition include (1) *dialectical behavior therapy* (Linehan, 1993a, 1993b), which has become a recognized treatment for borderline personality disorder; (2) *mindfulness-based stress reduction* (Kabat-Zinn, 1990, 2003), which involves an 8- to 10-week group program applying mindfulness techniques to coping with stress and promoting physical and psychological health; (3) *mindfulness-based cognitive therapy* (Segal et al., 2002), which is aimed primarily at treating depression; and (4) *acceptance and commitment therapy* (Hayes, Strosahl, & Houts, 2005; Hayes, Strosahl, & Wilson, 2011), which is based on encouraging clients to accept, rather than attempt to control or change, unpleasant sensations. All four of these approaches use mindfulness strategies that have been subjected to empirical scrutiny, which is a hallmark of the behavioral tradition.

DIALECTICAL BEHAVIOR THERAPY (DBT) Formulated by Linehan (1993a, 1993b), DBT is a promising blend of behavioral and psychoanalytic techniques for treating borderline personality disorders. Like analytic therapy, DBT emphasizes the importance of the psychotherapeutic relationship, validation of the client, the etiologic importance of the client having experienced an "invalidating environment" as a child, and confrontation of resistance.

DBT treatment strategies include both acceptance- and change-oriented strategies. The treatment program is geared toward helping clients make changes in their behavior and environment, and at the same time communicating acceptance of their current state (Robins & Rosenthal, 2011). To help clients who have particular problems with emotional regulation, DBT teaches clients to recognize and accept the existence of simultaneous, opposing forces. By acknowledging this fundamental dialectic relationship—such as not wanting to engage in a certain behavior, yet knowing they have to engage in the behavior if they want to achieve a desired goal—clients can learn to integrate the opposing notions of acceptance and change, and the therapist can teach clients how to regulate their emotions and behaviors. Mindfulness procedures are taught and practiced to develop an attitude of acceptance (Fishman, Rego, & Muller, 2011).

DBT employs behavioral and cognitive behavioral techniques, including a form of exposure therapy in which the client learns to tolerate painful emotions without enacting self-destructive behaviors. DBT integrates its cognitive behaviorism not only with analytic concepts but also with the mindfulness training of "Eastern psychological and spiritual practices (primarily Zen practice)" (Linehan, 1993b, p. 6). Many of the treatment strategies used and skills taught in DBT have roots in Zen Buddhist principles and practices. These include being aware of the present moment, seeing reality without distortion, accepting reality without judgment, letting go of attachments that result in suffering, developing a greater degree of acceptance of self and others, and entering fully into present activities without separating oneself from ongoing events and interactions (Robins & Rosenthal, 2011).

DBT is highly structured, but goals are tailored to each individual. Therapists assist clients in using whatever skills they possess or are learning to navigate crises more effectively and to address problem behaviors (Robins & Rosenthal, 2011). Skills are taught in four modules: mindfulness, interpersonal effectiveness, emotional regulation, and distress tolerance (Simpson, 2011). *Mindfulness* is a fundamental skill in DBT and is considered the basis for other skills taught. Mindfulness helps clients to embrace and tolerate the intense emotions they experience when facing distressing situations. *Interpersonal effectiveness* involves learning to ask for what one needs and learning to cope with interpersonal conflict. This skill entails increasing the chances that a client's goals will be met, while at the same time not damaging the relationship. *Emotion regulation* includes identifying emotions, identifying obstacles to changing emotions, reducing vulnerability, and increasing positive emotions. Clients learn the benefits of regulating emotions such as anger, depression, and anxiety. *Distress tolerance* is aimed at helping individuals to calmly recognizing emotions associated with negative situations without becoming overwhelmed by these situations. Clients learn how to tolerate pain or discomfort skillfully. These skills are the route clients can take in achieving their goals. "The therapy aims to assist clients to learn to control behavior, fully experience emotions, improve daily living skills, and achieve a sense of completeness" (Simpson, 2011, p. 230).

DBT skills training is not a "quick fix" approach. It generally involves a minimum of one year of treatment and includes both individual therapy and skills training done in a group. DBT requires a behavioral contract. To competently practice DBT, it is essential to obtain training in this approach. Because DBT places heavy emphasis on didactic instruction and teaching mindfulness skills, therapists must be competent in applying these skills and be able to model specific strategies and attitudes for clients. Therapists who want to employ mindfulness strategies must also have personal understanding and experience of these interventions to be able to effectively use them with clients (Dimidjian & Linehan, 2008). A useful resource for a more detailed discussion of DBT is Robins and Rosenthal (2011).

MINDFULNESS-BASED STRESS REDUCTION (MBSR) The essence of mindfulness-based stress reduction (MBSR) consists of the notion that much of our distress and suffering results from continually wanting things to be different from how they actually are (Salmon, Sephton, & Dreeben, 2011). MBSR aims to assist people in learning how to live more fully in the present rather than ruminating about the past or being overly concerned about the future. MBSR does not actively teach cognitive modification techniques, nor does it label certain cognitions as "dysfunctional," because this is not consistent with the nonjudgmental attitude one strives to cultivate in mindfulness practice.

The approach adopted in the MBSR program is to develop the capacity for sustained directed attention through formal meditation practice. The skills taught include sitting meditation and mindful yoga, which are aimed at cultivating mindfulness. The program includes a body scan meditation, which helps clients to observe all the sensations in their body. Clients are encouraged to bring mindfulness into all of their daily activities, including standing, walking, and eating. Those who are involved in the program are encouraged to practice formal mindfulness meditation for 45 minutes daily. The MBSR program is designed to teach participants to relate to external and internal sources of stress in constructive ways. MBSR places a heavy emphasis on experiential learning and the process of client self-discovery (Dimidjian & Linehan, 2008). MBSR has many clinical applications, and it is expected that the approach will evolve to address a range of negative psychological states, such as anxiety, stress, and depression. This approach has many applications in the area of health and wellness and in promoting healthy lifestyle changes. An excellent resource for a more detailed treatment of MBSR is Salmon, Sephton, and Dreeben (2011).

MINDFULNESS-BASED COGNITIVE THERAPY (MBCT) This program is a comprehensive integration of the principles and skills of mindfulness applied to the treatment of depression (Segal, Williams, & Teasdale, 2002). MBCT is an 8-week group treatment program adapted from Kabat-Zinn's (1990) mindfulness-based stress reduction program, and it includes components of cognitive behavior therapy. MBCT represents an integration of techniques from MBSR and teaching cognitive behavioral interventions to clients. The primary aim is to change clients' awareness of and relation to their negative thoughts. Participants are taught how to respond in skillful and intentional ways to their automatic negative thought patterns. Fesco, Flynn, Mennin, and Haigh (2011) describe the essence of the seven sessions in the MBCT program:

- Therapy begins by identifying negative automatic thinking of people experiencing depression and by introducing some basic mindfulness practices.
- In the second session, participants learn about the reactions they have to life experiences and learn more about mindfulness practices.
- The third session is devoted to teaching breathing techniques and focused attention on their present experiencing.
- In session four, the emphasis is on learning to experience the moment without becoming attached to outcomes as a way to prevent relapse.
- The fifth session teaches participants how to accept their experiencing without holding on.
- Session six is used to describe thoughts as "merely thoughts;" clients learn that they do not have to act on their thoughts. They can tell themselves, "I am not my thoughts" and "Thoughts are not facts."
- In the final sessions, participants learn how to take care of themselves, to prepare for relapse, and to generalize their mindfulness practices to daily life.

MBCT emphasizes experiential learning, in-session practice, learning from feedback, completing homework assignments, and applying what is learned in the program to challenging situations encountered outside of the sessions. The brevity of MBCT makes this approach an efficient and cost-effective treatment. For a more detailed review of MBCT, see Fresco, Flynn, Mennin, and Haigh (2011).

ACCEPTANCE AND COMMITMENT THERAPY (ACT) Another mindfulness-based approach is *acceptance and commitment therapy* (Hayes et al., 2005, 2011), which involves fully accepting present experience and mindfully letting go of obstacles. In this approach "acceptance is not merely tolerance—rather it is the active nonjudgmental embracing of experience in the here and now" (Hayes, 2004, p. 32). Acceptance is a stance or posture from which to conduct therapy and from which a client can conduct life that provides an alternative to contemporary forms of cognitive behavioral therapy (Eifert & Forsyth, 2005). In contrast to the cognitive behavioral approaches discussed in Chapter 10, in which dysfunctional thoughts are identified and challenged, in ACT there is little emphasis on changing the content of a client's thoughts. Instead, the emphasis is on *acceptance* (nonjudgmental awareness) of cognitions. The goal is for individuals to become aware of and examine their thoughts. Clients learn how to change their relationship to their thoughts. They learn how to accept and distance themselves from the thoughts and feelings they may have been trying to deny. Hayes has found that confronting maladaptive cognitions actually strengthens rather than reduces these cognitions. The goal of ACT is to allow for increased psychological flexibility. Values are a basic part of the therapeutic process, and ACT practitioners might ask clients, "What do you want your life to stand for?" Therapy involves assisting clients to choose values they want to live by, designing specific goals, and taking steps to achieve their goals (Wilson, 2011).

In addition to acceptance, commitment to action is essential. *Commitment* involves making mindful decisions about what is important in life and what the person is willing to do to live a valued and meaningful life (Wilson, 2011). ACT makes use of concrete homework and behavioral exercises as a way to create larger patterns of effective action that will help clients live by their values (Hayes, 2004). For example, one form of homework given to clients is asking them to write down life goals or things they value in various aspects of their lives. The focus of ACT is allowing experience to come and go while pursuing a meaningful life.

ACT is an effective form of therapy (Eifert & Forsyth, 2005) that continues to influence the practice of behavior therapy. Germer (2005a) suggests "mindfulness might become a construct that draws clinical theory, research, and practice closer together, and helps integrate the private and professional lives of therapists" (p. 11). According to Wilson (2011), ACT emphasizes common processes across clinical disorders, which makes it easier to learn basic treatment skills. Practitioners can then implement basic principles in diverse and creative ways. ACT has been effective for treatment of a variety of disorders, including for substance abuse, depression, anxiety, phobias, posttraumatic stress disorder, and panic disorder (Eifert & Forsyth, 2005).

For an in-depth discussion of the role of mindfulness in psychotherapeutic practice, three highly recommended readings are *Acceptance and Mindfulness in Cognitive Behavior Therapy: Understanding and Applying the New Therapies* (Herbert & Forman, 2011), *Mindfulness and Acceptance: Expanding the Cognitive-Behavioral Tradition* (Hayes et al., 2004), and *Mindfulness and Psychotherapy* (Germer et al., 2005).

Application to Group Counseling

Group-based behavioral approaches emphasize teaching clients self-management skills and a range of new coping behaviors, as well as how to restructure their thoughts. Clients can learn to use these techniques to control their lives, deal effectively with present and future problems, and function well after they complete their group experience. Many groups are designed primarily to increase the client's degree of control and freedom in specific aspects of daily life.

Group leaders who function within a behavioral framework may develop techniques from various theoretical viewpoints. Behavioral practitioners make use of a brief, active, directive, structured, collaborative, psychoeducational model of therapy that relies on empirical validation of its concepts and techniques. The leader follows the progress of group members through the ongoing collection of data *before*, *during*, and *after* all interventions. Such an approach provides both the group leader and the members with continuous feedback about therapeutic progress. Today, many groups in community agencies demand this kind of accountability.

Behavioral group therapy has some unique characteristics that set it apart from most of the other group approaches. A distinguishing characteristic of behavioral practitioners is their systematic adherence to specification and measurement. The specific unique characteristics of behavioral group therapy include (1) conducting a behavioral assessment, (2) precisely spelling out collaborative treatment goals, (3) formulating a specific treatment procedure appropriate to a particular problem, and (4) objectively evaluating the outcomes of therapy. Behavior therapists tend to utilize short-term, time-limited interventions aimed at efficiently and effectively solving problems and assisting members in developing new skills.

Behavioral group leaders assume the role of teacher and encourage members to learn and practice skills in the group that they can apply to everyday living. Group leaders typically assume an active, directive, and supportive role in the group and apply their knowledge of behavioral principles and skills to the resolution of problems. They model active participation and collaboration by their involvement with members in creating an agenda, designing homework, and teaching skills and new behaviors. Leaders carefully observe and assess behavior to determine the conditions that are related to certain problems and the conditions that will facilitate change. Members in behavioral groups identify specific skills that they lack or would like to enhance. Assertiveness and social skills training fit well into a group format (Wilson, 2011). Relaxation procedures, behavioral rehearsal, modeling, coaching, meditation, and mindfulness techniques are often incorporated in behavioral groups. The experience of being mindful is expanded in the group setting where people meditate and are still in the presence of others. Most of the other techniques described earlier in this chapter can be applied to group work.

There are many different types of groups with a behavioral twist, or groups that blend both behavioral and cognitive methods for specific populations. Structured groups, with a psychoeducational focus, are especially popular in various settings today. At least five general approaches can be applied to the practice of behavioral groups: (1) social skills training groups, (2) psychoeducational groups with specific themes, (3) stress management groups, (4) multimodal group therapy, and (5) mindfulness and acceptance-based behavior therapy in groups.

For a more detailed discussion of cognitive behavioral approaches to groups, see Corey (2012, chap.13).

BEHAVIOR THERAPY FROM A MULTICULTURAL PERSPECTIVE

Strengths From a Diversity Perspective

Behavior therapy has some clear advantages over many other theories in counseling culturally diverse clients. Because of their cultural and ethnic backgrounds, some clients hold values that are contrary to the free expression of feelings and the sharing of personal concerns. Behavioral counseling does not generally place emphasis on experiencing catharsis. Rather, it stresses changing specific behaviors and developing problem-solving skills. Some potential strengths of the behavioral approaches in working with diverse client populations include its specificity, task orientation, focus on objectivity, focus on cognition and behavior, action orientation, dealing with the present more than the past, emphasis on brief interventions, teaching coping strategies, and problem-solving orientation. The attention given to transfer of learning and the principles and strategies for maintaining new behavior in daily life are crucial. Clients who are looking for action plans and specific behavioral change are likely to cooperate with this approach because they can see that it offers them concrete methods for dealing with their problems of living.

Behavior therapy focuses on environmental conditions that contribute to a client's problems. Social and political influences can play a significant role in the lives of people of color through discriminatory practices and economic problems, and the behavioral approach takes into consideration the social and cultural dimensions of the client's life. Behavior therapy is based on an experimental analysis of behavior in the client's own social environment and gives special attention to a number of specific conditions: the client's cultural conception of problem behaviors, establishing specific therapeutic goals, arranging conditions to increase the client's expectation of successful therapeutic outcomes, and employing appropriate social influence agents (Tanaka-Matsumi et al., 2002). The foundation of ethical practice involves a therapist's familiarity with the client's culture, as well as the competent application of this knowledge in formulating assessment, diagnostic, and treatment strategies.

The behavioral approach has moved beyond treating clients for a specific symptom or behavioral problem. Instead, it stresses a thorough assessment of the person's life circumstances to ascertain not only what conditions give rise to the client's problems but also whether the target behavior is amenable to change and whether such a change is likely to lead to a significant improvement in the client's total life situation.

In designing a change program for clients from diverse backgrounds, effective behavioral practitioners conduct a functional analysis of the problem situation. This assessment includes the cultural context in which the problem behavior occurs, the consequences both to the client and to the client's sociocultural environment, the resources within the environment that can promote change, and the impact that change is likely to have on others in the client's social surroundings. Assessment methods should be chosen with the client's cultural background in mind (Spiegler & Guevremont, 2010; Tanaka-Matsumi et al., 2002). Counselors must be knowledgeable as well as open and sensitive to issues such as these: What is considered normal and abnormal behavior in the client's culture? What are the client's culturally based conceptions of his or her problems? What is the potential role of spirituality or religion in the client's life? What kind of information about the client is essential in making an accurate assessment?

Shortcomings From a Diversity Perspective

According to Spiegler and Guevremont (2010), a future challenge for behavior therapists is to develop empirically based recommendations for how behavior therapy can optimally serve culturally diverse clients. Although behavior therapy is sensitive to differences among clients in a broad sense, behavior therapists need to become more responsive to *specific* issues pertaining to all forms of diversity. Because race, gender, ethnicity, and sexual orientation are critical variables that influence the process and outcome of therapy, it is essential that behavior therapists pay careful attention to these factors and address social justice issues as they arise in a client's therapy.

Some behavioral counselors may focus on using a variety of techniques in narrowly treating specific behavioral problems. Instead of viewing clients in the context of their sociocultural environment, these practitioners concentrate too much on problems within the individual. In doing so they may overlook significant issues in the lives of clients. Such practitioners are not likely to bring about beneficial changes for their clients.

The fact that behavioral interventions often work well raises an interesting issue in multicultural counseling. When clients make significant personal changes, it is very likely that others in their environment will react to them differently. Before deciding too quickly on goals for therapy, the counselor and client need to discuss the complexity inherent in change. It is essential for therapists to conduct a thorough assessment of the interpersonal and cultural dimensions of the problem. Clients should be helped in assessing the possible consequences of some of their newly acquired social skills. Once goals are determined and therapy is under way, clients should have opportunities to talk about the problems they encounter as they bring new skills and behaviors into their home and work settings.

Behavior Therapy Applied to the Case of Stan

In Stan's case many specific and interrelated problems can be identified through an assessment process. *Behaviorally*, he is defensive, avoids eye contact, speaks hesitantly, uses alcohol excessively, has a poor sleep pattern, and displays various avoidance behaviors in social and interpersonal situations. In the *emotional* area, Stan has a number of specific problems, some of which include anxiety, panic attacks, depression, fear of criticism and rejection, feeling worthless and stupid, and feeling isolated and alienated. He experiences a range of physiological complaints such as dizziness, heart palpitations, and headaches. *Cognitively*, he worries about death and dying, has many self-defeating thoughts and beliefs, is governed by categorical imperatives ("shoulds," "oughts," "musts"), engages in fatalistic thinking, and compares himself negatively with others. In the *interpersonal* area, Stan is unassertive, has an unsatisfactory relationship with his parents, has few friends, is afraid of contact with women and fears intimacy, and feels socially inferior.

After completing this assessment, I focus on helping Stan define the specific areas where he would like to make changes. Before developing a treatment plan, I assist Stan in understanding the purposes of his behavior. I then educate Stan about how the therapy sessions (and his work outside of the sessions) can help him reach his goals. Early during treatment I help Stan translate some of his general goals into concrete and measurable ones. When Stan says, "I want to feel better about myself," I help him define more specific goals. When he says, "I want to get rid of my inferiority complex," I reply: "What exactly do you mean by this?" "What are some situations in which you feel inferior?" "What do you actually do that leads to feelings of inferiority?" Stan's concrete aims include his desire to function without drugs or alcohol. I suggest that he keep a record of when he drinks and what events lead to drinking. My hope is that Stan will establish goals that are based on positive markers, not negative goals. Instead of focusing on what Stan would like to get rid of, I am more interested in what he would like to acquire and develop.

Stan indicates that he does not want to feel apologetic for his existence. I introduce behavioral skills training because he has trouble talking with his boss and coworkers. I demonstrate specific skills that he can use in approaching them more directly and confidently. This procedure includes modeling, role playing, and behavior rehearsal. He then tries more effective behaviors with me as I play the role of the boss. I give him feedback on how strong or apologetic he seemed.

Imaginal exposure and systematic desensitization are appropriate in working with Stan's fear of failing. Before using these procedures, I explain the procedure to Stan and get his informed consent. Stan first learns relaxation procedures during the sessions and then practices them daily at home. Next, he lists his specific fears relating to failure, and he then generates a hierarchy of fear items. Stan identifies his greatest fear as fear of dating and interacting with women. The least fearful situation he identifies is being with a female student for whom he does not feel an attraction. I first do some systematic desensitization on Stan's hierarchy. Stan begins repeated, systematic exposure to items that he finds frightening, beginning at the bottom of the fear hierarchy. He continues with repeated exposure to the next fear hierarchy item when exposure to the previous item generates only mild fear. Part of the process involves exposure exercises for practice in various situations away from the therapy office.

The goal of therapy is to help Stan modify the behavior that results in his feelings of guilt and anxiety. By learning more appropriate coping behaviors, eliminating unrealistic anxiety and guilt, and acquiring more adaptive responses, Stan's presenting symptoms decrease, and he reports a greater degree of satisfaction.

Follow-Up: You Continue as Stan's Behavior Therapist

Use these questions to help you think about how you would work with Stan using a behavioral approach:

- How would you collaboratively work with Stan in identifying specific behavioral goals to give a direction to your therapy?
- What behavioral techniques might be most appropriate in helping Stan with his problems?
- Stan indicates that he does not want to feel apologetic for his existence. How might you help him translate this wish into a specific behavioral goal? What behavioral techniques might you draw on in helping him in this area?
- What homework assignments are you likely to suggest for Stan?

See DVD for Theory and Practice of Counseling and Psychotherapy: The Case of Stan and Lecturettes (Session 7 on behavior therapy) for a demonstration of my approach to counseling Stan from this perspective. This session involves collaboratively working on homework and behavior rehearsals to experiment with assertive behavior.

SUMMARY AND EVALUATION

Summary

Behavior therapy is diverse with respect not only to basic concepts but also to techniques that can be applied in coping with specific problems with a wide range of clients. The behavioral movement includes four major areas of development: classical conditioning, operant conditioning, social-cognitive theory, and increasing attention to the cognitive factors influencing behavior (see Chapter 10). A unique characteristic of behavior therapy is its strict reliance on the principles of the scientific method. Concepts and procedures are stated explicitly, tested empirically, and revised continually. Treatment and assessment are interrelated and occur simultaneously. Research is considered to be a basic aspect of the approach, and therapeutic techniques are continually refined.

A cornerstone of behavior therapy is identifying specific goals at the outset of the therapeutic process. In helping clients achieve their goals, behavior therapists typically assume an active and directive role. Although the client generally determines *what* behavior will be changed, the therapist typically determines *how* this behavior can best be modified. In designing a treatment plan, behavior therapists employ techniques and procedures from a wide variety of therapeutic systems and apply them to the unique needs of each client.

Contemporary behavior therapy places emphasis on the interplay between the individual and the environment. Behavioral strategies can be used to attain both individual goals and societal goals. Because cognitive factors have a place in the practice of behavior therapy, techniques from this approach can be used to attain humanistic ends. It is clear that bridges can connect humanistic and behavioral therapies, especially with the current focus of attention on self-management approaches and also with the incorporation of mindfulness and acceptance-based approaches into behavioral practice. Mindfulness practices rely of experiential learning as opposed to didactic instruction and client discovery rather than formal teaching (Dimidjian & Linehan, 2008).

Contributions of Behavior Therapy

Behavior therapy challenges us to reconsider our global approach to counseling. Some may assume they know what a client means by the statement, "I feel unloved; life has no meaning." A humanist might nod in acceptance to such a statement, but the behaviorist may respond with: "Who specifically do you feel is not loving you?" "What is going on in your life to make you think it has no meaning?" "What are some specific things you might be doing that contribute to the state you are in?" "What would you most like to change?" The specificity of the behavioral approaches helps clients translate unclear goals into concrete plans of action, and it helps both the counselor and the client to keep these plans clearly in focus. Ledley and colleagues (2010) state that therapists can help clients to learn about the contingencies that maintain their problematic thoughts and behaviors and then teach them ways to make the changes they want. Techniques such as role playing, relaxation procedures, behavioral rehearsal, coaching, guided practice, modeling, feedback, learning by successive approximations, mindfulness skills, and homework assignments can be included in any therapist's repertoire, regardless of theoretical orientation.

An advantage behavior therapists have is the wide variety of specific behavioral techniques at their disposal. Because behavior therapy stresses *doing*, as opposed to merely talking about problems and gathering insights, practitioners use many behavioral strategies to assist clients in formulating a plan of action for changing behavior. The basic therapeutic conditions stressed by person-centered therapists—active listening, accurate empathy, positive regard, genuineness, respect, and immediacy—need to be integrated in a behavioral framework.

A major contribution of behavior therapy is its emphasis on research into and assessment of treatment outcomes. It is up to practitioners to demonstrate that therapy is working. If progress is not being made, therapists look carefully at the original analysis and treatment plan. Of all the therapies presented in this book, this approach and its techniques have been subjected to the most empirical research. Behavioral practitioners are put to the test of identifying specific interventions that have been demonstrated to be effective. Fishman, Rego, and Muller (2011) acknowledge the evolving nature of these therapies but conclude:

> We believe the core of behavior therapy will endure in a commitment to theory that is scholarly, logically clear, directly linked to data, and primarily rooted in the interactional worldview; to therapy principles and procedures that are evidenced-based; to measurement methods designed to ensure accountability; and to a focus on outcomes that result in concrete improvement in patients' lives. (p. 135)

Evidence-based therapies (EBT) are a hallmark of both behavior therapy and cognitive behavior therapy. To their credit, behavior therapists are willing to examine the effectiveness of their procedures in terms of the generalizability, meaningfulness, and durability of change. Most studies show that behavior therapy methods are more effective than no treatment. Moreover, a number of behavioral and cognitive behavioral procedures are currently the best treatment strategies available for depression, obsessive-compulsive disorder, panic disorder, social phobia, hypochondriasis, generalized anxiety disorder, posttraumatic stress disorder, eating disorders, borderline personality disorder, bipolar disorder, and childhood disorders (Hollon & DiGiuseppe, 2011).

A strength of the behavioral approaches is the emphasis on ethical accountability. Behavior therapy is ethically neutral in that it does not dictate whose behavior or what behavior should be changed. At least in cases of voluntary counseling, the behavioral practitioner only specifies *how* to change those behaviors the client targets for change. Clients have a good deal of control and freedom in deciding *what* the goals of therapy will be.

Limitations and Criticisms of Behavior Therapy

Behavior therapy has been criticized for a variety of reasons. Let's examine four common criticisms and misconceptions people often have about behavior therapy, together with my reactions.

1. *Behavior therapy may change behaviors, but it does not change feelings.* Some critics argue that feelings must change before behavior can change. Behavioral practitioners hold that empirical evidence has not shown that feelings must be changed first, and behavioral clinicians do in actual practice deal with feelings as an overall part of the treatment process. A general criticism of both the behavioral and the cognitive approaches is that clients are not encouraged to experience their emotions. In concentrating on how clients are behaving or thinking, some behavior therapists tend to play down the working through of emotional issues. Generally, I favor initially focusing on what clients are feeling and then working with the behavioral and cognitive dimensions. My reasoning here is that I find when clients are feeling they are engaged and this seems to me to be a good point of departure. I can still tie a discussion of what clients are feeling with how this is affecting their behavior and I can later inquire about their cognitions.

2. *Behavior therapy does not provide insight.* If this assertion is indeed true, behavior therapists would probably respond that insight is not a necessary requisite for behavior change. Follette and Callaghan (2011) state that contemporary behavior therapists tend to be leery of the role of insight in favor of alterable, controllable, causal variables. It is possible for therapy to proceed without a client knowing how change is taking place. Although change may be taking place, clients often cannot explain precisely why. Furthermore, insights may result after clients make a change in behavior. Behavioral shifts often lead to a change in understanding or to insight, which may lead to emotional changes as well.

3. *Behavior therapy treats symptoms rather than causes.* The psychoanalytic assumption is that early traumatic events are at the root of present dysfunction. Behavior therapists may acknowledge that deviant responses have historical origins, but they contend that history is less important in the maintenance of current problems than environmental events such as antecedents and consequences. However, behavior therapists emphasize changing current environmental circumstances to change behavior.

Related to this criticism is the notion that, unless historical causes of present behavior are therapeutically explored, new symptoms will soon take the place of those that were "cured." Behaviorists rebut this assertion on both theoretical and empirical grounds. They contend that behavior therapy directly changes the maintaining conditions, which are the causes of problem behaviors (symptoms). Furthermore, they assert that there is no empirical evidence that symptom substitution occurs after behavior therapy has successfully eliminated unwanted behavior because they have changed the conditions that give rise to those behaviors (Kazdin & Wilson, 1978; Spiegler & Guevremont, 2010).

4. *Behavior therapy involves control and social influence by the therapist.* All therapists have a power relationship with the client and thus have control. According to Wilson (2011), all forms of therapy involve social influence; the ethical issue relates to the therapist's degree of awareness of this influence and how it is addressed in therapy. Behavior therapy recognizes the importance of making the social influence process explicit, and it emphasizes client-oriented behavioral goals. Therapists collaborate with clients to make sure there is a mutual agreement regarding treatment goals (Antony & Roemer, 2011b), and the client is encouraged to become an active participant in his or her therapy. Therapy progress is continually assessed and treatment is modified to ensure that the client's goals are being met.

Behavior therapists address ethical issues by stating that therapy is basically a psychoeducational process (Tanaka-Matsumi et al., 2002). At the outset of behavior therapy, clients learn about the nature of counseling, the procedures that may be employed, and the benefits and risks. Clients are given information about the specific therapy procedures appropriate for their particular problems. To some extent, they also participate in the choice of techniques that will be used in dealing with their problems. With this information clients become informed, fully enfranchised partners in the therapeutic venture.

The literature in the field of behavior therapy is so extensive and diverse that it is not possible in one brief survey chapter to present a comprehensive, in-depth discussion of behavioral techniques. I hope I have encouraged you to examine any misconceptions you may hold about behavior therapy. I urge you to examine some of the selected sources in the following section to further your knowledge of this complex approach.

WHERE TO GO FROM HERE

In the *DVD for Integrative Counseling: The Case of Ruth and Lecturettes,* Session 8 ("Behavioral Focus in Counseling"), I demonstrate a behavioral way to assist Ruth in developing an exercise program. It is crucial that Ruth makes her own decisions about specific behavioral goals she wants to pursue. This applies to my attempts to work with her in developing methods of relaxation, increasing her self-efficacy, and designing an exercise plan.

Other Resources

DVDs offered by the American Psychological Association that are relevant to this chapter include the following:

> Antony, M. M. (2009). *Behavioral Therapy Over Time* (APA Psychotherapy Video Series)
>
> Hayes, S. C. (2011). *Acceptance and Commitment Therapy* (Systems of Psychotherapy Video Series)

Psychotherapy.net is a comprehensive resource for students and professionals that offers videos and interviews on behavior therapy. New video and editorial content is made available monthly. DVDs relevant to this chapter are available at www.psychotherapy.net and include the following:

> Stuart, R. (1998). *Behavioral Couples Therapy* (Couples Therapy With the Experts Series)

Association for Behavioral and Cognitive Therapies (ABCT)

305 Seventh Avenue, 16th Floor
New York, NY 10001-6008
Telephone: (212) 647-1890
Fax: (212) 647-1865
E-mail: membership@abct.org
Website: www.abct.org

If you have an interest in further training in behavior therapy, the Association for Behavioral and Cognitive Therapies (ABCT) is an excellent resource. ABCT (formerly AABT) is a membership organization of more than 4,500 mental health professionals and students who are interested in behavior therapy, cognitive behavior therapy, behavioral assessment, and applied behavioral analysis. Full and associate memberships are $199 and include one journal subscription (to either *Behavior Therapy* or *Cognitive and Behavioral Practice*), and a subscription to the *Behavior Therapist* (a newsletter with feature articles, training updates, and association news). Membership also includes reduced registration and continuing education course fees for ABCT's annual convention held in November, which features workshops, master clinician programs, symposia, and other educational presentations. Student memberships are $49. Members receive discounts on all ABCT publications, some of which are:

- *Directory of Graduate Training in Behavior Therapy and Experimental-Clinical Psychology* is an excellent source for students and job seekers who want information on programs with an emphasis on behavioral training.

- *Directory of Psychology Internships: Programs Offering Behavioral Training* describes training programs having a behavioral component.
- *Behavior Therapy* is an international quarterly journal focusing on original experimental and clinical research, theory, and practice.
- *Cognitive and Behavioral Practice* is a quarterly journal that features clinically oriented articles.

Cognitive Behavior Therapy

ALBERT ELLIS / AARON T. BECK / JUDITH S. BECK / DONALD MEICHENBAUM

Photo Courtesy of Albert Ellis Institute

ALBERT ELLIS (1913–2007) was born in Pittsburgh but escaped to the wilds of New York at the age of 4 and lived there (except for a year in New Jersey) for the rest of his life. He was hospitalized nine times as a child, mainly with nephritis, and developed renal glycosuria at the age of 19 and diabetes at the age of 40. Despite his many physical challenges, he lived an unusually robust, active, and energetic life until his death at age 93. As he put it, "I am busy spreading the gospel according to St. Albert."

Realizing that he could counsel people skillfully and that he greatly enjoyed doing so, Ellis decided to become a psychologist. Believing psychoanalysis to be the deepest form of psychotherapy, Ellis was analyzed and supervised by a training analyst. He then practiced psychoanalytically oriented psychotherapy, but eventually he became disillusioned with the slow progress of his clients. He observed that they improved more quickly once they changed their ways of thinking about themselves and their problems. Early in 1955 he developed an approach to psychotherapy he called rational therapy and later rational emotive therapy, and which is now known as rational emotive behavior therapy (REBT). Ellis has rightly been referred to as the grandfather of cognitive behavior therapy.

To some extent Ellis developed his approach as a method of dealing with his own problems during his youth. At one point in his life, for example, he had exaggerated fears of speaking in public. During his adolescence he was extremely shy around young women. At age 19 he forced himself to talk to 100 different women in the Bronx Botanical Gardens over a period of one month. Although he never managed to get a date from these brief encounters, he does report that he desensitized himself to his fear of rejection by women. By applying rational and behavioral methods, he managed to conquer some of his strongest emotional blocks (Ellis, 1994, 1997).

People who heard Ellis lecture often commented on his abrasive, humorous, and flamboyant style. In his workshops it seemed that he took delight in giving vent to his eccentric side, such as peppering his speech with four-letter words. He greatly enjoyed his work and teaching REBT, which was his passion and primary commitment in life. It seems that his work was his life, and he gave workshops wherever he went in his travels. Ellis proclaimed, "I wouldn't go to the Taj Mahal unless they asked me to do a workshop there!"

Ellis married Australian psychologist Debbie Joffe in November 2004, whom he has called "the greatest love of my life" (Ellis, 2008). They shared the same life goals and ideals, and they worked as a team presenting workshops. If you are interested in learning more about the life and work of Albert Ellis, I recommend two of his books: *Rational Emotive Behavior Therapy: It Works for Me—It Can Work for You* (Ellis, 2004a) and *All Out! An Autobiography* (Ellis, 2010).

Courtesy of Beck Institute for Cognitive Behavior Therapy, Bala Cynwyd, PA.

AARON TEMKIN BECK (b. 1921) was born in Providence, Rhode Island. His childhood, although happy, was interrupted by a life-threatening illness when he was 8 years old. As a consequence, he experienced blood injury fears, fear of suffocation, and anxiety about his health. Beck used his personal problems as a basis for understanding others and for developing his cognitive theory.

A graduate of Brown University and Yale School of Medicine, Beck initially was trained as a neurologist, but he switched to psychiatry during his residency. Beck attempted to validate Freud's theory of depression, but his research resulted in his parting company with Freud's motivational model and the explanation of depression as self-directed anger. As a result of this decision, Beck endured isolation and rejection from many in the psychiatric community for many years. Through his research, Beck developed a cognitive theory of depression, which represents one of the most comprehensive conceptualizations. He found the cognitions of depressed individuals to be characterized by errors in interpretation that he called "cognitive distortions." For Beck, negative thoughts reflect underlying dysfunctional beliefs and assumptions. When these beliefs are triggered by situational events, a depressive pattern is put in motion. Beck believes clients can assume an active role in modifying their dysfunctional thinking and thereby gain relief from a range of psychiatric conditions. His continuous research in the areas of psychopathology and the utility of cognitive therapy has earned him a place of prominence in the scientific community in the United States. Beck is the pioneering figure in cognitive therapy, one of the most influential and empirically validated approaches to psychotherapy.

Beck joined the Department of Psychiatry of the University of Pennsylvania in 1954, where he currently holds the position of University Professor (Emeritus) of Psychiatry. Beck's pioneering research established the efficacy of cognitive therapy for

Courtesy of Beck Institute for Cognitive Behavior Therapy, Bala Cynwyd, PA.

JUDITH S. BECK (b. 1954) was born in Philadelphia, the second of four children. Both her parents were quite notable in their fields: her father, as "the father of cognitive therapy," and her mother, as the first female judge on the appellate court of the Commonwealth of Pennsylvania. From an early age, Beck wanted to be an educator, and she began her professional career teaching children with learning disabilities. Her ability to break down complex subjects into easily understandable ideas, so critical in the education of children with learning differences, is characteristic of all her work.

Beck later returned to graduate school, studied education and psychology, and completed a postdoctoral fellowship at the Center for Cognitive Behavior Therapy at the University of Pennsylvania. In 1994 she and her father opened the nonprofit Beck Institute for Cognitive Therapy in suburban Philadelphia, and she is currently president of the institute. A premier training organization, the institute is devoted to national and international training in cognitive therapy through workshop

depression. He has successfully applied cognitive therapy to depression, generalized anxiety and panic disorders, suicide, alcoholism and drug abuse, eating disorders, marital and relationship problems, psychotic disorders, and personality disorders. He has developed assessment scales for depression, suicide risk, anxiety, self-concept, and personality.

He is the founder of the Beck Institute, which is a research and training center directed by one of his four children, Dr. Judith Beck. He has eight grandchildren and two great-grandchildren and has been married for more than 60 years. To his credit, Aaron Beck has focused on developing the cognitive therapy skills of thousands of clinicians throughout the world. In turn, many of them have established their own cognitive therapy centers. Beck has a vision for the cognitive therapy community that is global, inclusive, collaborative, empowering, and benevolent. He continues to remain active in writing and research; he has published 21 books and more than 450 articles and book chapters. For more on the life of Aaron T. Beck, see *Aaron T. Beck* (Weishaar, 1993).

and supervision programs for students and faculty, deployed and returning military families, health and mental health professionals at all levels, and organizations.

Beck travels extensively in the United States and abroad, teaching and disseminating cognitive behavior therapy and assisting a wide variety of organizations in developing or strengthening their CT programs. She writes a number of CT-oriented blogs and edits "Cognitive Therapy Today," an e-newsletter. She is coauthor of the widely adopted self-report scales, the *Personality Belief Questionnaire* and the *Beck Youth Inventories II*, which screens children aged 7–18 for symptoms of depression, anxiety, disruptive behavior, self-concept, and anger.

Beck is Clinical Associate Professor at the University of Pennsylvania and was instrumental in founding the Academy of Cognitive Therapy, the "home" organization for cognitive therapists worldwide. She has written nearly a hundred articles and chapters on a variety of CT topics and authored several books on cognitive therapy, including *Cognitive Behavior Therapy: Basics and Beyond* (2011a), *Cognitive Therapy for Challenging Problems: What to Do When the Basics Don't Work*

(2005), and the *Cognitive Therapy Worksheet Packet* (2011b), as well as trade books with a cognitive behavioral program for diet and mainte-

DONALD MEICHEN-BAUM (b. 1940) was born in New York City (the Bronx) and learned early to be "street smart" and to be on the lookout for high-risk situations. He attended City College of New York and received his PhD in clinical psychology from the University of Illinois. At the University of Waterloo in Ontario, Canada, he conducted research on the development of cognitive behavior therapy (CBT). He is the recipient of a Lifetime Achievement Award from the Clinical Division of the American Psychological Association for his work on suicide prevention. In 1995 Meichenbaum retired from the University of Waterloo to become the research director of the Melissa Institute for Violence Prevention, which is designed to "give science away" in order to reduce violence and to treat victims of violence.

Meichenbaum attributes the origin of CBT to his mother, who had a knack for telling stories

nance. Judith Beck has been married for 34 years and has three adult children, one of whom is a social worker specializing in CT.

about her daily activities that were peppered with her thoughts, feelings, and a running commentary. This childhood experience contributed to Meichenbaum's psychotherapeutic approach of constructivist narrative therapy, in which clients to tell their stories and describe what they did to "survive and cope." Meichenbaum's recent work with returning service members using iPod technology to bolster resilience is modeled on this approach. When therapy is successful, Meichenbaum ensures that clients take credit for the changes they have achieved. As he observes, "I am at my therapeutic best when the clients I see are one step ahead of me offering the observations or suggestions that I would otherwise offer" (Donald Meichenbaum, personal communication, October 21, 2010).

Meichenbaum has published extensively, including *Cognitive Behavior Modification: An Integrative Approach* (1977), *Stress Inoculation Training* (1985), and *Treatment of Individuals with Anger-Control Problems and Aggressive Behaviors* (2002). He has lectured and consulted internationally and frequently presents workshops at professional conferences.

INTRODUCTION

As you saw in Chapter 9, traditional behavior therapy has broadened and largely moved in the direction of cognitive behavior therapy. Several of the more prominent cognitive behavioral approaches are featured in this chapter, including Albert Ellis's rational emotive behavior therapy (REBT), Aaron T. Beck's and Judith Beck's cognitive therapy (CT), and Donald Meichenbaum's cognitive behavior therapy (CBT). The cognitive behavior therapies, which combine both cognitive and behavioral principles and methods in a short-term treatment approach, have generated more empirical research than any other psychotherapy model (Dattilio, 2000a). These approaches all fall under the general umbrella of cognitive behavior therapies, which is the reason they are grouped together in this chapter.

All of the cognitive behavioral approaches share the same basic characteristics and assumptions as traditional behavior therapy described in Chapter 9. Although the approaches are quite diverse, they do share these attributes: (1) a collaborative relationship between client and therapist, (2) the premise that psychological distress is largely a function of disturbances in cognitive processes, (3) a focus on changing cognitions to produce desired changes in affect and behavior, (4) a present-centered, time-limited focus, (5) an active and directive stance by the therapist, and (6) an educational treatment focusing on specific and structured target problems (Beck & Weishaar, 2011). In addition, both cognitive therapy and the cognitive behavioral therapies are based on a structured psychoeducational model, emphasize the role of homework, place responsibility on the client to assume an active role both during and outside therapy sessions, emphasize developing a strong therapeutic alliance, and draw from a variety of cognitive and behavioral strategies to bring about change. Therapists help clients to examine the manner in which they understand themselves and their world and to experiment with new ways of behaving (Dienes, Torres-Harding, Reinecke, Freeman, & Sauer, 2011).

To a large degree, both cognitive therapy and cognitive behavior therapy are based on the assumption that a reorganization of one's self-statements will result in a corresponding reorganization of one's behavior. Behavioral techniques such as operant conditioning, modeling, and behavioral rehearsal can be applied to the more subjective processes of thinking and internal dialogue. Cognitive therapy and the cognitive behavioral approaches include a variety of behavioral strategies (discussed in Chapter 9) as a part of their integrative repertoire.

 See the video program for Chapter 10, *DVD for Theory and Practice of Counseling and Psychotherapy: The Case of Stan and Lecturettes*. I suggest that you view the brief lecture for each chapter prior to reading the chapter.

ALBERT ELLIS'S RATIONAL EMOTIVE BEHAVIOR THERAPY

Rational emotive behavior therapy (REBT) was the first of the cognitive behavior therapies, and today it continues to be a major cognitive behavioral approach. REBT has a great deal in common with the therapies that are oriented toward cognition and behavior as it also stresses thinking, judging, deciding, analyzing, and doing. The basic assumption of REBT is that people contribute to their own psychological problems, as well as to specific symptoms, by the rigid and extreme beliefs they hold about events and situations. REBT is based on the assumption that cognitions, emotions, and behaviors interact significantly and have a reciprocal cause-and-effect relationship. REBT has consistently emphasized all three of these modalities and their interactions, thus qualifying it as an integrative approach (Ellis, 2001a, 2001b, 2002, 2011; Ellis & Dryden, 2007; Wolfe, 2007).

Although REBT is generally conceded to be the parent of today's cognitive behavioral approaches, it was preceded by earlier schools of thought. Ellis gave credit to Alfred Adler as an influential precursor of REBT, and Karen Horney's (1950) ideas on the "tyranny of the shoulds" are apparent in the conceptual framework of REBT. Ellis also acknowledged his debt to the ancient Greeks, especially the Stoic philosopher Epictetus, who said around 2,000 years ago: "People are disturbed not by events, but by the views which they take of them" (as cited in Ellis, 2001a, p. 16). Ellis's reformulation of Epictetus's dictum can be stated as, "People disturb themselves by the rigid and extreme beliefs they hold about events."

REBT's basic hypothesis is that our emotions stem mainly from our beliefs, which influence the evaluations and interpretations we make of the reactions we have to life situations. Through the therapeutic process, clients learn skills that give them the tools to identify and dispute irrational beliefs that have been acquired and self-constructed and are now maintained by self-indoctrination. They learn how to replace such ineffective ways of thinking with effective and rational cognitions, and as a result they change their emotional reactions to situations. The therapeutic process allows clients to apply REBT principles of change not only to a particular presenting problem but also to many other problems in life or future problems they might encounter.

Several therapeutic implications flow from these assumptions: The focus is on working with *thinking* and *acting* rather than primarily with expressing feelings. Therapy is seen as an *educational process*. The therapist functions in many ways like a teacher, especially in collaborating with a client on homework assignments and in teaching strategies for straight thinking; and the client is a learner who practices these new skills in everyday life.

REBT differs from many other therapeutic approaches in that it does not place much value on free association, working with dreams, focusing on the client's past history, expressing and exploring feelings, or dealing with transference phenomena. Ellis (2011) maintains that transference is not encouraged, and when it does occur, the therapist is likely to confront it. Ellis believes the transference relationship is based on the irrational belief that the client must be liked and loved by the therapist, or parent figure. Although transference and countertransference may spontaneously occur in therapy, Ellis claims "they are quickly analyzed, the philosophies behind them are revealed, and they tend to evaporate in the process" (p. 221). Furthermore, when a client's deep feelings emerge, "the client is not given too much chance to revel in these feelings or abreact strongly about them" (p. 221). Ellis believes that such cathartic work may result in clients *feeling* better, but it will rarely aid them in *getting* better.

KEY CONCEPTS

View of Human Nature

Rational emotive behavior therapy is based on the assumption that human beings are born with a potential for both rational, or "straight," thinking and irrational, or "crooked," thinking. People have predispositions for self-preservation, happiness, thinking and verbalizing, loving, communion with others, and growth and self-actualization. They also have propensities for self-destruction, avoidance of thought, procrastination, endless repetition of mistakes, superstition, intolerance, perfectionism and self-blame, and avoidance of actualizing growth potentials. REBT encourages people accept themselves even though they will make mistakes.

View of Emotional Disturbance

REBT is based on the premise that we learn irrational beliefs from significant others during childhood and then re-create these irrational beliefs throughout our lifetime. We actively reinforce our self-defeating beliefs through the processes of autosuggestion and self-repetition, and we then behave in ways that are consistent with these beliefs. Hence, it is largely our own repetition of early-indoctrinated irrational beliefs, rather than a parent's repetition, that keeps dysfunctional attitudes alive and operative within us.

Ellis contends that people do not *need* to be accepted and loved, even though this may be highly desirable. The therapist teaches clients how to feel sad, but not depressed, even when they are unaccepted and unloved by significant others. A major goal of the REBT therapist is to encourage clients to be less emotionally reactive, for example, by feeling sadness and disappointment about life's adversities rather than by feeling anxiety, depression, and shame.

Ellis insists that blame is at the core of most emotional disturbances. If we want to become psychologically healthy, we had better stop blaming ourselves and others and learn to fully and unconditionally accept ourselves despite our imperfections. Ellis (Ellis & Blau, 1998; Ellis & Harper, 1997) hypothesizes that we have strong tendencies to transform our desires and preferences into dogmatic "shoulds," "musts," "oughts," demands, and commands. When we are disturbed, it is a good idea to look to our hidden dogmatic "musts" and absolutist "shoulds." Such demands underpin disruptive feelings and dysfunctional behaviors (Ellis, 2001a, 2004a).

Here are *three basics musts* (or irrational beliefs) that we internalize that inevitably lead to self-defeat (Ellis & Dryden, 2007):

- "I *must* do well and win the approval of others for my performances or else I am no good."
- "Other people *must* treat me considerately, fairly, kindly, and in exactly the way I want them to treat me. If they don't, they are no good and they deserve to be condemned and punished."
- "I *must* get what I want, when I want it; and I *must* not get what I don't want. If I don't get what I want, it's terrible, I can't stand it, and life is no good for depriving me of what I must have."

We have a strong tendency to make and keep ourselves emotionally disturbed by internalizing and perpetuating self-defeating beliefs such as these, which is why it is a real challenge to achieve and maintain good psychological health (Ellis, 2001a, 2001b).

A-B-C Framework

The A-B-C framework is central to REBT theory and practice. This model provides a useful tool for understanding the client's feelings, thoughts, events, and behavior (Wolfe, 2007). A is the existence of a fact, or an activating event, or an inference about an event, of an individual. C is the emotional and behavioral consequence or reaction of the individual; the reaction can be either healthy or unhealthy. A (the activating event) does not cause C (the emotional consequence). Instead, B, which is the person's belief about A, largely creates C, the emotional reaction.

The interaction of the various components can be diagrammed like this:

A (activating event) ← B (belief) → C (emotional and behavioral consequence)

↑

D (disputing intervention) → E (effect) → F (new feeling)

If a person experiences depression after a divorce, for example, it may not be the divorce itself that causes the depressive reaction nor his inference that he has failed, but the person's *beliefs* about his divorce or about his failure. Ellis maintains that the beliefs about the rejection and failure (at point B) are what mainly cause the depression (at point C)—not the actual event of the divorce or the person's inference of failure (at point A). Believing that human beings are largely responsible for creating their own emotional reactions and disturbances and showing people how they can change their irrational beliefs that directly "cause" their disturbed emotional consequences is at the heart of REBT (Ellis & Dryden, 2007; Ellis & Harper, 1997).

How is an emotional disturbance fostered? It is fed by the self-defeating sentences clients continually repeat to themselves, such as "I am totally to blame for the divorce," "I am a miserable failure, and everything I did was wrong," "I am a worthless person." Ellis repeatedly makes the point that "you mainly feel the way you think." Disturbed emotional reactions such as depression and anxiety are initiated and perpetuated by clients' self-defeating belief systems, which are based on irrational ideas clients have incorporated and invented.

After A, B, and C comes D (disputing). Essentially, D is the application of methods to help clients challenge their irrational beliefs. There are three components of this disputing process: detecting, debating, and discriminating. First, clients learn how to *detect* their irrational beliefs, particularly their absolutist "shoulds" and "musts," their "awfulizing," and their "self-downing." Then clients *debate* their dysfunctional beliefs by learning how to logically and empirically question them and to vigorously argue themselves out of and act against believing them. Finally, clients learn to *discriminate* irrational (self-defeating) beliefs from rational (self-helping) beliefs (Ellis, 1994, 1996). **Cognitive restructuring** is a central technique of cognitive therapy that teaches people how to improve themselves by replacing irrational beliefs with rational beliefs (Ellis, 2008). *Restructuring* involves helping clients learn to monitor their self-talk, identify maladaptive self-talk, and substitute adaptive self-talk for their negative self-talk (Spiegler, 2008).

Ellis (1996, 2001b) maintains that we have the capacity to significantly change our cognitions, emotions, and behaviors. We can best accomplish this goal by avoiding preoccupying ourselves with A and by acknowledging the futility of dwelling endlessly on emotional consequences at C. Rather, we can choose to examine, challenge, modify, and uproot B—the irrational beliefs we hold about the activating events at A.

Although REBT uses many other cognitive, emotive, and behavioral methods to help clients minimize their irrational beliefs, it stresses the process of disputing (D) such beliefs both during therapy sessions and in everyday life. Eventually clients arrive at E, an effective philosophy, which has a practical side. A new and effective belief system consists of replacing unhealthy thoughts with healthy ones. If we are successful in doing this, we also create F, a new set of feelings. Instead of feeling seriously anxious and depressed, we feel healthily sorry and disappointed in accord with a situation.

In sum, *philosophical restructuring* to change our dysfunctional personality involves these steps: (1) fully acknowledging that we are largely responsible for creating our own emotional problems; (2) accepting the notion that we have the ability to change these disturbances significantly; (3) recognizing that our emotional problems largely stem from irrational beliefs; (4) clearly perceiving these beliefs; (5) seeing the value of disputing such self-defeating beliefs; (6) accepting the fact that if we expect to change we had better work hard in emotive and behavioral ways to counteract our beliefs and the dysfunctional feelings and actions that follow; (7) understanding what the rational alternative to these irrational beliefs are; and (8) practicing REBT methods of uprooting or changing disturbed consequences and practicing their healthy alternatives for the rest of our life (Ellis, 1999, 2001b, 2002).

THE THERAPEUTIC PROCESS

Therapeutic Goals

According to Ellis (2001b; Ellis & Harper, 1997), we have a strong tendency not only to rate our acts and behaviors as "good" or "bad," "worthy" or "unworthy," but also to rate ourselves as a total person on the basis of our performances. These ratings constitute one of the main sources of our emotional disturbances. Therefore, most rational emotive behavior therapists have the general goal of teaching clients how to separate the evaluation of their behaviors from the evaluation of themselves—their essence and their totality—and how to accept themselves in spite of their imperfections.

The many roads taken in rational emotive behavior therapy lead toward the destination of clients minimizing their emotional disturbances and self-defeating behaviors by acquiring a more realistic and workable philosophy of life. The process of REBT involves a collaborative effort on the part of both the therapist and the client in choosing realistic and self-enhancing therapeutic goals. The therapist's task is to help clients differentiate between realistic and unrealistic goals and also self-defeating and self-enhancing goals (Dryden, 2007). A basic goal is to teach clients how to change their dysfunctional emotions and behaviors into healthy ones. Ellis (2001b) states that two of the main goals of REBT are to assist clients in the process of achieving *unconditional self-acceptance* (USA) and *unconditional other acceptance* (UOA), and to see how these are interrelated. As clients become more able to accept themselves, they are more likely to unconditionally accept others.

Therapist's Function and Role

The therapist has specific tasks, and the first step is to show clients how they have incorporated many irrational absolute "shoulds," "oughts," and "musts." The therapist disputes clients' irrational beliefs and encourages clients to engage in activities that will counter their self-defeating beliefs and to replace their rigid "musts" with preferences.

A second step in the therapeutic process is to demonstrate how clients are keeping their emotional disturbances active by continuing to think illogically and unrealistically. In other words, because clients keep reindoctrinating themselves, they are largely responsible for their own psychological problems.

To get beyond mere recognition of irrational thoughts, the therapist takes a third step—helping clients modify their thinking and minimize their irrational ideas. Although it is unlikely that we can entirely eliminate the tendency to think irrationally, we can reduce the frequency of such thinking. The therapist encourages clients to identify the irrational beliefs they originally unquestioningly accepted and demonstrates how they are continuing to indoctrinate themselves with these beliefs.

The fourth step in the therapeutic process is to challenge clients to develop a rational philosophy of life so that in the future they can avoid becoming the victim of other irrational beliefs. Tackling only specific problems or symptoms can give no assurance that new illogical fears will not emerge. It is desirable, then, for the therapist to dispute the core of the irrational thinking and to teach clients how to substitute rational beliefs and behaviors for irrational ones.

The therapist takes the mystery out of the therapeutic process, teaching clients about the cognitive hypothesis of disturbance and showing how rigid and extreme irrational beliefs lead to disturbed negative consequences. Insight alone does not typically lead to psychotherapeutic change, but it helps clients to see how they are continuing to sabotage themselves and what they can do to change.

Client's Experience in Therapy

Once clients begin to accept that their beliefs underpin their emotions and behaviors, they are able to participate effectively in the cognitive restructuring process (Ellis, Gordon, Neenan, & Palmer, 1997; Ellis & MacLaren, 2005). Because psychotherapy is viewed as a reeducative process, clients learn how to apply logical thought, participate in experiential exercises, and carry out behavioral homework as a way to bring about change. Clients can realize that life does not always work out the way that they would like it to. Even though life is not always pleasant, clients learn that life can be bearable and that even suffering can be honorable.

The therapeutic process largely focuses on clients' experiences in the present. Like the person-centered and existential approaches to therapy, REBT mainly emphasizes here-and-now experiences and clients' present ability to change the patterns of thinking and emoting that they constructed earlier. The therapist does not devote much time to exploring clients' early history and making connections between their past and present behavior unless doing so will aid the therapeutic process. Nor does the therapist usually explore clients' early relationships with their parents or siblings. Instead, the therapeutic process stresses to clients that they are presently disturbed because they still believe in and act upon their self-defeating view of themselves, other people, and the world.

Clients are expected to actively work outside the therapy sessions. By working hard and carrying out behavioral homework assignments, clients can learn to minimize faulty thinking, which leads to disturbances in feeling and behaving. **Homework** is carefully designed and agreed upon and is aimed at getting clients to carry out positive actions that induce emotional and attitudinal change. These assignments are checked in later sessions, and clients learn effective ways to dispute self-defeating thinking. Toward the end of therapy, clients review their progress, make plans, and identify strategies for dealing with continuing or potential problems.

Relationship Between Therapist and Client

Because REBT is essentially a cognitive and directive behavioral process, a warm relationship between therapist and client is not required. As with the person-centered therapy of Rogers, REBT practitioners strive to unconditionally accept all clients and to teach them to unconditionally accept others and themselves. However, Ellis believes that too much warmth and understanding can be counterproductive and foster a sense of dependence for approval from the therapist. REBT practitioners accept their clients as imperfect beings who can be helped through a variety of techniques such as teaching, bibliotherapy, and behavior modification (Ellis, 2011).

Rational emotive behavior therapists are often open and direct in disclosing their own beliefs and values. Some are willing to share their own imperfections as a way of disputing clients' unrealistic notions that therapists are "completely put together" persons. On this point, Wolfe (2007) claims "it is important to establish as much as possible an egalitarian relationship, as opposed to presenting yourself as a nondisclosing authority figure" (p. 186).

APPLICATION: THERAPEUTIC TECHNIQUES AND PROCEDURES

The Practice of Rational Emotive Behavior Therapy

Rational emotive behavior therapists are multimodal and integrative. REBT generally starts with clients' disturbed feelings and intensely explores these feelings in connection with thoughts and behaviors. REBT practitioners tend to use a number of different modalities (cognitive, imagery, emotive, behavioral, and interpersonal) to dispel these self-defeating cognitions and to teach people how to acquire a rational approach to living. Therapists are encouraged to be flexible and creative in their use of methods, making sure to tailor the techniques to the unique needs of each client (Dryden, 2007).

For a concrete illustration of how Dr. Ellis works with the client Ruth, drawing from cognitive, emotive, and behavioral techniques, see *Case Approach to Counseling and Psychotherapy* (Corey, 2013a, chap. 8). What follows is a brief summary of the major cognitive, emotive, and behavioral techniques Ellis describes (Ellis, 2004a; Ellis & Crawford, 2000; Ellis & Dryden, 2007; Ellis & MacLaren, 2005).

COGNITIVE METHODS REBT practitioners usually incorporate a persuasive cognitive methodology in the therapeutic process. They demonstrate to clients in a quick and direct manner what it is that they are continuing to tell themselves. Then they teach clients how to deal with these self-statements so that they no longer believe them, encouraging them to acquire a philosophy based on reality. REBT relies heavily on thinking, disputing, debating, challenging, interpreting, explaining, and teaching. The most efficient way to bring about lasting emotional and behavioral change is for clients to change their way of thinking (Dryden, 2007). Here are some cognitive techniques available to the therapist.

• *Disputing irrational beliefs.* The most common cognitive method of REBT consists of the therapist actively disputing clients' irrational beliefs and teaching them how to do this challenging on their own. Clients go over a particular "must," absolute "should," or "ought" until they no longer hold that irrational belief, or at least until it is diminished in strength. Here are some examples of questions or statements clients learn to tell themselves: "Why *must* people treat me fairly?" "How do I become a total flop if I don't succeed at important tasks I try?" "If I don't get the job I want, it may be disappointing, but I can certainly stand it." "If life doesn't always go the way I would like it to, it isn't *awful*, just inconvenient."

• *Doing cognitive homework.* REBT clients are expected to make lists of their problems, look for their absolutist beliefs, and dispute these beliefs. They often fill out the REBT Self-Help Form, which is reproduced in Corey's (2013b) *Student Manual for Theory and Practice of Counseling and Psychotherapy.* They can bring this form to their therapy sessions and critically evaluate the disputation of some of their beliefs. Homework assignments are a way of tracking down the "shoulds" and "musts" that are part of their internalized self-messages. Part of this homework consists of applying the A-B-C model to many of the problems clients encounter in daily life. Work in the therapy session can be designed in such a way that out-of-office tasks are feasible and the client has the skills to complete these tasks.

In carrying out homework, clients are encouraged to put themselves in risk-taking situations that will allow them to challenge their self-limiting beliefs. For example, a client with a talent for acting who is afraid to act in front of an audience because of fear of failure may be asked to take a small part in a stage play. The client is helped to replace irrational beliefs—"If I look foolish, this proves I am a fool." "If I am not liked, that would be awful." "I will fail and therefore be a failure."—with more positive messages such as these: "Even if I do behave foolishly at times, this does not make me a foolish *person*." "I can act." "I will do the best I can." "It's nice to be liked, but not everybody has to like me, and if they don't, that isn't the end of the world." "If I fail, I am human, not a failure."

The theory behind this and similar assignments is that clients often create a negative, self-fulfilling prophecy and actually fail because they told themselves in advance that they would. Clients are encouraged to carry out specific assignments during the sessions and, especially, in everyday situations between sessions. Clients are expected to take the time to record and think about how their beliefs contribute to their personal problems. In addition, they need to work hard at uprooting these self-defeating cognitions. In this way clients gradually learn to deal with anxiety and to challenge basic irrational thinking. Making changes is hard work, and doing work outside the sessions is of real value in revising clients' thinking, feeling, and behaving.

• *Bibliotherapy.* REBT, and other CBT approaches, can be delivered to some degree in a bibliotherapeutic format. It is probably best to utilize bibliotherapy as an adjunctive form of treatment. There are advantages of bibliotherapy, such as cost-effectiveness, widespread availability, and the potential of reaching a broad spectrum of populations. Bibliotherapeutic approaches have empirical support for the treatment of depression, for a variety of anxiety disorders, and for a range of clinical problems (Jacobs, 2008). Because therapy is seen as an educational process, clients are encouraged to read REBT self-help books such as *Rational Emotive Behavior Therapy: It Works for Me—It Can Work for You* (Ellis, 2004a) and other books by Ellis (1999, 2000, 2001a, 2001b).

- *Changing one's language.* REBT rests on the premise that imprecise language is one of the causes of distorted thinking processes. Clients learn that "musts," "oughts," and absolute "shoulds" can be replaced by *preferences*. Instead of saying "It would be absolutely awful if . . .", they learn to say "It would be inconvenient if . . .". Clients who use language patterns that reflect helplessness and self-condemnation can learn to employ new self-statements, which help them think and behave differently. As a consequence, they also begin to feel differently.

- *Psychoeducational methods.* REBT programs introduce clients to various educational materials. Therapists educate clients about the nature of their problems and how treatment is likely to proceed. They ask clients how particular concepts apply to them. Clients are more likely to cooperate with a treatment program if they understand how the therapy process works and if they understand why particular techniques are being used (Ledley, Marx, & Heimberg, 2010).

EMOTIVE TECHNIQUES REBT practitioners use a variety of emotive procedures, including unconditional acceptance, rational emotive role playing, modeling, rational emotive imagery, and shame-attacking exercises. Clients are taught the value of unconditional self-acceptance. Even though their behavior may be difficult to accept, they can decide to see themselves as fallible human beings. Clients are taught how destructive it is to engage in "putting oneself down" for perceived deficiencies.

Although REBT employs a variety of emotive techniques, which tend to be vivid and evocative in nature, the main purpose is to dispute clients' irrational beliefs (Dryden, 2007). These strategies are used both during the therapy sessions and as homework assignments in daily life. Their purpose is not simply to provide a cathartic experience but to help clients *change* some of their thoughts, emotions, and behaviors (Ellis, 2001b, 2011; Ellis & Dryden, 2007). Let's look at some of these evocative and emotive therapeutic techniques in more detail.

- *Rational emotive imagery.* This technique is a form of intense mental practice designed to establish new emotional patterns (see Ellis, 2001a, 2001b). Using the technique of **rational emotive imagery (REI)**, clients are asked to vividly imagine one of the worst things that might happen to them. They imagine themselves in specific situations where they experience disturbing feelings. Then they are shown how to train themselves to develop healthy emotions in place of disruptive ones. As clients change their feelings about adversities, they stand a better chance of changing their behavior in the situation. Such a technique can be usefully applied to interpersonal and other situations that are problematic for the individual. Ellis (2001a, 2011) maintains that if we keep practicing rational emotive imagery several times a week for a few weeks, we can reach the point that we no longer feel upset over negative events.

- *Using humor.* REBT contends that emotional disturbances often result from taking oneself too seriously, thus, this approach employs a good deal of humor. One appealing aspect of REBT is that it fosters the development of a better sense of humor and helps put life into perspective (Wolfe, 2007). Humor has both cognitive and emotional benefits in bringing about change. Humor shows the absurdity of certain ideas that clients steadfastly maintain, and it can be of value in helping clients take themselves much less seriously. It teaches clients to laugh—not at themselves, but at their self-defeating ways of thinking.

• *Role playing.* Role playing has emotive, cognitive, and behavioral components, and the therapist often interrupts to show clients what they are telling themselves to create their disturbances and what they can do to change their unhealthy feelings to healthy ones. Clients can rehearse certain behaviors to bring out what they feel in a situation. The focus is on working through the underlying irrational beliefs that are related to unpleasant feelings. For example, Dawson may put off applying to a graduate school because of his fears of not being accepted. Just the thought of not being accepted to the school of his choice brings out intense feelings of "being stupid." Dawson role-plays an interview with the dean of graduate students, notes his anxiety and the specific beliefs leading to it, and challenges his conviction that he absolutely must be accepted and that not gaining such acceptance means that he is a stupid and incompetent person.

• *Shame-attacking exercises.* The rationale underlying **shame-attacking exercises** is that emotional disturbance related to the self is often characterized by feelings of shame, guilt, anxiety, and depression. Ellis (1999, 2000, 2001a, 2001b) developed exercises to help people reduce shame and anxiety over behaving in certain ways. Ellis asserts that we can stubbornly refuse to feel ashamed by telling ourselves that it is not catastrophic if someone thinks we are foolish. The exercises are aimed at increasing self-acceptance and mature responsibility, as well as helping clients see that much of what they think of as being shameful has to do with the way they define reality for themselves. Clients may accept a homework assignment to take the risk of doing something that they are ordinarily afraid to do because of what others might think. For example, clients may wear "loud" clothes designed to attract attention, sing loudly, ask a silly question at a lecture, or ask for a left-handed monkey wrench in a grocery store. By carrying out such assignments, clients are likely to find out that other people are not really that interested in their behavior. They work on themselves so that they do not feel ashamed or humiliated, even when they acknowledge that some of their acts will lead to judgments by others. They continue practicing these exercises until they realize that their feelings of shame are self-created and until they are able to behave in less inhibited ways. Clients eventually learn that they often have no reason for continuing to let others' reactions or possible disapproval stop them from doing the things they would like to do. Note that these exercises do not involve illegal activities or acts that will be harmful to oneself or to others or that will unduly alarm other people.

BEHAVIORAL TECHNIQUES REBT practitioners use most of the standard behavior therapy procedures, especially operant conditioning, self-management principles, systematic desensitization, relaxation techniques, and modeling. Behavioral homework assignments to be carried out in real-life situations are particularly important. These assignments are done systematically and are recorded and analyzed on a form. Homework gives clients opportunities to practice new skills outside of the therapy session, which may be even more valuable for clients than work done during the therapy hour (Ledley et al., 2010). Doing homework may involve desensitization and live exposure in daily life situations. Clients can be encouraged to desensitize themselves gradually but also, at times, to perform the very things they dread doing implosively. For example, a person with a fear of elevators may decrease this fear by going up and down in an elevator 20 or 30 times in a day. Clients actually do new and difficult things, and in this way they put their insights to use in the form of concrete action. By acting differently, they also tend to incorporate functional beliefs.

Applications of REBT to Various Settings

With its clear structure (A-B-C framework), REBT is applicable to a wide range of settings and populations, including elementary and secondary schools. REBT can be applied to couples counseling and family therapy. In working with couples, the partners are taught the principles of REBT so that they can work out their differences or at least become less disturbed about them. In family therapy, individual family members are encouraged to consider letting go of the demand that others in the family behave in ways they would like them to. Instead, REBT teaches family members that they are primarily responsible for their own actions and for changing their own reactions to the family situation.

Application of REBT as a Brief Therapy

REBT is well suited as a brief form of therapy, whether it is applied to individuals, groups, couples, or families. Ellis originally developed REBT to try to make psychotherapy shorter and more efficient than most other systems of therapy, and it is often used as a brief therapy. Ellis has always maintained that the best therapy is efficient, quickly teaching clients how to tackle practical problems of living. Clients learn how to apply REBT techniques to their present as well as future problems. A distinguishing characteristic of REBT that makes it a brief form of therapy is that it is a self-help approach (Vernon, 2007). The A-B-C approach to changing basic disturbance-creating attitudes can be learned in 1 to 10 sessions and then practiced at home.

Application to Group Counseling

Cognitive behavior therapy (CBT) groups are among the most popular in clinics and community agency settings. Two of the most common CBT group approaches are based on the principles and techniques of REBT and cognitive therapy (CT).

REBT practitioners employ an active role in getting members to commit themselves to practicing in everyday situations what they are learning in the group sessions. They view what goes on during the group as being valuable, yet they know that the consistent work between group sessions and after a group ends is even more crucial. The group context provides members with tools they can use to become self-reliant and to accept themselves unconditionally as they encounter new problems in daily living.

REBT is also suitable for group therapy because the members are taught to apply its principles to one another in the group setting. Ellis recommends that most clients experience group therapy as well as individual therapy at some point. This form of group therapy focuses on specific techniques for changing a client's self-defeating thoughts in various concrete situations. In addition to modifying beliefs, this approach helps group members see how their beliefs influence what they feel and what they do. This model aims to minimize symptoms by bringing about a profound change in philosophy. Ellis (2011) contends that REBT is particularly applicable to group therapy and is frequently the treatment of choice. Group work affords many opportunities to agree on homework assignments, to practice assertiveness skills, to take risks by practicing different behaviors, to challenge self-defeating thinking, to learn from the experiences of others, and to interact therapeutically and socially with each other in after-group sessions. All of the cognitive, emotive, and behavioral techniques described earlier are applicable to group counseling as are the techniques covered in Chapter 9 on behavior therapy. Behavioral homework and skills training are just two useful methods for a group format.

A major strength of REBT and cognitive behavioral groups is the emphasis placed on education and prevention. Because CBT and REBT are based on broad principles of learning, these approaches can be used to meet the requirements of a wide variety of groups with a range of different purposes. The specificity of CBT allows for links among assessment, treatment, and evaluation strategies. CBT groups have targeted problems ranging from anxiety and depression to parent education and relationship enhancement. Cognitive behavioral group therapy has been demonstrated to have beneficial applications for some of the following specific problems: depression, anxiety, panic and phobia, obesity, eating disorders, dual diagnoses, dissociative disorders, and adult attention deficit disorders (see White & Freeman, 2000). Based on his survey of outcome studies of cognitive behavioral group therapy, Petrocelli (2002) concludes that this approach to groups is effective for treating a wide range of emotional and behavioral problems. For a more detailed discussion of REBT applied to group counseling, see Corey (2012, chap. 14).

AARON BECK'S COGNITIVE THERAPY
Introduction

Aaron T. Beck developed an approach known as **cognitive therapy** (CT) as a result of his research on depression (Beck 1963, 1967). Beck developed cognitive therapy about the same time that Ellis was developing REBT, yet they appear to have created their approaches independently. Beck's observations of depressed clients revealed that they had a negative bias in their interpretation of certain life events, which contributed to their cognitive distortions (Beck, 1967). Cognitive therapy has a number of similarities to both rational emotive behavior therapy and behavior therapy. All of these therapies are active, directive, time-limited, present-centered, problem-oriented, collaborative, structured, and empirical. They make use of homework and require explicit identification of problems and the situations in which they occur (Beck & Weishaar, 2011).

Cognitive therapy (CT) perceives psychological problems as stemming from commonplace processes such as faulty thinking, making incorrect inferences on the basis of inadequate or incorrect information, and failing to distinguish between fantasy and reality. Like REBT, CT is an insight-focused therapy with a strong psychoeducational component that emphasizes recognizing and changing unrealistic negative thoughts and maladaptive beliefs. Cognitive therapy is highly collaborative and involves designing specific learning experiences to help clients monitor their automatic thoughts; examine the validity of their automatic thoughts; understand the relationship among cognition, feelings, and behavior; develop more accurate and realistic cognitions; and change underlying beliefs and assumptions (Dobson & Dozois, 2010; Dozois & Beck, 2011). Cognitive therapy is based on the theoretical rationale that the way people feel and behave is influenced by how they perceive and structure their experience. The theoretical assumptions of cognitive therapy are (1) that people's internal communication is accessible to introspection, (2) that clients' beliefs have highly personal meanings, and (3) that these meanings can be discovered by the client rather than being taught or interpreted by the therapist (Weishaar, 1993).

Basic Principles of Cognitive Therapy

Beck, formerly a practicing psychoanalytic therapist for many years, grew interested in his clients' **automatic thoughts** (personalized notions that are triggered by particular stimuli that lead to emotional responses). As a part of a psychoanalytic research study, he was examining the dream content of depressed clients for anger that they were turning back on themselves. He began to notice that rather than retroflected anger, as Freud theorized with depression, clients exhibited a negative bias in their interpretation or thinking. Beck asked clients to observe their negative automatic thoughts that persisted even though they were contrary to objective evidence, and from this beginning he developed one of the most comprehensive theories of psychopathology in the world.

Individuals tend to maintain their core beliefs about themselves, their world, and their future. A primary focus of cognitive therapy is to assist clients in examining and restructuring their core beliefs (or core schema) (Dozois & Beck, 2011). By encouraging clients to gather and weigh the evidence in support of their beliefs, therapists help clients bring about enduring changes in their mood and their behavior.

Beck contends that people with emotional difficulties tend to commit characteristic "logical errors" that distort objective reality. Let's examine some of the systematic errors in reasoning that lead to faulty assumptions and misconceptions, which are termed **cognitive distortions** (J. Beck, 2011; Beck & Weishaar, 2011).

• *Arbitrary inferences* refer to making conclusions without supporting and relevant evidence. This includes "catastrophizing," or thinking of the absolute worst scenario and outcomes for most situations. You might begin your first job as a counselor with the conviction that you will not be liked or valued by either your colleagues or your clients. You are convinced that you fooled your professors and somehow just managed to get your degree, but now people will certainly see through you!

• *Selective abstraction* consists of forming conclusions based on an isolated detail of an event. In this process other information is ignored, and the significance of the total context is missed. The assumption is that the events that matter are those dealing with failure and deprivation. As a counselor, you might measure your worth by your errors and weaknesses, not by your successes.

• *Overgeneralization* is a process of holding extreme beliefs on the basis of a single incident and applying them inappropriately to dissimilar events or settings. If you have difficulty working with one adolescent, for example, you might conclude that you will not be effective counseling any adolescents. You might also conclude that you will not be effective working with *any* clients!

• *Magnification and minimization* consist of perceiving a case or situation in a greater or lesser light than it truly deserves. You might make this cognitive error by assuming that even minor mistakes in counseling a client could easily create a crisis for the individual and might result in psychological damage.

• *Personalization* is a tendency for individuals to relate external events to themselves, even when there is no basis for making this connection. If a client does not return for a second counseling session, you might be absolutely convinced that this absence is due to your terrible performance during the initial session. You might tell yourself, "This situation proves that I really let that client down, and now she may never seek help again."

• *Labeling and mislabeling* involve portraying one's identity on the basis of imperfections and mistakes made in the past and allowing them to define one's true identity. Thus, if you are not able to live up to all of a client's expectations, you might say to yourself, "I'm totally worthless and should turn my professional license in right away."

• *Dichotomous thinking* involves categorizing experiences in either-or extremes. With such polarized thinking, events are labeled in black or white terms. You might give yourself no latitude for being an imperfect person and imperfect counselor. You might view yourself as either being the perfectly competent counselor (which means you always succeed with all clients) or as a total flop if you are not fully competent (which means there is no room for any mistakes).

The cognitive therapist operates on the assumption that an important way to produce lasting change in dysfunctional emotions and behaviors is to modify inaccurate and dysfunctional thinking. The cognitive therapist teaches clients how to identify these distorted and dysfunctional cognitions through a process of evaluation. Through a collaborative effort, clients learn the influence that cognition has on their feelings and behaviors and even on environmental events. In cognitive therapy, clients learn to engage in more realistic thinking, especially if they consistently notice times when they tend to get caught up in catastrophic thinking.

After they have gained insight into how their unrealistic negative thoughts are affecting them, clients are taught to test these automatic thoughts against reality by examining and weighing the evidence for and against them. They can begin to monitor the frequency with which these beliefs intrude in situations in everyday life. The frequently asked question is, "What is the evidence for _____?" This process of critically examining their automatic thoughts and core beliefs involves empirically testing them by actively engaging in a Socratic dialogue with the therapist, carrying out homework assignments, doing behavioral experiments, gathering data on assumptions they make, and forming alternative interpretations (Dattilio, 2000a; Freeman & Dattilio, 1994; Tompkins, 2004, 2006). From the start of treatment, clients learn to employ specific problem-solving and coping skills. Through a process of guided discovery, clients acquire insight about the connection between their thinking and the ways they act and feel.

Cognitive therapy is focused on present problems, regardless of a client's diagnosis. The past may be brought into therapy when the therapist considers it essential to understand how and when certain core dysfunctional beliefs originated and how these ideas have a current impact on the client's specific schema (Dattilio, 2002a). The goals of this brief therapy include providing symptom relief, assisting clients in resolving their most pressing problems, and teaching clients relapse prevention strategies.

SOME DIFFERENCES BETWEEN CT AND REBT In both CT and REBT, reality testing is highly organized. Clients come to realize on an experiential level that they have misconstrued situations. Yet there are some important differences between these two approaches, especially with respect to therapeutic methods and style.

REBT is often highly directive, persuasive, and confrontational; it also focuses on the teaching role of the therapist. The therapist models rational thinking and helps clients to identify and dispute irrational beliefs. In contrast, CT uses a Socratic dialogue by posing open-ended questions to clients with the aim of getting clients to reflect on personal issues and arrive at their own conclusions. CT places more emphasis on helping clients identify their misconceptions for themselves than does REBT. Through this reflective questioning process, the cognitive therapist attempts to collaborate with clients in testing the validity of their cognitions (a process termed **collaborative empiricism**). Therapeutic change is the result of clients confronting faulty beliefs with contradictory evidence that they have gathered and evaluated.

There are also differences in how Ellis and Beck view faulty thinking. Through a process of rational disputation, Ellis works to persuade clients that certain of their beliefs are irrational and nonfunctional. Beck views his clients' beliefs as being more inaccurate than irrational and asks his clients to conduct behavioral experiments to test the accuracy of their beliefs (Hollon & DiGiuseppe, 2011). Cognitive therapists view dysfunctional beliefs as being problematic when they are irrational, or when they are too absolute, broad, and extreme (Beck & Weishaar, 2011). For Beck, people live by *rules* (premises or formulas); they get into trouble when they label, interpret, and evaluate by a set of rules that are unrealistic or when they use the rules inappropriately or excessively. If clients make the determination that they are living by rules that are likely to lead to misery, the therapist may suggest alternative rules for them to consider, without indoctrinating them. Although cognitive therapy often begins by recognizing the client's frame of reference, the therapist continues to ask for evidence for a belief system.

The Client-Therapist Relationship

One of the main ways the practice of cognitive therapy differs from the practice of rational emotive behavior therapy is its emphasis on the therapeutic relationship. As you will recall, Ellis views the therapist largely as a teacher and does *not* think that a warm personal relationship with clients is essential. In contrast, Beck (1987) emphasizes that the quality of the therapeutic relationship is basic to the application of cognitive therapy. Through his writings, it is clear that Beck believes that effective therapists must combine empathy and sensitivity, along with technical competence. The core therapeutic conditions described by Rogers in his person-centered approach are viewed by cognitive therapists as being *necessary*, but *not sufficient*, to produce optimum therapeutic effect. A therapeutic alliance is a necessary first step in cognitive therapy, especially in counseling difficult-to-reach clients. Without a working alliance, applying techniques will not be effective (Dienes et al., 2011). Therapists must also have a cognitive conceptualization of cases, be creative and active, be able to engage clients through a process of Socratic questioning, and be knowledgeable and skilled in the use of cognitive and behavioral strategies aimed at guiding clients in significant self-discoveries that will lead to change (Beck & Weishaar, 2011). Macy (2007) states that effective cognitive therapists strive to create "warm, empathic relationships with clients while at the same time effectively using cognitive therapy techniques that will enable clients to create change in their thinking, feeling, and behaving" (p. 171).

Cognitive therapists are continuously active and deliberately interactive with clients, helping clients frame their conclusions in the form of testable hypotheses. Therapists engage clients' active participation and collaboration throughout all phases of therapy, including deciding how often to meet, how long therapy should last, what problems to explore, and setting an agenda for each therapy session (J. Beck & Butler, 2005).

Aaron and Judith Beck conceptualize a partnership to devise personally meaningful evaluations of the client's negative assumptions (J. Beck, 2005, 2011a). The therapist functions as a catalyst and a guide who helps clients understand how their beliefs and attitudes influence the way they feel and act. Clients are expected to identify the distortions in their thinking, summarize important points in the session, and collaboratively devise homework assignments that they agree to carry out. Cognitive therapists emphasize the client's role in self-discovery. The assumption is that lasting changes in the client's thinking and behavior will be most likely to occur with the client's initiative, understanding, awareness, and effort (J. Beck, 2005, 2011a; J. Beck & Butler, 2005; Beck & Weishaar, 2011).

In cognitive therapy, the aim is to identify specific, measurable goals and to move directly into the areas that are causing the most difficulty for clients (Dienes et al. 2011). Cognitive therapists aim to teach clients how to be their own therapist. Typically, a therapist will educate clients about the nature and course of their problem, about the process of cognitive therapy, and how thoughts influence their emotions and behaviors. The educative process includes providing clients with information about their presenting problems and about relapse prevention. One way of educating clients is through bibliotherapy, in which clients complete readings dealing with the philosophy of cognitive therapy. These readings are assigned as an adjunct to therapy and are designed to enhance the therapeutic process by providing an educational focus (Dattilio & Freeman, 2007; Jacobs, 2008). Cognitive therapy self-help books also provide an educational focus, such as *The Beck Diet Solution: Train Your Brain to Think Like a Thin Person* (J. Beck, 2007a) and *The Complete Beck Diet for Life* (J. Beck, 2008).

Homework is often used as a part of cognitive therapy because practicing cognitive behavioral skills outside of the office facilitates more rapid gains (Dienes et al., 2011). Homework is tailored to the client's specific problem and arises out of the collaborative therapeutic relationship. Tompkins (2004, 2006) outlines the key steps to successful homework assignments and the steps involved in collaboratively designing homework. The purpose of homework is not merely to teach clients new skills but also to enable them to test their beliefs and experiment with different behaviors in daily-life situations. Homework is generally presented to clients as an experiment, which increases the openness of clients to get involved in an assignment. Emphasis is placed on self-help assignments that serve as a continuation of issues addressed in a therapy session (Dattilio, 2002b). Cognitive therapists realize that clients are more likely to complete homework if it is tailored to their needs, if they participate in designing the homework, if they begin the homework in the therapy session, and if they talk about potential problems in implementing the homework (J. Beck, 2005). Tompkins (2006) points out that there are clear advantages to the therapist and the client working in a collaborative manner in negotiating mutually agreeable homework tasks. One indicator of a good therapeutic alliance is whether homework is done and done well.

Applications of Cognitive Therapy

Cognitive therapy initially gained recognition as an approach to treating depression, but extensive research has also been devoted to the study and treatment of many other psychiatric disorders. One of the reasons for the popularity of cognitive therapy is due to "strong empirical support for its theoretical framework and to the large number of outcome studies with clinical populations" (Beck & Weishaar, 2011, p. 305). According to J. Beck (personal communication, January 1, 2011), hundreds of research studies have confirmed the theoretical underpinnings of CT, and hundreds of outcome trials have established its efficacy for a wide range of psychiatric disorders, psychological problems, and medical conditions with psychological components.

Cognitive therapy has been successfully used to treat phobias, psychosomatic disorders, eating disorders, anger, panic disorders, and generalized anxiety disorders (Chambless & Peterman, 2006; Dattilio & Kendall, 2007; Riskind, 2006); posttraumatic stress disorder, suicidal behavior, borderline personality disorders, narcissistic personality disorders, and schizophrenic disorders (Dattilio & Freeman, 2007); personality disorders (Pretzer & Beck, 2006); substance abuse (Newman, 2006); chronic pain (Beck, 1987); medical illness (Dattilio & Castaldo, 2001); crisis intervention (Dattilio & Freeman, 2007); couples and families therapy (Dattilio, 1993, 1998, 2001, 2005, 2010; Dattilio & Padesky, 1990; Epstein, 2006); child abusers, divorce counseling, skills training, and stress management (Dattilio, 1998; Granvold, 1994; Reinecke, Dattilio, & Freeman, 2002). Clearly, cognitive therapy programs have been designed for all ages and for a variety of client populations.

For an excellent resource on the clinical applications of cognitive therapy to a wide range of disorders and populations, see *Contemporary Cognitive Therapy* (Leahy, 2006a).

APPLYING COGNITIVE TECHNIQUES Beck and Weishaar (2011) describe both cognitive and behavioral techniques that are part of the overall strategies used by cognitive therapists. Cognitive techniques focus on identifying and examining a client's beliefs, exploring the origins of these beliefs, and modifying them if the client cannot support these beliefs. Examples of behavioral techniques typically used by cognitive therapists include activity scheduling, behavioral experiments, skills training, role playing, behavioral rehearsal, and exposure therapy. Regardless of the nature of the specific problem, the cognitive therapist is mainly interested in applying procedures that will assist individuals in making alternative interpretations of events in their daily living. Think about how you might apply the principles of CT to yourself in this classroom situation and change your feelings surrounding the situation:

> Your professor does not call on you during a particular class session. You *feel* depressed. *Cognitively*, you are telling yourself: "My professor thinks I'm stupid and that I really don't have much of value to offer the class. Furthermore, she's right, because everyone else is brighter and more articulate than I am. It's been this way most of my life!"

Some possible *alternative interpretations* are that the professor wants to include others in the discussion, that she is short on time and wants to move ahead, that she already knows your views, or that she believes you are self-conscious about being singled out or called on.

The therapist would have you become aware of the distortions in your thinking patterns by examining your automatic thoughts. The therapist would ask you to look at your inferences, which may be faulty, and may investigate whether these inferences can be traced back to earlier experiences in your life. Then the therapist would help you see how you sometimes come to a conclusion (your decision that you are stupid, with little of value to offer) when evidence for such a conclusion is either lacking or based on distorted information from the past.

As a client in cognitive therapy, you would also learn about the process of magnification or minimization of thinking, which involves either exaggerating the meaning of an event (you believe the professor thinks you are stupid because she did not acknowledge you on this one occasion) or minimizing it (you belittle your value as a student in the class). The therapist would assist you in learning how you disregard important aspects of a situation, engage in overly simplified and rigid thinking, and generalize from a single incident of failure. Can you think of other situations where you could apply CT procedures?

TREATMENT OF DEPRESSION Based on his research, Beck (1963) challenged the notion that depression results from anger turned inward. Instead, he focuses on the content of the depressive's negative thinking and biased interpretation of events. Beck (1987) writes about the *cognitive triad* as a pattern that triggers depression. In the first component of the triad, clients hold a negative view of themselves. They blame their setbacks on personal inadequacies without considering circumstantial explanations. They are convinced that they lack the qualities essential to bring them happiness. The second component of the triad consists of the tendency to interpret their personal world in a negative manner. Depressed people focus on certain facts that conform to their negative conclusions, a process referred to as selective abstraction by Beck. The third component of the triad pertains to depressed clients' gloomy vision and projections about the future. They expect their present difficulties to continue, and they anticipate only failure in the future.

Depression-prone people often set rigid, perfectionist goals for themselves that are impossible to attain. Their negative expectations are so strong that even if they experience success in specific tasks they anticipate failure the next time. They screen out successful experiences that are not consistent with their negative self-concept. The thought content of depressed individuals often centers on a sense of irreversible loss that results in emotional states of sadness, disappointment, and apathy.

The cognitive therapy approach to treating depressed clients focuses on specific problem areas and the reasons clients give for their symptoms. To assess the depth of depression, Beck (1967) designed a standardized device known as the Beck Depression Inventory (BDI). Some of the behavioral symptoms of depression are inactivity, withdrawal, and avoidance. The therapist is likely to probe with Socratic questioning such as this: "What would be lost by trying a specific activity? Will you feel worse if you are passive? How do you know that it is pointless to try?" Therapy procedures include setting up an activity schedule with graded tasks to be completed. Clients are asked to complete easy tasks first, so that they will meet with some success and become slightly more optimistic. The point is to enlist the client's cooperation with the therapist on the assumption that *doing something* is more likely to lead to feeling better than *doing nothing*.

A central characteristic of most depressive people is self-criticism. Underneath the person's negative self-attitudes are themes of weakness, inadequacy, and lack of responsibility. A number of therapeutic strategies can be used. Clients can be asked to identify and provide reasons for their excessively self-critical thinking. The therapist may ask the client, "If your friend were to make a mistake the way you do, would you be as critical of her as you are of yourself?" The therapist may also discuss with the client how the "tyranny of shoulds" can lead to increased distress.

Depressed clients typically experience painful emotions. They may say that they cannot stand the pain or that nothing can make them feel better. One procedure that may be helpful is to ask them to speak more conversationally about events in the past week in which their mood lifted even just a little.

Another specific characteristic of depressed people is an exaggeration of external demands, problems, and pressures. They may express thoughts of being overwhelmed and that there is so much to accomplish that they can never do it. A cognitive therapist might ask clients to list things that need to be done, set priorities, check off tasks that have been accomplished, and break down an external problem into manageable units. When problems are discussed, clients often become aware of how they are magnifying the importance of these difficulties. Through rational exploration, clients are able to regain a perspective on defining and accomplishing tasks.

The therapist typically has to take the lead in helping clients make a list of their responsibilities, set priorities, and develop a realistic plan of action. Because carrying out such a plan is often inhibited by negative automatic thoughts, it is well for therapists to use cognitive rehearsal techniques in both identifying and changing negative thoughts. If clients can learn to combat their self-doubts in the therapy session, they may be able to apply their newly acquired cognitive and behavioral skills in real-life situations.

APPLICATION TO FAMILY THERAPY The cognitive behavioral approach focuses on family interaction patterns, and family relationships, cognitions, emotions, and behavior are viewed as exerting a mutual influence on one another. A cognitive inference can evoke emotion and behavior, and emotion and behavior can likewise influence cognition in a reciprocal process that sometimes serves to maintain the dysfunction of the family unit.

Cognitive therapy, as set forth by Beck (1976), places a heavy emphasis on **schema**, or what have elsewhere been defined as core beliefs. A key aspect of the therapeutic process involves restructuring distorted beliefs (or schema), which has a pivotal impact on changing dysfunctional behaviors. Some cognitive behavior therapists place a strong emphasis on examining cognitions among individual family members as well as on what may be termed the "family schemata" (Dattilio, 1993, 1998, 2001, 2010). These are jointly held beliefs about the family that have formed as a result of years of integrated interaction among members of the family unit. It is the experiences and perceptions from the family of origin that shape the schema about both the immediate family and families in general. These schemata have a major impact on how the individual thinks, feels, and behaves in the family system (Dattilio, 2001, 2005, 2010).

For a concrete illustration of how Dr. Dattilio applies cognitive principles and works with family schemata, see his cognitive behavioral approach with Ruth in *Case Approach to Counseling and Psychotherapy* (Corey, 2013a, chap. 8). For a discussion of myths and misconceptions of cognitive behavior family therapy, see Dattilio (2001); for a concise presentation on the cognitive behavioral model of family therapy, see Dattilio (2010). Also, for an expanded treatment of applications of cognitive behavioral approaches to working with couples and families, see Dattilio (1998).

DONALD MEICHENBAUM'S COGNITIVE BEHAVIOR MODIFICATION

Introduction

Another major alternative to rational emotive behavior therapy is Donald Meichenbaum's **cognitive behavior modification** (CBM), which focuses on changing the client's self-verbalizations. Meichenbaum's cognitive behavioral approach combines some of the best elements of behavior therapy and cognitive therapy. According to Meichenbaum (1977), self-statements affect a person's behavior in much the same way as statements made by another person. A basic premise of CBM is that clients, as a prerequisite to behavior change, must notice how they think, feel, and behave and the impact they have on others. For change to occur, clients need to interrupt the scripted nature of their behavior so that they can evaluate their behavior in various situations (Meichenbaum, 1993, 2007).

This approach shares with REBT and Beck's cognitive therapy the assumption that distressing emotions are typically the result of maladaptive thoughts. REBT is more direct and confrontational in uncovering and disputing irrational thoughts, whereas Meichenbaum's *self-instructional training* focuses more on helping clients become aware of their self-talk and the stories they tell about themselves. Both REBT and CT focus on changing thinking processes, but Meichenbaum suggests that it may be easier and more effective to *behave* our way into a new way of thinking rather than to *think* our way into a new way of behaving. Furthermore, our emotions and thinking are two sides of the same coin: the way we feel can affect our way of thinking, just as how we think can influence how we feel. The therapeutic process consists of teaching clients to make self-statements and training clients to modify the instructions they give to themselves so that they can cope more effectively with the problems they encounter. Cognitive restructuring plays a central role in Meichenbaum's (1977, 1993) self-instructional training. He describes cognitive structure as the organizing aspect of thinking, which seems to monitor and direct the choice of thoughts through an "executive processor" that "holds the blueprints of thinking" that determine when to continue, interrupt, or change thinking. Together, therapist and client practice the self-instructions and the desirable behaviors in role-play situations that simulate problem situations in the client's daily life. The emphasis is on acquiring practical coping skills for problematic situations such as impulsive and aggressive behavior, anxiety in social situations, fear of taking tests, eating problems, and fear of public speaking.

How Behavior Changes

Meichenbaum (1977) proposes that "behavior change occurs through a sequence of mediating processes involving the interaction of inner speech, cognitive structures, and behaviors and their resultant outcomes" (p. 218). He describes a three-phase process of change in which those three aspects are interwoven. According to him, focusing on only one aspect will probably prove insufficient.

Phase 1: Self-observation. The beginning step in the change process consists of clients learning how to observe their own behavior. When clients begin therapy, their internal dialogue is characterized by negative self-statements and imagery. A critical factor is their willingness and ability to *listen* to themselves. This process involves an increased sensitivity to their thoughts, feelings, actions, physiological reactions, and ways of reacting to others. If depressed clients hope to make constructive changes, for example, they must first realize that they are not "victims" of negative thoughts and feelings. Rather, they are actually contributing to their depression through the things they tell themselves. Although self-observation is necessary if change is to occur, it is not sufficient for change. As therapy progresses, clients acquire new cognitive structures that enable them to view their problems in a new light. This reconceptualization process comes about through a collaborative effort between client and therapist.

Phase 2: Starting a new internal dialogue. As a result of the early client–therapist contacts, clients learn to notice their maladaptive behaviors, and they begin to see opportunities for adaptive behavioral alternatives. If clients hope to change what they are telling themselves, they must initiate a new behavioral chain, one that is incompatible with their maladaptive behaviors. Clients learn that psychological distress is a function of the interdependence of cognitions, emotions, behaviors, and resultant consequences. In therapy, clients learn to change their internal dialogue, which serves as a guide to new behavior.

Phase 3: Learning new skills. The third phase of the modification process consists of helping clients interrupt the downward spiral of thinking, feeling, and behaving and teaching them more adaptive ways of coping using the resources they bring to therapy. Clients learn more effective coping skills, which are practiced in real-life situations. For example, clients who can't cope with failure may avoid appealing activities for fear of not succeeding at them. Cognitive restructuring can help them change their negative view, thus making them more willing to engage in desired activities. At the same time, clients continue to focus on telling themselves new sentences and observing and assessing the outcomes. As they behave differently in situations, they typically get different reactions from others. The stability of what they learn is greatly influenced by what they say to themselves about their newly acquired behavior and its consequences.

Stress Inoculation Training

A particular application of a coping skills program is teaching clients stress management techniques by way of a strategy known as **stress inoculation training** (SIT). Using cognitive techniques, Meichenbaum (1985, 2007, 2008) has developed stress inoculation procedures that are a psychological and behavioral analog to immunization on a biological level. Individuals are given opportunities to deal with relatively mild stress stimuli in successful ways, so that they gradually develop a tolerance for stronger stimuli. This training is based on the assumption that we can affect our ability to cope with stress by modifying our beliefs and self-statements about our performance in stressful situations. Meichenbaum's stress inoculation training is concerned with more than merely teaching people specific coping skills. His program is designed to prepare clients for intervention and motivate them to change, and it deals with issues such as resistance and relapse.

Stress inoculation training consists of a combination of information giving, Socratic discovery-oriented inquiry, cognitive restructuring, problem solving, relaxation training, behavioral rehearsals, self-monitoring, self-instruction, self-reinforcement, and modifying environmental situations (Meichenbaum, 2008). SIT involves collaborative goal setting that nurtures hope, direct-action skills, and acceptance-based coping skills. These coping skills are designed to be applied to both present problems and future difficulties. Clients are assisted in generalizing what they learn in the training to daily living, and relapse prevention strategies are taught. Meichenbaum (2008) describes stress inoculation training as a complex, multifaceted cognitive behavioral intervention that is both a preventive and a treatment approach.

Clients can acquire more effective strategies in dealing with stressful situations by learning how to modify their cognitive "set," or core beliefs. The following procedures are designed to teach these coping skills:

- Expose clients to anxiety-provoking situations by means of role playing and imagery
- Require clients to evaluate their anxiety level

- Teach clients to become aware of the anxiety-provoking cognitions they experience in stressful situations
- Help clients examine these thoughts by reevaluating their self-statements
- Have clients note the level of anxiety following this reevaluation

THE PHASES OF STRESS INOCULATION TRAINING Meichenbaum (2007, 2008) has designed a three-stage model for stress inoculation training: (1) the conceptual-educational phase, (2) the skills acquisition and consolidation phase, and (3) the application and follow-through phase.

During the *conceptual-educational phase*, the primary focus is on creating a working relationship and therapeutic alliance with clients. This is mainly done by helping them gain a better understanding of the nature of stress and reconceptualizing it in social-interactive terms. The therapist enlists the client's collaboration during this early phase and together they rethink the nature of the problem or the individual's stress concerns. Initially, clients are provided with a conceptual framework in simple terms designed to educate them about ways of responding to a variety of stressful situations. They learn about the role cognitions and emotions play in creating and maintaining stress through didactic presentations, by curious questioning, and by a process of guided self-discovery.

Clients often begin treatment feeling that they are the victims of external circumstances, thoughts, feelings, and behaviors over which they have no control. As a way to understand the subjective world of clients, the therapist generally elicits stories that clients tell themselves. Training includes teaching clients to become aware of their own role in creating their stress and their life stories. They acquire this awareness by systematically observing the statements they make internally as well as by monitoring the maladaptive behaviors that flow from this inner dialogue. Such self-monitoring continues throughout all the phases. As is true in cognitive therapy, clients typically keep an open-ended diary in which they systematically monitor and record their specific thoughts, feelings, and behaviors. In teaching these coping skills, therapists strive to be flexible in their use of techniques and to be sensitive to the individual, cultural, and situational circumstances of their clients.

During the *skills acquisition and consolidation phase*, the focus is on giving clients a variety of behavioral and cognitive coping skills to apply to stressful situations. This phase involves direct actions, such as gathering information about their fears, learning specifically what situations bring about stress, arranging for ways to lessen the stress by doing something different, and learning methods of physical and psychological relaxation. The training involves cognitive coping; clients are taught that adaptive and maladaptive behaviors are linked to their inner dialogue. Through this training, clients acquire and rehearse a new set of self-statements. Meichenbaum (1986) provides some examples of coping statements that are rehearsed in this phase of SIT:

- "How can I prepare for a stressor?" ("What do I have to do? Can I develop a plan to deal with the stress?")
- "How can I confront and deal with what is stressing me?" ("What are some ways I can handle a stressor? How can I meet this challenge?")

- "How can I cope with feeling overwhelmed?" ("What can I do right now? How can I keep my fears in check?")
- "How can I make reinforcing self-statements?" ("How can I give myself credit?")

Clients also are exposed to various behavioral interventions, such as relaxation training, social skills training, time-management instruction, and self-instructional training. They are helped to make lifestyle changes by reevaluating priorities, developing support systems, and taking direct action to alter stressful situations. Through teaching, demonstration, and guided practice, clients learn the skills of progressive relaxation and practice them regularly to decrease arousal due to stress.

During the *application and follow-through phase*, the focus is on carefully arranging for transfer and maintenance of change from the therapeutic situation to everyday life. Clients practice their new self-statements and apply their new skills to everyday life. To consolidate the lessons learned in the training sessions, clients participate in a variety of activities, including imagery and behavior rehearsal, role playing, modeling, and graded in vivo exposure. Once clients have become proficient in cognitive and behavioral coping skills, they practice behavioral assignments, which become increasingly demanding. They are asked to write down the homework assignments they are willing to complete. The outcomes of these assignments are carefully checked at subsequent meetings, and if clients do not follow through with them, the therapist and the client collaboratively consider the reasons for the failure.

Relapse prevention, which consists of procedures for dealing with the inevitable setbacks clients are likely to experience as they apply what they are learning to daily life, is taught at this stage (Marlatt & Donovan, 2005). Part of relapse prevention involves teaching clients to view any lapses that occur as "learning opportunities" rather than "catastrophic failures." Clients explore a variety of possible high-risk stressful situations that they may reexperience. Then they rehearse and practice in a collaborative fashion with the therapist, and with other clients in a group, ways of applying skills they have learned in the training to maintain the gains they have made. Follow-up and booster sessions typically take place at 3-, 6-, and 12-month periods as an incentive for clients to continue practicing and refining their coping skills. SIT can be considered part of an ongoing stress management program that extends the benefits of training into the future.

Stress inoculation training has potentially useful applications for a wide variety of problems and clients and for both remediation and prevention. The clinical application of SIT has been individually tailored to specific target populations and includes anger control, anxiety management, assertion training, improving creative thinking, treating depression, and dealing with health problems. Stress inoculation training has been employed with medical patients and with psychiatric patients. SIT has been successfully used with children, adolescents, and adults who have anger problems, anxiety disorders, phobias, social incompetence, addictions, alcoholism, sexual dysfunctions, social withdrawal, or posttraumatic stress disorder (PTSD), including use with veterans who experience combat-related PTSD (Meichenbaum, 1993, 1994a, 1994b, 2007, 2008). Meichenbaum (2007) contends that the flexibility of the SIT format has contributed to its robust effectiveness.

The Constructivist Approach to Cognitive Behavior Therapy

Meichenbaum (1997) has developed his approach by incorporating the **constructivist narrative perspective** (CNP), which focuses on the stories people tell about themselves and others regarding significant events in their lives. Therapists elicit stories from their clients that are explored in the therapy process. This approach begins with the assumption that there are multiple realities. One of the therapeutic tasks is to help clients appreciate how they construct their realities and how they author their own stories (see Chapter 13). Meichenbaum describes the constructivist approach to cognitive behavior therapy as less structured and more discovery-oriented than standard cognitive therapy. The constructivist approach gives more emphasis to past development, tends to target deeper core beliefs, and explores the behavioral impact and emotional toll a client pays for clinging to certain root metaphors.

Meichenbaum (personal communication, October 21, 2010) claims that we are all "story tellers" and that we should beware of the stories that we tell ourselves and others. For example, victimized clients might see themselves as "prisoners of the past" or as "stubborn victims." These phrases are not idle metaphors; they are the organizing schemas that color the ways individuals view themselves, their world, and their future. Therapists help clients appreciate how they construct reality (story tell) and examine the implications and conclusions clients draw from their stories. Telling the "rest of the story"—what they did to survive and cope—bolsters clients' strengths and helps them develop resilient-engendering behaviors. In this way, clients can move from being "stubborn victims" to becoming "tenacious survivors" and perhaps "impressive thrivers." Meichenabum works in a collaborative fashion with clients to develop the coping skills necessary to achieve these treatment goals. He uses a Socratic discovery-oriented approach and the art of questioning to assist clients in reaching their goals.

Meichenbaum (1997) uses these questions to evaluate the outcomes of therapy:

- Are clients now able to tell a new story about themselves and the world?
- Do clients now use more positive metaphors to describe themselves?
- Are clients able to predict high-risk situations and employ coping skills in dealing with emerging problems?
- Are clients able to take credit for the changes they have been able to bring about?

In successful therapy clients develop their own voices, take pride in what they have accomplished, and take ownership of the changes they are bringing about. In short, clients become their own therapists and take the therapists' voice with them.

COGNITIVE BEHAVIOR THERAPY FROM A MULTICULTURAL PERSPECTIVE

Strengths From a Diversity Perspective

There are several strengths of cognitive behavioral approaches in working with individuals from diverse cultural, ethnic, and racial backgrounds. If therapists understand the core values of their culturally diverse clients, they can help clients explore these values and gain a full awareness of their conflicting feelings. Then the client and the therapist can work together to modify selected beliefs and practices. Cognitive behavior therapy tends to be culturally sensitive because it uses the individual's belief system, or worldview, as part of the method of self-exploration.

Because counselors with a cognitive behavioral orientation function as teachers, clients are actively involved in learning skills to deal with the problems of living. In speaking with colleagues who work with culturally diverse populations, I have learned that their clients tend to appreciate the emphasis on cognition and action, as well as the stress on relationship issues. The collaborative approach of CBT offers clients the structure they may want, yet the therapist still makes every effort to enlist clients' active cooperation and participation. According to Spiegler (2008), because of its basic nature and the way CBT is practiced, it is inherently suited to treating diverse clients. Some of the factors that Spiegler identifies that makes CBT diversity effective include individualized treatment, focusing on the external environment, active nature, emphasis on learning, reliance on empirical evidence, concern with present behavior, and brevity. A strength of CBT is integrating assessment throughout therapy, which communicates respect for clients' viewpoints regarding their progress.

According to Hays (2009), there is an "almost perfect fit" between cognitive behavior therapy and multicultural therapy because these perspectives share common assumptions that make integration possible. Some aspects that contribute to an integrative framework follow:

- Interventions are tailored to the unique needs and strengths of the individual.
- Clients are empowered by learning specific skills they can apply in daily life (CBT) and by the emphasis on cultural influences that contribute to clients' uniqueness (multicultural therapy).
- Inner resources and strengths of clients are activated to bring about change.
- Clients make changes that minimize stressors, increase personal strengths and supports, and establish skills for dealing more effectively with their physical and social (cultural) environments.

Shortcomings From a Diversity Perspective

Exploring values and core beliefs plays an important role in all of the cognitive behavioral approaches, and it is crucial for therapists to have some understanding of the cultural background of clients and to be sensitive to their struggles. Therapists would do well to use caution in confronting clients about their beliefs and behaviors until they clearly understand their cultural context. On this matter, Wolfe (2007) suggests that the therapist's job is to help clients examine and challenge long-standing cultural assumptions only if they result in dysfunctional emotions or behaviors. She writes that the therapist assists clients in critically thinking about "potential conflicts with the values of the dominant culture so they can work toward achieving their own personal goals within their own sociocultural context" (p. 188).

A potential limitation of REBT is its negative view of dependency. Many cultures view interdependence as necessary to good mental health. According to Ellis (1994), REBT is aimed at inducing people to examine and change some of their most basic values. Clients with certain long-cherished cultural values pertaining to interdependence are not likely to respond favorably to such forceful methods of persuasion toward independence. "REBT practitioners often employ a rapid-fire active-directive-persuasive philosophical methodology. In most instances, they quickly pin clients down to a few basic dysfunctional beliefs" (Ellis, 2011, p. 214). This style may intimidate or alienate clients who value being reflective. Modifications in a therapist's style need to be made depending on the client's culture.

Hays (2009) suggests that therapists avoid challenging the core cultural beliefs of clients, unless the client is clearly open to this. By emphasizing collaboration over confrontation, the therapist can avoid seeming to be disrespectful. Hays recommends drawing on the client's culturally related strengths in developing helpful ways of thinking to replace unhelpful cognitions. For example, consider an Asian American client, Sung, from a culture that stresses values such as doing one's best, cooperation, interdependence, and working hard. It is likely that Sung may feel that she is bringing shame to her family if she is going through a divorce, and she may feel guilt if she perceives that she is not living up to the expectations and standards set for her by her family and her community. The rules for Sung are likely to be different than are the rules for a male member of her culture. The counselor could assist Sung in understanding and exploring how both her gender and her culture are factors to consider in her situation. If Sung is confronted too quickly on living by the expectations or rules of others, the results are likely to be counterproductive. Sung might even leave counseling feeling that she has been misunderstood.

Cormier, Nurius, and Osborn (2013) suggest that therapists refrain from jargon and use of disrespectful language when describing clients' cognitions, avoiding terms such as *rational* and *irrational*, or *maladaptive* and *dysfunctional*. This is especially important when interacting with individuals who feel marginalized by the mainstream culture. They recommend adapting the language presented in cognitive restructuring to the client's primary language, age, and educational level. These guidelines can certainly be applied to REBT practitioners who might do well to reflect on the words they use and their tone, especially when zeroing in on a client's core beliefs.

The emphasis of CBT on assertiveness, independence, verbal ability, rationality, cognition, and behavioral change may limit its use in cultures that value subtle communication over assertiveness, interdependence over personal independence, listening and observing over talking, and acceptance over behavior change (Hayes, 2009). In CBT the focus is on the present, which can result in the therapist failing to recognize the role of the past in a client's development. Cognitive behavioral assessments involve the investigation of a client's *personal* history. If the therapist is unaware of a client's *cultural* beliefs, which are rooted in the past, the therapist may have difficulty interpreting the client's personal experiences accurately. Another limitation of CBT from a multicultural perspective involves its individualistic orientation. An inexperienced therapist may overemphasize cognitive restructuring to the neglect of environmental interventions. Hays points out that these potential limitations do not preclude the integration of CBT and multicultural counseling. Instead, being aware of these limitations "presents opportunities for rethinking, refining, adapting and increasing the relevance and effectiveness of psychotherapy" (p. 356).

From a cognitive behavioral perspective, I want Stan to critically evaluate and modify his self-defeating beliefs, which will likely result in Stan acquiring more effective behavior. As his therapist, I am both goal oriented and problem focused. From the initial session, I ask Stan to identify his problems and formulate specific goals and help him reconceptualize his problems in a way that will increase his chances of finding solutions.

I follow a clear structure for every session. The basic procedural sequence includes (1) preparing him by providing a cognitive rationale for treatment and demystifying treatment; (2) encouraging him to monitor the thoughts that accompany his distress; (3) implementing behavioral and cognitive techniques; (4) assisting him in identifying and examining some basic beliefs and ideas; (5) teaching him ways to examine his beliefs and assumptions by testing them in reality; and (6) teaching him basic coping skills that will enable him to avoid relapsing into old patterns.

As a part of the structure of the therapy sessions, I ask Stan for a brief review of the week, elicit feedback from the previous session, review homework assignments, collaboratively create an agenda for the session, discuss topics on the agenda, and set new homework for the week. I encourage Stan to perform personal experiments and practice coping skills in daily life.

Stan tells me that he would like to work on his fear of women and would hope to feel far less intimidated by them. He reports that he feels threatened by most women, but especially by women he perceives as powerful. In working with Stan's fears, I proceed with four steps: educating him about his self-talk; having him monitor and evaluate his faulty beliefs; using cognitive and behavioral interventions; and collaboratively designing homework with Stan that will give him opportunities to practice new behaviors in daily life.

First, I educate him about the importance of examining his automatic thoughts, his self-talk, and the many "shoulds," "oughts," and "musts" he has accepted without questioning. Working with Stan as a collaborative partner in his therapy, I guide him in discovering some basic cognitions that influence what he tells himself and how he feels and acts. This is some of his self-talk:

- "I always have to be strong, tough, and perfect."
- "I'm not a man if I show any signs of weakness."
- "If everyone didn't love me and approve of me, things would be catastrophic."
- "If a woman rejected me, I really would be reduced to a 'nothing.'"
- "If I fail, I am then a failure as a person."
- "I'm apologetic for my existence because I don't feel equal to others."

Second, I assist Stan in monitoring and evaluating the ways in which he keeps telling himself these self-defeating sentences. I assist him in clarifying specific problems and learning how to critically evaluate some of his faulty thinking:

> You're not your father. I wonder why you continue telling yourself that you're just like him? Do you think you need to continue accepting without question your parents' value judgments about your worth? Where is the evidence that they were right in their assessment of you? You say you're such a failure and that you feel inferior. Do your present activities support this? If you were not so hard on yourself, how might your life be different?

Third, once Stan more fully understands the nature of his cognitive distortions and his self-defeating beliefs, I draw on a variety of cognitive and behavioral techniques to help Stan make the changes he most desires. Through various cognitive techniques, he learns to identify, evaluate, and respond to his dysfunctional beliefs. I rely heavily on cognitive techniques such as *Socratic questioning, guided discovery,* and *cognitive restructuring* to assist Stan in examining the evidence that seems to support or contradict his core beliefs. I work with Stan so he will view his basic beliefs and automatic thinking as hypotheses to be tested. In a way, he will become a personal scientist by checking out the validity of many of the conclusions and basic assumptions that contribute to his personal difficulties. By the use of guided discovery, Stan learns to evaluate the validity and functionality of his beliefs and conclusions. Stan can also profit from cognitive restructuring, which would entail his observing his own behavior in various situations. For example, during the week he can take a particular situation that is problematic for him, paying particular attention to his automatic thoughts and internal dialogue. What is he telling himself as he approaches a difficult situation? How is he setting himself up for failure with his self-talk? As he learns to attend to his maladaptive behaviors, he begins to see that what he tells himself has as much impact as others' statements about him. He also sees the connections between his thinking and his behavioral problems. With this awareness he is in an ideal place to begin to learn a new, more functional internal dialogue.

Fourth, I work collaboratively with him in creating specific homework assignments to help him deal with his fears. It is expected that Stan will learn new coping skills, which he can practice first in the sessions and then in daily life situations. It is not enough for him to merely say new things to himself; Stan needs to apply his new cognitive and behavioral coping skills in various daily situations. At one point, for instance, I ask Stan to explore his fears of powerful women and his reasons for continuing to tell himself: "They expect me to be strong and perfect. If I'm not careful, they'll dominate me." His homework includes approaching a woman for a date. If he succeeds in getting the date, he can think about his catastrophic expectations of what might happen. What would be so terrible if she did not like him or if she refused the date? Stan tells himself over and over that he must be *approved of* by women and that if any woman rebuffs him the consequences are more than he can bear. With practice, he learns to label distortions and is able to automatically identify his dysfunctional thoughts and monitor his cognitive patterns. Through a variety of cognitive and behavioral strategies, he is able to acquire new information, change his basic beliefs, and implement new and more effective behavior.

Follow-Up: You Continue as Stan's Cognitive Behavior Therapist

Use these questions to help you think about how to counsel Stan using a cognitive behavior approach:

- My therapeutic style is characterized as an integrative form of cognitive behavioral therapy. I borrow concepts and techniques from the approaches of Ellis, Beck, and Meichenbaum. In your work with Stan, what specific concepts would you borrow from these approaches? What cognitive behavioral techniques would you use? What possible advantages do you see, if any, in applying an integrative cognitive behavioral approach in your work with Stan?

- What are some things you would most want to teach Stan about how cognitive behavior therapy works? How would you explain to him the therapeutic alliance and the collaborative therapeutic relationship?

- What are some of Stan's most prominent faulty beliefs that get in the way of his living fully? What cognitive and behavioral techniques might you use in helping him examine his core beliefs?

- Stan lives by many "shoulds" and "oughts." His automatic thoughts seem to impede him from getting what he wants. What techniques would you use to encourage guided discovery on his part?

- What are some homework assignments that would be useful for Stan to carry out? How would you collaboratively design homework with Stan? How would you encourage him to develop action plans to test the validity of his thinking and his conclusions?

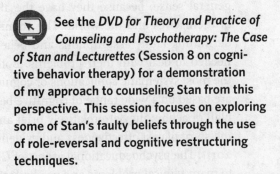 **See the *DVD for Theory and Practice of Counseling and Psychotherapy: The Case of Stan and Lecturettes* (Session 8 on cognitive behavior therapy) for a demonstration of my approach to counseling Stan from this perspective. This session focuses on exploring some of Stan's faulty beliefs through the use of role-reversal and cognitive restructuring techniques.**

SUMMARY AND EVALUATION

Summary

REBT has evolved into a comprehensive and integrative approach that emphasizes thinking, judging, deciding, and doing. This approach is based on the premise of the interconnectedness of thinking, feeling, and behaving. Therapy begins with clients' problematic behaviors and emotions and disputes the thoughts that directly create them. To block the self-defeating beliefs that are reinforced by a process of self-indoctrination, REBT therapists employ active and directive techniques such as teaching, suggestion, persuasion, and homework assignments, and they challenge clients to substitute a rational belief system for an irrational one. Therapists demonstrate how and why dysfunctional beliefs lead to negative emotional and behavioral results. They teach clients how to dispute self-defeating beliefs and behaviors that might occur in the future. REBT stresses action—doing something about the insights one gains in therapy. Change comes about mainly by a commitment to consistently practice new behaviors that replace old and ineffective ones.

Rational emotive behavior therapists are typically eclectic in selecting therapeutic strategies. They have the latitude to develop their own personal style and to exercise creativity; they are not bound by fixed techniques for particular problems. Cognitive therapists also practice from an integrative stance, using many methods to assist clients in modifying their self-talk. The working alliance is given special importance in cognitive therapy as a way of forming a collaborative partnership. Although the client–therapist relationship is viewed as necessary, it is not sufficient for successful outcomes. In cognitive therapy, it is presumed that clients are helped by the skillful use of a range of cognitive and behavioral interventions and by their willingness to perform homework assignments between sessions.

All of the cognitive behavioral approaches stress the importance of cognitive processes as determinants of behavior. It is assumed that how people feel and what they actually do is largely influenced by their subjective assessment and interpretation of situations. Because this appraisal of life situations is influenced by beliefs, attitudes, assumptions, and internal dialogue, such cognitions become the major focus of therapy.

Contributions of the Cognitive Behavioral Approaches

Most of the therapies discussed in this book can be considered "cognitive," in a general sense, because they have the aim of changing clients' subjective views of themselves and the world. The cognitive behavioral approaches focus on undermining faulty assumptions and beliefs and teaching clients the coping skills needed to deal with their problems. Both Ellis's REBT and Beck's CT represent the most systematic applications of cognitive behavior therapy. Both REBT and CT are based on a wide range of cognitive behavioral techniques and follow a defined plan of action; they are relatively brief and structured treatments in keeping with the spirit of cost effectiveness and evidence-based practice (Hollon & DiGiuseppe, 2011). The psychoeducational aspect of CBT is a clear strength that can be applied to many clinical problems and used effectively in many settings with diverse client populations.

ELLIS'S REBT I find aspects of REBT very valuable in my work because I believe we are responsible for maintaining self-destructive ideas and attitudes that influence our daily transactions. I see value in asking clients questions such as "What are your assumptions and basic beliefs?" and "Have you examined the core ideas you live by to determine if they are your own values or merely introjects?" REBT has built on the Adlerian notion that events themselves do not have the power to determine us; rather, it is our interpretation of these events that is crucial. The A-B-C framework simply and clearly illustrates how human disturbances occur and the ways in which problematic behavior can be changed. Rather than focusing on events themselves, therapy stresses how clients interpret and react to what happens to them and the necessity of actively disputing a range of faulty beliefs.

One of the strengths of REBT is the focus on teaching clients ways to carry on their own therapy without the direct intervention of a therapist. I particularly like the emphasis that REBT puts on supplementary and psychoeducational approaches such as listening to tapes, reading self-help books, keeping a record of what they are doing and thinking, carrying out homework assignments, and attending workshops. In this way clients can further the process of change in themselves without becoming excessively dependent on a therapist.

BECK'S COGNITIVE THERAPY Beck's key concepts share similarities with REBT, but differ in underlying philosophy, the process by which therapy proceeds, and the formulation and treatment for different disorders. Beck made pioneering efforts in the treatment of anxiety, phobias, and depression. Today, empirically validated treatments for both anxiety and depression have revolutionized therapeutic practice; research has demonstrated the efficacy of cognitive therapy for a variety of problems (Leahy, 2002; Scher, Segal, & Ingram, 2006). Beck developed specific cognitive procedures to help depressive clients evaluate their assumptions and beliefs and to create a new cognitive perspective that can lead to optimism and changed behavior. The effects of cognitive therapy on depression and hopelessness have been demonstrated through research to be maintained for at least one year after treatment. Cognitive therapy has been applied to a wide range of clinical populations that Beck did not originally believe were appropriate for this model, including treatment for posttraumatic stress disorder, schizophrenia, delusional disorders, bipolar disorder, and various personality disorders (Leahy, 2002, 2006a). The credibility of the cognitive model grows out of the fact that many of its propositions have been empirically tested.

Beck demonstrated that a structured therapy that is present centered and problem oriented can be very effective in treating depression and anxiety in a relatively short time. One of Beck's major theoretical contributions has been bringing private experience back into the realm of legitimate scientific inquiry (Weishaar, 1993). A strength of cognitive therapy is its focus on developing a detailed case conceptualization as a way to understand how clients view their world.

A key strength of all the cognitive behavioral therapies is that they are integrative forms of psychotherapy, and this is particularly true of cognitive therapy. Beck considers cognitive therapy to be *the* integrative psychotherapy because it draws from so many different modalities of psychotherapy (Alford & Beck, 1997).

MEICHENBAUM'S COGNITIVE BEHAVIOR MODIFICATION Meichenbaum's work in self-instruction and stress inoculation training has been applied successfully to a variety of client populations and specific problems. Of special note is his contribution to understanding how stress is largely self-induced through inner dialogue. Meichenbaum's integration of the constructivist perspective is a key strength in that he is able to combine elements of the postmodern interest in stories clients tell with assisting clients in changing their cognitions, feelings, and behaviors by drawing on a cognitive behavioral conceptual framework.

A contribution of all of the cognitive behavioral approaches is the emphasis on putting newly acquired insights into action. Homework assignments are well suited to enabling clients to practice new behaviors and assisting them in the process of learning more effective coping skills. Adlerian therapy, reality therapy, behavior therapy, and solution-focused brief therapy all share with the cognitive behavioral approaches this action orientation. It is important that homework be a natural outgrowth of what is taking place in the therapy session. Clients are more likely to carry out their homework if the assignments are collaboratively created. Meichenbaum's stress inoculation training places special emphasis on practicing new skills both in the training itself and in daily life, and homework is a key part of the training process. Clients learn how to generalize coping skills to various problem situations and acquire relapse prevention strategies to ensure that their gains are consolidated.

A major contribution made by Ellis, the Becks, and Meichenbaum is the demystification of the therapy process. The cognitive behavioral approaches are based on an educational model that stresses a working alliance between therapist and client. The models encourage self-help, provide for continuous feedback from the client on how well treatment strategies are working, and provide a structure and direction to the therapy process that allows for evaluation of outcomes. Clients are active, informed, and responsible for the direction of therapy because they are partners in the enterprise.

Limitations and Criticisms of the Cognitive Behavioral Approaches

The cognitive behavioral approaches focus only limited attention on the role of emotions in treatment. Although Dattilio (2001) admits that CBT places central emphasis on cognition and behavior, he maintains that emotion is not ignored in the therapy process; rather, he believes that emotion is a by-product of cognition and behavior and is addressed in a different fashion. Some potential limitations of the various CBT approaches follow.

ELLIS'S REBT I value paying attention to a client's past without getting lost in this past and without assuming a fatalistic stance about earlier traumatic experiences. I question the REBT assumption that exploring the past is ineffective in helping clients change faulty thinking and behavior. From my perspective, exploring past childhood experiences can have a great deal of therapeutic power if the discussion is connected to our present functioning.

Another potential limitation involves the misuse of the therapist's power by imposing ideas of what constitutes rational thinking. Due to the active and directive nature of this approach, it is particularly important for practitioners to know themselves well and to avoid imposing their own philosophy of life on their clients. Because the therapist has a large amount of power by virtue of persuasion, psychological harm is more possible in REBT than in less directive approaches.

As Ellis practiced it, REBT is a forceful and confrontational therapy. Some clients will have trouble with a confrontational style, especially if a strong therapeutic alliance has not been established. It is well to underscore that REBT can be effective when practiced in a style different from Ellis's. Indeed, a therapist can be soft-spoken and gentle and still use REBT concepts and methods effectively. Janet Wolfe, who has supervised hundreds of practitioners in her 30 years at the Albert Ellis Institute, makes the point that therapists do not need to emulate Ellis's style to effectively incorporate REBT into their own repertoire of interventions. Wolfe (2007) encourages practitioners to embrace this useful therapy approach, but to develop a style that is consistent with their own personality.

For practitioners who value a spiritual dimension of psychotherapy, Ellis's views on religion and spirituality are likely to raise some problems. Historically, Ellis has declared himself as an atheist and has long been critical of dogmatic religions that instill guilt in people. Ellis (2004b) has written about the core philosophies that can either improve our mental health or can lead to disturbances. Although his tone softened over the years, he was still critical of any philosophies that promoted rigid beliefs. Personally, I think that a spiritual and a religious orientation can be incorporated into the practice of REBT if this is meaningful to the client and if this is done in a thoughtful manner by the therapist. Throughout his life, Ellis was driven by his passion to teach people about REBT, and he always chuckled when he said in his workshops that his mission was to spread the gospel according to St. Albert. Indeed, I would say that his "religion" is embodied in the principles and practices of REBT. For more on this topic, see *The Road to Tolerance* (Ellis, 2004b).

BECK'S COGNITIVE THERAPY Cognitive therapy has been criticized for focusing too much on the power of positive thinking; being too superficial and simplistic; denying the importance of the client's past; being too technique oriented; failing to use the therapeutic relationship; working only on eliminating symptoms, but failing to explore the underlying causes of difficulties; ignoring the role of unconscious factors; and neglecting the role of feelings (Freeman & Dattilio, 1992; Weishaar, 1993).

Freeman and Dattilio (1992, 1994; Dattilio, 2001) do a good job of debunking the myths and misconceptions about cognitive therapy. Weishaar (1993) concisely addresses a number of criticisms leveled at the approach. Although the cognitive therapist is straightforward and looks for simple rather than complex solutions, this does not imply that the practice of cognitive therapy is simple. Cognitive therapists do not explore the unconscious or underlying conflicts but work with clients in the present to bring about changes in their core beliefs. However, they do recognize that clients' current problems are often a product of earlier life experiences, and thus, they may explore with clients, especially those with Axis II disorders, the ways their past is presently influencing them.

MEICHENBAUM'S COGNITIVE BEHAVIOR MODIFICATION Some practitioners who apply stress inoculation training focus more on techniques to change a client's reaction to stress or pay too much attention to the client's internal dialogue. Meichenbaum is a high-energy person and is very charismatic in his workshop presentations. I suspect that much of the success of his approach has to do with his level of caring and his creativity in implementing CBT interventions. Practitioners without his wit, energy, personal flair, and direct therapeutic style may not get the same results even though they follow his treatment protocol. This emphasizes the importance of each therapist developing his or her own unique therapeutic style. Meichenbaum (1986) cautions cognitive behavioral practitioners against the tendency to become overly preoccupied with techniques. If progress is to be made, he suggests that cognitive behavior therapy must develop a testable theory of behavior change. He reports that some attempts have been made to formulate a cognitive social learning theory that will explain behavior change and specify the best methods of intervention.

A potential limitation of any of the cognitive behavioral approaches is the therapist's level of personal development, training, knowledge, skill, and perceptiveness. Although this is true of all therapeutic approaches, it is especially true for CBT practitioners because they tend to be active, highly structured, and offer clients psychoeducational information and teach life skills. According to Judith Beck (personal communication, May 27, 2011), a limitation in learning cognitive therapy is that therapists need to learn the specific cognitive formulation for each disorder they treat and learn how to address the key cognitions and behavioral strategies for each disorder. Macy (2007) stresses that the effective use of cognitive behavior therapy interventions requires extensive study, training, and practice: "Effective implementation of these interventions requires that the practitioner be fully grounded in the therapy's theory and premises, and be able to use a range of associated techniques and interventions" (p. 159).

WHERE TO GO FROM HERE

In the *DVD for Integrative Counseling: The Case of Ruth and Lecturettes,* I work with Ruth from a cognitive behavioral perspective in a number of therapy sessions. In Sessions 6, 7, and 8, I demonstrate my way of working with Ruth from a cognitive, emotive, and behavioral focus. See also Session 9 ("Integrative Perspective"), which illustrates the interactive nature of working with Ruth on thinking, feeling, and doing levels.

Other Resources

DVDs relevant to this chapter offered by the American Psychological Association from their Systems of Psychotherapy Video Series include the following:

Beck, J. (2005). *Cognitive Therapy*

Meichenbaum, D. (2007). *Cognitive Behavioral Therapy With Donald Meichenbaum*

Vernon, A. (2010). *Rational Emotive Behavior Therapy Over Time*

Dobson, K. S. (2010). *Cognitive Therapy Over Time*

Persons, J. (2006). *Cognitive-Behavior Therapy*

Dobson, K. S. (2008). *Cognitive-Behavioral Therapy for Perfectionism Over Time*

Dobson, K. S. (2011). *Cognitive-Behavioral Therapy Strategies*

Psychotherapy.net is a comprehensive resource for students and professionals that offers videos and interviews on cognitive behavior therapy. New video and editorial content is made available monthly. DVDs relevant to this chapter are available at www.psychotherapy.net and include the following:

Beck, J. (2010). *Cognitive Therapy for Weight Loss: A Coaching Session*

Ellis, A. (1996). *Rational-Emotive Therapy for Addictions*

Ellis, A. (1996). *Coping With the Suicide of a Loved One: An REBT Approach*

Freeman, A. (1994). *Depression: A Cognitive Therapy Approach*

Krumboltz, J. (1997). *Cognitive-Behavioral Therapy With John Krumboltz* (Psychotherapy With the Experts Series)

Lazarus, A. (1997). *Multimodal Therapy* (Psychotherapy With the Experts Series)

Liese, B. (2000). *Cognitive Therapy for Addictions* (Brief Therapy for Addictions Series)

Masek, B. (2002). *Cognitive-Behavioral Child Therapy* (Child Therapy With the Experts Series)

Meichenbaum, D. (1996). *Mixed Anxiety and Depression: A Cognitive-Behavioral Approach*

Meichenbaum, D. (2000). *Cognitive-Behavioral Therapy With Donald Meichenbaum* (Psychotherapy With the Experts Series)

The *Journal of Rational-Emotive and Cognitive-Behavior Therapy* is published by Kluwer Academic/Human Sciences Press. This quarterly journal is an excellent way to keep informed of a wide variety of cognitive behavioral specialists.

For information about the work of Albert Ellis, and current training opportunities, contact:

Debbie Joffe
Telephone: (917) 887-2006
Website: www.rebtnetwork.org/

The *International Journal of Cognitive Therapy*, edited by John Riskind, also provides information on theory, practice, and research in cognitive behavior therapy. Information about the journal is available from the International Association of Cognitive Psychotherapy or by contacting John Riskind directly.

Dr. John Riskind
George Mason University
Department of Psychology, MSN 3F5
Fairfax, VA 22030-4444
Telephone: (703) 993-4094
Private Practice Telephone: (703) 280-8060

Fax: (703) 993-1359
E-mail: jriskind@gmu.edu
Website: www.the-iacp.com

The Center for Cognitive Therapy, Newport Beach, California, maintains a website for mental health professionals. They list cognitive therapy books, audio and video training tapes, current advanced training workshops, and other cognitive therapy resources and information.

Center for Cognitive Therapy
E-mail: mooney@padesky.com
Website: http://www.padesky.com

For more information about CBT workshops, supervision, a CBT blog, and newsletter, contact the Beck Institute.

Beck Institute for Cognitive Behavior Therapy
One Belmont Avenue, Suite 700
Bala Cynwyd, PA 19004-1610
Telephone: (610) 664-3020
Fax: (610) 709-5336
E-mail: info@beckinstitute.org
Website: www.beckinstitute.org

The "home" organization for cognitive therapists worldwide is the Academy of Cognitive Therapy, which Judith S. Beck was instrumental in founding.

Academy of Cognitive Therapy
Website: www.academyofct.org

The American Institute for Cognitive Therapy is an internationally recognized group of clinical psychologists and psychotherapists who provide the highest quality cognitive behavioral treatment for depression, anxiety, phobias, eating disorders, personality disorders, child and adolescent problems, and family and marital problems.

American Institute for Cognitive Therapy
Robert L. Leahy, PhD
136 E 57th St., Suite 1101
New York, NY 10022
Telephone: (212) 308-2440
Fax: (212) 308-3099
E-mail: AICT@aol.com
Website: www.cognitivetherapynyc.com

Donald Meichenbaum is research director of the Melissa Institute for Violence Prevention, a nonprofit organization designed to "give science away" in order to reduce violence and to treat victims of violence. The institute is dedicated to the study and prevention of violence through education, community service, research support, and consultation.

Melissa Institute for Violence Prevention
Website: www.melissainstitute.org

Reality Therapy

WILLIAM GLASSER

(b. 1925), currently retired, was educated at Case Western Reserve University in Cleveland, Ohio. Initially a chemical engineer, he turned to psychology (MA, Clinical Psychology, 1948) and then to psychiatry, attending medical school (MD, 1953) with the intention of becoming a psychiatrist. By 1957 he had completed his psychiatric training at the Veterans Administration and UCLA in Los Angeles and in 1961 was board certified in psychiatry.

Glasser was married to Naomi for 47 years, and she was very involved with the William Glasser Institute until her death in 1992. In 1995 Glasser married Carleen, who is an instructor at the institute. Glasser played tennis often until recently, and now, at age 86, he enjoys watching basketball on television.

Very early Glasser rejected the Freudian model, partly due to his observation of psychoanalytically trained therapists who did not seem to be implementing Freudian principles. Rather, they tended to hold people responsible for their behavior. Early in his career, Glasser was a psychiatrist at the Ventura School, a prison and school for girls operated by the California Youth Authority. He became convinced that his psychoanalytic training was of limited utility in counseling these young people. From these observations, Glasser thought it best to talk to the sane part of clients, not their disturbed side. Glasser was also influenced by G. L. Harrington, a psychiatrist and mentor. Harrington believed in getting his patients involved in projects in the real world, and by the end of his residency Glasser began to put together ideas that would later be known as reality therapy.

In 1962 Glasser began to present public lectures on "reality psychiatry," but few psychiatrists were in the audience. Most of those attending were educators, social workers, counselors, and correctional workers, so Glasser changed the name of his system to "reality therapy," which became the title of his groundbreaking book published in 1965. Educators found the principles of reality therapy helpful, and he was asked to apply it to the classroom and the school as an organization. As a result of this experience, he wrote *Schools Without Failure* in 1968, which had a major impact on the administration of schools, the training of teachers, and the way learning is conducted in schools. Glasser took the position that schools needed to be structured in ways to help students achieve a *success identity* as opposed to a *failure identity*. He advocated for a curriculum geared to the lives of learners. Glasser made significant contributions through in-service workshops for teachers and administrators. Since the late 1960s, reality therapy has been further applied to education and to virtually all other human relationships, especially intimate relationships.

Glasser became convinced that it was of paramount importance that clients accept personal responsibility for their behavior. By the early 1980s, Glasser was looking for a theory that could explain all his work. Glasser learned about *control theory* from William Powers, and he believed this theory had great potential. He spent the next 10 years expanding, revising, and clarifying what he was initially taught. By 1996 Glasser had become convinced that these revisions had so changed the theory that it was misleading to continue to call it control theory, and he changed the name to *choice theory* to reflect all that he had developed. The essence of reality therapy, now taught all over the world, is that we are all responsible for what we choose to do. We are internally motivated by current needs and wants, and we control our present behavioral choices.

ROBERT E. WUBBOLDING, EdD

(b. 1936), born and raised in Cincinnati, Ohio, is the youngest of six children. He received his doctorate in counseling from the University of Cincinnati, is a member of several professional organizations, and has licenses as a counselor and as a psychologist. He taught high school history, worked as a high school and elementary school counselor, and served as a consultant to drug and alcohol abuse programs of the U.S. Army and Air Force. In addition, Bob Wubbolding began a career in the Catholic priesthood but later "left the clergy freely and honorably." He is married to Sandra Trifilio, a former French teacher, who shares his passion for his work and is administrator of the Center for Reality Therapy, as well as editor of his writings.

He is now the director of the Center for Reality Therapy in Cincinnati and professor emeritus of Xavier University, where he taught counselor education for 32 years. He loved teaching and viewed his students as being highly motivated, eager to learn, and experienced. One of his most meaningful experiences was teaching graduate students in the counseling department at Xavier University.

After completing his doctorate, Wubbolding attended training sessions representing a wide range of counseling approaches, yet he found reality therapy to be best suited to his interests. He attended many intensive training workshops conducted by William Glasser in Los Angeles, and in 1988 Glasser appointed him director of training for the William Glasser Institute.

Wubbolding served as visiting professor at the University of Southern California in their overseas programs in Japan, Korea, and Germany, thus fulfilling his lifelong desire to travel and to live in other countries. He has become an internationally known teacher, author, and practitioner of reality therapy and has introduced choice theory and reality therapy in Europe, Asia, and the Middle East. Among his specialties is adapting choice theory and reality therapy to various cultures and ethnic groups. He received the Gratitude Award (2009) for Initiating Reality Therapy in the United Kingdom and the Certificate of Reality Therapy Psychotherapist by the European Association for Psychotherapy (2009).

Wubbolding has extended the theory and practice of reality therapy with his conceptualization of the WDEP system, which is described later in the chapter. He has written 11 books and more than 145 articles, essays, and chapters in textbooks as well as preparing 12 videos/DVDs, some of which are referenced in this chapter. His religious commitment and his life of service to others are apparent in his work, and he continues his vocation of teacher, counselor, psychologist, and active member of his church.

INTRODUCTION

Reality therapists believe the underlying problem of most clients is the same: they are either involved in a present unsatisfying relationship or lack what could even be called a relationship. Many of the problems of clients are caused by their inability to connect, to get close to others, or to have a satisfying or successful relationship with at least one significant person in their lives. The therapist guides clients toward a satisfying relationship and teaches them more effective ways of behaving. The more clients are able to connect with people, the greater chance they have to experience happiness.

Few clients understand that their problem, which is unhappiness, results from the way they are choosing to behave. What they do know is that they feel a great deal of pain or that they are unhappy because they have been sent for counseling by someone with authority who is not satisfied with their behavior—typically a court official, a school administrator, an employer, a spouse, or a parent. Reality therapists recognize that clients choose their behaviors as a way to deal with the frustrations caused by unsatisfying relationships.

Glasser (2003) contends that clients should not be labeled with a diagnosis except when it is necessary for insurance purposes. From Glasser's perspective, diagnoses are descriptions of the behaviors people choose in their attempt to deal with the pain and frustration that is endemic to their unsatisfying present relationships. Labeling these ineffective behaviors as mental illness is inaccurate. Glasser believes mental illnesses are conditions such as Alzheimer's disease, epilepsy, head trauma, and brain infections—conditions associated with tangible brain damage. Because these people are suffering from a brain abnormality, he contends they should be treated primarily by neurologists.

Reality therapy is based on choice theory as it is explained in several of Glasser's (1998, 2001, 2003) books. (In this chapter, the discussion of Glasser's ideas pertains to these three books, unless otherwise specified.) **Choice theory** is the theoretical basis for reality therapy; it explains why and how we function. **Reality therapy** provides a delivery system for helping individuals take more effective control of their lives. If choice theory is the highway, reality therapy is the vehicle delivering the product (Wubbolding, 2011a). Therapy consists mainly of helping and sometimes teaching clients to make more effective choices as they deal with the people they need in their lives. Glasser maintains that it is essential for the therapist to establish a satisfying relationship with clients as a prerequisite for effective therapy. Once this relationship is developed, the skill of the therapist as a teacher assumes a central role.

Reality therapy has been used in a variety of settings. The approach is applicable to counseling, social work, education, crisis intervention, corrections and rehabilitation, institutional management, and community development. Reality therapy is popular in schools, general hospitals, state mental hospitals, halfway houses, and alcohol and drug abuse centers. Many of the military clinics that treat substance abusers use reality therapy as their preferred therapeutic approach.

 See the video program for Chapter 11, *DVD for Theory and Practice of Counseling and Psychotherapy: The Case of Stan and Lecturettes.* I suggest that you view the brief lecture for each chapter prior to reading the chapter.

KEY CONCEPTS

View of Human Nature

Choice theory posits that we are not born blank slates waiting to be *externally motivated* by forces in the world around us. Rather, we are born with five genetically encoded needs that drive us all our lives: *survival,* or self-preservation; *love and belonging; power,* or inner control; *freedom,* or independence; and *fun,* or enjoyment. Each of us has all five needs, but they vary in strength. For example, we all have a need for love and belonging, but some of us need more love than others. Choice theory is based on the premise that because we are by nature social creatures we need to both receive and give love. Glasser (2001, 2005) believes the need *to love and to belong* is the primary need because we need people to satisfy the other needs. It is also the most difficult need to satisfy because we must have a cooperative person to help us meet it.

Our brain functions as a control system. It continually monitors our feelings to determine how well we are doing in our lifelong effort to satisfy these needs. Whenever we feel bad, one or more of these five needs is unsatisfied. Although we may not be aware of our needs, we know that we want to feel better. Driven by pain, we try to figure out how to feel better. Reality therapists teach clients choice theory, sometimes subtly and indirectly, so clients can identify unmet needs and try to satisfy them.

Choice theory teaches that we do not satisfy our needs directly. What we do, beginning shortly after birth and continuing all our lives, is to keep close track of anything we do that feels very good. We store information inside our minds and build a file of wants, called our **quality world**, which is at the core of our life. It is our personal Shangri-la—the world we would like to live in if we could. It is completely based on our wants and needs, but unlike the needs, which are general, it is very specific. The quality world consists of specific images of people, activities, events, beliefs, possessions, and situations that fulfill our needs (Wubbolding, 2000, 2011a). Our quality world is like a picture album. We develop an inner **picture album** of specific wants as well as precise ways to satisfy these wants. We are attempting to behave in a way that gives us the most effective control over our lives. Some pictures may be blurred, and the therapist's role is to help the client clarify them. Pictures exist in priority for most people, yet clients may have difficulty identifying their priorities. Part of the process of reality therapy is assisting clients in prioritizing their wants and uncovering what is most important to them (Wubbolding, 2011a).

People are the most important component of our quality world, and these are the people we most want to connect with. It contains the people we are closest to and most enjoy being with. Those who enter therapy generally have no one in their quality world or, more often, someone in their quality world that they are unable to relate to in a satisfying way. For therapy to have a chance of success, a therapist must be the kind of person that clients would consider putting in their quality world. Getting into the clients' quality world is the art of therapy. It is from this relationship with the therapist that clients begin to learn how to get close to the people they need.

Choice Theory Explanation of Behavior

Choice theory explains that all we ever do from birth to death is behave and, with rare exceptions, everything we do is chosen. Every total behavior is our best attempt to get what we want to satisfy our needs. **Total behavior** teaches that all behavior is made up of four inseparable but distinct components—*acting, thinking, feeling,* and *physiology*—that necessarily accompany all of our actions, thoughts, and feelings. Choice theory emphasizes thinking and acting, which makes this a general form of cognitive behavior therapy. The primary emphasis is on what the client is doing on and how the doing component influences the other aspects of total behavior. Behavior is purposeful because it is designed to close the gap between what we want and what we perceive we are getting. Specific behaviors are always generated from this discrepancy. Our behaviors come from the inside, and thus we choose our destiny.

Glasser says that to speak of being depressed, having a headache, being angry, or being anxious implies passivity and lack of personal responsibility, and it is inaccurate. It is more accurate to think of these as parts of total behaviors and to use the verb forms *depressing, headaching, angering,* and *anxietying* to describe them. It is more accurate to think of people depressing or angering themselves rather than being depressed or being angry. When people choose misery by developing a range of "paining" behaviors, it is because these are the best behaviors they are able to devise at the time, and these behaviors often get them what they want.

When a reality therapist starts teaching choice theory, the client will often protest and say, "I'm suffering; don't tell me I'm choosing to suffer like this." As painful as depressing is, the therapist explains that people do not choose pain and suffering directly; rather, it is an unchosen part of their total behavior. The behavior of the person is the best effort, ineffective as it is, to satisfy needs.

Robert Wubbolding (personal communication, September 7, 2010) has added a new idea to choice theory. He believes that behavior is a language, and that we send messages by what we are doing. The purpose of behavior is to influence the world to get what we want. Therapists ask clients what messages they are sending to the world by way of their actions: "What message do you want others to get?" "What message are others getting whether or not you intended to send them?" By considering the messages that clients send to others, counselors can help clients indirectly gain a greater appreciation of messages they unintentionally send to others.

Characteristics of Reality Therapy

Contemporary **reality therapy** focuses quickly on the unsatisfying relationship or the lack of a relationship, which is often the cause of clients' problems. Glasser has given increasing attention to the role of meaningful relationships in fostering emotional health. Clients may complain of a problem such as not being able to keep a job, not doing well in school, or not having a meaningful relationship. When clients complain about how other people are causing them pain, the therapist does not get involved with finding fault. Reality therapists ask clients to consider how effective their choices are, especially as these choices affect their relationships with significant people in their lives. Choice theory teaches that talking about what clients cannot control is of minimal value; the emphasis is on what clients *can* control in their relationships. The basic axiom of choice theory, which is crucial for clients to understand, is this: "The only person you can control is yourself." Two books devoted to how choice theory can help people deal with their relationship problems and enhance their relationships are *Getting Together and Staying Together* (Glasser & Glasser, 2000) and *Eight Lessons for a Happier Marriage* (Glasser & Glasser, 2007).

Reality therapists do not listen very long to complaining, blaming, and criticizing, for these are the most ineffective behaviors in our behavioral repertoire. Because reality therapists give little attention to these self-defeating *total behaviors,* Glasser maintains that they tend to disappear from therapy. What do reality therapists focus on? Here are some underlying characteristics of reality therapy.

EMPHASIZE CHOICE AND RESPONSIBILITY If we choose all we do, we must be responsible for what we choose. This does not mean we should be blamed or punished, unless we break the law, but it does mean the therapist should never lose sight of the fact that clients are responsible for what they do. Choice theory changes the focus of responsibility to choice and choosing.

Reality therapists deal with people "as if" they have choices. Therapists focus on those areas where clients have choice, for doing so gets them closer to the people they need. For example, being involved in meaningful activities, such as work, is a good way to gain the respect of other people, and work can help clients fulfill their need for power. It is very difficult for adults to feel good about themselves if they don't engage in some form of meaningful activity. As clients begin to feel good about themselves, it is less necessary for them to continue to choose ineffective and self-destructive behaviors.

REJECT TRANSFERENCE Reality therapists strive to be themselves in their professional work. By being themselves, therapists can use the relationship to teach clients how to relate to others in their lives. Glasser contends that transference is a way that both therapist and client avoid being who they are and owning what they are doing right now. It is unrealistic for therapists to go along with the idea that they are anyone but themselves. Assume the client claims, "I see you as my father or mother and this is why I'm behaving the way I am." In such a situation a reality therapist is likely to say clearly and firmly, "I am not your mother, father, or anyone but myself."

KEEP THE THERAPY IN THE PRESENT Some clients come to counseling convinced that they must revisit the past if they are to be helped. Many therapeutic models teach that to function well in the present people must understand and revisit their past. Glasser (2001) disagrees with this assumption and contends that whatever mistakes were made in the past are not pertinent now. An axiom of choice theory is that the past may have contributed to a current problem but that the past is never the problem. To function effectively, people need to live and plan in the present and take steps to create a better future. We can only satisfy our needs in the present.

The reality therapist does not totally reject the past. If the client wants to talk about past successes or good relationships in the past, the therapist will listen because these may be repeated in the present. Reality therapists will devote only enough time to past failures to assure clients that they are not rejecting them. As soon as possible, therapists tell clients, "What has happened is over; it can't be changed. The more time we spend looking back, the more we avoid looking forward." Although the past has propelled us to the present, reality therapists contend that it does not have to determine our future. We are free to make choices, even though our external world limits our choices (Wubbolding, 2011b).

AVOID FOCUSING ON SYMPTOMS In traditional therapy a great deal of time is spent focusing on symptoms by asking clients how they feel and why they are obsessing. Focusing on the past "protects" clients from facing the reality of unsatisfying present relationships, and focusing on symptoms does the same thing. Glasser (2003) contends that people who have symptoms believe that if they could only be symptom-free they would find happiness. Whether people are depressing or paining, they tend to think that what they are experiencing is happening to them. They are reluctant to accept the reality that their suffering is due to the total behavior they are choosing. Their symptoms can be viewed as the body's way of warning them that the behavior they are choosing is not satisfying their basic needs. The reality therapist spends as little time as he or she can on the symptoms because they will last only as long as they are needed to deal with an unsatisfying relationship or the frustration of basic needs.

According to Glasser, if clients believe that the therapist wants to hear about their symptoms or spend time talking about the past, they are more than willing to comply. Engaging in long journeys into the past or exploring symptoms results in lengthy therapy. Glasser (2005) maintains that almost all symptoms are caused by a present unhappy relationship. By focusing on present problems, especially interpersonal concerns, therapy can generally be shortened considerably.

CHALLENGE TRADITIONAL VIEWS OF MENTAL ILLNESS Choice theory rejects the traditional notion that people with problematic physical and psychological symptoms are mentally ill. Glasser (2003) has warned people to be cautious of psychiatry, which can be hazardous to both one's physical and mental health. He criticizes the traditional psychiatric establishment for relying heavily on the *DSM-IV-TR* (American Psychiatric Association, 2000) for both diagnosis and treatment. Glasser (2003) challenges the traditionally accepted views of mental illness and treatment by the use of medication, especially the widespread use of psychiatric drugs that often result in negative side effects both physically and psychologically. Wubbolding (personal communication, September 7, 2010) emphasizes that reality therapy is a mental health system rather than a remediating system. He incorporates the Ericksonian principle that "people don't have problems, they have solutions that have not worked." By reframing diagnostic categories and negative behaviors, the counselor helps the client to perceive his or her behaviors in a very different light, which facilitates the search for more effective solutions and choices.

THE THERAPEUTIC PROCESS
Therapeutic Goals

A primary goal of contemporary reality therapy is to help clients get connected or reconnected with the people they have chosen to put in their quality world. In addition to fulfilling this need for love and belonging, a basic goal of reality therapy is to help clients learn better ways of fulfilling all of their needs, including achievement, power or inner control, freedom or independence, and fun. The basic human needs serve to focus treatment planning and setting both short- and long-term goals. Reality therapists assist clients in making more effective and responsible choices related to their wants and needs.

In many instances, clients come voluntarily for therapy, and these clients are the easiest to help. However, another goal entails working with an increasing number of involuntary clients who may actively resist the therapist and the therapy process. These individuals often engage in violent behavior, addictions, and other kinds of antisocial behaviors. It is essential for counselors to do whatever they can to get connected with involuntary clients. If the counselor is unable to make a connection, there is no possibility of providing significant help. If the counselor *can* make a connection, the goal of teaching the client how to fulfill his or her needs can slowly begin.

Therapist's Function and Role

Therapy is often considered as a mentoring process in which the therapist is the teacher and the client is the student. Reality therapists teach clients how to engage in self-evaluation, which is done by raising the question, "Is what you are choosing to do getting you what you want and need?" Here are some other questions that therapists tend to ask clients:

- How would you most like to change your life?
- What do you want in your life that you are not getting?
- What would you have in your life if you were to change?
- What do you have to do now to make the changes happen?

The role of the reality therapist is not to make the evaluation for clients but to challenge clients to examine what they are doing. Reality therapists assist clients in evaluating their own behavioral direction, specific actions, wants, perceptions, level of commitment, possibilities for new directions, and action plans. Clients then decide what to change and formulate a plan to facilitate the desired changes. The outcome is better relationships, increased happiness, and a sense of inner control of their lives (Wubbolding, 2011b).

It is the job of therapists to convey the idea that no matter how bad things are there is hope. If therapists are able to instill this sense of hope, clients feel that they are no longer alone and that change is possible. The therapist functions as an advocate, or someone who is on the client's side. Together they can creatively address a range of concerns and options.

Client's Experience in Therapy

Clients are not expected to backtrack into the past or get sidetracked into talking about symptoms. Neither will much time be spent talking about feelings separate from the acting and thinking that are part of the total behaviors over which clients have direct control. The emphasis in on actions. When clients change what they are doing, they often change how they are feeling and thinking.

Therapists will gently, but firmly confront clients. Reality therapists often ask clients questions such as these: "Is what you are choosing to do bringing you closer to the people you want to be closer to right now?" "Is what you are doing getting you closer to a new person if you are presently disconnected from everyone?" These questions are part of the self-evaluation process, which is the cornerstone of reality therapy.

Clients can expect to experience some urgency in therapy. Time is important, as each session may be the last. Clients should be able to say to themselves, "I can begin to use what we talked about today in my life. I am able to bring my present experiences to therapy as my problems are in the present, and my therapist will not let me escape from that fact."

Relationship Between Therapist and Client

Reality therapy emphasizes an understanding and supportive relationship, or therapeutic alliance, which is the foundation for effective outcomes (Wubbolding & Brickell, 2005; Wubbolding, Robey, & Brickell, 2010). The therapist's skill in establishing a trusting relationship is critical. It is also important that the client perceives the therapist as being skilled and knowledgeable. Although the therapeutic relationship is paramount, it is not an end in itself, and it is not automatically curative or healing (Wubbolding, 2011a).

For involvement between the therapist and the client to occur, the counselor must have certain personal qualities, including warmth, sincerity, congruence, understanding, acceptance, concern, respect for the client, openness, and the willingness to be challenged by others. (For other personal characteristics, see Chapter 2.) Wubbolding (2010, 2011a, 2011b) identifies specific ways for counselors to create a climate that leads to involvement with clients. Some of these ways entail using attending behavior, listening to clients, suspending judgment, doing the unexpected, using humor appropriately, being oneself as a counselor, engaging in facilitative self-disclosure, listening for metaphors in the client's mode of self-expression, listening for themes, summarizing and focusing, allowing consequences, allowing silence, and being an ethical practitioner. The basis for therapeutic interventions to work effectively rests on a fair, firm, friendly, and trusting environment. Once involvement has been established, the counselor assists clients in gaining a deeper understanding of the consequences of their current behavior.

APPLICATION: THERAPEUTIC TECHNIQUES AND PROCEDURES

The Practice of Reality Therapy

The practice of reality therapy can best be conceptualized as the *cycle of counseling*, which consists of two major components: (1) creating the counseling environment and (2) implementing specific procedures that lead to changes in behavior. The art of counseling is to weave these components together in ways that lead clients to evaluate their lives and decide to move in more effective directions.

How do these components blend in the counseling process? The cycle of counseling begins with creating a working relationship with clients, which was described in the previous section. The process proceeds through an exploration of clients' wants, needs, and perceptions. Clients explore their total behavior and make their own evaluation of how effective they are in getting what they want. If clients decide to try new behavior, they make plans that will lead to change, and they commit themselves to those plans. The cycle of counseling includes following up on how well clients are doing and offering further consultation as needed.

It is important to keep in mind that although the concepts may seem simple as they are presented here, being able to translate them into actual therapeutic practice takes considerable skill and creativity. Although the principles will be the same when used by any counselor who is certified in reality therapy, the manner in which these principles are applied does vary depending on the counselor's style and personal characteristics. These principles are applied in a progressive manner, but they should not be thought of as discrete and rigid categories. The art of practicing reality therapy involves far more than following procedures in a step-by-step, cookbook fashion. Although these procedures are described in jargon-free language, they can be challenging to implement (Wubbolding, 2007, 2011b). Counseling is not a simplistic method that is applied in the same way with every client. With choice theory in the background of practice, the counselor tailors the counseling to what the client presents. Although the counselor is prepared to work in a way that is meaningful to the client, the move toward satisfying relationships remains in the foreground.

Robert Wubbolding is a reality therapist who has extended the practice of reality therapy (WDEP system) for both implementing and teaching reality therapy (Wubbolding, 2009). Over the years he has played a major role in the development of reality therapy. I especially value Wubbolding's contributions to teaching reality therapy and to conceptualizing therapeutic procedures. His ideas render choice theory practical and useable by counselors, and his system provides a basis for conceptualizing and applying the theory. Although reality therapists operate within the spirit of choice theory, they practice in their own unique ways and develop their own individual therapeutic style. This section is based on an integrated summary and adaptation of material from various sources (Glasser, 1992, 1998, 2001; Wubbolding, 1988, 1991, 2000, 2007, 2008, 2011a, 2011b; Wubbolding et al., 1998, 2004). The *Student Manual* that accompanies this textbook contains Wubbolding's (2010) chart, which highlights issues and tasks to be accomplished throughout the cycle of counseling.

The Counseling Environment

The practice of reality therapy rests on the assumption that a supportive and challenging environment allows clients to begin making life changes. The therapeutic relationship is the foundation for effective practice; if this is lacking, there is little hope that the system can be successfully implemented. Counselors who hope to create a therapeutic alliance strive to avoid behaviors such as arguing, attacking, accusing, demeaning, bossing, criticizing, finding fault, coercing, encouraging excuses, holding grudges, instilling fear, and giving up easily (Wubbolding, 2010, 2011a, 2011b). In a short period of time, clients generally begin to appreciate the caring, accepting, noncoercive choice theory environment. It is from this mildly confrontive yet always noncriticizing, nonblaming, noncomplaining, caring environment that clients learn to create the satisfying environment that leads to successful relationships. In this coercion-free atmosphere, clients feel free to be creative and to begin to try new behaviors.

Procedures That Lead to Change

Reality therapists operate on the assumption that we are motivated to change (1) when we are convinced that our present behavior is not meeting our needs and (2) when we believe we can choose other behaviors that will get us closer to what we want. Reality therapists begin by asking clients what they want from therapy. Therapists take the mystery and uncertainty out of the therapeutic process. They also inquire about the choices clients are making in their relationships. In most instances, there is a major unsatisfied relationship, and clients usually do not believe they have any choice in what is going on in this relationship. In the beginning the client may deny this is the case. For example, the client might say, "I'm depressed. My depression is the problem. Why are you talking about my relationships?" The client often does not want to talk about the real problem, which is the unsatisfying relationship or lack thereof.

In the first session a skilled therapist looks for and defines the wants of the client. The therapist also looks for a key unsatisfying present relationship—usually with a spouse, a child, a parent, or an employer. The therapist might ask, "Whose behavior can you control?" This question may need to be asked several times during the next few sessions to deal with the client's resistance to looking at his or her own behavior. The emphasis is on encouraging clients to focus on what they can control.

When clients begin to realize that they can control only their own behavior, therapy is under way. The rest of therapy focuses on how clients can make better choices. There are more choices available than clients realize, and the therapist explores these possible choices. Clients may be stuck in misery, blaming, and the past, but they can choose to change—even if the other person in the relationship does not change. Wubbolding (2011a) makes the point that clients can learn that they are not at the mercy of others, are not victims, are capable of gaining a sense of inner control, and have a range of choices open to them. In short, clients in reality therapy often acquire a sense of hope for a better future.

Reality therapists explore the tenets of choice theory with clients, helping clients identify basic needs, discovering clients' quality world, and finally, helping clients understand that they are choosing the total behaviors that are their symptoms. In every instance when clients make a change, it is their choice. With the therapist's help, clients learn to make better choices than they did when they were on their own. Through choice theory, clients can acquire and maintain successful relationships.

The "WDEP" System

Wubbolding (2000) uses the acronym WDEP to describe key procedures in the practice of reality therapy. The WDEP system of reality therapy can be described as "effective, practical, usable, theory-based, cross-cultural, and founded on universal human principles" (Wubbolding, 2007, p. 204). The WDEP system can be used to help clients explore their *wants*, possible things they can *do*, opportunities for *self-evaluation*, and design *plans* for improvement (Wubbolding, 2007, 2011a, 2011b). Grounded in choice theory, the WDEP system assists people in satisfying their basic needs. Each of the letters refers to a cluster of strategies: W = wants, needs, and perceptions; D = direction and doing; E = self-evaluation; and P = planning. These strategies are designed to promote change. Let's look at each one in more detail.

WANTS (EXPLORING WANTS, NEEDS, AND PERCEPTIONS) Reality therapists assist clients in discovering their wants and hopes. All wants are related to the five basic needs. The key question asked is, "What do you want?" Through the therapist's skillful questioning, clients are assisted in defining what they want from the counseling process and from the world around them. It is useful for clients to define what they expect and want from the counselor and from themselves. Part of counseling consists of exploring the "picture album," or **quality world**, of clients and how their behavior is aimed at moving their perception of the external world closer to their inner world of wants.

Clients are given the opportunity to explore every facet of their lives, including what they want from their family, friends, and work. Furthermore, this exploration of wants, needs, and perceptions should continue throughout the counseling process as clients' pictures change.

Here are some useful questions to help clients pinpoint what they want:

- If you were the person that you wish you were, what kind of person would you be?
- What would your family be like if your wants and their wants matched?
- What would you be doing if you were living as you want to?
- Do you really want to change your life?
- What is it you want that you don't seem to be getting from life?
- What do you think stops you from making the changes you would like?

Wubbolding and Brickell (2009) now include questions focusing on perceptions: "How do you look at the situation?" "Where do you see your control?" (p. 51). People have a great deal more control than they often perceive, and these questions help clients move from a sense of external control to a sense of internal control. This line of questioning sets the stage for applying other procedures in reality therapy. It is an art for counselors to know *what* questions to ask, *how* to ask them, and *when* to ask them. Relevant questions help clients gain insights and arrive at plans and solutions. Although well-timed, open-ended questions can help clients identify their counseling goals, excessive questioning can result in resistance and defensiveness. Part of this phase of counseling involves eliciting a commitment to counseling. Personal growth will occur to the degree that clients are committed to making changes in their actions (Wubbolding, 2011b).

DIRECTION AND DOING The focus on the present is characterized by the key question asked by the reality therapist: "What are you doing?" Even though problems may be rooted in the past, clients need to learn how to deal with them in the present by learning better ways of getting what they want. Problems must be solved either in the present or through a plan for the future. The therapist's challenge is to help clients make more need-satisfying choices.

Early in counseling it is essential to discuss with clients the overall direction of their lives, including where they are going and where their behavior is taking them. This exploration is preliminary to the subsequent evaluation of whether it is a desirable direction. The therapist holds a mirror before the client and asks, "What do you see for yourself now and in the future?" It often takes some time for this reflection to become clearer to clients so they can verbally express their perceptions.

Reality therapy focuses on gaining awareness of and changing current total behavior. To accomplish this, reality therapists focus on questions like these: "What are you doing now?" "What did you actually do yesterday?" "What did you want to do differently this past week?" "What stopped you from doing what you said you wanted to do?" "What will you do tomorrow?"

Listening to clients talk about feelings can be productive, but only if it is linked to what they are doing. When an emergency light on the car dashboard lights up, the driver is alerted that something is wrong and that immediate action is necessary to remedy a problem. In a similar way, when clients talk about problematic feelings, most reality therapists affirm and acknowledge these feelings. Rather than focusing mainly on these feelings, however, reality therapists encourage clients to take action by changing what they are doing and thinking. It is easier to change what we are doing and thinking than to change our feelings. From a choice theory perspective, discussions centering on feelings, without strongly relating them to what people are doing and thinking, are counterproductive.

SELF-EVALUATION **Self-evaluation** is the cornerstone of reality therapy procedures. The core of reality therapy, as we have seen, is to ask clients to make the following self-evaluation: "Does your present behavior have a reasonable chance of getting you what you want now, and will it take you in the direction you want to go?" Specifically, evaluation involves the client examining behavioral direction, specific actions, wants, perceptions, new directions, and plans (Wubbolding, 2011b). According to Wubbolding (2007), clients often present a problem with a significant relationship, which is at the root of much of their dissatisfaction. The counselor can help clients evaluate their behavior by asking this question: "Is your current behavior bringing you closer to people important to you or is it driving you further apart?" Through skillful questioning, the counselor helps clients determine if what they are doing is helping them. Artful questioning assists clients in evaluating their present behavior and the direction this is taking them. Wubbolding (2000, 2011a) suggests questions like these:

- Is what you are doing helping or hurting you?
- Is what you are doing now what you want to be doing?
- Is your behavior working for you?
- Is there a healthy congruence between what you are doing and what you believe?
- Is what you are doing against the rules?
- Is what you want realistic or attainable?
- Does it help you to look at it that way?
- Is it really true that you have no control over your situation?
- How committed are you to the therapeutic process and to changing your life?
- After carefully examining what you want, does it appear to be in your best interests and in the best interest of others?

Asking clients to evaluate each component of their total behavior is a major task in reality therapy. It is the counselor's task to assist clients in evaluating the quality of their actions and to help them make responsible choices and devise effective plans. Individuals will not change until they first decide that a change would be more advantageous. Without an honest self-assessment, it is unlikely that clients will change. Reality therapists are relentless in their efforts to help clients conduct explicit self-evaluations of each behavioral component. When therapists ask a depressing client if this behavior is helping in the long run, they introduce the idea of choice to the client. The process of evaluation of the doing, thinking, feeling, and physiological components of total behavior is within the scope of the client's responsibility.

Reality therapists may be directive with certain clients at the beginning of treatment. This is done to help clients recognize that some behaviors are not effective. In working with clients who are in crisis, for example, it is sometimes necessary to suggest straightforwardly what will work and what will not. Other clients, such as alcoholics and children of alcoholics, need direction early in the course of treatment, for they often do not have the thinking behaviors in their control system to be able to make consistent evaluations of when their lives are seriously out of effective control. These clients are likely to have blurred pictures and, at times, to be unaware of what they want or whether their wants are realistic. As they grow and continue to interact with the counselor, they learn to make evaluations with less and less help from the counselor (Wubbolding, 2011a; Wubbolding & Brickell, 2005).

PLANNING AND ACTION Much of the significant work of the counseling process involves helping clients identify specific ways to fulfill their wants and needs. Once clients determine what they want to change, they are generally ready to explore other possible behaviors and formulate an action plan. The key question is, "What is your plan?" The process of creating and carrying out plans enables people to begin to gain effective control over their lives. If the plan does not work, for whatever reason, the counselor and client work together to devise a different plan. The plan gives the client a starting point, a toehold on life, but plans can be modified as needed. Throughout this planning phase, the counselor continually urges the client to be willing to accept the consequences for his or her own choices and actions. Not only are plans discussed in light of how they can help the client personally, but plans are also designed in terms of how they are likely to affect others in the client's life.

Wubbolding (2000, 2007, 2008, 2011a, 2011b) discusses the central role of planning and commitment. The culmination of the cycle of counseling rests with a plan of action. Although planning is important, it is effective only if the client has made a self-evaluation and determined that he or she wants to change a behavior. Wubbolding uses the acronym SAMIC to capture the essence of a good plan: simple, attainable, measurable, immediate, involved, controlled by the planner, committed to, and consistently done. Wubbolding contends that clients gain more effective control over their lives with plans that have the following characteristics:

- The plan is within the limits of the motivation and capacities of the client. Skillful counselors help clients identify plans that involve greater need-fulfilling payoffs. Clients may be asked, "What plans could you make now that would result in a more satisfying life?"
- Good plans are simple and easy to understand. They are realistically doable, positive rather than negative, dependent on the planner, specific, immediate, and repetitive. Although they need to be specific, concrete, and measurable, plans should be flexible and open to revision as clients gain a deeper understanding of the specific behaviors they want to change.
- The plan involves a positive course of action, and it is stated in terms of what the client is willing to do. Even small plans can help clients take significant steps toward their desired changes.
- Counselors encourage clients to develop plans that they can carry out independently of what others do. Plans that are contingent on others lead clients to sense that they are not steering their own ship but are at the mercy of the ocean.

- Effective plans are repetitive and, ideally, are performed daily.
- Plans are carried out as soon as possible. Counselors can ask the question, "What are you willing to do today to begin to change your life?"
- Plans involve process-centered activities. For example, clients may plan to do any of the following: apply for a job, write a letter to a friend, take a yoga class, substitute nutritious food for junk food, devote 2 hours a week to volunteer work, or take a vacation that they have been wanting.
- Before clients carry out their plan, it is a good idea for them to evaluate it with their therapist to determine whether it is realistic and attainable and whether it relates to what they need and want. After the plan has been carried out in real life, it is useful to evaluate it again and make any revisions that may be necessary.
- To help clients commit themselves to their plan, it is useful for them to firm it up in writing.

Resolutions and plans are empty unless there is a commitment to carry them out. It is up to clients to determine how to take their plans outside the restricted world of therapy and into the everyday world. Effective therapy can be the catalyst that leads to self-directed, responsible living.

Asking clients to determine what they want for themselves, to make a self-evaluation, and to follow through with action plans includes assisting them in determining how intensely they are willing to work to attain the changes they desire. Commitment is not an all-or-nothing matter; it exists in degrees. Wubbolding (2007, 2011a, 2011b) maintains that it is important for a therapist to express concern about clients' level of commitment, or how much they are willing to work to bring about change. This communicates in an implicit way to clients that they have within them the power to take charge of their lives. It is essential that those clients who are reluctant to make a commitment be helped to express and explore their fears of failing. Clients are helped by a therapist who does not easily give up believing in their ability to make better choices, even if they are not always successful in completing their plans. In his workshops, Wubbolding often mentions this axiom of reality therapy: "To fail to plan is to plan to fail."

Application to Group Counseling

With the emphases on connection and interpersonal relationships, reality therapy is well suited for various kinds of group counseling. Groups provide members with many opportunities for exploring ways to meet their needs through the relationships formed within the group. In particular, the WDEP system can be applied to helping group members satisfy their basic needs. If members talk about their past experiences or make excuses for their current behavior, the group leader redirects them to what they are presently doing. From the very beginning of a group, the members can be asked to take an honest look at what they are doing and to clarify whether their behavior is getting them what they say they want. Once group members get a clearer picture of what they have in their lives now and what they want to be different, they can use the group as a place to explore an alternative course of behavior.

This model lends itself to expecting the members to carry out homework assignments between the group meetings. However, it is the members, with the help of the leader, who evaluate their own behavior and decide whether they want to change. Members also take the lead in deciding what kinds of homework tasks they will set for themselves as a way to achieve their goals. Group leaders often meet with resistance if they make poorly timed suggestions and plans for how the members should best live their lives. To their credit, reality therapists keep asking the members to evaluate for themselves whether what they are doing is getting them what they want. If the members concede that what they are doing is not working for them, their resistance is much more likely to melt, and they tend to be more open to trying different behaviors.

Once the members make some changes, reality therapy provides the structure for them to formulate specific plans for action and to evaluate their level of success. Feedback from the members and the leader can help individuals design realistic and attainable plans. Considerable time is devoted during the group sessions for developing and implementing plans. If people don't carry out a plan, it is important to discuss with them what stopped them. Perhaps they set their goals unrealistically high, or perhaps there is a discrepancy between what they *say* they want to change and the steps they are willing to take to bring about change.

I also like reality therapy's insistence that change will not come by insight alone; rather, members have to begin doing something different once they determine that their behavior is not working for them. I am skeptical about the value of catharsis as a therapeutic vehicle unless the release of pent-up emotions is eventually put into some kind of cognitive framework and is followed up with an action plan. In the groups that I facilitate, group members are challenged to look at the futility of waiting for others to change. I ask members to assume that the significant people in their life may never change, which means that they will have to take a more active stance in shaping their own destiny. I appreciate the emphasis of reality therapy on teaching clients that the only life they can control is their own and the focus placed on helping group members change their own patterns of acting and thinking.

For a more detailed discussion of reality therapy in groups, see Corey (2012, chap. 15).

REALITY THERAPY FROM A MULTICULTURAL PERSPECTIVE

Strengths From a Diversity Perspective

The core principles of choice theory and reality therapy have much to offer in the area of multicultural counseling. In cross-cultural therapy it is essential that counselors respect the differences in worldview between themselves and their clients.

Counselors demonstrate their respect for the cultural values of their clients by helping them explore how satisfying their current behavior is both to themselves and to others. Once clients make this assessment, they can formulate realistic plans that are consistent with their cultural values. It is a further sign of respect that the counselor refrains from deciding what behavior should be changed. Through skillful questioning on the counselor's part, clients from diverse ethnic backgrounds can be helped to determine the degree to which they have become acculturated into the dominant society. Is it possible for them to find a balance, retaining their ethnic identity and values while integrating some of the values and practices of the dominant group? Again, the counselor does not determine this balance for clients, but works with them to arrive at their own answers. With this focus on thinking and acting rather than on exploring feelings, many clients are less likely to display resistance to counseling.

Glasser (1998) contends that reality therapy and choice theory can be applied both individually and in groups to anyone with any psychological problem in any cultural context. We are all members of the same species and have the same genetic structure; therefore, relationships are the problem in all cultures. Wubbolding (2007, 2011a, 2011b) asserts that the principles underlying choice theory are universal, which makes choice theory applicable to all people. All of us have internal needs, we all make choices, and we all seek to influence the world around us. Putting the principles of choice theory into action demands creativity, sensitivity to cultures and individuals, and flexibility in implementing the procedures of reality therapy. Reality therapy principles and procedures need to be applied differently in various cultures and must be adapted to the psychological and developmental levels presented by individuals (Wubbolding, 2011b).

Based on the assumption that reality therapy must be modified to fit the cultural context of people other than North Americans, Wubbolding (2000, 2011a) and Wubbolding and colleagues (1998, 2004) have expanded the practice of reality therapy to multicultural situations. Wubbolding's experience in conducting reality therapy workshops in Japan, Taiwan, Hong Kong, Singapore, Korea, India, Kuwait, Australia, Slovenia, Croatia, and countries in western Europe has taught him the difficulty of generalizing about other cultures. Growing out of these multicultural experiences, Wubbolding (2000) has adapted the cycle of counseling in working with Japanese clients. He points to some basic language differences between Japanese and Western cultures. North Americans are inclined to say what they mean and to be assertive. In Japanese culture, assertive language is not appropriate between a child and a parent or between an employee and a supervisor. Ways of communicating are more indirect. To ask some Japanese clients what they want may seem harsh and intrusive to them. Because of these style differences, adaptations such as those listed below are needed to make the practice of reality therapy relevant to Japanese clients:

- The reality therapist's tendency to ask direct questions may need to be softened, with questions being raised more elaborately and indirectly. It may be a mistake to ask individualistic questions built around whether specific behaviors meet the client's need. Confrontation should be done only after carefully considering the context.

- There is no exact Japanese translation for the word "plan," nor is there an exact word for "accountability," yet both of these are key dimensions in the practice of reality therapy and are central to Japanese culture.
- In asking clients to make plans and commit to them, Western counselors do not settle for a response of "I'll try." Instead, they tend to push for an explicit pledge to follow through. In Japanese culture, however, the counselor is likely to accept "I'll try" as a firm commitment.

These are but a few illustrations of ways in which reality therapy might be adapted to non-Western clients. Although this approach assumes that all people have the same basic needs (survival, love and belonging, power, freedom, and fun), the way these needs are expressed depends largely on the cultural context. In working with culturally diverse clients, the therapist must allow latitude for a wide range of acceptable behaviors to satisfy these needs. As with other theories and the techniques that flow from them, flexibility is a foremost requirement.

A key strength of reality therapy is that it provides clients with tools to make the changes they desire. This is especially true during the planning phase, which is central to the process of reality therapy. The focus is on positive steps that can be taken, not on what cannot be done. Clients identify those problems that are causing them difficulty, and these problems become the targets for change. This type of specificity and the direction that is provided by an effective plan are certainly assets in working with diverse client groups.

Reality therapy needs to be used artfully and to be applied in different ways with a variety of clients. Many of its principles and concepts can be incorporated in a dynamic and personal way in the style of counselors, and there is a basis for integrating these concepts with most of the other therapeutic approaches covered in this book.

Shortcomings From a Diversity Perspective

One of the shortcomings of reality therapy in working with clients from certain ethics groups is that it may not take fully into account some very real environmental forces that operate against them in their everyday lives. Reality therapy gives only limited attention to helping people address environmental and social problems. Discrimination, racism, sexism, homophobia, heterosexism, ageism, negative attitudes toward disabilities, and other social injustices are unfortunate realities, and these forces do limit many individuals in getting what they want from life. It is important that therapists acknowledge that people do not choose to be the victims of various forms of discrimination and oppression. If therapists do not accept these environmental restrictions or are not interested in bringing about social justice as well as individual change, clients are likely to feel misunderstood. There is a danger that some reality therapists may overstress the ability of these clients to take charge of their lives and not pay enough attention to systemic and environmental factors that can limit the potential for choice.

Some reality therapists may make the mistake of too quickly or too forcefully stressing the ability of their clients to take charge of their lives. On this point,

Wubbolding (2008) maintains that because of oppression and discrimination, some people have fewer choices available to them, yet they do have choices. Wubbolding sees reality therapy as helping clients to focus on those choices they *do* have. Although focusing on choices clients do have is useful, I believe clients may need to talk about the ways their choices are restricted by environmental circumstances. Therapists would do well to consider how both they and their clients could take even small steps toward bringing about societal changes, as do feminist therapists (see Chapter 12).

Another shortcoming associated with reality therapy is that some clients are very reluctant to directly verbally express what they need. Their cultural values and norms may not reinforce them in assertively asking for what they want. In fact, they may be socialized to think more of what is good for the social group than of their individual wants. In working with people with these values, counselors must "soften" reality therapy somewhat. If reality therapy is to be used effectively with clients from other cultures, the procedures must be adapted to the life experiences and values of members from various cultures (Wubbolding, 2000, 2011a; Wubbolding et al., 2004).

Reality Therapy Applied to the Case of Stan

As a reality therapist, I am guided by the key concepts of choice theory to identify Stan's behavioral dynamics, to provide a direction for him to work toward, and to teach him about better alternatives for achieving what he wants. Stan has not been effective in getting what he needs—a satisfying relationship.

Stan has fallen into a victim role, blaming others, and looking backward instead of forward. Initially, he wants to tell me about the negative aspects of his life, which he does by dwelling on his major symptoms: depression, anxiety, inability to sleep, and other psychosomatic symptoms. I listen carefully to his concerns, but I hope he will come to realize that he has many options for acting differently. I operate on the premise that therapy will offer the opportunity to explore with Stan what he can build on—successes, productive times, goals, and hopes for the future.

After creating a relationship with Stan, I am able to show him that he does not have to be a victim of his past unless he chooses to be, and I assure him that he has rehashed his past miseries enough. As counseling progresses,

Stan learns that even though most of his problems did indeed begin in childhood, there is little he can now do to undo his childhood. He eventually recognizes that all of his symptoms and avoidances keep him from getting what he most wants. He eventually realizes that he has a great deal of control over what he can do for himself now.

I have Stan describe how his life would be different if he were symptom free. I am interested in knowing what he would be doing if he were meeting his needs for belonging, achievement, power, freedom, and fun. I explain to him that he has an ideal picture of what he wants his life to be, yet he does not possess effective behaviors for meeting his needs. I talk to him about all of his basic psychological needs and how this type of therapy will teach him to satisfy them in effective ways. I also explain that his *total behavior* is made up of acting, thinking, feeling, and physiology. Even though he says he hates feeling anxious most of the time, Stan learns that much of what he is doing and thinking is directly leading to his unwanted feelings and physiological reactions. When he complains of feeling depressed much of the time, anxious at night, and overcome by panic attacks, I let him know that I am more interested in what he is *doing* and *thinking* because these are the behavioral components that can be directly changed.

I help Stan understand that his *depressing* is the feeling part of his choice. Although he may think he has little control over how he feels, over his bodily sensations, and over his thoughts, I want him to understand that he can begin to take different action, which is likely to change his depressing experience. I frequently ask this question, "Is what you are choosing to do getting you what you want?" I lead Stan to begin to recognize that he does have *some,* indirect control over his feelings. This is best done after he has made some choices about doing something different from what he has been doing. At this point he is in a better place to see that the choice to take action has contributed to feeling better, which helps him realize that he has some power to change.

Stan tells me about the pictures in his head, a few of which are becoming a counselor, acting confident in meeting people, thinking of himself as a worthwhile person, and enjoying life. Through therapy he makes the evaluation that much of what he is doing is not getting him closer to these pictures or getting him what he wants. After he decides that he is willing to work on himself to be different, the majority of time in the sessions is devoted to making plans and discussing their implementation. We both focus on the specific steps he can take right now to begin the changes he would like.

As Stan continues to carry out plans in the real world, he gradually begins to experience success. When he does backslide, I do not put him down but help him refocus. We then develop a new plan that we both feel more confident about. I am not willing to give up on Stan even when he does not make major progress, and Stan lets me know that my support is a source of real inspiration for him to keep working on himself.

I teach Stan about choice theory, and, if he is willing to engage in some reading, I suggest that he read and reflect on the ideas in *Counseling With Choice Theory: The New Reality Therapy* (Glasser, 2001) and *A Set of Directions for Putting and Keeping Yourself Together* (Wubbolding & Brickell, 2001). Stan brings some of what he is learning from his reading into his sessions, and eventually he is able to achieve some of his goals. The combination of working with a reality therapist, his reading, and his willingness to put what he is learning into practice by engaging in new behaviors in the world assist him in replacing ineffective choices with life-affirming choices. Stan comes to accept that he is the only person who can control his own destiny.

Follow-Up: You Continue as Stan's Reality Therapist

Use these questions to help you think about how you would counsel Stan using reality therapy:

- If Stan complains of feeling depressed most of the time and wants you to "fix" him, how would you proceed?
- If Stan persists, telling you that his mood is getting the best of him and that he wants you to work with his physician in getting him on an antidepressant drug, what would you say or do?
- What are some of Stan's basic needs that are not being met? What action plans can you think of to help Stan find better ways of getting what he wants?
- Would you be inclined to do a checklist on alcoholism with Stan? Why or why not? If you determined that he was addicted to alcohol, would you insist that he attend a program such as Alcoholics Anonymous in conjunction with therapy with you? Why or why not?
- What interventions would you make to help Stan explore his total behavior?

See *DVD for Theory and Practice of Counseling and Psychotherapy: The Case of Stan and Lecturettes* (Session 9 on reality therapy) for a demonstration of my approach to counseling Stan from this perspective. This session deals with assisting Stan in forming an action plan.

SUMMARY AND EVALUATION

Summary

The reality therapist functions as a teacher, a mentor, and a model, confronting clients in ways that help them evaluate what they are doing and whether their behavior is fulfilling their basic needs without harming themselves or others. The heart of reality therapy is learning how to make better and more effective choices and gain more effective control. People take charge of their lives rather than being the victims of circumstances beyond their control. Practitioners of reality therapy focus on what clients are *able and willing to do in the present* to change their behavior. Practitioners teach clients how to make significant connections with others. Therapists continue to ask clients to evaluate the effectiveness of what they are choosing to do to determine if better choices are possible.

The practice of reality therapy weaves together two components, the counseling environment and specific procedures that lead to changes in behavior. This therapeutic process enables clients to move in the direction of getting what they want. The goals of reality therapy include behavioral change, better decision making, improved significant relationships, enhanced living, and more effective satisfaction of all the psychological needs.

Contributions of Reality Therapy

Among the advantages of reality therapy are its relatively short-term focus and the fact that it deals with conscious behavioral problems. Insight and awareness are not enough; the client's self-evaluation, a plan of action, and a commitment to following through are the core of the therapeutic process. I like the focus on strongly encouraging clients to engage in self-evaluation, to decide if what they are doing is working or not, and to commit themselves to doing what is required to make changes. The existential underpinnings of choice theory are a major strength of this approach, which accentuates taking responsibility for what we are doing. People are not viewed as being hopelessly and helplessly depressed. Instead, people are viewed as doing the best they can, or making the choices they hope will result in fulfilling their needs. With the emphasis on responsibility and choice, individuals can acquire a sense of self-direction and empowerment.

Too often counseling fails because therapists have an agenda for clients. The reality therapist helps clients conduct a searching inventory of what they are doing. If clients determine that their present behavior is not working, they are then much more likely to consider acquiring a new behavioral repertoire. Many clients approach counseling with a great deal of skepticism. Reality therapy can be used effectively with individuals who manifest reluctance and who are often highly resistant. For example, in working with people with addictions, reality therapy strategies can be used to help clients evaluate where their behavior is leading them and to provide clients with options to bring about positive changes in their behavior. Reality therapy has been effectively used in addiction treatment and recovery programs for more than 30 years (Wubbolding & Brickell, 2005). In many situations with these populations, it would be inappropriate to embark on long-term therapy that delves into unconscious dynamics and an intensive exploration of one's past. Reality therapy focuses on making changes in the present and is an effective, short-term approach, often in 10 sessions or less.

Limitations and Criticisms of Reality Therapy

From my perspective, one of the main limitations of reality therapy is that it does not give adequate emphasis to the role of the following aspects of the counseling process: the role of insight, the unconscious, the power of the past and the effect of traumatic experiences in early childhood, the therapeutic value of dreams, and the place of transference. Because reality therapy focuses almost exclusively on consciousness, it does not take into account factors such as repressed conflicts and the power of the unconscious in influencing how we think, feel, behave, and choose.

Dealing with dreams is not part of the reality therapist's repertoire. According to Glasser (2001), it is not therapeutically useful to explore dreams. For him, spending time discussing dreams can be a defense used to avoid talking about one's behavior and, thus, is time wasted. From my perspective, dreams are powerful tools in helping people recognize their internal conflicts. I believe that there is richness in dreams, which can be a shorthand message of clients' central struggles, wants, hopes, and visions of the future. Asking clients to recall, report, share, and relive their dreams in the here and now of the therapeutic session can help unblock them and can pave the way for clients to take a different course of action.

Similarly, I have a difficult time accepting Glasser's view of transference as a misleading concept, for I find that clients are able to learn that significant people in their lives have a present influence on how they perceive and react to others. To rule out an exploration of transference that distorts accurate perception of others seems narrow in my view.

As you will recall, Glasser (2001, 2003) contends that chronic depression and profound psychosis are chosen behaviors. Apart from specific brain pathology, Glasser argues that mental illness is the result of an individual's unsatisfying present relationships or general unhappiness. I have trouble viewing all psychological disorders as behavioral choices. People suffering from chronic depression or schizophrenia are struggling to cope with a real illness. In reality therapy these people may have additional guilt to carry if they accept the premise that they are *choosing* their condition.

I believe reality therapy is vulnerable to the practitioner who assumes the role of an expert in deciding for others how life should be lived and what constitutes responsible behavior. Wubbolding (2008) admits that reality therapy can lend itself to fixing problems and imposing a therapist's values on clients, especially by inexperienced or inadequately trained counselors. Wubbolding adds that it is not the therapist's role to evaluate the behavior of clients. Generally, clients need to engage in a process of courageous self-evaluation to determine how well certain behaviors are working and what changes they may want to make. It is critical that therapists monitor any tendency to judge clients' behavior, but instead to do all that is possible to get clients to make their own evaluation of their behavior.

Finally, reality therapy makes use of concrete language and simple concepts. This can erroneously be viewed as a simple approach that does not require a high level of competence. Because reality therapy is easily understood, it might appear to be easy to implement. However, the effective practice of reality therapy requires practice, supervision, and continuous learning (Wubbolding, 2007b, 2011a). Competent reality therapists have a thorough understanding of choice theory and have mastered the art of applying reality therapy procedures to working with diverse clients with a range of clinical problems.

WHERE TO GO FROM HERE

In the *DVD for Integrative Counseling: The Case of Ruth and Lecturettes,* Session 8 ("Behavioral Focus in Counseling"), you will note ways that I attempt to assist Ruth in specifying concrete behaviors that she will target for change. In this session I am drawing heavily from principles of reality therapy in assisting Ruth to develop an action plan to make the changes she desires.

Free Podcasts for ACA Members

You can download ACA Podcasts (prerecorded interviews) at www.counseling.org; click on the Resource button and then the Podcast Series. For Chapter 11, Reality Therapy, look for Podcast 18, "Reality Therapy, Choice Theory: What's the Difference?" by Dr. Robert Wubbolding.

Other Resources

DVDs offered by the American Psychological Association that are relevant to this chapter include the following:

> Wubbolding, R. (2007). *Reality Therapy*

Psychotherapy.net is a comprehensive resource for students and professionals that offers videos and interviews on demonstrating reality therapy working with addictions, adults, and children. New video and editorial content is made available monthly. DVDs relevant to this chapter are available at www.psychotherapy.net and include the following:

> Wubbolding, R. (2000). *Reality Therapy* (Psychotherapy With the Experts Series)
> Wubbolding, R. (2000). *Reality Therapy for Addictions* (Brief Therapy for Addictions Series)
> Wubbolding, R. (2002). *Reality Therapy With Children* (Child Therapy With the Experts Series)

The programs offered by the William Glasser Institute are designed to teach the concepts of choice theory and the practice of reality therapy. More than 7,800 therapists have completed the training in reality therapy and choice theory. The institute offers a certification process, which starts with a 3-day introductory course known as "basic training" in which participants are involved in discussions, demonstrations, and role playing. For those wishing to pursue more extensive training, the institute offers a five-part sequential course of study leading to certification in reality therapy, which includes basic training, a basic practicum, advanced training, an advanced practicum, and a certification week. This 18-month training program culminates in a Certificate of Completion. Complete information on this program can be obtained directly from the institute.

The William Glasser Institute

William Glasser, MD, President and Founder
Attention: Executive Director
22024 Lassen Street, Suite #118
Chatsworth, CA 91311-3600
Telephone: (818) 700-8000
Toll free: (800) 899-0688
Fax: (818) 818-700-0555
E-mail: wginst@wglasser.com
Website: www.wglasser.com

Center for Reality Therapy

Dr. Robert E. Wubbolding, Director
7672 Montgomery Road #383
Cincinnati, OH 45236-4204
Telephone: (513) 561-1911
Fax: (513) 561-3568
E-mail: wubsrt@fuse.net
Website: www.realitytherapywub.com

The *International Journal of Choice Theory and Reality Therapy* (online journal) focuses on concepts of internal control psychology, with particular emphasis on research, development, and practical applications of choice theory and reality therapy principles in various settings. To subscribe, contact:

Dr. Tom Parish

International Journal of Choice Theory and Reality Therapy
4606 SW Moundview Drive
Topeka, Kansas 66610
Telephone: (785) 862-1379
E-mail: Parishts@gmail.com

Feminist Therapy

Coauthored by Barbara Herlihy and Gerald Corey

Feminist therapy does not have a single founder. Rather, it has been a collective effort by many. We have selected a few individuals who have made significant contributions to feminist therapy for inclusion here, recognizing full well that many other equally influential scholar-practitioners could have appeared in this space. Feminist therapy is truly founded on a theory of inclusion.

JEAN BAKER MILLER / CAROL ZERBE ENNS / OLIVA M. ESPIN / LAUARA S. BROWN

Courtesy of Jean Baker Miller Training Institute

JEAN BAKER MILLER, MD (1928–2006), was a clinical professor of psychiatry at Boston University School of Medicine and director of the Jean Baker Miller Training Institute at the Stone Center, Wellesley College. She wrote *Toward a New Psychology of Women* (1986) and coauthored *The Healing Connection: How Women Form Relationships in Therapy and in Life* (Miller & Stiver, 1997) and *Women's Growth in Connection* (Jordan et al., 1991). Dr. Miller collaborated with diverse groups of scholars and colleagues on the development of relational-cultural theory. She made important contributions toward expanding this theory and exploring new applications to complex issues in psychotherapy and beyond, including issues of diversity, social action, and workplace change.

Courtesy of Carolyn Zerbe Enns

CAROLYN ZERBE ENNS, PhD, is Professor of Psychology and participant in the Women's Studies and Ethnic Studies programs at Cornell College in Mt. Vernon, Iowa. Enns became interested in feminist therapy while she was completing her PhD in Counseling Psychology at the University of California, Santa Barbara. She devotes much of her work to exploring the profound impact feminist theory has on the manner in which therapists implement therapeutic practices, and she discusses this impact in *Feminist Theories and Feminist Psychotherapies: Origins, Themes, and Diversity* (2004). The relationship of theory to feminist pedagogy is another major interest area and is the topic of a co-edited book (with Ada Sinacore) of *Teaching and Social Justice: Integrating Multicultural and Feminist Theories in the Classroom* (2005). Dr. Enns was one of three co-chairs (with Roberta Nutt and Joy Rice) of the task force that developed APA's (2007) "Guidelines for Psychological Practice with Girls and Women." Her most recent efforts are directed toward articulating the importance of multicultural feminist therapy, exploring the practice of feminist therapy around the world (especially in Japan), and writing about multicultural feminist pedagogies.

Courtesy of Dr. Oliva Espin, Professor Emerita of Women's Studies, San Diego State University

OLIVA M. ESPIN, PhD, is Professor Emerita in the Department of Women's Studies at San Diego State University and at the California School of Professional Psychology of Alliant International University. A native of Cuba, she did her undergraduate work in psychology at the Universidad de Costa Rica and received her PhD from the University of Florida, specializing in counseling and therapy with women from different cultures and in Latin American Studies. She is a pioneer in the theory and practice of feminist therapy with women from different cultural backgrounds and has done extensive research, teaching, and training on multicultural issues in psychology. Dr. Espin has published on psychotherapy with Latinas, women immigrants and refugees, the sexuality of Latinas, language in therapy with fluent bilinguals, and training clinicians to work with multicultural populations. Espin co-edited *Refugee Women and Their Mental Health: Shattered Societies, Shattered Lives* (Cole, Espin, & Rothblum, 1992) and has written *Latina Healers: Lives of Power and Tradition* (1996) , *Latina Realities: Essays on Healing, Migration, and Sexuality* (1997), and *Women Crossing Boundaries: A Psychology of Immigration and the Transformation of Sexuality* (1999), which is based on a study of women immigrants from all over the world.

LAURA S. BROWN, PhD, is a founding member of the Feminist Therapy Institute, an organization dedicated to the support of advanced practice in feminist therapy, and a member of the theory workgroup at the National Conference on Education and Training in Feminist Practice. She has written several books considered core to feminist practice in psychotherapy and counseling, and *Subversive Dialogues: Theory in Feminist Therapy* (1994) is considered by many to be the foundation book addressing how theory informs practice in feminist therapy. Her most recent book is *Feminist Therapy* (2010). Dr. Brown has made particular contributions to thinking about ethics and boundaries, and the complexities of ethical practice in small communities. Her current interests include feminist forensic psychology and the application of feminist principles to treatment of trauma survivors.

INTRODUCTION

This chapter provides an alternative perspective to the models considered thus far in this book.* As you will see, feminist therapy puts intersections of gender, social location, and power at the core of the therapeutic process. Feminist therapy is built on the premise that it is essential to consider the social, cultural, and political context that contributes to a person's problems in order to understand that person. This perspective has significant implications for the development of counseling theory and for how practitioners intervene with diverse client populations.

A central concept in feminist therapy is the importance of understanding and acknowledging the psychological oppression of women and the constraints imposed by the sociopolitical status to which women have been relegated. The feminist perspective offers a unique approach to understanding the roles that both women and men have been socialized to accept and to bringing this understanding into the therapeutic process. The socialization of women inevitably affects their identity development, self-concept, goals and aspirations, and emotional well-being (Belenky, Clinchy, Goldberger, & Tarule, 1987/1997; Gilligan, 1982; Turner & Werner-Wilson, 2008). As Natalie Rogers (1995) has observed, socialization patterns tend to result in women giving away their power in relationships, often without being aware of it. Feminist therapy keeps knowledge about gender socialization in mind in the work with all clients.

The majority of clients in counseling are women, and the majority of psychotherapy practitioners at the master's level are women. However, most theories that

---

*I invited a colleague and friend, Barbara Herlihy, a professor of counselor education at the University of New Orleans, to coauthor this chapter. We have coauthored two books (Herlihy & Corey, 2006a, 2006b), which seems like a natural basis for collaboration on a project that we both consider valuable.

are traditionally taught—including all of the other theories in this book—were founded by White males from Western (American or European) cultures, with only Adler taking a pro-feminist stance in early theory development. The need for a theory that evolves from the thinking and experiencing of women seems self-evident. Theories are developed from the experiences of the "developer," and feminist theory is the first therapeutic theory from a female perspective.

Feminist therapists have challenged male-oriented assumptions regarding what constitutes a mentally healthy individual. Early feminist therapy efforts focused on valuing women's experiences, political realities, and the unique issues facing women within a patriarchal system. Current feminist practice emphasizes a diverse approach that includes an understanding of multiple oppressions, multicultural competence, and social justice (American Psychological Association, 2007; Beardsley, Morrow, Castillo, & Weitzman, 1998; Brown & Root, 1990; Enns & Byars-Winston, 2010). Today's feminists believe that gender cannot be considered apart from other identities related to race, ethnicity, socioeconomic class, and sexual orientation. The contemporary version of feminist therapy and the multicultural and social justice approaches to counseling practice have a great deal in common (Crethar, Torres Rivera, & Nash, 2008). All three of these approaches provide a systemic perspective based on understanding the social context of clients' lives and are aimed toward affecting social change as well as individual change.

 See the video program for Chapter 12, *DVD for Theory and Practice of Counseling and Psychotherapy: The Case of Stan and Lecturettes.* I suggest that you view the brief lecture for each chapter prior to reading the chapter.

History and Development

Feminist therapy has developed in a grassroots manner, responding to challenges and to the emerging needs of women (Brabeck & Brown, 1997). No single individual can be identified as the founder of this approach, reflecting a central theme of feminist collaboration. Its history is relatively brief. The beginnings of feminism can be traced to the late 1800s, but it is the women's movement of the 1960s that laid the foundation for the development of feminist therapy. In the 1960s women began uniting their voices to express their dissatisfaction with the limiting and confining nature of traditional female roles. Consciousness-raising groups, in which women came together to share their experiences and perceptions, helped individual women become aware that they were not alone. A sisterhood developed, and some of the services that evolved from women's collective desires to improve society included shelters for battered women, rape crisis centers, and women's health and reproductive health centers.

Changes in psychotherapy occurred when women therapists participated in consciousness-raising groups and were changed by their experiences. They formed feminist therapy groups that operated from the same norms as consciousness-raising groups, including nonhierarchical structures, equal sharing of resources and power, and empowerment of women. These women also realized in their sharing that they were already working with clients from a feminist lens that had never been formally defined.

Believing that personal counseling was a legitimate means to effect change, they viewed therapy as a partnership between equals and built mutuality into the therapeutic process. They took the stance that therapy needed to move away from an intrapsychic perspective on psychopathology (in which the sources of a woman's unhappiness reside within her) to a focus on understanding the social, political, and cultural forces in society that damage and constrain girls and women, as well as boys and men.

A profusion of research on gender-bias emerged in the 1970s, which helped further feminist therapy ideas, and formal organizations began to foster the development and definition of feminist therapy. Among them were the Association for Women in Psychology (AWP) and various efforts by the American Psychological Association (APA).

The 1980s were marked by efforts to define feminist therapy as an entity in its own right (Enns, 1993), and individual therapy became the most frequently practiced form of feminist therapy (Kaschak, 1981). Gilligan's (1982) work on the development of a morality of care in women, and the work of Miller (1986) and the Stone Center scholars in developing the *self-in-relation* model (now called the "relational-cultural" model) were influential in the evolution of a feminist personality theory. New theories emerged that honored the relational and cooperative dimensions of women's experiencing (Enns, 1991, 2000, 2004; Enns & Sinacore, 2001). Feminist therapists began to formally examine the relationship of feminist theory to traditional psychotherapy systems, and integrations with various existing systems were proposed.

By the 1980s feminist group therapy had changed dramatically, becoming more diverse as it focused increasingly on specific problems and issues such as body image, abusive relationships, eating disorders, incest, and other forms of sexual abuse (Enns, 1993). The feminist philosophies that guided the practice of therapy also became more diverse. According to Enns (2004), in the field of feminist therapy "there is room for diversity of practice and the opportunity for individuals to articulate a set of beliefs which are personally meaningful and which guide transformational practice" (p. 10). Brown (2010) maintains that feminist therapy is a technically integrative approach that stresses tailoring interventions to meet clients with their strengths. Feminist therapists also draw upon strategies from many other therapy models. There are feminists who identify themselves as person-centered, Gestalt, Adlerian, cognitive, cognitive-behavioral, existential, and psychoanalytic, but most feminist therapists do not feel a need to position themselves in a particular philosophical place.

Enns (1993, 2004; Enns & Sinacore, 2001) identifies four enduring feminist philosophies, which are often described as the "second wave" of feminism: liberal, cultural, radical, and socialist feminism. These philosophies all advocate social activism and changing society as goals in feminist practice.

Liberal feminists focus on helping individual women overcome the limits and constraints of traditional gender-role socialization patterns. Liberal feminists argue for a transformation from accepting traditional gender roles to creating equal opportunities for both women and men. These feminists tend to believe the differences between women and men will be less problematic as work and social environments become increasingly bias free. For liberal feminists, the major goals of therapy include personal empowerment of individual women, dignity, self-fulfillment, shared power in decision making in relationships, and equality. Another key goal is to eliminate psychotherapy practices that have supported traditional socialization and are based on biased views about women and men (Enns, 2004).

Cultural feminists believe oppression stems from society's devaluation of women's strengths, values, and roles. They emphasize the differences between women and men and believe the solution to oppression lies in feminization of the culture so that society becomes more nurturing, intuitive, subjective, cooperative, and relational. Cultural feminism highlights the value of interdependence over individualism (Enns, 2004). For cultural feminists, the major goal of therapy is social transformation through the infusion of feminine values (such as cooperation, altruism, and connectedness) into the culture.

Radical feminists focus on the oppression of women that is embedded in patriarchy and seek to change society through activism and equalizing power. Radical feminists strive to identify and question the many ways in which patriarchy dominates every area of life including household chores, paid employment, intimate partnerships, violence, and parenting. They challenge the many ways that women are denied power. The major goals are to transform gender relationships, transform societal institutions, and increase women's sexual and procreative self-determination.

Socialist feminists share with radical feminists the goal of societal change. Their emphasis differs, however, in that they focus on multiple oppressions and believe solutions to society's problems must include considerations of class, race, sexual orientation, economics, nationality, and history. Socialist feminists pay close attention to the ways that work, education, and family roles affect their lives. For socialist feminists, the major goal of therapy is to transform social relationships and institutions.

During the past 20 years feminist women of color and postmodern feminists have found classic feminist theories wanting and have offered new theoretical perspectives focused on issues of diversity, the complexity of sexism, and the centrality of social context in understanding gender issues. In 1993 psychologists who embraced a diversity of feminist perspectives met at the National Conference on Education and Training in Feminist Practice. They reached consensus on basic themes and premises underlying feminist practice, thus taking a significant step toward integration of a number of feminist perspectives. Enns (2004) states that this "third wave" of feminism embraces diversity with its inclusion of women of color, lesbians, and the postmodern and constructivist viewpoints espoused by many of the most recent generation of feminist women. New developments in feminism also include global and international perspectives. Enns (2004) describes some of the key characteristics associated with contemporary feminist approaches.

Postmodern feminists provide a model for critiquing other traditional and feminist approaches, addressing the issue of what constitutes reality and proposing multiple truths as opposed to a single truth. The postmodern perspective is based on the assumption that "reality is embedded in social relationships and historical contexts, is socially created or invented, and is reproduced through power relationships" (Enns, 2004, p. 271). This approach calls attention to the limitation of knowledge and the fallibility of "knowers." Polarities such as masculine–feminine are deconstructed, which involves an analysis of how such constructs are created.

Women of color feminists believe it is essential that feminist theory be broadened and made more inclusive. Women of color have criticized some White feminists who overgeneralize the experiences of White women to fit the experiences of all women. They challenge feminist theory to include an analysis of the intersections of multiple oppressions, an assessment of access to privilege and power, to recognize the importance of the spiritual dimension of human experience, and to emphasize activism.

Lesbian feminists share commonalities with many aspects of radical feminism. Both perspectives view women's oppression as related to heterosexism and sexualized images of women. Lesbians who define themselves as feminists sometimes feel excluded by heterosexual feminists who do not understand discrimination based on sexual orientation. This perspective calls for feminist theory to include an analysis of the intersections of a person's multiple identities and their relationship to oppression and to recognize the diversity that exists among lesbians. In recent years, lesbian feminism has been enriched through interaction with queer theory, which emphasizes the fluidity, flexibility, and multiple meanings associated with sex, sexual orientation, and gender. Some individuals identify "lesbian feminism" with 1970s and 1980s movements. Although queer theory and lesbian theory are not identical, queer theory seems to be increasingly integrated with lesbian feminism.

Global international feminists take a worldwide perspective and seek to understand the ways in which racism, sexism, economics, and classism affect women in different countries. Western feminists are challenged to recognize their ethnocentrism and stereotyping of women in different parts of the world. Global feminists assume that each woman lives under unique systems of oppression. They see a need to address those cultural differences that directly contribute to women's oppression.

The variety in feminist theories provides a range of different but overlapping perspectives from which to work (Enns & Sinacore, 2001). Brown (2010) defines feminist therapy as a postmodern, technically integrative approach that emphasizes the analysis of gender, power, and social location as strategies for facilitating change. Feminist therapists, both male and female, believe that understanding and confronting gender-role stereotypes and power are central to therapeutic practice and that addressing a client's problems requires adopting a sociocultural perspective: namely, understanding the impact of the society and culture in which a client lives.

View of Human Nature

The feminist view of human nature is fundamentally different from that of most other therapeutic models. Many of the traditional theories grew out of a historical period in which social arrangements were assumed to be rooted in one's biologically based gender. Men were assumed to be the norm and were the only group studied or understood within the normative construct. It also was assumed that because of biological gender differences women and men would pursue different directions in life. Worell and Remer (2003) are critical of traditional theories for being **androcentric** (using male-oriented constructs to draw conclusions about human, including female, nature), **gendercentric** (proposing two separate paths of development for women and men), **heterosexist** (viewing a heterosexual orientation as normative and desirable and devaluing lesbian, gay male, and bisexual orientations), **deterministic** (assuming that personality patterns and behavior are fixed at an early stage of development), and having an **intrapsychic orientation** (attributing behavior to internal causes, which often results in blaming the victim and ignoring sociocultural and political factors). To the degree that traditional theories contain these biased elements, they have clear limitations for counseling females and members of marginalized groups.

Worell and Remer (2003) describe the constructs of feminist theory as being gender fair, flexible–multicultural, interactionist, and life-span-oriented. **Gender-fair approaches** explain differences in the behavior of women and men in terms of socialization processes rather than on the basis of our "innate" natures, thus avoiding stereotypes in social roles and interpersonal behavior. A **flexible–multicultural perspective** uses concepts and strategies that apply equally to individuals and groups regardless of age, race, culture, gender, ability, class, or sexual orientation. The **interactionist** view contains concepts specific to the thinking, feeling, and behaving dimensions of human experience and accounts for contextual and environmental factors. A **life-span perspective** assumes that human development is a lifelong process and that personality and behavioral changes can occur at any time rather than being fixed during early childhood.

Feminist Perspective on Personality Development

Feminist therapists emphasize that societal gender-role expectations profoundly influence a person's identity from the moment of birth and become deeply ingrained in adult personality. Because gender politics are embedded in the fabric of American society, they influence how we see ourselves as girls and boys and as women and men throughout the course of our lives. Prochaska and Norcross (2010) point out that gender-role expectations tend to generate a false sense of self and force women to accept stereotyped gender roles. "Women are expected to be a lady, to never swear, hit, or get angry. They should strive to please men and, above all, never offend or best a man" (p. 379).

Gilligan (1977) recognized that theories of moral development were based almost exclusively on research with males. As a result of her studies on women's moral and psychosocial development, Gilligan came to believe women's sense of self and morality is based in issues of responsibility and care for other people and is embedded in a cultural context. She posited that the concepts of connectedness and interdependence—virtually ignored in male-dominated developmental theories— are central to women's development.

Most models of human growth and development emphasize a struggle toward independence and autonomy, but feminists recognize that women are searching for a connectedness with others. In feminist therapy women's relational qualities are seen as strengths and as pathways for healthy growth and development instead of being identified as weaknesses or defects.

The founding scholars of **relational-cultural theory** have elaborated on the vital role that relationships and connectedness with others play in the lives of women (Jordan, Kaplan, Miller, Stiver, & Surrey, 1991; Miller, 1986, 1991; Miller et al., 1999; Miller & Stiver, 1997; Surrey, 1991; Trepal, 2010). These scholars suggest that a woman's sense of identity and self-concept develop in the context of relation- ships. They describe a process of relational movement in which women move through connections, disconnections, and enhanced transformative relationships throughout their lives (Comstock et al., 2008). As you will see, many of the tech- niques of feminist therapy foster mutuality, relational capacities, and growth in connection.

Bem (1993) posits that even very young children develop *gender schemas*, which are internalizations of the gender roles perpetuated in a sexist society. In a similar vein, Kaschak (1992) used the term *engendered lives* to describe her belief that gen- der is the organizing principle in people's lives. She has studied the role gender plays in shaping the identities of females and males and believes the masculine defines the feminine. For instance, because men pay great attention to women's bodies, women's appearance is given tremendous importance in Western society. It is easy to see how this perspective gets reified in both eating disorders and vari- ous forms of depression. Men, as the dominant group, define and determine the roles that women play. Because women occupy a subordinate position, to survive and thrive in society they must be able to interpret the needs and behaviors of the dominant group. To that end, women have developed "women's intuition" and have included in their gender schema an internalized belief that women are less important than men. Females are raised in a culture grounded in sexism, and they internalize the oppression. Understanding and acknowledging internalized oppression is central in feminist work.

Feminist therapists remind us that traditional gender stereotypes of women are still prevalent in cultures throughout the world. They teach their clients that uncritical acceptance of traditional roles can greatly restrict their range of freedom. Today many women and men are resisting being so narrowly defined. Women and men in therapy learn that, if they choose to, they can experience mutual behavioral characteristics such as accepting themselves as being interdependent, giving to others, being open to receiving, thinking and feeling, and being tender and tough. Rather than being cemented to a single behavioral style, women and men who reject traditional roles are saying that they are entitled to express the complex range of characteristics that are appropriate for different situations and that they are open to their vulnerability as human beings.

Principles of Feminist Therapy

A number of feminist writers have articulated core principles that form the foundation for the practice of feminist therapy. These principles are interrelated and overlapping.

1. *The personal is political.* This principle is based on the assumption that the personal or individual problems that individuals bring to counseling originate in a political and social context. For females this is often a context of marginalization, oppression, subordination, and stereotyping. Acknowledgment of the political and societal impact on an individual's life is perhaps the most fundamental tenet that lies at the core of feminist therapy. Although feminist therapists emphasize social context, they also work from a biopsychosocial perspective, attending to the intersection of the biological, psychological, and social aspects of people's lives (Brown, 1994).

2. *Commitment to social change.* Feminist therapy aims not only for individual change but for social change. Feminists view their therapy practice as existing not only to help individual clients in their struggles but also to advance a transformation in society. Direct action for social change is part of their responsibility as therapists. It is important that women who engage in the therapy process—clients and therapists alike—recognize that they have suffered from oppression as members of a subordinate group and that they can join with other women to right these wrongs. The goal is to advance a different vision of societal organization that frees both women and men from the constraints imposed by gender-role expectations. This vision of counseling, which moves away from the traditional focus on change from within the individual out into the realm of social activism, distinguishes feminist therapy from other historically accepted approaches.

3. *Women's and girl's voices and ways of knowing are valued and their experiences are honored.* Women's perspectives are considered central in understanding their distress. Traditional therapies that operate on androcentric norms compare women to the male norm and find them deviant. Much of psychological theory and research tends to conceptualize women and men in a polarized way, forcing a male–female split in most aspects of human experience (Bem, 1993). A goal of feminist therapy is to replace patriarchal "objective truth" with feminist consciousness, which acknowledges diverse ways of knowing. Women are encouraged to value their emotions and their intuition and to use their personal experience as a touchstone for determining what is "reality." Their voices are acknowledged as authoritative and invaluable sources of knowledge. The valuing and facilitation of women's voices in or out of therapy directly counteracts the often forced silence of women and contributes to an ultimate change in the body politic of society.

4. *The counseling relationship is egalitarian.* Attention to power is central in feminist therapy. Feminist therapists recognize that there is a power imbalance in the therapeutic relationship, so they strive for an **egalitarian relationship**, keeping in mind that clients are the experts on their own lives. The intent is to shift power and privilege to the voices and experiences of those who come to counseling and away from those who deliver it (Brown, 2010). An open discussion of power and role differences in the therapeutic relationship helps clients to understand how power dynamics influence both counseling and other relationships and also invites a dialogue about ways to reduce power differentials (Enns, 2004). Finding ways to share power with clients and to demystify therapy is essential because feminist therapists believe all relationships should strive for equality, or mutuality (a condition of authentic connection between the client and the therapist).

5. *A focus on strengths and a reformulated definition of psychological distress.* Feminist therapy has a "conflicted and ambivalent relationship" with diagnostic labeling and the "disease model" of mental illness (Brown, 2010, p. 50). Psychological distress is reframed, not as disease but as a communication about unjust systems. When contextual variables are considered, symptoms can be reframed as survival strategies. Feminist therapists talk about problems in the context of living and coping skills rather than pathology (Enns, 2004; Worell & Remer, 2003). If a formal diagnosis is used, it is arrived at collaboratively with the client.

6. *All types of oppression are recognized.* Clients can best be understood in the context of their sociocultural environments. Feminist therapists acknowledge that social and political inequities have a negative effect on *all* people. Feminist therapists work to help individuals make changes in their lives, but they also are committed to working toward social change that will liberate all members of society from stereotyping, marginalization, and oppression. Diverse sources of oppression, not simply gender, are identified and interactively explored as a basis for understanding the concerns that clients bring to therapy. Framing clients' issues within a cultural context leads to empowerment, which can be fully realized only through social change (Worell & Remer, 2003).

THE THERAPEUTIC PROCESS
Therapeutic Goals

According to Enns (2004), some goals of feminist therapy include empowerment, valuing and affirming diversity, striving for change rather than adjustment, equality, balancing independence and interdependence, social change, and self-nurturance. Enns adds that a key goal of feminist therapy is to assist individuals in viewing themselves as active agents on their own behalf and on behalf of others. A goal of feminist therapy is to empower all people to create a world of equality that is reflected at individual, interpersonal, institutional, national, and global levels (Enns & Byars-Winston, 2010). Perhaps the ultimate goal of this approach is to create the kind of society where sexism and other forms of discrimination and oppression are no longer a reality (Worell & Remer, 2003). Feminist therapy strives for transformation for both the individual client and society as a whole.

At the individual level, feminist therapists work to help females and males recognize, claim, and embrace their personal power. Empowering the client is at the heart of feminist therapy, which is the overarching long-term therapeutic goal (Gilbert & Rader, 2007). Through this empowerment, clients are able to free themselves from the constraints of their gender-role socialization and to challenge ongoing institutional oppression.

According to Worell and Remer (2003), feminist therapists help clients:

- Become aware of their own gender-role socialization process
- Identify their internalized messages and replace them with more self-enhancing beliefs
- Understand how sexist and oppressive societal beliefs and practices influence them in negative ways
- Acquire skills to bring about change in the environment
- Restructure institutions to rid them of discriminatory practices
- Develop a wide range of behaviors that are freely chosen
- Evaluate the impact of social factors on their lives
- Develop a sense of personal and social power
- Recognize the power of relationships and connectedness
- Trust their own experience and their intuition

Feminist therapists also work toward reinterpreting women's mental health. Their aim is to depathologize women's experiencing and to influence society so that female voices are honored and relational qualities are valued. Women's and girls' experiences are examined without the bias of patriarchal values, and their life skills and accomplishments are acknowledged.

Therapist's Function and Role

Feminist therapy rests on a set of philosophical assumptions that can be applied to various theoretical orientations. Any theory can be evaluated against the criteria of being gender fair, flexible–multicultural, interactionist, and life-span-oriented. The therapist's role and functions will vary to some extent depending on the particular therapist and client in the therapeutic relationship. In *Case Approach to Counseling and Psychotherapy* (Corey, 2013, chap. 10) three feminist therapists (Drs. Evans, Kincade, and Seem) team up to demonstrate a variety of feminist interventions in their work with Ruth. They also conceptualize the case of Ruth from a feminist therapy perspective.

Feminist therapists have integrated feminism into their approach to therapy and into their lives. Their actions and beliefs and their personal and professional lives are congruent. They are committed to monitoring their own biases and distortions, especially the social and cultural dimensions of women's experiences. Feminist therapists are also committed to understanding oppression in all its forms—including but not limited to sexism, racism, heterosexism—and they consider the impact of oppression and discrimination on psychological well-being. They value being emotionally present for their clients, being willing to share themselves during the therapy hour, modeling proactive behaviors, and being committed to their own consciousness-raising process. Finally, although feminist therapists may use techniques and strategies from other theoretical orientations, they are unique in the feminist assumptions they hold.

Feminists share common ground with Adlerian therapists in their emphasis on social equality and social interest, and with existential therapists who emphasize therapy as a shared journey, one that is life changing for both client and therapist, and with their basic trust in the client's ability to move forward in a positive and constructive manner (Bitter, Robertson, Healey, & Cole, 2009). Feminist therapists believe the therapeutic relationship should be a nonhierarchical, person-to-person relationship, and they aim to empower clients to live according to their own values and to rely on an internal (rather than external or societal) locus of control in determining what is right for them. Like person-centered therapists, feminist therapists convey their genuineness and strive for mutual empathy between client and therapist. Unlike person-centered therapists, however, feminist therapists do not see the therapeutic relationship alone as being sufficient to produce change. Insight, introspection, and self-awareness are springboards to action.

Some feminist therapists share with postmodern therapists (see Chapter 13) an emphasis on the politics and power relationships in the therapy process and a concern about power relations in the world in general. Both feminist and postmodern thought asserts that psychotherapists must not replicate societal power imbalances or foster dependency in the client. Rather, therapist and client take active and equal roles, working together to determine goals and procedures. A common denominator of both feminist and postmodern approaches is the avoidance of assuming a therapist role of all-knowing expert.

Client's Experience in Therapy

Clients are active participants in the therapeutic process. Feminist therapists are committed to ensuring that this does not become another arena in which women remain passive and dependent. It is important that clients tell their stories and give voice to their experiencing.

Appropriate self-disclosure is affirmed within feminist therapy. The female therapist may share some of her own experiences including gender-role oppression. As an analysis of gender-role stereotyping is conducted, the client's consciousness is raised.

Feminist therapists do not restrict their practice to female clients; they also work with males, couples, families, and children. The therapeutic relationship is always a partnership, and the client, male or female, will be the expert in determining what he or she needs and wants from therapy. A male client will explore ways in which he has been limited by his gender-role socialization, becoming more aware of how he is constrained in his ability to express a range of emotions. In the safe environment of the therapeutic sessions, he may be able to fully experience such feelings as sadness, tenderness, uncertainty, and empathy. As he transfers these ideas to daily living, he may find that relationships change in his family, his social world, and at work.

As mentioned earlier, a major goal of feminist therapy is empowerment, which involves acquiring a sense of self-acceptance, self-confidence, joy, and authenticity. Worell and Remer (2003) write that clients acquire a new way of looking at and responding to their world. They add that the shared journey of empowerment can be both frightening and exciting—for both client and therapist. Clients need to be prepared for major shifts in their way of viewing the world around them, changes in the way they perceive themselves, and transformed interpersonal relationships.

Relationship Between Therapist and Client

Feminist therapists view the therapeutic relationship as being based on mutuality, equality, and empowerment (Evans, Kincade, & Seem, 2011). The very structure of the client–therapist relationship models how to identify and use power responsibly. Feminist therapists clearly state their values to reduce the chance of value imposition. This allows clients to make a choice regarding whether or not to work with the therapist. It also is a step in demystifying the process.

As mentioned, although there is an inherent power differential in the therapy relationship, feminist therapists work to equalize the power base in the relationship by employing a number of strategies (Thomas, 1977). First, they are acutely sensitive to ways they might abuse their own power in the relationship, such as by diagnosing unnecessarily, by interpreting or giving advice, by staying aloof behind an "expert" role, or by discounting the impact the power imbalance between therapist and client has on the relationship.

Second, therapists actively focus on the power their clients have in the therapeutic relationship and make this part of their informed consent processes. Therapists encourage clients to identify and express their feelings, to become aware of the ways they relinquish power in relationships with others as a result of socialization or as a means for survival, and to make decisions with this knowledge as the basis.

Third, feminist therapists work to demystify the counseling relationship by sharing with the client their own perceptions about what is going on in the relationship, by making the client an active partner in determining any diagnosis, and by making use of appropriate self-disclosure. Some feminist therapists use contracts as a way to make the goals and processes of therapy overt rather than covert and mysterious.

A defining theme of the client–counselor relationship is the inclusion of clients in both the assessment and the treatment process, keeping the therapeutic relationship as egalitarian as possible. Walden (2006) emphasizes the value of educating and empowering clients. When counselors keep their clients uninformed about the nature of the therapeutic process, they deny them the potential for active participation in their therapy. When counselors make decisions about a client *for* the client rather than *with* the client, they rob the client of power in the therapeutic relationship. Collaboration with the client in all aspects of therapy leads to a genuine partnership with the client.

APPLICATION: THERAPEUTIC TECHNIQUES AND PROCEDURES

The Role of Assessment and Diagnosis

Feminist therapists have been sharply critical of the DSM classification system, and research indicates that gender, culture, and race may influence assessment of clients' symptoms (Enns, 2000; Eriksen & Kress, 2005). To the degree that assessment is influenced by subtle forms of sexism, racism, ethnocentrism, heterosexism, ageism, or classism, it is extremely difficult to arrive at a meaningful assessment or diagnosis. For a thoughtful discussion of feminist challenges to DSM diagnosis, see Eriksen and Kress (2005, 2008) and Evans, Kincade, and Seem (2011).

From the perspective of feminist therapy, diagnostic criteria were established through a system that views male gender-role traits as "normative." Thus women's behaviors are more prone to becoming pathologized. Feminist therapists refer to distress rather than psychopathology (Brown, 2010), and they use diagnostic labels quite carefully, if at all. They believe diagnostic labels are severely limiting for these reasons: (1) they focus on the individual's symptoms and not the social factors that cause dysfunctional behavior; (2) as part of a system developed mainly by White male psychiatrists, they may represent an instrument of oppression; (3) they (especially the personality disorders) may reinforce gender-role stereotypes and encourage adjustment to the norms of the status quo; (4) they may reflect the inappropriate application of power in the therapeutic relationship; (5) they can lead to an overemphasis on individual solutions rather than social change; and (6) they have the potential to dehumanize the client through the label. Using diagnostic categories may contribute to a victim-blaming stance and dull the therapist's sensitivity to external factors that contribute to a client's symptoms (Enns, 2000; Eriksen & Kress, 2005).

The feminist approach emphasizes the importance of considering the gender-normative context of men and women's lives and points out that many symptoms can be understood as coping or survival strategies rather than as evidence of pathology (Bitter, 2008; Worell & Remer, 2003). Due to the cultural and gender limitations of diagnoses, Eriksen and Kress (2005) encourage therapists "to be tentative in diagnosing those from diverse backgrounds, and to, as a part of a more egalitarian relationship, co-construct an understanding of the problem *with* the client, rather than imposing a diagnosis *on* the client" (p. 104). In keeping with the focus on client empowerment, diagnosis is a shared process in which clients are the experts on the meaning of their distress. Reframing symptoms as resistance to oppression and as coping skills or strategies for survival and shifting the etiology of the problem to the environment avoids "blaming the victim" for her or his problems. Assessment is viewed as an ongoing process between client and therapist and is connected to treatment interventions (Enns, 2000). In the feminist therapy process, diagnosis of distress becomes secondary to identification and assessment of strengths, skills, and resources (Brown, 2010). If a DSM diagnosis is discussed, feminist therapists may ask questions aimed at deconstructing the diagnosis: "Who benefits from using this label?" "How might this label contribute to disempowering the person to whom it is assigned?"

Using the *DSM-IV-TR* (American Psychiatric Association, 2000), depression is diagnosed twice as often in women as in men. Feminist therapists believe women have many more reasons to experience depression than do men, and they often frame depression as a normative experience for women. Women are often financially disadvantaged or dependent, relationally submissive, and strive to please others by anticipating their needs. Depression may result from women's sense of powerlessness in their subordinate position, along with their experiences of domestic violence, sexual abuse, poverty, or sexual harassment in the workplace. Similarly, with eating disorders feminist therapists focus on messages given by society, and by the mass media in particular, about women's bodies. The therapist uses a gender-role analysis to help clients who suffer from anorexia or bulimia to examine these societal injunctions and how they have come to accept them. Therapist and client work together on ways to challenge and change these messages.

Perhaps the potentially most damaging diagnosis is *borderline personality disorder* (American Psychiatric Association, 2000), a diagnosis usually assigned to and critical of women (Bitter, 2008). Since very few women who receive this diagnosis have escaped physical abuse or sexual molestation, Herman (1992) has argued that the more appropriate diagnosis would be complex posttraumatic stress disorder. The latter diagnosis would certainly generate more compassion and sympathy in therapists than does the diagnosis of borderline personality disorder.

Feminist therapists do not refuse to use the *DSM-IV-TR* in this age of managed care and the prevalence of the medical model of mental health, but therapists who participate in the process of diagnosis have a responsibility to challenge the current diagnostic system (Eriksen & Kress, 2008). Diagnosis, when used, results from a shared dialogue between client and therapist. The therapist is careful to review with the client any implications of assigning a diagnosis so the client can make an informed choice, and discussion focuses on helping the client understand the role of socialization and culture in the etiology of her problems.

Techniques and Strategies

Feminist therapy does not prescribe any particular set of interventions; rather, feminist therapists tailor interventions to clients' strengths with the goal of empowering clients while evoking their feminist consciousness (Brown, 2010). Nonetheless, they have developed several unique techniques, and have borrowed others from traditional approaches. Particularly important are consciousness-raising techniques that help women to differentiate between what they have been taught is socially acceptable or desirable and what is actually healthy for them. Some of the techniques described by Worell and Remer (2003) and Enns (1993, 2004) are discussed in this section, using the case example of Alma to illustrate how these techniques might be applied.

> Alma, age 22, comes to counseling reporting general anxiety about a new job she began a month ago. She states that she has struggled with depression off and on throughout her life because of bullying as a child and rejection from much of her family after coming out as a lesbian at age 14. Alma identifies as Dominican and continues to struggle with the loss of her place within her family of origin. She now believes coming out was a selfish mistake and is trying to make amends by keeping her feelings regarding her sexual and affectional orientation hidden. Due in part to past experiences, she is worried that if she comes out to her coworkers the company might find a reason to fire her. Alma says, "I would like to cut my hair short again because it is more manageable and I also prefer to wear what is considered to be more masculine clothing, but I am worried this will cause people at work to question my femininity. I really like my job, and I worked very hard to get it. I am afraid if I show them who I really am, they won't want me there anymore."

EMPOWERMENT Enns and Byars-Winston (2010) point out that many of the strategies of multicultural feminist therapy are part of the general umbrella of empowerment, which enables people to see themselves as active agents on behalf of themselves and others. At the heart of feminist strategies is the goal of empowering the client. Feminist therapists work in an egalitarian manner and use empowerment strategies that are tailored to each client (Brown, 2010; Evans, Kincade, & Seem, 2011). Alma's therapist will pay careful attention to *informed consent* issues, discussing ways Alma can get the most from the therapy session, clarifying expectations, identifying goals, and working toward a contract that will guide the therapeutic process.

The process of feminist therapy begins with the informed consent process, which Brown (2010) refers to as "empowerment consent." Informed consent offers a place to begin a relationship that is egalitarian and collaborative. By explaining how therapy works and enlisting Alma as an active partner in the therapeutic venture, the therapy process is demystified and Alma becomes an equal participant. Alma will learn that she is in charge of the direction, length, and procedures of her therapy. Alma's therapist might ask her, "What is the most powerful thing you could do right now?" The intent of this question is to "interrupt the trance of powerlessness" (Brown, 2010, p. 35) by inviting Alma to notice how power is actually available to her. Given Alma's cultural background, it may be particularly important to address power within the therapeutic relationship because Alma may view the therapist as an expert who holds the answers she is seeking. In addition, Alma may view counseling as a weakness and may feel shame associated with her need for help.

SELF-DISCLOSURE Feminist therapists use therapeutic self-disclosure in the best interests of the client to equalize the client–therapist relationship, to provide modeling, to normalize women's collective experiences, to empower clients, and to establish informed consent. Believing that there is no such thing as therapist neutrality or objectivity, therapists who disown the reality of being knowable and known to clients are at greater risk of abusing their power (Brown, 2010). For example, Alma's therapist may disclose her own difficulties in relating to members of her family of origin, acknowledging that at times hiding information seems important in order to keep the peace. The therapist can share how she decides when to be open about her personal life and how to balance relating in a less open way. The counselor could then discuss with Alma ways in which they have both experienced cultural and social pressures to conform to a hetero-normative ideal. Alma benefits from this modeling by a woman who does not meet society's expectations for female behavior and appearance but is comfortable with the image she has developed and how it has worked for her, not against her.

Self-disclosure is not just sharing information and experiences. It also involves a certain quality of presence the therapist brings to the therapeutic sessions. Effective therapist self-disclosure is grounded in authenticity and a sense of mutuality. The therapist considers how the disclosures may affect the client by using what relational-cultural theorists refer to as "anticipatory empathy." Feminist therapists, like counselors who subscribe to other theoretical orientations, are ethically committed to using self-disclosure appropriately to enhance the therapeutic process.

The therapist also clearly states her relevant values and beliefs about society to allow Alma to make an informed choice about whether or not to enter into a professional relationship with this therapist. The therapist explains to Alma the therapeutic interventions that are likely to be employed. Alma, as an informed consumer, will be involved in evaluating how well these strategies are working and the degree to which her personal goals in therapy are being met.

GENDER-ROLE ANALYSIS A hallmark of feminist therapy, gender-role analysis explores the impact of gender-role expectations on the client's psychological well-being and draws upon this information to make decisions about future gender-role behaviors (Enns, 2004). Some feminist therapists prefer the term "social identity analysis" because it reflects the importance of assessing all relevant aspects of a client's identity, including multiple memberships in both socially disempowered and privileged groups. Hayes (2008) proposes an ADDRESSING model that includes the elements of age, disability status, religion, ethnicity, race, social class, and sexual orientation along with gender.

Gender-role analysis begins with clients identifying the societal messages they received about how women and men should be and act (Remer, 2008). The therapist begins by asking Alma to identify messages she has received related to sexuality and appearance from her culture, society, her peers, the media, and her family. The therapist talks about how body image expectations differ between females and males in our culture and how they may differ in other cultures. The therapist explains how expectations related to appearance could intersect with beliefs about what it means to be gay or straight in Alma's culture, family, and society as it relates to her working environment. Alma decides what messages she would prefer to have in her mind and keeps an open awareness when the discounting messages play in her head.

GENDER-ROLE INTERVENTION Using this technique, the therapist responds to Alma's concern by placing it in the context of society's role expectations for women. The aim is to provide Alma with insight into the ways social issues are affecting her. Alma's therapist responds to her statement with, "Our society really focuses on sometimes unrealistic beauty ideals with females. The media bombards girls and women with the message that they must be thin, have long straight hair, and wear attractive clothing. The message is so ingrained that many girls are struggling with self-esteem issues related to their appearance as early as elementary school to avoid being bullied or to fit in." By placing Alma's concern in the context of societal expectations, the therapist gives Alma insight into how these expectations have affected her psychological condition and have contributed to her feeling depressed and anxious about judgment from others. The therapist's statement also paves the way for Alma to think more positively about her unity with other women and even to think about how she might contribute as a role model for girls and young women in the future.

POWER ANALYSIS Power analysis refers to the range of methods aimed at helping clients understand how unequal access to power and resources can influence personal realities. Together therapists and clients explore how inequities or institutional barriers often limit self-definition and well-being (Enns, 2004). With this technique, Alma will become aware of the power difference between men and women as well as the power differences associated with sexual orientation in our society. Specific issues related to Alma's cultural perspective also are explored. In Alma's case the power analysis may focus on helping Alma identify alternate kinds of power she may exercise and to challenge the gender-role messages that prohibit the exercise of that kind of power. Interventions are aimed at helping Alma learn to appreciate herself as she is, regain her self-confidence based on the personality attributes she possesses, and set goals that will be fulfilling to her within the context of her cultural values.

BIBLIOTHERAPY Nonfiction books, psychology and counseling textbooks, autobiographies, self-help books, educational videos, films, and even novels can all be used as bibliotherapy resources. Reading about feminist perspectives on common issues in women's lives (incest, rape, battering, and sexual harassment) may challenge a woman's tendency to blame herself for these problems (Remer, 2008). The therapist describes a number of books that address issues of relevance to Alma, and she selects one to read over the next few weeks. Providing Alma with reading material increases knowledge and decreases the power difference between Alma and her therapist. Reading can supplement what is learned in the therapy sessions, and Alma can enhance her therapy by exploring her reactions to what she is reading.

ASSERTIVENESS TRAINING By teaching and promoting assertive behavior, women become aware of their interpersonal rights, transcend stereotypical gender roles, change negative beliefs, and implement changes in their daily lives. The therapist and client consider what is culturally appropriate, and the client makes decisions about when and how to use the new skill of assertion.

Through learning and practicing assertive behaviors and communication, Alma may increase her own power, which will ameliorate her depression and anxiety. Alma learns that it is her right to ask for what she wants and needs in the workplace. The therapist helps Alma to evaluate and anticipate the consequences of behaving assertively, which might range from criticism to actually getting what she wants.

REFRAMING AND RELABELING Like bibliotherapy, therapist self-disclosure, and assertiveness training, reframing is not unique to feminist therapy. However, reframing is applied uniquely in feminist therapy. **Reframing** includes a shift from "blaming the victim" to a consideration of social factors in the environment that contribute to a client's problem. In reframing, rather than dwelling exclusively on intrapsychic factors, the focus is on examining societal or political dimensions. Alma may come to understand that her depression and anxiety are linked to social pressures to behave within hetero-normative gender-role expectations and to develop an appearance that matches these culturally and societally prescribed ideals.

Relabeling is an intervention that changes the label or evaluation applied to some behavioral characteristic. Alma can change certain labels she has attached to herself, such as being inadequate or socially unwanted because she does not conform to ideals commonly associated with feminism. An example might be that Alma is encouraged to talk about herself as a strong and healthy woman rather than as being "selfish" or too "masculine."

SOCIAL ACTION Social action, or social activism, is an essential quality of feminist therapy (Enns, 2004). As clients become more grounded in their understanding of feminism, therapists may suggest that clients become involved in activities such as volunteering at a rape crisis center, lobbying lawmakers, or providing community education about gender issues. Participating in such activities can empower clients and help them see the link between their personal experiences and the sociopolitical context in which they live. Alma might decide to join and participate in organizations that are working to change societal stereotypes about beauty expectations for women or social groups that affirm people who identify with a variety of sexual and affectional orientations. Taking this kind of social action is another way for Alma to feel more empowered.

GROUP WORK Group work became popular as a way for women to discuss their lack of voice in many aspects of society. Historically, group work has been used for both consciousness-raising and support (Herlihy & McCollum, 2011). Consciousness-raising groups initially provided an avenue for women to share their experiences of oppression and powerlessness. Eventually, these groups evolved into self-help groups that empowered women and challenged many of the social patterns of the time (Evans, Kincade, Marbley, & Seem, 2005; Evans et al., 2011). Feminist therapists often encourage their clients to make the transition from individual therapy to a group format such as joining a support group or a political action group as soon as this is realistic (Herlihy & McCollum, 2011). Although these groups are as diverse as the women who comprise them, they share a common denominator emphasizing support for the experience of women. The literature reveals that women who join these groups eventually realize that they are not alone and gain validation for their experiences by participating in the group. These groups can provide women with a social network, decrease feelings of isolation, create an environment that encourages sharing of experiences, and help women realize that they are not alone in their experiences (Eriksen & Kress, 2005). Groups provide a supportive context where women can share and begin to critically explore the messages they have internalized about their self-worth and their place in society. The self-disclosures of both the members and the leader foster deeper self-exploration, a sense of universality, and increased levels of cohesion. Members learn to use power effectively by providing support to one another, practicing behavioral skills, considering social/political actions, and by taking interpersonal risks in a safe setting (Enns, 2004). Through their group participation, women learn that their individual experiences are frequently rooted in problems within the system. In conjunction with the group members, the group facilitator's job is to design a group that results in both individual and systemic change (Kees & Leech, 2004). Participation in a group experience can inspire women to take up some form of social action. Indeed, a form of homework can be to carry out what women are learning in the group to bring about changes in their lives outside of the group.

Alma and her therapist will likely discuss the possibility of Alma joining a women's support group, a gay-straight alliance, or another type of group as a part of the process of terminating individual therapy. By joining a group Alma will have opportunities to discover that she is not alone in her struggles. Other women can provide her with nurturance and support, and Alma will have the chance to be significant to other women as they engage in their healing process.

The Role of Men in Feminist Therapy

Men can be feminist therapists, and feminist therapy can be practiced with male clients. It is an erroneous perception that feminist therapy is conducted only by women and for women, or that feminist therapy is anti-men because it is pro-women (Herlihy & McCollum, 2011). Although the original feminist therapists were exclusively women, men are now included among their ranks. Male feminist therapists are willing to understand and "own" their male privilege, confront sexist behavior in themselves and others, redefine masculinity and femininity according to other than traditional values, work toward establishing egalitarian relationships, and actively support women's efforts to create a just society.

The principles and practices of feminist psychotherapy are useful in working with male clients, individuals from diverse racial and cultural backgrounds, and people who are committed to addressing social justice issues in counseling practice (Enns, 2000, 2004; Worell & Remer, 2003). Social mandates about masculinity such as restrictive emotionality, overvaluing power and control, the sexualization of emotion, and obsession with achievement can be limiting to males (Gilbert & Scher, 1999; Pleck, 1995; Pollack, 1995, 1998; Real, 1998).

Some feminist therapists routinely work with men, especially with abusive men and in batterers' groups. According to Ganley (1988), issues that men can deal with productively in feminist therapy include learning how to increase their capacity for intimacy, expressing their emotions and learning self-disclosure, balancing achievement and relationship needs, accepting their vulnerabilities, and creating collaborative relationships at work and with significant others that are not based on a "power-over" model of relating. Any presenting issue can be dealt with from a feminist perspective.

FEMINIST THERAPY FROM A MULTICULTURAL AND SOCIAL JUSTICE PERSPECTIVE

Strengths From a Diversity Perspective

Of all the theoretical approaches to counseling and psychotherapy in this book, feminist therapy has the most in common with the multicultural and social justice perspectives. Historically, multicultural approaches evolved in response to societal oppression, discrimination, and marginalization faced by people of color. Over time, multicultural counseling has become more inclusive, and contemporary multicultural counselors work to address inequities created not only by racism but also by other "isms" that limit full participation in society. Social justice counseling aims to empower the individual as well as to confront injustice and inequality in society.

Although multicultural, feminist, and social justice counseling have been viewed as disparate models, they have many common threads (Crethar, Torres Rivera, & Nash, 2008). All three approaches emphasize the need to promote social, political, and environmental changes within the counseling context. Practitioners of all three theories strive to create an egalitarian relationship in which counselor and client co-construct the client's problems from a contextual perspective and collaborate in setting goals and choosing strategies. All three approaches reject the "disease model" of psychopathology; they view clients' problems as symptoms of their experiences of living in an unjust society rather than as having an intrapsychic origin.

The "personal is political" principle is embraced equally in each of the approaches. None of the approaches rests solely on individual change; they all emphasize direct action for social change as a part of the role of therapists.

Culture encompasses the sociopolitical reality of people's lives, including how the privileged dominant group (in Western societies: White, Protestant, heterosexual, rich males) treats those who are different from them. Feminist therapists believe psychotherapy is inextricably bound to culture, and, increasingly, they are being joined by thoughtful leaders in the field of counseling practice. All cultures include feminist voices from within them today.

The women's movement and the multicultural movement, and more recently the social justice movement, have called to our attention the negative effects of discrimination and oppression on their targets and also on those doing the discriminating and oppressing. Culturally competent feminist therapists look for ways to work within the client's culture by exploring consequences and alternatives. They appreciate the complexities involved in changing within one's culture but do not view culture as sacrosanct (Worell & Remer, 2003). It is important to understand and respect diverse cultures, but most cultural contexts have both positive and toxic aspects. Feminist therapists are committed to taking a critical look at cultural beliefs and practices that discriminate against, subordinate, and restrict the potential of groups of individuals, which can be either a strength or a shortcoming.

Shortcomings From a Diversity Perspective

Feminist therapists advocate for change in the social structure, especially in the areas of inequality, power in relationships, the right to self-determination, freedom to pursue a career outside or inside the home, and the right to an education. This agenda could pose some problems when working with women who do not share these beliefs. Remer (2008) acknowledges this practice of critically evaluating societal values and structures that subordinate certain groups as a shortcoming of the approach. If therapists do not fully understand and respect the cultural values of clients from diverse groups, they run the risk of imposing their own values. Remer claims "a potential danger inherent in feminist counseling is that counselors' values will too strongly influence clients or will conflict with clients' values" (p. 431).

Being aware of the cultural context is especially important when feminist therapists work with women from cultures that endorse culturally prescribed roles that keep women in a subservient place or that are grounded in patriarchy. Consider this scenario. You are a feminist therapist working with a Vietnamese woman who is struggling to find a way to be true to her culture and also to follow her own educational and career aspirations. Your client is a student in a helping profession who is being subjected to extreme pressure from her father to return home and take care of her family. Although she wants to complete a degree and eventually help others in the Vietnamese community, she feels a great deal of guilt when she considers "selfishly" pursuing her education when her family at home needs her.

In this complex situation, the therapist is challenged to work together with the client to find a path that enables her to consider her own individual goals without ignoring or devaluing her collectivistic cultural values. The therapist's job is not to take away her pain or struggle, nor to choose for the client, but to be present in such a way that the client will truly be empowered to make significant decisions. The feminist counselor must remain aware that the price may be very high if this woman chooses to go against what is culturally expected of her, and that the client is the one to ultimately decide which path to follow. As can be seen from this example, to minimize this potential shortcoming of imposing cultural values on a client, it is essential that therapists understand how their own cultural perspectives are likely to influence their interventions, especially when they are working with culturally diverse clients. A safeguard against value imposition is for feminist therapists to clearly present their values to clients early in the course of the counseling relationship so that clients can make an informed choice about continuing this relationship (Remer, 2008).

Feminist Therapy Applied to the Case of Stan

 Stan's fear of women and his gender-role socialization experiences make him an excellent candidate to benefit from feminist therapy. A therapeutic relationship that is egalitarian will be a new kind of experience for Stan.

Stan has indicated that he is willing and even eager to change. Despite his low self-esteem and negative self-evaluations, he is able to identify some positive attributes. These include his determination, his ability to articulate his feelings, and his gift for working with children. Stan knows what he wants out of therapy and has clear goals: to stop drinking, to feel better about himself, to relate to women on an equal basis, and to learn to love and trust himself and others. Operating from a feminist orientation, I will build on these strengths.

In the first session I focus on establishing an egalitarian working relationship to help Stan begin to regain his personal power. It is important that the therapeutic relationship does not replicate other relationships Stan has had with significant figures in his life. I consciously work to demystify the therapeutic process and equalize the relationship, conveying to Stan that he is in charge of the direction of his therapy. I spend time explaining my view of the therapy process and how it works.

A gender-role analysis is conducted to help Stan become aware of the influence of gender-role expectations in the development of his problems. First, I ask him to identify gender-role messages he received while growing up from a variety of societal sources including his parents, teachers, the media, faith community, and peers. In his autobiography Stan has written about some of the messages his parents gave him, and this provides a natural starting point for his analysis. He remembers his father calling him "dumb" and his mother saying, "Why can't you grow up and be a man?" Stan wrote about his mother "continually harping at" his father and telling Stan how she wished she hadn't had him. He describes his father as weak, passive, and mousy in relating to his mother and remembers that his father compared him unfavorably with his siblings. Stan internalized these messages, often crying himself to sleep and feeling very hopeless.

I ask Stan to identify the damaging self-statements he makes now that are based on these early experiences. As we review his writings, Stan sees how societal messages he received about what a man "should" be were reinforced by parental messages and have shaped his view of himself today. For example, he wrote that he feels sexually inadequate. It appears that he has introjected the societal notion that men should always initiate sex, be ready for sex, and be able to achieve and sustain an erection. Stan also sees that he has already identified and written about how he wants to change those messages, as exemplified in his statements that he wants to "feel equal with others" and not "feel apologetic" for his existence and develop a loving relationship with a woman. Stan begins to feel capable and empowered as I acknowledge the important work he has already done, even before he entered therapy.

I follow this gender-role analysis with a gender-role intervention to place Stan's concerns in the context of societal role expectations. I say, "Indeed, it is a burden to try to live up to society's notion of what it means to be a man, always having to be strong and tough. Those aspects of yourself that you would like to value—your ability to feel your feelings, being good with children—are qualities society tends to label as 'feminine.'" Stan replies wistfully, "Yeah, it would be a better world if women could be strong without being seen as domineering and if men could be sensitive and nurturing without being seen as weak." I raise the question, "Are you sure that's not possible? Have you ever met a woman or a man who was like that?" Stan ponders for a minute and then with some animation describes the college professor who taught his Psychology of Adjustment class. Stan saw her as very accomplished and strong but also as someone who empowered him by encouraging him to find his own voice through writing his autobiography. He also remembers a male counselor at the youth rehabilitation facility where he spent part of his adolescence as a man who was strong as well as sensitive and nurturing.

As the first session draws to a close, I invite Stan to talk about what he learned from our time together. Stan says two things stand out for him.

First, he is beginning to believe he doesn't need to keep blaming himself. He knows that many of the messages he has received from his parents and from society about what it means to be a man have been undesirable and one-dimensional. He acknowledges that he has been limited and constrained by his gender-role socialization. Second, he feels hopeful because there are alternatives to those parental and societal definitions—people he admires have been able to successfully combine "masculine" and "feminine" traits. If they can do it, so can he. I ask Stan whether he chooses to return for another session. When he answers in the affirmative, I give him W. S. Pollack's (1998) book *Real Boys* to read. I explain that this book descriptively captures the gender-role socialization that many boys experience.

Stan comes to the following session eager to talk about his homework assignment. He tells me that he gained some real insights into his own attitudes and beliefs by reading *Real Boys*. What Stan learned from reading this book leads to a further exploration of his relationship with his mother. He finds it helpful to understand his parents' behavior in the context of societal expectations and stereotypes rather than continuing to blame them. I help Stan to see how our culture tends to hold extreme positions about mothers—that they are either perfect or wicked—and that neither of these extremes is true. As Stan learns to reframe his relationship with his mother, he develops a more realistic picture of her. He comes to realize, too, that his father has been oppressed by his own socialization experiences and by an idealistic view of masculinity that he may have felt unable to achieve.

Stan continues to work at learning to value the nurturing and sensitive aspects of himself. He is learning to value the "feminine" aspects of himself as well as the "masculine" side of his personality. He also continues to monitor and make changes in his self-talk about what it means to be a man. He is involved in gaining ongoing awareness of these messages that come from current sources such as the media and friends. Since a number of Stan's sessions were devoted to exploring his relationship with his mother, along with his resentment toward her, I suggest another reading assignment—Caplan's (1989) book, *Don't Blame Mother*. The aim of this assignment is to assist Stan in exploring alternatives to blaming his mother for his present problems.

Throughout our therapeutic relationship, we discuss with immediacy how we are communicating and relating to each other during the sessions. I am self-disclosing and treat Stan as an equal, continually acknowledging that he is the "expert" on his life.

Follow-Up: You Continue as Stan's Feminist Therapist

Use these questions to help you think about how you would counsel Stan using a feminist therapy model:

- What unique values do you see in working with Stan from a feminist perspective as opposed to working from the other therapeutic approaches you've studied thus far?

- If you were to continue working with Stan, what self-statements regarding his view of himself as a man might you

focus on, and what alternatives might you offer?

- In what ways could you integrate cognitive behavior therapy with feminist therapy in Stan's case? What possibilities do you see for integrating Gestalt therapy methods with feminist therapy? What other therapies might you combine with a feminist approach?

- I used bibliotherapy as a form of homework assignment. Would you suggest books or films for Stan? If so, which ones? What other homework might you suggest to Stan? What other feminist therapy strategies would you utilize in counseling Stan?

 See *DVD for Theory and Practice of Counseling and Psychotherapy: The Case of Stan and Lecturettes* (Session 10 on feminist therapy) for a demonstration of my approach to counseling Stan from this perspective. This session deals with Stan's exploration of his gender-role identity and messages he has incorporated about being a man.

SUMMARY AND EVALUATION
Summary

The origins of feminist therapy are connected with the women's movements of the late 1800s and the 1960s, when women united in vocalizing their dissatisfaction over the restrictive nature of traditional female roles. Feminist therapy largely grew out of the recognition by women that the traditional models of therapy suffer from basic limitations due to the inherent bias of earlier theoreticians. Feminist therapy emphasizes these concepts:

- Viewing problems in a sociopolitical and cultural context rather than on an individual level

- Recognizing that clients know what is best for their lives and are experts on their own lives

- Striving to create a therapeutic relationship that is egalitarian through the process of self-disclosure and informed consent

- Demystifying the therapeutic process by including the client as much as possible in all phases of assessment and treatment, which increases client empowerment

- Viewing women's experiences from a unique perspective
- Understanding and appreciating the lives and perspectives of diverse women
- Understanding that gender never exists in isolation from other aspects of identity
- Challenging traditional ways of assessing the psychological health of women
- Emphasizing the role of the therapist as advocate as well as facilitator
- Encouraging clients to get involved in social action to address oppressive aspects of the environment

Feminist therapy is aimed at both personal and social change. The theory is not static but is continually evolving and maturing. The major goal is to replace the current patriarchal system with feminist consciousness and thus create a society that values equality in relationships, values diversity, stresses interdependence rather than dependence, and encourages both women and men to define themselves rather than being defined by societal demands.

Instead of being a singular and unified approach to psychotherapy, feminist practice tends to be diverse. As feminist therapy has matured, it has become more self-critical and varied. Feminist therapists share a number of basic assumptions and roles: they engage in appropriate self-disclosure; they make their values and beliefs explicit so that the therapy process is clearly understood; they establish egalitarian roles with clients; they work toward client empowerment; they emphasize the commonalities among women while honoring their diverse life experiences; and they all have an agenda to bring about social change.

Feminist therapists are committed to actively breaking down the hierarchy of power in the therapeutic relationship through the use of various interventions. Some of these strategies are unique to feminist therapy, such as gender-role analysis and intervention, power analysis, assuming a stance of advocate in challenging conventional attitudes toward appropriate roles for women, and encouraging clients to take social action. Other therapeutic strategies are borrowed from various therapy models, including bibliotherapy, assertiveness training, cognitive restructuring, reframing and relabeling, counselor self-disclosure, role playing, identifying and challenging untested beliefs, and journal writing. Feminist therapy principles and techniques can be applied to a range of therapeutic modalities such as individual therapy, couples counseling, family therapy, group counseling, and community intervention. Regardless of the specific techniques used, the overriding goals are client empowerment and social transformation.

Contributions of Feminist Therapy

One of the major contributions feminists have made to the field of counseling and psychotherapy is paving the way for gender-sensitive practice and an awareness of the impact of the cultural context and multiple oppressions. By focusing attention on our attitudes and biases pertaining to gender and culture, feminist therapists have expanded the awareness of therapists of all theoretical orientations regarding how social justice issues may touch clients. Feminists have had a major influence on therapeutic practice with women and girls; for example, feminist perspectives are reflected throughout the American Psychological Association's *Guidelines for Psychological Practice with Girls and Women* (2007). A significant contribution of feminist therapy is the emphasis on social change, which can lead to a transformation in society. Therapists with a feminist orientation understand how important it is to be fully aware of typical gender-role messages clients have grown up with, and they are skilled in helping clients identify and examine these messages (Philpot, Brooks, Lusterman, & Nutt, 1997).

According to Gilbert and Rader (2007), feminist therapists have brought about significant theoretical and professional advances in counseling practice. Some of these contributions include power sharing with clients, cultural critiques of both assessment and treatment approaches, and the validation of women and their normative experiences. Feminist therapists have also made important contributions by questioning traditional counseling theories and models of human development. Most theories place the cause of problems within individuals rather than with external circumstances and the environment. This has led to holding individuals responsible for their problems and not giving full recognition to social and political realities that create problems. A key contribution feminists continue to make is reminding all of us that the proper focus of therapy includes addressing oppressive factors in society rather than expecting individuals to merely adapt to expected role behaviors. This emphasis on social justice issues has expanded the role of therapists to be advocates for clients. For a discussion of adaptations to traditional approaches to counseling women, see Enns (2003).

Another major contribution of the feminist movement is in the areas of ethics in psychology and counseling practice (Brabeck, 2000) and ethical decision making in therapy (Rave & Larsen, 1995). The unified feminist voice called attention to the extent and implications of child abuse, incest, rape, sexual harassment, and domestic violence. Feminists pointed out the consequences of failing to recognize and take action when children and women were victims of physical, sexual, and psychological abuse. Feminist therapists work with male clients who are abusive, and increasing numbers of groups composed of male batterers are led or co-led by feminist therapists.

Feminist therapists demanded action in cases of sexual misconduct at a time when male therapists misused the trust placed in them by their female clients. Not too long ago the codes of ethics of all the major professional organizations were silent on the matter of therapist and client sexual liaisons. Now, virtually all of the professional codes of ethics prohibit sexual intimacies with current clients and with former clients for a specified time period. Furthermore, the professions agree that a sexual relationship cannot later be converted into a therapeutic relationship. Largely due to the efforts and input of women on ethics committees, the existing codes are explicit with respect to sexual harassment and sexual relationships with clients, students, and supervisees (Herlihy & Corey, 2006b).

Feminist therapy principles have been applied to supervision, teaching, consultation, ethics, research, and theory building as well as to the practice of psychotherapy. Building community, providing authentic mutual empathic relationships, creating a sense of social awareness, and addressing social injustices are all significant strengths of this approach.

The principles and techniques of feminist therapy can be incorporated in many other contemporary therapy models and vice versa (Enns, 2003). Both feminist and

Adlerian therapists view the therapeutic relationship as egalitarian. Both feminist and person-centered therapists agree on the importance of therapist authenticity, modeling, and self-disclosure; empowerment is the basic goal of both orientations. When it comes to making choices about one's destiny, existential and feminist therapists are speaking the same language—both emphasize choosing for oneself instead of living a life determined by societal dictates.

Although feminist therapists have been critical of psychoanalysis as a sexist orientation, a number of feminist therapists believe psychoanalysis can be an appropriate approach to helping women. Object-relations theory may help clients examine internalized object representations that are based on their relationships with their parents. Therapy might include an examination of unconscious learning about women's roles through the mother–daughter relationship to provide insights into why gender roles are so deeply ingrained and difficult to change.

Gestalt therapy and feminist therapy share the goal of increasing the client's awareness of personal power. Gestalt therapy also is useful for increasing a woman's sense of herself as a powerful person (Enns, 2003). In many ways the dialogic, relational, and collaborative model of Gestalt therapy fits well with the philosophy of a feminist perspective (Enns, 1987, 2004).

Cognitive behavioral therapies and feminist therapy are compatible in that they view the therapeutic relationship as a collaborative partnership, with the client being in charge of setting goals and selecting strategies for change. These approaches are committed to demystifying therapy, and both aim to help clients take charge of their own lives. Both the cognitive behavior therapist and the feminist therapist assume a range of information-giving and teaching functions so clients can become active partners in the therapy process. A feminist therapist could employ action-oriented strategies such as assertiveness training and behavioral rehearsal, and suggest homework assignments for clients to practice in their everyday lives. A useful source for further discussion of feminist cognitive behavior therapy is Worell and Remer (2003).

Limitations and Criticisms of Feminist Therapy

Feminist therapists do not take a neutral stance; they believe therapy is a value-oriented process. They emphasize the importance of counselors clarifying their personal and professional values and being aware of the potential impact of these values on clients. However, there is a danger that therapists may unduly influence clients, especially those who lack a strong sense of their own values. Feminist therapists must remain aware of their own values and explicitly share these values with clients in an appropriate, timely, and respectful manner to reduce the risk of value imposition.

Feminist therapists call attention to clients' unexamined choices, but they must honor clients' choices as long as those choices are indeed informed. Once clients understand the impact of gender and cultural factors on their choices, the therapist must guard against providing specific directions for client growth. Feminist therapists are committed to helping clients weigh the costs and benefits of their current life choices but should not push clients too quickly toward changes they feel are beyond their reach. Lenore Walker (1994) raised this issue with regard to working with abused women. Although Walker focuses on the importance of asking questions that enable women to think through their situations in new ways and of helping women develop "safety plans," she emphasizes how critical it is to understand those factors in a woman's life that often pose difficulties for her in making changes.

Looking at contextual or environmental factors that contribute to a woman's problems and moving away from exploring the intrapsychic domain can be both a strength and a limitation. Instead of being blamed for her depression, the client is able to come to an understanding of external realities that are indeed oppressive. However, viewing the source of a client's problem as being in the environment could contribute to the client not taking personal responsibility to act in the face of an unfair world. A client can make some internal changes even in those circumstances where external realities may largely be contributing to her problems. Therapists must balance an exploration of the outer and inner worlds of the client if the client is to find a way to take action in her own life.

Because feminist therapists do not assume a neutral stance, they need to identify any sources of bias and work toward restructuring or eliminating biased aspects in any theories or techniques they employ. This is indeed a demanding endeavor, and it should be considered an ongoing process.

Factors that inhibit the growth of feminist therapy include training that is often offered only sporadically in a nonsystematic way (Brown, 2010) and the lack of quality control. No credentialing organization confers official status as a qualified feminist therapist, so formalized training and credentialing need to be addressed in the future. In addition, evidence-based research on the efficacy of feminist therapy is lacking, as is an understanding of feminist therapy as an integrative approach that can inform therapeutic practice for counselors of varied theoretical orientations.

WHERE TO GO FROM HERE

The *DVD for Integrative Counseling: The Case of Ruth and Lecturettes* is especially useful as a demonstration of interventions I make with Ruth that illustrate some principles and procedures of feminist therapy. For example, in Session 1 ("Beginning of Counseling") I ask Ruth about her expectations and initiate the informed consent process. I attempt to engage Ruth as a collaborative partner in the therapeutic venture, and I teach her how counseling works. Clearly, Ruth is the expert on her own life and my job is to assist her in attaining the goals we collaboratively identify as a focus of therapy. In Session 4 ("Understanding and Addressing Diversity") Ruth brings up gender differences, and she also mentions our differences in religion, education, culture, and socialization. Ruth and I explore the degree to which she feels comfortable with me and trusts me.

Other Resources

DVDs offered by the American Psychological Association that are relevant to this chapter include the following:

> Brown, L. S. (2009). *Feminist Therapy Over Time* (APA Psychotherapy Video Series)

Psychotherapy.net is a comprehensive resource for students and professionals that offers videos and interviews on feminist therapy. New video and editorial content is made available monthly. DVDs relevant to this chapter are available at www.psychotherapy.net and include the following:

Walker, L.(1994). *The Abused Woman: A Survivor Therapy Approach*
Walker, L. (1997). *Feminist Therapy* (Psychotherapy With the Experts Series)

The Jean Baker Miller Training Institute offers workshops, courses, professional training, publications, and ongoing projects that explore applications of the relational-cultural approach and integrate research, psychological theory, and social action. This relational-cultural model is based on the assumption that growth-fostering relationships and disconnections are constructed within specific cultural contexts.

Jean Baker Miller Training Institute

Stone Center, Wellesley College
106 Central Street
Wellesley, MA 02481
Telephone: (781) 283-3800
Fax: (781) 283-3646
Website: www.wellesley.edu/JBMTI/

The American Psychological Association has two divisions devoted to special interests in women's issues: Division 17 (Counseling Psychology's Section on Women) and Division 35 (Psychology of Women).

American Psychological Association

750 First Street, N.E.
Washington, DC 20002-4242
Telephone: (202) 336-5500 or (800) 374-2721
Fax: (202) 336-5568
Association Website: www.apa.org
Division 17 Website: www.div17.org
Division 35 Website: www.apa.org/divisons/div35

The Association for Women in Psychology (AWP) sponsors an annual conference dealing with feminist contributions to the understanding of life experiences of women. AWP is a scientific and educational feminist organization devoted to reevaluating and reformulating the role that psychology and mental health research generally play in women's lives.

Association for Women in Psychology

Website: www.awpsych.org

The Psychology of Women Resource List, or POWR online, is cosponsored by APA Division 35, Society for the Psychology of Women, and the Association for Women in Psychology. This public electronic network facilitates discussion of current topics, research, teaching strategies, and practice issues among people interested in the discipline of psychology of women. Most people with computer access to Bitnet or the Internet can subscribe to POWR-L at no cost. To subscribe, send the command below via e-mail to:

LISTSERV@URIACC (Binet) or LISTSERV@URIACC.URI.EDU
Subscribe POWR-L Your name (Use first and last name)

The University of Kentucky offers a minor specialty area in counseling women and feminist therapy within the Counseling Psychology graduate programs. For information, contact:

Dr. Pam Remer
University of Kentucky
Department of Educational and Counseling Psychology
251-C Dickey Hall
Lexington, KY 40506-0017
Telephone: (859) 257-4158
E-mail: Premer@uky.edu
Website: www.uky.edu/Education/edphead.html

Texas Women's University offers a training program with emphasis in women's issues, gender issues, and family psychology. For information, contact:

Dr. Roberta Nutt
Texas Women's University
Counseling Psychology Program
P. O. Box 425470
Denton, Texas 76204-5470
Telephone: (940) 898-2313
E-mail: rnutt@mail.twu.edu
Website: www.twu.edu/as/psyphil/Counseling_Home.htm

Postmodern Approaches

SOME CONTEMPORARY FOUNDERS OF POSTMODERN THERAPIES

The postmodern approaches do not have a single founder. Rather, it has been a collective effort by many. I have highlighted two cofounders of solution-focused brief therapy and two cofounders of narrative therapy who have had a major impact on the development of these therapeutic approaches.

INSOO KIM BERG / STEVE DE SHAZER / MICHAEL WHITE / DAVID EPSTON

INSOO KIM BERG (1935–2007) was a co-developer of the solution-focused approach. Until her death in 2007, she was the director of the Brief Family Therapy Center in Milwaukee, Wisconsin. As a leader in the practice of solution-focused brief therapy (SFBT), she provided workshops in the United States, Japan, South Korea, Australia, Denmark, England, and Germany. Among her writings are *Family Based Services: A Solution-Focused Approach* (1994), *Working With the Problem Drinker: A Solution-Focused Approach* (Berg & Miller, 1992), and *Interviewing for Solutions* (De Jong & Berg, 2008).

STEVE de SHAZER (1940-2005) was one of the pioneers of solution-focused brief therapy. For many years he was the director of research at the Brief Family Therapy Center in Milwaukee, where solution-focused brief therapy was developed. He wrote several books on SFBT, including *Keys to Solutions in Brief Therapy* (1985), *Clues: Investigating Solutions in Brief Therapy* (1988), *Putting Difference to Work* (1991), and *Words Were Originally Magic* (1994). He presented workshops, trained, and consulted widely in North America, Europe, Australia, and Asia. He died in September 2005 while on a teaching tour in Europe.

MICHAEL WHITE (1949-2008) was the cofounder, with David Epston, of the narrative therapy movement. He founded the Dulwich Centre in Adelaide, Australia, and his work with families and communities has attracted widespread international interest. Among his many books are *Narrative Means to Therapeutic Ends* (White & Epston, 1990), *Reauthoring Lives: Interviews and Essays* (1995), *Narrative of Therapists' Lives* (1997), and *Maps of Narrative Practice* (2007). Michael White died in April 2008 while visiting San Diego for a teaching workshop.

DAVID EPSTON (b. 1944) is one of the co-developers of narrative therapy. He is co-director of the Family Therapy Centre in Auckland, New Zealand. He is an international traveler, presenting lectures and workshops in Australia, Europe, and North America. He is a coauthor of *Narrative Means to Therapeutic Ends* (White & Epston, 1990) and *Playful Approaches to Serious Problems: Narrative Therapy With Children and Their Families* (Freeman, Epston, & Lobovits, 1997). He is well known for his work with persons affected by eating disorders and was a coauthor of *Biting the Hand That Starves You* (Maisel, Epston, & Borden, 2004).

INTRODUCTION TO SOCIAL CONSTRUCTIONISM

Each of the models of counseling and psychotherapy we have studied so far has its own version of "reality." The simultaneous existence of multiple and often conflicting "truths" has led to increasing skepticism of the possibility that a singular, universal theory will one day explain human beings and the systems in which they live. We have entered a postmodern world in which truth and reality are often understood as points of view bounded by history and context rather than as objective, immutable facts.

Modernists believe in objective reality and assume that it can be observed and systematically known through the scientific method. They further believe reality exists independent of any attempt to observe it. Modernists believe people seek therapy for a problem when they have deviated too far from some objective norm. For example, clients may think they are abnormally depressed when they experience sadness for longer than they think is normal. They might then seek help to return to "normal" behavior.

Postmodernists, in contrast, believe that realities do not exist independent of observational processes. **Social constructionism** is a psychological expression of this postmodern worldview; it values the client's reality without disputing whether it is accurate or rational (Gergen, 1991, 1999; Weishaar, 1993). To social constructionists, any understanding of reality is based on the use of language and is largely a function of the situations in which people live. Our knowledge about realities is socially constructed. A person is depressed when he or she adopts a definition of self as depressed. Once a definition of self is adopted, it is hard to recognize behaviors counter to that definition; for example, it is hard for someone who is suffering from depression to acknowledge the value of a periodic good mood in his or her life.

In postmodern thinking, forms of language and the use of language in stories create meaning. There may be as many meanings as there are people to tell the stories, and each of these stories expresses a truth for the person telling it. Every person involved in a situation has a perspective on the "reality" of that situation, but the range of truths is limited due to the effects of specific historical events and the language uses that dominate particular social contexts. In practice, therefore, the range of possible meanings is not infinite. When Kenneth Gergen (1985, 1991, 1999) and others began to emphasize the ways in which people make meaning in social relationships, the field of social constructionism was born. Berger and Luckman (1967) are reputed to be the first who used the term *social constructionism*, and it signaled a shift in emphasis for individual and family systems psychotherapy.

In social constructionism the therapist disavows the role of expert, preferring a more collaborative or consultative stance. Clients are viewed as experts about their own lives. De Jong and Berg (2008) put this notion about the therapist's task well:

> We do not view ourselves as expert at scientifically assessing client problems and then intervening. Instead, we strive to be expert at exploring clients' frames of reference and identifying those perceptions that clients can use to create more satisfying lives. (p. 19)

The collaborative partnership in the therapeutic process is considered more important than assessment or technique. Understanding narratives and deconstructing language processes (linguistics) are the focus for both understanding individuals and helping them construct desired change.

Social constructionist theory is grounded on four key assumptions (Burr, 2003), which form the basis of the difference between postmodernism and traditional psychological perspectives. First, social constructionist theory invites a critical stance toward taken-for-granted knowledge. Social constructionists challenge conventional knowledge that has historically guided our understanding of the world, and they caution us to be suspicious of assumptions of how the world appears to be. Second, social constructionists believe the language and concepts we use to generally understand the world are historically and culturally specific. Knowledge is time- and culture-bound, and our ways of understanding are not necessarily better than other ways. Third, social constructionists assert that knowledge is constructed through social processes. What we consider to be "truth" is a product of daily interactions between people in daily life. Thus there is not a single or "right" way to live one's life. Fourth, negotiated understandings (social constructions) are considered to be practices that affect social life rather than being abstractions from it. Therefore, knowledge and social action go together.

 See the video program for Chapter 13, *DVD for Theory and Practice of Counseling and Psychotherapy: The Case of Stan and Lecturettes*. I suggest that you view the brief lecture for each chapter prior to reading the chapter.

Historical Glimpse of Social Constructionism

A mere hundred years ago, Freud, Adler, and Jung were part of a major paradigm shift that transformed psychology as well as philosophy, science, medicine, and even the arts. In the 21st century, postmodern constructions of alternative knowledge sources seem to be one of the paradigm shifts most likely to affect the field of psychotherapy. Postmodernist thought is influencing the development of many psychotherapy theories and contemporary psychotherapeutic practice. The creation of the self, which so dominated the modernist search for human essence and truth, is being replaced with the concept of socially *storied lives*. Diversity, multiple frameworks, and integration—collaboration of the knower with the known—are all part of this new social movement, which provides a wider range of perspectives in counseling practice. For some social constructionists, the process of "knowing" includes a distrust of the dominant cultural positions that permeate families and society today (White & Epston, 1990), particularly when the dominant culture exerts a destructive impact on the lives of those who live beyond the margins of what is generally considered normal. Change begins by deconstructing the power of cultural narratives and then proceeds to the co-construction of a new life of meaning.

Among the best-known postmodern perspectives on therapy practice are the collaborative language systems approach (Anderson & Goolishian, 1992), solution-focused brief therapy (de Shazer, 1985, 1988, 1991, 1994), solution-oriented therapy (Bertolino & O'Hanlon, 2002; O'Hanlon & Weiner-Davis, 2003), narrative therapy (White & Epston, 1990), and feminist therapy (Brown, 2010). The next section examines the collaborative language systems approach, but the heart of this chapter addresses two of the most significant postmodern approaches: solution-focused brief therapy and narrative therapy.

The Collaborative Language Systems Approach

A relatively unstructured social constructionist dialogue has been suggested by Harlene Anderson and the late Harold Goolishian (1992) of the Houston Galveston Institute. Rejecting the more therapist-controlled and theory-based interventions of other North American therapeutic approaches, Anderson and Goolishian developed a therapy of caring and being with the client. Their stance is similar to the person-centered way of being that originated with Carl Rogers, but without the theory of self-actualization. Informed by and contributing to the field of social constructionism, they came to believe human life is constructed in personal and family narratives that maintain both process and meaning in people's lives. These narratives are constructed in social interaction over time. The sociocultural systems in which people live are a product of social interaction, not the other way around. In this sense, therapy is also a system process created in the therapeutic conversations of the client and the listener-facilitator.

When people seek therapy, they are often "stuck" in a dialogic system that has a unique language, meaning, and process related to "the problem." Therapy is another conversational system that becomes therapeutic through its "problem-organizing, problem-dissolving" nature (Anderson & Goolishian, 1992, p. 27). It is therapists' willingness to enter the therapeutic conversation from a "not-knowing" position that facilitates this caring relationship with the client. In the *not-knowing position,* therapists still retain all of the knowledge and personal, experiential capacities they have gained over years of living, but they allow themselves to enter the conversation with curiosity and with an intense interest in discovery. The aim here is to enter a client's world as fully as possible. Clients become the experts who are informing and sharing with the therapist the significant narratives of their lives. The not-knowing position is empathic and is most often characterized by questions that "come from an honest, continuous therapeutic posture of not understanding too quickly" (Anderson, 1993, p. 331).

Based on the referral or intake process, the therapist enters the session with some sense of what the client may wish to address. The questions the therapist asks are always informed by the answers the client-expert has provided. The client's answers provide information that stimulates the interest of the therapist, still in a posture of inquiry, and another question proceeds from each answer given. The process is similar to the Socratic method without any preconceived idea about how or in which direction the development of the stories should go. The intent of the conversation is not to confront or challenge the narrative of the client but to facilitate the telling and retelling of the story until opportunities for new meaning and new stories develop: "Telling one's story is a representation of experience; it is constructing history in the present" (Anderson & Goolishian, 1992, p. 37). By staying with the story, the therapist–client conversation evolves into a dialogue of new meaning, constructing new narrative possibilities. This not-knowing position of the therapist has been infused as a key concept for both the solution-focused and the narrative therapeutic approaches.

SOLUTION-FOCUSED BRIEF THERAPY

Introduction

Solution-focused brief therapy (SFBT) is a future-focused, goal-oriented therapeutic approach to brief therapy developed initially by Steve de Shazer and Insoo Kim Berg at the Brief Family Therapy Center in Milwaukee in the early 1980s. SFBT emphasizes strengths and resiliencies of people by focusing on exceptions to their problems and their conceptualized solutions.

Having grown dissatisfied with the constraints of the strategic model, in the 1980s de Shazer collaborated with a number of therapists, including Eve Lipchik, John Walter, Jane Peller, Michelle Weiner-Davis, and Bill O'Hanlon, who each wrote extensively about solution-focused therapy and started their own solution-focused training institutes. Both O'Hanlon and Weiner-Davis were influenced by de Shazer and Berg's original work, and they expanded on this foundation to create what they called *solution-oriented therapy*. In this chapter when I discuss *solution-focused brief therapy*, *solution-focused therapy*, and *solution-oriented therapy*, I am focusing on what these approaches have in common rather than looking at their differences.

Key Concepts

UNIQUE FOCUS OF SFBT Solution-focused brief therapy (SFBT) differs from traditional therapies by eschewing the past in favor of both the present and the future. Therapists focus on what is possible, and they have little or no interest in gaining an understanding of how the problem emerged. Behavior change is viewed as the most effective approach to assisting people in enhancing their lives. De Shazer (1988, 1991) suggests that it is not necessary to know the cause of a problem to solve it and that there is no necessary relationship between the causes of problems and their solutions. Assessing problems is not necessary for change to occur. If knowing and understanding problems are unimportant, so is searching for "right" or absolute solutions. Any person might consider multiple solutions, and what is right for one person may not be right for others. In solution-focused brief therapy, clients choose the goals they wish to accomplish; little attention is given to diagnosis, history taking, or exploring the emergence of the problem (Berg & Miller, 1992; Gingerich & Eisengart, 2000; O'Hanlon & Weiner-Davis, 2003).

POSITIVE ORIENTATION Solution-focused brief therapy is grounded on the optimistic assumption that people are healthy and competent and have the ability to construct solutions that can enhance their lives. An underlying assumption of SFBT is that we already have the ability to resolve the challenges life brings us, but at times we lose our sense of direction or our awareness of our competencies. Regardless of what shape clients are in when they enter therapy, solution-focused therapists believe clients are competent. The therapist's role is to help clients recognize the competencies they already possess and apply them toward solutions. The essence of therapy involves building on clients' hope and optimism by creating positive expectations that change is possible. SFBT is a nonpathologizing approach that emphasizes competencies rather than deficits, and strengths rather than weaknesses

(Metcalf, 2001). The solution-focused model requires a philosophical stance of accepting people where they are and assisting them in creating solutions. Solution-focused brief therapy has parallels with **positive psychology**, which concentrates on what is right and what is working for people rather than dwelling on deficits, weaknesses, and problems (Murphy, 2008). By emphasizing positive dimensions, clients quickly become involved in resolving their problems, which makes this a very empowering approach.

Because clients often come to therapy in a "problem-oriented" state, even the few solutions they have considered are wrapped in the power of the problem orientation. Clients often have a story that is rooted in a deterministic view that what has happened in their past will certainly shape their future. Solution-focused practitioners counter this negative client presentation with optimistic conversations that highlight a belief in achievable and usable goals. Therapists can be instrumental in assisting clients in making a shift from a fixed problem state to a world with new possibilities. One of the goals of SFBT is to shift clients' perceptions by reframing what White and Epston (1990) refer to as clients' *problem-saturated stories* through the counselor's skillful use of language.

LOOKING FOR WHAT IS WORKING The emphasis of SFBT is to focus on what is working in clients' lives, which stands in stark contrast to the traditional models of therapy that tend to be problem-focused. Individuals bring stories to therapy. Some stories are used to justify the client's belief that life can't be changed or, worse, that life is moving them further and further away from their goals. Solution-focused brief therapists assist clients in paying attention to the exceptions to their problem patterns. They promote hope by helping clients discovering exceptions, or times when the problem is less intrusive in their life (Metcalf, 2001). SFBT focuses on finding out what people are doing that is working and then helping them apply this knowledge to eliminate problems in the shortest amount of time possible. Identifying what is working and encouraging clients to replicate these patterns is extremely important (Murphy, 2008). A key concept is, "Once you know what works, do more of it." If something is not working, clients are encouraged to do something different, which typically involves drawing on their unique strengths and successes.

There are various ways to assist clients in thinking about what has worked for them. De Shazer (1991) prefers to engage clients in conversations that lead to progressive narratives whereby people create situations in which they can make steady gains toward their goals. De Shazer might say, "Tell me about times when you felt a little better and when things were going your way." It is in these stories of life worth living that the power of problems is deconstructed and new solutions are manifest and made possible.

BASIC ASSUMPTIONS GUIDING PRACTICE Walter and Peller (1992, 2000) think of solution-focused therapy as a model that explains how people change and how they can reach their goals. Here are some of their basic assumptions about solution-focused therapy:

- Individuals who come to therapy do have the capability of behaving effectively, even though this effectiveness may be temporarily blocked by negative cognitions. Problem-focused thinking prevents people from recognizing effective ways they have dealt with problems.

- There are advantages to a positive focus on solutions and on the future. If clients can reorient themselves in the direction of their strengths using solution-talk, there is a good chance therapy can be brief.
- There are exceptions to every problem, or times when the problem was absent. By talking about these exceptions, clients can get clues to effective solutions and can gain control over what had seemed to be an insurmountable personal difficulty. Rapid changes are possible when clients identify exceptions to their problems and begin to organize their thinking around these exceptions instead of around the problem.
- Clients often present only one side of themselves. Solution-focused therapists invite clients to examine another side of the story they are presenting.
- No problem is constant, and change is inevitable. What people need to do is become aware of any positive changes that are happening. Small changes pave the way for larger changes. Oftentimes, small changes are all that are needed to resolve problems that clients bring to therapy. Like tipping the first domino, one small change leads to another, then another, and so on until the "solution momentum" outweighs the problem momentum.
- Clients want to change, have the capacity to change, and are doing their best to make change happen. Therapists should adopt a cooperative stance with clients rather than devising strategies to control resistant patterns. When therapists find ways to cooperate with people, resistance does not occur.
- Clients can be trusted in their intention to solve their problems. Therapists assume that clients want to change, can change, and will change under cooperative and empowering therapeutic conditions. There are no "right" solutions to specific problems that can be applied to all people. Each individual is unique and so, too, is each solution.

Walter and Peller (2000) have moved away from the term *therapy* and refer to what they do as *personal consultation*. They facilitate conversations around the preferences and possibilities of their clients to help them create a positive future. By avoiding the stance of the expert, Walter and Peller believe they can be interested, curious, and encouraging in jointly exploring the desires of their clients.

The Therapeutic Process

Bertolino and O'Hanlon (2002) stress the importance of creating collaborative therapeutic relationships and see doing so as necessary for successful therapy. Acknowledging that therapists have expertise in creating a context for change, they stress that clients are the experts on their own lives and often have a good sense of what has or has not worked in the past and, as well, what might work in the future. Solution-focused counseling assumes a collaborative approach with clients in contrast to the educative stance that is typically associated with most traditional models of therapy. If clients are involved in the therapeutic process from beginning to end, the chances are increased that therapy will be successful. In short, collaborative and cooperative relationships tend to be more effective than hierarchical relationships in therapy.

Walter and Peller (1992) describe four steps that characterize the process of SFBT: (1) Find out what clients want rather than searching for what they do not want. (2) Do not look for pathology, and do not attempt to reduce clients by giving them a diagnostic label. Instead, look for what clients are doing that is already working and encourage them to continue in that direction. (3) If what clients are doing is not working, encourage them to experiment with doing something different. (4) Keep therapy brief by approaching each session as if it were the last and only session. Although these steps seem fairly obvious, the collaborative process of the client and therapist constructing solutions is not merely a matter of mastering a few techniques.

De Shazer (1991) believes clients can generally build solutions to their problems without any assessment of the nature of their problems. Given this framework, the structure of solution building differs greatly from traditional approaches to problem solving as can be seen in this brief description of the steps involved (De Jong & Berg, 2008):

1. Clients are given an opportunity to describe their problems. The therapist listens respectfully and carefully as clients answer the therapist's question, "How can I be useful to you?"
2. The therapist works with clients in developing well-formed goals as soon as possible. The question is posed, "What will be different in your life when your problems are solved?"
3. The therapist asks clients about those times when their problems were not present or when the problems were less severe. Clients are assisted in exploring these exceptions, with special emphasis on what they did to make these events happen.
4. At the end of each solution-building conversation, the therapist offers clients summary feedback, provides encouragement, and suggests what clients might observe or do before the next session to further solve their problem.
5. The therapist and clients evaluate the progress being made in reaching satisfactory solutions by using a rating scale. Clients are asked what needs to be done before they see their problem as being solved and also what their next step will be.

THERAPEUTIC GOALS SFBT reflects some basic notions about change, about interaction, and about reaching goals. The solution-focused therapist believes people have the ability to define meaningful personal goals and that they have the resources required to solve their problems. Goals are unique to each client and are constructed by the client to create a richer future (Prochaska & Norcross, 2010). A lack of clarity regarding client preferences, goals, and desired outcomes can result in a rift between therapist and client. During the early phase of therapy, it is important that clients be given the opportunity to express what they want from therapy and what concerns they are willing to explore. From the first contact with clients, the therapist strives to create a climate that will facilitate change and encourage clients to think in terms of a range of possibilities.

Solution-focused therapists concentrate on small, realistic, achievable changes that can lead to additional positive outcomes. Because success tends to build upon itself, modest goals are viewed as the beginning of change. Solution-focused practitioners join with the language of their clients, using similar words, pacing, and tone. Therapists use questions such as these that presuppose change, posit multiple answers, and remain goal-directed and future-oriented: "What did you do, and what has changed since last time?" or "What did you notice that went better?" (Bubenzer & West, 1993).

Walter and Peller (1992) and Murphy (2008) emphasize the importance of assisting clients in creating well-defined goals that are (1) stated positively in the client's language; (2) are process- or action-oriented; (3) are structured in the here and now; (4) are attainable, concrete, specific, and measurable; and (5) are controlled by the client. Counselors should not too rigidly impose an agenda of getting precise goals before clients have a chance to express their concerns. Clients must feel that their concerns are heard and understood before they can formulate meaningful personal goals. In a therapist's zeal to be solution-focused, it is possible to get lost in the mechanics of therapy and not attend sufficiently to the interpersonal aspects.

Solution-oriented therapy offers several forms of goals: changing the *viewing* of a situation or a frame of reference, changing the *doing* of the problematic situation, and tapping client *strengths* and *resources* (O'Hanlon & Weiner-Davis, 2003). Therapists note the language they use, so they can increase their clients' hope and optimism and their openness to possibilities and change. Clients are encouraged to engage in change- or solution-talk, rather than problem-talk, on the assumption that what we talk about most will be what we produce. Talking about problems can produce ongoing problems. Talk about change can produce change.

THERAPIST'S FUNCTION AND ROLE Clients are much more likely to fully participate in the therapeutic process if they perceive themselves as determining the direction and purpose of the conversation (Walter & Peller, 1996). Much of what the therapeutic process is about involves clients' thinking about their future and what they want to be different in their lives. Consistent with the postmodern and social constructionist perspective, solution-focused brief therapists adopt a *not-knowing position* to put clients in the position of being the experts about their own lives. Therapists do not assume that by virtue of their expert frame of reference they know the significance of the client's actions and experiences (Anderson & Goolishian, 1992). This model casts the role and function of a therapist in quite a different light from traditionally oriented therapists who view themselves as experts in assessment and treatment. The therapist-as-expert is replaced by the client-as-expert, especially when it comes to what the client wants in life and in therapy. It is important that therapists actually believe that their clients are the true experts on their own lives. According to Guterman (2006), therapists have expertise in the process of change, but clients are the experts on *what* they want changed. The therapist's task is to point clients in the direction of change without dictating what to change.

Therapists strive to create a climate of mutual respect, dialogue, and affirmation in which clients experience the freedom to create, explore, and coauthor their evolving stories. A key therapeutic task consists of helping clients imagine how they would like life to be different and what it would take to make this transformation happen. One of the functions of the therapist is to ask questions and, based on the answers, generate further questions. Examples of some useful questions are "What do you hope to gain from coming here?" "If you were to make the changes you desire, how would that make a difference in your life?" and "What steps can you take now that will lead to these changes?"

THE THERAPEUTIC RELATIONSHIP The quality of the relationship between therapist and client is a determining factor in the outcomes of SFBT, so relationship building or engagement is a basic step in SFBT. The attitude of the therapist is crucial to the effectiveness of the therapeutic process. It is essential to create a sense of trust so clients will return for further sessions and will follow through on homework suggestions. The therapeutic process works best when clients become actively involved, when they experience a positive relationship with the therapist, and when counseling addresses what clients see as being important (Murphy, 2008). One way of creating an effective therapeutic partnership is for the therapist to show clients how they can use the strengths and resources they already have to construct solutions. Clients are encouraged to do something different and to be creative in thinking about ways to deal with their present and future concerns.

De Shazer (1988) has described three kinds of relationships that may develop between therapists and their clients:

1. *Customer:* the client and therapist jointly identify a problem and a solution to work toward. The client realizes that to attain his or her goals, personal effort will be required.
2. *Complainant:* the client describes a problem but is not able or willing to assume a role in constructing a solution, believing that a solution is dependent on someone else's actions. In this situation, the client generally expects the therapist to change the other person to whom the client attributes the problem.
3. *Visitor:* the client comes to therapy because someone else (a spouse, parent, teacher, or probation officer) thinks the client has a problem. This client may not agree that he or she has a problem and may be unable to identify anything to explore in therapy.

De Jong and Berg (2008) recommend using caution so that therapists do not box clients into static identities. These three roles are only starting points for conversation. Rather than categorizing clients, therapists can reflect on the kinds of relationships that are developing between their clients and themselves. For example, clients who tend to place the cause of their problems on another person or persons in their lives (complainants) may be helped by skilled intervention to begin to see their own role in their problems and the necessity for taking active steps in creating solutions. A visitor client may be willing to work with the therapist to create a customer relationship by exploring what the client needs to do to satisfy the other person or "get them off their back." Initially, some clients will feel powerless and overwhelmed by their problems. Even clients who are unable to articulate a problem may change as the result of developing an effective therapeutic alliance. How the therapist responds to different behaviors of clients has a lot to do with bringing about a shift in the relationship. In short, both complainants and visitors have the capacity for becoming customers.

Application: Therapeutic Techniques and Procedures

Some of the key techniques that solution-focused practitioners are likely to employ include looking for differences in doing, exception questions, scaling questions, and the miracle question. If these techniques are used in a routine way without developing a collaborative working alliance, they will not lead to effective results. Murphy (2008) reminds us that these solution-focused techniques should be used flexibly and tailored to the unique circumstances of each client. Therapy is best guided by the client's goals, perceptions, resources, and feedback. Therapy should not be determined by any absolutes or rigid standards outside the therapeutic relationship (namely, evidence-based treatments).

PRETHERAPY CHANGE Simply scheduling an appointment often sets positive change in motion. During the initial therapy session, it is common for solution-focused therapists to ask, "What have you done since you called for the appointment that has made a difference in your problem?" (de Shazer, 1985, 1988). By asking about such changes, the therapist can elicit, evoke, and amplify what clients have already done by way of making positive change. These changes cannot be attributed to the therapy process itself, so asking about them tends to encourage clients to rely less on their therapist and more on their own resources to accomplish their treatment goals (McKeel, 1996; Weiner-Davis, de Shazer, & Gingerich, 1987).

EXCEPTION QUESTIONS SFBT is based on the notion that there were times in clients' lives when the problems they identify were not problematic. These times are called *exceptions* and represent *news of difference* (Bateson, 1972). Solution-focused therapists ask **exception questions** to direct clients to times when the problem did not exist, or when the problem was not as intense. **Exceptions** are those past experiences in a client's life when it would be reasonable to have expected the problem to occur, but somehow it did not (de Shazer, 1985; Murphy, 2008). By helping clients identify and examine these exceptions, the chances are increased that they will work toward solutions (Guterman, 2006). Once identified by an individual, these instances of success can be useful in making further changes. *Change-focused questions* explore what clients believe to be important goals and how they can tap their strengths and resources to reach their goals (Murphy, 2008). This exploration reminds clients that problems are not all-powerful and have not existed forever; it also provides a field of opportunity for evoking resources, engaging strengths, and positing possible solutions. The therapist asks clients what has to happen for these exceptions to occur more often.

THE MIRACLE QUESTION Therapy goals are developed by using what de Shazer (1988) calls the **miracle question**, which is a main SFBT technique. The therapist asks, "If a miracle happened and the problem you have was solved overnight, how would you know it was solved, and what would be different?" Clients are then encouraged to enact "what would be different" in spite of perceived problems. If a client asserts that she wants to feel more confident and secure, the therapist might say: "Let yourself imagine that you leave the office today and that you are on track to acting more confidently and securely. What will you be *doing* differently?" This process of considering hypothetical solutions reflects O'Hanlon and

Weiner-Davis's (2003) belief that changing the *doing* and *viewing* of the perceived problem changes the problem.

De Jong and Berg (2008) identify several reasons the miracle question is a useful technique. Asking clients to consider that a miracle takes place opens up a range of future possibilities. Clients are encouraged to allow themselves to dream as a way of identifying the kinds of changes they most want to see. This question has a future focus in that clients can begin to consider a different kind of life that is not dominated by a particular problem. This intervention shifts the emphasis from both past and current problems toward a more satisfying life in the future.

SCALING QUESTIONS Solution-focused therapists also use **scaling questions** when change in human experiences are not easily observed, such as feelings, moods, or communication, and to assist clients in noticing that they are not completely defeated by their problem (de Shazer & Berg, 1988). For example, a woman reporting feelings of panic or anxiety might be asked: "On a scale of zero to 10, with zero being how you felt when you first came to therapy and 10 being how you feel the day after your miracle occurs and your problem is gone, how would you rate your anxiety right now?" Even if the client has only moved away from zero to 1, she has improved. How did she do that? What does she need to do to move another number up the scale? Scaling questions enable clients to pay closer attention to what they are doing and how they can take steps that will lead to the changes they desire.

FORMULA FIRST SESSION TASK The **formula first session task** (FFST) is a form of homework a therapist might give clients to complete between their first and second sessions. The therapist might say: "Between now and the next time we meet, I would like you to observe, so that you can describe to me next time, what happens in your (family, life, marriage, relationship) that you want to continue to have happen" (de Shazer, 1985, p. 137). At the second session, clients can be asked what they observed and what they would like to have happen in the future. This kind of assignment offers clients hope that change is inevitable. It is not a matter of *if* change will occur, but *when* it will happen. According to de Shazer, this intervention tends to increase clients' optimism and hope about their present and future situation. The FFST technique emphasizes future solutions rather than past problems (Murphy, 2008). Bertolino and O'Hanlon (2002) suggest that the FFST intervention be used after clients have had a chance to express their present concerns, views, and stories. It is important that clients feel understood before they are directed to make changes.

THERAPIST FEEDBACK TO CLIENTS Solution-focused practitioners generally take a break of 5 to 10 minutes toward the end of each session to compose a summary message for clients. During this break therapists formulate feedback that will be given to clients after the break. De Jong and Berg (2008) describe three basic parts to the structure of the summary feedback: compliments, a bridge, and suggesting a task. *Compliments* are genuine affirmations of what clients are already doing that is leading toward effective solutions. It is important that complimenting is not done in a routine or mechanical way, but in an encouraging manner that creates hope and conveys the expectation to clients that they can achieve their goals by drawing on their strengths and successes. Second, a *bridge* links the initial compliments to the suggested tasks that will be given. The bridge provides the rationale for the suggestions. The third aspect of feedback consists of *suggesting tasks* to clients, which can be considered as homework. Observational tasks ask clients to simply pay attention to some aspect of their lives. This self-monitoring process helps clients note the differences when things are better, especially what was different about the way they thought, felt, or behaved. Behavioral tasks require that clients actually do something the therapist believes would be useful to them in constructing solutions. De Jong and Berg (2008) stress that a therapist's feedback to clients addresses what they need to do more of and do differently in order to increase the chances of obtaining their goals.

TERMINATING From the very first solution-focused interview, the therapist is mindful of working toward termination. Once clients are able to construct a satisfactory solution, the therapeutic relationship can be terminated. The initial goal-formation question that a therapist often asks is, "What needs to be different in your life as a result of coming here for you to say that meeting with me was worthwhile?" Another question to get clients thinking is, "When the problem is solved, what will you be doing differently?" Through the use of scaling questions, therapists can assist clients in monitoring their progress so clients can determine when they no longer need to come to therapy (De Jong & Berg, 2008). Prior to ending therapy, therapists assist clients in identifying things they can do to continue the changes they have already made into the future. Clients can also be helped to identify hurdles or perceived barriers that could get in the way of maintaining the changes they have made.

Guterman (2006) maintains that the ultimate goal of solution-focused counseling is to end treatment. He adds, "If counselors are not proactive in making their treatment brief by design, then in many cases counseling will be brief by default" (p. 67). Because this model of therapy is brief, present-centered, and addresses specific complaints, it is very possible that clients will experience other developmental concerns at a later time. Clients can ask for additional sessions whenever they feel a need to get their life back on track or to update their story. Dr. John Murphy puts many SFBT techniques into action as he illustrates assessment and treatment from a solution-focused brief therapy approach in the case of Ruth in *Case Approach to Counseling and Psychotherapy* (Corey, 2013, chap. 11).

APPLICATION TO GROUP COUNSELING The solution-focused group practitioner believes that people are competent, and that given a climate where they can experience their competency, they are able to solve their own problems, enabling them to live a richer life. From the beginning, the group facilitator sets a tone of focusing on solutions (Metcalf, 1998) in which group members are given an opportunity to describe their problems briefly. A facilitator might begin a new group by requesting, "I would like each of you to introduce yourself. As you do, give us a brief idea as to why you are here and tell us what you would like for us to know about you." Facilitators help members to keep the problem external in conversations, which tends to be a relief because it gives members an opportunity to see themselves as less problem-saturated. It is the facilitator's role to create opportunities for the members to view themselves as being resourceful. Because SFBT is designed to be brief, the leader has the task of keeping group members on a solution track rather than a problem track, which helps members to move in a positive direction.

The group leader works with members in developing well-formed goals as soon as possible. Leaders concentrate on small, realistic, achievable changes that may lead to additional positive outcomes. Because success tends to build upon itself, modest goals are viewed as the beginning of change. Questions used to assist members in formulating clear goals might include "What will be different in your life when each of your problems is solved?" and "What will be going on in the future that will tell you and the rest of us in the group that things are better for you?" Sometimes members talk about what others will be doing or not doing and forget to pay attention to their own goals or behavior. At times such as this they can be asked, "And what about yourself? What will you be doing differently in that picture? As a result of your doing things differently, how would you imagine others responding to you?"

The facilitator asks members about times when their problems were not present or when the problems were less severe. The members are assisted in exploring these exceptions, and special emphasis is placed on what they did to make these events happen. The participants engage in identifying exceptions with each other. This improves the group process and promotes a solution focus, which can become quite powerful. Exceptions are real events that take place outside of the problem context. In individual counseling, only the therapist and the client are observers of competency. An advantage of group counseling is that the audience widens and more input is possible (Metcalf, 1998).

The art of questioning is a main intervention used in solution-focused groups. Questions are asked from a position of respect, genuine curiosity, sincere interest, and openness. Group leaders use questions such as these that presuppose change and remain goal-directed and future-oriented: "What did you do and what has changed since last time?" or "What did you notice that went better?" Other group members are encouraged to respond along with the group leader to promote group interaction. Facilitators may pose questions like these: "Someday, when the problems that brought you to this group are less problematic to you, what will you be doing?" "As each of you listened to others today, is there someone in our group who could be a source of encouragement for you to do something different?" The leader is attempting to help the members identify exceptions and begin to recognize personal resiliency and competency. Creating a group context in which the members are able to learn more about their personal abilities is key to members learning to resolve their own concerns.

Solution-focused group counseling offers a great deal of promise for practitioners who want a practical and time-effective approach to interventions in school settings. As a cooperative approach, SFBT shifts the focus from what's wrong in students' lives to what's working for them (Murphy, 2008; Sklare, 2005). Rather than being a cookbook of techniques for removing students' problems, this approach offers school counselors a collaborative framework aimed at achieving small, concrete changes that enable students to discover a more productive direction. This model has much to offer to school counselors who are responsible for serving large caseloads of students in a K–12 school system. For a more detailed treatment of how SFBT can be applied to group work in the schools, see Sklare (2005) and Murphy (2008). They give special attention to the process of goal setting and provides many concrete examples of how counselors can assist students in identifying well-established goals. For a more detailed discussion of SFBT in groups, see Corey (2012, chap. 16).

NARRATIVE THERAPY

Introduction

Of all the social constructionists, Michael White and David Epston (1990) are best known for their use of narrative in therapy. According to White (1992), individuals construct the meaning of life in interpretive stories, which are then treated as "truth." Because of the power of dominant culture narratives, individuals tend to internalize the messages from these dominant discourses, which often work against the life opportunity of the individual.

Adopting a postmodern, narrative, social constructionist view sheds light on how power, knowledge, and "truth" are negotiated in families and other social and cultural contexts (Freedman & Combs, 1996). Therapy is, in part, a reestablishment of personal agency from the oppression of external problems and the dominant stories of larger systems.

Key Concepts

The key concepts and therapeutic process sections are adapted from several different works, but primarily from these sources: Winslade and Monk (2007), Monk (1997), Winslade, Crocket, and Monk (1997), McKenzie and Monk (1997), and Freedman and Combs (1996).

FOCUS OF NARRATIVE THERAPY The narrative approach involves adopting a shift in focus from most traditional theories. Therapists are encouraged to establish a collaborative approach with a special interest in listening respectfully to clients' stories; to search for times in clients' lives when they were resourceful; to use questions as a way to engage clients and facilitate their exploration; to avoid diagnosing and labeling clients or accepting a totalizing description based on a problem; to assist clients in mapping the influence a problem has had on their lives; and to assist clients in separating themselves from the dominant stories they have internalized so that space can be opened for the creation of alternative life stories (Freedman & Combs, 1996).

THE ROLE OF STORIES We live our lives by stories we tell about ourselves and that others tell about us. These stories actually shape reality in that they construct and constitute what we see, feel, and do. The stories we live by grow out of conversations in a social and cultural context. Therapy clients do not assume the role of pathologized victims who are leading hopeless and pathetic lives; rather, they emerge as courageous victors who have vivid stories to recount. The stories not only change the person telling the story, but also change the therapist who is privileged to be a part of this unfolding process (Monk, 1997).

LISTENING WITH AN OPEN MIND All social constructionist theories emphasize listening to clients without judgment or blame, affirming and valuing them. Narrative practice goes further in deconstructing the systems of normalizing judgment that are found in medical, psychological, and educational discourse. *Normalizing judgment* is any kind of judgment that locates a person on a normal curve and is used to assess intelligence, mental health, or normal behavior. Because these kinds of judgments claim to be objective measures, they are difficult for individuals to resist and usually are internalized. Narrative therapists argue that suspending personal judgment is of little value if you participate in normalizing judgment. Deconstruction involves turning the tables and inquiring what clients think of the judgments they have been assigned. Narrative practitioners might be said to invite people to pass judgment on the judgments that have been working them over.

Lindsley (1994) emphasizes that therapists can encourage their clients to reconsider absolutist judgments by moving toward seeing both "good" and "bad" elements in situations. Narrative therapists make efforts to enable clients to modify painful beliefs, values, and interpretations without imposing their value systems and interpretations. They want to create meaning and new possibilities from the stories clients share rather than out of a preconceived and ultimately imposed theory of importance and value.

Although narrative therapists bring to the therapy venture certain attitudes such as optimism, respectful curiosity and persistence, and a valuing for the client's knowledge, they seek to listen to the problem-saturated story of the client without getting stuck. As narrative therapists listen to the client's story, they stay alert for details that give evidence of the client's competence in taking stands against oppressive problems. Winslade and Monk (2007) maintain that the therapist believes that clients have abilities, talents, positive intentions, and life experiences that can be the catalysts for new possibilities for action. The counselor needs to demonstrate faith that these strengths and competencies can be identified, even when the client is having difficulty seeing them.

During the narrative conversation, attention is given to avoiding totalizing language, which reduces the complexity of the individual by assigning an all-embracing, single description to the essence of the person. Therapists begin to separate the person from the problem in their mind as they listen and respond (Winslade & Monk, 2007).

The narrative perspective focuses on the capacity of humans for creative and imaginative thought, which is often found in their resistance to dominant discourse. Narrative practitioners do not assume that they know more about the lives of clients than their clients do. Clients are the primary interpreters of their own experiences. People are viewed as active agents who are able to derive meaning from their experiential world, and they are encouraged to join with others who might share in the development of a counter story.

The Therapeutic Process

This brief overview of the steps in the narrative therapeutic process illustrates the structure of the narrative approach (O'Hanlon, 1994, pp. 25–26):

- Collaborate with the client to come up with a mutually acceptable name for the problem.
- Personify the problem and attribute oppressive intentions and tactics to it.
- Investigate how the problem has been disrupting, dominating, or discouraging to the client.
- Invite the client to see his or her story from a different perspective by offering alternative meanings for events.
- Discover moments when the client wasn't dominated or discouraged by the problem by searching for exceptions to the problem.
- Find historical evidence to bolster a new view of the client as competent enough to have stood up to, defeated, or escaped from the dominance or oppression of the problem. (At this phase the person's identity and life story begin to be rewritten.)
- Ask the client to speculate about what kind of future could be expected from the strong, competent person who is emerging. As the client becomes free of problem-saturated stories of the past, he or she can envision and plan for a less problematic future.
- Find or create an audience for perceiving and supporting the new story. It is not enough to recite a new story. The client needs to live the new story outside of therapy. Because the person's problem initially developed in a social context, it is essential to involve the social environment in supporting the new life story that has emerged in the conversations with the therapist.

Winslade and Monk (2007) stress that narrative conversations do not follow the linear progression described here; it is better to think of these steps in terms of cyclical progression containing the following elements:

- Move problem stories toward externalized descriptions of problems
- Map the effects of a problem on the individual
- Listen to signs of strength and competence in an individual's problem-saturated stories
- Build a new story of competence and document these achievements

THERAPY GOALS A general goal of narrative therapy is to invite people to describe their experience in new and fresh language. In doing this, they open up new vistas of what is possible. This new language enables clients to develop new meanings for problematic thoughts, feelings, and behaviors (Freedman & Combs, 1996). Narrative therapy almost always includes an awareness of the impact of various aspects of dominant culture on human life. Narrative practitioners seek to enlarge the perspective and focus and facilitate the discovery or creation of new options that are unique to the people they see.

THERAPIST'S FUNCTION AND ROLE Narrative therapists are active facilitators. The concepts of care, interest, respectful curiosity, openness, empathy, contact, and even fascination are seen as a relational necessity. The not-knowing position, which allows therapists to follow, affirm, and be guided by the stories of their clients, creates participant-observer and process-facilitator roles for the therapist and integrates therapy with a postmodern view of human inquiry.

A main task of the therapist is to help clients construct a preferred story line. The narrative therapist adopts a stance characterized by respectful curiosity and works with clients to explore both the impact of the problem on them and what they are doing to reduce the effects of the problem (Winslade & Monk, 2007). One of the main functions of the therapist is to ask questions of clients and, based on the answers, to generate further questions.

White and Epston (1990) start with an exploration of the client in relation to the presenting problem. It is not uncommon for clients to present initial stories in which they and the problem are fused, as if one and the same. White uses questions aimed at separating the problem from the people affected by the problem. This shift in language begins the deconstruction of the original narrative in which the person and the problem were fused; now the problem is objectified as external to the client.

Like the solution-focused therapist, the narrative therapist assumes the client is the expert when it comes to what he or she wants in life. The narrative therapist tends to avoid using language that embodies diagnosis, assessment, treatment, and intervention. Functions such as diagnosis and assessment often grant priority to the practitioner's "truth" over clients' knowledge about their own lives. The narrative approach gives emphasis to understanding clients' lived experiences and de-emphasizes efforts to predict, interpret, and pathologize. Narrative practitioners are careful not to ascribe the major role of taking initiative in another person's life or usurping the agency (power) of the client in bringing about change (Winslade et al., 1997).

When it comes to the effective practice of narrative therapy, there are no set formulas or recipes to follow (Freedman & Combs, 1996; Monk, Winslade, Crocket, & Epston, 1997; Winslade & Monk, 2007). Monk (1997) emphasizes that narrative therapy will vary with each client because each person is unique. For Monk, narrative conversations are based on a way of being, and if narrative counseling "is seen as a formula or used as a recipe, clients will have the experience of having things done *to* them and feel left out of the conversation" (p. 24).

THE THERAPEUTIC RELATIONSHIP Narrative therapists place great importance on the values and ethical commitments a therapist brings to the therapy venture. Some of these attitudes include optimism and respect, curiosity and persistence, valuing the client's knowledge, and creating a special kind of relationship characterized by a real power-sharing dialogue (Winslade & Monk, 2007). Collaboration, compassion, reflection, and discovery characterize the therapeutic relationship. If this relationship is to be truly collaborative, the therapist needs to be aware of how power manifests itself in his or her professional practice. This does not mean that the therapist does not have authority as a professional. He or she uses this authority, however, by treating clients as experts in their own lives. Furthermore, the therapist is interested in facilitating the articulation of the values and ethical commitments of the client.

Winslade, Crocket, and Monk (1997) describe this collaboration as coauthoring or sharing authority. Clients function as authors when they have the authority to speak on their own behalf. In the narrative approach, the therapist-as-expert is replaced by the client-as-expert. This notion challenges the stance of the therapist as being an all-wise and all-knowing expert. Winslade and Monk (2007) state: "The integrity of the counseling relationship is thus maintained while the client is honored as the senior author in the construction of an alternative narrative (pp. 57–58).

Clients are often stuck in a pattern of living a problem-saturated story that does not work. When a client has a limited perception of his or her capacities due to being saturated in problem thinking, it is the job of the therapist to elicit other strength-related stories to modify the client's perception. The therapist assists the client in this pursuit by entering into a dialogue and asking questions in an effort to elicit the perspectives, resources, and unique experiences of the client. The past is history, but it sometimes provides a foundation for understanding and discovering news of differences or unique outcomes that will make a difference. The history of the problem often dominates understanding, but there is another history that narrative therapists argue should not be neglected. It is the history of the counter story to the problem story, which is constructed in conversation and becomes the foundation for a different future. The narrative therapist supplies the optimism and sometimes a process, but the client generates what is possible and contributes the movement that actualizes it.

Application: Therapeutic Techniques and Procedures

The effective application of narrative therapy is more dependent on therapists' attitudes or perspectives than on techniques. In the practice of narrative therapy, there is no recipe, no set agenda, and no formula that the therapist can follow to assure positive results (Drewery & Winslade, 1997). When externalizing questions are approached mainly as a technique, the intervention will be shallow, forced, and unlikely to produce significant therapeutic effects (Freedman & Combs, 1996; O'Hanlon, 1994).

Narrative therapists are in agreement with Carl Rogers on the notion of the therapist's way of being as opposed to being technique driven. A narrative approach to counseling is more than the application of skills; it is based on the therapist's personal characteristics that create a climate that encourages clients to see their stories from different perspectives. However, a series of "maps" of narrative conversational trajectories can help give structure and direction to a therapeutic conversation (White, 2007). The approach is also an expression of an ethical stance, which is grounded in a postmodern framework. It is from this conceptual framework that practices are applied to assist clients in finding new meanings and new possibilities in their lives (Winslade & Monk, 2007).

QUESTIONS . . . AND MORE QUESTIONS The questions narrative therapists ask may seem embedded in a unique conversation, part of a dialogue about earlier dialogues, a discovery of unique events, or an exploration of dominant culture processes and imperatives. Whatever the purpose, the questions are often circular, or relational, and they seek to empower clients in new ways. To use Gregory Bateson's (1972) famous phrase, they are questions in search of a difference that will make a difference.

Narrative therapists use questions as a way to generate experience rather than to gather information. The aim of questioning is to progressively discover or construct the client's experience so that the client has a sense of a preferred direction. Questions are always asked from a position of respect, curiosity, and openness. Therapists ask questions from a not-knowing position, meaning that they do not pose questions that they think they already know the answers to. Monk (1997) describes this stance as follows:

> In contrast to the normative, knowing stance, a narrative way of working invites the counselor to take up the investigative, exploratory, archaeological position. She demonstrates to the client that being a counselor does not imply any privileged access to the truth. The counselor is consistently in the role of seeking understanding of the client's experience. (p. 25)

Through the process of asking questions, therapists provide clients with an opportunity to explore various dimensions of their life situations. This questioning process helps bring out the unstated cultural assumptions that contribute to the original construction of the problem. The therapist is interested in finding out how the problems first became evident, and how they have affected clients' views of themselves (Monk, 1997). Narrative therapists attempt to engage people in deconstructing problem-saturated stories, identifying preferred directions, and creating alternative stories that support these preferred directions (Freedman & Combs, 1996). For a more complete discussion of the use of questions in narrative therapy, see Madigan (2011).

EXTERNALIZATION AND DECONSTRUCTION Narrative therapists believe it is not the person that is the problem, but the problem that is the problem (White, 1989). These problems often are products of the cultural world or of the power relations in which this world is located. Living life means relating to problems, not being fused with them.. Narrative therapists help clients deconstruct these problematic stories by disassembling the taken-for-granted assumptions that are made about an event, which then opens alternative possibilities for living (Winslade & Monk, 2007).

Externalization is one process for deconstructing the power of a narrative. This process separates the person from identification with the problem. When clients view themselves as "being" the problem, they are limited in the ways they can effectively deal with the problem. When clients experience the problem as being located outside of themselves, they create a relationship with the problem. For example, there is quite a difference between labeling someone an alcoholic and indicating that alcohol has invaded his or her life. Separating the problem from the individual facilitates hope and enables clients to take a stand against specific story lines, such as self-blame. By understanding the cultural invitations to blame oneself, clients can deconstruct this story line and generate a more positive, healing story.

The method used to separate the person from the problem is referred to as externalizing conversation, which opens up space for new stories to emerge. This method is particularly useful when people have internalized diagnoses and labels that have not been validating or empowering of the change process (Bertolino & O'Hanlon, 2002). **Externalizing conversations** counteract oppressive, problem-saturated stories and empower clients to feel competent to handle the problems they face. Two stages of structuring externalizing conversations are (1) to map the influence of the problem in the person's life, and (2) to map the influence of the person's life back on the problem (McKenzie & Monk, 1997).

Mapping the influence of the problem on the person generates a great deal of useful information and often results in people feeling less shamed and blamed. People feel listened to and understood when the problem's influences are explored in a systematic fashion. A common question is, "When did this problem first appear in your life?" When this mapping is done carefully, it lays the foundation for coauthoring a new story line for the client. Often clients feel outraged when they see for the first time how much the problem is affecting them. The job of the therapist is to assist clients in tracing the problem from when it originated to the present. Therapists may put a future twist on the problem by asking, "If the problem were to continue for a month (or any time period), what would this mean for you?" This question can motivate the client to join with the therapist in combating the impact of the problem's effects. Other useful questions are "To what extent has this problem influenced your life?" and "How deeply has this problem affected you?"

It is important to identify instances when the problem did not completely dominate a client's life. This kind of mapping can help the client who is disillusioned by the problem see some hope for a different kind of life. Therapists look for these "sparkling moments" as they engage in externalizing conversations with clients (White & Epston, 1990).

The case of Brandon illustrates an externalizing conversation. Brandon says that he gets angry far too much, especially when he feels that his wife is criticizing him unjustly: "I just flare! I pop off, get upset, fight back. Later, I wish I hadn't, but it's too late. I've messed up again." Questions about how his anger occurs, complete with specific examples and events, can help chart the influence of the problem. However, it is questions like the ones that follow that *externalize* the problem: "What is the mission of the anger, and how does it recruit you into this mission?" "How does the anger get you, and how does it trick you into letting it become so powerful?" "What does the anger require of you, and what happens to you when you meet its requirements?" "What cultural supports (in your family/community/world) have shaped the role that anger plays for you?"

SEARCH FOR UNIQUE OUTCOMES In the narrative approach, externalizing questions are followed by questions searching for unique outcomes. The therapist talks to the client about moments of choice or success regarding the problem. This is done by selecting for attention any experience that stands apart from the problem story, regardless of how insignificant it might seem to the client. The therapist may ask: "Was there ever a time in which anger wanted to take you over, and you resisted? What was that like for you? How did you do it?" These questions are aimed at highlighting moments when the problem has not occurred or when the problem has been dealt with successfully. Unique outcomes can often be found in the past or the present, but they can also be hypothesized for the future: "What form would standing up against your anger take?" Exploring questions such as these enables clients to see that change is possible. Linking a series of such unique outcomes together starts to form a counter story. It is within the account of unique outcomes that a gateway is provided for alternative versions of a person's life (White, 1992).

Following the description of a unique outcome, White (1992) suggests posing questions, both direct and indirect, that lead to the elaboration of preferred identity stories:

- What do you think this tells me about what you have wanted for your life and about what you have been trying for in your life?
- How do you think knowing this has affected my view of you as a person?
- Of all those people who have known you, who would be least surprised that you have been able to take this step in addressing your problem's influence in your life?
- What actions might you commit yourself to if you were to more fully embrace this knowledge of who you are? (p. 133)

The development of unique outcome stories into solution stories is facilitated by what Epston and White (1992) call "circulation questions":

- Now that you have reached this point in life, who else should know about it?
- I guess there are a number of people who have an outdated view of who you are as a person. What ideas do you have about updating these views?
- If other people seek therapy for the same reasons you did, can I share with them any of the important discoveries you have made? (p. 23)

These questions are not asked in a barrage-like manner. Questioning is an integral part of the context of the narrative conversation, and each question is sensitively attuned to the responses brought out by the previous question (White, 1992).

McKenzie and Monk (1997) suggest that therapists seek permission from the client before asking a series of questions. By letting a client know that they do not have answers to the questions they raise, therapists are putting the client in control of the therapeutic process. Asking permission of the client to use persistent questioning tends to minimize the risk of inadvertently pressuring the client.

ALTERNATIVE STORIES AND REAUTHORING Constructing new stories goes hand in hand with deconstruction, and the narrative therapist listens for openings to new stories. People can continually and actively reauthor their lives, and narrative therapists invite clients to author alternative stories through "unique outcomes," defined as events that could not be predicted from listening to the dominant problem-saturated story. The narrative therapist asks for openings: "Have you ever been able to escape the influence of the problem?" The therapist listens for clues to competence in the midst of a problematic story and builds a story of competence around it. Madigan (2011) suggests that a person's life story is probably much more interesting than the story being told. He maintains a therapist's main task is "to help people to remember, reclaim and reinvent a richer, thicker, and more meaningful alternative story" (p. 159).

A turning point in the narrative interview comes when clients make the choice of whether to continue to live by a problem-saturated story or create an alternative story (Winslade & Monk, 2007). Through the use of unique possibility questions, the therapist moves the focus into the future. For example: "Given what you have learned about yourself, what is the next step you might take?" "When you are acting from your preferred identity, what actions will it lead you to do more of?" Such questions encourage people to reflect upon what they have presently achieved and what their next steps might be.

The therapist works with clients collaboratively by helping them construct more coherent and comprehensive stories (Neimeyer, 1993). Whether involved in a free-flowing conversation or engaged in a series of questions in a relatively consistent process, narrative therapists seek to elicit new possibilities and embed them in the life narratives and processes of the people they serve. White and Epston's (1990) inquiry into unique outcomes is similar to the exception questions of solution-focused therapists. Both seek to build on the competence already present in the person. The development of alternative stories, or narratives, is an enactment of ultimate hope: Today is the first day of the rest of your life. Refer to *Case Approach to Counseling and Psychotherapy* (Corey, 2013, chap. 11) for two concrete examples of a narrative approach to working with Ruth from the perspectives of Dr. Gerald Monk and Dr. John Winslade.

DOCUMENTING THE EVIDENCE Narrative practitioners believe that new stories take hold only when there is an audience to appreciate and support them. Gaining an audience for the news that change is taking place needs to occur if alternative stories are to stay alive (Andrews & Clark, 1996), and an appreciative audience to new developments is consciously sought.

One technique for consolidating the gains a client makes is by writing letters. Narrative therapists have pioneered the development of therapeutic letter writing. These letters that the therapist writes provide a record of the session and may include an externalizing description of the problem and its influence on the client, as well as an account of the client's strengths and abilities that are identified in a session. Letters can be read again at different times, and the story that they are part of can be reinspired. The letter highlights the struggle the client has had with the problem and draws distinctions between the problem-saturated story and the developing new and preferred story (McKenzie & Monk, 1997).

Epston has developed a special facility for carrying on therapeutic dialogues between sessions through the use of letters (White & Epston, 1990). His letters may be long, chronicling the process of the interview and the agreements reached, or short, highlighting a meaning or understanding reached in the session and asking a question that has occurred to him since the end of the previous therapy visit. These letters are used to encourage clients, noting their accomplishments in relation to handling problems or speculating on the meaning of their accomplishments for others in their community. Letters documenting the changes clients have achieved tend to strengthen the significance of the changes, both for the client and for others in the client's life (Winslade & Monk, 2007).

David Nylund, a clinical social worker, uses narrative letters as a basic part of his practice. Nylund describes a conceptual framework he has found useful in structuring letters to his clients (Nylund & Thomas, 1994):

- The introductory paragraph reconnects the client to the previous therapy session.
- Statements summarize the influence the problem has had and is having on the client.
- Questions the therapist thought about after the session that pertain to the alternative story that is developing may be posed to the client.
- The letter documents unique outcomes or exceptions to the problematic story that emerged during the session. Where possible, the client's words are quoted verbatim. Using the client's words enhances the therapeutic relationship, resulting in the client feeling empowered and understood. This connection leads to a more comfortable opportunity for the client to rethink descriptions and stories and to create new images, leading to change.

Nylund and Thomas (1994) contend that narrative letters reinforce the importance of carrying what is being learned in the therapy office into everyday life. The message conveyed is that participating fully in the world is more important than being in the therapy office. In an informal survey of the perceptions of the value of narrative letters by past clients, the average worth of a letter was equal to more than three individual sessions. This finding is consistent with McKenzie and Monk's (1997) statement: "Some narrative counselors have suggested that a well-composed letter following a therapy session or preceding another can be equal to about five regular sessions" (p. 113).

APPLICATION TO GROUP COUNSELING Many of the techniques described in this chapter can be applied to group counseling. Winslade and Monk (2007) claim that the narrative emphasis on creating an appreciative audience for new developments in an individual's life lends itself to group counseling. They state: "Groups provide a ready-made community of concern and many opportunities for the kind of interaction that opens possibilities for new ways of living. New identities can be rehearsed and tried out into a wider world" (p. 135). They give several examples of working in a narrative way with groups in schools: getting back on track in schoolwork; an adventure-based program; an anger management group; and a grief counseling group. For a detailed description of these narrative groups, see Winslade and Monk (2007, chap. 5).

POSTMODERN APPROACHES FROM A MULTICULTURAL PERSPECTIVE

Strengths From a Diversity Perspective

Social constructionism is congruent with the philosophy of multiculturalism. One of the problems that culturally diverse clients often experience is the expectation that they should conform their lives to the truths and reality of the dominant society of which they are a part. With the emphasis on multiple realities and the assumption that what is perceived to be a truth is the product of social construction, the postmodern approaches are a good fit with diverse worldviews.

The social constructionist approach to therapy provides clients with a framework to think about their thinking and to determine the impact stories have on what they do. Clients are encouraged to explore how their realities are being constructed out of cultural discourse and the consequences that follow from such constructions. Within the framework of their cultural values and worldview, clients can explore their beliefs and provide their own reinterpretations of significant life events. The practitioner with a social constructionist perspective can guide clients in a manner that respects their underlying values. This dimension is especially important in those cases where counselors are from a different cultural background or do not share the same worldview as their clients.

Narrative therapy is grounded in a sociocultural context, which makes this approach especially relevant for counseling culturally diverse clients. Narrative therapists operate on the premise that problems are identified within social, cultural, political, and relational contexts rather than existing within individuals. They are very much concerned with considering the specifications of gender, ethnicity, race, disability, sexual orientation, social class, and spirituality and religion as therapeutic issues. Furthermore, therapy becomes a place to reauthor the social constructions and identity narratives that clients are finding problematic.

Narrative therapy is a relational and anti-individualistic practice. Michael White believes that to address a person's struggles in therapy without a relational and contextual understanding of his or her story is entirely absurd (Madigan, 2011). Narrative therapists concentrate on problem stories that dominate and subjugate at the personal, social, and cultural levels. The sociopolitical conceptualization of problems sheds light on those cultural notions and practices that produce dominant and oppressive narratives. From this orientation, practitioners take apart the cultural assumptions that are a part of a client's problem situation. People are able to come to an understanding of how oppressive social practices have affected them. This awareness can lead to a new perspective on dominant themes of oppression that have been such an integral part of a client's story, and with this cultural awareness new stories can be generated.

In their discussion of the multicultural influences on clients, Bertolino and O'Hanlon (2002) make the point that they do not approach clients with a preconceived notion about their experience. Instead, they learn from their clients about their experiential world. Bertolino and O'Hanlon practice multicultural curiosity by listening respectfully to their clients, who become their best teachers. Here are some questions these authors suggest as a way to more fully understand multicultural influences on a client:

- Tell me more about the influence that [some aspect of your culture] has played in your life.
- What can you share with me about your background that will enable me to more fully understand you?
- What challenges have you faced growing up in your culture?
- What, if anything, about your background has been difficult for you?
- How have you been able to draw on strengths and resources from your culture? What resources can you draw from in times of need?

Questions such as these can shed light on specific cultural influences that have been sources of support or that contributed to a client's problem.

Shortcomings From a Diversity Perspective

A potential shortcoming of the postmodern approaches pertains to the not-knowing stance the therapist assumes, along with the assumption of the client-as-expert. Individuals from many different cultural groups tend to elevate the professional as the expert who will offer direction and solutions for the person seeking help. If the therapist is telling the client, "I am not really an expert; you are the expert; I trust in your resources for you to find solutions to your problems," then this may engender lack of confidence in the therapist. To avoid this situation, the therapist using a solution-focused or a narrative orientation needs to convey to clients that he or she has expertise in the process of therapy but clients are the experts in knowing what they want in their lives. The postmodern approaches stress being transparent with clients and honoring their hopes and expectations in therapy. This emphasis creates a context for providing culturally responsive services.

Postmodern Approaches Applied to the Case of Stan

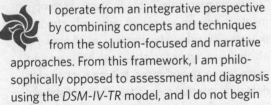 I operate from an integrative perspective by combining concepts and techniques from the solution-focused and narrative approaches. From this framework, I am philosophically opposed to assessment and diagnosis using the *DSM-IV-TR* model, and I do not begin therapy with a formal assessment. Instead, I engage Stan in collaborative conversations centered on change, competence, preferences, possibilities, and ideas for making changes in the future.

I begin my work with Stan by inviting him to tell me about the concerns that brought him to therapy and what he expects to accomplish in his sessions. I also provide Stan with a brief orientation of some of the basic ideas that guide my practice and describe my view of counseling as a collaborative partnership in which he is the senior partner. Stan is somewhat surprised by this because he expected that I was the person with the experience and expertise. He informs me that he has very little confidence in knowing how to proceed with his life, especially since he has "messed up" so often. I am aware that he has self-doubts when it comes to assuming the role of senior partner. However, I work to demystify the therapeutic process and establish a collaborative relationship, conveying to Stan that he is in charge of the direction his therapy will take.

Soon after this orientation to how therapy works, I inquire about some specific goals that Stan would like to reach through the therapy sessions. Stan gives clear signs that he is willing and eager to change. However, he adds that he has become convinced that he suffers from low self-esteem. I begin to externalize the idea of low self-esteem and inquire into its effects in his life. Then I start to focus Stan on looking for exceptions to the problem of low self-esteem. I pose an exception question (solution-focused therapy): "What is different about the contexts or times when you have not experienced low self-esteem?" Stan is able to identify some positive characteristics: his courage, determination, and willingness to try new things in spite of his self-doubts, and his gift for working with children. Stan knows what he wants out of therapy and has clear goals: to achieve his educational goals, to enhance his belief in himself, to relate to women without fear, and to feel more joy instead of sadness and anxiety. I invite Stan to talk more about how he has managed to make the gains he has in spite of struggling with the problem of self-doubt and low self-esteem.

I allow Stan to share his problem-saturated story, but I do not get stuck in this narrative. I invite Stan to think of his problems as external to the core of his selfhood. I help him to notice the cultural forces that have recruited him into a story of thinking less about himself. Even during the early sessions, I encourage Stan to separate his being from his problems by posing questions that externalize his problem.

Although Stan presents several problem areas that are of concern to him, I work with him on identifying one particular problem. Stan says he is depressed a great deal of the time, and he worries that his depression might someday overwhelm him. After listening to Stan's fears and concerns, I ask Stan the miracle question (solution-focused technique): "Let's suppose that a miracle were to happen while you are asleep tonight. When you wake up tomorrow, the problems you are mentioning are gone. What would be the signs to you that this miracle actually occurred and that your problems were solved? How would your life be different?" With this intervention, I am shifting the focus from talking about problems to talking about solutions. I explain to Stan that much of his therapy will deal with finding both present and future solutions rather than dwelling on past problems. Together we engage in a conversation that features change-talk rather than problem-talk.

To a great extent, Stan has linked his identity with his problems, especially depression. He doesn't think of his problems as being separate from himself. I want Stan to realize that he personally is not his problem, but instead that the problem is the problem. When I ask Stan to give a name to his problem, he eventually comes up with "Disabling depression!" He then relates how his depression has kept him from functioning the way he would like in many areas of his life. I then use *externalizing questions* (narrative technique) as a way to separate Stan from his problem: "How long has depression gotten the best of you?" "What has depression cost you?" "Have there been times when you stood up to depression and did not let it win?" Of course, I briefly explain to him what I am doing by using externalizing language, lest he think this is a strange way to counsel. I talk more about the advantages of engaging in externalizing conversations. I also talk with Stan about the importance

of mapping the effects of the problem on his life. This process involves exploring how long the problem has been around, the extent to which the problem has influenced various aspects of his life, and how deeply the problem continues to affect him.

As the sessions progress, there is a collaborative effort aimed at investigating how the problem has been a disrupting, dominating, and discouraging influence. Stan comes to view his story from a different perspective. I continue talking with Stan about those moments when he has not been dominated or discouraged by depression and anxiety and continue to search for exceptions to these problematic experiences. Stan and I participate in conversations about unique outcomes, or occasions when he has demonstrated courage and persistence in the face of discouraging events. Some of these "sparkling moments" include Stan's accomplishments in college, volunteer work with children, progress in curbing his tendencies to abuse alcohol, willingness to challenge his fears and make new acquaintances, talking back to self-defeating internal messages, accomplishments in securing employment, and his willingness to create a vision of a productive future.

With my help, Stan accumulates evidence from his past to bolster a new view of himself as competent enough to have escaped from the dominance of problematic stories. At this phase in his therapy, Stan makes a decision to create an alternative narrative. Several sessions are devoted to reauthoring Stan's story in ways that are lively, creative, and colorful. Along with the process of creating an alternative story, I explore with Stan the possibilities of recruiting an audience who will reinforce his positive changes. I ask, "Who do you know who would be least surprised to hear of your recent changes, and what would this person know about you that would lead to him or her not being so surprised?" Stan identifies one of his early teachers who served as a mentor to him and who believed in him when Stan had little belief in himself. Some therapy time is devoted to discussing how new stories take root only when there is an audience to appreciate them.

After five therapy sessions, Stan brings up the matter of termination. At the sixth and final session, I introduce scaling questions, asking Stan to rate his degree of improvement on a range of problems we explored in the past weeks. On a scale of zero to 10, Stan ranks how he saw himself prior to his first session and how he sees himself today on various specific dimensions. We also talked about Stan's goals for his future and what kinds of improvements he will need to make to attain what he wants. I then give Stan a letter I wrote summarizing both the problem story and its effects and also the counter story that we have been developing in therapy. In my narrative letter, I describe Stan's determination and cooperation in his own words and encourage him to circulate the news of the differences he has brought about in his life. I also ask some questions that invite him to develop the new story of identity more fully.

Follow-Up: You Continue as Stan's Postmodern Therapist

Use these questions to help you think about how to counsel Stan from a postmodernist approach:

- As Stan's therapist, I borrowed key concepts and techniques common to both solution-focused and narrative orientations. In your work with Stan, what specific concepts would you borrow from each of these approaches? What techniques would you draw from each of the approaches? What possible advantages do you see, if any, in applying an integration of

solution-focused and narrative models in your work with Stan?

- What unique values, if any, do you see in working with Stan from a postmodern perspective as opposed to working with Stan from the other therapeutic approaches you've studied thus far?

- I asked many questions of Stan. List some additional questions you would be particularly interested in pursuing with Stan.

- In what ways could you integrate SFBT and narrative therapy with feminist therapy in Stan's case? What other therapies might you combine with the postmodern approaches? What other therapies would not combine so well with these postmodern therapies?

- At this point, you are very familiar with the themes in Stan's life. If you were to write a narrative letter that you would then give to Stan, what would you most want to include? What would you want to talk to him about regarding his future?

See *DVD for Theory and Practice of Counseling and Psychotherapy: The Case of Stan and Lecturettes* (Session 11 on SFBT and Session 12 on narrative therapy) for a demonstration of my approach to counseling Stan from this perspective. Session 11 illustrates techniques such as identifying exceptions, the miracle question, and scaling. Session 12 focuses on Stan's work in creating a new story of his life.

SUMMARY AND EVALUATION

Summary

In social constructionist theory the therapist-as-expert is replaced by the client-as-expert. Although clients are viewed as experts on their own lives, they are often stuck in patterns that are not working well for them. Both solution-focused and narrative therapists enter into dialogues in an effort to elicit the perspectives, resources, and unique experiences of their clients. The therapeutic endeavor is a highly collaborative relationship in which the client is the senior partner. The qualities of the therapeutic relationship are at the heart of the effectiveness of both SFBT and narrative therapy. This has resulted in many therapists giving increased attention to creating a collaborative relationship with clients. Collaborative therapists adjust their approach to each client or group instead of requiring clients to adapt to their approach. Thus therapy may look very different for one client than for another.

The not-knowing position of the therapist has been infused as a key concept of both the solution-focused and narrative therapeutic approaches. The not-knowing position, which allows therapists to be curious about, affirm, and be guided by the stories of their clients, creates participant-observer and process-facilitator roles for the therapist and integrates therapy with a postmodern perspective of human inquiry.

Both solution-focused brief therapy and narrative therapy are based on the optimistic assumption that people are healthy, competent, resourceful, and possess the ability to construct solutions and alternative stories that can enhance their lives. In SFBT the therapeutic process provides a context whereby individuals focus on creating solutions rather than talking about their problems. Some common techniques include the use of miracle questions, exception questions, and scaling questions. In narrative therapy the therapeutic process attends to the sociocultural context wherein clients are assisted in separating themselves from their problems and are afforded the opportunity of authoring new stories.

Practitioners with solution-focused or narrative orientations tend to engage clients in conversations that lead to progressive narratives that help clients make steady gains toward their goals. Therapists often ask clients: "Tell me about times when your life was going the way you wanted it to." These conversations illustrate stories of life worth living. On the basis of these conversations, the power of problems is taken apart (deconstructed) and new directions and solutions are manifest and made possible.

Contributions of Postmodern Approaches

Social constructionism, SFBT, and narrative therapy are making many contributions to the field of psychotherapy. I especially value the optimistic orientation of these postmodern approaches that rest on the assumptions that people are competent and can be trusted to use their resources in creating better solutions and more life-affirming stories. Many postmodern practitioners and writers have found that clients are able to make significant moves toward building more satisfying lives in a relatively short period of time (Bertolino & O'Hanlon, 2002; De Jong & Berg, 2008; de Shazer, 1991; Freedman & Combs, 1996; Miller, Hubble, & Duncan, 1996; O'Hanlon & Weiner-Davis, 2003; Walter & Peller, 1992, 2000; Winslade & Monk, 2007).

To its credit, solution-focused therapy is a brief approach, of about five sessions, that seems to show promising results (de Shazer, 1991). In de Shazer's summary of two outcome studies at the Brief Family Therapy Center, he reports that 91% of the clients who attended four or more sessions were successful in achieving their treatment goals. SFBT tends to be very brief, even among the time-limited therapies. In one study, Rothwell (2005) reports the average number of solution-focused sessions to be two, in comparison to five sessions for cognitive therapy. Brevity is a main appeal of SFBT in an era of managed care, which places a premium on short-term therapy. It should be noted that the brevity comes from the client being in charge of goal setting and determining which issues are of immediate concern. This differs from many other models in which the therapist determines the direction therapy should take. The narrative approach to counseling also tends to be based on brief methods.

I think the nonpathologizing stance characteristic of practitioners with a social constructionist, solution-focused, or narrative orientation is a major contribution to the counseling profession. Rather than dwelling on what is wrong with a person, these approaches view the client as being competent and resourceful. People cannot be reduced to a specific problem nor accurately labeled and identified with a disorder. Even practitioners who are expected to formulate a diagnosis can learn the value of a respectful way to relate to clients.

Research from an "empirical generalizable" perspective is somewhat antithetical to the social constructionist approach, but how effective is solution-focused brief therapy? Regardless of the specific theoretical orientation of the therapist, brief therapy has been shown to be effective for a wide range of clinical problems. Studies that have compared brief therapies with long-term therapies have generally found no difference in outcomes (McKeel, 1996). In a review of research of SFBT, McKeel concludes that when SFBT techniques have been tested, the results are generally favorable. Although only a few studies of SFBT exist, outcome studies generally show that most clients receiving SFBT report accomplishing their treatment goals.

One particular area where the solution-focused approach shows promise is in group treatment with domestic violence offenders. Lee, Sebold, and Uken (2003) describe a cutting-edge treatment approach that seems to create effective, positive change in domestic violence offenders. This approach is dramatically different from traditional approaches in that there is virtually no emphasis on the presenting problem of domestic violence. The approach focuses on holding offenders accountable and responsible for building solutions rather than emphasizing their problems and deficits. The process described by Lee and colleagues is brief when measured against traditional program standards, lasting only eight sessions over a 10- to 12-week period. Lee, Sebold, and Uken report research that indicates a recidivism rate of 16.7% and completion rates of 92.9%. In contrast, more traditional approaches typically generate recidivism rates between 40 and 60% and completion rates of less than 50%.

In their review of 15 outcome studies of SFBT, Gingerich and Eisengart (2000) found that 5 studies were well controlled, and all showed positive outcomes. The other 10 studies, which were only moderately controlled, supported a hypothesis of the effectiveness of SFBT. The review of these studies provided preliminary support for the idea that SFBT may be beneficial to clients, but methodological flaws did not permit a definitive conclusion. For a more detailed review of early research and outcome measurement of SFBT, see De Jong and Berg (2008, chap. 11).

A major strength of both solution-focused and narrative therapies is the use of questioning, which is the centerpiece of both approaches. Open-ended questions about the client's attitudes, thoughts, feeling, behaviors, and perceptions are one of the main interventions. Especially useful are future-oriented questions that get clients thinking about how they are likely to solve potential problems in the future. Questions can assist clients in developing their story and discovering better ways to deal with their concerns. Effective questioning can help individuals examine their story and find new ways to present their story. Winslade and Monk (2007) note that a therapist's careful questioning about clients' early experiences of their capabilities and resources tends to strengthen the foundation for clients in building a new sense of direction and for them to create alternative stories.

Limitation and Criticisms of Postmodern Approaches

To effectively practice solution-focused brief therapy, it is essential that therapists are skilled in brief interventions. Although it may appear that SFBT is simple and easy to implement, therapists practicing within this framework must be able to make assessments, assist clients in formulating specific goals, and effectively use a range of appropriate interventions. Some inexperienced or untrained therapists may be enamored by the variety of techniques: the miracle question, scaling questions, the exception question, and externalizing questions. But effective therapy is not simply a matter of relying on any of these interventions. The attitudes of the therapist and his or her ability to use questions that are reflective of genuine respectful interest are crucial to the therapeutic process.

McKenzie and Monk (1997) express their concerns over those counselors who attempt to employ narrative ideas in a mechanistic fashion. They caution that a risk in describing a map of a narrative orientation lies in the fact that some beginners will pay more attention to following the map than they will to following the lead of the client. In such situations, McKenzie and Monk are convinced that mechanically using techniques will not be effective. They add that although narrative therapy is based on some simple ideas, it is a mistake to assume that the practice is simple.

McKeel (1996) observes that recent research on the importance of the therapeutic relationship is consistent with the SFBT view that positive treatment outcomes are linked to therapists developing effective and collaborative working relationships with clients. He cautions practitioners that losing sight of the potency of the therapeutic relationship "will only doom SFBT to be remembered as a disembodied set of clever techniques" (p. 265). Some solution-focused practitioners now acknowledge the problem of relying too much on a few techniques, and they are placing increased importance on the therapeutic relationship and the overall philosophy of the approach (Lipchik, 2002; Nichols, 2013).

Despite these limitations, the postmodern approaches have much to offer practitioners, regardless of their theoretical orientation. Many of the basic concepts and techniques of both solution-focused brief therapy and narrative therapy can be integrated into the other therapeutic orientations discussed in this book.

WHERE TO GO FROM HERE
Free Podcasts for ACA Members

You can download ACA Podcasts (prerecorded interviews) at www.counseling.org; click on the Resource button and then the Podcast Series. For Chapter 13, Postmodern Approaches, look for the following:

> Interview with Dr. John Murphy on *Solution-Focused Counseling in Schools* (Podcast 5) Lorraine Hedtke, L. & Winslade, J., *Remembering Lives, Conversations With the Dying and Bereaved*

Other Resources

Psychotherapy.net is a comprehensive resource for students and professionals that offers videos and interviews on the postmodern approaches. New video and editorial content is made available monthly. DVDs relevant to this chapter are available at www.psychotherapy.net and include the following:

Madigan, S. (2002). *Narrative Therapy With Children* (Child Therapy With the Experts)

Madigan, S. (1998). *Narrative Family Therapy* (Family Therapy With the Experts)

If you are interested in keeping up to date with the developments in brief therapy, the *Journal of Brief Therapy* is a useful resource. It is devoted to developments, innovations, and research related to brief therapy with individuals, couples, families, and groups. The articles deal with brief therapy related to all theoretical approaches, but especially to social constructionism, solution-focused therapy, and narrative therapy. For subscription information, contact:

Springer Publishing Company
11 West 42nd Street, 15th Floor
New York, NY 10036
Toll-Free Telephone: (877) 687-7476
Website: www.springerpub.com

Another useful journal is the *International Journal of Narrative Therapy and Community Work*. For more information, contact:

Dulwich Centre
345 Carrington Street
Adelaide, South Australia 5000
Website: www.dulwichcentre.com.au/

Training in Solution-Focused Therapy Approaches

Center for Solution-Focused Brief Therapy

John Walter and Jane Peller
2320 Thayer Street
Evanston, IL 60201
Telephone: (847) 475-2691
E-mail: John Walter@aol.com

O'Hanlon and O'Hanlon Inc.

223 N. Guadalupe #278
Santa Fe, NM 87501
Telephone: (505) 983-2843
Fax: (505) 983-2761
E-mail: PossiBill@brieftherapy.com
Website: www.brief.org.uk

The Solution Focused Institute (SFI) at Texas Wesleyan University was founded in January 2009 in Fort Worth, Texas, to provide training to mental health practitioners and school teachers and counselors who want to implement a solution-focused approach in their work. The institute provides training on- and off-site in solution-focused therapy and offers supervision to individuals and groups. For information on SFI services, contact:

Linda Metcalf, PhD

Solution Focused Institute

3001 Avenue D
Fort Worth, TX 76105
Telephone: (817) 690-2229
Fax: (817) 531-4935
E-mail: lmetcalf@txwes.edu
Website:www.Solutionfocusedinstitute.com

Change-Focused Practice in Schools (CFPS) was initiated by John Murphy in 2005 to translate psychotherapy research into practical applications in schools and other settings. CFPS offers international training, supervision, and consultation on solution-focused/outcome-informed approaches to helping young people change in ways that honor their strengths and resources. For more information, contact:

John Murphy, PhD

Department of Psychology & Counseling

University of Central Arkansas
Conway, AR 72035-0001
Telephone: (501) 450-5450
Fax: (501) 450-5424
E-mail: jmurphy@uca.edu
Website: www.drjohnmurphy.com

Training in Narrative Therapy

Evanston Family Therapy Institute

Jill Freedman and Gene Combs
820 Davis Street, Suite 504
Evanston, Illinois 60201

Dulwich Centre

Cheryl White
345 Carrington Street
Adelaide, South Australia 5000
http://www.dulwichcentre.com.au/

Bay Area Family Therapy Training Associates

Jeffrey L. Zimmerman and Marie-Nathalie Beaudoin
21760 Stevens Creek Blvd., Suite 102
Cupertino, CA 95015
Telephone: (408) 257-6881
Fax: (408) 257-0689
E-mail: baftta@aol.com
Website: www.baftta.com

The Houston-Galveston Institute

3316 Mount Vernon
Houston, TX 77006
Telephone: (713) 526-8390
Fax: (713) 528-2618
E-mail: admin@talkhgi.com
Website: www.talkhgi.com

Family Systems Therapy

Coauthored by James Robert Bitter and Gerald Corey

CONTRIBUTORS TO FAMILY SYSTEMS THEORY

Family systems therapy is represented by a variety of theories and approaches, all of which focus on the relational aspects of human problems. Some of the individuals most closely associated with the origins of these systemic approaches are featured here.

ALFRED ADLER / MURRAY BOWEN / VIRGINIA SATIR / CARL WHITAKER / SALVADOR MINUCHIN / JAY HALEY AND CLOÉ MADANES

Hulton Archive/Getty Images

ALFRED ADLER (1870–1937) was the first psychologist of the modern era to do family therapy using a systemic approach. He set up more than 30 child guidance clinics in Vienna after World War I, and later Rudolf Dreikurs brought this concept to the United States in the form of family education centers. Adler and Dreikurs conducted family counseling sessions in an open public forum, educating parents and professionals in greater numbers; they believed the problems of any one family were common to all others in the community (Christensen, 2004). As we have seen in the chapter on Adlerian therapy, the focus of interventions is on the purposes or goals of behavior—and Adlerian family therapists extend this teleological focus to family interactions and patterns of communication.

Courtesy of The Bowen Center for the Study of the Family; photo by Andrea Schara

MURRAY BOWEN (1913–1990) was one of the original developers of mainstream family therapy. Much of his theory and practice grew out of his work at the National Institute of Mental Health (and later at Georgetown University) with schizophrenic individuals in families. He believed families could best be understood when analyzed from a three-generation perspective because patterns of interpersonal relationships connect family members across generations. Two of his objectives in therapy were to help family members develop a rational, nonreactive approach to living (called a differentiation of self) and to de-tangle family interactions that involved two people pulling a third person into the couples' problems and arguments (or triangulation). Bowen's emphasis on a multigenerational perspective led to the development of genograms (McGoldrick, Gerson, & Petry, 2008), family life cycle development (McGoldrick, Carter, & Garcia-Preto, 2011), and a comprehensive focus on a multicultural perspective in family therapy (McGoldrick, Giordano, & Garcia-Preto, 2005).

Courtesy of The Virginia Satir Global Network

VIRGINIA SATIR (1916–1988) developed conjoint family therapy, a human validation process model that emphasizes communication and emotional experiencing. Like Bowen, she used an intergenerational model, but she worked to bring family patterns to life in the present through sculpting and family reconstructions. Claiming that techniques were secondary to relationship, she concentrated on the personal relationship between therapist and family to achieve change. The core of Satir's model relied on the power of congruence to help family members communicate with emotional honesty. Her presence with people encouraged them to get in touch with what was significant within, to become more fully human, to share the individual's best self with a significant other: Satir called this experience "making contact," and she believed that it extended the peace one had within to a peace between people, and eventually, to a peace among people. From Satir, family therapy gets it model for empathic listening, therapeutic presence, and nurturance (Satir, Banmen, Gerber, & Gomori, 1991).

University of Wisconsin Madison Archives

CARL WHITAKER (1912–1995) is the creator of symbolic-experiential family therapy, a freewheeling, intuitive approach to helping families open channels of interaction. His goal was to facilitate individual autonomy while retaining a sense of belonging in the family. He saw the therapist as an active participant and coach who enters the family process with creativity, putting enough pressure on this process to produce change in the status quo. From Whitaker, the field of family therapy learned to tolerate and sometimes create anxiety in families—and then how to join families in their struggle to become more real and more transparent.

Courtesy of The Minuchin Center for the Family

SALVADOR MINUCHIN (b. 1921) began to develop structural family therapy in the 1960s through his work with delinquent boys from poor families at the Wiltwyck School in New York. Working with colleagues at the Philadelphia Child Guidance Clinic in the 1970s, Minuchin refined the theory and practice of structural family therapy. Focusing on the structure, or organization, of the family, the therapist helps the family modify its stereotyped patterns and redefine relationships among family members. He believes structural changes in families must occur before individual members' symptoms can be reduced or eliminated. From Minuchin and his colleagues, family therapy developed an understanding of power, organization, and alignments in family life, and family therapists learned how to use themselves to set boundaries and even unbalance dysfunctional family systems.

Courtesy of Chloe Madanes

JAY HALEY (1923–2007) and **CLOÉ MADANES** (b. 1941) founded the Washington School of strategic family therapy in the 1970s, after Haley had left the Mental Research Institute in Palo Alto, California, and later the Philadelphia Child Guidance Center, where he spent a brief period with Salvador Minuchin and colleagues. Haley blended structural family therapy with the concepts of hierarchy, power, and strategic interventions. Madanes contributed to the development of a brief, solution-oriented therapy approach. The strategic interventions most favored by Haley and Madanes were reframing, family directives, and paradoxical interventions. Strategic family therapy became the most popular family therapy approach in the 1980s. It is a pragmatic approach that focuses on solving problems in the present; understanding and insight are neither required nor sought. The problem brought by the family to therapy is treated as "real"—not a symptom of underlying issues—and is solved. When the problem is solved, therapy is finished.

INTRODUCTION

Although the seeds of a North American family therapy movement were planted in the 1940s, it was during the 1950s that systemic family therapy began to take root (Becvar & Becvar, 2009). During the early years of its evolution, working with families was considered to be a revolutionary approach to treatment. In the 1960s and 1970s, psychodynamic, behavioral, and humanistic approaches (called the first, second, and third force, respectively) dominated counseling and psychotherapy.

Today, the various approaches to family systems represent a paradigm shift that we might even call the "fourth force."

The Family Systems Perspective

Perhaps the most difficult adjustment for counselors and therapists from Western cultures is the adoption of a "systems" perspective. Our personal experience and Western culture often tell us that we are autonomous individuals, capable of free and independent choice. And yet we are born into families—and most of us live our entire lives attached to one form of family or another. Within these families, we discover who we are; we develop and change; and we give and receive the support we need for survival. We create, maintain, and live by often unspoken rules and routines that we hope will keep the family (and each of its members) functional.

In this sense, a family systems perspective holds that individuals are best understood through assessing the interactions between and among family members. The development and behavior of one family member is inextricably interconnected with others in the family. Symptoms are often viewed as an expression of a set of habits and patterns within a family. It is revolutionary to conclude that the identified client's problem might be a symptom of how the system functions, not just a symptom of the individual's maladjustment, history, and psychosocial development. This perspective is grounded on the assumptions that a client's problematic behavior may (1) serve a function or purpose for the family; (2) be unintentionally maintained by family processes; (3) be a function of the family's inability to operate productively, especially during developmental transitions; or (4) be a symptom of dysfunctional patterns handed down across generations. All these assumptions challenge the more traditional intrapsychic frameworks for conceptualizing human problems and their formation.

The one central principle agreed upon by family therapy practitioners, regardless of their particular approach, is that the client is connected to living systems. Attempts at change are best facilitated by working with and considering the family or set of relationships as a whole. Therefore, a treatment approach that comprehensively addresses the family as well as the "identified" client is required. Because a family is an interactional unit, it has its own set of unique traits. It is not possible to accurately assess an individual's concern without observing the interaction of the other family members, as well as the broader contexts in which the person and the family live. Because the focus is on interpersonal relationships, Becvar and Becvar (2009) maintain that family therapy is a misnomer and that *relationship therapy* is a more appropriate label.

Family therapy perspectives call for a conceptual shift because the family is viewed as a functioning unit that is more than the sum of the roles of its various members. Actions by any individual family member will influence all the others in the family, and their reactions will have a reciprocal effect on the individual. Goldenberg and Goldenberg (2013) point to the need for therapists to view all behavior, including all symptoms expressed by the individual, within the context of the family and society. They add that a systems orientation does not preclude dealing with the dynamics within the individual, but that this approach broadens the traditional emphasis on individual internal dynamics.

See the video program for Chapter 14, *DVD for Theory and Practice of Counseling and Psychotherapy: The Case of Stan and Lecturettes.* I suggest that you view the brief lecture for each chapter prior to reading the chapter.

Differences Between Systemic and Individual Approaches

There are significant differences between individual therapeutic approaches and systemic approaches. A case may help to illustrate these differences. Ann, age 22, sees a counselor because she is suffering from a depression that has lasted for more than 2 years and has impaired her ability to maintain friendships and work productively. She wants to feel better, but she is pessimistic about her chances. How will a therapist choose to help her?

Both the individual therapist and the systemic therapist are interested in Ann's current living situation and life experiences. Both discover that she is still living at home with her parents, who are in their 60s. They note that she has a very successful older sister, who is a prominent lawyer in the small town in which the two live. The therapists are impressed by Ann's loss of friends who have married and left town over the years while she stayed behind, often lonely and isolated. Finally, both therapists note that Ann's depression affects others as well as herself. It is here, however, that the similarities tend to end:

The individual therapist may:	The systemic therapist may:
• Focus on obtaining an accurate diagnosis, perhaps using the *DSM-IV-TR* (American Psychiatric Association, 2000)	• Explore the system for family process and rules, perhaps using a genogram
• Begin therapy with Ann immediately	• Invite Ann's mother, father, and sister into therapy with her
• Focus on the causes, purposes, and cognitive, emotional, and behavioral processes involved in Ann's depression and coping	• Focus on the family relationships within which the continuation of Ann's depression "makes sense"
• Be concerned with Ann's individual experiences and perspectives	• Be concerned with transgenerational meanings, rules, cultural, and gender perspectives within the system, and even the community and larger systems affecting the family
• Intervene in ways designed to help Ann cope	• Intervene in ways designed to help change Ann's context

Systemic therapists do not deny the importance of the individual in the family system, but they believe an individual's systemic affiliations and interactions have more power in the person's life than a single therapist could ever hope to have. By working with the whole family(or even community) system, the therapist has a chance to observe how individuals act within the system and participate in maintaining the status quo; how the system influences (and is influenced by) the individual; and what interventions might lead to changes that help the couple, family, or larger system as well as the individual expressing pain.

In Ann's case, her depression may have organic, genetic, or hormonal components. It may also involve cognitive, experiential, or behavioral patterns that interfere with effective coping. Even if her depression can be explained in this manner, however, the systemic therapist is very interested in how her depression affects others in the family and how it influences family process. Her depression may signal both her own pain and the unexpressed pain of the family. Indeed, many family system approaches would investigate how the depression serves other family members; distracts from problems in the intimate relationships of others; or reflects her need to adjust to family rules, to cultural injunctions, or to processes influenced by gender or family life-cycle development. Rather than losing sight of the individual, family therapists understand the person as specifically embedded in larger systems.

DEVELOPMENT OF FAMILY SYSTEMS THERAPY AND PERSONAL DEVELOPMENT OF THE FAMILY THERAPIST

Family systems theory has evolved throughout the past 100 years, and today therapists creatively employ various perspectives when tailoring therapy to a particular family. This section presents a brief historical overview of some of the key figures associated with the development of family systems therapy—with special attention to those aspects of family theory that speak to the development of the family therapist as a person and a professional. Who one is, the person's way of being, is intimately connected to the development of the practitioner and the kind of therapy that she or he provides. So let's start by taking a look at the most prominent models and what they indicate is significant in the development of the therapist.

Adlerian Family Therapy

Alfred Adler was the first psychologist of the modern era to do family therapy (Christensen, 2004). His approach was systemic long before systems theory had been applied to psychotherapy. Adler's original conceptualizations can still be found within the principles and practice of other models.

Adler (1927) was the first to notice that the development of children within the family constellation (his phrase for family system) was heavily influenced by birth order. Adler was a phenomenologist, and even though birth order appeared to have some constancy to each position, he believed it was the interpretations children assigned to their birth positions that counted. Adler also noted that all behavior was purposeful—and that children often acted in patterns motivated by a desire to belong, even when these patterns were useless or mistaken.

It was Rudolf Dreikurs (1950, 1973), however, who refined Adler's concepts into a typology of mistaken goals and created an organized approach to family therapy. A basic assumption of modern Adlerian family therapy is that both parents and children often become locked in repetitive, negative interactions based on mistaken goals that motivate all parties involved (Bitter, 2009a). Adlerian family therapy starts with forming a relationship based on mutual respect, just as an Adlerian therapist does with an individual client. Assessment is based on the subjective descriptions that family members use to define themselves and the interactions that occur in everyday life. It is within these interactions that Adlerians seek to discover the purposes and goals of behavior (Bitter, Roberts, & Sonstegard, 2002).

Take a moment and think about two different family experiences in your own life. When you were little, what descriptions would you have used for your parents? What do these descriptions tell you about what was important to you? Now, think about your current family situation—either with your family of origin or with a new family you have started. What descriptions would be used by family members for you? What does that tell you about your place or role in the family? Finally, think about a recent family interaction that was difficult for you. What goals or purposes did you have for your part of the interaction? What goals or purposes might have been involved for those interacting with you? You can generally discover the goal or purpose of behavior by looking at the consequence of that behavior in the responses of others. What do people do when I act in one way or another?

Multigenerational Family Therapy

Murray Bowen (1978) was one of the developers of mainstream family therapy. His family systems theory, which is a theoretical and clinical model that evolved from psychoanalytic principles and practices, is sometimes referred to as multigenerational family therapy. Bowen and his associates implemented an innovative approach to schizophrenia at the National Institute of Mental Health where Bowen actually hospitalized entire families so that the family system could be the focus of therapy.

Bowen's observations led to his interest in patterns across multiple generations. He contended that problems manifested in one's current family will not significantly change until relationship patterns in one's family of origin are understood and directly challenged. His approach operates on the premise that a predictable pattern of interpersonal relationships connects the functioning of family members across generations. According to Kerr and Bowen (1988), the cause of an individual's problems can be understood only by viewing the role of the family as an emotional unit. Within the family unit, unresolved emotional reactivity to one's family must be addressed if one hopes to achieve a mature and unique personality. Emotional problems will be transmitted from generation to generation until unresolved emotional attachments are dealt with effectively. Change must occur with other family members and cannot be done by an individual in a counseling room.

One of Bowen's key concepts is *triangulation*, a process in which triads result in a *two-against-one* experience. Bowen assumed that triangulation could easily happen between family members and the therapist, which is why Bowen placed so much emphasis on his trainees becoming aware of their own family-of-origin issues (Kerr & Bowen, 1988). Later in the chapter we show you how to construct a basic genogram of your extended family. Take some time to gather this information and use it as an opportunity to explore the stories in your family's life.

Another major contribution of Bowen's theory is the notion of **differentiation of self**, which involves both the psychological separation of intellect and emotion and independence of the self from others. In the process of individuation, individuals acquire a sense of self-identity. The opposite of a differentiated self is experienced as emotional reactivity, which is what happens when others "push your buttons." The response, whatever it might be (anger, hurt, panic), is automatic. Similar to cognitive behaviorists, Bowen felt that people could learn to use their intellect to respond rationally. Bowen asked his trainees to go to significant family events and to adopt an observer role, to practice noting what happens and to not react. This differentiation from the family of origin enabled his trainees to accept personal responsibility for their thoughts, feelings, perceptions, and actions. After you construct your genogram, you might want to note on it which people were good at pushing your buttons. How did they do it? What were the issues involved? Was there a sequence to the interactions that escalated into emotional reactivity?

It is also important to note that two of Bowen's most prominent colleagues, Betty Carter and Monica McGoldrick, almost single-handedly initiated both a developmental and a multicultural perspective in family therapy. Indeed, McGoldrick's work includes the field's most important work on genograms (McGoldrick et al., 2008), family life cycle (McGoldrick et al., 2011), and gender (McGoldrick, Anderson, & Walsh, 1991).

Human Validation Process Model

At about the same time that Bowen was developing his approach, Virginia Satir (1983) began emphasizing family connection. Her therapeutic work had already led her to believe in the value of a strong, nurturing relationship based on interest and fascination with those in her care. Unlike Bowen, Satir could envision and sought to support the development of a nurturing triad: two people, for example parents, working for the well-being of another, perhaps a child. Satir thought of herself as a detective who sought out and listened for the reflections of self-esteem in the communication of her clients. Indeed, she placed a very strong emphasis on the importance of communication and meta-communication in family interactions, and the value of therapeutic validation in the process of change (Satir & Bitter, 2000).

Satir (1988) outlined four communication stances that people tended to adopt under stress: blaming, placating, super reasonable, and irrelevant. *Blaming* is when one shifts responsibility to someone else in an effort to preserve the self. *Placating* is just the opposite, taking the blame to protect someone else from being held responsible—or trying to make everyone happy so others will be happy with that person. Adopting a *super reasonable* position is done to maintain control of one's messy or painful emotions; this person will respond with facts and sound very much like a computer. *Irrelevance* is any distracting communication used to avoid stress or pain altogether; it is what people say when they are ignoring problems right in front of them. The antidote to these stress communications is *congruence*, by which Satir meant emotional honesty, in which one speaks for oneself, stays grounded (or centered), and is able to both share what she or he is feeling and ask for what is needed. Families in therapy are almost never congruent, but it helps a great deal if the counselor or therapist is.

Think about a time when people in your family were under a lot of stress. What communication stance did your family members use? On which stance did you most rely? Was there a dance to the stress communications, maybe first super reasonable, then blaming, and then placating? What is it like to think about communication as an interactive stress dance? How did people respond to you when you were under stress? Do you know anyone, maybe even yourself, who responds to stress in a congruent manner?

Experiential Family Therapy

Carl Whitaker (1976) was a pioneer in symbolic-experiential family therapy. Clearly an application of existential therapy to family systems, Whitaker stressed choice, freedom, self-determination, growth, and actualization (Whitaker & Bumberry, 1988). Like Satir and other experiential approaches, Whitaker stressed the importance of the relationship between the family and the therapist. Whitaker was clearly more confrontive in his "realness" than Satir, who was more nurturing. His goal was not to eliminate anxiety in the family but to maintain or enhance it so that it would serve as a motivation for change. Whitaker's interventions were almost always enacted with co-therapists. Toward the end of his life, he would only see whole families, never individuals or parts of families, and he even tried to get community and work associates of the family to come in.

Whitaker's freewheeling, intuitive approach sought to unmask pretense and create new meaning while liberating family members to be themselves. Whitaker did not propose a set of methods; rather, it is the personal involvement of the therapist with a family that makes a difference. When techniques are employed, they arise from the therapist's intuitive and spontaneous reactions to the present situation and are designed to increase clients' awareness of their inner potential and to open channels of family interaction (see Bitter, 2009b).

From Whitaker, we learn the importance of using yourself in therapy. What are some things you could imagine thinking or feeling about a family but which you would feel constrained not to say? How would you go about finding your own way of confronting families in a therapeutic way? Whitaker's "intuition" was informed by more than 50 years of practice. How will you go about training your intuition, and do you think it would be wise to have a co-therapist while you do that? What would you expect in your relationship with a co-therapist?

Structural-Strategic Family Therapy

The origins of **structural family therapy** can be traced to the early 1960s when Salvador Minuchin was conducting therapy, training, and research with delinquent boys from poor families at the Wiltwyck School in New York. Minuchin's (1974) central idea was that an individual's symptoms are best understood from the vantage point of interactional patterns, or sequences, within a family, and further, structural changes must occur in a family before an individual's symptoms can be reduced or eliminated. The goals of structural family therapy are twofold: (1) reduce symptoms of dysfunction and (2) bring about structural change within the system by modifying the family's transactional rules and developing more appropriate boundaries.

In the late 1960s, Jay Haley joined Minuchin at the Philadelphia Child Guidance Clinic. The work of Haley and Minuchin shared so many similarities in goals and process that many clinicians in the 1980s and 1990s began to question whether the two models were distinct schools of thought. Indeed, by the late 1970s, **structural-strategic approaches** were the most used models in family systems therapy. The interventions generated in these models became synonymous with a systems approach; they included joining, boundary setting, unbalancing, reframing, ordeals, paradoxical interventions, and enactments.

If you divided your family of origin into subsystems, who would be in the parental subsystem? The spousal subsystem? The sibling subsystem? In your family, did the parental subsystem and the spousal subsystem contain the same people or different people at different times? What rules and boundaries were set around each subsystem? Were the boundaries ever crossed? By whom and with what result? What were common interactional sequences in your family? What were the routines that made up your early life, and what rules governed these routines? How accommodating were your family members to change and transitions brought on by family development or when all of you had to face an external challenge or ordeal? Who had the power in your family, and how was it exercised? Who was aligned with whom—and what did they use that alignment to achieve? These are just a few of the assessments that structural-strategic therapists taught us to consider.

Minuchin and other structural family therapists initiated their work with the poor. They have always been engaged in multicultural settings and worked with multicultural clients. Indeed, many of the most prominent structural family therapists have dedicated their efforts to working predominantly with African American and Hispanic families. It was only in Haley's most recent work that he emphasized the importance of cultural embeddedness (Haley & Richeport-Haley, 2003).

Recent Innovations in Family Therapy

In the last decade, *feminism, multiculturalism,* and *postmodern social constructionism* have all entered the family therapy field. These models are more collaborative, treating clients—individuals, couples, or families—as experts in their own lives. The therapeutic conversations start with the counselor in a "not-knowing" position in which clients are approached with curiosity and interest. The therapist is socially active and aids clients in taking a preferred stand in relation to the dominant culture that may be oppressing them. Therapy often incorporates "reflecting teams" and "definitional ceremonies" to bring multiple perspectives to the work (see West, Bubenzer, & Bitter, 1998).

These more recent approaches to family therapy challenge what Becvar and Becvar (2009) call first-order cybernetics, a perspective that has been part of family therapy since the time of Adler. *First-order cybernetics* views the counselor and therapist as an observer who is outside of the system, can assess what is going on, and can promote change—all without ever becoming part of the system. This perspective is inherent in the medical model and is the way in which many professions function. Feminist and postmodern models of family therapy are based on the perspective of *second-order cybernetics;* that is, the family practitioner becomes part of the family system and just by being present with the family changes it. Feminist, multicultural, and postmodern therapists are extremely aware of the power they have entering into already established systems, and they work to promote understanding through curiosity and interest rather than through formal assessments. Adopting a decentered position allows them to be part of the system without taking it over.

POSTMODERN PERSPECTIVES IN FAMILY THERAPY In Chapter 13 you were introduced to pioneers in the postmodern approaches. We return here to briefly discuss some of the contributions of these individuals in developing postmodern models of family therapy.

Steve de Shazer (1985) and his spouse/partner Insoo Kim Berg turned strategic family therapy as it was practiced at the Mental Research Institute on its head. Rather than focusing on the problem, de Shazer developed methods that focused only on solutions, calling his approach *solution-focused therapy*. Indeed, de Shazer was so solution-focused that he actually suggested he did not even need to know what the problem was that brought the family to therapy. Using interventions like the miracle question, scaling questions, exception questions, and even compliments, solution-focused therapists helped families create their preferred ways of being. One of de Shazer and Berg's former students, Michele Weiner-Davis, joined with Bill O'Hanlon to modify the solution-focused approach slightly (O'Hanlon & Weiner-Davis, 2003). They created solution-oriented therapy and believed that family solutions were often embedded within the problems that their clients reported. Solution-focused and solution-oriented therapies were part of a new orientation to family therapy based on a postmodern perspective and what Gergen (1999) called social constructionism.

Michael White and David Epston (1990) created the most influential of the postmodern approaches, *narrative therapy*. White and Epston believed that people and families did not merely live life but lived the stories of their lives. Each member of the family had his or her own personal narrative as well as the family narrative. When these stories became problem saturated, neither individuals nor families functioned very well. White and Epston adopted a decentered position with families, which came to be known as a "not-knowing" position (Anderson & Goolishian, 1992). They approached the members of a family with curiosity and interest, and they treated these individuals as experts in their own lives. Narrative therapists seek to map the influence problems have on people and then externalize those problems so that individuals and families can adopt a preferred stand in relation to the problem— as well as seeking a preferred outcome. You can see in this latter emphasis the relationship of the narrative model to solution-oriented therapy. Postmodern approaches to family therapy, like narrative therapy, seek to reduce or eliminate the power and impact of the family therapist. Taken together, postmodern approaches represent a real paradigm shift in the field of family therapy.

Now that you have taken this brief tour of some of the major approaches to family therapy, which approach most interests you and which one would you want to learn more about? What do you believe is the best approach to families in difficulty? Are you more comfortable with formal assessments, directives, paradoxical interventions, and challenging the family system? Or are you more interested in family stories and individual perspectives that are both an influence on and have been influenced by culture, gender, and societal prerogatives? Do you see yourself as an outside observer or a person who enters the system and becomes part of it in some way? Neither perspective is right or wrong, good or bad; they are just different. Knowing the perspective with which you are most comfortable can make all the difference in the development of your career.

This brief discussion of the various systemic viewpoints in family therapy provides a context for understanding the development of family therapy. Table 14.1

TABLE 14.1 A Comparison of Six Systemic Viewpoints in Family Therapy

	ADLERIAN FAMILY THERAPY	MULTI-GENERATIONAL FAMILY THERAPY	HUMAN VALIDATION PROCESS MODEL	EXPERIENTIAL/ SYMBOLIC FAMILY THERAPY	STRUCTURAL FAMILY THERAPY	STRATEGIC FAMILY THERAPY
Key figures	Afred Adler, Rudolf Dreikurs, Oscar Christensen, & Manford Sonstegard	Murray Bowen	Virginia Satir	Carl Whitaker	Salvador Minuchin	Jay Haley & Cloé Madanes
Time focus	Present with some reference to the past	Present and past: family of origin; three generations	Here and now	Present	Present and past	Present and Future
Therapy goals	Enable parents as leaders; unlock mistaken goals and inter-actional patterns in family; promotion of effective parenting	Differentiate the self; change the individual within the context of the system; decrease anxiety	Promote growth, self-esteem, and connection; help family reach congruent communication and interaction	Promote spontaneity, creativity, autonomy, and ability to play	Restructure family organization; change dysfunctional transactional patterns	Eliminate presenting problem; change dysfunctional patterns; interrupt sequence

Role and function of the therapist	Educator; motivational investigator; collaborator	Guide, objective researcher, teacher; monitor of own reactivity	Active facilitator; resource detective; model for congruence	Family coach; challenger; model for change through play	"Friendly uncle"; stage manager; promoter of change in family structure	Active director of change; problem solver
Process of change	Formation of relationship based on mutual respect; investigation of birth order and mistaken goals, reeducation	Questions and cognitive processes lead to differentiation and understanding of family of origin	Family is helped to move from status quo through chaos to new possibilities and new integrations	Awareness and seeds of change are planted in therapy confrontations	Therapist joins the family in a leadership role; changes structure; sets boundaries	Change occurs through actionoriented directives and paradoxical interventions
Techniques and innovations	Family constellation; typical day; goal disclosure; natural/logical consequences	Genograms; dealing with family-of-origin issues; detriangulating relationships	Empathy; touch, communication; sculpting; role playing; family-life chronology	Co-therapy; self-disclosure; confrontation; use of self as change agent	Joining & accommodating; unbalancing; tracking; boundary making; enactments	Reframing; directives and paradox; amplifying; pretending; enactments

outlines the differences in these historical perspectives. For an in-depth treatment of the schools of family therapy, see Bitter's (2009b) *Theory and Practice of Family Therapy and Counseling*. See also the recommended readings at the end of the chapter.

A MULTILAYERED PROCESS OF FAMILY THERAPY

Families are multilayered systems that both affect and are affected by the larger systems in which they are embedded. Families can be described in terms of their individual members and the various roles they play, the relationships between the members, and the sequential patterns of the interactions and the purposes these sequences serve. Both the members and the system can be assessed based on power, alignment, organization, structure, development, culture, and gender (Breunlin, Schwartz, & MacKune-Karrer, 1997). Even individuals can be considered from the perspective of an internal family system (Schwartz, 1995). In addition, nuclear families in a global community are often part of extended, if distant, families; multiple families make up a community; multiple communities make up both regions and cultures, which in turn constitute nations (or societies). The power of these macrosystems to influence family life—especially in the areas of gender and culture—is significant. Given our presuppositions about families and the larger systems in which families are embedded, a multilayered approach to family therapy is essential.

Several forms and structures have been proposed for integrative models of family counseling and therapy (e.g., Carlson, Sperry, & Lewis, 2005; Gladding, 2010; Hanna, 2007; Nichols, 2010, 2013). The integrative model we have chosen to present here allows for an enlarged integration of ideas from multiple models of family therapy. Similar to a piece of classical music, the process of family therapy, it seems to us, has movements. These movements can be described as separate experiences embedded in the larger flow of therapy. In this section we describe four general movements, each with different tasks: forming a relationship, conducting an assessment, hypothesizing and sharing meaning, and facilitating change. In rare instances, these four movements might occur within a single session; in most cases, however, each movement requires multiple sessions.

Forming a Relationship

Over the years, family systems therapists have used a wide range of metaphors to describe the role of the therapist and the therapeutic relationship. The emergence of feminist and postmodern models in therapy has moved the field of family therapy toward more egalitarian, collaborative, cooperative, co-constructing relationships (see T. Andersen, 1987, 1991; H. Anderson, 1993; Anderson & Goolishian, 1992; Epston & White, 1992; Luepnitz, 1988).

The debate Carl Rogers (1980) first introduced to individual therapy in the 1940s has reemerged within family therapy in the form of these questions:

- What expertise does the therapist have in relation to the family, and how should that expertise be used?

- How directive should therapists be in relation to families, and what does that say about the uses of power in therapy?

We believe a multilayered approach to family therapy is best supported by a collaborative therapist–client relationship in which mutual respect, caring, empathy, and a genuine interest in others is primary. In addition, we believe directed actions and enactments are most useful when they are a joint venture of both the therapist and the family.

Therapists begin to form a relationship with clients from the moment of first contact. In most cases, we believe therapists should make their own appointments, answer initial questions clients may have, and give clients a sense of what to expect when they come. This is also a time when counselors can let families know their position on whether all members should be present. Some family therapists will work with any of those members of the family who wish to come; others will only see the family if everyone is a part of the therapy session.

From the moment of first face-to-face contact, good therapeutic relationships start with efforts at making contact with each person present (Satir & Bitter, 2000). Whether it is called *joining, engagement,* or simple *care and concern,* it is the therapist's responsibility to meet each person with openness and warmth. Generally, a focused interest on each family member helps to reduce the anxiety the family may be feeling.

Therapeutic process and structure are part of the therapist's job description. It is important for family members to introduce themselves and to express their concerns, but the therapist should not focus too tightly on content issues. Understanding family process is almost always facilitated by *how* questions. Questions that begin with *what, why, where,* or *when* tend to overemphasize content details (Gladding, 2010).

All change in human systems starts with understanding and accepting things just as they are (Satir & Baldwin, 1983). The family practitioner's skill in communicating that understanding and empathy through active listening lays the foundation for an effective working relationship. Those counselors and therapists who use validation and encouragement, who support family resilience, and who elicit cooperation experience the greatest amount of success in therapy.

Conducting an Assessment

The multiple layers we have noted above provide numerous entry points for conducting family assessments, but beginning counselors and therapists will often find that more formal assessment procedures, such as genograms (McGoldrick et al., 2008), will allow the family structure and stories to be presented in a clearer, more orderly manner. In some cases, formal tests and rating scales (see, for example, Gottman, 1999) also can be useful.

Let's start with the process for co-constructing a genogram. Most family practitioners start with a map of the family that comes to therapy. The parents are listed with their name, age, and date of birth in either a rectangle (for men) or a circle (for women). If there are multiple relationships involved in the parental subsystem, they are generally indicated in chronological order with men listed on the left and women on the right.

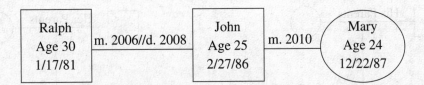

In the above genogram, Mary married Ralph when she was 20 and Ralph was 26; their marriage lasted about 2 years, and then they were divorced. In 2010, Mary and John were married. If John and Mary had decided to live together, but not commit to a formal marriage, the genogram would use a broken line (or dashes) to indicate an informal relationship, like this:

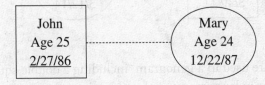

If Ralph had died instead of divorcing Mary, it would look like this:

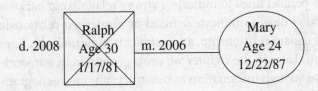

When Mary and John have children, their genogram may look like this:

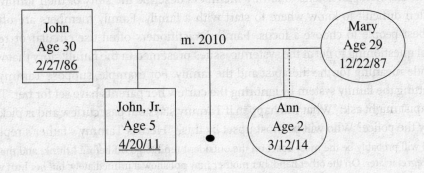

In the above genogram, it is now 2016, and John and Mary have been married for 6 years. When they had been married for 1 year, Mary gave birth to their first child, a boy that they named John Jr. A year later, Mary had a miscarriage, indicated by a black oval at the end of a child line. Two years ago, they adopted (indicated by a solid line next to a broken line) their daughter Ann. If we extend John and Mary's genogram to three generations and if we assume that both John and Mary were only children, the basic three generation family genogram would look like this:

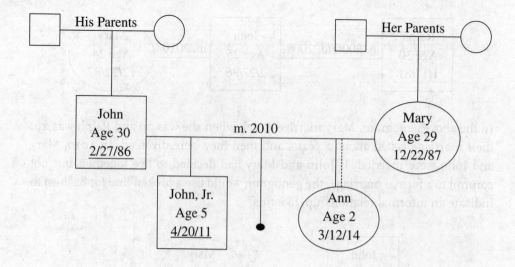

Many other symbols are used in a genogram, including a double square or a double circle to indicate the index person or person on whom the genogram is a focus. An upside down triangle in a square or circle is used to indicate a gay man or a lesbian woman. We shade the bottom half of a square or circle to indicate substance abuse. We use double parallel lines to indicate a strong relationship between two people and three parallel lines to indicate a fused or enmeshed relationship. A dotted line indicates a distant relationship, and conflict is indicated with lines that look like this: /\/\/\/\/\. Later in the chapter we use a genogram in our work with Stan, but you now have enough information to construct your own genogram, and we highly recommend that you get a large piece of paper and get started. It works best if two people interview each other so that you are both drawing the genogram and telling each other the story of your family.

As the therapist listens to family members describe the story of their family, it is often difficult to know where to start with a family. Family members are often the best people to choose a focus. Family practitioners often use circular or relational questioning to get at the systemic issues presented in the family story that will provide meaning for the therapist and the family. For example, suppose Tammy is upsetting the family system by ignoring the curfew her parents have set for her. The therapist might ask: "What will happen if Tammy stays out past curfew and is picked up by the police? Who will be most upset by this?" Here is Tammy's father's reply:

> I will probably be the most upset on the outside. I tend to go off before I think, and then I regret it later. On the other hand, her mother may not show it immediately, but her hurt will stay with her longer, and then she will get mad at me for "letting Tammy off the hook." She will say that Tammy is manipulating me, but I just don't see why we should keep fighting about things. It doesn't do any good. We fight, and Tammy disappears. She wants to run with the big kids, some of whom are in college, over 18, and have no curfew.

From this father's response, the therapist can choose from a number of points of entry into the life of this family. The counselor might choose to work with the anger or guilt expressed by the members and present in their interactions. Sequential patterns were clearly articulated by the father when the family members are trying to resolve conflict and handle problems. His description also includes implied positions on the roles of men, women, and female children in families—as well as developmental issues related to Tammy wanting to be older than she is.

In the assessment process, it is helpful to inquire about family perspectives on issues inherent in each of these layers. In addition to the points of entry we have noted, here are some other questions that might be included in a more detailed assessment.

- What does each family member bring to the session?
- How does each person describe who he or she is?
- What are the goals of each family member? What goals does each family member have for the other people in the family?
- What routines support the daily living of each member of the family?
- Who makes decisions? How are conflicts resolved or problems handled?
- What parts are involved in the most common sequences in the family?
- What is a typical day like?
- Are the parents effective leaders of the family, and is the process of leadership balanced or imbalanced?
- How do the children respond to parental leadership? What are the children's goals in responding the way they do?
- Where is each person in the family in relation to personal biological, cognitive, emotional, and social development?
- Where is the family in the family life cycle, and how are they handling transitions?
- What cultures are in the family backgrounds of each of the family members?
- In what culture or region is the family currently living, and is immigration or migration a recent family experience?
- How do economics, education, ethnicity, religion, race, regional background, gender, sexual orientation, ableness, and age affect family processes—and how is the fit between the family practitioner and the family with regard to these aspects of family life?
- What effects has racism, patriarchy, or heterosexism had on this family and its members?
- What ideas in relation to gender need to be affirmed or challenged?
- Where is this family in the process of change?
- What resources (internal or external) need to be accessed?

Hypothesizing and Sharing Meaning

To hypothesize is to form a set of ideas about people, systems, and situations that focus meaning in a useful way. In family therapy, hypothesizing flows from the ideas and understandings generated in the assessment process. Two questions are germane to the form of hypothesizing one chooses to do: (1) How much faith do the therapist and the family have in the ideas they generate? (2) How much of an influence is the therapist willing to be in the lives of people and families?

Family counselors, like individual therapists, cannot avoid influencing the family and its members. But what kind of influence will the therapist bring to the session? Satir and Bitter (2000) suggest that family therapists cannot be in charge of the people, but they need to be in charge of the process; that is, they own the responsibility for how therapy is conducted. Feminists and social constructionists are, perhaps, the most expressive of their concerns about the misuse of power in therapy. They are joined by multiculturalists, person-centered therapists, Adlerians, and existentialists, to name a few, who have also witnessed the often unconscious imposition of "dominant culture" in therapy. In the early days of family therapy, the mostly male therapists often ignored the effects on family life of patriarchy, poverty, racism, cultural discrimination and marginalization, homo-prejudice, and other societal problems. At the strategic-structural end of the continuum, therapists were more likely to claim a certain expertise in systems work that allowed them to make direct interventions in the enactment of "needed" changes in the family. To counteract therapeutic abuses and what some perceived to be an ongoing misuse of power in therapy, some narrative therapists adopted a *decentered* position in relation to the family (White, 1997, 2007). Like person-centered therapists before them, decentered therapists seek to keep families and family members at the center of the therapeutic process.

It is important for families to be invited into respectful, essentially collaborative dialogues in therapeutic work. The different perspectives discovered in this work tend to coalesce into working hypotheses, and sharing these ideas provides the family with a window into the heart and mind of the therapist as well as themselves. Sharing hypotheses almost immediately invites and invokes feedback from various family members. And it is this feedback that allows the therapist and the family to develop a good fit with each other, which in turn tends to cement a working relationship.

The tentative hypothesizing and sharing process that Dreikurs (1950, 1997) developed is well designed for the kind of collaborative work envisioned here. Dreikurs would use a passionate interest and curiosity to ask questions and gather together the subjective perspectives of family members. Indeed, he would honor the ideas that individuals brought to their joint understanding. When he had an idea that he wanted to share, he would often seek permission for his disclosure:

- I have an idea I would like to share with you. Would you be willing to hear it?
- Could it be that . . .

The value of this way of presenting hypotheses is that it invites families and family members to consider and to engage without giving up their right to discard anything that does not fit. When a suggested idea does not fit, the therapist is then clear about letting it go and letting the family redirect the conversation toward more useful conceptualizations.

Facilitating Change

Facilitating change is what happens when family therapy is viewed as a joint or collaborative process. Techniques are more important to models that see the therapist-as-expert and in charge of *making change happen*. Collaborative approaches require *planning*. "Planning can still include what family therapy has called *techniques* or *interventions*, but with the family's participation" (Breunlin et al., 1997, p. 292). Two of the most common forms for facilitation of change are enactments and assignment of tasks. Both of these processes work best when the family co-constructs them with the therapist—or at least accepts the rationale for their use.

Within the change process, the number of possible outcomes is only limited by the resources available internally and externally to the family. This does not mean, however, that the family practitioner is without a guide for preferred or desired outcomes. In general, the internal parts of family members function best when they are balanced (not polarized) and when the individual experiences personal parts as resources. Being able to think is usually more useful than emotional reactivity; being able to feel is better than not feeling; good contact with others is more rewarding than isolation or self-absorption; and taking reasonable risks in the service of growth and development is more beneficial than stagnation or a retreat into fear.

Further, knowing the goals and purposes for our behaviors, feelings, and interactions tends to give us choices about their use. And understanding the patterns we enact in face-to-face relationships, the ebbs and flows of life, or across generations provide multiple avenues for challenging patterns and the enactment of new possibilities.

FAMILY SYSTEMS THERAPY FROM A MULTICULTURAL PERSPECTIVE

Strengths From a Diversity Perspective

One of the strengths of the systemic perspective in working from a multicultural framework is that many ethnic and cultural groups place great value on the extended family. If therapists are working with an individual from a cultural background that gives special value to including grandparents, aunts, and uncles in the treatment, it is easy to see that family approaches have a distinct advantage over individual therapy. Family therapists can do some excellent networking with members of the extended family.

Within the field of family therapy, Monica McGoldrick has been the most influential leader in the development of both gender and cultural perspectives and frameworks in family practice (see McGoldrick et al., 1991, 2005; McGoldrick, & Hardy, 2008). In many ways, McGoldrick and her colleagues approach families like systems anthropologists. They see each family as a unique culture whose particular characteristics must be understood. Like larger cultural systems, families have a unique language that governs behavior, communication, and even how to feel about and experience life. Families have celebrations and rituals that mark transitions, protect them against outside interference, and connect them to their past as well as to a projected future.

Similarly, families cannot escape the sexism and patriarchy that are inherent in all cultures. The roles for men and women are prescribed in different societies, but in every culture women tend to come out on the short end more often than not. The roles that women as mothers play in the family, in the world of work, and in the community set the model for female children often for generations to come. Because family life is where the roles of women can be most limited, a consideration of gender issues in families is an essential framework for family therapy (McGoldrick et al., 1991). Perhaps the most difficult integration of all is figuring out how to honor different cultures in therapy without supporting marginalization or oppression of women. Toward this end, it is important to remember that there are feminist voices in every culture throughout the world.

Just as differentiation means coming to understand our family well enough to be a part of it—to belong—and also to separate and be our own person, understanding cultures allows therapists and families to appreciate diversity and to contextualize family experiences in relation to the larger cultures. Today, family therapists explore the individual culture of the family, the larger cultures to which the family members belong, and the host culture that dominates the family's life. They look for ways in which culture can both inform and modify family work. Interventions are no longer applied universally, regardless of the cultures involved: rather, they are adapted and even designed to join with the cultural systems.

Shortcomings From a Diversity Perspective

Given the multicultural focus and collaborative approach of family systems therapy, it is difficult to find shortcomings from a diversity perspective. This model of family therapy embraces attitudes, knowledge, and skills that are essential to a multicultural perspective. Perhaps the major concern for non-Western cultures would be with regard to the balance that this model advocates for the individual versus the collective. The process of differentiation occurs in most cultures, but it takes on a different shape due to cultural norms. For instance, a young person may become separate from her parents yet not move out of the house. When ethnic-minority families immigrate to North America, their children often adapt to a Western concept of differentiation. In such cases, the intergenerational process of therapy is appropriate if the therapist is sensitive to the family-of-origin's cultural roots. Although a multilayered approach addresses the notion of togetherness and individuality from a balanced perspective, many non-Western cultures would not embrace a theory that valued individuality above loyalty to family in any form. Nor would non-Western cultures have the same conceptualizations of time or even emotions. Therapists, regardless of their model of therapy, must find ways to enter the family's world and honor the traditions that support the family.

A possible shortcoming of the practice of family therapy involves practitioners who assume Western models of family are universal. Indeed, there are many cultural variations to family structure, processes, and communication. Family therapists are finding ways to broaden their views of individuation, appropriate gender roles, family life cycles, and extended families. Some family therapists focus primarily on the nuclear family, which is based on Western notions, and this could clearly be a shortcoming in working with clients in extended families.

Family Therapy Applied to the Case of Stan

In our work with Stan in this modality, we include examples of forming a relationship and joining, reading Stan's genogram, a multilayered assessment, reframing, boundary setting in therapy, and facilitating change. There are many useful models and ways to work with families; this discussion represents some possible ways to work with Stan from a multilayered perspective.

At an intake interview, a family therapist meets with Stan to explore his issues and concerns and to learn more about him and his life situation. As they talk, the therapist brings an intense interest and curiosity to the interview and wonders out loud about the familial roots of some of Stan's problems. It does not take much of an inquiry to learn that Stan is still very much engaged with his parents and siblings, no matter how difficult these relationships have been for him. This initial conversation involves the development of a genogram of Stan's family of origin (see Figure 14.1). This map will serve both Stan and the therapist as a guide to the people and the processes that influence Stan's life.

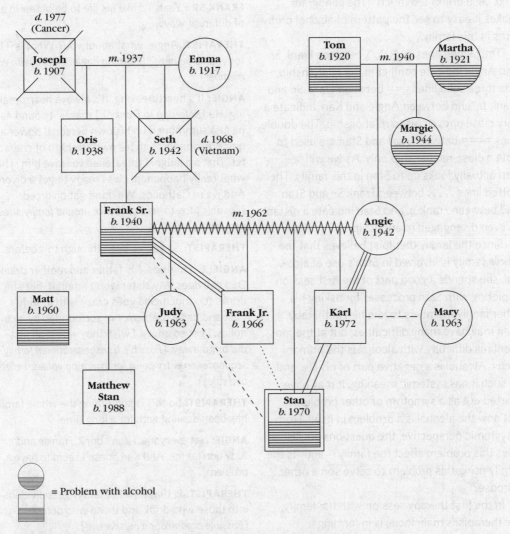

FIGURE 14.1 Three-Generation Genogram of Stan's Family

Stan's genogram is really a family picture, or map, of his family-of-origin system. In this genogram, we learn that Stan's grandparents tend to have lived fairly long lives. Stan's maternal grandparents are both alive. The shaded lower half of their square and circle indicates that each had some problem with alcohol. In the case of Tom, Stan reports that he was an admitted alcoholic who recommitted himself to Christ and found help through Alcoholics Anonymous. Stan's maternal grandmother always drank a little socially and with her husband, but she never considered herself to have a problem. In her later years, however, she seems to secretly use alcohol more and more, and it is a source of distress in her marriage. Stan also knows that Margie drinks a lot, because he has been drinking with his aunt for years. She is the one who gave him his first drink.

Angie, Stan's mother, married Frank Sr. after he had stopped drinking, also with the help of AA. He still goes to meetings. Angie is suspicious of all men around alcohol. She is especially upset with Stan and with Judy's husband, Matt, who "also drinks too much." The genogram makes it easy to see the pattern of alcohol problems in this family.

The jagged lines /\/\/\ between Frank Sr. and Angie indicate conflict in the relationship. The three solid lines === between Frank Sr. and Frank Jr., and between Angie and Karl, indicate a very close or even fused relationship. The double lines ==== between Karl and Stan are used to note a close relationship only. As we will see, Karl actually looks up to Stan in this family. The dotted lines ..... between Frank Sr. and Stan and between Frank Jr. and Stan indicate a distant or even disengaged relationship.

Since the family therapist believes that the whole family is involved in Stan's use of alcohol, she spends a good part of the first session exploring with Stan processes for asking his other family members to join him in therapy. Stan may have many difficulties, but at the moment his difficulty with alcohol is the primary focus. Alcohol is a negative part of his life, and as such it has systemic meaning. It may have started out as a symptom of other problems, but now the alcohol is a problem in itself. From a systemic perspective, the questions are "How does this problem affect the family?" and "Is the family using this problem to serve some other purpose?"

In the first therapy session with the family, the therapist's main focus is in forming a relationship with each of the family members, but even here, a variety of approaches present themselves.

THERAPIST [*to Frank sr.*]: I know coming here was an inconvenience for you, but I want you to know how appreciative I am that you came. Can you tell me what it's like for you to be here? [*Forming a relationship through joining*]

FRANK SR.: Well, I have to tell you that I don't like it much. [*Pause*] Things are a lot different today than they used to be. We didn't have counseling 20 years ago. I had a problem with drinking at one point, but I got over it. I just quit—on my own.

That's what Stan needs to do. He just needs to stop.

THERAPIST: So I'm hearing that life is better for you without alcohol, and you would like Stan's life to be better too. [*Reframing*]

FRANK SR.: Yeah. I'd like his life to be better in a lot of different ways.

THERAPIST: Angie, what about you? What is it like for you to be here? [*Forming a relationship with each member*]

ANGIE: It's heartbreaking. It's always heartbreaking. He [*Referring to Frank Sr.*] makes it sound as if he just summoned up his own personal power and quit drinking through his own strength of character. That's a laugh. I threatened to leave him. That's what really happened. I was ready to get a divorce! And we're Catholics. We don't get divorced. [*Possible face-to-face sequence around family stress and coping*]

THERAPIST: So you've been through this before.

ANGIE: Oh my, yes. My father and mother drank. Dad still does. My sister won't admit it, but she drinks too much. She goes crazy with it. Judy's husband has a problem. I'm surrounded by alcoholics. I get so angry. I wish they would all just die or go away. [*Possible transgenerational family sequence: an entry point for exploring values, beliefs, and rules*]

THERAPIST: So this is something the whole family has been dealing with for a long time.

ANGIE: Not everyone. I don't drink. Frankie and Judy don't drink. And Karl doesn't seem to have a problem.

THERAPIST: Is that how the family gets divided: into those who drink and those who don't? [*Possible organization perspective*]

JUDY: Drinking isn't the only problem we have. It's probably not even the most important.

THERAPIST: Say more about that.

JUDY: Stan has always had it hard. I feel sorry for him. Frankie is clearly Dad's favorite [*Frank Sr. protests, saying he doesn't have favorites*], and things have always come easily for me. And Karl, he gets whatever he wants. He's Mom's favorite. Mom and Dad have fought a lot over the years. None of us have been that happy, but Stan seems to have the worst of it. [*Again, possible sequence and organization perspectives*]

FRANK JR.: As I remember it, Stan gave Dad and Mom a lot to fight about. He was always messing up in one way or another.

THERAPIST: Frankie, when your father was talking earlier, I sensed he had some disappointment about Stan too, but he also wanted to see things work out better for him. Is that true for you too? [*Reframing Frankie's comment, maintaining a focus on new possibilities and new relations that might be developed*]

FRANK JR.: Yes. I would like his life to be better.

The initial part of this counseling session has been devoted to meeting family members, listening intently to the multiple perspectives they present, and reframing Stan's problem into a family desire for a positive outcome. Although there is a long way to go, the seeds of change have already been planted. There is evidence in these early interactions that Stan's problem has a multigenerational context. If this context is explored, family sequences that support and maintain alcohol as a problem may be identified. It is possible to track these interactions and to work toward more congruent communications. Evolving relational, organizational, developmental sequences might be explored as a means of freeing family members for new possibilities in their life together. Among other possibilities still to be explored are perspectives related to gender and culture. If the therapist were just listening to Stan, only one point of view would be evident. In this family session, multiple perspectives and the entire interactive process become clear in a very short time.

As the family interview proceeds, a number of possibilities are presented for consideration. The therapist considers and may structure therapy around any or all of the following possibilities:

1. Stan's parents have not been a well-functioning leadership team for a long time, and both their spousal relationship and their parenting have suffered.
2. The adult siblings need a new opportunity to function together without the influence and distractions continually imposed by the parents.

3. Stan has been reduced to a single part (his alcoholic part), and his description and experience of himself needs to be enlarged—both for his own perspective and in the eyes of others.

A new place for Stan in the family, a better way of relating, and an ability to access "lost" parts of his internal system are all critical to winning his battle with alcohol. As therapy continues, it becomes clear that two separate relational–organization hypotheses must be explored. One is that the spousal relationship has been defined by the problem of alcohol too, and it has not evolved or developed in any kind of positive way over the years. Second, the transgenerational sequences have targeted Stan and assigned him to a fixed role that he has been expected to play that has blocked development past his middle to late adolescence, which was the period in which he started drinking.

Follow-Up: You Continue as Stan's Family Therapist

Use these questions to help you think about how you would counsel Stan from a family systems perspective:

- What unique values do you see in working with Stan from a multilayered, systemic perspective as opposed to an individual therapy approach?
- What internal parts might Stan re-access as he continues in therapy? What parts of him might be polarized?
- Assuming that Stan was successful in getting at least some of his family members to another session, where would you begin? Would you get everyone involved in the sessions? If so, how would you do that?
- What are some specific ways to explore other perspectives with this family?
- What hypotheses are you developing, and how would you share them with the family?
- Are there systemic interventions that you would find hopeful in terms of facilitating change?

SUMMARY AND EVALUATION
Summary

Let's first review the themes that unite the many approaches to family therapy, with particular emphasis on the multilayered approach.

BASIC ASSUMPTION If we hope to work therapeutically with an individual, it is critical to consider him or her within the family system. An individual's problematic behavior grows out of the interactional unit of the family as well as the larger community and societal systems.

FOCUS OF FAMILY THERAPY Most of the family therapies tend to be brief because families who seek professional help typically want resolution of some problematic symptom. Changing the system can stimulate change quickly. In addition to being short-term, solution-focused, and action-oriented, family therapy tends to deal with present interactions. The main focus of family therapy is on here-and-now interactions in the family system. One way in which family therapy differs from many individual therapies is its emphasis on how current family relationships contribute to the development and maintenance of symptoms.

ROLE OF GOALS AND VALUES Specific goals are determined by the practitioner's orientation or by a collaborative process between family and therapist. Global goals include using interventions that enable individuals and the family to change in ways that will reduce their distress. Tied to the question of what goals should guide a therapist's interventions is the question of the therapist's values. Family therapy is grounded on a set of values and theoretical assumptions. Ultimately, every intervention a therapist makes is an expression of a value judgment. It is critical for therapists, regardless of their theoretical orientation, to be aware of their values and monitor how these values influence their practice with families.

HOW FAMILIES CHANGE An integrative approach to the practice of family therapy includes guiding principles that help the therapist organize goals, interactions, observations, and ways to promote change. Some perspectives of family systems therapy focus on perceptual and cognitive change, others deal mainly with changing feelings, and still other theories emphasize behavioral change. Regardless of the perspectives that a family therapist operates from, change needs to happen in relationships, not just within the individual.

TECHNIQUES OF FAMILY THERAPY The intervention strategies therapists employ are best considered in conjunction with their personal characteristics. Bitter (2009b), Goldenberg and Goldenberg (2013), and Nichols (2010, 2013) emphasize that techniques are tools for achieving therapeutic goals but that these intervention strategies do not make a family therapist. Personal characteristics such as respect for clients, compassion, empathy, and sensitivity are human qualities that influence the manner in which techniques are delivered. It is also essential to have a rationale for the techniques that are used, with some sense of the expected outcomes. Faced with meeting the demands of clinical practice, practitioners will need to be flexible in selecting intervention strategies. The central consideration is what is in the best interests of the family.

A multilayered approach to family therapy is more complex than models with a singular focus. At least initially, some of the confidence and clarity that might be gained from a single approach may be lost, but in time the flexibility to change directions is an asset. We have presented a structure for therapy that is useful across models. We have integrated a multilayered process of family therapy in assessment, hypothesizing, and facilitating change. This chapter has described a collaborative process for therapy in which both the family and the therapist share influence according to the needs of the situation.

Contributions of Family Systems Approaches

One of the key contributions of most systemic approaches is that neither the individual nor the family is blamed for a particular dysfunction. The family is empowered through the process of identifying and exploring internal, developmental, and purposeful interactional patterns. At the same time, a systems perspective recognizes that individuals and families are affected by external forces and systems, among them illness, shifting gender patterns, culture, and socioeconomic considerations. If change is to occur in families or with individuals, therapists must be aware of as many systems of influence as possible.

Most of the individual therapies considered in this textbook fail to give a primary focus to the systemic factors influencing the individual. Family therapy redefines the individual as a system embedded within many other systems, which brings an entirely different perspective to assessment and treatment. An advantage to this viewpoint is that an individual is not scapegoated as the "bad person" in the family. Rather than blaming either the "identified patient" or a family, the entire family has an opportunity (a) to examine the multiple perspectives and interactional patterns that characterize the unit and (b) to participate in finding solutions.

Limitations and Criticisms of Family Systems Approaches

In the early days of family therapy, therapists all too often got lost in their consideration of the "system." In adopting the language of systems, therapists began to describe and think of families as being made up of "dyads" and "triads"; as being "functional" or "dysfunctional," "stuck" or "unstuck," and "enmeshed" or "disengaged"; and as displaying "positive" and "negative" outcomes and "feedback loops." It was as if the family was a well-oiled machine or perhaps a computer that occasionally broke down. Just as it was easy to fix a machine without an emotional consideration of the parts involved, some therapists approached family systems work with little concern for the individuals as long as the "whole" of the family "functioned" better. Enactments, ordeals, and paradoxical interventions were often "done to" clients—sometimes even without their knowledge (see Haley, 1963, 1976, 1984; Minuchin & Fishman, 1981; Selvini Palazzolli, Boscolo, Cecchin, & Prata, 1978).

Feminists were perhaps the first, but not the only group to lament the loss of a personal perspective within a systemic framework. As the field moves now toward an integration of individual and systemic frameworks, it is important to reinvest the language of therapy with human emotional terminology that honors the place real people have always held in families. It is our hope that this chapter gives you enough of an introduction to the diverse field of family therapy that you will want to learn more through reading as well as watching the many videotapes currently available.

WHERE TO GO FROM HERE
Other Resources

Psychotherapy.net is a comprehensive resource for students and professionals that offers videos and interviews on family therapy. New video and editorial content is made available monthly. DVDs relevant to this chapter are available at www.psychotherapy.net and include the following:

Aponte, H. (1998). *Structural Family Therapy* (Family Therapy With the Experts Series)

Hardy, K. (1997). *Family Systems Therapy* (Psychotherapy With the Experts Series)

McGoldrick, M. (1996). *The Legacy of Unresolved Loss: A Family Systems Approach*

Schwartz, R. (2001). *Internal Family Systems* (Couples Therapy With the Experts Series)

You may want to consider joining the American Association for Marriage and Family Therapy, which has a student membership category. You must obtain an official application, including the names of at least two Clinical Members from whom the association can request official endorsements. You also need a statement signed by the coordinator or director of a graduate program in marital and family therapy in a regionally accredited educational institution, verifying your current enrollment. Student membership may be held until receipt of a qualifying graduate degree or for a maximum of 5 years. Members receive the *Journal of Marital and Family Therapy,* which is published four times a year, and a subscription to six issues yearly of *The Family Therapy Magazine.* For a copy of the AAMFT Code of Ethics, membership applications, and further information, contact:

American Association for Marriage and Family Therapy
112 South Alfred Street
Alexandria, VA 22314-3061
Telephone: (703) 838-9808
Fax: (703) 838-9805
Website: www.aamft.org

PART 3

Integration and Application

An Integrative Perspective

INTRODUCTION

This chapter will help you think about areas of convergence and divergence among the II therapeutic systems covered in this book. Although these approaches all have some goals in common, they have many differences when it comes to the best route to achieve these goals. Some therapies call for an active and directive stance on the therapist's part, and others place value on clients being the active agent. Some therapies focus on experiencing *feelings,* others stress identifying *cognitive patterns,* and still others concentrate on actual *behavior.* The key task is to find ways to integrate certain features of each of these approaches so that you can work with clients on all three levels of human experience.

The field of psychotherapy is characterized by a diverse range of specialized models. With all this diversity, is there any hope that a practitioner can develop skills in all of the existing techniques? How does a student decide which theories are most relevant to practice? Looking for commonalities among the systems of psychotherapy is relatively new (Norcross & Beutler, 2011). Practitioners have been battling over the "best" way to bring about personality change dating back to the work of Freud. For decades, counselors resisted integration, often to the point of denying the validity of alternative theories and of ignoring effective methods from other theoretical schools. The early history of counseling is full of theoretical wars.

Since the early 1980s, psychotherapy integration has developed into a clearly delineated field. It is now an established and respected movement that is based on combining the best of differing orientations so that more complete theoretical models can be articulated and more efficient treatments developed (Goldfried, Pachankis, & Bell, 2005). The Society for the Exploration of Psychotherapy Integration, formed in 1983, is an international organization whose members are professionals working toward the development of therapeutic approaches that transcend single theoretical orientations. As the field of psychotherapy has matured, the concept of integration has emerged as a mainstay (Norcross & Beutler, 2011).

In this chapter I consider the advantages of developing an integrative perspective for counseling practice. I also present a framework to help you begin to integrate concepts and techniques from various approaches. As you read, start to formulate your own personal perspective for counseling. Look for ways to synthesize diverse elements from different theoretical perspectives. As much as possible, be alert to how these systems can function in harmony.

 See the video program for Chapter 15, *DVD for Theory and Practice of Counseling and Psychotherapy: The Case of Stan and Lecturettes.* **I suggest that you view the brief lecture for each chapter prior to reading the chapter.**

THE MOVEMENT TOWARD PSYCHOTHERAPY INTEGRATION

A large number of therapists identify themselves as "eclectic," and this category covers a broad range of practice. At its worst, eclectic practice consists of haphazardly picking techniques without any overall theoretical rationale. This is known as **syncretism,** wherein the practitioner, lacking in knowledge and skill in selecting interventions, looks for anything that seems to work, often making little attempt to determine whether the therapeutic procedures are indeed effective. Such an uncritical and unsystematic combination of techniques is no better than a narrow and dogmatic orthodoxy. This pulling of techniques from many sources without a sound rationale results in syncretistic confusion (Lazarus, 1996b; Norcross & Beutler, 2011).

Pathways Toward Psychotherapy Integration

Psychotherapy integration is best characterized by attempts to look beyond and across the confines of single-school approaches to see what can be learned from other perspectives and how clients can benefit from a variety of ways of conducting therapy. The majority of psychotherapists do not claim allegiance to a particular therapeutic school but prefer, instead, some form of integration (Norcross, 2005; Norcross & Beutler, 2011). In a survey conducted by the *Psychotherapy Networker* (2007), only 4.2% of respondents identified themselves as being aligned with one therapy model exclusively. The remaining 95.8% claimed to be *integrative*, meaning they combined a variety of methods or approaches in their counseling practice.

The integrative approach is characterized by openness to various ways of integrating diverse theories and techniques, and there is a decided preference for the term *integrative* over *eclectic* (Norcross, Karpiak, & Lister, 2005). Although different terms are sometimes used—eclecticism, integration, convergence, and rapprochement—the goals are very similar. The ultimate goal of integration is to enhance the efficiency and applicability of psychotherapy. Norcross and Beutler (2011) and Stricker (2010) describe four of the most common pathways toward the integration of psychotherapies: *technical integration, theoretical integration, assimilative integration*, and *common factors approach*. All of these approaches to integration look beyond the restrictions of single approaches, but they do so in distinctive ways.

Technical integration aims at selecting the best treatment techniques for the individual and the problem. It tends to focus on differences, chooses from many approaches, and is a collection of techniques. This path calls for using techniques from different schools without necessarily subscribing to the theoretical positions that spawned them. For those who practice from the perspective of technical integration, there is no necessary connection between conceptual foundations and techniques. One of the best-known forms of technical integration, which he refers to as *technical eclecticism*, is Lazarus's (1997a) *multimodal therapy* (see Chapter 9). Multimodal therapists borrow from many other therapeutic models, using techniques that have been demonstrated to be effective in dealing with specific clinical problems. Whenever feasible, multimodal therapists employ empirically supported techniques (Lazarus, 2008a).

In contrast, **theoretical integration** refers to a conceptual or theoretical creation beyond a mere blending of techniques. This route has the goal of producing a conceptual framework that synthesizes the best aspects of two or more theoretical approaches under the assumption that the outcome will be richer than either theory alone. This approach emphasizes integrating the underlying theories of therapy along with techniques from each. Examples of this form of integration are *dialectical behavior therapy* (DBT) and *acceptance and commitment therapy* (ACT), both of which were described in Chapter 9. *Emotion-focused therapy* (EFT), which is informed by the role of emotion in psychotherapeutic change, also can be considered a form of theoretical integration. Greenberg (2011), a key figure of the development of EFT, conceptualizes the model as an empirically supported, integrative, experiential approach to treatment. EFT synthesizes concepts of person-centered therapy, Gestalt therapy, experiential therapy, and existential therapy, viewed through the lens of modern cognitive and emotion theory.

The **assimilative integration** approach is grounded in a particular school of psychotherapy, along with an openness to selectively incorporate practices from other therapeutic approaches. Assimilative integration combines the advantages of a single coherent theoretical system with the flexibility of a variety of interventions from multiple systems. An example of this form of integration is *mindfulness-based cognitive therapy* (MBCT), which integrates aspects of cognitive therapy and mindfulness-based stress reduction procedures. As you may recall from Chapter 9, MBCT is a comprehensive integration of the principles and skills of mindfulness applied to the treatment of depression (Segal, Williams, & Teasdale, 2002).

The **common factors approach** searches for common elements across different theoretical systems. Despite many differences among the theories, a recognizable core of counseling practice is composed of nonspecific variables common to all therapies. Lambert (2011) concludes that common factors can be a basis for psychotherapy integration:

> The common factors explanation for the general equivalence of diverse therapeutic interventions has resulted in the dominance of integrative practice in routine care by implying that the dogmatic advocacy of a particular theoretical school is not supported by research. Research also suggests that *common factors* can become the focal point for integration of seemingly diverse therapy techniques. (p. 314)

Some of these common factors include empathic listening, developing a working alliance, opportunity for catharsis, practicing new behaviors, positive expectations of clients, working through one's own conflicts, understanding interpersonal and intrapersonal dynamics, and learning to be self-reflective about one's work (Norcross & Beutler, 2011; Prochaska & Norcross, 2010). Other common factors that have been shown to be curative include support, warmth, feedback, reassurance, and credibility (Lambert, 2011). These common factors are thought to be at least as important in accounting for therapeutic outcomes as the unique factors that differentiate one theory from another. Among the approaches to psychotherapy integration, the common factors approach has the strongest empirical support (Duncan, Miller, Wampold, & Hubble, 2010).

Of all of the common factors investigated in psychotherapy, none has received more attention and confirmation than a facilitative therapeutic relationship (Lambert, 2011). The importance of the therapeutic alliance is a well-established critical component of effective therapy, and research confirms that the client–therapist relationship is central to therapeutic change.

Advantages of Psychotherapy Integration
One reason for the movement toward psychotherapy integration is the recognition that no single theory is comprehensive enough to account for the complexities

of human behavior, especially when the range of client types and their specific problems are taken into consideration. Because no one theory contains all the truth, and because no single set of counseling techniques is always effective in working with diverse client populations, integrative approaches hold promise for counseling practice. Norcross and Wampold (2011b) maintain that effective clinical practice requires a flexible and integrative perspective. Psychotherapy should be flexibly tailored to the unique needs and contexts of the individual client. Norcross and Wampold contend that using an identical therapy relationship style and treatment method for all clients is inappropriate and can be unethical.

The 11 systems discussed in this book have evolved in the direction of broadening their theoretical and practical bases and have become less restrictive in their focus. Many practitioners who claim allegiance to a particular system of therapy are expanding their theoretical outlook and developing a wider range of therapeutic techniques to fit a more diverse population of clients. There is a growing recognition that psychotherapy can be most effective when contributions from various approaches are integrated (Goldfried, Glass, & Arnkoff, 2011). Although to date the bulk of psychotherapy integration has been based on theoretical and clinical foundations, Goldfried and colleagues suggest that evidence-based practice will increasingly become the organizing force for integration. Empirical pragmatism, not theory, will be the integrative theme of the 21st century.

Practitioners who are open to an integrative perspective will find that several theories play a crucial role in their personal counseling approach. Each theory has its unique contributions and its own domain of expertise. By accepting that each theory has strengths and weaknesses and is, by definition, "different" from the others, practitioners have some basis to begin developing a theory that fits for them and their clients. It takes considerable time to learn the various theories in depth. It is not realistic for any of us to expect that we can integrate all the theories. Instead, integration of some aspects of some of the theories is a more realistic goal. Developing an integrative perspective is a lifelong endeavor that is refined with clinical experience, reflection, reading, and discourse with colleagues.

Integration of Multicultural Issues in Counseling

Multiculturalism is a reality that cannot be ignored by practitioners if they hope to meet the needs of diverse client groups. I believe current theories, to varying degrees, can and should be expanded to incorporate a multicultural dimension. I have consistently pointed out that if contemporary theories do not account for the cultural dimension, they will have limited applicability in working with diverse client populations. For some theories, this transition is easier than for others.

Clients can be harmed if they are expected to fit all the specifications of a given theory, whether or not the values espoused by the theory are consistent with their own cultural values. Rather than stretching the client to fit the dimensions of a single theory, practitioners need to tailor their theory and practice to fit the unique needs of the client. This calls for counselors to possess knowledge of various cultures, to be aware of their own cultural heritage, and to have skills to assist a wide spectrum of clients in dealing with the realities of their culture. Psychotherapy integration stresses tailoring interventions to the individual client rather than to an overarching theory, making this approach particularly well suited to considering cultural factors and the unique perspective of each client. Comas-Diaz (2011) asserts that cultural competence enables counselors to work effectively in most clinical settings. Practitioners demonstrate their cultural competence by becoming aware of their own and their clients' worldviews, and by being able to use culturally appropriate interventions to reflect their cultural beliefs, knowledge, and skills. She adds:

> Culturally competent therapists develop the capacities to value diversity and manage the dynamics of difference. They also acquire and incorporate cultural knowledge into their interventions, plus adapt to diversity and the cultural contexts of their clients. (p. 251)

This is a good time to review the discussion of the culturally skilled counselor in Chapter 2 and to consult Tables 15.7 and 15.8, which appear later in this chapter.

In your role as a counselor, you need to be able to assess the special needs of clients. Depending on the client's ethnicity and culture and on the concerns that bring this person to counseling, you are challenged to develop flexibility in utilizing an array of therapeutic strategies. Some clients will need more direction, and even advice. Others will be very hesitant in talking about themselves in personal ways, especially during the early phase of the counseling process. What you may see as resistance could be the client's response to years of cultural conditioning and respect for certain values and traditions. Basically, it comes down to your familiarity with a variety of theoretical approaches and your ability to employ and adapt your techniques to fit the person-in-the-environment. It is not enough to merely assist your clients in gaining insight, expressing suppressed emotions, or making certain behavioral changes. The challenge is to find practical strategies for adapting the techniques you have developed to enable clients to examine the impact their culture continues to have on their lives and to make decisions about what, if anything, they want to change.

Being an effective counselor involves reflecting on how your own culture influences you and your interventions in your counseling practice. This awareness is critical in becoming more sensitive to the cultural backgrounds of the clients who seek your help. Using an integrative perspective, therapists can encompass social, cultural, spiritual, and political dimensions in their work with clients.

Integration of Spirituality and Religion in Counseling

The counseling process can help clients gain insight into the ways their core beliefs and values are reflected in their behavior. Current interest in spiritual and religious beliefs has implications for how such beliefs might be incorporated in therapeutic relationships (Young & Cashwell, 2011a; Frame, 2003). Survey data from members of both the American Psychological Association and the American Counseling Association indicate that spiritual and religious matters are therapeutically relevant, ethically appropriate, and potentially significant topics for the practice of counseling in secular settings (Delaney, Miller, & Bisono, 2007; Young, Wiggins-Frame, & Cashwell, 2007).

Worthington (2011) asserts that the increasing openness of therapists to clients' spiritual and religious concerns and interests has been fueled by the multicultural evolution. The emphasis on multiculturalism has empowered people to define themselves from a cultural perspective, which includes their spiritual, religious, and ethnic contexts.

Clients who are experiencing a crisis situation may find a source of comfort, support, and strength in drawing upon their spiritual resources. For some clients spirituality entails embracing a religion, which can have many different meanings. Other clients value spirituality, yet do not have any ties to a formal religion. Whatever one's particular view of spirituality, it is a force that can help the individual to find a purpose (or purposes) for living. Spirituality or religious beliefs can be a major sustaining power that supports clients when all else fails. Other clients may be affected by depression and a sense of worthlessness due to guilt, anger, or sadness created by their unexamined acceptance of spiritual or religious dogma. Counselors must remain open and nonjudgmental in conversations about religion or spirituality. Furthermore, counselors cannot ignore a client's spiritual and religious perspectives if they want to practice in a culturally sensitive and ethical manner (Young & Cashwell, 2011a; 2011b).

COMMON GOALS In some ways spirituality and counseling have similar goals. Both emphasize learning to accept oneself, forgiving others and oneself, learning to love oneself and others, admitting one's shortcomings, accepting personal responsibility, letting go of hurts and resentments, dealing with guilt, and learning to let go of self-destructive patterns of thinking, feeling, and acting.

Spiritual/religious values have a major part to play in human life and struggles, which means that exploring these values has a great deal to do with providing solutions for clients' struggles. Because spiritual and therapeutic paths converge in some ways, integration is possible, and dealing with a client's spirituality will often enhance the therapy process. Themes that have healing influences include loving, caring, learning to listen with compassion, challenging clients' basic life assumptions, accepting human imperfection, and going outside of self-oriented interests (social interest). Both religion and counseling help people ponder questions of "Who am I?" and "What is the meaning of my life?" At their best, both counseling and religion can foster healing.

IMPLICATIONS FOR ASSESSMENT AND TREATMENT Traditionally, when clients come to a therapist with a problem, the therapist explores all the factors that contributed to the development of the problem. A background of involvement in religion can be part of clients' history, and thus it can be a part of the intake assessment and can be explored in counseling sessions. Frame (2003) presents many reasons for including spirituality in the assessment process: understanding clients' worldviews and the contexts in which they live, assisting clients in grappling with questions regarding the purpose of their lives and what they most value, exploring religion and spirituality as client resources, and uncovering religious and spiritual problems. This information will assist the therapist in choosing appropriate interventions. Young and Cashwell (2011a) maintain that counselors must assess clients' spiritual or religious beliefs if they may be exacerbating clients' psychological problems.

YOUR ROLE AS A COUNSELOR It is critical that counselors not be judgmental when it comes to their clients' beliefs and that they create an inviting and safe climate for clients to explore their values and beliefs. There are many paths toward fulfilling spiritual needs, and it is not your role as a counselor to prescribe any particular pathway. By conducting a thorough assessment on a client's background, you will obtain many clues regarding personal themes for potential exploration. If you remain finely tuned to clients' stories and to the purpose for which they sought therapy, clients' concerns about spiritual or religious values, beliefs, and practices will surface.

To assist clients in clarifying their values and in making their own decisions requires that you have a clear sense of your own spiritual perspective. Spiritual self-awareness is the basis for competence in dealing with the worldviews of your clients (Hagedorn & Moorhead, 2011). Worthington (2011) reminds therapists of their responsibility to provide informed and sensitive care to all clients, whether or not they embrace a spiritual or religious worldview:

> Given the social changes and openness of both clients and therapists to religion and spirituality, it is a reasonable supposition that spirituality tailored therapies will increase to meet clients' needs. There will also need to be continuing sensitivity to clients who do not want to attend religiously or spiritually tailored therapy. (p. 541)

Robertson and Young (2011) stress the need to work with a client's spiritual and religious concerns, and state that "failure to address these issues, may, in some cases, be incompetent or unethical practice" (p. 38).

If you are to effectively serve diverse client populations, it is essential that you pay attention to your training and competence in addressing spiritual and religious concerns your clients bring to therapy. Ethically, it is important to monitor yourself for subtle ways that you might be inclined to influence clients to embrace a spiritual perspective or to give up certain religious beliefs that you think are no longer functional for them. It is important to keep in mind that clients should determine the specific values they want to retain, replace, or modify.

From my vantage point, the emphasis on spirituality will continue to be important in counseling practice, which makes it imperative that you prepare yourself to work competently with the spiritual and religious concerns that your clients bring up. For further reading on the topic of integrating spirituality and religion into counseling, I highly recommend *Integrating Spirituality and Religion into Counseling: A Guide to Competent Practice* (Cashwell & Young, 2011).

The Challenge of Developing an Integrative Perspective

A survey of approaches to counseling and psychotherapy reveals that no common philosophy unifies them. Many of the theories have different basic philosophies and views of human nature (Table 15.1). As the postmodern therapists remind us, our philosophical assumptions are important because they influence which "reality" we perceive, and they direct our attention to the variables that we are "set" to see. A word of caution, then: Beware of subscribing exclusively to any one view of human nature. Remain open and selectively incorporate a framework for counseling that is consistent with your own personality and your belief system.

TABLE 15.1 The Basic Philosophies

Psychoanalytic therapy	Human beings are basically determined by psychic energy and by early experiences. Unconscious motives and conflicts are central in present behavior. Early development is of critical importance because later personality problems have their roots in repressed childhood conflicts.
Adlerian therapy	Humans are motivated by social interest, by striving toward goals, by inferiority and superiority, and by dealing with the tasks of life. Emphasis is on the individual's positive capacities to live in society cooperatively. People have the capacity to interpret, influence, and create events. Each person at an early age creates a unique style of life, which tends to remain relatively constant throughout life.
Existential therapy	The central focus is on the nature of the human condition, which includes a capacity for self-awareness, freedom of choice to decide one's fate, responsibility, anxiety, the search for meaning, being alone and being in relation with others, striving for authenticity, and facing living and dying.
Person-centered therapy	Positive view of people; we have an inclination toward becoming fully functioning. In the context of the therapeutic relationship, the client experiences feelings that were previously denied to awareness. The client moves toward increased awareness, spontaneity, trust in self, and inner-directedness.
Gestalt therapy	The person strives for wholeness and integration of thinking, feeling, and behaving. Some key concepts include contact with self and others, contact boundaries, and awareness. The view is nondeterministic in that the person is viewed as having the capacity to recognize how earlier influences are related to present difficulties. As an experiential approach, it is grounded in the here and now and emphasizes awareness, personal choice, and responsibility.
Behavior therapy	Behavior is the product of learning. We are both the product and the producer of the environment. Traditional behavior therapy is based on classical and operant principles. Contemporary behavior therapy has branched out in many directions.
Cognitive behavior therapy	Individuals tend to incorporate faulty thinking, which leads to emotional and behavioral disturbances. Cognitions are the major determinants of how we feel and act. Therapy is primarily oriented toward cognition and behavior, and it stresses the role of thinking, deciding, questioning, doing, and redeciding. This is a psychoeducational model, which emphasizes therapy as a learning process, including acquiring and practicing new skills, learning new ways of thinking, and acquiring more effective ways of coping with problems.

Reality therapy	Based on choice theory, this approach assumes that we need quality relationships to be happy. Psychological problems are the result of our resisting the control by others or of our attempt to control others. Choice theory is an explanation of human nature and how to best achieve satisfying interpersonal relationships.
Feminist therapy	Feminists criticize many traditional theories to the degree that they are based on gender-biased concepts, such as being androcentric, gendercentric, ethnocentric, heterosexist, and intrapsychic. The constructs of feminist therapy include being gender fair, flexible, interactionist, and life-span-oriented. Gender and power are at the heart of feminist therapy. This is a systems approach that recognizes the cultural, social, and political factors that contribute to an individual's problems.
Postmodern approaches	Based on the premise that there are multiple realities and multiple truths, postmodern therapies reject the idea that reality is external and can be grasped. People create meaning in their lives through conversations with others. The postmodern approaches avoid pathologizing clients, take a dim view of diagnosis, avoid searching for underlying causes of problems, and place a high value on discovering clients' strengths and resources. Rather than talking about problems, the focus of therapy is on creating solutions in the present and the future.
Family systems therapy	The family is viewed from an interactive and systemic perspective. Clients are connected to a living system; a change in one part of the system will result in a change in other parts. The family provides the context for understanding how individuals function in relationship to others and how they behave. Treatment deals with the family unit. An individual's dysfunctional behavior grows out of the interactional unit of the family and out of larger systems as well.

Despite the divergences in the various theories, creative syntheses among some models are possible. For example, an existential orientation does not necessarily preclude using techniques drawn from behavior therapy or from some of the cognitive theories. Each point of view offers a perspective for helping clients in their search for self. I encourage you to study all the major theories and to remain open to what you might take from the various orientations as a basis for an integrative perspective that will guide your practice.

In developing a personal integrative perspective, it is important to be alert to the problem of attempting to mix theories with incompatible underlying assumptions. Lazarus (1995) asks, "How is it possible to blend two systems that rest on totally different assumptions about the meaning, origins, development, maintenance, significance, and management of problems?" (p. 156). An advocate of *technical eclecticism*, Lazarus (2008b) has consistently emphasized that a blend of different theories is likely to result in confusion and argued against the notion of theoretical integration. He adds that basic concepts that may seem compatible often are, upon closer scrutiny, quite irreconcilable (see Table 15.2). Lazarus stresses that psychotherapy integration does not have to rely on a theoretical amalgamation. Clinicians can be *technically eclectic* (or technically integrative) in that they can select methods from any discipline without necessarily endorsing any of the theories that spawned them.

TABLE 15.2 Key Concepts

Psychoanalytic therapy	Normal personality development is based on successful resolution and integration of psychosexual stages of development. Faulty personality development is the result of inadequate resolution of some specific stage. Anxiety is a result of repression of basic conflicts. Unconscious processes are centrally related to current behavior.
Adlerian therapy	Key concepts include the unity of personality, the need to view people from their subjective perspective, and the importance of life goals that give direction to behavior. People are motivated by social interest and by finding goals to give life meaning. Other key concepts are striving for significance and superiority, developing a unique lifestyle, and understanding the family constellation. Therapy is a matter of providing encouragement and assisting clients in changing their cognitive perspective and behavior.
Existential therapy	Essentially an experiential approach to counseling rather than a firm theoretical model, it stresses core human conditions. Interest is on the present and on what one is becoming. The approach has a future orientation and stresses self-awareness before action.
Person-centered therapy	The client has the potential to become aware of problems and the means to resolve them. Faith is placed in the client's capacity for self-direction. Mental health is a congruence of ideal self and real self. Maladjustment is the result of a discrepancy between what one wants to be and what one is. In therapy attention is given to the present moment and on experiencing and expressing feelings.
Gestalt therapy	Emphasis is on the "what" and "how" of experiencing in the here and now to help clients accept all aspects of themselves. Key concepts include holism, figure-formation process, awareness, unfinished business and avoidance, contact, and energy.
Behavior therapy	Focus is on overt behavior, precision in specifying goals of treatment, development of specific treatment plans, and objective evaluation of therapy outcomes. Present behavior is given attention. Therapy is based on the principles of learning theory. Normal behavior is learned through reinforcement and imitation. Abnormal behavior is the result of faulty learning.

Cognitive behavior therapy	Although psychological problems may be rooted in childhood, they are reinforced by present ways of thinking. A person's belief system is the primary cause of disorders. Internal dialogue plays a central role in one's behavior. Clients focus on examining faulty assumptions and misconceptions and on replacing these with effective beliefs.
Reality therapy	The basic focus is on what clients are doing and how to get them to evaluate whether their present actions are working for them. People are mainly motivated to satisfy their needs, especially the need for significant relationships. The approach rejects the medical model, the notion of transference, the unconscious, and dwelling on one's past.
Feminist therapy	Core principles of feminist therapy are that the personal is political, therapists have a commitment to social change, women's voices and ways of knowing are valued and women's experiences are honored, the counseling relationship is egalitarian, therapy focuses on strengths and a reformulated definition of psychological distress, and all types of oppression are recognized.
Postmodern approaches	Therapy tends to be brief and addresses the present and the future. The person is not the problem; the problem is the problem. The emphasis is on externalizing the problem and looking for exceptions to the problem. Therapy consists of a collaborative dialogue in which the therapist and the client co-create solutions. By identifying instances when the problem did not exist, clients can create new meanings for themselves and fashion a new life story.
Family systems therapy	Focus is on communication patterns within a family, both verbal and nonverbal. Problems in relationships are likely to be passed on from generation to generation. Key concepts vary depending on specific orientation but include differentiation, triangles, power coalitions, family-of-origin dynamics, functional versus dysfunctional interaction patterns, and dealing with here-and-now interactions. The present is more important than exploring past experiences.

By remaining theoretically consistent, but technically integrative, practitioners can spell out precisely the interventions they will employ with various clients, as well as the means by which they will select these procedures. Lazarus (1997a, 1997b) contends that therapists who hope to be effective with a wide range of problems and with different client populations must be flexible and versatile. Therapists should ask these basic questions when devising a treatment program: "What works for whom under which particular circumstances?" "Why are some procedures helpful and others unhelpful?" "What can be done to ensure long-term success and positive follow-ups?" Lazarus (1993) believes some clients respond to warm, informal counselors but that others want more formal counselors. Some clients work well with therapists who are quiet and nonforceful, whereas others work best with directive and outgoing therapists. Furthermore, the same client may respond favorably to various therapeutic techniques and styles at different times.

Lazarus (1996a) mentions the value of a therapist assuming an active role in blending a flexible repertoire of relationship styles with a wide range of techniques as a way to enhance therapeutic outcomes. He maintains that a skilled therapist is able to determine when to be confrontational, when to be directive, when to allow the client to struggle, when to be formal or informal, when to self-disclose or remain anonymous, and when to be gentle or tough. Lazarus (1993) asserts that relationships of choice are at least as important as techniques of choice. (For a review of multimodal procedures and their rationale, see Chapter 9.)

One of the challenges you will face as a counselor is to deliver therapeutic services in a brief, comprehensive, effective, and flexible way. Many of the theoretical orientations addressed in this book can be applied to brief forms of therapy. One of the driving forces of the psychotherapy integration movement has been the increase of brief therapies and the pressures to do more for a variety of client populations within the limitations of 6 to 20 sessions. Most forms of short-term psychotherapy are active in nature, collaborative in relationship, and integrative in orientation (Norcross & Beutler, 2011).

The main goal of brief therapy is to help clients resolve problems and to move forward as quickly as possible. Some of the defining characteristics of brief therapy include the following (Hoyt, 2011):

- Rapid working alliance between therapist and client
- Clear specification of achievable treatment goals
- Clear division of responsibilities between client and therapist, with active client participation and a high level of therapist activity
- Emphasis on client's strengths, competencies, and adaptive capacities
- Expectation that change is possible and realistic
- Here-and-now orientation with a primary focus on current functioning in thinking, feeling, and behaving
- Specific, integrated, and eclectic techniques
- Time sensitive, including making the most of each session and ending therapy as soon as possible

The core task is for integrative practitioners to learn how to rapidly and systematically identify problems, create a collaborative relationship with clients, and intervene with a range of specific methods. Hoyt puts the challenge to therapists concisely: "The simple truth is that most therapy is brief therapy and will be increasingly so; for the sake of our patients and our profession, we should learn to practice it well" (p. 419).

An integrative perspective at its best entails a *systematic integration* of underlying principles and methods common to a range of therapeutic approaches. The strengths of systematic integration are based on its ability to be taught, replicated, and evaluated (Norcross & Beutler, 2011). To develop this kind of integration, you will eventually need to be thoroughly conversant with a number of theories, be open to the idea that these theories can be connected in some ways, and be willing to continually test your hypotheses to determine how well they are working. Developing a systematic integrative perspective is the product of a great deal of study, clinical practice, research, and theorizing.

ISSUES RELATED TO THE THERAPEUTIC PROCESS

Therapeutic Goals

The goals of counseling are almost as diverse as are the theoretical approaches. Some goals include restructuring the personality, uncovering the unconscious, creating social interest, finding meaning in life, curing an emotional disturbance, examining old decisions and making new ones, developing trust in oneself, becoming more self-actualizing, reducing anxiety, reducing maladaptive behavior and learning adaptive patterns, becoming grounded in the present moment, managing intense emotions, gaining more effective control of one's life, and reauthoring the story of one's life (Table 15.3). Is there a common denominator in this range of goals?

TABLE 15.3 Goals of Therapy

Psychoanalytic therapy	To make the unconscious conscious. To reconstruct the basic personality. To assist clients in reliving earlier experiences and working through repressed conflicts. To achieve intellectual and emotional awareness.
Adlerian therapy	To challenge clients' basic premises and life goals. To offer encouragement so individuals can develop socially useful goals and increase social interest. To develop the client's sense of belonging.
Existential therapy	To help people see that they are free and to become aware of their possibilities. To challenge them to recognize that they are responsible for events that they formerly thought were happening to them. To identify factors that block freedom.
Person-centered therapy	To provide a safe climate conducive to clients' self-exploration, so that they can recognize blocks to growth and can experience aspects of self that were formerly denied or distorted. To enable them to move toward openness, greater trust in self, willingness to be a process, and increased spontaneity and aliveness. To find meaning in life and to experience life fully. To become more self-directed.
Gestalt therapy	To assist clients in gaining awareness of moment-to-moment experiencing and to expand the capacity to make choices. To foster integration of the self.

Behavior therapy	To eliminate maladaptive behaviors and learn more effective behaviors. To identify factors that influence behavior and find out what can be done about problematic behavior. To encourage clients to take an active and collaborative role in clearly setting treatment goals and evaluating how well these goals are being met.
Cognitive behavior therapy	To teach clients to confront faulty beliefs with contradictory evidence that they gather and evaluate. To help clients seek out their faulty beliefs and minimize them. To become aware of automatic thoughts and to change them.
Reality therapy	To help people become more effective in meeting all of their psychological needs. To enable clients to get reconnected with the people they have chosen to put into their quality worlds and teach clients choice theory.
Feminist therapy	To bring about transformation both in the individual client and in society. To assist clients in recognizing, claiming, and using their personal power to free themselves from the limitations of gender-role socialization. To confront all forms of institutional policies that discriminate or oppress on any basis.
Postmodern approaches	To change the way clients view problems and what they can do about these concerns. To collaboratively establish specific, clear, concrete, realistic, and observable goals leading to increased positive change. To help clients create a self-identity grounded on competence and resourcefulness so they can resolve present and future concerns. To assist clients in viewing their lives in positive ways, rather than being problem saturated.
Family systems therapy	To help family members gain awareness of patterns of relationships that are not working well and to create new ways of interacting.

This diversity can be simplified by considering the degree of generality or specificity of goals. Goals exist on a continuum from specific, concrete, and short term on one end, to general, global, and long term on the other. The cognitive behavioral approaches stress the former; the relationship-oriented therapies tend to stress the latter. The goals at opposite ends of the continuum are not necessarily contradictory; it is a matter of how specifically they are defined.

Therapist's Function and Role

In working toward an integrative perspective, ask yourself these questions:

- How do the counselor's functions change depending on the stage of the counseling process?
- Does the therapist maintain a basic role, or does this role vary in accordance with the characteristics of the client?

- How does the counselor determine how active and directive to be?
- How is structuring handled as the course of therapy progresses?
- What is the optimum balance of responsibility in the client–therapist relationship?
- What is the most effective way to monitor the therapeutic alliance?
- What, when, and how much does the counselor self-disclose?

As you saw through your study of the 11 therapeutic approaches, a central issue of each system is the degree to which the therapist exercises control over clients' behavior both during and outside the session. Cognitive behavior therapists and reality therapists, for example, operate within a present-centered, directive, didactic, structured, and psychoeducational context. As a collaborative endeavor, they frequently design homework assignments to assist clients in practicing new behavior outside therapy sessions. In contrast, person-centered therapists operate with a much looser and less defined structure. Solution-focused and narrative therapists view the client as the expert on his or her own life; they assist clients in reflection outside of the session that might result in self-directed change. Although they are active questioners, they are not prescriptive in their practice.

Structuring depends on the particular client and the specific circumstances he or she brings to the therapy situation. From my perspective, clear structure is most essential during the early phase of counseling because it encourages the client to talk about the problems that led to seeking therapy. In a collaborative way, it is useful for both counselor and client to make some initial assessment that can provide a focus for the therapy process. As soon as possible, the client should be given a significant share of the responsibility for deciding on the content and agenda of the sessions. From early in the therapy process the client can be empowered if the counselor expects the client to become an active participant in the process.

Client's Experience in Therapy

Most clients share some degree of suffering, pain, or at least discontent. There is a discrepancy between how they would like to be and how they are. Some individuals initiate therapy because they hope to cure a specific symptom or set of symptoms. They want to get rid of migraine headaches, free themselves of chronic anxiety attacks, lose weight, or get relief from depression. They may have conflicting feelings and reactions, may struggle with low self-esteem, or may have limited information and skills. Many seek to resolve conflicts in their close relationships. I believe people are increasingly entering therapy with existential problems. Their complaints often relate to the these existential issues: a sense of emptiness, meaninglessness in life, routine ways of living, unsatisfying personal relationships, anxiety over uncertainty, a lack of intense feelings, and a loss of their sense of self.

The initial expectation of many clients is that results will come quickly. They often have great hope for major changes in their life and rely on direction from the therapist. As therapy progresses, clients discover that they must be active in the process, selecting their own goals and working toward them, both in the sessions and in daily living. Some clients can benefit from recognizing and expressing pent-up feelings, others will need to examine their beliefs and thoughts, others will most need to begin behaving in different ways, and others will benefit from talking with you about their relationships with the significant people in their lives. Most clients will need to do some work in all three dimensions—feelings, thoughts, and behaviors—because these dimensions are interrelated.

In deciding what interventions are most likely to be helpful, it is important to take into account the client's cultural, ethnic, and socioeconomic background. Moreover, the focus of counseling may change as clients enter different phases in the counseling process. Although some clients initially feel a need to be listened to and allowed to express deep feelings, they can profit later from examining the thought patterns that are contributing to their psychological pain. Certainly at some point in therapy it is essential that clients translate what they are learning about themselves into concrete action. The client's given situation in the environment provides a framework for selecting interventions that are most appropriate.

Listening to client feedback about the therapy process is of the utmost importance. One of the best ways to improve the effectiveness of psychotherapy is through client-directed, outcome-informed therapy (Duncan, Miller, & Sparks, 2004). Therapists need to take direction from their clients. If therapists learn to listen to clients' feedback throughout the therapeutic process, clients can become full and equal participants in all aspects of their therapy. In their book, *The Heroic Client*, Duncan and his colleagues (2004) emphasize that "it is time to recast the client as not only the hero or heroine of the therapy drama but also the director of the change endeavor" (p. 12). Client strengths and perceptions are the foundation of therapy work, and these authors advocate for systematic and consistent assessment of the client's perceptions of progress, which allows the therapist to tailor the therapy to the individual needs and characteristics of each client. Using client feedback, therapists can adjust and accommodate to maximize beneficial outcomes. In essence, Duncan and colleagues are arguing for *practice-based evidence* rather than evidence-based practice: "Becoming outcome informed not only amplifies the client's voice but offers the most viable, research-tested method to improve clinical effectiveness" (p. 16).

Relationship Between Therapist and Client

Most approaches share common ground in accepting the importance of the therapeutic relationship. The existential, person-centered, Gestalt, Adlerian, and postmodern views emphasize the personal relationship as *the* crucial determinant of treatment outcomes. Rational emotive behavior therapy, reality therapy, cognitive behavior therapy, and behavior therapy certainly do not ignore the relationship factor, yet they place less emphasis on the relationship and more on the effective use of techniques (Table 15.4).

Counseling is a personal matter that involves a personal relationship, and evidence indicates that honesty, sincerity, acceptance, understanding, and spontaneity are basic ingredients for successful outcomes. Therapists' degree of caring, their interest and ability in helping their clients, and their genuineness influence the relationship. Norcross and Wampold (2011a) stress that psychotherapy is primarily a human relationship. Both client and therapist bring origins, culture, expectations, biases, defenses, and strengths to this relationship. They claim that how we

TABLE 15.4 The Therapeutic Relationship

Psychoanalytic therapy	The classical analyst remains anonymous, and clients develop projections toward him or her. Focus is on reducing the resistances that develop in working with transference and on establishing more rational control. Clients undergo long-term analysis, engage in free association to uncover conflicts, and gain insight by talking. The analyst makes interpretations to teach clients the meaning of current behavior as it relates to the past. In contemporary relational psychoanalytic therapy, the relationship is central and emphasis is given to here-and-now dimensions of this relationship.
Adlerian therapy	The emphasis is on joint responsibility, on mutually determining goals, on mutual trust and respect, and on equality. Focus is on identifying, exploring, and disclosing mistaken goals and faulty assumptions within the person's lifestyle.
Existential therapy	The therapist's main tasks are to accurately grasp clients' being in the world and to establish a personal and authentic encounter with them. The immediacy of the client–therapist relationship and the authenticity of the here-and-now encounter are stressed. Both client and therapist can be changed by the encounter.
Person-centered therapy	The relationship is of primary importance. The qualities of the therapist, including genuineness, warmth, accurate empathy, respect, and nonjudgmentalness— and communication of these attitudes to clients—are stressed. Clients use this genuine relationship with the therapist to help them transfer what they learn to other relationships.
Gestalt therapy	Central importance is given to the I/Thou relationship and the quality of the therapist's presence. The therapist's attitudes and behavior count more than the techniques used. The therapist does not interpret for clients but assists them in developing the means to make their own interpretations. Clients identify and work on unfinished business from the past that interferes with current functioning.
Behavior therapy	The therapist is active and directive and functions as a teacher or mentor in helping clients learn more effective behavior. Clients must be active in the process and experiment with new behaviors. Although a quality client–therapist relationship is not viewed as sufficient to bring about change, it is considered essential for implementing behavioral procedures.

Cognitive behavior therapy	In REBT the therapist functions as a teacher and the client as a student. The therapist is highly directive and teaches clients an A-B-C model of changing their cognitions. In CT the focus is on a collaborative relationship. Using a Socratic dialogue, the therapist assists clients in identifying dysfunctional beliefs and discovering alternative rules for living. The therapist promotes corrective experiences that lead to learning new skills. Clients gain insight into their problems and then must actively practice changing self-defeating thinking and acting.
Reality therapy	A fundamental task is for the therapist to create a good relationship with the client. Therapists are then able to engage clients in an evaluation of all their relationships with respect to what they want and how effective they are in getting this. Therapists find out what clients want, ask what they are choosing to do, invite them to evaluate present behavior, help them make plans for change, and get them to make a commitment. The therapist is a client's advocate, as long as the client is willing to attempt to behave responsibly.
Feminist therapy	The therapeutic relationship is based on empowerment and egalitarianism. Therapists actively break down the hierarchy of power and reduce artificial barriers by engaging in appropriate self-disclosure and teaching clients about the therapy process. Therapists strive to create a collaborative relationship in which clients can become their own expert.
Postmodern approaches	Therapy is a collaborative partnership. Clients are viewed as the experts on their own life. Therapists use questioning dialogue to help clients free themselves from their problem-saturated stories and create new life-affirming stories. Solution-focused therapists assume an active role in guiding the client away from problem-talk and toward solution-talk. Clients are encouraged to explore their strengths and to create solutions that will lead to a richer future. Narrative therapists assist clients in externalizing problems and guide them in examining self-limiting stories and creating new and more liberating stories.
Family systems therapy	The family therapist functions as a teacher, coach, model, and consultant. The family learns ways to detect and solve problems that are keeping members stuck, and it learns about patterns that have been transmitted from generation to generation. Some approaches focus on the role of therapist as expert; others concentrate on intensifying what is going on in the here and now of the family session. All family therapists are concerned with the process of family interaction and teaching patterns of communication.

create and nurture this powerful human relationship can be guided by the fruits of research.

As you think about developing your personal counseling perspective, give consideration to the issue of the match between client and counselor. I certainly do not advocate changing your personality to fit your perception of what each client is expecting; it is important that you be *yourself* as you meet clients. You also need to consider the reality that you will probably not be able to work effectively with every client. Some clients will work better with counselors who have another type of personal and therapeutic style than yours. Be sensitive in assessing what your client needs, and use good judgment when determining the appropriateness of the match between you and a potential client.

Although you do not have to be like your clients or have experienced the same problems to be effective with them, it is critical that you be able to understand their world and respect them. Ask yourself how well prepared you are to counsel clients from a different cultural background. To what degree do you think you can successfully establish a therapeutic relationship with a client of a different race? Ethnic group? Gender? Age? Sexual orientation? Spiritual/religious orientation? Socioeconomic group? Do you see any potential barriers that would make it difficult for you to form a working relationship with certain clients? It is also important to consider the client's diagnosis, resistance level, treatment preferences, and stages of change. Different types of clients respond better to different types of treatments and relationship styles. Therapeutic techniques and styles should be selected to fit the client's personal characteristics. Norcross and Beutler (2011) suggest that therapists create a new therapy for each client:

> We believe that the purpose of integrative psychotherapy is *not* to create a single or unitary treatment. Rather, we select different treatment methods according to the patient's response to the treatment goals, following an established set of integrative principles. The result is a more efficient and efficacious therapy—and one that fits both the client and the clinician. (p. 509)

THE PLACE OF TECHNIQUES AND EVALUATION IN COUNSELING
Drawing on Techniques From Various Approaches

Effective therapists incorporate a wide range of procedures into their therapeutic style. Much depends on the purpose of therapy, the setting, the personality and style of the therapist, the qualities of the particular client, and the problems selected for intervention. Regardless of the therapeutic model you may be working with, you must decide *what* relationship style to adopt, *what* techniques, procedures, or intervention methods to use, *when* to use them, and with *which* clients. Take time to review Table 15.5 and Table 15.6 on therapeutic techniques and applications of techniques. Pay careful attention to the focus of each type of therapy and how that focus might be useful in your practice.

It is critical to be aware of how clients' cultural backgrounds contribute to their perceptions of their problems. Each of the 11 therapeutic approaches has both strengths and limitations when applied to culturally diverse client populations

TABLE 15.5 Techniques of Therapy

Psychoanalytic therapy	The key techniques are interpretation, dream analysis, free association, analysis of resistance, analysis of transference, and countertransference. Techniques are designed to help clients gain access to their unconscious conflicts, which leads to insight and eventual assimilation of new material by the ego.
Adlerian therapy	Adlerians pay more attention to the subjective experiences of clients than to using techniques. Some techniques include gathering life-history data (family constellation, early recollections, personal priorities), sharing interpretations with clients, offering encouragement, and assisting clients in searching for new possibilities.
Existential therapy	Few techniques flow from this approach because it stresses understanding first and technique second. The therapist can borrow techniques from other approaches and incorporate them in an existential framework. Diagnosis, testing, and external measurements are not deemed important. Issues addressed are freedom and responsibility, isolation and relationships, meaning and meaninglessness, living and dying.
Person-centered therapy	This approach uses few techniques but stresses the attitudes of the therapist and a "way of being." Therapists strive for active listening, reflection of feelings, clarification, "being there" for the client, and focusing on the moment-to-moment experiencing of the client. This model does not include diagnostic testing, interpretation, taking a case history, or questioning or probing for information.
Gestalt therapy	A wide range of experiments are designed to intensify experiencing and to integrate conflicting feelings. Experiments are co-created by therapist and client through an I/Thou dialogue. Therapists have latitude to creatively invent their own experiments. Formal diagnosis and testing are not a required part of therapy.
Behavior therapy	The main techniques are reinforcement, shaping, modeling, systematic desensitization, relaxation methods, flooding, eye movement and desensitization reprocessing, cognitive restructuring, assertion and social skills training, self-management programs, mindfulness and acceptance methods, behavioral rehearsal, coaching, and various multimodal therapy techniques. Diagnosis or assessment is done at the outset to determine a treatment plan. Questions concentrate on "what," "how," and "when" (but not "why"). Contracts and homework assignments are also typically used.

Cognitive behavior therapy	Therapists use a variety of cognitive, emotive, and behavioral techniques; diverse methods are tailored to suit individual clients. This is an active, directive, time-limited, present-centered, psychoeducational, structured therapy. Some techniques include engaging in Socratic dialogue, collaborative empiricism, debating irrational beliefs, carrying out homework assignments, gathering data on assumptions one has made, keeping a record of activities, forming alternative interpretations, learning new coping skills, changing one's language and thinking patterns, role playing, imagery, confronting faulty beliefs, self-instructional training, and stress inoculation training.
Reality therapy	This is an active, directive, and didactic therapy. Skillful questioning is a central technique used for the duration of the therapy process. Various techniques may be used to get clients to evaluate what they are presently doing to see if they are willing to change. If clients decide that their present behavior is not effective, they develop a specific plan for change and make a commitment to follow through.
Feminist therapy	Although techniques from traditional approaches are used, feminist practitioners tend to employ consciousness-raising techniques aimed at helping clients recognize the impact of gender-role socialization on their lives. Other techniques frequently used include gender-role analysis and intervention, power analysis and intervention, demystifying therapy, bibliotherapy, journal writing, therapist self-disclosure, assertiveness training, reframing and relabeling, cognitive restructuring, identifying and challenging untested beliefs, role playing, psychodramatic methods, group work, and social action.
Postmodern approaches	In solution-focused therapy the main technique involves change-talk, with emphasis on times in a client's life when the problem was not a problem. Other techniques include creative use of questioning, the miracle question, and scaling questions, which assist clients in developing alternative stories. In narrative therapy, specific techniques include listening to a client's problem-saturated story without getting stuck, externalizing and naming the problem, externalizing conversations, and discovering clues to competence. Narrative therapists often write letters to clients and assist them in finding an audience that will support their changes and new stories.
Family systems therapy	A variety of techniques may be used, depending on the particular theoretical orientation of the therapist. Techniques include genograms, teaching, asking questions, joining the family, tracking sequences, issuing directives, use of countertransference, family mapping, reframing, restructuring, enactments, and setting boundaries. Techniques may be experiential, cognitive, or behavioral in nature. Most are designed to bring about change in a short time.

TABLE 15.6 Applications of the Approaches

Psychoanalytic therapy	Candidates for analytic therapy include professionals who want to become therapists, people who have had intensive therapy and want to go further, and those who are in psychological pain. Analytic therapy is not recommended for self-centered and impulsive individuals or for people with psychotic disorders. Techniques can be applied to individual and group therapy.
Adlerian therapy	Because the approach is based on a growth model, it is applicable to such varied spheres of life as child guidance, parent–child counseling, marital and family therapy, individual counseling with all age groups, correctional and rehabilitation counseling, group counseling, substance abuse programs, and brief counseling. It is ideally suited to preventive care and alleviating a broad range of conditions that interfere with growth.
Existential therapy	This approach is especially suited to people facing a developmental crisis or a transition in life and for those with existential concerns (making choices, dealing with freedom and responsibility, coping with guilt and anxiety, making sense of life, and finding values) or those seeking personal enhancement. The approach can be applied to both individual and group counseling, and to couples and family therapy, crisis intervention, and community mental health work.
Person-centered therapy	Has wide applicability to individual and group counseling. It is especially well suited for the initial phases of crisis intervention work. Its principles have been applied to couples and family therapy, community programs, administration and management, and human relations training. It is a useful approach for teaching, parent–child relations, and for working with groups of people from diverse cultural backgrounds.
Gestalt therapy	Addresses a wide range of problems and populations: crisis intervention, treatment of a range of psychosomatic disorders, couples and family therapy, awareness training of mental health professionals, behavior problems in children, and teaching and learning. It is well suited to both individual and group counseling. The methods are powerful catalysts for opening up feelings and getting clients into contact with their present-centered experience.
Behavior therapy	A pragmatic approach based on empirical validation of results. Enjoys wide applicability to individual, group, couples, and family counseling. Some problems to which the approach is well suited are phobic disorders, depression, trauma, sexual disorders, children's behavioral disorders, stuttering, and prevention of cardiovascular disease. Beyond clinical practice, its principles are applied in fields such as pediatrics, stress management, behavioral medicine, education, and geriatrics.

Cognitive behavior therapy	Has been widely applied to treatment of depression, anxiety, relationship problems, stress management, skill training, substance abuse, assertion training, eating disorders, panic attacks, performance anxiety, and social phobias. CBT is especially useful for assisting people in modifying their cognitions. Many self-help approaches utilize its principles. CBT can be applied to a wide range of client populations with a variety of specific problems.
Reality therapy	Geared to teaching people ways of using choice theory in everyday living to increase effective behaviors. It has been applied to individual counseling with a wide range of clients, group counseling, working with youthful law offenders, and couples and family therapy. In some instances it is well suited to brief therapy and crisis intervention.
Feminist therapy	Principles and techniques can be applied to a range of therapeutic modalities such as individual therapy, relationship counseling, family therapy, group counseling, and community intervention. The approach can be applied to both women and men with the goal of bringing about empowerment.
Postmodern approaches	Solution-focused therapy is well suited for people with adjustment disorders and for problems of anxiety and depression. Narrative therapy is now being used for a broad range of human difficulties including eating disorders, family distress, depression, and relationship concerns. These approaches can be applied to working with children, adolescents, adults, couples, families, and the community in a wide variety of settings. Both solution-focused and narrative approaches lend themselves to group counseling and to school counseling.
Family systems therapy	Useful for dealing with marital distress, problems of communicating among family members, power struggles, crisis situations in the family, helping individuals attain their potential, and enhancing the overall functioning of the family.

(Table 15.7 and Table 15.8). Although it is unwise to stereotype clients because of their cultural heritage, it is useful to assess how the cultural context has a bearing on their concerns. Some techniques may be contraindicated because of a client's socialization. The client's responsiveness (or lack of it) to certain techniques is a critical barometer in judging the effectiveness of these methods.

Effective counseling involves proficiency in a combination of cognitive, affective, and behavioral techniques. Such a combination is necessary to help clients *think* about their beliefs and assumptions, to experience on a *feeling* level their conflicts and struggles, and to translate their insights into *action* programs by

TABLE 15.7 Contributions to Multicultural Counseling

Therapy	Contributions
Psychoanalytic therapy	Its focus on family dynamics is appropriate for working with many cultural groups. The therapist's formality appeals to clients who expect professional distance. Notion of ego defense is helpful in understanding inner dynamics and dealing with environmental stresses.
Adlerian therapy	Its focus on social interest, helping others, collectivism, pursuing meaning in life, importance of family, goal orientation, and belonging is congruent with the values of many cultures. Focus on person-in-the-environment allows for cultural factors to be explored.
Existential therapy	Focus is on understanding client's phenomenological world, including cultural background. This approach leads to empowerment in an oppressive society. Existential therapy can help clients examine their options for change within the context of their cultural realities. The existential approach is particularly suited to counseling diverse clients because of the philosophical foundation that emphasizes the human condition.
Person-centered therapy	Focus is on breaking cultural barriers and facilitating open dialogue among diverse cultural populations. Main strengths are respect for clients' values, active listening, welcoming of differences, nonjudgmental attitude, understanding, willingness to allow clients to determine what will be explored in sessions, and prizing cultural pluralism.
Gestalt therapy	Its focus on expressing oneself nonverbally is congruent with those cultures that look beyond words for messages. Provides many experiments in working with clients who have cultural injunctions against freely expressing feelings. Can help to overcome language barrier with bilingual clients. Focus on bodily expressions is a subtle way to help clients recognize their conflicts.
Behavior therapy	Focus on behavior, rather than on feelings, is compatible with many cultures. Strengths include a collaborative relationship between counselor and client in working toward mutually agreed-upon goals, continual assessment to determine if the techniques are suited to clients' unique situations, assisting clients in learning practical skills, an educational focus, and stress on self-management strategies.
Cognitive behavior therapy	Focus is on a collaborative approach that offers clients opportunities to express their areas of concern. The psychoeducational dimensions are often useful in exploring cultural conflicts and teaching new behavior. The emphasis on thinking (as opposed to identifying and expressing feelings) is likely to be acceptable to many clients. The focus on teaching and learning tends to avoid the stigma of mental illness. Clients may value the active and directive stance of the therapist.

Reality therapy	Focus is on clients making their own evaluation of behavior (including how they respond to their culture). Through personal assessment clients can determine the degree to which their needs and wants are being satisfied. They can find a balance between retaining their own ethnic identity and integrating some of the values and practices of the dominant society.
Feminist therapy	Focus is on both individual change and social transformation. A key contribution is that both the women's movement and the multicultural movement have called attention to the negative impact of discrimination and oppression for both women and men. Emphasizes the influence of expected cultural roles and explores client's satisfaction with and knowledge of these roles.
Postmodern approaches	Focus is on the social and cultural context of behavior. Stories that are being authored in the therapy office need to be anchored in the social world in which the client lives. Therapists do not make assumptions about people and honor each client's unique story and cultural background. Therapists take an active role in challenging social and cultural injustices that lead to oppression of certain groups. Therapy becomes a process of liberation from oppressive cultural values and enables clients to become active agents of their destinies.
Family systems therapy	Focus is on the family or community system. Many ethnic and cultural groups place value on the role of the extended family. Many family therapies deal with extended family members and with support systems. Networking is a part of the process, which is congruent with the values of many clients. There is a greater chance for individual change if other family members are supportive. This approach offers ways of working toward the health of the family unit and the welfare of each member.

TABLE 15.8 Limitations in Multicultural Counseling

Psychoanalytic therapy	Its focus on insight, intrapsychic dynamics, and long-term treatment is often not valued by clients who prefer to learn coping skills for dealing with pressing daily concerns. Internal focus is often in conflict with cultural values that stress an interpersonal and environmental focus.
Adlerian therapy	This approach uses a detailed interview about one's family background; this can conflict with cultures that have injunctions against disclosing family matters. Some clients may view the counselor as an authority who will provide answers to problems, which conflicts with the egalitarian, person-to-person spirit as a way to reduce social distance.

Existential therapy	Values of individuality, freedom, autonomy, and self-realization often conflict with cultural values of collectivism, respect for tradition, deference to authority, and interdependence. Some may be deterred by the absence of specific techniques. Others will expect more focus on surviving in their world.
Person-centered therapy	Some of the core values of this approach may not be congruent with the client's culture. Lack of counselor direction and structure are unacceptable for clients who are seeking help and immediate answers from a knowledgeable professional.
Gestalt therapy	Clients who have been culturally conditioned to be emotionally reserved may not embrace Gestalt experiments. Some may not see how "being aware of present experiencing" will lead to solving their problems.
Behavior therapy	Family members may not value clients' newly acquired assertive style, so clients must be taught how to cope with resistance by others. Counselors need to help clients assess the possible consequences of making behavioral changes.
Cognitive behavior therapy	Before too quickly attempting to change the beliefs and actions of clients, it is essential for the therapist to understand and respect their world. Some clients may have serious reservations about questioning their basic cultural values and beliefs. Clients could become dependent on the therapist for deciding what are appropriate ways to solve problems.
Reality therapy	This approach stresses taking charge of one's own life, yet some clients are more interested in changing their external environment. Counselor needs to appreciate the role of discrimination and racism and help clients deal with social and political realities.
Feminist therapy	This model has been criticized for its bias toward the values of White, middle-class, heterosexual women, which are not applicable to many other groups of women nor to men. Therapists need to assess with their clients the price of making significant personal change, which may result in isolation from extended family as clients assume new roles and make life changes.
Postmodern approaches	Some clients come to therapy wanting to talk about their problems and may be put off by the insistence on talking about exceptions to their problems. Clients may view the therapist as an expert and be reluctant to view themselves as experts. Certain clients may doubt the helpfulness of a therapist who assumes a "not-knowing" position.

Family systems therapy	Family therapy rests on value assumptions that are not congruent with the values of clients from some cultures. Western concepts such as individuation, self-actualization, self-determination, independence, and self-expression may be foreign to some clients. In some cultures, admitting problems within the family is shameful. The value of "keeping problems within the family" may make it difficult to explore conflicts openly.

behaving in new ways in day-to-day living. Table 15.9 and Table 15.10 outline the contributions and limitations of the various therapeutic approaches. These tables will help you identify elements from the various approaches that you may want to incorporate in your own counseling perspective.

Evaluating the Effectiveness of Counseling and Therapy

Mental health providers must be accountable and be able to demonstrate the efficacy of their services. In the era of managed care, it is even more essential for practitioners to demonstrate the degree to which their interventions are both clinically sound and cost-effective. Does therapy make a significant difference? Are people substantially better after therapy than they were without it? Can therapy actually be more harmful than helpful? A thorough discussion of these questions is beyond the scope of this book, but I will address a few basic issues related to evaluating the effectiveness of counseling.

TABLE 15.9 Contributions of the Approaches

Psychoanalytic therapy	More than any other system, this approach has generated controversy as well as exploration and has stimulated further thinking and development of therapy. It has provided a detailed and comprehensive description of personality structure and functioning. It has brought into prominence factors such as the unconscious as a determinant of behavior and the role of trauma during the first 6 years of life. It has developed several techniques for tapping the unconscious and shed light on the dynamics of transference and countertransference, resistance, anxiety, and the mechanisms of ego defense.
Adlerian therapy	A key contribution is the influence that Adlerian concepts have had on other systems and the integration of these concepts into various contemporary therapies. This is one of the first approaches to therapy that was humanistic, unified, holistic, and goal-oriented and that put an emphasis on social and psychological factors.
Existential therapy	Its major contribution is recognition of the need for a subjective approach based on a complete view of the human condition. It calls attention to the need for a philosophical statement on what it means to be a person. Stress on the I/Thou relationship lessens the chances of dehumanizing therapy. It provides a perspective for understanding anxiety, guilt, freedom, death, isolation, and commitment.

Person-centered therapy	Clients take an active stance and assume responsibility for the direction of therapy. This unique approach has been subjected to empirical testing, and as a result both theory and methods have been modified. It is an open system. People without advanced training can benefit by translating the therapeutic conditions to both their personal and professional lives. Basic concepts are straightforward and easy to grasp and apply. It is a foundation for building a trusting relationship, applicable to all therapies.
Gestalt therapy	The emphasis on direct experiencing and doing rather than on merely talking about feelings provides a perspective on growth and enhancement, not merely a treatment of disorders. It uses clients' behavior as the basis for making them aware of their inner creative potential. The approach to dreams is a unique, creative tool to help clients discover basic conflicts. Therapy is viewed as an existential encounter; it is process-oriented, not technique-oriented. It recognizes nonverbal behavior as a key to understanding.
Behavior therapy	Emphasis is on assessment and evaluation techniques, thus providing a basis for accountable practice. Specific problems are identified, and clients are kept informed about progress toward their goals. The approach has demonstrated effectiveness in many areas of human functioning. The roles of the therapist as reinforcer, model, teacher, and consultant are explicit. The approach has undergone extensive expansion, and research literature abounds. No longer is it a mechanistic approach, for it now makes room for cognitive factors and encourages self-directed programs for behavioral change.
Cognitive behavior therapy	Major contributions include emphasis on a comprehensive and eclectic therapeutic practice; numerous cognitive, emotive, and behavioral techniques; an openness to incorporating techniques from other approaches; and a methodology for challenging and changing faulty thinking. Most forms can be integrated into other mainstream therapies. REBT makes full use of action-oriented homework, various psychoeducational methods, and keeping records of progress. CT is a structured therapy that has a good track record for treating depression and anxiety in a short time.
Reality therapy	This is a positive approach with an action orientation that relies on simple and clear concepts that are easily grasped in many helping professions. It can be used by teachers, nurses, ministers, educators, social workers, and counselors. Due to the direct methods, it appeals to many clients who are often seen as resistant to therapy. It is a short-term approach that can be applied to a diverse population, and it has been a significant force in challenging the medical model of therapy.

Feminist therapy	The feminist perspective is responsible for encouraging increasing numbers of women to question gender stereotypes and to reject limited views of what a woman is expected to be. It is paving the way for gender-sensitive practice and bringing attention to the gendered uses of power in relationships. The unified feminist voice brought attention to the extent and implications of child abuse, incest, rape, sexual harassment, and domestic violence. Feminist principles and interventions can be incorporated in other therapy approaches.
Postmodern approaches	The brevity of these approaches fit well with the limitations imposed by a managed care structure. The emphasis on client strengths and competence appeals to clients who want to create solutions and revise their life stories in a positive direction. Clients are not blamed for their problems but are helped to understand how they might relate in more satisfying ways to such problems. A strength of these approaches is the question format that invites clients to view themselves in new and more effective ways.
Family systems therapy	From a systemic perspective, neither the individual nor the family is blamed for a particular dysfunction. The family is empowered through the process of identifying and exploring interactional patterns. Working with an entire unit provides a new perspective on understanding and working through both individual problems and relationship concerns. By exploring one's family of origin, there are increased opportunities to resolve other conflicts in systems outside of the family

TABLE 15.10 Limitations of the Approaches

Psychoanalytic therapy	Requires lengthy training for therapists and much time and expense for clients. The model stresses biological and instinctual factors to the neglect of social, cultural, and interpersonal ones. Its methods are less applicable for solving specific daily life problems of clients and may not be appropriate for some ethnic and cultural groups. Many clients lack the degree of ego strength needed for regressive and reconstructive therapy. It may be inappropriate for certain counseling settings.
Adlerian therapy	Weak in terms of precision, testability, and empirical validity. Few attempts have been made to validate the basic concepts by scientific methods. Tends to oversimplify some complex human problems and is based heavily on common sense.

Existential therapy	Many basic concepts are fuzzy and ill-defined, making its general framework abstract at times. Lacks a systematic statement of principles and practices of therapy. Has limited applicability to lower functioning and nonverbal clients and to clients in extreme crisis who need direction.
Person-centered therapy	Possible danger from the therapist who remains passive and inactive, limiting responses to reflection. Many clients feel a need for greater direction, more structure, and more techniques. Clients in crisis may need more directive measures. Applied to individual counseling, some cultural groups will expect more counselor activity.
Gestalt therapy	Techniques lead to intense emotional expression; if these feelings are not explored and if cognitive work is not done, clients are likely to be left unfinished and will not have a sense of integration of their learning. Clients who have difficulty using imagination may not profit from certain experiments.
Behavior therapy	Major criticisms are that it may change behavior but not feelings; that it ignores the relational factors in therapy; that it does not provide insight; that it ignores historical causes of present behavior; that it involves control by the therapist; and that it is limited in its capacity to address certain aspects of the human condition.
Cognitive behavior therapy	Tends to play down emotions, does not focus on exploring the unconscious or underlying conflicts, de-emphasizes the value of insight, and sometimes does not give enough weight to the client's past. REBT, being a confrontational therapy, might lead to premature termination. CBT might be too structured for some clients.
Reality therapy	Discounts the therapeutic value of exploration of the client's past, dreams, the unconscious, early childhood experiences, and transference. The approach is limited to less complex problems. It is a problem-solving therapy that tends to discourage exploration of deeper emotional issues.
Feminist therapy	A possible limitation is the potential for therapists to impose a new set of values on clients—such as striving for equality, power in relationships, defining oneself, freedom to pursue a career outside the home, and the right to an education. Therapists need to keep in mind that clients are their own best experts, which means it is up to them to decide which values to live by.

Postmodern approaches	There is little empirical validation of the effectiveness of therapy outcomes. Some critics contend that these approaches endorse cheerleading and an overly positive perspective. Some are critical of the stance taken by most postmodern therapists regarding assessment and diagnosis, and also react negatively to the "not-knowing" stance of the therapist. Because some of the solution-focused techniques are relatively easy to learn, practitioners may use these interventions in a mechanical way or implement these techniques without a sound rationale.
Family systems therapy	Limitations include problems in being able to involve all the members of a family in the therapy. Some family members may be resistant to changing the structure of the system. Therapists' self-knowledge and willingness to work on their own family-of-origin issues is crucial, for the potential for countertransference is high. It is essential that the therapist be well trained, receive quality supervision, and be competent in assessing and treating individuals in a family context.

Evaluating how well psychotherapy works is far from simple. Therapeutic systems are applied by practitioners who have unique individual characteristics, and clients themselves have much to do with therapeutic outcomes. For example, effects resulting from unexpected and uncontrollable events in the environment can lessen the impact of gains made in psychotherapy. Moreover, practitioners who adhere to the same approach are likely to use techniques in various ways and to relate to clients in diverse fashions, functioning differently with different clients and in different clinical settings. Norcross and Beutler (2011) note that evidence-based practice reflects a commitment on "what works, not on what theory applies" (p. 510).

Most of the outcome studies have been done by two divergent groups: (1) the behavior and cognitive therapists, who have based their therapeutic practice on empirical studies, and (2) the person-centered researchers, who have made significant contributions to understanding both process and outcome variables. Significant empirical research dealing with how well the therapy works has not been produced for most of the other models covered in this book.

How effective is psychotherapy? A meta-analysis of psychotherapy outcome literature conducted by Smith, Glass, and Miller (1980) concluded that psychotherapy was highly effective. Prochaska and Norcross (2010) note that controlled outcome research consistently supports the effectiveness of psychotherapy. They point out that more than 5,000 individual studies and 500 meta-analyses have been conducted on the effectiveness of psychotherapy; these studies demonstrate that well-developed therapy interventions have meaningful, positive effects on the intended outcome variables. In short, not only does psychotherapy work, but research demonstrates that therapy is remarkably effective.

A summary of the research data shows that the various treatment approaches achieve roughly equivalent results (Duncan et al., 2004). Lambert's (2011) review of psychotherapy research makes it clear that the similarities rather than the differences among models account for the effectiveness of psychotherapy. Reviews of comparative outcome studies reveal the same general conclusion: there is relative equivalence among the various therapeutic approaches. Interpersonal, social, and affective factors common across therapeutic orientations are more critical than techniques employed when it comes to facilitating therapeutic gains. Lambert believes the future direction of theory, practice, and training will see (1) the decline of single-theory practice and the growth of integrative therapies, and (2) the increase in short-term, time-limited, and group treatments that seem to be as effective as long-term individual treatments with many client populations.

Although it is clear that therapy works, there are no simple explanations of how it works, and it appears that we must look to factors that are common to all therapeutic approaches. Hubble, Duncan, Miller, and Wampold (2010) summarized research studies in the field and found that the following four factors account for change in therapy:

- Client factors: 40%
- Alliance factors (the therapeutic relationship): 30%
- Expectancy factors (hope and allegiance): 15%
- Theoretical models and techniques: 15%

Common factors that are part of all theoretical orientations are critical to therapeutic outcome. Wampold (2010) concludes that "there is little evidence that the specific ingredients of any treatment are responsible for the benefits of therapy" (p. 71). Research indicates that a variety of treatments are equally effective—when administered by therapists who believe in them and when they are accepted by the client.

The various therapy approaches and techniques work equally well because they share the most important ingredient accounting for change—the client. Data point to the conclusion that the engine of change is the client (Bohart & Tallman, 2010), and we can most productively direct our efforts toward ways of employing the client in the process of change (Duncan et al., 2004). Duncan and colleagues further state that therapists can translate this research into their clinical work by purposefully working to do the following:

- Enhance the common factors across all theories that account for successful outcomes
- Focus on the client's perspective and theory of change as a guide to selecting techniques and integrating various therapy models
- Obtain systematic client feedback regarding the client's experience of the process and outcome of therapy

Hubble, Duncan, Miller, and Wampold (2010) note that monitoring outcome and adjusting accordingly on the basis of feedback from the client must become routine practice. Duncan and colleagues (2004) claim that the client's theory of change can be used as a basis for determining which approach, by whom, can be most effective for this person, with his or her specific problem, under this particular set of circumstances. This approach to practicing therapy places emphasis on continuous client input into the therapy process. Doing this increases the chances of active client participation in therapy, which is the most important determinant of the outcome of treatment.

SUMMARY

Creating an integrative stance is truly a challenge. Therapists cannot simply pick bits and pieces from theories in a random and fragmented manner. In forming an integrated perspective, it is important to ask: Which theories provide a basis for understanding the *cognitive* dimensions? What about the *feeling* aspects? And how about the *behavioral* dimension? Most of the 11 therapeutic orientations discussed here focus on one of these dimensions of human experience. Although the other dimensions are not necessarily ignored, they are often given short shrift.

Developing an integrated theoretical perspective requires an accurate, in-depth knowledge of the various theories. Without such knowledge, you cannot formulate a true synthesis. Simply put, you cannot integrate what you do not know (Norcross & Beutler, 2011). A central message of this book has been to remain open to each theory, to do further reading, and to reflect on how the key concepts of each approach fit your personality. Building your personalized orientation to counseling, which is based on what you consider to be the best features of several theories, is a long-term venture.

Besides considering your own personality, think about what concepts and techniques work best with a range of clients. It requires knowledge, skill, art, and experience to be able to determine what techniques are suitable for particular problems. It is also an art to know when and how to use a particular therapeutic intervention. Although reflecting on your personal preferences is important, I would hope that you also balance your preferences with evidence from the research studies. Developing a personal approach to counseling practice does not imply that anything goes. Indeed, in this era of managed care and evidence-based practice, your personal preferences will not likely be the sole determinant of your psychotherapy practice. In counseling clients with certain clinical problems (such as depression and generalized anxiety), specific techniques have demonstrated their effectiveness. For instance, behavior therapy, cognitive behavior therapy, mindfulness-based cognitive therapy, and short-term psychodynamic therapy have repeatedly proved successful in treating depression. Your use of techniques must be grounded on solid theoretical constructs. Ethical practice implies that you employ efficacious procedures in dealing with clients and their problems, and that you are able to provide a theoretical rationale for the interventions you make in your clinical work.

This is a good time to review what you have learned about counseling theory and practice. Identify a particular theory that you might adopt as a foundation for establishing your counseling perspective. Consider from which therapies you would be most inclined to draw (1) underlying assumptions, (2) major concepts, (3) therapeutic goals, (4) therapeutic relationship, and (5) techniques and procedures.

Also, consider the major applications of each of the therapies as well as their basic limitations and major contributions. The tables presented in this chapter are designed to assist you in conceptualizing your view of the counseling process.

WHERE TO GO FROM HERE

In the *DVD for Integrative Counseling: The Case of Ruth and Lecturettes* (Session 9, "An Integrative Perspective") you will view my ways of working with Ruth by drawing on techniques from various theoretical models. I demonstrate how the foundation of my integrative approach rests on existential therapy. In this session I am drawing heavily from principles of the action-oriented therapies.

Other Resources

DVDs offered by the American Psychological Association that are relevant to this chapter include the following:

> Stricker, G. (2009). *Psychotherapy Integration Over Time* (Psychotherapy Video Series)

A private group of clinicians and researchers is dedicated to studying "what works" in behavioral mental health. Members and associates translate the latest research into guidelines for clinical practice and publish the information in clinically friendly terms on their website. The Institute for the Study of Therapeutic Change has also developed an outcome management system that uses ongoing client feedback to monitor and improve retention in therapy and improve outcome of treatment services.

Scott D. Miller, PhD, Co-director
Institute for the Study of Therapeutic Change
P. O. Box 180147
Chicago, IL 60618-0573
Telephone: (773) 404-5130
Fax: (847) 841-4874
Mobile: (773) 454-8511
Website: www.talkingcure.com

The International Center for Clinical Excellence (ICCE) is a worldwide community of practitioners, health care managers, educators, and researchers dedicated to promoting excellence in behavioral health care services. This online community facilitates sharing of best practices and innovative ideas specifically designed to improve behavioral health care practice and enable practitioners and managers to achieve their personal best as helping professionals.

The International Center for Clinical Excellence
www.centerforclinicalexcellence.com

Scott D. Miller's website has additional information on workshops on clinical excellence:

Scott D. Miller
Website: www.scottdmiller.com

Case Illustration: An Integrative Approach in Working With Stan

COUNSELING STAN: INTEGRATION OF THERAPIES

The purpose of this chapter is to bring together in an integrative fashion the 11 approaches you have studied by combining thinking, feeling, and acting models in counseling Stan. The material in Chapter 15 provides a conceptual framework for my way of counseling from an integrative perspective. Many of the key points made in Chapter 15 will become clearer as you read about the interventions I am making with Stan in this chapter. At this point it would be helpful for you to review the background material and themes in Stan's life presented in Chapter 1. In addition, I suggest you consult the *Student Manual for Theory and Practice of Counseling and Psychotherapy* (Chapter 16) for an overview and review of the major areas I focus on for each of the theoretical approaches in my work with Stan.

In this section, I describe how I would integrate concepts and techniques from the 11 theoretical perspectives in counseling Stan on the levels of *thinking, feeling,* and *doing.* I use information presented in Stan's autobiography, and I indicate what aspects from the various theories I would draw on in working with Stan at the various stages of his therapy. As you read, think about the interventions you would make with Stan that would be either similar to or different from mine. Questions in the "Follow-Up" section near the end of the chapter will guide you as you reflect on being Stan's counselor and working with him from your own integrative perspective.

 See the video program for Chapter 16, *DVD for Theory and Practice of Counseling and Psychotherapy: The Case of Stan and Lecturettes*. I suggest that you view the brief lecture for each chapter prior to reading the chapter.

A Place to Begin

I start by giving Stan a chance to say how he feels about coming to the initial session. To begin to understand why Stan has sought therapy, I might explore his thoughts regarding any of the following questions:

- What brings you here? What has been going on in your life recently that made you want to seek professional help?
- What expectations do you have of therapy? Of me? What are your hopes, fears, and any reservations? What goals do you have for yourself through therapy?
- Give me a picture of some significant turning points in your life? Who have been the important people in your life? What significant decisions have you made? What are some of the struggles you've dealt with, and what are some of these issues that are current for you?
- How would you describe your life in your family? How did you view your parents? How did they react to you? What do you remember about your early years? (It would be useful to administer the Adlerian lifestyle questionnaire.)

Clarifying the Therapeutic Relationship

I will work with Stan to develop a contract, which involves a discussion of our mutual responsibilities and a clear statement of what he wants from these sessions and what he is willing to do to obtain his goals. I believe it is important to discuss any factors that might perpetuate a client's dependency on the therapist, so I invite Stan's questions about this therapeutic relationship. One goal is to demystify the therapy process; another is to get some focus for the direction of our sessions by developing clear goals for the therapy.

In establishing the therapeutic relationship, I am influenced by the person-centered, existential, Gestalt, feminist, postmodern, and Adlerian approaches. They do not view therapy as something that the therapist *does* to a passive client. I will apply my knowledge of these therapies to establish a working relationship with Stan that is characterized by mutual trust and respect. I will ask myself these questions: "To what degree am I able to listen to and hear Stan in a nonjudgmental way? Am I able to respect and care for him? Do I have the capacity to enter his subjective world without losing my own identity? Am I able to share with him my own thoughts and reactions as they pertain to our relationship?" I begin by being as honest as I can be with Stan as the basis for creating this relationship. This relationship is critical at the initial stages of therapy, but it must be maintained during all stages if therapy is to be effective. I operate on the assumption that the quality of our relationship will be critical to the therapeutic outcome.

Clarifying the Goals of Therapy

It is not enough to simply ask Stan what he hopes to gain by the conclusion of therapy. Clients are oftentimes vague, global, and unfocused about what they want. With respect to goals, precision and clarity are essential. There is no progress when you have directionless sessions. Thus, specificity is a must. Once we have identified some goals, Stan can begin to observe and measure his own behavior, both in the sessions and in his daily life. This self-monitoring is a vital step in any effort to bring about change. I will be asking for Stan's feedback throughout the therapeutic process and will use his feedback as a basis for making modifications in our therapeutic alliance.

Here are a few interchanges that focus on the process of defining goals that will give direction to Stan's therapy:

JERRY: What would you most hope for, through our work together?

STAN: Well, I know I put myself down a lot. I'd like to feel better about myself.

JERRY: If you had what you want in your life today, what would that be like? What would it take for you to feel good about yourself?

STAN: For one thing, I'd have people in my life, and I would be closer to people.

JERRY: Is this an area you'd be willing to explore in our sessions?

STAN: Yes.

JERRY: I'll be glad to provide suggestions of ways to begin, if I know what you want.

STAN: For sure I'd like to get over my dumb fears of being with people.

JERRY: I like it that you're willing to challenge your fears. Are you aware that you just put yourself down by labeling your fears as dumb?

STAN: It's almost a reflex response for me. But I would like to feel more comfortable when I'm with others.

JERRY: How is it for you to be here with me now?

STAN: It's not like me to do something like this, but I feel good. I'm talking, and I'm saying what's on my mind.

JERRY: I hope you will continue to give yourself credit for being different in our conversation right now.

Goal setting is not accomplished in a single session. Throughout our time together, I ask Stan to decide time and again what he wants from his therapy and to assess the degree to which our work together is resulting in his meeting his goals. As his therapist, I expect to be active, yet it is important that Stan provide the direction in which he wants to travel on his journey. Once I have a clear sense of the specific ways Stan wants to change how he is thinking, feeling, and acting, I am likely to take an active role in co-creating experiments with Stan that he can do both in the therapy sessions and on his own away from our sessions.

Working With Stan's Past, Present, and Future

DEALING WITH THE PAST Reality therapy, solution-focused brief therapy, behavior therapy, and rational emotive behavior therapy place very little emphasis on the client's history. The rationale for this lack of attention to the past is that early childhood experiences do not necessarily have much to do with the maintenance of present ineffective behavior. My inclination, in contrast, is to give weight to understanding, exploring, and working with Stan's early history and to connect his past with what he is doing today. My view is that themes running through our life can become evident if we come to terms with significant experiences in our childhood. The use of an Adlerian lifestyle questionnaire would indicate some of these themes that originate from Stan's childhood. The psychoanalytic approach, of course, emphasizes uncovering and reexperiencing traumas in early childhood, working through the places where we have become "stuck," and resolving conflicts that are often out of our awareness.

Although I agree that Stan's childhood experiences were influential in contributing to his present personality (including his ways of thinking, feeling, and behaving), it does not make sense to me to assume that these factors have *determined* him. I favor the Gestalt approach of asking Stan to bring into the here and now those people in his life with whom he feels unfinished. A variety of role-playing techniques in which Stan addresses significant others through symbolic work in our sessions will bring Stan's past intensely to life in the present moment of our sessions.

DEALING WITH THE PRESENT Being interested in Stan's past does not mean that we get lost in history or that we dwell on reliving traumatic situations. By paying attention to what is going on in the here and now during the counseling session, I get excellent clues about what is unfinished from Stan's past. He and I can direct attention to his immediate feelings as well as to his thoughts and actions. It seems essential to me that we work with all three dimensions—what he is thinking, what he is actually doing, and how his thoughts and behaviors affect his feeling states. Again, by directing Stan's attention to what is going on with him during our sessions, I can show him how he interacts in his world apart from therapy.

DEALING WITH THE FUTURE Adlerians are especially interested in where the client is heading. Humans are pulled by goals, strivings, and aspirations. It would help to know what Stan's goals in life are. What does he want for himself? If he decides that his present behavior is not getting him what he wants, he is in a good position to think ahead about the changes he would like to make and what he can do now to actualize his aspirations. The present-oriented behavioral focus of reality therapy is a good reference point for getting Stan to dream about what he would like to say about his life 5 years hence. Connecting present behavior with future plans is an excellent way to help Stan formulate a concrete plan of action. He will actually create his future.

Identifying Feelings

The person-centered approach stresses the first stage in the therapy process, which involves identifying, clarifying, and learning how to express feelings. Because of the therapeutic relationship I have built with Stan, I expect him to feel increasingly free to talk about feelings that he has kept to himself. In some cases these feelings are out of his awareness, and I encourage Stan to talk about any feelings that are a source of difficulty.

During the early stages of our sessions, I rely on empathic listening. I need to do more than merely reflect what I hear Stan saying; I need to share with him my reactions as I listen to him because doing so helps to build a good therapeutic alliance. When Stan senses that he is being understood and accepted for the feelings he has, he has less need to deny or distort his feelings. His capacity for clearly identifying what he is feeling at any moment will gradually increase.

There is a great deal of value in letting Stan tell his story in a way he chooses. The way he walks into the office, his gestures, his style of speech, the details he chooses to go into, and what he decides to relate and not to relate—to mention just a few elements—provide me with clues to his world. If I do too much structuring too soon, I will interfere with his typical style of presenting himself.

Expressing and Exploring Feelings

The authenticity of my relationship with Stan encourages him to begin to identify and share with me a range of feelings. But I do not believe an open and trusting relationship between us is sufficient to change Stan's personality and behavior. I must also use my knowledge, skills, and experiences although my clinical expertise is not the sole determinant of therapeutic change. Stan is the best expert on his own life, and I will assist him in coming to value the ways in which he is the expert in the therapeutic endeavor.

As a way of helping Stan express and explore his feelings, I draw heavily on Gestalt experiments. Eventually, I ask him to avoid merely talking about situations and about feelings. Rather, I encourage him to bring whatever reactions he is having into the present. For instance, if Stan reports feeling tense, I ask him *how* he experiences this tension right now and *where* it is located in his body. I encourage him to "be that feeling." Thus, if he has a knot in his stomach, he can intensify his feeling of tension by "becoming the knot, giving it voice and personality." If I notice tears in his eyes, I may direct him to "be his tears now." By putting words to his tears, he avoids abstract intellectualization about all the reasons he is sad or tense. Before he can change his feelings, Stan must allow himself to *fully experience* them. The experiential therapies provide valuable tools for guiding him to the expression of his feelings.

Here are some segments of our dialogue in a session where Stan becomes quite aware of what he is feeling as he talks about his relationship with his father:

JERRY: You mentioned that your father often compared you with your brother Frank and your sister Judy. What was that like for you?

STAN: I hated it! He told me that I'd never amount to anything.

JERRY: And when he said that, how did that affect you?

STAN: It made me feel that I could never measure up to all the great things that Judy and Frank were accomplishing. I felt like a failure. [*As he says this, he begins to tear up, and his voice changes.*]

JERRY: Stan, what is going on right now?

STAN: All of a sudden a wave of sadness is coming over me. I'm getting all choked up. This is hard!

JERRY: Stay with your feeling. What's going on?

STAN: My chest is tight, like something wants to come out.

JERRY: Say more.

STAN: I'm feeling very sad and hurt.

JERRY: Would you be willing to try something? I'd like you to talk to me as though I were your father. Are you willing to do that?

STAN: Well, you're not mean the way he was, but I can try.

JERRY: How old are you feeling now?

STAN: Oh, maybe 12 years old—just like when I had to be around my father and listen to all the stuff he told me about how useless I was.

JERRY: Let yourself be 12 again, and tell me what it's like for you to be you—speaking to me as your father.

STAN: There was nothing that I could ever do that was good enough for you. No matter how hard I tried, I couldn't get you to notice me. [*Crying*] Why didn't I count, and why did you ignore me?

JERRY: Stan, I'll just let you talk for a while, and I'll listen. So keep on telling me all the things you may be feeling as that 12-year-old now.

STAN: All I ever wanted was to know that I mattered to you. But no matter how hard I tried, all you'd do was put me down. Nothing I did was worth anything. I just wanted you to love me. Why didn't you ever do anything with me? [*Stan stops talking and just cries for a while.*]

JERRY: What's happening with you now?

STAN: I'm feeling so sad. As if it's hopeless. Nothing I can do will ever get his approval.

JERRY: At 12 it was important for you to get his acceptance and his love. There is still that part in you that wants his love.

STAN: Yes, and I don't think I'll ever get it.

JERRY: Tell him more of what that's like.

Stan continues talking to his "father" and recounts some of the ways in which he tried to live up to his expectations. No matter what he did, there was no way to get the acceptance that Frank and Judy got from him.

JERRY: Having said all that, what are you aware of now?

STAN: I'm feeling embarrassed.

JERRY: You say you're embarrassed. Whom are you aware of now?

STAN: Well, right now of you. I feel like a wimp. You're probably thinking that I'm weak and dumb for letting this get to me.

JERRY: Tell me more about feeling weak and dumb.

Stan expresses that he should be stronger and that he is afraid I'll think he is hopeless. He goes into some detail in belittling himself for what he has just experienced and expressed. I avoid quickly reassuring him that he "shouldn't feel that way." Instead, I let him express whatever he is feeling. After telling me many of the ways in which he is feeling embarrassed, he wonders if I still want to work with him. At this point I let him know that I respect his struggle and encourage him to continue revealing aspects that he typically keeps hidden. Because this session is coming to an end, I talk with Stan about the value of releasing feelings that he has been carrying around for a long time, suggesting that this is a good beginning. I am also interested in getting him to do some homework before the next session. By focusing on his feelings both in the therapy office and in daily life, I hope Stan can eventually learn to avoid judging himself so harshly.

JERRY: Stan, I'd like to suggest that you write a letter to your father . . .

STAN: [*Interrupting*] Oh no! I'm not going to give that guy the satisfaction of knowing that I need anything from him!

JERRY: Wait. I was about to say that I hope you'll write him a letter that you don't mail.

STAN: What's the point of a letter that won't be sent?

JERRY: Writing him a letter is an opportunity for further release and to gain some new insights. I hope you'll let yourself write about all the ways you tried to live up to his expectations. Let him know what it felt like to be around him. Tell him more about you, especially how it felt in not getting those things that you so much wanted.

STAN: OK, I'll do that.

In this session I might have made many different interventions. For the moment, I chose to let him "borrow my eyes" and talk to me as his father while he was 12 years old. I asked him to stay with whatever he was experiencing, paying particular attention to his body and to the emotions that were welling up within him. It would be premature to suggest problem-solving strategies or to attempt to figure everything out. My intent in offering him the homework assignment of writing a letter is to provide an avenue for Stan to continue thinking about the impact his father has had on him and to further promote his work during the week. Writing the letter may trigger memories, and he may experience further emotional release.

At our next session I will ask Stan about the letter and what it was like for him to write it. What did he say to his father? How was it to read the letter later? Is there anything that he wants to share with me? The direction of our next session will depend on his response. Again, Stan will provide clues to where he needs to go next.

The Thinking Dimension in Therapy

Once Stan has experienced some intense feelings and perhaps released pent-up feelings, some cognitive work is essential. To bring in this cognitive dimension, I focus Stan's attention on messages he incorporated as a child and on the decisions he made. I get him to think about the reason he made certain early decisions. Finally, I challenge Stan to look at these decisions about life, about himself, and about others and to make necessary revisions that can lead him to creating a life of his own choosing.

After getting basic information about Stan's life history (by means of the Adlerian lifestyle assessment form), I summarize and interpret it with Stan in a session. For example, I find some connections between his present fears of developing intimate relationships and his history of rejection by his siblings and his parents. I am interested in his family constellation and his early recollections. Rather than working exclusively with his feelings, I want Stan to begin to understand (cognitively) how these early experiences affected him then and how they still influence him today. My emphasis is on having Stan begin to question the conclusions he came to about himself, others, and life. What is his private logic? What are some of his mistaken, self-defeating perceptions that grew out of his family experiences? An Adlerian perspective provides tools for doing some productive cognitive work both in and out of the therapy sessions.

From rational emotive behavior therapy I especially value the emphasis on learning to think rationally and am interested in having Stan assess whether or not his thoughts are rational. I am not imposing my views of rational thinking; rather, I hope to help Stan examine his behavior and his beliefs about his behavior. I look for the ways in which Stan contributes to his painful feelings by the process of self-indoctrination with faulty beliefs that no longer serve him well. I ask him to test the validity of the dire consequences he predicts. I value the stress put on doing hard work in demolishing beliefs that have no validity and replacing them with sound and rational beliefs. I do not think Stan can merely think his way through life or that examining his faulty logic is enough by itself for personality change. But I do see this process as an essential component of therapy.

The cognitive behavioral therapies have a range of cognitive techniques that can help Stan recognize connections between his cognitions and his behaviors. He should also learn about his inner dialogue and the impact it has on his day-to-day behavior. Eventually, our goal is some cognitive restructuring work by which Stan can learn new ways to think, new things to tell himself, and new assumptions about life. This provides a basis for change in his behavior.

I have given Stan a number of homework assignments aimed at helping him identify a range of feelings and thoughts that may be problematic for him. Following are sample pieces of a session in which we focus on his cognitions.

JERRY: Several times now you've brought up how you're sure you'd be judged critically if you allowed yourself to get close to a woman. Is this a topic you want to explore in more depth?

STAN: Yes. I'm tired of avoiding women, but I'm still scared of approaching a woman. I'm convinced that if any woman gets to know me, she'll eventually reject me.

JERRY: Have you checked out this assumption? How many women have you approached, and how many of them have actually rejected you?

STAN: They never tell me these things. But in my head I keep telling myself that if they get to know the real me they'll be turned off by my weakness, and then they wouldn't want anything to do with me.

JERRY: How about telling me some of the things you tell yourself when you think of meeting a woman? Just let yourself free associate, listing out loud some of the statements you make to yourself internally. Ready?

STAN: So often I say to myself that I'm not worth knowing. [*Pause*]

JERRY: Just rattle off as many of these self-statements as you can. Don't worry about how it sounds.

STAN: What a nerd! Every time you open your mouth, you put your foot in it. Why don't you just shut up and hide? When you do talk to people, you freeze up. They're judging you, and if you say much of anything, they'll find out what a complete and utter failure you are. Anything you try, you fail in. You are not very interesting. You're a weak and a scared kid. Why don't you keep to yourself so that others won't reject you?

Stan continues with this list, and I listen. After he seems finished, I tell him how I'm affected by hearing his typical self-talk. I let him know that it saddens me. Although I like Stan, I don't have the sense that he will emotionally believe that I care about him. I let him know that I respect the way he doesn't run from his fears and that I admire his willingness to talk openly about his troubles.

Stan has acquired a wide range of critical internal dialogues that he has practiced for many years. As he begins to challenge those thoughts, he will discover that his thinking is grossly inaccurate. Eventually I hope he will change many of the beliefs that are resulting in problems for him. Along this line, I work with him to pinpoint specific beliefs and then do my best to get him to examine them. I am influenced by the constructivist trend in cognitive behavior therapy. Applied to Stan, constructivism holds that his subjective framework and interpretations are far more important than the objective bases that may be at the origin of his faulty beliefs. Thus, rather than imposing my version of what may constitute faulty, irrational, and dysfunctional beliefs on his part, I pursue a line of Socratic questioning whereby I get Stan to evaluate his own thinking processes and his conclusions.

JERRY: Let's take one statement that you've made a number of times: "When I'm with other people, I feel stupid." What goes on within you when you say this?

STAN: I hear critical voices, like people are in my head or are sitting on my shoulder.

JERRY: Name one person who often sits on your shoulder and tells you you're stupid.

STAN: My dad, for one. I hear his voice in my head a lot.

JERRY: Let me be Stan for a moment, and you be your dad, saying to me some of those critical things that you hear him saying inside your head.

STAN: Why are you going to college? Why don't you quit and give your seat to someone who deserves it? You're not a good student. You're wasting your time and the taxpayers' money by pretending to be a college student. Do yourself a favor and wake up to the fact that you are just a dumb kid.

JERRY: How much truth is there in what you just said as your dad?

STAN: You know, it sounds stupid that I let him convince me that I'm totally stupid.

JERRY: Instead of saying that you're stupid for letting him tell you that you're stupid, can you give yourself credit for being smart enough to come to this realization?

STAN: OK, but he's right that I've failed at most of the things I've tried.

JERRY: Does failing at a task mean that you're right holding to the label of being a failure in life? I'd like to hear you produce the evidence that supports your interpretation of being stupid and of being a failure.

STAN: How about the failure in my marriage? I couldn't make it work, and I was responsible for the divorce. That's a pretty big failure.

JERRY: And were you totally responsible for the divorce? Did your wife have any part in it?

STAN: She always told me that no woman could ever live with me. She convinced me that I couldn't have a satisfying relationship with her or any other woman.

JERRY: Although she could speak for herself, I'm wondering what qualifies her to determine your future with all women. What study did she conduct that proves that Stan is utterly destined to be allergic to all women forever?

STAN: I suppose I just bought into what she told me. After all, if I couldn't live with her, what makes me think I could have a satisfying life with any woman?

At this point, there are many directions to go with Stan to explore the origin of his beliefs and to assess the validity of his interpretations about life situations and his conclusions about his basic worth. In this and other sessions, we explore what cognitive therapists call "cognitive distortions." Here are some of Stan's cognitive distortions:

- *Arbitrary inferences.* Stan makes conclusions without supporting and relevant evidence. He often engages in "catastrophizing," or thinking about the worst possible scenario for a given situation.
- *Overgeneralization.* Stan holds extreme beliefs based on a single incident and applies them inappropriately to other dissimilar events or settings. For instance, because he and his wife divorced, he is convinced he is destined to be a failure with any woman.
- *Personalization.* Stan has a tendency to relate external events to himself, even when there is no basis for making the connection. He relates an incident in which a female classmate did not show up for a lunch date. He agonized over this event and convinced himself that she would have been humiliated to be seen in his presence. He did not consider any other possible explanations for her absence.
- *Labeling and mislabeling.* Stan presents himself in light of his imperfections and mistakes. He allows his past failures to define his total being.
- *Polarized thinking.* Stan frequently engages in thinking and interpreting in all-or-nothing terms. Through this process of dichotomous thinking, he has created self-defeating labels that keep him restricted.

Over a number of sessions we work on specific beliefs. The aim is for Stan to critically evaluate the evidence for many of his conclusions. My role is to promote corrective experiences that will lead to changes in his thinking. I am striving to create a collaborative relationship, one in which he will discover for himself how to distinguish between functional and dysfunctional beliefs. He can learn this by testing his conclusions.

Doing: Another Essential Component of Therapy

Stan can spend countless hours gathering interesting insights about why he is the way he is. He can learn to express feelings that he kept hidden for many years. He can think about the things he tells himself that lead to defeat. Yet in my view feeling and thinking are not a complete therapy process. *Doing* is a way of bringing these feelings and thoughts together by applying them to real-life situations in various action programs. I am indebted to Adlerian therapy, behavior therapy, reality therapy, rational emotive behavior therapy, cognitive therapy, narrative therapy, and solution-focused brief therapy, all of which give central emphasis to the role of action as a prerequisite for change.

Behavior therapy offers a multitude of techniques for behavioral change. In Stan's case I am especially inclined to work with him in developing self-management programs. For example, he complains of often feeling tense and anxious. Daily relaxation procedures are one way Stan can gain more control of his physical and psychological tension. I have been teaching him a variety of mindfulness techniques, including a combination of meditation and relaxation procedures. Through mindfulness practice, Stan can get himself centered before he goes to his classes, meets women, or talks to friends. He can also begin to monitor his behavior in everyday situations to gain increased awareness of what he tells himself, what he does, and then how he feels. When he gets depressed, he tends to drink to alleviate his symptoms. He can carry a small notebook with him and actually record events that lead up to his feeling depressed (or anxious or hurt). He might also record what he actually did in these situations and what he might have done differently. By paying attention to what he is doing in daily life, he is already beginning to gain more control of his behavior.

This behavioral monitoring can be coupled with both Adlerian and cognitive approaches. My guess is that Stan gets depressed, engages in self-destructive behavior (drinking, for one), and then feels even worse. I work very much on both his behaviors and cognitions and show him how many of his actions are influenced by what he is telling himself. Together we work on how he is setting himself up for failure by his self-defeating expectations. True to the spirit of rational emotive behavior therapy, we explore his faulty assumptions that he *must* be perfect and that if he does not get the job, life will be unbearable. There are many opportunities for Stan to see connections between his cognitive processes and his daily behavior. I encourage him to begin to behave differently and then look for changes in his feeling states and his thinking.

With this in mind, I ask Stan to think of as many ways as possible of actually bringing into his daily living the new learning he is acquiring in our sessions. Practice is essential. Homework assignments (preferably ones that Stan gives himself) are an excellent way for Stan to become an active agent in his therapy. He must *do* something himself for change to occur. The degree to which he will change is directly proportional to his willingness to experiment. I want Stan to learn from his new behavior in life. Thus, each week we discuss his progress toward meeting his goals, and we review how well he is completing his assignments. If he does not like the way he carried out an assignment, we can use this as an opportunity to talk about how he can adjust his behavior. I hold firm about expecting a commitment from him to have an action plan for change and to continually look at how well his plan is working.

In the following dialogue, our interchanges deal primarily with Stan learning a more assertive style of behavior with one of his professors. Although this session focuses on Stan's behavior, we are also dealing with what he is thinking and feeling. These three dimensions are interactive.

JERRY: Last week we role-played different ways you could approach a professor with whom you were having a difficulty. You learned several assertive skills that you used quite effectively when I assumed the role of the critical professor. Before you left last week, you agreed to set up a time to meet with your professor and let her know about your difficulty. When we did the role playing, you were very clear about what you wanted to say and strong in staying with your feelings. Did you carry out your plan?

STAN: The next day I tried to talk to her before class. She said she didn't have time to talk but that we could talk after class.

JERRY: And how did that go?

STAN: After class all I wanted to do was make an appointment with her so that I could talk in private and without feeling hurried. When I tried to make the appointment, she very brusquely said that she had to go to a meeting and that I should see her during her office hours.

JERRY: How did that affect you?

STAN: I was mad. All I wanted to do was make an appointment.

JERRY: Did you go to her office hours?

STAN: I did, that very afternoon. She was 20 minutes late for her office hours, and then some students were waiting to ask her questions. All I got to do was make an appointment with her in a couple of days.

JERRY: Did that appointment actually take place?

STAN: Yes, but she was 10 minutes late and seemed preoccupied. I had a hard time at the beginning.

JERRY: How so? Tell me more.

STAN: I feel stupid in her class, and I wanted to talk to her about it. When I ask questions, she gets a funny look on her face—as if she's impatient.

JERRY: Did you check out these assumptions with her?

STAN: Yes I did, and I feel proud of myself. She told me that at times she does get a bit impatient because I seem to need a lot of her time and reassurance. Then I let her know how much I was studying for her class and how serious I was about doing well in my major. It was good for me to challenge my fears, instead of avoiding her because I felt she was judgmental.

JERRY: It's good to hear you give yourself credit for the steps you took. Even though it was tough, you hung in there and said what you wanted to say. Is there anything about this exchange with her that you wish you could have changed?

STAN: For the most part, I was pretty assertive. Generally, I blame people in authority like her for making me feel stupid. I give them a lot of power in judging me. But this time I remembered what we worked on in our session, and I stayed focused on myself rather than telling her what she was doing or not doing.

JERRY: How did that go?

STAN: The more I talked about myself, the less defensive she became. I learned that part of how she reacts to me is influenced by my behavior and when I changed she also changed. I can still feel good about myself, even if the other person doesn't change. That was powerful.

JERRY: Great! Did you notice any difference in how you felt in her class after you had this talk?

STAN: For a change, I didn't feel so self-conscious, especially when I asked questions or took part in class discussions. I was not so concerned about what she might think about me, and she seemed more at ease with me.

JERRY: What did your meeting with her teach you about yourself?

STAN: For one thing, I'm learning to check out my assumptions. That freed me up to act much more spontaneously. Also, I learned that I could be clear, direct, and assertive without getting nasty. It was possible for me to take care of myself without being critical of her. Normally, I'd just swallow all my feelings and walk away feeling dumb. This time I was assertive and was able to let her know that I needed some unhurried time from her.

Practicing assertive behavior is associated with working with the feeling and thinking domains. Had Stan not done as well as he did in engaging his professor, we could have examined what had gone wrong from his vantage point. We could have continued role-playing various approaches in our sessions, and then with new knowledge and skills and more practice, he could have tried again. It is essential that Stan be willing to experiment with new ways of acting, especially outside of the therapy sessions. In a sense, counseling can be like a dress rehearsal for living. He exhibited courage and determination in carrying out a specific action plan, and change did take place.

Working Toward Revised Decisions

When Stan has identified and explored both his feelings and his faulty beliefs and thinking processes, it does not mean that therapy is over. Becoming aware of early decisions, including some of his basic mistakes and his self-defeating ideas, is the starting point for change. It is essential that Stan find ways to translate his emotional and cognitive insights into new ways of thinking, feeling, and behaving. Therefore, as much as possible I structure situations in the therapy sessions that will facilitate new decisions on his part on both the emotional and cognitive levels. In encouraging Stan to make these new decisions, I draw on cognitive, emotive, and behavioral techniques. A few techniques I employ are role playing, imagery work, assertion training procedures, and behavioral rehearsals. Both reality therapy and

Adlerian therapy have a lot to offer on getting clients to decide on a plan of action and then make a commitment to carry out their program for change.

Here are some examples of experiments I suggest for Stan during the therapy sessions and homework assignments.

• I engage in reverse role-playing situations in which I "become" Stan and have Stan assume the role of his mother, father, former wife, sister, older brother, and a professor. Through this process Stan gets a clearer picture of ways in which he allowed others to define him, and he acquires some skills in arguing back to self-defeating voices.

• To help Stan deal with his anxiety, I teach him meditation and other mindfulness techniques and encourage him to practice them daily. Stan learns to employ these relaxation strategies in anxiety-arousing situations. I also teach him a range of coping skills, such as assertiveness and disputing faulty beliefs. Stan is able to apply these skills in several life situations.

• Stan agrees to keep a journal in which he records impressions and experiences. After encountering difficult situations, he writes about his reactions, both on a thinking and a feeling level. He also records how he behaved in these situations, how he felt about his actions, and how he might have behaved differently. He also agrees to read a few self-help books in areas that are particularly problematic for him.

• As a homework assignment that we collaboratively design, Stan agrees to meet with people whom he would typically avoid. For instance, he is highly anxious over his performance in a couple of his classes. He decides to make an appointment with each professor to discuss his progress. In one case, a professor took an increased interest in him, and now he does very well in her class. In the other case, the professor is rather abrupt and not too helpful. He is able to recognize that this is more the professor's problem than anything he is doing.

• Stan wants to put himself in situations where he can make new friends. Together we work on a clear plan of action that involves joining a club, going to social events, and asking a woman in his class for a date. Although he is anxious in each of these situations, he follows through with his plans. In our sessions we explore some of his self-talk and actions at these events.

Encouraging Stan to Work With His Family of Origin

After working with Stan for a time, I suggest that he take the initiative to invite his entire family for a session. My assumption is that many of his problems stem from his family-of-origin experiences and that he is still being affected by these experiences. I think it will be useful to have at least one session with the family so that I can get a better idea of the broader context. The following dialogue illustrates my attempt to introduce this idea to Stan.

JERRY: Our sessions are certainly revealing a good deal of difficulties with several members of your family. I think it would be useful to bring in as many of them as you can for a session.

STAN: No way! That's way too much.

JERRY: Are you willing to talk with me more about this idea?

STAN: I'll talk, but I don't think it will change my mind.

JERRY: Why is that?

STAN: They already think I'm nutty, and if they find out I'm seeing a psychologist, that will be one more thing they can throw in my face.

JERRY: Would they use this against you?

STAN: Yes. Besides, I can't see how it would help much. My mother and father don't think they have any problems. I don't see them wanting to change much.

JERRY: Changing them is not my goal. It is more to give you a chance to express yourself respectfully to people who are still an important part of your life.

STAN: Maybe, but I'm not ready for that one yet!

JERRY: I can respect that you don't feel ready yet. I hope you'll remain open to the idea, and if you change your mind, let me know.

My rationale for including at least some of Stan's family members is to provide him with a context for understanding how his behavior is being influenced by what he learned as a child. He is a part of this system, and as he changes, it is bound to influence others in his family with whom he has contact. From what he has told me, I am assuming that his unclear boundaries with his mother have had an impact on his relationships with other women. If he can gain a clearer understanding of his relationship with his mother, he may be able to apply some of these insights with other women. In many ways Stan has allowed himself to be intimidated by his father, and he still hears Dad's voice in his head a lot. In much of his present behavior, Stan compares himself unfavorably with others, which is a pattern that was established in early childhood with his siblings. If he is able to deal with the members of his family about some of their past and present struggles, there is a good chance that he will be able to form the kind of intimate relationships that he says he would like to have in his life. (For a more complete description of working with Stan from a family systems perspective, see Stan's case in Chapter 14.)

The Spiritual Dimension

Although I do not have an agenda to impose religious or spiritual values on Stan, I want to assess the role spirituality plays, if any, in his life currently—and to assess beliefs, attitudes, and practices from his earlier years. When I ask Stan if religion was a factor in his childhood or adolescence, he informs me that his mother was a practicing Lutheran and his father was rather indifferent to religion. His mother made sure that he went to church each week. He tells me what he mainly remembers from his church experiences is feeling a sense of guilt. Stan recalls that his attitudes about religion fit in with his low self-esteem. Not only was he not good enough in the eyes of his parents, but he was also not good enough in the eyes of God. He also adds that when he went to college he developed a new interest in spirituality.

Although formal religion does not seem to play a key role for Stan now, he is struggling to find a spiritual core as this is missing in his life. He also lets me know that he is pleasantly surprised that I am even mentioning religion and spirituality. He was under the impression that counselors would not be too interested in these areas. Upon further discussion of this area, he informs me of his intention to bring up his concerns about his spirituality at a future session.

Working With Stan's Drinking Problem

Although each of the 11 therapeutic approaches address drug and alcohol abuse in different ways, all probably agree that it is imperative at some point in Stan's therapy to confront him on the probability that he is a chemically dependent person. In this section, I describe my approach to working with his dependence as well as giving some brief background information on the alcoholic personality and on treatment approaches.

SOME BASIC ASSUMPTIONS Stan has given me a number of significant clues suggesting that he is a chemically dependent person. From the information he has provided, it is clear that Stan has many of the personality traits typically associated with addictions, including low self-concept, anxiety, underachievement, feelings of social isolation, inability to receive love from others, hypersensitivity, impulsivity, dependence, fear of failure, feelings of guilt, and suicidal ideation. He has used drugs and alcohol as a way of blunting anxiety and attempting to control what he perceives as a painful reality.

Once our therapeutic relationship is firmly established, I confront Stan (in a caring and concerned manner) on the self-deception that drinking is less problematic than taking drugs. He needs to see that alcohol *is* a drug. I think it is important that he make an honest evaluation of his behavior so that he can recognize the degree to which his drinking is interfering in his living.

A SUPPLEMENTARY TREATMENT PROGRAM Stan eventually recognizes and acknowledges that he does indeed have a problem with alcoholism, and he says he is willing to do something about this problem. Stan needs to know that long-term recovery is based on the principle of total abstinence from all drugs and alcohol and that such abstinence is a prerequisite to effective counseling. In addition to his weekly individual therapy sessions with me, I provide Stan with a referral to deal with his chemical dependence.

I encourage Stan to join Alcoholics Anonymous and attend their meetings. The 12-step program of AA has worked very well for many alcoholics. Once Stan understands the nature of his chemical dependence and no longer uses drugs, the chances are greatly increased that we can focus on the other aspects of his life that he sees as problematic and would like to change. In short, it is possible to treat his alcoholism and at the same time carry out a program of individual therapy geared to changing Stan's ways of thinking, feeling, and behaving.

Moving Toward Termination of Therapy

The process I have been describing will probably take months. During this time, I will continue to draw simultaneously on a variety of therapeutic systems in working with Stan's thoughts, feelings, and behaviors. Eventually this process will lead to a time when Stan can continue what he has learned in therapy without my assistance.

Termination of therapy is as important as the initial phase, for now the key task is to put into practice what he has learned in the sessions by applying new skills and attitudes to daily social situations without professional assistance. When Stan brings up a desire to "go it alone," we talk about his readiness to end therapy and his reasons for thinking about termination. I also share with him my perceptions of the directions I have seen him take. This is a good time to talk about where he can go from here. We spend time developing an action plan and talking about how he can best maintain his new learning. He may want to join a therapeutic group. He could find support in a variety of social networks. In essence, he can continue to challenge himself by doing things that are difficult for him yet at the same time broaden his range of choices. Now he can take the risk and be his own therapist, dealing with feelings as they arise in new situations.

In a behavioral spirit, evaluating the process and outcomes of therapy seems essential. This evaluation can take the form of devoting some time to discussing Stan's specific changes in therapy. A few questions for focus are: "What stands out the most for you, Stan? What did you learn that you consider the most valuable? How did you learn these lessons? What can you do now to keep practicing new behaviors? What will you do if you experience a setback?" We explore potential difficulties he expects to face when he no longer comes to weekly counseling sessions. At this point, I introduce some relapse prevention strategies to help Stan cope constructively with future problems. By addressing potential problems and stumbling blocks that he might have to deal with, Stan is less likely to become discouraged if he experiences any setbacks. If any relapses do occur, we talk about seeing these as "learning opportunities" rather than as signs that he has failed. I let Stan know that his termination of formal therapy does not mean that he cannot return for a visit or session when he considers it appropriate. Rather than coming for weekly sessions, Stan might well decide to come in at irregular intervals for follow-up sessions.

Encouraging Stan to Join a Therapy Group

As Stan and I talk about termination, he gives me clear indications that he has learned a great deal about himself through individual counseling. Although Stan has been doing well on his own, I believe he would benefit from a group experience. I suggest that Stan consider joining a 16-week therapy group that will begin in 2 months.

To me, progressing from individual therapy to a group seems useful for a client like Stan. Because many of his problems are interpersonal, a group is an ideal place for him to deal with them. The group will give Stan a context for practicing the very behaviors he says he wants to acquire. Stan wants to feel freer in being himself, to be able to approach people even when he is fearful, and to be able to trust people more fully. In addition to a group experience, I will be working with Stan to find some other ways to continue his growth.

Commentary on the Thinking, Feeling, and Doing Perspective

In applying my integrative perspective to Stan, I've dealt separately with the cognitive, affective, and behavioral dimensions of human experience. Although the steps I outlined may appear relatively structured and even simple, actually working with clients is more complex and less predictable. If you are practicing from an integrative perspective, it would be a mistake to assume that it is best to always begin working with what clients are thinking (or feeling or doing). Effective counseling begins where the client is, not where a theory indicates a client should be.

In summary, depending on what clients need at the moment, I may focus initially on what they are thinking and how this is affecting them, or I may focus on how they feel, or I may choose to direct them to pay attention to what they are doing. Thinking and feeling are two sides of the same coin, and if Stan can change his thoughts, I believe he is likely to change some of his behaviors and his feelings. If he changes his feelings, he might well begin to think and act differently. If he changes certain behaviors, he may begin thinking and feeling differently. Because these facets of human experience are interrelated, one route generally leads to the other dimensions.

A person-centered focus respects the wisdom within the client and uses it as a lead for where to go next. My guess is that counselors often make the mistake of getting too far ahead of their clients, thinking, "What should I do next?" By staying with our clients and asking them what they want, they will tell us which direction to take either directly or indirectly. We can learn to pay attention to our own reactions to our clients and to our own energy. By doing so we can engage in a therapeutic connection that is helpful for both parties in the relationship.

Follow-Up: You Continue Working With Stan in an Integrative Style

Think about these questions to help you decide how to counsel Stan from your own integrative approach:

- What themes in Stan's life do you find most significant, and how might you draw on these themes during the initial phase of counseling?
- What specific concepts from the various theoretical orientations would you be most inclined to utilize in your work with Stan?
- Identify some key techniques from the various therapies that you are most likely to employ in your therapy with Stan.
- How would you develop experiments for Stan to carry out both inside and outside the therapy sessions?
- Knowing what you do about Stan, what do you imagine it would be like to be his therapist? What problems, if any, might you expect to encounter in your counseling relationship with him?

 See *DVD for Theory and Practice of Counseling and Psychotherapy: The Case of Stan and Lecturettes* (Session 13 on an integrative approach) for a demonstration of my approach to counseling Stan from this perspective. This session deals with termination and takes an integrative view of Stan's work. This is also a good time to review the entire program of the 13 sessions with Stan as a way to think about how you might counsel Stan from your integrative perspective.

CONCLUDING COMMENTS

At the beginning of the introductory course in counseling, my students typically express two reactions: "How will I ever be able to learn all these theories?" and "How can I make sense out of all this information?" By the end of the course, these students are often surprised by how much work they have done *and* by how much they have learned. Although an introductory survey course will not turn students into accomplished counselors, it generally provides the basis for selecting from among the many models to which they are exposed.

At this point you may be able to begin putting the theories together in some meaningful way for yourself. This book will have served its central purpose if it has encouraged you to read further and to expand your knowledge of the theories that most caught your interest. I hope you have seen something of value that you can use from each of the approaches described. You will not be in a position to conceptualize a completely developed integrative perspective after your first course in counseling theory, but you now have the tools to begin the process of integration. With additional study and practical experience, you will be able to expand and refine your emerging personal philosophy of counseling.

Finally, the book will have been put to good use if it has stimulated you to think about the ways in which your philosophy of life, your values, your life experiences, and the person you are becoming are vitally related to the caliber of counselor you can become. This book and your course may have raised questions for you regarding your decision to become a counselor. Seeking out at least one of your professors to explore these questions can be the next step.

Now that you have finished this book, I would be very interested in hearing about your experience with it and with your course. The comments readers have sent me over the years have been helpful in revising each edition, and I welcome your feedback. You can complete the reaction sheet at the end of the book and mail it to Brooks/Cole, Cengage Learning, 20 Davis Drive, Belmont, California 94002.

Recommended Supplementary Readings for Part 1

Leaving It at the Office: A Guide to Psychotherapist Self-Care (Norcross & Guy, 2007) addresses 12 self-care strategies that are supported by empirical evidence. The authors develop the position that self-care is personally essential and professionally ethical. This is one of the most useful books on therapist self-care and on prevention of burnout.

Psychotherapy Relationships That Work: Evidence-based Responsiveness (Norcross, 2011) is a comprehensive treatment of the effective elements of the therapy relationship. Many different contributors address ways of tailoring the therapy relationship to individual clients. Implications from research for effective clinical practice are presented.

Ethics Desk Reference for Counselors (Barnett & Johnson, 2010) is a practical guide to understanding and applying the *ACA Code of Ethics*. It is a reference that is easy to read, interesting, and has appeal for both students and practitioners.

The Gift of Therapy: An Open Letter to a New Generation of Therapists and Their Patients (Yalom, 2003) is a highly readable, insightful, and useful resource. It includes 85 short chapters on a wide variety of topics that pertain to the counselor as a person and as a professional.

ACA Ethical Standards Casebook (Herlihy & Corey, 2006a) contains a variety of useful cases that are geared to the *ACA Code of Ethics*. The examples illustrate and clarify the meaning and intent of the standards.

Boundary Issues in Counseling: Multiple Roles and Responsibilities (Herlihy & Corey, 2006b) puts the multiple-relationship controversy into perspective. The book focuses on dual relationships in a variety of work settings.

Boundaries in Psychotherapy: Ethical and Clinical Explorations (Zur, 2007) examines the complex nature of boundaries in professional practice by offering a decision-making process to help practitioners deal with a range of topics such as gifts, nonsexual touch, home visits, bartering, and therapist self-disclosure.

Issues and Ethics in the Helping Professions (Corey, Corey, & Callanan, 2011) is devoted entirely to the issues that were introduced briefly in Chapter 3. The book is designed to involve readers in a personal and active way, and many open-ended cases are presented to help readers formulate their thoughts on a wide range of ethical issues.

Becoming a Helper (M. Corey & Corey, 2011) has separate chapters that expand on issues dealing with the personal and professional lives of helpers and ethical issues in counseling practice.

Ethics in Action: CD-ROM (Corey, Corey, & Haynes, 2003) is a self-instructional program divided into three parts: (1) ethical decision making, (2) values and the helping relationship, and (3) boundary issues and multiple relationships. The program includes video clips of vignettes demonstrating ethical situations aimed at stimulating discussion.

Student Manual for Theory and Practice of Counseling and Psychotherapy (Corey, 2013c) is designed to help you integrate theory with practice and to make the concepts covered in this book come alive. It consists of self-inventories, overview summaries of the theories, a glossary of key concepts, study questions, issues and questions for personal application, activities and exercises, comprehension checks and quizzes, and case examples. The manual is fully coordinated with the textbook to make it a personal study guide.

Case Approach to Counseling and Psychotherapy (Corey, 2013b) provides case applications of how each of the theories presented in this book works in action. A hypothetical client, Ruth, experiences counseling from all of the therapeutic vantage points.

The Art of Integrative Counseling (Corey, 2013a) is a presentation of concepts and techniques from the various theories of counseling. The book provides guidelines for readers in developing their own approaches to counseling practice.

DVD for Theory and Practice of Counseling and Psychotherapy: The Case of Stan and Lecturettes (Corey, 2013) is an interactive self-study tool that consists of two programs. Part 1 includes 13 sessions in which Gerald Corey counsels Stan using a few selected techniques from each theory. Part 2 consists of brief lectures by the author for each chapter in *Theory and Practice of Counseling and Psychotherapy*. Both programs emphasize the practical applications of the various theories.

DVD for Integrative Counseling: The Case of Ruth and Lecturettes (Corey & Haynes, 2013) is an interactive self-study tool that contains video segments and interactive questions designed to teach students ways of working with a client (Ruth) by drawing concepts and techniques from diverse theoretical approaches. The topics in this video program parallel the topics in the book *The Art of Integrative Counseling*.

Creating Your Professional Path: Lessons From My Journey (Corey, 2010) is a personal book that deals with a range of topics pertaining to the counselor as a person and as a professional. In addition to the author's discussion of his personal and professional journey, 18 contributors share their personal stories regarding turning points in their lives and lessons they learned.

The Counselor as Person and Professional (DVD) elaborates on the themes in Chapter 2 and is available from the American Counseling Association. This program is a keynote address that was given by Gerald Corey at the ACA conference in 2010 in Pittsburgh.

References and Suggested Readings for Chapter 3

American Counseling Association. (2005). *ACA code of ethics*. Alexandria, VA: Author.

American Psychiatric Association. (2000). *Diagnostic and statistical manual of mental disorders, text revision* (4th ed.). Washington, DC: Author.

*Books and articles marked with an asterisk are suggested for further study.

American Psychological Association. (2002). Ethical principles of psychologists and code of conduct. *American Psychologist, 57*(12), 1060-1073.

American Psychological Association. (2003). Guidelines on multicultural education, training, research, practice, and organizational change for psychologists. *American Psychologist, 58*(5), 377-402.

*American Psychological Association Presidential Task Force on Evidence-Based Practice. (2006). Evidence-based practice in psychology. *American Psychologist, 61*, 271-285.

Arredondo, P., Toporek, R., Brown, S., Jones, J., Locke, D., Sanchez, J., & Stadler, H. (1996). Operationalization of multicultural counseling competencies. *Journal of Multicultural Counseling and Development, 24*(1), 42-78.

*Baker, E. K. (2003). *Caring for ourselves: A therapist's guide to personal and professional well-being.* Washington, DC: American Psychological Association.

*Barnett, J. E., & Johnson, W. B. (2008). *Ethics desk reference for psychologists.* Washington, DC: American Psychological Association.

*Barnett, J. E., & Johnson, W. B. (2010). *Ethics desk reference for counselors.* Alexandria, VA: American Counseling Association.

Cardemil, E. V., & Battle, C. L. (2003). Guess who's coming to therapy? Getting comfortable with conversations about race and ethnicity in psychotherapy. *Professional Psychology: Research and Practice, 34*(3), 278-286.

Codes of Ethics for the Helping Professions (4Th Ed.). (2011). Belmont, CA: Brooks/Cole, Cengage Learning.

Comas-Diaz, L. (2011). Multicultural approaches to psychotherapy. In J. C. Norcross, G. R. Vandenbos, & D. K. Freedheim (Eds.), *History of psychotherapy* (2nd ed., pp. 243-268). Washington, DC: American Psychological Association.

Committee on Professional Practice and Standards. (2003). Legal issues in the professional practice of psychology. *Professional Psychology: Research and Practice, 34*(6), 595-600.

*Corey, G. (2010). *Creating your professional path: Lessons from my journey.* Alexandria, Va: American Counseling Association.

*Corey, G. (2013a). *The art of integrative counseling* (3rd ed.). Belmont, CA: Brooks/Cole, Cengage Learning.

*Corey, G. (2013b). *Case approach to counseling and psychotherapy* (8th ed.). Belmont, CA: Brooks/Cole, Cengage Learning.

*Corey, G. (2013c). *Student manual for theory and practice of counseling and psychotherapy* (9th ed.). Belmont, CA: Brooks/Cole, Cengage Learning.

*Corey, G., & Corey, M. (2010). *I never knew I had a choice* (9th ed.). Belmont, CA: Brooks/Cole, Cengage Learning.

*Corey, G., Corey, M., & Callanan, P. (2011). *Issues and ethics in the helping professions* (8th ed.). Belmont, CA: Brooks/Cole, Cengage Learning.

*Corey, G., Corey, M., & Haynes, R. (2003). *Ethics in action: CD-ROM.* Belmont, CA: Brooks/Cole, Cengage Learning.

*Corey, G., & Haynes, R. (2013). *DVD for integrative counseling: The case of Ruth and lecturettes.* Belmont, CA: Brooks/Cole, Cengage Learning.

*Corey, M., & Corey, G. (2011). *Becoming a helper* (6th ed.). Belmont, CA: Brooks/Cole, Cengage Learning.

Cukrowicz, K. C., White, B. A., Reitzel, L. R., Burns, A. B., Driscoll, K. A., Kemper, T. S., & Joiner, T. E. (2005). Improved treatment outcome associated with the shift to empirically supported treatments in a graduate training clinic. *Professional Psychology: Research and Practice, 36*(3), 330-337.

Deegear, J., & Lawson, D. M. (2003). The utility of empirically supported treatments. *Professional Psychology: Research and Practice, 34*(3), 271-277.

*Duncan, B. L., Miller, S. D., & Sparks, J. A. (2004). *The heroic client: A revolutionary way to improve effectiveness through client-directed, outcome-informed therapy.* San Francisco: Jossey-Bass.

*Duncan, B. L., Miller, S. D., Wampold, B. E. & Hubble, M. A. (Eds.). (2010). *The heart and *soul of change: Delivering what works in therapy* (2nd ed.). Washington, DC: American Psychological Association.

Edwards, J. A., Dattilio, F. M., & Bromley, D. B. (2004). Developing evidence-based practice: The role of case-based research. *Professional Psychology: Research and Practice, 35*(6), 589–597.

Elkins, D. N. (2009). *Humanistic psychology: A clinical manifesto.* Colorado Springs, CO: University of the Rockies Press.

*Falender, C. A., & Shafranske, E. P. (2004). *Clinical supervision: A competency-based approach.* Washington, DC: American Psychological Association.

*Geller, J. D., Norcross, J. C., & Orlinsky, D. E. (Eds.). (2005a). *The psychotherapist's own psychotherapy: Patient and clinician perspectives.* New York: Oxford University Press.

*Geller, J. D., Norcross, J. C., & Orlinsky, D. E. (2005b). The question of personal therapy: Introduction and prospectus. In J. D. Geller, J. C. Norcross, & D. E. Orlinsky (Eds.), *The psychotherapist's own psychotherapy: Patient and clinician perspectives* (pp. 3–11). New York: Oxford University Press.

Gutheil, T. G., & Brodsky, A. (2008). *Preventing boundary violations in clinical practice.* New York: Guilford Press.

*Herlihy, B., & Corey, G. (2006a). *ACA ethical standards casebook* (6th ed.). Alexandria, VA: American Counseling Association.

*Herlihy, B., & Corey, G. (2006b). *Boundary issues in counseling: Multiple roles and responsibilities* (2nd ed.). Alexandria, VA: American Counseling Association.

*Knapp, S. J., & Vandecreek, L. (2006). *Practical ethics for psychologists: A positive approach.* Washington, DC: American Psychological Association.

Lambert, M. J. (2011). Psychotherapy research and its achievements. In J. C. Norcross, G. R. Vandenbos, & D. K. Freedheim (Eds.), *History of psychotherapy* (2nd ed., pp. 299–332). Washington, DC: American Psychological Association.

*Lazarus, A. A., & Zur, O. (2002). *Dual relationships and psychotherapy.* New York: Springer.

*Lum, D. (2011). *Culturally competent practice: A framework for understanding diverse groups and justice issues* (4th ed.). Belmont, CA: Brooks/Cole, Cengage Learning.

*Miller, S. D., Duncan, B. L., & Hubble, M. A. (2004) Beyond integration: The triumph of outcome over process in clinical practice. *Psychotherapy in Australia, 10*(2), 2–19.

*Nagy, T. F. (2011). *Essential ethics for psychologists: A primer for understanding and mastering core issues.* Washington, DC: American Psychological Association.

*Norcross, J. C. (2005). The psychotherapist's own psychotherapy: Educating and developing psychologists. *American Psychologist, 60*(8), 840–850.

*Norcross, J. C. (Ed.). (2011). *Psychotherapy relationships that work: Evidence-based responsiveness* (2nd ed.). New York: Oxford University Press.

Norcross, J. C., Beutler, L. E., & Levant, R. F. (2006). *Evidence-based practices in mental health: Debate and dialogue on the fundamental questions.* Washington, DC: American Psychological Association.

*Norcross, J. C., & Goldfried, M. R. (Eds.). (2005). *Handbook of psychotherapy integration* (2nd ed.). New York: Oxford University Press.

*Norcross, J. C., & Guy, J. D. (2007). *Leaving it at the office: Psychotherapist self-care.* New York: Guilford Press.

*Norcross, J. C., Hogan, T. P., & Koocher, G. P. (2008). *Clinician's guide to evidence-based practices.* New York: Oxford University Press.

Norcross, J. C., & Lambert, M. J. (2011). Evidence-based therapy relationships. In J.C. Norcross (Ed.), *Psychotherapy relationships that work: Evidence-based responsiveness* (2nd ed., pp. 3–21). New York: Oxford University Press.

Norcross, J. C., Vandenbos, G. R., & Freedheim, D. K. (2011). *History of psychotherapy* (2nd ed.). Washington, DC: American Psychological Association.

Norcross, J. C., & Wampold, B. E. (2011). Evidence-based therapy relationships: Research conclusions and clinical practices. In J.C. Norcross (Ed.), *Psychotherapy relationships that work: Evidence-based responsiveness* (2nd ed., pp. 423–430). New York: Oxford University Press.

Orlinsky, D. E., Norcross, J. C., Ronnestad, M. H., & Wiseman, H. (2005). Outcomes and impacts of the psychotherapists' own psychotherapy. In J. D. Geller, J. C. Norcross, & D. E. Orlinsky (Eds.), *The psychotherapist's own psychotherapy: Patient and clinician perspectives* (pp. 214–230). New York: Oxford University Press.

*Pedersen, P. (2000). *A handbook for developing multicultural awareness* (3rd ed.). Alexandria, VA: American Counseling Association.

*Remley, T. P., & Herlihy, B. (2010). *Ethical, legal, and professional issues in counseling* (3rd ed.). Upper Saddle River, NJ: Merrill/Prentice-Hall.

*Schank, J. A., & Skovholt, T. M. (2006). *Ethical practice in small communities: Challenges and rewards for psychologists.* Washington, DC: American Psychological Association.

Shallcross, L. (2010). Putting clients ahead of personal values. *Counseling Today, 53*(5), 32–34.

Shallcross, L. (2011). Taking care of yourself as a counselor. *Counseling Today, 53*(7), 30–37.

*Skovholt, T. M., & Jennings, L. (2004). *Master therapists: Exploring expertise in therapy and counseling.* Boston: Pearson Education.

*Sperry, L. (2007). *The ethical and professional practice of counseling and psychotherapy.* Boston: Allyn & Bacon (Pearson).

*Stebnicki, M. A. (2008). *Empathy fatigue: Healing the mind, body, and spirit of professional counselors.* New York: Springer.

Sue, D. W., Arredondo, P., & Mcdavis, R. J. (1992). Multicultural counseling competencies and standards. A call to the profession. *Journal of Counseling and Development, 70*(4), 477–486.

*Sue, D. W., & Sue, D. (2008). *Counseling the culturally diverse: Theory and practice* (5th ed.). New York: Wiley.

Toporek, R. L., Gerstein, L. H., Fouad, N. A., Roysircar, G., & Israel, T. (2006). *Handbook for social justice counseling in counseling psychology: Leadership, vision, and action.* Thousand Oaks, CA: Sage.

Wampold, B. E. (2001). *The great psychotherapy debate: Models, methods, and findings.* Hillsdale, NJ: Erlbaum.

Wampold, B. E., & Bhati, K. S. (2004). Attending to the omissions: A historical examination of evidence-based practice movements. *Professional Psychology: Research and Practice, 35*(6), 563–570.

*Yalom, I. D. (2003). *The gift of therapy: An open letter to a new generation of therapists and their patients.* New York: HarperCollins (Perennial).

*Zur, O. (2007). *Boundaries in psychotherapy: Ethical and clinical explorations.* Washington, DC: American Psychological Association.

Recommended Supplementary Readings for chapter 4

Psychoanalytic Theory: An Introduction (Elliott, 1994) provides thorough coverage of the psychoanalytic implications for "postmodern" theories, systems approaches, and feminist thought.

Brief Dynamic Therapy (Levenson, 2010) describes a model of psychodynamic therapy that fits the reality of time-limited therapy and outlines the steps toward clinical work that is both focused and deep. The book deals with how psychoanalytic concepts and techniques can be modified to suit the needs of many clients who cannot participate in long-term therapy.

Psychodynamic Psychiatry in Clinical Practice (Gabbard, 2005) offers an excellent account of various psychoanalytic perspectives on borderline and narcissistic disorders.

Object Relations and Self Psychology: An Introduction (St. Clair, with Wigren, 2004) provides an overview and critical assessment of two streams of psychoanalytic theory and practice: object-relations theory and self psychology. Especially useful are the chapters discussing the approaches of Margaret Mahler, Otto Kernberg, and Heinz Kohut.

References and Suggested Readings for Chapter 4

*Ainslie, R. (2007). Psychoanalytic psychotherapy. In A. B. Rochlen (Ed.), *Applying counseling theories: An online case-based approach* (pp. 5–20). Upper Saddle River, NJ: Pearson Prentice-Hall.

Atkinson, D. R., Thompson, C. E., & Grant, S. K. (1993). A three-dimensional model for counseling racial/ethnic minorities. *The Counseling Psychologist, 2*(2), 257–277.

Clarkin, J., Yeomans, F., & Kernberg, O. (2006). *Psychotherapy for borderline personality: Focusing on object relations.* Washington DC: American Psychiatric Press.

Corey, G. (2012). *Theory and practice of group counseling* (8th ed.). Belmont, CA: Brooks/Cole, Cengage Learning.

*Corey, G. (2013). *Case approach to counseling and psychotherapy* (8th ed.). Belmont, CA: Brooks/Cole, Cengage Learning.

*Curtis, R. C., & Hirsch, I. (2011). Relational psychoanalytic psychotherapy. In S. B. Messer & A. S. Gurman, (Eds.), *Essential psychotherapies: Theory and practice* (3rd ed., pp. 72–104). New York: Guilford Press.

*Elliot, A. (1994). *Psychoanalytic theory: An introduction.* Oxford UK & Cambridge USA: Blackwell.

Enns, C. Z. (1993). Twenty years of feminist counseling and therapy: From naming biases to implementing multifaceted practice. *The Counseling Psychologist, 21*(1), 3–87.

*Erikson, E. H. (1963). *Childhood and society* (2nd ed.). New York: Norton.

Freud, S. (1949). *An outline of psychoanalysis.* New York: Norton.

*Books and articles marked with an asterisk are suggested for further study.

*Freud, S. (1955). *The interpretation of dreams*. London: Hogarth Press.

*Gabbard, G. (2005). *Psychodynamic psychiatry in clinical practice* (4th ed.). Washington, DC: American Psychiatric Press.

*Gelso, C. J., & Hayes, J. A. (2002). The management of countertransference. In J. C. Norcross (Ed.), *Psychotherapy relationships that work* (pp. 267–283). New York: Oxford University Press.

*Harris, A. S. (1996). *Living with paradox: An introduction to Jungian psychology*. Belmont, CA: Brooks/Cole, Cengage Learning.

Hayes, J. A., (2004). Therapist know thyself: Recent research on countertransference. *Psychotherapy Bulletin, 39*(4), 6–12.

Hayes, J. A., Gelso, C. J., & Hummel, A. M. (2011). Management of countertransference. In J.C. Norcross (Ed.), *Psychotherapy relationships that work: Evidence-based responsiveness* (2nd ed., pp. 239–258). New York: Oxford University Press.

*Hedges, L. E. (1983). *Listening perspectives in psychotherapy*. New York: Aronson.

*Jung, C. G. (1961). *Memories, dreams, reflections*. New York: Vintage.

Kernberg, O. F. (1975). *Borderline conditions and pathological narcissism*. New York: Aronson.

Kernberg, O. F. (1976). *Object-relations theory and clinical psychoanalysis*. New York: Aronson.

Kernberg, O. F. (1997). Convergences and divergences in contemporary psychoanalytic technique and psychoanalytic psychotherapy. In J. K. Zeig (Ed.), *The evolution of psychotherapy: The third conference* (pp. 3–22). New York: Brunner/Mazel.

Kernberg, O. F., Yeomans, F. E., Clarkin, J. F., & Levy, K. N. (2008). Transference focused psychotherapy: Overview and update. *International Journal of Psychoanalysis, 89,* 601–620.

Klein, M. (1975). *The psychoanalysis of children*. New York: Dell.

Kohut, H. (1971). *The analysis of self*. New York: International Universities Press.

Kohut, H. (1977). *Restoration of the self*. New York: International Universities Press.

Kohut, H. (1984). *How does psychoanalysis cure?* Chicago: University of Chicago Press.

*Levenson, H. (2007). Time-limited dynamic psychotherapy. In A. B. Rochlen (Ed.), *Applying counseling theories: An online case-based approach* (pp. 75–90). Upper Saddle River, NJ: Pearson Prentice-Hall.

Levenson, H. (2010). *Brief dynamic therapy*. Washington, DC: American Psychological Association.

Linehan, M. M. (1993a). *Cognitive-behavioral treatment of borderline personality disorder*. New York: Guilford Press.

Linehan, M. M. (1993b). *Skills training manual for treating borderline personality disorder*. New York: Guilford Press.

*Luborsky, E. B., O'Reilly-Landry, M., & Arlow, J. A. (2011). Psychoanalysis. In R. J. Corsini & D. Wedding (Eds.), *Current psychotherapies* (9th ed., pp. 15–66). Belmont, CA: Brooks/Cole, Cengage Learning.

Mahler, M. S. (1968). *On human symbiosis or the vicissitudes of individuation*. New York: International Universities Press.

Masterson, J. F. (1976). *Psychotherapy of the borderline adult: A developmental approach*. New York: Brunner/Mazel.

Messer, S. B., & Gurman, A. S. (2011). *Essential psychotherapies: Theory and practice* (3rd ed.). New York: Guilford Press.

Messer, S. B., & Warren, C. S. (2001). Brief psychodynamic therapy. In R. J. Corsini (Ed.), *Handbook of innovative therapies* (2nd ed., pp. 67–85). New York: Wiley.

Mitchell, S. A. (1988). *Relational concepts in psychoanalysis: An integration*. Cambridge, MA: Harvard University Press.

*Mitchell, S. A. (2000). *Relationality: From attachment to intersubjectivity*. Hillsdale, NJ: The Analytic Press.

Mitchell, S. A., & Black, M. J. (1995). *Freud and beyond: A history of modern psychoanalytic thought*. New York: Basic Books.

Prochaska, J. O., & Norcross, J. C. (2010). *Systems of psychotherapy: A transtheoretical analysis* (7th ed.). Belmont, CA: Brooks/Cole, Cengage Learning.

Reik, T. (1948). *Listening with the third ear.* New York: Pyramid.

*Rutan, J. S., Stone, W. N., & Shay, J. J. (2007). *Psychodynamic group psychotherapy* (4th ed.). New York: Guilford Press.

*Schultz, D., & Schultz, S. E. (2009). *Theories of personality* (9th ed.). Belmont, CA: Wadsworth, Cengage Learning.

Smith, L. (2005). Psychotherapy, classism, and the poor. *American Psychologist, 60*(7), 687–696.

*St. Clair, M. (with Wigren, J.). (2004). *Object relations and self psychology: An introduction* (4th ed.). Belmont, CA: Brooks/Cole, Cengage Learning.

Stern, D. N. (1985). *The interpersonal world of the infant: A view from psychoanalysis and developmental psychology.* New York: Basic Books.

Strupp, H. H. (1992). The future of psychodynamic psychotherapy. *Psychotherapy, 29*(l), 21–27.

Wolitzsky, D. L. (2011a). Contemporary Freudian psychoanalytic psychotherapy. In S. B. Messer & A. S. Gurman (Eds.), *Essential psychotherapies: Theory and practice* (3rd ed., pp. 33–71). New York: Guilford Press.

Wolitzsky, D. L. (2011b). Psychoanalytic theories in psychotherapy. In J. C. Norcross, G. R. Vandenbos, & D. K. Freedheim (Eds.), *History of psychotherapy* (2nd ed., pp. 65–100). Washington, DC: American Psychological Association.

Yalom, I. D. (2003). *The gift of therapy: An open letter to a new generation of therapists and their patients.* New York: HarperCollins (Perennial).

Recommended Supplementary Readings for Chapter 5

Adlerian Therapy: Theory and Practice (Carlson, Watts, & Maniacci, 2006) clearly presents a comprehensive overview of Adlerian therapy in contemporary practice. There are chapters on the therapeutic relationship, brief individual therapy, brief couples therapy, group therapy, play therapy, and consultation. This book lists Adlerian intervention videos that are available.

Adlerian Counseling and Psychotherapy: A Practitioner's Approach (Sweeney, 2009) is one of the most comprehensive books written on the wide range of Adlerian applications to therapy and wellness.

Adlerian Psychotherapy: An Advanced Approach to Individual Psychology (Oberst & Stewart, 2003) is an up-to-date and in-depth presentation of Adlerian psychotherapeutic process, including chapters on family therapy and the relevance of this model to postmodern approaches.

Early Recollections: Interpretative Method and Application (Mosak & Di Pietro, 2006) is an extensive review of the use of early recollections as a way to understand an individual's dynamics and behavioral style. This book addresses the theory, research, and clinical applications of early recollections.

Understanding Life-Style: The Psycho-Clarity Process (Powers & Griffith, 1987) is a useful source of information for doing a lifestyle assessment. Separate chapters deal with interview techniques, lifestyle assessment, early recollections, the family constellation, and methods of summarizing and interpreting information.

References and Suggested Readings for Chapter 5

Adler, A. (1958). *What life should mean to you.* New York: Capricorn. (Original work published 1931)

---

*Books and articles marked with an asterisk are suggested for further study.

Adler, A. (1959). *Understanding human nature.* New York: Premier Books. (Original work published 1927)

Adler, A. (1964). *Social interest. A challenge to mankind.* New York: Capricorn. (Original work published 1938)

Adler, A. (1978). *The education of children.* Chicago: Regnery Publishing. (Original work published 1930)

Albert, L. (1996). *Cooperative discipline.* Circle Pines, MN: American Guidance Service.

American Psychiatric Association. (2000). *Diagnostic and statistical manual of mental disorders, text revision* (4th ed.). Washington, DC: Author.

Ansbacher, H. L. (1974). Goal-oriented individual psychology: Alfred Adler's theory. In A. Burton (Ed.), *Operational theories of personality* (pp. 99–142). New York: Brunner/Mazel.

*Ansbacher, H. L. (1979). The increasing recognition of Adler. In. H. L. Ansbacher & R. R. Ansbacher (Eds.), *Superiority and social interest. Alfred Adler, A collection of his later writings* (3rd rev. ed., pp. 3–20). New York: Norton.

*Ansbacher, H. L. (1992). Alfred Adler's concepts of community feeling and social interest and the relevance of community feeling for old age. *Individual Psychology, 48*(4), 402–412.

*Ansbacher, H. L., & Ansbacher, R. R. (Eds.). (1964). *The individual psychology of Alfred Adler.* New York: Harper & Row/Torchbooks. (Original work published 1956)

*Ansbacher, H. L., & Ansbacher, R. R. (Eds.). (1979). *Superiority and social interest. Alfred Adler: A collection of his later writings* (3rd rev. ed.). New York: Norton.

Arciniega, G. M., & Newlon, B. J. (2003). Counseling and psychotherapy: Multicultural considerations. In D. Capuzzi & D. F. Gross (Eds.), *Counseling and psychotherapy: Theories and interventions* (3rd ed., pp. 417–441). Upper Saddle River, NJ: Merrill/Prentice-Hall.

Bitter, J. R. (2006, May 25). *Am I an Adlerian?* Ansbacher Lecture, 54th annual convention of the North American Society of Adlerian Psychology (NASAP), Chicago, IL.

Bitter, J. R. (2008). Reconsidering narcissism: An Adlerian-feminist response to the articles in the special section of the *Journal of Individual Psychology*, volume 63, number 2. *Journal of Individual Psychology, 64*(3), 270–279.

Bitter, J. R. (2009). *Theory and practice of family therapy and counseling.* Belmont, CA: Brooks/Cole, Cengage Learning.

*Bitter, J. R., Christensen, O. C., Hawes, C., & Nicoll, W. G. (1998). Adlerian brief therapy with individuals, couples, and families. *Directions in Clinical and Counseling Psychology, 8*(8), 95–111.

*Bitter, J. R., & Nicoll, W. G. (2000). Adlerian brief therapy with individuals: Process and practice. *Journal of Individual Psychology, 56*(1), 31–44.

*Bitter, J. R., & Nicoll, W. G. (2004). Relational strategies: Two approaches to Adlerian brief therapy. *Journal of Individual Psychology, 60*(1), 42–66.

Bitter, J. R., Robertson, P. E., Healey, A., & Cole, L. (2009). Reclaiming a pro-feminist orientation in Adlerian therapy. *Journal of Individual Psychology, 65*(1), 13–33.

*Carlson, J. M., & Carlson, J. D. (2000). The application of Adlerian psychotherapy with Asian-American clients. *Journal of Individual Psychology, 56*(2), 214–225.

Carlson, J., & Dinkmeyer, D. (2003). *Time for a better marriage.* Atascadero, CA: Impact Publishers.

*Carlson, J. D., & Englar-Carlson, M. (2008). Adlerian therapy. In J. Frew & M. D. Spiegler (Eds.), *Contemporary psychotherapies for a diverse world* (pp. 93–140). Boston: Lahaska Press.

*Carlson, J., & Slavik, S. (Eds.). (1997). *Techniques in Adlerian psychology.* Philadelphia, PA: Taylor & Francis.

*Carlson, J., Watts, R. E., & Maniacci, M. (2006). *Adlerian therapy: Theory and practice.* Washington DC: American Psychological Association.

Clark, A. (2002). *Early recollections: Theory and practice in counseling and psychotherapy.* New York: Brunner Routledge.

*Corey, G. (2010). *Creating your professional path: Lessons from my journey.* Alexandria, VA: American Counseling Association.

*Corey, G. (2012). *Theory and practice of group counseling* (8th ed.). Belmont, CA: Brooks/Cole, Cengage Learning.

*Corey, G. (2013). *Case approach to counseling and psychotherapy* (8th ed.). Belmont, CA: Brooks/Cole, Cengage Learning.

Dinkmeyer, D. C., & Mc Kay, G. D. (1997). *Systematic training for effective parenting [STEP].* Circle Pines, MN: American Guidance Service.

Dinkmeyer, D., Jr., & Sperry, L. (2000). *Counseling and psychotherapy: An integrated Individual Psychology approach* (3rd ed.). Upper Saddle River, NJ: Merrill/Prentice-Hall.

*Disque, J. G., & Bitter, J. R. (1998). Integrating narrative therapy with Adlerian lifestyle assessment: A case study. *Journal of Individual Psychology, 54*(4), 431–450.

Dreikurs, R. (1953). *Fundamentals of Adlerian psychology.* Chicago: Alfred Adler Institute.

Dreikurs, R. (1967). *Psychodynamics, psychotherapy, and counseling. Collected papers.* Chicago: Alfred Adler Institute.

Dreikurs, R. (1968). *Psychology in the classroom* (2nd ed.). New York: Harper & Row.

Dreikurs, R. (1969). Group psychotherapy from the point of view of Adlerian psychology. In H. M. Ruitenbeck (Ed.), *Group therapy today: Styles, methods, and techniques* (pp. 37–48). New York: Aldine-Atherton. (Original work published 1957)

Dreikurs, R. (1971). *Social equality: The challenge of today.* Chicago: Regnery.

Dreikurs, R. (1997). Holistic medicine. *Individual Psychology, 53*(2), 127–205.

Hawes, E. C. (1993). Marriage counseling and enrichment. In O. C. Christensen (Ed.), *Adlerian family counseling* (Rev. ed., pp. 125–163). Minneapolis, MN: Educational Media Corporation.

Hawes, C., & Blanchard, L. M. (1993). Life tasks as an assessment technique in marital counseling. *Individual Psychology, 49,* 306–317.

Hoffman, E. (1996). *The drive for self: Alfred Adler and the founding of Individual Psychology.* Reading, MA: Addison-Wesley.

Hood, A. B., & Johnson, R. W. (2007). *Assessment in counseling: A guide to the use of psychological assessment procedures* (4th ed.). Alexandria, VA: American Counseling Association.

Kefir, N. (1981). Impasse/priority therapy. In R. J. Corsini (Ed.), *Handbook of innovative psychotherapies* (pp. 401–415). New York: Wiley.

Milliren, A. P., & Clemmer, F. (2006). Introduction to Adlerian psychology: Basic principles and methodology. In S. Slavik & J. Carlson (Eds.), *Readings in the theory and practice of Individual Psychology* (pp. 17–43). New York: Routledge (Taylor & Francis).

Milliren, A. P., Evans, T. D., & Newbauer, J. F. (2007). Adlerian theory. In D. Capuzzi & D. R. Gross (Eds.), *Counseling and psychotherapy: Theories and interventions* (4th ed., pp. 123–163). Upper Saddle River, NJ: Merrill Prentice-Hall.

*Mosak, H. H., & Di Pietro, R. (2006). *Early recollections: Interpretative method and application.* New York: Routledge.

*Mosak, H. H., & Maniacci, M. P. (2011). Adlerian psychotherapy. In R. J. Corsini & D. Wedding (Eds.), *Current psychotherapies* (9th ed., pp. 67–112). Belmont, CA: Brooks/Cole, Cengage Learning.

Mosak, H. H., & Shulman, B. H. (1988). *Lifestyle inventory.* Muncie, IN: Accelerated Development.

Mozdzierz, G. J., Lisiecki, J., Bitter, J. R., & Williams, A. L. (1986). Role-functions for Adlerian therapists. *Individual Psychology, 42*(2), 154–177.

Mozdzierz, G. J., Peluso, P. R., & Lisiecki, J. (2009). *Principles of counseling and psychotherapy: Learning the essential domains and non-linear thinking of master practitioners.* New York: Routledge.

Nystul, M. S. (1999a). An interview with Gerald Corey. *Journal of Individual Psychology, 55*(1), 15–25.

Nystul, M. S. (1999b). An interview with Paul Pedersen. *Journal of Individual Psychology, 55*(2), 216–224.

Oberst, U. E., & Stewart, A. E. (2003). *Adlerian psychotherapy: An advanced approach to individual psychology.* New York: Brunner-Routledge.

Popkin, M. (1993). *Active parenting today.* Atlanta, GA: Active Parenting.

*Powers, R. L., & Griffith, J. (1987). *Understanding life-style. The psycho-clarity process.* Chicago: Americas Institute of Adlerian Studies.

Powers, R. L., & Griffith, J. (1995). *IPCW: The individual psychology client workbook with supplements.* Chicago: Americas Institute of Adlerian Studies. (Original work published 1986)

Schultz, D., & Schultz, S. E. (2009). *Theories of personality* (9th ed.). Belmont, CA: Wadsworth, Cengage Learning.

Sherman, R., & Dinkmeyer, D. (1987). *Systems of family therapy. An Adlerian integration.* New York: Brunner/Mazel.

Shulman, B. H., & Mosak, H. H. (1988). *Manual for life style assessment.* Muncie, IN: Accelerated Development.

*Sonstegard, M. A., & Bitter, J. R. (with Pelonis, P.). (2004). *Adlerian group counseling and therapy: Step-by-step.* New York: Brunner/Routledge (Taylor & Francis).

Sonstegard, M. A., Bitter, J. R., Pelonis-Peneros, P. P., & Nicoll, W. G. (2001). Adlerian group psychotherapy: A brief therapy approach. *Directions in Clinical and Counseling Psychology, 11*(2), 11–12.

*Sperry, L., Carlson, J., & Peluso, P. (2006). *Couples therapy.* Denver, CO: Love.

Sweeney, T. J. (2009). *Adlerian counseling and psychotherapy: A practitioner's approach* (5th ed.). New York: Routledge (Taylor & Francis).

Vaihinger, H. (1965). *The philosophy of "as if."* London: Routledge & Kegan Paul.

Watts, R. E. (1999). The vision of Adler: An introduction. In R. E. Watts & J. Carlson (Eds.), *Interventions and strategies in counseling and psychotherapy* (pp. 1–13). Philadelphia, PA: Accelerated Development (Taylor & Francis).

Watts, R. E. (2000). Entering the new millennium: Is Individual Psychology still relevant? *Journal of Individual Psychology, 56*(1), 21–30.

Watts, R. E. (2003). *Adlerian, cognitive, and constructivist therapies: An integrative dialogue.* New York: Springer.

Watts, R. E., & Holden, J. M. (1994). Why continue to use "fictional finalism"? *Individual Psychology, 50,* 161–163.

Watts, R. E., Peluso, P. R., & Lewis, T. F. (2005). Expanding the acting as if technique: An Adlerian/constructive integration. *Journal of Individual Psychology, 61*(4), 380–387.

Watts, R. E., & Pietrzak, D. (2000). Adlerian "encouragement" and the therapeutic process of solution-focused brief therapy. *Journal of Counseling and Development, 78*(4), 442–447.

Watts, R. E., & Shulman, B. H. (2003). Integrating Adlerian and constructive therapies: An Adlerian perspective. In R. E. Watts (Ed.), *Adlerian, cognitive, and constructivist therapies: An integrative dialogue* (pp. 9–37). New York: Springer.

Recommended Supplementary Readings for Chapter 6

Everyday Mysteries: A Handbook of Existential Psychotherapy (van Deurzen, 2010) provides a framework for practicing counseling from an existential perspective. The author puts into clear perspective topics such as anxiety, authentic living, clarifying one's worldview, determining values, discovering meaning, and coming to terms with life.

Existential Therapies (Cooper, 2003) provides a useful and clear introduction to the existential therapies. There are separate chapters on logotherapy, the British school of existential analysis, the U.S. existential-humanistic approach, dimensions of existential therapeutic practice, and brief existential therapies.

Existential Psychotherapy (Yalom, 1980) is a superb treatment of the ultimate human concerns of death, freedom, isolation, and meaninglessness as these issues relate to therapy. This book has depth and clarity, and it is rich with clinical examples that illustrate existential themes.

Existential-Humanistic Therapy (Schneider & Krug, 2010) is a clear presentation of the theory and practice of existential-humanistic therapy. This approach incorporates techniques from other contemporary therapeutic approaches.

Existential-Integrative Psychotherapy: Guideposts to the Core of Practice (Schneider, 2008) is an edited book that offers recent and future trends in existential-integrative therapy and case illustrations of this model.

I Never Knew I Had a Choice (Corey & Corey, 2010) is a self-help book written from an existential perspective. Topics include our struggle to achieve autonomy; the meaning of loneliness, death, and loss; and how we choose our values and philosophy of life.

References and Suggested Readings for Chapter 6

Binswanger, L. (1975). *Being-in-the-world: Selected papers of Ludwig Binswanger.* London: Souvenir Press.

Boss, M. (1963). *Daseinanalysis and psychoanalysis.* New York: Basic Books.

Buber, M. (1970). *I and thou* (W. Kaufmann, Trans.). New York: Scribner's.

Bugental, J.F.T. (1986). Existential-humanistic psychotherapy. In I. L. Kutash & A. Wolf (Eds.), *Psychotherapist's casebook* (pp. 222–236). San Francisco: Jossey-Bass.

---

*Books and articles marked with an asterisk are suggested for further study.

*Bugental, J.F.T. (1987). *The art of the psychotherapist.* New York: Norton.

Bugental, J.F.T. (1997). There is a fundamental division in how psychotherapy is conceived. In J. K. Zeig (Ed.), *The evolution of psychotherapy: The third conference* (pp. 185–196). New York: Brunner/Mazel.

*Bugental, J.F.T. (1999). *Psychotherapy isn't what you think: Bringing the psychotherapeutic engagement into the living moment.* Phoenix, AZ: Zeig, Tucker.

Bugental, J.F.T. (2008). Preliminary sketches for a short-term existential-humanistic therapy. In K. J. Schneider (Ed.), *Existential-integrative psychotherapy: Guideposts to the core of practice* (pp. 165–168). New York: Routledge.

Bugental, J.F.T., & Bracke, P. E. (1992). The future of existential-humanistic psychotherapy. *Psychotherapy, 29*(I), 28–33.

*Cooper, M. (2003). *Existential therapies.* London: Sage.

Corey, G. (2012). *Theory and practice of group counseling* (8th ed.). Belmont, CA: Brooks/Cole, Cengage Learning.

*Corey, G. (2013). *Case approach to counseling and psychotherapy* (8th ed.). Belmont, CA: Brooks/Cole, Cengage Learning.

*Corey, G., & Corey, M. (2010). *I never knew I had a choice* (9th ed.). Belmont, CA: Brooks/Cole, Cengage Learning.

Dattilio, F. M. (2002, January-February). Cognitive-behaviorism comes of age: Grounding symptomatic treatment in an existential approach. *The Psychotherapy Networker, 26*(1), 75–78.

*Deurzen, E., van. (2002a). *Existential counselling and psychotherapy in practice* (2nd ed.). London: Sage.

*Deurzen, E., van. (2002b). Existential therapy. In W. Dryden (Ed.), *Handbook of individual therapy* (4th ed., pp. 179–208). London: Sage.

Deurzen, E., van. (2009). *Psychotherapy and the quest for happiness.* London: Sage.

*Deurzen, E., van. (2010). *Everyday mysteries: A handbook of existential psychotherapy* (2nd ed). London: Routledge.

*Elkins, D. N. (2009). *Humanistic psychology: A clinical manifesto.* Colorado Springs, CO: University of the Rockies Press.

Farha, B. (1994). Ontological awareness: An existential/cosmological epistemology. *The Person-Centered Periodical, 1*(1), 15–29.

*Frankl, V. (1963). *Man's search for meaning.* Boston: Beacon.

*Frankl, V. (1965). *The doctor and the soul.* New York: Bantam Books.

*Frankl, V. (1978). *The unheard cry for meaning.* New York: Simon & Schuster (Touchstone).

Gould, W. B. (1993). *Viktor E. Frankl: Life with meaning.* Pacific Grove, CA: Brooks/Cole.

Heidegger, M. (1962). *Being and time.* New York: Harper & Row.

May, R. (1950). *The meaning of anxiety.* New York: Ronald Press.

*May, R. (1953). *Man's search for himself.* New York: Dell.

May, R. (1958). The origins and significance of the existential movement in psychology. In R. May, E. Angel, & H. R. Ellenberger (Eds.), *Existence: A new dimension in psychiatry and psychology.* New York: Basic Books.

*May, R. (Ed.). (1961). *Existential psychology.* New York: Random House.

May, R. (1969). *Love and will.* New York: Norton.

May, R. (1975). *The courage to create.* New York: Norton.

May, R. (1981). *Freedom and destiny.* New York: Norton. .

*May, R. (1983). *The discovery of being: Writings in existential psychology.* New York: Norton.

May, R., Angel, E., & Ellenberger, H. F. (Eds.). (1958). *Existence: A new dimension in psychiatry and psychology.* New York: Basic Books.

Russell, J. M. (1978). Sartre, therapy, and expanding the concept of responsibility. *American Journal of Psychoanalysis, 38,* 259–269.

*Russell, J. M. (2007). Existential psychotherapy. In A. B. Rochlen (Ed.), *Applying coun-seling theories: An online case-based approach* (pp. 107–125). Upper Saddle River, NJ: Pearson Prentice-Hall.

Sartre, J. P. (1971). *Being and nothingness.* New York: Bantam Books.

*Schneider, K. J. (Ed.). (2008). *Existential-integrative psychotherapy: Guideposts to the core of practice.* New York: Routledge.

*Schneider, K. J. (2011). Existential-humanistic psychotherapies. In S. B. Messer & A. S. Gurman, (Eds.), *Essential psychotherapies: Theory and practice* (3rd ed., pp. 261–294). New York: Guilford Press.

*Schneider, K. J., & Krug, O. T. (2010). *Existential-humanistic therapy.* Washington, DC: American Psychological Association.

*Schneider, K. J., & May, R. (Eds.). (1995). *The psychology of existence: An integrative, clinical perspective.* New York: McGraw-Hill.

Sharf, R. S. (2012). *Theories of psychotherapy and counseling: Concepts and cases* (5th ed.). Belmont, CA: Brooks/Cole, Cengage Learning.

*Sharp, J. G., & Bugental, J.F.T. (2001). Existential-humanistic psychotherapy. In R. J. Corsini (Ed.), *Handbook of innovative therapies* (2nd ed., pp. 206–217). New York: Wiley.

*Strasser, F., & Strasser, A. (1997). *Existential time-limited therapy: The wheel of existence.* Chichester: Wiley.

Tillich, P. (1952). *The courage to be.* New Haven, CT: Yale University Press.

*Vontress, C. E. (1996). A personal retrospective on cross-cultural counseling. *Journal of Multicultural Counseling and Development, 24*(3), 156–166.

*Vontress, C. E. (2008). Existential therapy. In J. Frew & M. D. Spiegler (Eds.), *Contemporary psychotherapies for a diverse world* (pp. 141–176). Boston: Lahaska Press.

*Vontress, C. E., Johnson, J. A., & Epp, L. R. (1999). *Cross-cultural counseling: A casebook.* Alexandria, VA: American Counseling Association.

*Walsh, R. A., & McElwain, B. (2002). Existential psychotherapies. In D. J. Cain & J. Seeman

(Eds.), *Humanistic psychotherapies: Handbook of research and practice* (pp. 253–278). Washington, DC: American Psychological Association.

*Watson, J. C., Goldman, R. N., & Greenberg, L. S.** (2011). Humanistic and experiential theories in psychotherapy. In J. C. Norcross, G. R. Vandenbos, & D. K. Freedheim (Eds.), *History of psychotherapy* (2nd ed., pp. 141–172). Washington, DC: American Psychological Association.

Wampold, B. (2008, February 6). Existential-integrative psychotherapy comes of age [Review of Existential-integrative psychotherapy: Guideposts to the core of practice]. *PsycCritiques*, 53, Release 6, Article 1, p. 6.

*Yalom, I. D.** (1980). *Existential psychotherapy.* New York: Basic Books.

*Yalom, I. D.** (1987). *Love's executioner: And other tales of psychotherapy.* New York: Harper Perennial.

Yalom, I. D. (1992). *When Nietzsche wept.* New York: Basic Books.

*Yalom, I. D.** (1997). *Lying on the couch: A novel.* New York: Harper Perennial.

*Yalom, I. D.** (2000). *Momma and the meaning of life: Tales of psychotherapy.* New York: Harper Perennial.

*Yalom, I. D.** (2003). *The gift of therapy: An open letter to a new generation of therapists and their patients.* New York: HarperCollins (Perennial).

Yalom, I. D. (2005a). *The Schopenhauer cure: A novel.* New York: HarperCollins.

*Yalom, I. D.** (with Leszcz, M.). (2005b). *The theory and practice of group psychotherapy* (5th ed.). New York: Basic Books. (Original work published 1970)

*Yalom, I. D.** (2008). *Staring at the sun: Overcoming the terror of death.* San Francisco: Jossey-Bass.

*Yalom, I. D., & Josselson, R.** (2011). Existential psychotherapy. In R. Corsini & D. Wedding (Eds.), *Current psychotherapies* (9th ed., pp. 310–341). Belmont, CA: Brooks/Cole, Cengage Learning.

Recommended Supplementary Readings for Chapter 7

On Becoming a Person (Rogers, 1961) is one of the best primary sources for further reading on person-centered therapy. This is a collection of Rogers's articles on the process of psychotherapy, its outcomes, the therapeutic relationship, education, family life, communication, and the nature of the healthy person.

A Way of Being (Rogers, 1980) contains a series of writings on Rogers's personal experiences and perspectives, as well as chapters on the foundations and applications of the person-centered approach.

The Creative Connection: Expressive Arts as Healing (N. Rogers, 1993) is a practical, spirited book lavishly illustrated with color and action photos and filled with fresh ideas to stimulate creativity, self-expression, healing, and transformation. Natalie Rogers combines the philosophy of her father with the expressive arts to enhance communication between client and therapist.

The Life and Work of Carl Rogers (Kirschenbaum, 2009) is a definitive biography of Carl Rogers that follows his life from his early childhood through his death. This book illustrates the legacy of Carl Rogers and shows his enormous influence on the field of counseling and psychotherapy.

Person-Centered Psychotherapies (Cain, 2010) contains a clear discussion of person-centered theory, the therapeutic process, evaluation of the approach, and future developments.

Humanistic Psychology: A Clinical Manifesto (Elkins, 2009) offers an insightful critique of the medical model of psychotherapy and the myth of empirically supported treatments. The author calls for a relationship-based approach to psychotherapy that can provide both individual and social transformation.

References and Suggested Readings for Chapter 7

*Arkowitz, H., & Miller, W. R. (2008). Learning, applying, and extending motivational interviewing. In H. Arkowitz, H. A. Westra, W. R. Miller, & S. Rollnick (Eds.), *Motivational interviewing in the treatment of psychological disorders* (pp. 1–25). New York: Guilford Press.

Arkowitz, H., & Westra, H. A. (2009). Introduction to the special series on motivational interviewing and psychotherapy. *Journal of Clinical Psychology, 65*(11), 1149–1155.

*Arkowitz, H., Westra, H. A., Miller, W. R., & Rollnick, S. (Eds.). (2008). *Motivational interviewing in the treatment of psychological problems*. New York: Guilford Press.

Axline, V. (1964). *Dibs: In search of self.* New York: Ballantine.

Axline, V. (1969). *Play therapy* (Rev. ed.). New York: Ballantine.

*Bohart, A. C., & Greenberg, L. S. (Eds.). (1997). *Empathy reconsidered: New directions in psychotherapy*. Washington, DC: American Psychological Association.

*Bohart, A. C., & Tallman, K. (1999). *How clients make therapy work: The process of active self-healing*. Washington, DC: American Psychological Association.

*Bohart, A. C., & Tallman, K. (2010). Clients: The neglected common factor in psychotherapy. In B. L. Duncan, S. D. Miller, B. E. Wampold, & M. A. Hubble (Eds.), *The heart and soul of change: Delivering what works in therapy* (2nd ed., pp. 83–111). Washington, DC: American Psychological Association.

Bohart, A. C., & Watson, J. C. (2011). Person-centered psychotherapy and related experiential approaches. In S. B. Messer & A. S. Gurman, (Eds.), *Essential psychotherapies: Theory and practice* (3rd ed., pp. 223–260). New York: Guilford Press.

*Bozarth, J. D., Zimring, F. M., & Tausch, R. (2002). Client-centered therapy: The evolution of a revolution. In D. J. Cain & J. Seeman (Eds.), *Humanistic psychotherapies: Handbook of research and practice* (pp. 147–188). Washington, DC: American Psychological Association.

Brodley, B. T. (1999). The actualizing tendency concept in client-centered theory. *The Person-Centered Journal, 6*(2), 108–120.

Cain, D. J. (1986). Editorial: A call for the "write stuff." *Person-Centered Review, 1*(2), 117–124.

Cain, D. J. (1987a). Carl Rogers' life in review. *Person-Centered Review, 2*(4), 476–506.

Cain, D. J. (1987b). Carl R. Rogers: The man, his vision, his impact. *Person-Centered Review, 2*(3), 283–288.

Cain, D. J. (1987c). Our international family. *Person-Centered Review, 2*(2), 139–149.

*Cain, D. J. (2002a). Defining characteristics, history, and evolution of humanistic psychotherapies. In D. J. Cain & J. Seeman (Eds.), *Humanistic psychotherapies: Handbook of research and practice* (pp. 3–54). Washington, DC: American Psychological Association.

Cain, D. J. (2002b). Preface. In D. J. Cain & J. Seeman (Eds.), *Humanistic psychotherapies: Handbook of research and practice* (pp. xix–xxvi). Washington, DC: American Psychological Association.

*Cain, D. J. (2008). Person-centered therapy. In J. Frew & M. D. Spiegler (Eds.), *Contemporary psychotherapies for a diverse world* (pp. 177–227). Boston: Lahaska Press.

*Cain, D. J. (2010). *Person-centered psychotherapies*. Washington, DC: American Psychological Association.

*Books and articles marked with an asterisk are suggested for further study.

*Cain, D. J., & Seeman, J. (Eds.). (2002). *Humanistic psychotherapies: Handbook of research and practice.* Washington, DC: American Psychological Association.

Clark, A. J. (2010). Empathy: An integral model in the counseling process. *Journal of Counseling & Development, 88*(3), 348–356.

Combs, A. W. (1988). Some current issues for person-centered therapy. *Person-Centered Review, 3*(3), 263–276.

Combs, A. W. (1989). *A theory of therapy: Guidelines for counseling practice.* Newbury Park, CA: Sage.

Combs, A. W. (1999). *Being and becoming.* New York: Springer.

Corey, G. (2012). *Theory and practice of group counseling* (8th ed.). Belmont, CA: Brooks/Cole, Cengage Learning.

Corey, G. (2013). *Case approach to counseling and psychotherapy* (8th ed.). Belmont, CA: Brooks/Cole, Cengage Learning.

*Duncan, B. L., Miller, S. D., Wampold, B. E., & Hubble, M. A. (Eds.). (2010). *The heart and soul of change* (2nd ed.). Washington, DC: American Psychological Association.

*Elkins, D. N. (2009). *Humanistic psychology: A clinical manifesto.* Colorado Springs, CO: University of the Rockies Press.

Elliott, R., Bohart, A. C., Watson, J. C., & Greenberg, L. S. (2011). Empathy. In J.C. Norcross (Ed.), *Psychotherapy relationships that work: Evidence-based responsiveness* (2nd ed., pp. 132–152). New York: Oxford University Press.

Farber, B. A., & Doolin, E. M. (2011). Positive regard and affirmation. In J.C. Norcross (Ed.), *Psychotherapy relationships that work: Evidence-based responsiveness* (2nd ed., pp. 168–186). New York: Oxford University Press.

Fairhurst, I. (Ed.). (1999). *Women writing in the person-centred approach.* Ross-on-Wye: PCCS Books.

*Gendlin, E. T. (1996). *Focusing-oriented psychotherapy: A manual of the experiential method.* New York: Guilford Press.

*Greenberg, L. S. (2011). *Emotion-focused therapy.* Washington, DC: American Psychological Association.

*Greenberg, L. S., Korman, L. M., & Paivio, S. C. (2002). Emotion in humanistic psychotherapy. In D. J. Cain & J. Seeman (Eds.), *Humanistic psychotherapies: Handbook of research and practice* (pp. 499–530). Washington, DC: American Psychological Association.

*Greenberg, L. S., Rice, L. N., & Elliott, R. (1993). *Facilitating emotional change: The moment-by-moment process.* New York: Guilford Press.

Keys, S. (Ed.). (2003). *Idiosyncratic person-centred therapy: From the personal to the universal.* Ross-on-Wye: PCCS Books.

*Kirschenbaum, H. (2009). *The life and work of Carl Rogers.* Alexandria, VA: American Counseling Association.

*Kirschenbaum, H., & Henderson, V. (Eds.) (1989). *The Carl Rogers reader.* Boston: Houghton Mifflin.

Koldon, G. G., Klein, M. H., Wang, C., & Austin, S. B. (2011). Congruence/genuineness. In J. C. Norcross (Ed.), *Psychotherapy relationships that work: Evidence-based responsiveness* (2nd ed., pp. 187–202). New York: Oxford University Press.

Lago, C., & Smith, B. (Eds.). (2003). *Anti-discriminatory counselling practice.* London: Sage.

Levensky, E. R., Kersh, B. C., Cavasos, L. L., & Brooks, J. A. (2008). Motivational interviewing. In W. O'Donohue, & J. E. Fisher (Eds.), *Cognitive behavior therapy: Applying empirically supported techniques in your practice* (2nd ed., pp. 357–366). Hoboken, NJ: Wiley.

Maslow, A. (1968). *Toward a psychology of being.* New York: Van Nostrand Reinhold.

Maslow, A. (1970). *Motivation and personality* (2nd ed.). New York: Harper & Row.

Maslow, A. (1971). *The farther reaches of human nature.* New York: Viking.

Mearns, D. (2003). *Developing person-centred counselling* (2nd ed.). London: Sage.

*Mearns, D., & Cooper, M. (2005). *Working at relational depth in counselling and psychotherapy.* London: Sage.

*Mearns, D., & Thorne, B. (2000). *Person-centred therapy today: New frontiers in theory and practice.* London: Sage.

*Mearns, D., & Thorne, B. (2007). *Person-centred counselling in action* (3rd ed.). London: Sage.

Merry, T. (1999). *Learning and being in person-centred counselling.* Ross-on-Wye: PCCS Books.

*Miller, W. R., & Rollnick, S. (2002). *Motivational interviewing: Preparing people for change* (2nd ed.). New York: Guilford Press.

*Natiello, P. (2001). *The person-centred approach: A passionate presence.* Ross-on-Wye: PCCS Books.

*Norcross, J. C. (2010). The therapeutic relationship. In B. L. Duncan, S. D. Miller, B. E. Wampold, & M. A. Hubble (Eds.), *The heart and soul of change: Delivering what works in therapy* (2nd ed., pp. 113-141). Washington, DC: American Psychological Association.

*Norcross, J. C., Hogan, T. P., & Koocher, G. P. (2008). *Clinician's guide to evidence-based practices.* New York: Oxford University Press.

Norcross, J. C., Krebs, P. M., & Prochaska, J. O. (2011). Stages of change. In J.C. Norcross (Ed.), *Psychotherapy relationships that work: Evidence-based responsiveness* (2nd ed., pp. 279-300). New York: Oxford University Press.

Patterson, C. H. (1995). A universal system of psychotherapy. *The Person-Centered Journal, 2*(1), 54-62.

Prochaska, J., & Norcross, J. (2010). *Systems of psychotherapy: A transtheoretical analysis* (7th ed.). Belmont, CA: Brooks/Cole, Cengage Learning.

Raskin, N. J., Rogers, C. R., & Witty, M. (2008). Client-centered therapy. In R. Corsini & D. Wedding (Eds.), *Current psychotherapies* (8th ed., pp. 141-186). Belmont, CA: Thomson Brooks/Cole.

Rennie, D. L. (1998). *Person-centered counseling: An experiential approach.* London: Sage.

Rice, L. N., & Greenberg, L. (1984). *Patterns of change.* New York: Guilford Press.

Rogers, C. (1942). *Counseling and psychotherapy: Newer concepts in practice.* Boston: Houghton Mifflin.

Rogers, C. (1951). *Client-centered therapy.* Boston: Houghton Mifflin.

Rogers, C. (1957). The necessary and sufficient conditions of therapeutic personality change. *Journal of Consulting Psychology, 21,* 95-103.

*Rogers, C. (1961). *On becoming a person.* Boston: Houghton Mifflin.

Rogers, C. (1967). The conditions of change from a client-centered viewpoint. In B. Berenson & R. Carkhuff (Eds.), *Sources of gain in counseling and psychotherapy.* New York: Holt, Rinehart & Winston.

Rogers, C. (1970). *Carl Rogers on encounter groups.* New York: Harper & Row.

Rogers, C. (1977). *Carl Rogers on personal power: Inner strength and its revolutionary impact.* New York: Delacorte Press.

*Rogers, C. (1980). *A way of being.* Boston: Houghton Mifflin.

Rogers, C. (1986a). Carl Rogers on the development of the person-centered approach. *Person-Centered Review, 1*(3), 257-259.

Rogers, C. (1986b). Client-centered therapy. In I. L. Kutash & A. Wolf (Eds.), *Psychotherapists casebook* (pp. 197-208). San Francisco: Jossey-Bass.

Rogers, C. R. (1987a). Rogers, Kohut, and Erickson: A personal perspective on some similarities and differences. In J. K. Zeig (Ed.), *The evolution of psychotherapy* (pp. 179-187). New York: Brunner/Mazel.

Rogers, C. R. (1987b). Steps toward world peace, 1948-1986: Tension reduction in theory and practice. *Counseling and Values, 32*(1), 12-16.

Rogers, C. R. (1987c). The underlying theory: Drawn from experiences with individuals and groups. *Counseling and Values, 32*(I), 38-45.

*Rogers, C. R., & Freiberg, H. J. (1994). *Freedom to learn* (3rd ed.). Upper Saddle River, NJ: Prentice-Hall.

*Rogers, C. R., & Russell, D. E. (2002). *Carl Rogers: The quiet revolutionary.* Roseville, CA: Penmarin Books.

*Rogers, N. (1993). *The creative connection: Expressive arts as healing.* Palo Alto, CA: Science & Behavior Books.

*Rogers, N. (1995). *Emerging woman: A decade of midlife transitions.* Manchester, UK: PCCS Books.

Rogers, N. (2002). *Carl Rogers: A Daughter's Tribute* (CD ROM). Mingarden Media, Inc. www.nrogers.com

*Rogers, N. (2011). *The creative connection for groups: Person-centered expressive arts for healing and social change.* Palo Alto, CA: Science and Behavior Books.

Rollnick, S., & Miller, W. R. (1995). What is motivational interviewing? *Behavioural & Cognitive Psychotherapy, 23,* 325–334.

*Rollnick, S., Miller, W. R., & Butler, C. C. (2008). *Motivational interviewing in health care: Helping patients change behavior.* New York: Guilford Press.

*Schneider, K. J., & Krug, O. T. (2010). *Existential-humanistic therapy.* Washington, DC: American Psychological Association.

Sommers-Flanagan, J. (2007). The development and evolution of person-centered expressive art therapy: A conversation with Natalie Rogers. *Journal of Counseling and Development, 85*(1), 120–125.

*Thorne, B. (1992). *Carl Rogers.* London: Sage.

*Thorne, B. (2002a). *The mystical power of person-centred therapy: Hope beyond despair.* London: Whurr Publishers.

Thorne, B. (2002b). Person-centred therapy. In W. Dryden (Ed.), *Handbook of individual therapy* (4th ed., pp. 131–157). London: Sage.

*Watson, J. C. (2002). Re-visioning empathy. In D. J. Cain & J. Seeman (Eds.), *Humanistic psychotherapies: Handbook of research and practice* (pp. 445–471). Washington, DC: American Psychological Association.

*Watson, J. C. (Ed.). (2003). *Client-centered and experiential psychotherapy: Advances in theory research, and practice.* Ross-on-Wye: PCCS Books.

Watson, J. C., Goldman, R. N., & Greenberg, L. S. (2011). Humanistic and experiential theories in psychotherapy. In J. C. Norcross, G. R. Vandenbos, & D. K. Freedheim (Eds.), *History of psychotherapy* (2nd ed., pp. 141–172). Washington, DC: American Psychological Association.

Zimring, F. M., & Raskin, N. J. (1992). Carl Rogers and client/person-centered therapy. In D. K. Freedheim (Ed.), *History of psychotherapy: A century of change* (pp. 629–656). Washington, DC: American Psychological Association.

Recommended Supplementary Readings for Chapter 8

Gestalt Therapy Verbatim (Perls, 1969a) provides a firsthand account of the way Fritz Perls worked. It contains many verbatim transcripts of workshop demonstrations.

Gestalt Therapy: History, Theory, and Practice (Woldt & Toman, 2005) introduces the historical underpinnings and key concepts of Gestalt therapy and features applications of those concepts to therapeutic practice. This is a significant recent publication in the field of Gestalt therapy that contains pedagogical learning activities and experiments, review questions, and photographs of all contributors.

Gestalt Therapy Integrated: Contours of Theory and Practice (Polster & Polster, 1973) is a classic in the field and an excellent source for those who want a more advanced and theoretical treatment of this model.

References and Suggested Readings for Chapter 8

*Barber, P. (2006). *Becoming a practitioner researcher: A Gestalt approach to holistic inquiry.* London: Middlesex University Press.

Beisser, A. R. (1970). The paradoxical theory of change. In J. Fagan & I. L. Shepherd (Eds.), *Gestalt therapy now* (pp. 77–80). New York: Harper & Row (Colophon).

*Bowman, C. (2005). The history and development of Gestalt therapy. In A. Woldt & S. Toman (Eds.), *Gestalt therapy: History, theory, and practice* (pp. 3–20). Thousand Oaks, CA: Sage.

*Books and articles marked with an asterisk are suggested for further study.

Breshgold, E. (1989). Resistance in Gestalt therapy: An historical theoretical perspective. *The Gestalt Journal, 12*(2), 73–102.

*Brown, J. R. (2007). Gestalt therapy. In A. B. Rochlen (Ed.), *Applying counseling theories: An online case-based approach* (pp. 127–141). Upper Saddle River, NJ: Pearson Prentice-Hall.

*Brownell, P. (2008). *Handbook for theory, research and practice in Gestalt therapy.* Newcastle, UK: Cambridge Scholar Publishing.

*Cain, D. J. (2002). Defining characteristics, history, and evolution of humanistic psychotherapies. In D. J. Cain & J. Seeman (Eds.), *Humanistic psychotherapies: Handbook of research and practice* (pp. 3–54). Washington, DC: American Psychological Association.

Clarkson, P., & Mackewn, J. (1993). *Fritz Perls.* Newbury Park, CA: Sage.

Corey, G. (2012). *Theory and practice of group counseling* (8th ed.). Belmont, CA: Brooks/ Cole, Cengage Learning.

*Corey, G. (2013). *Case approach to counseling and psychotherapy* (8th ed.). Belmont, CA: Brooks/Cole, Cengage Learning.

Elliott, R., Watson, J. C., Goldman, R. N., & Greenberg, L. S. (2004). *Learning emotion-focused therapy: A process-experiential approach to change.* Washington, DC: American Psychological Association.

*Feder. B. (2006). *Gestalt group therapy: A practical guide.* New Orleans: Gestalt Institute Press.

*Feder, B., & Frew, J. (Eds.). (2008). *Beyond the hot seat revisited: Gestalt approaches to group.* New Orleans: Gestalt Institute Press.

Feder, B., & Ronall, R. (Eds.). (1996). *A living legacy of Fritz and Laura Perls: Contemporary case studies.* Montclair, NJ: Walden.

Fernbacher, S., & Plummer, D. (2005). Cultural influences and considerations in Gestalt therapy. In A. Woldt & S. Toman (Eds.), *Gestalt therapy: History, theory, and practice* (pp. 117–132). Thousand Oaks, CA: Sage.

Frew, J. E. (1986). The functions and patterns of occurrence of individual contact styles during the development phase of the Gestalt group. *The Gestalt Journal, 9*(1), 55–70.

Frew, J. E. (1997). A Gestalt therapy theory application to the practice of group leadership. *Gestalt Review, 1*(2), 131–149.

*Frew, J. (2008). Gestalt therapy. In J. Frew & M. D. Spiegler (Eds.), *Contemporary psychotherapies for a diverse world* (pp. 228–274). Boston: Lahaska Press.

*Greenberg, L. S. (2011). *Emotion-focused therapy.* Washington, DC: American Psychological Association.

Humphrey, K. (1986). Laura Perls: A biographical sketch. *The Gestalt Journal, 9*(1), 5–11.

*Hycner, R., & Jacobs, L. (1995). *The healing relationship in Gestalt therapy.* Highland, NY: Gestalt Journal Press.

Jacobs, L. (1989). Dialogue in Gestalt theory and therapy. *The Gestalt Journal, 12*(1), 25–67.

*Latner, J. (1986). *The Gestalt therapy book.* Highland, NY: Center for Gestalt Development.

*Lee, R. G. (Ed.). (2004). *The values of connection: A relational approach to ethics.* Cambridge, MA: Gestalt Press.

Levitsky, A., & Perls, F. (1970). The rules and games of Gestalt therapy. In J. Fagan & I. Shepherd (Eds.), *Gestalt therapy now* (pp. 140–149). New York: Harper & Row (Colophon).

Maurer, R. (2005). Gestalt approaches with organizations and large systems. In A. Woldt & S. Toman (Eds.), *Gestalt therapy: History, theory, and practice.* (pp. 237–256). Thousand Oaks, CA: Sage.

Melnick, J., & Nevis, S. (2005). Gestalt therapy methodology. In A. Woldt & S. Toman (Eds.), *Gestalt therapy: History, theory, and practice.* (pp. 101–116). Thousand Oaks, CA: Sage.

Parlett, M. (2005). Contemporary Gestalt therapy: Field theory. In A. Woldt & S. Toman (Eds.), *Gestalt therapy: History, theory, and practice* (pp. 41–64). Thousand Oaks, CA: Sage.

Passons, W. R. (1975). *Gestalt approaches in counseling.* New York: Holt, Rinehart & Winston.

*Perls, F. (1969a). *Gestalt therapy verbatim.* Moab, UT: Real People Press.

Perls, F. (1969b). *In and out of the garbage pail.* Moab, UT: Real People Press.

Perls, F., Hefferline, R., & Goodman, R. (1951). *Gestalt therapy: Excitement and growth in the human personality.* New York: Dell.

Perls, L. (1976). Comments on new directions. In E.W.L. Smith (Ed.), *The growing edge of Gestalt therapy* (pp. 221–226). New York: Brunner/Mazel.

Perls, L. (1990). A talk for the 25th anniversary. *The Gestalt Journal, 13*(2), 15–22.

Polster, E. (1987a). Escape from the present: Transition and storyline. In J. K. Zeig (Ed.), *The evolution of psychotherapy* (pp. 326–340). New York: Brunner/Mazel.

*Polster, E. (1987b). *Every person's life is worth a novel: How to cut through emotional pain and discover the fascinating core of life.* New York: Norton.

*Polster, E. (1995). *A population of selves: A therapeutic exploration of personality diversity.* San Francisco: Jossey-Bass.

*Polster, E., & Polster, M. (1973). *Gestalt therapy integrated: Contours of theory and practice.* New York: Brunner/Mazel.

Polster, E., & Polster, M. (1976). Therapy without resistance: Gestalt therapy. In A. Burton (Ed.), *What makes behavior change possible?* (pp. 259–277). New York: Brunner/Mazel.

Polster, M. (1987). Gestalt therapy: Evolution and application. In J. K. Zeig (Ed.), *The evolution of psychotherapy* (pp. 312–325). New York: Brunner/Mazel.

Polster, M., & Polster, E. (1990). Gestalt therapy. In J. K. Zeig & W. M. Munion (Eds.), *What is psychotherapy? Contemporary perspectives* (pp. 103–107). San Francisco: Jossey-Bass.

*Strumpfel, U., & Goldman, R. (2002). Contacting Gestalt therapy. In D. J. Cain & J. Seeman (Eds.), *Humanistic psychotherapies: Handbook of research and practice* (pp. 189–219). Washington, DC: American Psychological Association.

Watson, J. C., Goldman, R. N., & Greenberg, L. S. (2011). Humanistic and experiential theories in psychotherapy. In J. C. Norcross, G. R. Vandenbos, & D. K. Freedheim (Eds.), *History of psychotherapy* (2nd ed., pp. 141–172). Washington, DC: American Psychological Association.

*Woldt, A., & Toman, S. (Eds.). (2005). *Gestalt therapy: History, theory, and practice.* Thousand Oaks, CA: Sage.

*Yontef, G. M. (1993). *Awareness, dialogue and process: Essays on Gestalt therapy.* Highland, NY: Gestalt Journal Press.

*Yontef, G. (1995). Gestalt therapy. In A. S. Gurman & S. B. Messer (Eds.), *Essential psychotherapies: Theory and practice* (pp. 261–303). New York: Guilford Press.

Yontef, G. (1999). Awareness, dialogue and process: Preface to the 1998 German edition. *The Gestalt Journal, 22*(1), 9–20.

*Yontef, G. M. (2005). Gestalt therapy theory of change. In A. Woldt & S. Toman (Eds.), *Gestalt therapy: History, theory, and practice* (pp. 81–100). Thousand Oaks, CA: Sage.

*Yontef, G., & Jacobs, L. (2011). Gestalt therapy. In R. Corsini & D. Wedding (Eds.), *Current psychotherapies* (9th ed., pp. 342–382). Belmont, CA: Brooks/Cole, Cengage Learning.

Zahm, S. (1998). Therapist self-disclosure in the practice of Gestalt therapy. *The Gestalt Journal, 21,* 21–52.

*Zinker, J. (1978). *Creative process in Gestalt therapy.* New York: Random House (Vintage).

Recommended Supplementary Readings for Chapter 9

Contemporary Behavior Therapy (Spiegler & Guevremont, 2010) is a comprehensive and up-to-date treatment of basic principles and applications of the behavior therapies, as well as a fine discussion of ethical issues. Specific chapters deal with procedures that can be usefully applied to a range of client populations:

behavioral assessment, modeling therapy, systematic desensitization, exposure therapies, cognitive restructuring, and cognitive coping skills.

Interviewing and Change Strategies for Helpers (Cormier, Nurius, & Osborn, 2013) is a comprehensive and clearly written textbook dealing with training experiences and skill development. Its excellent documentation offers practitioners a wealth of material on a variety of topics, such as assessment procedures, selection of goals, development of appropriate treatment programs, and methods of evaluating outcomes.

Cognitive Behavior Therapy: Applying Empirically Supported Techniques in Your Practice (O'Donohue & Fisher, 2008) is a useful collection of edited short chapters describing empirically supported techniques for working with a wide range of presenting problems.

Behavior Therapy (Antony & Roemer, 2011a) offers a useful and updated overview of behavior therapy.

Behavior Modification: Principles and Procedures (Miltenberger, 2012) is an excellent resource for learning more about basic principles such as reinforcement, extinction, punishment, and procedures to establish new behavior.

Acceptance and Mindfulness in Cognitive Behavior Therapy: Understanding and Applying the New Therapies (Herbert & Forman, 2011) is one of the best resources for discussion of new developments in the behavior therapy tradition and the future trends of these therapies.

References and Suggested Readings for Chapter 9

*Alberti, R. E., & Emmons, M. L. (2008). *Your perfect right: A guide to assertive behavior* (9th ed.). Atascadero, CA: Impact.

*Antony, M. M., & Roemer, L. (2011a). *Behavior therapy*. Washington, DC: American Psychological Association.

Antony, M. M., & Roemer, L. (2011b). Behavior therapy: Traditional approaches. In S. B. Messer & A. S. Gurman (Eds.), *Essential psychotherapies: Theory and practice* (3rd ed., pp. 107–142). New York: Guilford Press.

Bandura, A. (1969). *Principles of behavior modification*. New York: Holt, Rinehart & Winston.

Bandura, A. (Ed.). (1971a). *Psychological modeling: Conflicting theories*. Chicago: Aldine-Atherton.

Bandura, A. (1971b). Psychotherapy based upon modeling principles. In A. E. Bergin & S. L. Garfield (Eds.), *Handbook of psychotherapy and behavior change*. New York: Wiley.

Bandura, A. (1977). *Social learning theory*. Englewood Cliffs, NJ: Prentice-Hall.

Bandura, A. (1982). Self-efficacy mechanisms in human agency. *American Psychologist, 37*, 122–147.

Bandura, A. (1986). *Social foundations of thought and action: A social cognitive theory*. Englewood Cliffs, NJ: Prentice-Hall.

*Bandura, A. (1997). *Self-efficacy: The exercise of self-control*. New York: Freeman.

Bandura, A., & Walters, R. H. (1963). *Social learning and personality development*. New York: Holt, Rinehart & Winston.

*Beck, A. T. (1976). *Cognitive therapy and emotional disorders*. New York: New American Library.

*Books and articles marked with an asterisk are suggested for further study.

Beck, A. T., & Weishaar, M. E. (2011). Cognitive therapy. In R. J. Corsini & D. Wedding (Eds.), *Current psychotherapies* (9th ed., pp. 276–309). Belmont, CA: Brooks/Cole, Cengage Learning.

*Corey, G. (2012). *Theory and practice of group counseling* (8th ed.). Belmont, CA: Brooks/Cole, Cengage Learning.

*Corey, G. (2013a). *Case approach to counseling and psychotherapy* (8th ed.). Belmont, CA: Brooks/Cole, Cengage Learning.

*Corey, G. (2013b). *Student manual for theory and practice of counseling and psychotherapy* (9th ed.). Belmont, CA: Brooks/Cole, Cengage Learning.

*Cormier, S., Nurius, P. S., & Osborn, C. (2013). *Interviewing and change strategies for helpers* (7th ed.). Belmont, CA: Brooks/Cole, Cengage Learning.

Dattilio, F. M. (2006). *Progressive muscle relaxation* (CD). www.dattilio.com

Dimidjian, S., & Linehan, M. M. (2008). Mindfulness practice. In W. O'Donohue & J. E. Fisher (Eds.), *Cognitive behavior therapy: Applying empirically supported techniques in your practice* (2nd ed., pp. 327–336). Hoboken, NJ: Wiley.

Dobson, D., & Dobson, K. S. (2009). *Evidence-based practice of cognitive-behavioral therapy.* New York: Guilford Press.

Dobson, K. S. (2010). *Handbook of cognitive-behavioral therapies* (3rd ed.). New York: Guilford Press.

Eifert, G. H., & Forsyth, J. P. (2005). *Acceptance and commitment therapy for anxiety disorders: A practitioner's treatment guide to using mindfulness, acceptance, and values-based behavior change strategies.* Oakland, CA: New Harbinger Publications.

Ferguson, K. E., & Sgambati, R. E. (2008). Relaxation. In W. O'Donohue & J. E. Fisher (Eds.), *Cognitive behavior therapy: Applying empirically supported techniques in your practice* (2nd ed., pp. 434–444). Hoboken, NJ: Wiley.

*Fishman, D. B., Rego, S. A., & Muller, K. L. (2011). Behavioral theories in psychotherapy. In J. C. Norcross, G. R. Vandenbos, & D. K. Freedheim (Eds.), *History of psychotherapy* (2nd ed., pp. 101–140). Washington, DC: American Psychological Association.

Follette, W. C., & Callaghan, G. M. (2011). Behavior therapy: Functional-contextual approaches. In S. B. Messer & A. S. Gurman, (Eds.), *Essential psychotherapies: Theory and practice* (3rd ed., pp. 184–220). New York: Guilford Press.

*Fresco, D. M., Flynn, J. J., Mennin, D. S., & Haigh, A. P. (2011). Mindfulness-based cognitive therapy. In J. D. Hebert & E. M. Forman (Eds.), *Acceptance and mindfulness in cognitive behavior therapy: Understanding and applying the new therapies* (pp. 57–82). Hoboken, NJ: Wiley.

Germer, C. K. (2005a). Mindfulness: What is it: What does it matter? In C. K. Germer, R. D. Siegel, & P. R. Fulton (Eds.), *Mindfulness and psychotherapy* (pp. 3–27). New York: Guilford Press.

Germer, C. K. (2005b). Teaching mindfulness in therapy. In C. K. Germer, R. D. Siegel, & P. R. Fulton (Eds.), *Mindfulness and psychotherapy* (pp. 113–129). New York: Guilford Press.

*Germer, C. K., Siegel, R. D., & Fulton, P. R. (Eds.). (2005). *Mindfulness and psychotherapy.* New York: Guilford Press.

Hayes, S. C. (2004). Acceptance and commitment therapy and the new behavior therapies: Mindfulness, acceptance, and relationship. In S. C. Hayes, V. M. Follette, & M. M. Linehan (Eds.), *Mindfulness and acceptance: Expanding the cognitive-behavioral tradition* (pp. 1–29). New York: Guilford Press.

*Hayes, S. C., Follette, V. M., & Linehan, M. M. (Eds.). (2004). *Mindfulness and acceptance: Expanding the cognitive-behavioral tradition.* New York: Guilford Press.

*Hayes, S. C., Strosahl, K. D., & Houts, A. (Eds.). (2005). *A practical guide to acceptance and commitment therapy.* New York: Springer.

*Hayes, S. C., Strosahl, K. D., & Wilson, K. G. (Eds.). (2011). *Acceptance and commitment therapy: The process and practice of mindful change* (2nd ed.). New York: Guilford Press.

Hazlett-Stevens, H., & Craske, M. G. (2008). Live (in vivo) exposure. In W. O'Donohue &

J. E. Fisher (Eds.), *Cognitive behavior therapy: Applying empirically supported techniques in your practice* (2nd ed., pp. 309–316). Hoboken, NJ: Wiley.

Head, L. S., & Gross, A. M. (2008). Systematic desensitization. In W. O'Donohue & J. E. Fisher (Eds.), *Cognitive behavior therapy: Applying empirically supported techniques in your practice* (2nd ed., pp. 542–549). Hoboken, NJ: Wiley.

Herbert, J. D., & Forman, E. M. (2011). *Acceptance and mindfulness in cognitive behavior therapy: Understanding and applying the new therapies.* Hoboken, NJ: Wiley.

Hollon, S. D., & Digiuseppe, R. (2011). Cognitive theories in psychotherapy. In J. C. Norcross, G. R. Vandenbos, & D. K. Freedheim (Eds.), *History of psychotherapy* (2nd ed., pp. 203–242). Washington, DC: American Psychological Association.

Jacobson, E. (1938). *Progressive relaxation.* Chicago: University of Chicago Press.

*Kabat-Zinn, J. (1990). *Full catastrophe living: Using the wisdom of your body and mind to face stress, pain, and illness.* New York: Dell.

*Kabat-Zinn, J. (1994). *Wherever you go there you are: Mindfulness meditation in everyday life.* New York: Hyperion.

Kabat-Zinn, J. (2003). Mindfulness-based interventions in context: Past, present and future. *Clinical Psychology: Science and Practice, 10,* 144–156.

Kazdin, A. E. (1978). *History of behavior modification: Experimental foundations of contemporary research.* Baltimore: University Park Press.

*Kazdin, A. E. (2001). *Behavior modification in applied settings* (6th ed.). Pacific Grove, CA: Brooks/Cole.

Kazdin, A. E., & Wilson, G. T. (1978). *Evaluation of behavior therapy: Issues, evidence, and research strategies.* Cambridge, MA: Ballinger.

Lazarus, A. A. (1989). *The practice of multimodal therapy.* Baltimore: Johns Hopkins University Press.

Lazarus, A. A. (1992a). The multimodal approach to the treatment of minor depression. *American Journal of Psychotherapy, 46*(l), 50–57.

Lazarus, A. A. (1992b). Multimodal therapy: Technical eclecticism with minimal integration. In J. C. Norcross & M. R. Goldfried (Eds.), *Handbook of psychotherapy integration* (pp. 231–263). New York: Basic Books.

*Lazarus, A. A. (1993). Tailoring the therapeutic relationship, or being an authentic chameleon. *Psychotherapy, 30,* 404–407.

*Lazarus, A. A. (1996a). Some reflections after 40 years of trying to be an effective psychotherapist. *Psychotherapy, 33*(1), 142–145.

*Lazarus, A. A. (1996b). The utility and futility of combining treatments in psychotherapy. *Clinical Psychology: Science and Practice, 3*(1), 59–68.

*Lazarus, A. A. (1997a). *Brief but comprehensive psychotherapy: The multimodal way.* New York: Springer.

Lazarus, A. A. (1997b). Can psychotherapy be brief, focused, solution-oriented, and yet comprehensive? A personal evolutionary perspective. In J. K. Zeig (Ed.), *The evolution of psychotherapy: The third conference* (pp. 83–94). New York: Brunner/Mazel.

Lazarus, A. A. (2000). Multimodal strategies with adults. In J. Carlson & L. Sperry (Eds.), *Brief therapy with individuals and couples* (pp. 106–124). Phoenix: Zeig & Tucker.

*Lazarus, A. A. (2005). Multimodal therapy. In J. C. Norcross & M. R. Goldfried (Eds.), *Handbook of psychotherapy integration* (2nd ed., pp. 105–120). New York: Oxford University Press.

Lazarus, A. A. (2006). Multimodal therapy: A seven-point integration. In G. Stricker & J. Gold (Eds.), *A casebook of psychotherapy integration* (pp. 17–28). Washington DC: American Psychological Association.

Lazarus, A. A. (2008a). Multimodal behavior therapy. In W. O'Donohue & J. E. Fisher (Eds.), *Cognitive behavior therapy: Applying empirically supported techniques in your practice* (2nd ed., pp. 342–346). Hoboken, NJ: Wiley.

Lazarus, A. A. (2008b). Technical eclecticism and multimodal therapy. In J. L. Lebow (Ed.), *Twenty-first century psychotherapies* (pp. 424–452). Hoboken, NJ: Wiley.

REFERENCES AND SUGGESTED READINGS FOR PART 2

Lazarus, A. A., & Lazarus, C. N. (2005). Multimodal life-history inventory. In G. P. Koocher, J. C. Norcross, & S. S. Hill III (Eds.), *Psychologist's desk reference* (2nd ed. pp. 16–23) Oxford: Oxford University Press.

Lazarus, A. A., & Zur, O. (2002). *Dual relationships and psychotherapy*. New York: Springer.

*Ledley, D. R., Marx, B. P., & Heimberg, R. G. (2010). *Making cognitive-behavioral therapy work: Clinical processes for new practitioners* (2nd ed.). New York: Guilford Press.

Linehan, M. M. (1993a). *Cognitive-behavioral treatment of borderline personality disorder*. New York: Guilford Press.

Linehan, M. M. (1993b). *Skills training manual for treating borderline personality disorder*. New York: Guilford Press.

Martell, C. R. (2007). Behavioral therapy. In A. B. Rochlen (Ed.), *Applying counseling theories: An online case-based approach* (pp. 143–156). Upper Saddle River, NJ: Pearson Prentice-Hall.

*Messer, S. B., & Gurman, A. S. (2011). *Essential psychotherapies: Theory and practice* (3rd ed.). New York: Guilford Press.

Miller, W. R. & Rollnick, S. (2002). *Motivational interviewing: Preparing people for change* (2nd ed.). New York: Guilford Press.

*Miltenberger, R. G. (2012). *Behavior modification: Principles and procedures* (5th ed.). Belmont, CA: Brooks/Cole, Cengage Learning.

*Norcross, J. C., Beutler, L. E., & Levant, R. F. (2006). *Evidence-based practices in mental health: Debate and dialogue on the fundamental questions*. Washington, DC: American Psychological Association.

Nye, R. D. (2000). *Three psychologies: Perspectives from Freud, Skinner, and Rogers* (6th ed.). Belmont, CA: Brooks/Cole, Cengage Learning.

*O'Donohue, W., & Fisher, J. E. (Eds.). (2008). *Cognitive behavior therapy: Applying empirically supported techniques in your practice* (2nd ed.). Hoboken, NJ: Wiley.

Panjares, F. (2004). *Albert Bandura: Biographical sketch*. Retrieved from http://des.emory. edu/mfp/bandurabio.html

Paul, G. L. (1967). Outcome research in psychotherapy. *Journal of Consulting Psychology, 31,* 109–188.

Prochaska, J. O., & Norcross, J. C. (2010). *Systems of psychotherapy: A transtheoretical analysis* (7th ed.). Belmont, CA: Brooks/Cole, Cengage Learning.

*Robins, C. J., & Rosenthal, M. Z. (2011). Dialectical behavior therapy. In J. D. Hebert & E. M. Forman (Eds.), *Acceptance and mindfulness in cognitive behavior therapy: Understanding and applying the new therapies* (pp. 164–209). Hoboken, NJ: Wiley.

*Salmon, P. G., Sephton, S. E., & Dreeben, S. J. (2011). Mindfulness-based stress reduction. In J. D. Hebert & E. M. Forman (Eds.), *Acceptance and mindfulness in cognitive behavior therapy: Understanding and applying the new therapies* (pp. 132–163). Hoboken, NJ: Wiley.

*Segal, Z. V., Williams, J. M. G., & Teasdale, J. D. (2002). *Mindfulness-based cognitive therapy for depression: A new approach to preventing relapse*. New York: Guilford Press.

Segrin, C. (2008). Social skills training. In W. O'Donohue & J. E. Fisher (Eds.), *Cognitive behavior therapy: Applying empirically supported techniques in your practice* (2nd ed., pp. 502–509). Hoboken, NJ: Wiley.

*Shapiro, F. (2001). *Eye movement desensitization and reprocessing: Basic principles, protocols, and procedures* (2nd ed.). New York: Guilford Press.

Shapiro, F. (2002a). *EMDR as an integrative psychotherapy approach*. Washington, DC: American Psychological Association.

Shapiro, F. (2002b). EMDR twelve years after its introduction: Past and future research. *Journal of Clinical Psychology, 58,* 1–22.

Simpson, L. R. (2011). Dialectical behavior theory. In D. Capuzzi & D. R. Gross (Eds.), *Counseling and psychotherapy: Theories and interventions* (5th ed., pp. 215–235). Alexandria, VA: American Counseling Association.

Skinner, B. F. (1948). *Walden II*. New York: Macmillan.

Skinner, B. F. (1953). *Science and human behavior*. New York: Macmillan.

Skinner, B. F. (1971). *Beyond freedom and dignity*. New York: Knopf.

Spiegler, M. D. (2008). Behavior therapy 1: Traditional behavior therapy. In J. Frew & M. D. Spiegler (Eds.), *Contemporary psychotherapies for a diverse world* (pp. 275–319). Boston: Lahaska Press.

*Spiegler, M. D., & Guevremont, D. C. (2010). *Contemporary behavior therapy* (5th ed.). Belmont, CA: Wadsworth, Cengage Learning.

Tanaka-Matsumi, J., Higginbotham, H. N., & Chang, R. (2002). Cognitive-behavioral approaches to counseling across cultures: A functional analytic approach for clinical applications. In P. B. Pedersen, J. G. Draguns, W. J. Lonner, & J. E. Trimble (Eds.), *Counseling across cultures* (5th ed., pp. 337–379). Thousand Oaks, CA: Sage.

Vujanovic, A. A., Niles, B., Pietrefesa, A., Schmertz, S. K., & Potter, C. M. (2011). Mindfulness in the treatment of posttraumatic stress disorder among military veterans. *Professional Psychology: Research and Practice, 42*(1), 24–31.

*Watson, D. L., & Tharp, R. G. (2007). *Self-directed behavior: Self-modification for personal adjustment* (9th ed.). Belmont, CA: Wadsworth, Cengage Learning.

*Wilson, G. T. (2011). Behavior therapy. In R. Corsini & D. Wedding (Eds.), *Current psychotherapies* (9th ed., pp. 235–275). Belmont, CA: Brooks/Cole, Cengage Learning.

Wolpe, J. (1990). *The practice of behavior therapy* (4th ed.). Elmsford, NY: Pergamon Press.

Worthington, E. L., Jr. (2011). Integration of spirituality and religion into psychotherapy. In J. C. Norcross, G. R. Vandenbos, & D. K. Freedheim (Eds.), *History of psychotherapy* (2nd ed., pp. 533–544). Washington, DC: American Psychological Association.

Recommended Supplementary Readings for Chapter 10

Rational Emotive Behavior Therapy: It Works for Me—It Can Work for You (Ellis, 2004a) is a personal book that describes the many challenges Ellis has faced in his life and how he has coped with these realities by applying REBT principles.

The Road to Tolerance: The Philosophy of Rational Emotive Behavior Therapy (Ellis, 2004b) is a companion book to the book listed above. In this book Ellis demonstrates that tolerance is a deliberate, rational choice that we can make, both for the good of ourselves and for others.

Cognitive Behavior Therapy: Basics and Beyond (J. Beck, 2011a) is a main text in cognitive therapy that presents a comprehensive overview of the approach. An earlier edition of this book was translated into 20 languages.

Cognitive Therapy for Challenging Problems (J. Beck, 2005) is a comprehensive account of cognitive therapy procedures applied to clients who present a multiplicity of difficult behaviors. It covers the nuts and bolts of cognitive therapy with various populations and cites important research on cognitive therapy since its inception. There are chapters dealing with topics such as the therapeutic alliance, setting goals, structuring sessions, homework, identifying cognitions, modifying thoughts and images, modifying assumptions, and modifying core beliefs.

Cognitive Behavior Therapy: Applying Empirically Supported Techniques in Your Practice (O'Donohue & Fisher, 2008) is a useful collection of short chapters on applying empirically supported techniques in working with a wide range of presenting problems. Most of these chapters can be applied to both individual and group therapy.

Mind Over Mood: Change How You Feel by Changing the Way You Think (Greenberger & Padesky, 1995) provides step-by-step worksheets to identify moods, solve problems, and test thoughts related to depression, anxiety, anger, guilt, and shame. This is a popular self-help workbook and a valuable tool for therapists and clients learning cognitive therapy skills.

Clinician's Guide to Mind Over Mood (Padesky & Greenberger, 1995) shows therapists how to integrate *Mind Over Mood* in therapy and use cognitive therapy treatment protocols for specific diagnoses. This succinct overview of cognitive therapy has troubleshooting guides, reviews cultural issues, and offers guidelines for individual, couples, and group therapy.

References and Suggested Readings for Chapter 10

*Alford, B. A., & Beck, A. T. (1997). *The integrative power of cognitive therapy.* New York: Guilford Press.

Arnkoff, D. B., & Glass, C. R. (1992). Cognitive therapy and psychotherapy integration. In D. K. Freedheim (Ed.), *History of psychotherapy: A century of change* (pp. 657–694). Washington, DC: American Psychological Association.

Beck, A. T. (1963). Thinking and depression: Idiosyncratic content and cognitive distortions. *Archives of General Psychiatry, 9,* 324–333.

Beck, A. T. (1967). *Depression: Clinical, experimental, and theoretical aspects.* New York: Harper & Row. (Republished as *Depression: Causes and treatment.* Philadelphia: University of Pennsylvania Press, 1972)

*Beck, A. T. (1976). *Cognitive therapy and emotional disorders.* New York: International Universities Press.

Beck, A. T. (1987). *Cognitive therapy.* In J. K. Zeig (Ed.), *The evolution of psychotherapy* (pp. 149–178). New York: Brunner/Mazel.

*Beck, A. T., Rush, A., Shaw, B., & Emery, G. (1979). *Cognitive therapy of depression.* New York: Guilford Press.

*Beck, A. T., & Weishaar, M. E. (2011). Cognitive therapy. In R. J. Corsini & D. Wedding (Eds.), *Current psychotherapies* (9th ed., pp. 276–309). Belmont, CA: Brooks/Cole, Cengage Learning.

Beck, A., Wright, E. D., Newman, C. E., & Liese, B. (1993). *Cognitive therapy of substance abuse.* New York: Guilford Press.

*Beck, J. S. (2005). *Cognitive therapy for challenging problems: What to do when the basics don't work.* New York: Guilford Press.

Beck, J. S. (2007a). *The Beck diet solution: Train your brain to think like a thin person.* New York: Oxmoor House.

Beck, J. S. (2007b). *Beck diet solution weight loss workbook.* New York: Oxmoor House.

Beck, J. S. (2008). *The complete Beck diet for life.* New York: Oxmoor House.

*Beck, J. S. (2011a). *Cognitive behavior therapy: Basics and beyond* (2nd ed.). New York: Guilford Press.

*Beck, J. S. (2011b). *Cognitive therapy worksheet packet* (Rev.). Bala Cynwyd, PA: Beck Institute for Cognitive Therapy.

Beck, J. S., & Butler, A. C. (2005). Treating psychotherapists with cognitive therapy. In J. D. Geller, J. C. Norcross, & D. E. Orlinsky (Eds.), *The psychotherapist's own psychotherapy: Patient and clinician perspectives* (pp. 254–264). New York: Oxford University Press.

*Bond, F., & Flaxman, P. (2010). *Acceptance and commitment therapy: Distinctive features.* New York: Routledge (Taylor & Francis Group).

*Burns, D. (1988). *Feeling good: The new mood therapy.* New York: Signet.

Burns, D. (1989). *The feeling good handbook.* New York: Morrow.

*Books and articles marked with an asterisk are suggested for further study.

Chambless, D. L., & Peterman, M. (2006). Evidence on cognitive-behavioral therapy for generalized anxiety disorder and panic disorder. In R. L. Leahy (Ed.), *Contemporary cognitive therapy: Theory, research, and practice* (pp. 86–115). New York: Guilford Press.

*Corey, G. (2012). *Theory and practice of group counseling* (8th ed.). Belmont, CA: Brooks/Cole, Cengage Learning.

*Corey, G. (2013a). *Case approach to counseling and psychotherapy* (8th ed.). Belmont, CA: Brooks/Cole, Cengage Learning.

Corey, G. (2013b). *Student manual for Theory and Practice of Counseling and Psychotherapy* (9th ed.). Belmont, CA: Brooks/Cole, Cengage Learning.

*Cormier, S., Nurius, P. S., & Osborn, C. J. (2013). *Interviewing and change strategies for helpers: Fundamental skills and cognitive behavioral interventions* (7th ed.). Belmont, CA: Brooks/Cole, Cengage Learning.

*Crane, R. (2008). *Mindfulness-based cognitive therapy: Distinctive features.* New York: Routledge (Taylor & Francis Group).

*Craske, M. G. (2010). *Cognitive-behavioral therapy.* Washington, DC: American Psychological Association.

*Dattilio, F. M. (1993). Cognitive techniques with couples and families. *The Family Journal, 1*(1), 51–65.

*Dattilio, F. M. (Ed.). (1998). *Case studies in couple and family therapy: Systemic and cognitive perspectives.* New York: Guilford Press.

Dattilio, F. M. (2000a). Cognitive-behavioral strategies. In J. Carlson & L. Sperry (Eds.), *Brief therapy with individuals and couples* (pp. 33–70). Phoenix, AZ: Zeig, Tucker & Theisen.

Dattilio, F. M. (2000b). Families in crisis. In F. M. Dattilio & A. Freeman (Eds.), *Cognitive-behavioral strategies in crisis intervention* (2nd ed., pp. 316–338). New York: Guilford Press.

Dattilio, F. M. (2001). Cognitive-behavior family therapy: Contemporary myths and misconceptions. *Contemporary Family Therapy, 23*(1), 3–18.

Dattilio, F. M. (2002a, January–February). Cognitive-behaviorism comes of age: Grounding symptomatic treatment in an existential approach. *The Psychotherapy Networker, 26*(1), 75–78.

Dattilio, F. M. (2002b). Homework assignments in couple and family therapy. *Journal of Clinical Psychology, 58*(5), 535–547.

Dattilio, F. M. (2005). Restructuring family schemas: A cognitive-behavioral perspective. *Journal of Marital and Family Therapy, 31*(1), 15–30.

Dattilio, F. M. (2010). *Cognitive-behavior therapy with couples and families: A comprehensive guide for clinicians.* New York: Guilford Press.

Dattilio, F. M., & Castaldo, J. E. (2001). Differentiating symptoms of anxiety from relapse of Guillain-Barre-syndrome. *Harvard Review of Psychiatry, 9*(5), 260–265.

*Dattilio, F. M., & Freeman, A. (Eds.). (2007). *Cognitive-behavioral strategies in crisis intervention* (3rd ed.). New York: Guilford Press.

Dattilio, F. M., & Kendall, P. C. (2007). Panic disorder. In F. M. Dattilio & A. Freeman (Eds.), *Cognitive-behavioral strategies in crisis intervention* (3rd ed., pp. 59–83). New York: Guilford Press.

*Dattilio, F. M., & Padesky, C. A. (1990). *Cognitive therapy with couples.* Sarasota, FL: Professional Resources Exchange.

Dienes, K. A., Torres-Harding, S., Reinecke, M. A., Freeman, A., & Sauer, A. (2011). Cognitive therapy. In S. B. Messer & A. S. Gurman (Eds.), *Essential psychotherapies: Theory and practice* (3rd ed., pp.143–183). New York: Guilford Press.

*Dobson, D., & Dobson, K. S. (2009). *Evidence-based practice of cognitive-behavioral therapy.* New York: Guilford Press.

Dobson, K. S., & Dozois, D. J. A. (2010). Historical and philosophical bases of the cognitive-behavioral therapies. In K. S. Dobson (Ed.), *Handbook of cognitive-behavioral therapies* (3rd ed., pp. 3–38). New York: Guilford Press.

Dozois, D. J. A., & Beck, A. T. (2011). Cognitive therapy. In J. D. Hebert & E. M. Forman (Eds.), *Acceptance and mindfulness in cognitive behavior therapy: Understanding and applying the new therapies* (pp. 26–56). Hoboken, NJ: Wiley.

*Dryden, W. (2006). *Getting started with REBT: A concise guide for clients.* New York: Routledge (Taylor & Francis Group).

Dryden, W. (2007). Rational emotive behaviour therapy. In *Dryden's handbook of individual therapy* (5th ed., pp. 352-378). London: Sage.

*Dryden, W. (2008). *Understanding emotional problems: The REBT perspective.* New York: Routledge (Taylor & Francis Group).

*Dryden, W. (2009a). *How to think and intervene like an REBT therapist.* New York: Routledge (Taylor & Francis Group).

*Dryden, W. (2009b). *Rational emotive behaviour therapy: Distinctive features.* New York: Routledge (Taylor & Francis Group).

*Dryden, W., & Neenan, M. (2006). *Rational emotive behaviour therapy: 100 key points and techniques.* New York: Routledge (Taylor & Francis Group).

*Ellis, A. (1994). *Reason and emotion in psychotherapy revised.* New York: Kensington.

*Ellis, A. (1996). *Better, deeper, and more enduring brief therapy: The rational emotive behavior therapy approach.* New York: Brunner/Mazel.

*Ellis, A. (1997). The evolution of Albert Ellis and rational emotive behavior therapy. In J. K. Zeig (Ed.), *The evolution of psychotherapy: The third conference* (pp. 69-82). New York: Brunner/Mazel.

*Ellis, A. (1999). *How to make yourself happy and remarkably less disturbable.* Atascadero, CA: Impact.

*Ellis, A. (2000). *How to control your anxiety before it controls you.* New York: Citadel Press.

*Ellis, A. (2001a). *Feeling better, getting better, and staying better.* Atascadero, CA: Impact.

*Ellis, A. (2001b). *Overcoming destructive beliefs, feelings, and behaviors.* Amherst, NY: Prometheus Books.

*Ellis, A. (2002). *Overcoming resistance: A rational emotive behavior therapy integrated approach* (2nd ed.). New York: Springer.

*Ellis, A. (2004a). *Rational emotive behavior therapy: It works for me—It can work for you.* Amherst, NY: Prometheus.

*Ellis, A. (2004b). *The road to tolerance: The philosophy of rational emotive behavior therapy.* Amherst, NY: Prometheus.

Ellis, A. (2008). Cognitive restructuring of the disputing of irrational beliefs. In W. O'Donohue & J. E. Fisher (Eds.), *Cognitive behavior therapy: Applying empirically supported techniques in your practice* (2nd ed., pp. 91-95). Hoboken, NJ: Wiley.

Ellis, A. (2010). *All out! An autobiography.* Amherst, NY: Prometheus Books.

Ellis, A. (2011). Rational emotive behavior therapy. In R. Corsini & D. Wedding (Eds.), *Current psychotherapies* (9th ed., pp. 196-234). Belmont, CA: Brooks/Cole, Cengage Learning.

*Ellis, A., & Blau, S. (Eds.). (1998). *The Albert Ellis reader.* New York: Kensington.

*Ellis, A., & Crawford, T. (2000). *Making intimate connections: Seven guidelines for great relationships and better communication.* Atascadero, CA: Impact.

*Ellis, A., & Dryden, W. (2007). *The practice of rational-emotive therapy* (2nd ed.). New York: Springer.

Ellis, A., & Ellis, D. J. (2011). *Rational emotive behavior therapy.* Washington, DC: American Psychological Association.

Ellis, A., Gordon, J., Neenan, M., & Palmer, S. (1997). *Stress counseling: A rational emotive behavior approach.* New York: Springer.

Ellis, A., & Harper, R. A. (1997). *A guide to rational living* (3rd ed.). North Hollywood, CA: Melvin Powers (Wilshire Books).

*Ellis, A., & MacLaren, C. (2005). *Rational emotive behavior therapy: A therapist's guide* (2nd ed.). Atascadero, CA: Impact.

Epstein, N. B. (2006). Cognitive-behavioral therapy with couples: Theoretical and empirical status. In R. L. Leahy (Ed.), *Contemporary cognitive therapy: Theory, research, and practice* (pp. 367-388). New York: Guilford Press.

Freeman, A., & Dattilio, F. M. (Eds.). (1992). *Comprehensive casebook of cognitive therapy.* New York: Plenum Press.

Freeman, A., & Dattilio, R. M. (1994). Cognitive therapy. In J. L. Ronch, W. Van Ornum, & N. C. Stilwell (Eds.), *The counseling sourcebook: A practical reference on contemporary issues* (pp. 60–71). New York: Continuum Press.

*Gilbert, P., & Leahy, R. L. (2009). *The therapeutic relationship in the cognitive behavioral psychotherapies.* New York: Routledge (Taylor & Francis Group).

Granvold, D. K. (Ed.). (1994). *Cognitive and behavioral treatment: Method and applications.* Pacific Grove, CA: Brooks/Cole.

*Greenberger, D., & Padesky, C. A. (1995). *Mind over mood: Change how you feel by changing the way you think.* New York: Guilford Press.

Hays, P. A. (2009). Integrating evidence-based practice, cognitive-behavior therapy, and multicultural therapy: Ten steps for culturally competent practice. *Professional Psychology: Research and Practice, 40*(4), 354–360.

Hollon, S. D., & DiGiuseppe, R. (2011). Cognitive theories in psychotherapy. In J. C. Norcross, G. R. Vandenbos, & D. K. Freedheim (Eds.), *History of psychotherapy* (2nd ed., pp. 203–242). Washington, DC: American Psychological Association.

Horney, K. (1950). *Neurosis and human growth.* New York: Norton.

Jacobs, N. N. (2008). Bibliotherapy utilizing CBT. In W. O'Donohue & J. E. Fisher (Eds.), *Cognitive behavior therapy: Applying empirically supported techniques in your practice* (2nd ed., pp. 60–67). Hoboken, NJ: Wiley.

Kalodner, C. R. (2011). Cognitive-behavioral theories. In D. Capuzzi & D. R. Gross (Eds.), *Counseling and psychotherapy: Theories and interventions* (5th ed., pp. 193–213). Alexandria, VA: American Counseling Association.

*Kazantzis, N., Deane, F. P., Ronan, K. R., & L'Abate, L. (2005). *Using homework assignments in cognitive behavior therapy.* New York: Routledge (Taylor & Francis Group).

Leahy, R. L. (2002). Cognitive therapy: Current problems and future directions. In R. L. Leahy & E. T. Dowd (Eds.), *Clinical advances in cognitive psychotherapy: Theory and application* (pp. 418–434). New York: Springer.

*Leahy, R. L. (2006a). (Ed.). *Contemporary cognitive therapy: Theory, research, and practice.* New York: Guilford Press.

*Leahy, R. L. (2006b). (Ed.). *Roadblocks in cognitive-behavioral therapy.* New York: Guilford Press.

*Ledley, D. R., Marx, B. P., & Heimberg, R. G. (2010). *Making cognitive-behavioral therapy work: Clinical processes for new practitioners* (2nd ed.). New York: Guilford Press.

Macy, R. J. (2007). Cognitive therapy. In A. B. Rochlen (Ed.), *Applying counseling theories: An online case-based approach* (pp. 157–176). Upper Saddle River, NJ: Pearson Prentice-Hall.

Marlatt, G., & Donovan, D. M. (Eds.). (2005). *Relapse prevention: Maintenance strategies in the treatment of addictive behaviors* (2nd ed.). New York: Guilford Press.

*Meichenbaum, D. (1977). *Cognitive behavior modification: An integrative approach.* New York: Plenum Press.

*Meichenbaum, D. (1985). *Stress inoculation training.* New York: Pergamon Press.

Meichenbaum, D. (1986). Cognitive behavior modification. In F. H. Kanfer & A. P. Goldstein (Eds.), *Helping people change: A textbook of methods* (pp. 346–380). New York: Pergamon Press.

Meichenbaum, D. (1993). Stress inoculation training: A 20 year update. In P. M. Lehrer & R. L. Woolfolk (Eds.), *Principles and practice of stress management* (2nd ed., pp 373–406). New York: Guilford Press.

Meichenbaum, D. (1994a). *A clinical handbook/practical therapist manual: For assessing and treating adults with post-traumatic stress disorder (PTSD).* Waterloo, Ontario, Canada: Institute Press.

Meichenbaum, D. (1994b). *Treating adults with PTSD.* Clearwater, FL: Institute Press.

Meichenbaum, D. (2002). *Treatment of individuals with anger-control problems and aggressive behaviors: A clinical handbook.* Clearwater, FL: Institute Press.

Meichenbaum, D. (2007). Stress inoculation training: A preventive and treatment approach.

In P. M. Lehrer, R. L. Woolfolk, & W. Sime (Eds.), *Principles and practices of stress management* (3rd ed., pp. 497–518). New York: Guilford Press.

*Meichenbaum, D. (2008). Stress inoculation training. In W. O'Donohue & J. E. Fisher (Eds.), *Cognitive behavior therapy: Applying empirically supported techniques in your practice* (2nd ed., pp. 529–532). Hoboken, NJ: Wiley.

Newman, C. (2006). Substance abuse. In R. L. Leahy (Ed.), *Contemporary cognitive therapy: Theory, research, and practice* (pp. 206–227). New York: Guilford Press.

*O'Donohue, W., & Fisher, J. E. (Eds.). (2008). *Cognitive behavior therapy: Applying empirically supported techniques in your practice* (2nd ed.). Hoboken, NJ: Wiley.

*Padesky, C. A., & Greenberger, D. (1995). *Clinician's guide to mind over mood.* New York: Guilford Press.

Petrocelli, J. V. (2002). Effectiveness of group cognitive-behavioral therapy for general symptomatology: A meta-analysis. *Journal for Specialists in Group Work, 27*(1), 92–115.

Pretzer, J., & Beck, J. (2006). Cognitive therapy of personality disorders. In R. L. Leahy (Ed.), *Contemporary cognitive therapy: Theory, research, and practice* (pp. 299–318). New York: Guilford Press.

Reinecke, M., Dattilio, F. M., & Freeman, A. (Eds.). (2002). *Casebook of cognitive behavior therapy with children and adolescents* (2nd ed.). New York: Guilford Press.

Riskind, J. H. (2006). Cognitive theory and research on generalized anxiety disorder. In R. L. Leahy (Ed.), *Contemporary cognitive therapy: Theory, research, and practice* (pp. 62–85). New York: Guilford Press.

*Roemer, L., & Orsillio, S. M. (2010). *Mindfulness and acceptance-based behavioral therapies in practice.* New York: Guilford Press.

Scher, C. D., Segal, Z. V., & Ingram, R. E. (2006). Beck's theory of depression: Origins, empirical status, and future directions for cognitive vulnerability. In R. L. Leahy (Ed.), *Contemporary cognitive therapy: Theory, research, and practice* (pp. 27–61). New York: Guilford Press.

Spiegler, M. D. (2008). Behavior therapy II: Cognitive-behavioral therapy. In J. Frew & M. D. Spiegler (Eds.), *Contemporary psychotherapies for a diverse world* (pp. 320–359). Boston: Lahaska Press.

*Spiegler, M. D., & Guevremont, D. C. (2010). *Contemporary behavior therapy* (5th ed.). Belmont, CA: Wadsworth, Cengage Learning.

*Swales, M. A., & Heard, H. L. (2008). *Dialectical behaviour therapy: Distinctive features.* New York: Routledge (Taylor & Francis Group).

Tompkins, M. A. (2004). *Using homework in psychotherapy: Strategies, guidelines, and forms.* New York: Guilford Press.

Tompkins, M. A. (2006). Effective homework. In R. L. Leahy (Ed.), *Roadblocks in cognitive-behavioral therapy* (pp. 49–66). New York: Guilford Press.

Vernon, A. (2007). Rational emotive behavior therapy. In D. Capuzzi & D. R. Gross (Eds.), *Counseling and psychotherapy: Theories and interventions* (4th ed., pp. 266–288). Upper Saddle River, NJ: Merrill Prentice-Hall.

Weishaar, M. E. (1993). *Aaron T. Beck.* London: Sage.

*White, J. R., & Freeman, A. (Eds.). (2000). *Cognitive-behavioral group therapy for specific problems and populations.* Washington, DC: American Psychological Association.

Wills, F. (2009). *Beck's cognitive therapy: Distinctive features.* New York: Routledge (Taylor & Francis Group).

Wolfe, J. L. (2007). Rational emotive behavior therapy (REBT). In A. B. Rochlen (Ed.), *Applying counseling theories: An online case-based approach* (pp. 177–191). Upper Saddle River, NJ: Pearson Prentice-Hall.

Recommended Supplementary Readings for Chapter 11

Counseling With Choice Theory: The New Reality Therapy (Glasser, 2001) represents the author's latest thinking about choice theory and develops the existential theme that we choose all of our total behaviors. Case examples demonstrate how choice theory principles can be applied in helping people establish better relationships.

Reality Therapy (Wubbolding, 2011a) updates and extends previous publications on choice theory and reality therapy. As a part of the APA theories of psychotherapy series, this is a well-written and comprehensive overview of reality therapy and choice theory.

Case Approach to Counseling and Psychotherapy (Corey, 2013) illustrates how prominent reality therapists Drs. William Glasser and Robert Wubbolding would counsel Ruth from their different perspectives of choice theory and reality therapy.

References and Suggested Readings for Chapter 11

American Psychiatric Association. (2000). *Diagnostic and statistical manual of mental disorders, text revision,* (4th ed.). Washington, DC: Author.

Corey, G. (2012). *Theory and practice of group counseling* (8th ed.). Belmont, CA: Brooks/Cole, Cengage Learning.

*Corey, G.** (2013). *Case approach to counseling and psychotherapy* (8th ed.). Belmont, CA: Brooks/Cole, Cengage Learning.

Glasser, W. (1965). *Reality therapy: A new approach to psychiatry.* New York: Harper & Row.

Glasser, W. (1968). *Schools without failure.* New York: Harper & Row.

Glasser, W. (1992). Reality therapy. *New York State Journal for Counseling and Development,* 7(1), 5–13.

*Glasser, W.** (1998). *Choice theory: A new psychology of personal freedom.* New York: HarperCollins.

*Glasser, W.** (2001). *Counseling with choice theory: The new reality therapy.* New York: HarperCollins.

Glasser, W. (2003). *Warning: Psychiatry can be hazardous to your mental health.* New York: HarperCollins.

Glasser, W. (2005). *Defining mental health as a public health issue: A new leadership role for the helping and teaching professions.* Chatsworth, CA: William Glasser Institute.

Glasser, W., & Glasser, C. (2000). *Getting together and staying together.* New York: HarperCollins.

Glasser, W., & Glasser, C. (2007). *Eight lessons for a happier marriage.* New York: HarperCollins.

*Wubbolding, R. E.** (1988). *Using reality therapy.* New York: Harper & Row (Perennial Library).

*Wubbolding, R. E.** (1991). *Understanding reality therapy.* New York: Harper & Row (Perennial Library).

*Wubbolding, R. E.** (2000). *Reality therapy for the 21st century.* Philadelphia, PA: Brunner-Routledge.

Wubbolding, R. E. (2007). Reality therapy. In A. B. Rochlen (Ed.), *Applying counseling theories: An online case-based approach* (pp. 193–207). Upper Saddle River, NJ: Pearson Prentice-Hall.

Wubbolding, R. E. (2008). Reality therapy. In J. Frew & M. D. Spiegler (Eds.), *Contemporary psychotherapies for a diverse world* (pp. 360–396). Boston: Houghton Mifflin.

Wubbolding, R. E. (2009). Headline or footnote? Mainstream or backwater? Cutting edge or trailing edge? Included or excluded from the professional world? *International Journal of Reality Therapy, 29*(1), 26–29.

Wubbolding, R. E. (2010). *Cycle of psychotherapy, counseling, coaching, managing and supervising* (chart, 17th revision). Cincinnati, OH: Center for Reality Therapy.

*Books and articles marked with an asterisk are suggested for further study.

*Wubbolding, R. E. (2011a). *Reality therapy*. Washington, DC: American Psychological Association.

*Wubbolding, R. E. (2011b). Reality therapy/choice theory. In D. Capuzzi & D. R. Gross (Eds.), *Counseling and psychotherapy: Theories and interventions* (5th ed., pp. 263–285). Alexandria, VA: American Counseling Association.

*Wubbolding, R. E., & Brickell, J. (2001). *A set of directions for putting and keeping yourself together*. Minneapolis, MN: Educational Media Corporation.

Wubbolding, R. E., & Brickell, J. (2005). Reality therapy in recovery. *Directions in Addiction Treatment and Prevention, 9*(1), 1–10. New York: The Hatherleigh Company.

Wubbolding, R. E., & Brickell, J. (2009). Perception: The orphaned component of choice theory. *International Journal of Reality Therapy, 28*(2), 50–54.

Wubbolding, R. E., & Colleagues. (1998). Multicultural awareness: Implications for reality therapy and choice theory. *International Journal of Reality Therapy, 17*(2), 4–6.

Wubbolding, R. E., Brickell, J., Imhof, L., Kim, R., Lojk, L., & Al-Rashidi, B. (2004). Reality therapy: A global perspective. *International Journal for the Advancement of Counselling, 26*(3), 219–228.

Wubbolding, R. E., Robey, P., & Brickell, J. (2010). A partial and tentative look at the future of choice theory, reality therapy and lead management. *International Journal of Choice Theory and Reality Therapy, 19*(2), 25–34.

Recommended Supplementary Readings for Chapter 12

Feminist Perspectives in Therapy: Empowering Diverse Women (Worell & Remer, 2003) is an outstanding text that clearly outlines the foundations of empowerment feminist therapy. The book covers a range of topics such as integrating feminist and multicultural perspectives on therapy, changing roles for women, feminist views of counseling practice, feminist transformation of counseling theories, and a feminist approach to assessment and diagnosis. There also are excellent chapters dealing with depression, surviving sexual assault, confronting abuse, choosing a career path, and lesbian and ethnic minority women.

Feminist Theories and Feminist Psychotherapies: Origins, Themes, and Diversity (Enns, 2004) describes the wide range of feminist theories that inform and influence feminist practice. The book includes short self-assessment questionnaires designed to help readers clarify their feminist theoretical perspective.

Feminist Therapy (Brown, 2010) provides an interesting perspective on the history of feminist therapy and speculates about future developments of the approach. Brown clearly explains key concepts of feminist theory and the therapeutic process.

Introduction to Feminist Therapy: Strategies for Social and Individual Change (Evans, Kincade, & Seem, 2011) emphasizes the practical applications of feminist theory to clinical practice. They provide useful information on social change and empowerment, the importance of establishing an egalitarian relationship, and intervention strategies when working with people from diverse cultural backgrounds.

The Healing Connection: How Women Form Relationships in Therapy and Life (Miller & Stiver, 1997) describes how connections are formed between people and how this leads to strong, healthy individuals. The authors also deal with disconnections between people that lead to anxiety, isolation, and depression.

Women's Growth in Diversity: More Writings From the Stone Center (Jordan, 1997) builds on the foundations laid by Women's Growth in Connection (Jordan et al., 1991). This work offers insights on issues such as sexuality, shame, anger, depression, power relations between women, and women's experiences in therapy.

References and Suggested Readings for Chapter 12

American Psychiatric Association. (2000). *Diagnostic and statistical manual of mental disorders, text revision* (4th ed.). Washington, DC: Author.

American Psychological Association. (2007). Guidelines for psychological practice with girls and women. *American Psychologist, 62,* 949–979.

Beardsley, B., Morrow, S. L., Castillo, L., & Weitzman, L. (1998, March). *Perceptions and behaviors of practicing feminist therapists: Development of the feminist multicultural practice instrument.* Paper presented at the 23rd annual conference of the Association for Women in Psychology, Baltimore.

Belenky, M., Clinchy, B., Goldberger, N., & Tarule, J. (1997). *Women's ways of knowing: The development of self, voice, and mind* (10th anniv. ed.). New York: HarperCollins. (Original work published 1987)

Bem, S. L. (1993). *The lenses of gender.* New Haven, CT: Yale University Press.

Bitter, J. R. (2008). Reconsidering narcissism: An Adlerian-feminist response to the articles in the special section of the Journal of Individual Psychology. *Journal of Individual Psychology, 64*(3), 270–279.

Bitter, J. R., Robertson, P. E., Healey, A., & Cole, L. (2009). Reclaiming a profeminist orientation in Adlerian therapy. *Journal of Individual Psychology, 65*(1), 13–33.

Brabeck, M. M. (Ed.). (2000). *Practicing feminist ethics in psychology.* Washington, DC: American Psychological Association.

Brabeck, M., & Brown, L. (1997). Feminist theory and psychological practice. In J. Worell & N. G. Johnson (Eds.), *Shaping the future of feminist psychology: Education, research, and practice* (pp. 15–35). Washington, DC: American Psychological Association.

*****Brown, L. S.** (1994). *Subversive dialogues: Theory in feminist therapy.* New York: Basic Books.

Brown, L. S. (2006). Still subversive after all these years: The relevance of feminist therapy in the age of evidence-based practice. *Psychology of Women Quarterly, 30,* 15–24.

*****Brown, L. S.** (2010). *Feminist therapy.* Washington, DC: American Psychological Association.

Brown, L. S., & Root, M. (1990). *Diversity and complexity in feminist therapy.* New York: Hayworth.

*****Caplan, P. J.** (1989). *Don't blame mother.* New York: Harper & Row.

Cole, E., Espín, O. M., & Rothblum, E. D. (1992). *Refugee women and their mental health: Shattered societies, shattered lives.* Binghamton, NY: Haworth Press.

Comstock, D. L., Hammer, T. R., Strentzsch, J., Cannon, K., Parsons, J., & Salazar, G. (2008). Relational-cultural theory: A framework for bridging relational, multicultural, and social justice competencies. *Journal of Counseling and Development, 86,* 279–287.

*****Corey, G.** (2013). *Case approach to counseling and psychotherapy* (8th ed.). Belmont, CA: Brooks/Cole, Cengage Learning.

Crethar, H. C., Torres Rivera, E., & Nash, S. (2008). In search of common threads: Linking multicultural, feminist, and social justice counseling paradigms. *Journal of Counseling and Development, 86,* 269–278.

Enns, C. Z. (1987). Gestalt therapy and feminist therapy: A proposed integration. *Journal of Counseling and Development, 66,* 93–95.

---

*Books and articles marked with an asterisk are suggested for further study.

Enns, C. Z. (1991). The "new" relationship models of women's identity: A review and critique for counselors. *Journal of Counseling and Development, 69*, 209–217.

Enns, C. Z. (1993). Twenty years of feminist counseling and therapy: From naming biases to implementing multifaceted practice. *The Counseling Psychologist, 21*(1), 3–87.

Enns, C. Z. (2000). Gender issues in counseling. In S. D. Brown & R. W. Lent (Eds.), *Handbook of counseling psychology* (3rd ed., pp. 601–638). New York: Wiley.

*Enns, C. Z. (2003). Contemporary adaptations of traditional approaches to the counseling of women. In M. Kopala & M. Keitel (Eds.), *Handbook of counseling women* (pp. 1–21). Thousand Oaks, CA: Sage.

*Enns, C. Z. (2004). *Feminist theories and feminist psychotherapies: Origins, themes, and diversity* (2nd ed.). New York: Haworth.

Enns, C. Z. (2010). Locational feminisms and feminist social identity analysis. *Professional Psychology: Research and Practice, 41*(4), 333–339.

Enns, C. Z. (2011). Feminist approaches to counseling. In E. M. Altmaier & J. C. Hansen (Eds.), *Oxford handbook of counseling psychology* (pp. 434–459). New York: Oxford University Press.

Enns, C.Z., & Byars-Winston, A. (2010). Multicultural feminist therapy. In H. Landrine & N.F. Russo (Eds.), *Handbook of diversity in feminist psychology* (pp. 367–388). New York: Springer.

*Enns, C. Z., & Sinacore, A. L. (2001). Feminist theories. In J. Worell (Ed.), *Encyclopedia of gender* (Vol. 1, pp. 469–480). San Diego, CA: Academic Press.

Enns, C. Z., & Sinacore, A. L. (Eds.). (2005). *Teaching and social justice: Integrating multicultural and feminist theories in the classroom.* Washington, DC: American Psychological Association.

*Eriksen, K., & Kress, V. E. (2005). *Beyond the DSM story: Ethical quandaries, challenges, and best practices.* Thousand Oaks, CA: Sage.

*Eriksen, K., & Kress, V. E. (2008). Gender and diagnosis: Struggles and suggestions for counselors. *Journal of Counseling & Development, 86*, 152–162.

Espín, O. M. (1996). *Latina healers: Lives of power and tradition.* Encino, CA: Floricanto Press.

Espín, O. M. (1997). *Latina realities: Essays on healing, migration, and sexuality.* Boulder, CO: Westview Press.

Espín, O. M. (1999). *Women crossing boundaries: A psychology of immigration and the transformation of sexuality.* New York: Routledge.

Evans, K. M., Kincade, E. A., Marbley, A. F., & Seem, S. R. (2005). Feminism and feminist therapy: Lessons from the past and hopes for the future. *Journal of Counseling & Development, 83*(3), 269–277.

Evans, K. M., Kincade, E. A., & Seem, S. R. (2011). *Introduction to feminist therapy: Strategies for social and individual change.* Thousand Oaks, CA: Sage.

Feminist Therapy Institute. (2000). *Feminist therapy code of ethics* (revised, 1999). San Francisco: Feminist Therapy Institute.

Ganley, A. L. (1988). Feminist therapy with male clients. In M. A. Dutton-Douglas & L. E. Walker (Eds.), *Feminist psychotherapies: Integration of therapeutic and feminist systems* (pp. 186–205). Norwood, NJ: Ablex.

*Gilbert, L. A., & Rader, J. (2007). Feminist counseling. In A. B. Rochlen (Ed.), *Applying counseling theories: An online case-based approach* (pp. 225–238). Upper Saddle River, NJ: Pearson Prentice-Hall.

Gilbert, L. A., & Scher, M. (1999). *Gender and sex in counseling and psychotherapy.* Boston: Allyn & Bacon.

Gilligan, C. (1977). In a different voice: Women's conception of self and morality. *Harvard Educational Review, 47*, 481–517.

*Gilligan, C. (1982). *In a different voice.* Cambridge, MA: Harvard University Press.

*Hays, P. A. (2008). *Addressing cultural complexities in practice* (2nd ed.). Washington DC: American Psychological Association.

Herlihy, B., & Corey, G. (2006a). *ACA ethical standards casebook* (6th ed.). Alexandria, VA: American Counseling Association.

Herlihy, B., & Corey, G. (2006b). *Boundary issues in counseling: Multiple roles and* responsibilities (2nd ed.). Alexandria, VA: American Counseling Association.

*Herlihy, B., & Mccollum, V. J. (2011). Feminist theory. In D. Capuzzi & D. R. Gross (Eds.), Counseling and psychotherapy: Theories and interventions (5th ed., pp. 313–333). Alexandria, VA: American Counseling Association.

Herman, J. (1992). Trauma and recovery. New York: Basic Books.

*Jordan, J. V. (Ed.). (1997). Women's growth in diversity: More writings from the Stone Center. New York: Guilford Press.

*Jordan, J. V., Kaplan, A. G., Miller, J. B., Stiver, I. P., & Surrey, J. L. (Eds.). (1991). Women's growth in connection: Writings from the Stone Center. New York: Guilford Press.

Kaschak, E. (1981). Feminist psychotherapy: The first decade. In S. Cox (Ed.), Female psychology: The emerging self (pp. 387–400). New York: St. Martins.

Kaschak, E. (1992). Engendered lives. New York: Basic Books.

Kees, N. L., & Leech, N. (2004). Practice trends in women's groups: An inclusive view. In J. L. DeLucia-Waack, D. Gerrity, C. R. Kalodner, & M. T. Riva (Eds.), Handbook of group counseling and psychotherapy (pp. 445–455). Thousand Oaks, CA: Sage.

Miller, J. B. (1986). Toward a new psychology of women (2nd ed.). Boston: Beacon.

Miller, J. B. (1991). The development of women's sense of self. In J. V. Jordan, A. G. Kaplan, J. B. Miller, I. P. Stiver, & J. L. Surrey (Eds.), Women's growth in connection (pp. 11–26). New York: Guilford Press.

Miller, J. B., Jordon, J., Stiver, I. P., Walker, M., Surrey, J., & Eldridge, N. S. (1999). Therapists' authenticity (Work in progress no. 82). Wellesley, MA: Stone Center Working Paper Series.

*Miller, J. B., & Stiver, I. P. (1997). The healing connection: How women form relationships in therapy and in life. Boston: Beacon Press.

*Philpot, C. L., Brooks, G. R., Lusterman, D. D., & Nutt, R. L. (1997). Bridging separate gender worlds: Why men and women clash and how therapists can bring them together. Washington, DC: American Psychological Association.

Pleck, J. H. (1995). The gender role strain paradigm: An update. In R. R. Levant & W. S. Pollack (Eds.), A new psychology of men (pp. 11–32). New York: Basic Books.

Pollack, W. S. (1995). No man is an island: Toward a new psychoanalytic psychology of men. In R. F. Levant & W. S. Pollack (Eds.), A new psychology of men (pp. 33–67). New York: Basic Books.

*Pollack, W. S. (1998). Real boys. New York: Henry Holt.

Prochaska, J. O., & Norcross, J. C. (2010). Systems of psychotherapy: A transtheoretical analysis (7th ed.). Belmont, CA: Brooks/Cole, Cengage Learning.

Rave, E. J., & Larsen, C. C. (Eds.). (1995). Ethical decision making in therapy: Feminist perspectives. New York: Guilford Press.

*Real, T. (1998). I don't want to talk about it: Overcoming the secret legacy of male depression. New York: Simon & Schuster (Fireside).

*Remer, P. (2008). Feminist therapy. In J. Frew & M. D. Spiegler (Eds.), Contemporary psychotherapies for a diverse world (pp. 397–441). Boston: Lahaska Press.

*Rogers, N. (1995). Emerging woman: A decade of midlife transitions. Manchester, England: PCCS Books.

*Surrey, J. L. (1991). The "self-in-relation": A theory of women's development. In J. V. Jordan, A. G. Kaplan, J. B. Miller, I. P. Stiver, & J. L. Surrey (Eds.), Women's growth in connection (pp. 51–66). New York: Guilford Press.

Thomas, S. A. (1977). Theory and practice in feminist therapy. Social Work, 22, 447–454.

Trepal, H. (2010). Exploring self-injury through a relational-cultural lens. Journal of Counseling and Development, 88(4), 492–499.

Turner, L. C., & Werner-Wilson, R. J. (2008). Phenomenological experiences of girls in a single-sex day treatment group. Journal of Feminist Family Therapy, 20(3), 220–250.

Walden, S. L. (2006). Inclusion of the client perspective in ethical practice. In B. Herlihy & G. Corey, Boundary issues in counseling: Multiple roles and responsibilities (2nd ed., pp. 46–52). Alexandria, VA: American Counseling Association.

Walker, L. (1994). *Abused women and survivor therapy: A practical guide for the psychotherapist.* Washington, DC: American Psychological Association.

*Worell, J., & Remer, P. (2003). *Feminist perspectives in therapy: Empowering diverse women* (2nd ed.). New York: Wiley.

Recommended Supplementary Readings for Chapter 13

Interviewing for Solutions (De Jong & Berg, 2008) is a practical text aimed at teaching and learning solution-focused skills. It is written in a conversational and informal style and contains many examples to solidify learning of skills.

Solution-Focused Counseling in Schools (Murphy, 2008) is a clearly written and practical book that offers efficient strategies for addressing a range of problems from preschool through high school. Numerous case examples illustrate the foundations, tasks, and techniques of solution-focused counseling. The book also describes how the principles of client-directed, outcome-informed practice can be integrated in solution-focused counseling.

Narrative Means to Therapeutic Ends (White & Epston, 1990) is the most widely known book on narrative therapy.

Maps of Narrative Practice (White, 2007) is Michael White's final book, which brings together much of his work over several decades in one accessible volume.

Narrative Therapy (Madigan, 2011) provides an updated discussion of the theory and therapeutic process of narrative therapy.

Narrative Counseling in Schools (Winslade & Monk, 2007) is a basic and easy-to-read guide to applying concepts and techniques of narrative therapy to school settings.

Narrative Therapy: The Social Construction of Preferred Realities (Freedman & Combs, 1996) is an exceptionally clear explanation of the basic ideas of narrative therapy. The authors emphasize key concepts and the application of specific clinical practices. This is one of the best sources on the theory and practice of narrative therapy.

References and Suggested Readings for Chapter 13

Anderson, H. (1993). On a roller coaster: A collaborative language system approach to therapy. In S. Friedman (Ed.), *The new language of change* (pp. 324–344). New York: Guilford Press.

*Anderson, H., & Goolishian, H. (1992). The client is the expert: A not-knowing approach to therapy. In S. McNamee & K. J. Gergen (Eds.), *Therapy as social construction* (pp. 25–39). Newbury Park, CA: Sage.

Andrews, J., & Clark, D. J. (1996). In the case of a depressed woman: Solution-focused or narrative therapy approaches? *The Family Journal, 4*(3), 243–250.

Bateson, G. (1972). *Steps to an ecology of mind.* New York: Ballantine.

Berg, I. K. (1994). *Family based services: A solution-focused approach.* New York: Norton.

Berg, I. K., & Miller, S. D. (1992). *Working with the problem drinker: A solution-focused approach.* New York: Norton.

Berger, P. L., & Luckman, T. (1967). *The social construction of reality: A treatise in the sociology of knowledge.* London: Penguin.

*Books and articles marked with an asterisk are suggested for further study.

*Bertolino, B., & O'Hanlon, B. (2002). *Collaborative, competency-based counseling and therapy.* Boston: Allyn & Bacon.

*Brown, L. S. (2010). *Feminist therapy.* Washington, DC: American Psychological Association.

Bubenzer, D. L., & West, J. D. (1993). William Hudson O'Hanlon: On seeking possibilities and solutions in therapy. *The Family Journal: Counseling and Therapy for Couples and Families, 1*(4), 365–379.

Burr, V. (2003). *Social constructionism.* London, UK: Routledge.

Corey, G. (2012). *Theory and practice of group counseling* (8th ed.). Belmont, CA: Brooks/Cole, Cengage Learning.

Corey, G. (2013). *Case approach to counseling and psychotherapy* (8th ed.). Belmont, CA: Brooks/Cole, Cengage Learning.

*De Jong, P., & Berg, I. K. (2008). *Interviewing for solutions* (3rd ed.). Belmont, CA: Brooks/Cole, Cengage Learning.

*De Shazer, S. (1985). *Keys to solutions in brief therapy.* New York: Norton.

*De Shazer, S. (1988). *Clues: Investigating solutions in brief therapy.* New York: Norton.

*De Shazer, S. (1991). *Putting difference to work.* New York: Norton.

*De Shazer, S. (1994). *Words were originally magic.* New York: Norton.

De Shazer, S., & Berg, I. (1988). Doing therapy: A post-structural revision. *Journal of Marital and Family Therapy, 18,* 71–81.

*De Shazer, S., & Dolan, Y. M. (with Korman, H., Trepper, T., McCullom, E., & Berg, I. K.). (2007). *More than miracles: The state of the art of solution-focused brief therapy.* New York: Haworth Press.

Drewery, W., & Winslade, J. (1997). The theoretical story of narrative therapy. In G. Monk, J. Winslade, K. Crocket, & D. Epston (Eds.), *Narrative therapy in practice: The archaeology of hope* (pp. 32–52). San Francisco: Jossey-Bass.

Epston, D., & White, M. (1992). Consulting your consultants: The documentation of alternative knowledges. In *Experience, contradiction, narrative and imagination: Selected papers of David Epston and Michael White, 1989–1991* (pp. 11–26). Adelaide, South Australia: Dulwich Centre.

*Freedman, J., & Combs, G. (1996). *Narrative therapy: The social construction of preferred realities.* New York: Norton.

Freedman, J., Epston, D., & Lobovits, D. (1997). *Playful approaches to serious problems: Narrative therapy with children and their families.* New York: Norton.

Gergen, K. (1985). The social constructionist movement in modern psychology. *American Psychologist, 40,* 266–275.

Gergen, K. (1991). *The saturated self.* New York: Basic Books.

Gergen, K. (1999). *An invitation to social construction.* Thousand Oaks, CA: Sage.

Gingerich, W. J., & Eisengart, S. (2000). Solution-focused brief therapy: A review of the outcome research. *Family Process, 39*(4), 477–498.

*Guterman, J. T. (2006). *Mastering the art of solution-focused counseling.* Alexandria, VA: American Counseling Association.

Lee, M. Y., Sebold, J., & Uken, A. (2003). *Solution-focused treatment of domestic violence offenders: Accountability for change.* New York: Oxford University Press.

Lindsley, J. R. (1994). Rationalist therapy in a constructivistic frame. *The Behavior Therapist, 17*(7), 160–162.

Lipchik, E. (2002). *Beyond technique in solution-focused therapy: Working with emotion and the therapeutic relationship.* New York: Guilford Press.

*Madigan, S. (2011). *Narrative therapy.* Washington, DC: American Psychological Association.

Maisel, R., Epston, D., & Borden, A. (2004). *Biting the hand that starves you: Inspiring resistance to anorexia/bulimia.* New York: Norton.

McKeel, A. J. (1996). A clinician's guide to research on solution-focused brief therapy. In S. D. Miller, M. A. Hubble, & B. L. Duncan (Eds.), *Handbook of solution-focused brief therapy* (pp. 251–271). San Francisco: Jossey-Bass.

McKenzie, W., & Monk, G. (1997). Learning and teaching narrative ideas. In G. Monk, J. Winslade, K. Crocket, & D. Epston (Eds.), *Narrative therapy in practice: The archaeology of hope* (pp. 82–117). San Francisco: Jossey-Bass.

*Metcalf, L. (1998). *Solution-focused group therapy: Ideas for groups in private practice, schools, agencies and treatment programs.* New York: The Free Press.

Metcalf, L. (2001). Solution focused therapy. In R. J. Corsini (Ed.), *Handbook of innovative therapy* (2nd ed., pp. 647–659). New York: Wiley.

Miller, S. D., Hubble, M. A., & Duncan, B. L. (Eds.). (1996). *Handbook of solution-focused brief therapy.* San Francisco: Jossey-Bass.

Monk, G. (1997). How narrative therapy works. In G. Monk, J. Winslade, K. Crocket, & D. Epston (Eds.), *Narrative therapy in practice: The archaeology of hope* (pp. 3–31). San Francisco: Jossey-Bass.

*Monk, G., Winslade, J., Crocket, K., & Epston, D. (Eds.). (1997). *Narrative therapy in practice: The archaeology of hope.* San Francisco: Jossey-Bass.

*Murphy, J. (2008). *Solution-focused counseling in schools* (2nd ed.). Alexandria, VA: American Counseling Association.

Neimeyer, R. A. (1993). An appraisal of constructivist psychotherapies. *Journal of Consulting and Clinical Psychology, 61*(2), 221–234.

Nichols, M. P. (with Schwartz, R. C.). (2010). *The essentials of family therapy* (4th ed.). Upper Saddle River, NJ: Prentice-Hall.

*Nichols, M. P. (with Schwartz, R. C.). (2013). *Family therapy: Concepts and methods* (10th ed.). Upper Saddle River, NJ: Prentice-Hall.

Nylund, D., & Thomas, J. (1994). The economics of narrative. *The Family Therapy Networker, 18*(6), 38–39.

O'Hanlon, W. H. (1999). *Do one thing different.* New York: HarperCollins.

*O'Hanlon, W. H., & Weiner-Davis, M. (2003). *In search of solutions: A new direction in psychotherapy* (Rev. ed.). New York: Norton.

Prochaska, J. O., & Norcross, J. C. (2010). *Systems of psychotherapy: A transtheoretical analysis* (7th ed.). Belmont, CA: Brooks/Cole, Cengage Learning.

Rothwell, N. (2005). How brief is solution-focused therapy? A comprehensive study. *Clinical Psychology & Psychotherapy, 12*(5), 402–405.

*Sklare, G. B. (2005). *Brief counseling that works: A solution-focused approach for school counselors and administrators* (2nd ed.). Thousand Oaks, CA: Corwin Press.

*Walter, J. L., & Peller, J. E. (1992). *Becoming solution-focused in brief therapy.* New York: Brunner/Mazel.

*Walter, J. L., & Peller, J. E. (1996). Rethinking our assumptions: Assuming anew in a postmodern world. In S. D. Miller, M. A. Hubble, & B. L. Duncan (Eds.), *Handbook of solution-focused brief therapy* (pp. 9–26). San Francisco: Jossey-Bass.

*Walter, J. L., & Peller, J. E. (2000). *Recreating brief therapy: Preferences and possibilities.* New York: Norton.

Weiner-Davis, M., De Shazer, S., & Gingerich, W. (1987). Using pre-treatment change to construct a therapeutic solution. *Journal of Marital and Family Therapy, 13*(4), 359–363.

Weishaar, M. E. (1993). *Aaron T. Beck.* London: Sage.

White, M. (1989). The externalizing of the problem in the reauthoring of lives and relationships. In *Selected Papers, Dulwich Centre Newsletter.* Adelaide, South Australia: Dulwich Centre.

White, M. (1992). Deconstruction and therapy. In *Experience, contradiction, narrative, and imagination: Selected papers of David Epston and Michael White, 1989–1991* (pp. 109–151). Adelaide, South Australia: Dulwich Centre.

White, M. (1995). *Reauthoring lives: Interviews and essays.* Adelaide, South Australia: Dulwich Centre.

White, M. (1997). *Narrative of therapists' lives.* Adelaide, South Australia: Dulwich Centre.

*White, M. (2007). *Maps of narrative practice.* New York: Norton.

*White, M., & Epston, D. (1990). *Narrative means to therapeutic ends.* New York: Norton.

*Winslade, J., Crocket, K., & Monk, G. (1997). The therapeutic relationship. In G. Monk, J. Winslade, K. Crocket, & D. Epston (Eds.), *Narrative therapy in practice: The archaeology of hope* (pp. 53–81). San Francisco: Jossey-Bass.

*Winslade, J., & Monk, G. (2007). *Narrative counseling in schools* (2nd ed.). Thousand Oaks, CA: Corwin Press (Sage).

Recommended Supplementary Readings for Chapter 14

Ethnicity and Family Therapy (McGoldrick, Giordano, & Garcia-Preto, 2005) is the seminal work on culture in family therapy. The authors review the importance of cultural considerations in relation to family therapy and provide chapters on the background, research, and therapy issues of more than 15 cultures.

Theory and Practice of Family Therapy and Counseling (Bitter, 2009b) is a comprehensive textbook that seeks to develop personal and professional growth in family practitioners as well as orient the reader to the theories that make up the field of family therapy and counseling.

Family Therapy: An Overview (Goldenberg & Goldenberg, 2013) provides an excellent basic overview of these contemporary perspectives on family therapy.

Family Therapy: Concepts and Methods (Nichols, 2013) is an AAMFT-based text that covers seven of the major contemporary family systems models. The final chapter presents an integration of key themes among diverse approaches to family therapy.

Family Therapy: History, Theory, and Practice (Gladding, 2010) is an overview of family therapy models and therapeutic interventions designed for counselors associated with the American Counseling Association.

References and Suggested Readings for Chapter 14

Adler, A. (1927). *Understanding human nature* (W. B. Wolfe, Trans.). New York: Fawcett.

American Psychiatric Association. (2000). *Diagnostic and statistical manual of mental disorders* (4th ed., text revision). Washington, DC: Author.

Andersen, T. (1987). The reflecting team: Dialogue and metadialogue in clinical work. *Family process, 26*(4), 415–428.

*Andersen, T.** (1991*). The reflecting team: Dialogues and dialogues about the dialogues.* New York: Norton.

Anderson, H. (1993). On a roller coaster: A collaborative language system approach to therapy. In S. Friedman (Ed.), *The new language of change* (pp. 324–344). New York: Guilford Press.

*Anderson, H., & Goolishian, H.** (1992). The client is the expert: A not-knowing approach to therapy. In S. McNamee & K. J. Gergen (Eds.), *Therapy as social construction* (pp. 25–39). Newbury Park, CA: Sage.

*Becvar, D. S., & Becvar, R. J.** (2009). *Family therapy: A systemic integration* (7th ed.). Boston, MA: Allyn & Bacon (Pearson).

Bitter, J. R. (2009a). The mistaken notions of adults with children. *Journal of Individual Psychology, 65*(4), 135–155.

*Bitter, J. R.** (2009b). *Theory and practice of family therapy and counseling.* Belmont, CA: Brooks/Cole, Cengage Learning.

Bitter, J. R., Roberts, A., & Sonstegard, M. A. (2002). Adlerian family therapy. In J. Carlson & D. Kjos (Eds.), *Theories and strategies of family therapy* (pp. 41–79). Boston: Allyn & Bacon.

---

*Books and articles marked with an asterisk are suggested for further study.

*Bowen, M. (1978). *Family therapy in clinical practice.* New York: Jason Aronson.

*Breunlin, D. C., Schwartz, R. C., & MacKune-Karrer, B. (1997). *Metaframeworks: Transcending the models of family therapy* (Rev. ed.). San Francisco: Jossey-Bass.

*Carlson, J., Sperry, L., & Lewis, J. A. (2005). *Family therapy techniques: Integrating and tailoring treatment.* Belmont, CA: Brooks/Cole, Cengage Learning.

*Christensen, O. C. (Ed.). (2004). *Adlerian family counseling* (3rd ed.). Minneapolis, MN: Educational Media Corp. (Original work published 1983)

De Shazer, S. (1985). *Keys to solutions in brief therapy.* New York: Norton.

Doherty, W. J., & McDaniel, S. H. (2010). *Family therapy.* Washington, DC: American Psychological Association.

Dreikurs, R. (1950). The immediate purpose of children's misbehavior, its recognition and correction. *Internationale Zeitschrift fur Individual-psychologie, 19,* 70–87.

Dreikurs, R. (1973). Counseling for family adjustment. In R. Dreikurs, *Psychodynamics, psychotherapy, and counseling* (Rev. ed.). Chicago: Alfred Adler Institute. (Original work published 1949)

Epston, D., & White, M. (1992). Consulting your consultants: The documentation of alternative knowledges. In *Experience, contradiction, narrative and imagination: Selected papers of David Epston and Michael White, 1989–1991* (pp. 11–26). Adelaide, South Australia: Dulwich Centre.

*Gergen, K. J. (1999). *An invitation to social construction.* Thousand Oaks, CA: Sage.

*Gladding, S. T. (2010). *Family therapy: History, theory, and practice* (5th ed.). Upper Saddle River, NJ: Merrill/Prentice-Hall.

*Goldenberg, H., & Goldenberg, I. (2013). *Family therapy: An overview* (8th ed.). Belmont, CA: Brooks/Cole, Cengage Learning.

Gottman, J. M. (1999). *The marriage clinic: A scientifically based marital therapy.* New York: Norton.

Haley, J. (1963). *Strategies of psychotherapy.* New York: Grune & Stratton.

Haley, J. (1976). *Problem-solving therapy: New strategies for effective family therapy.* San Francisco: Jossey-Bass.

Haley, J. (1984). *Ordeal therapy.* San Francisco: Jossey-Bass.

*Haley, J., & Richeport-Haley, M. (2003). *The art of strategic therapy.* New York: Brunner Routledge.

*Hanna, S. M. (2007). *The practice of family therapy: Key elements across models* (4th ed.). Belmont, CA: Brooks/Cole, Cengage Learning.

*Kerr, M. E., & Bowen, M. (1988). *Family evaluation: An approach based on Bowen theory.* New York: Norton.

*Luepnitz, D. A. (1988). *The family interpreted: Feminist theory in clinical practice.* New York: Basic Books.

*Madanes, C. (1981). *Strategic family therapy.* San Francisco: Jossey-Bass.

*McGoldrick, M., Anderson, C., & Walsh, F. (1991). *Women in families: A framework for family therapy.* New York: Norton.

*McGoldrick, M., Carter, B., & Garcia-Preto, N. (Ed.). (2011). *The expanded family life cycle: Individual, family and social perspectives* (4th ed.). Boston: Allyn & Bacon (Pearson).

*McGoldrick, M., Gerson, R., & Petry, S. (2008). *Genograms: Assessment and intervention* (3rd ed.). New York: Norton.

*McGoldrick, M., Giordano, J., & Garcia-Preto, N. (Eds.). (2005). *Ethnicity and family therapy* (3rd ed.). New York: Guilford Press.

*McGoldrick, M., & Hardy, K. V. (2008). *Revisioning family therapy: Race, culture, and gender in clinical practice* (2nd ed.). New York: Guilford Press.

*Minuchin, S. (1974). *Families and family therapy.* Cambridge, MA: Harvard University Press.

*Minuchin, S., & Fishman, H. C. (1981). *Family therapy techniques.* Cambridge, MA: Harvard University Press.

*Nichols, M. P. (2010). *The essentials of family therapy* (4th ed.). Upper Saddle River, NJ: Prentice-Hall.

*Nichols, M. P. (with Schwartz, R. C.). (2013). *Family therapy: Concepts and methods* (10th ed.). Upper Saddle River, NJ: Prentice-Hall.

O'Hanlon, W. H., & Weiner-Davis, M. (2003). *In search of solutions: A new direction in psychotherapy* (Rev. ed.). New York: Norton.

Richeport-Haley, M., & Carlson, J. (2010). *Jay Haley revisited.* New York: Routledge Books.

Rogers, C. R. (1980). *A way of being.* Boston: Houghton Mifflin.

*Satir, V. (1983). *Conjoint family therapy* (3rd ed.). Palo Alto, CA: Science and Behavior Books.

Satir, V. (1988). *The new peoplemaking.* Palo Alto, CA: Science and Behavior Books.

Satir, V., & Baldwin, M. (1983). *Satir: Step-by-step.* Palo Alto, CA: Science and Behavior Books.

*Satir, V. M., Banman, J., Gerber, J., & Gamori, M. (1991). *The Satir model: Family therapy and beyond.* Palo Alto, CA: Science and Behavior Books.

Satir, V. M., & Bitter, J. R. (2000). The therapist and family therapy: Satir's human validation process model. In A. M. Horne (Ed.), *Family counseling and therapy* (3rd ed., pp. 62–101). Itasca, IL: F. E. Peacock.

Schwartz, R. (1995). *Internal family systems therapy.* New York: Guilford Press.

Selvini Palazzoli, M., Boscolo, L., Cecchin, F. G., & Prata, G. (1978). *Paradox and counterparadox.* Northvale, NJ: Aronson.

West, J. D., Bubenzer, D. L., & Bitter, J. R. (Eds.). (1998). *Social construction in couple and family counseling.* Alexandria, VA: ACA/IAMFC.

Whitaker, C. A. (1976). The hindrance of theory in clinical work. In P. J. Guerin Jr. (Ed.), *Family therapy: Theory and practice.* New York: Gardner Press.

*Whitaker, C. A., & Bumberry, W. M. (1988). *Dancing with the family: A symbolic-experiential approach.* New York: Brunner/Mazel.

White, M. (1997). *Narratives of therapists' lives.* Adelaide, South Australia: Dulwich Centre.

*White, M. (2007). *Maps of narrative practice.* New York: Norton.

*White, M., & Epston, D. (1990). *Narrative means to therapeutic ends.* New York: Norton. (Original title *Linguistic means to therapeutic ends*)

Wilcoxon, S. A., Remley, T. P., & Gladding, S. T. (2012). *Ethical, legal, and professional issues in the practice of marriage and family therapy* (5th ed.). Upper Saddle River, NJ: Merrill/Prentice-Hall (Pearson).

Recommended Supplementary Readings for Chapter 15

Psychotherapy Integration (Stricker, 2010) is a concise presentation that deals with the theory, therapeutic process, evaluation, and future developments of integrative approaches.

A Casebook of Psychotherapy Integration (Stricker & Gold, 2006) features master therapists who demonstrate how they successfully apply their own integrative approaches.

Handbook of Psychotherapy Integration (Norcross & Goldfried, 2005) is an excellent resource for conceptual and historical perspectives on therapy integration. This edited volume gives a comprehensive overview of the major current approaches, such as theoretical integration and technical eclecticism.

The Art of Integrative Counseling (Corey, 2013a) is designed to assist students in developing their own integrative approach to counseling. This book is complemented by the *DVD for Integrative Counseling: The Case of Ruth and Lecturettes* (Corey, 2013c).

Case Approach to Counseling and Psychotherapy (Corey, 2013b) illustrates each of the 11 contemporary theories by applying them to the single case of Ruth. I also demonstrate my integrative approach in counseling Ruth in the final chapter. This book also is designed to fit well with the *DVD for Integrative Counseling: The Case of Ruth and Lecturettes* (Corey, 2013c).

Integrating Spirituality and Religion into Counseling: A Guide to Competent Practice (Cashwell & Young, 2011) offers a concrete perspective on how to provide counseling in an ethical manner, consistent with a client's spiritual beliefs and practices. The authors help practitioners develop a respectful stance that honors the client's worldview and works within this framework in a collaborative fashion to achieve the client's goals.

References and Suggested Readings for Chapter 15

Bohart, A. C., & Tallman, K. (2010). Clients: The neglected common factor in psychotherapy. In B. L. Duncan, S. D. Miller, B. E. Wampold, & M. A. Hubble (Eds.), *The heart and soul of change: Delivering what works in therapy* (2nd ed., pp. 83–111). Washington, DC: American Psychological Association.

*Cashwell, C. S., & Young, J. S.** (2011). *Integrating spirituality and religion into counseling: A guide to competent practice* (2nd ed.). Alexandria, VA: American Counseling Association.

Comas-Diaz, L. (2011). Multicultural approaches to psychotherapy. In J. C. Norcross, G. R. Vandenbos, & D. K. Freedheim (Eds.), *History of psychotherapy* (2nd ed., pp. 243–268). Washington, DC: American Psychological Association.

*Books and articles marked with an asterisk are recommended for further study.

*Corey, G. (2013a). *The art of integrative counseling* (3rd ed.). Belmont, CA: Brooks/Cole, Cengage Learning.

*Corey, G. (2013b). *Case approach to counseling and psychotherapy* (8th ed). Belmont, CA: Brooks/Cole, Cengage Learning.

*Corey, G. (with Haynes, R.). (2013c). *DVD for integrative counseling: The case of Ruth and lecturettes.* Belmont, CA: Brooks/Cole, Cengage Learning.

Delaney, H. D., Miller, W. R., & Bisono, A. M. (2007). Religiosity and spirituality among psychologists: A survey of clinician members of the American Psychological Association. *Professional Psychology: Research and Practice, 38*(5), 538–546.

*Duncan, B. L., Miller, S. D., & Sparks, J. A. (2004). *The heroic client: A revolutionary way to improve effectiveness through client-directed, outcome-informed therapy.* San Francisco: Jossey-Bass.

*Duncan, B. L., Miller, S. D., Wampold, B. E., & Hubble, M. A. (Eds.). (2010). *The heart and soul of change: Delivering what works in therapy* (2nd ed.). Washington DC: American Psychological Association.

*Frame, M. W. (2003). *Integrating religion and spirituality into counseling: A comprehensive approach.* Belmont, CA: Brooks/Cole, Cengage Learning.

*Goldfried, M. R., Glass, C. R., & Arnkoff, D. B. (2011). Integrative approaches to psychotherapy. In J. C. Norcross, G. R. Vandenbos, & D. K. Freedheim (Eds.), *History of psychotherapy* (2nd ed., pp. 269–296). Washington, DC: American Psychological Association.

Goldfried, M. R., Pachankis, J. E., & Bell, A. C. (2005). A history of psychotherapy integration. In J. C. Norcross & M. R. Goldfried (Eds.), *Handbook of psychotherapy integration* (2nd ed., pp. 24–60). New York: Oxford University Press.

*Greenberg, L. S. (2011). *Emotion-focused therapy.* Washington, DC: American Psychological Association.

Hagedorn, W. B., & Moorhead, H.J.H. (2011). Counselor self-awareness: Exploring attitudes, beliefs, and values. In C. S. Cashwell & J. S. Young (Eds.), *Integrating spirituality and religion into counseling: A guide to competent practice* (2nd ed., pp. 71–96). Alexandria, VA: American Counseling Association.

Hoyt, M. F. (2011). Brief psychotherapies. In S. B. Messer & A. S. Gurman, (Eds.), *Essential psychotherapies: Theory and practice* (3rd ed., pp. 387–425). New York: Guilford Press.

*Hubble, M. A., Duncan, B. L., Miller, S. D., & Wampold, B. E. (2010). Introduction. In B. L. Duncan, S. D. Miller, B. E. Wampold, & M. A. Hubble (Eds.), *The heart and soul of change: Delivering what works in therapy* (2nd ed., pp. 23–46). Washington DC: American Psychological Association.

Lambert, M. J. (2011). Psychotherapy research and its achievements. In J. C. Norcross, G. R. Vandenbos, & D. K. Freedheim (Eds.), *History of psychotherapy* (2nd ed., pp. 299–332). Washington, DC: American Psychological Association.

*Lazarus, A. A. (1993). Tailoring the therapeutic relationship, or being an authentic chameleon. *Psychotherapy, 30,* 404–407.

*Lazarus, A. A. (1995). Different types of eclecticism and integration: Let's be aware of the dangers. *Journal of Psychotherapy Integration, 5*(1), 27–39.

Lazarus, A. A. (1996a). Some reflections after 40 years of trying to be an effective psychotherapist. *Psychotherapy, 33*(1), 142–145.

Lazarus, A. A. (1996b). The utility and futility of combining treatments in psychotherapy. *Clinical Psychology: Science and Practice, 3*(1), 59–68.

*Lazarus, A. A. (1997a). *Brief but comprehensive psychotherapy: The multimodal way.* New York: Springer.

Lazarus, A. A. (1997b). Can psychotherapy be brief, focused, solution-oriented, and yet comprehensive? A personal evolutionary perspective. In J. K. Zeig (Ed.), *The evolution of psychotherapy: The third conference* (pp. 83–94). New York: Brunner/Mazel.

Lazarus, A. A. (2008a). Multimodal behavior therapy. In W. O'Donohue, & J. E. Fisher (Eds.),

Cognitive behavior therapy: Applying empirically supported techniques in your practice (2nd ed., pp. 342–346). Hoboken, NJ: Wiley.

Lazarus, A. A. (2008b). Technical eclecticism and multimodal therapy. In J. L. Lebow (Ed.), *Twenty-first century psychotherapies* (pp. 424–452). Hoboken, NJ: Wiley.

Norcross, J. C. (2005). A primer on psychotherapy integration. In J. C. Norcross & M. R. Goldfried (Eds.), *Handbook of psychotherapy integration* (2nd ed., pp. 3–23). New York: Oxford University Press.

*Norcross, J. C.** (2011). (Ed.). *Psychotherapy relationships that work: Evidence-based responsiveness* (2nd ed.). New York: Oxford University Press.

*Norcross, J. C., & Beutler, L. E.** (2011). Integrative psychotherapies. In R. J. Corsini & D. Wedding (Eds.), *Current psychotherapies* (9th ed., pp. 502–535). Belmont, CA: Brooks/Cole, Cengage Learning.

*Norcross, J. C., Beutler, L. E., & Levant, R. F. (Eds.).** (2006). *Evidence-based practice in mental health: Debate and dialogue on the fundamental questions.* Washington, DC: American Psychological Association.

*Norcross, J. C., Freedheim, D. K., & Vandenbos, G. R.** (2011). Into the future: Retrospect and prospect in psychotherapy. In J. C. Norcross, G. R. Vandenbos, & D. K. Freedheim (Eds.), *History of psychotherapy* (2nd ed., pp. 743–760). Washington, DC: American Psychological Association.

*Norcross, J. C., & Goldfried, M. R. (Eds.).** (2005). *Handbook of psychotherapy integration* (2nd ed.). New York: Oxford University Press.

Norcross, J. C., Karpiak, C. P., & Lister, K. M. (2005). What's an integrationist? A study of self-identified integrative and (occasionally) eclectic psychologists. *Journal of Clinical Psychology, 61,* 1587–1594.

Norcross, J. C., Krebs, P. M., & Prochaska, J. O. (2011). Stages of change. In J.C. Norcross (Ed.), *Psychotherapy relationships that work: Evidence-based responsiveness* (2nd ed., pp. 279–300). New York: Oxford University Press.

Norcross, J. C., & Lambert, M. J. (2011). Evidence-based therapy relationships. In J.C. Norcross (Ed.), *Psychotherapy relationships that work: Evidence-based responsiveness* (2nd ed., pp. 3–21). New York: Oxford University Press.

Norcross, J. C., & Wampold, B. E. (2011a). Evidence-based therapy relationships: Research conclusions and clinical practices. In J.C. Norcross (Ed.), *Psychotherapy relationships that work: Evidence-based responsiveness* (2nd ed., pp. 423–430). New York: Oxford University Press.

Norcross, J. C., & Wampold, J. C. (2011b). What works for whom: Tailoring psychotherapy to the person. *Journal of Clinical Psychology, 67*(2), 127–132.

*Prochaska, J. O., & Norcross, J. C.** (2010). *Systems of psychotherapy: A transtheoretical analysis* (7th ed.). Belmont, CA: Brooks/Cole, Cengage Learning.

Psychotherapy Networker. (2007, March). The top 10: The most influential therapists of the past quarter century. *Psychotherapy Networker, 31*(2), 24–68.

Robertson, L. A., & Young, M. E. (2011). The revised ASERVIC spirituality competencies. In C. S. Cashwell & J. S. Young (Eds.), *Integrating spirituality and religion into counseling: A guide to competent practice* (2nd ed., pp. 25–42). Alexandria, VA: American Counseling Association.

Segal, Z. V., Williams, J.M.G., & Teasdale, J. D. (2002). *Mindfulness-based cognitive therapy for depression: A new approach to preventing relapse.* New York: Guilford Press.

Smith, M. L., Glass, G. V., & Miller, T. I. (1980). *The benefits of psychotherapy.* Baltimore: Johns Hopkins University Press.

Stricker, G. (2010). *Psychotherapy integration.* Washington, DC: American Psychological Association.

*Stricker, G., & Gold, J.** (2006). *A casebook of psychotherapy integration.* Washington, DC: American Psychological Association.

Stricker, G., & Gold, J. (2011). Integrative approaches to psychotherapy. In S. B. Messer & A. S. Gurman (Eds.), *Essential psychotherapies:*

Theory and practice (3rd ed., pp. 426–459). New York: Guilford Press.

*Wampold, B. E. (2001). *The great psychotherapy debate: Models, methods, and findings.* Hillsdale, NJ: Erlbaum.

Wampold, B. E. (2010). The research evidence for the common factors models: A historical situated perspective. In B. L. Duncan, S. D. Miller, B. E. Wampold, & M. A. Hubble (Eds.), *The heart and soul of change: Delivering what works in therapy* (2nd ed., pp. 49–81). Washington DC: American Psychological Association.

Worthington, E. L., Jr. (2011). Integration of spirituality and religion into psychotherapy. In J. C. Norcross, G. R. Vandenbos, & D. K. Freedheim (Eds.), *History of psychotherapy* (2nd ed., pp. 533–544). Washington, DC: American Psychological Association.

Young, J. S., & Cashwell, C. S. (2011a). Integrating spirituality and religion into counseling: An introduction. In C. S. Cashwell & J. S. Young (Eds.), *Integrating spirituality and religion into counseling: A guide to competent practice* (2nd ed., pp. 1–24). Alexandria, VA: American Counseling Association.

Young, J. S., & Cashwell, C. S. (2011b). Where do we go from here? In C. S. Cashwell & J. S. Young (Eds.), *Integrating spirituality and religion into counseling: A guide to competent practice* (2nd ed., pp. 279–289). Alexandria, VA: American Counseling Association.

Young, J. S., Wiggins-Frame, M., & Cashwell, C. S. (2007). Spirituality and counselor competence: A national survey of American Counseling Association members. *Journal of Counseling and Development, 85*(1), 47–52.

Name Index

Adler, A., 10–11, 57, 78, 94–95, 98–100, 107, 112, 120, 131, 267, 395, 399
Ainslie, R., 69–71, 79
Alberti, R., 245
Alford, B., 298
Al-Rashidi, B., 313, 320, 322
American Counseling Association (ACA), 23, 48–49
American Psychiatric Association, 45, 99, 310, 342–343, 398
American Psychological Association, 331, 353
American Psychological Association Presidential Task Force on Evidence-Based Practice, 46
Andersen, T., 407
Anderson, C., 401, 413
Anderson, H., 362–363, 368, 404, 407
Andrews, J., 382
Angel, E., 131
Ansbacher, H., 95–100, 111, 120
Ansbacher, R., 96–100, 111
Antony, M., 227, 234, 243, 249, 260
Arciniega, G., 115–116
Arkowitz, H., 177–178
Arlow, J., 67–69, 90–91
Arnkoff, D., 426
Arredondo, P., 25
Astor-Lazarus, D., 227
Atkinson, D., 85
Austin, S., 168
Axline, V., 187

Baldwin, M., 408
Bandura, A., 10, 225–227, 229–230
Banman, J., 395
Barber, P., 219
Bateson, G., 370, 379
Beardsley, B., 331
Beck, A. T., 10, 120, 230, 264–265, 267, 278–279, 281–286, 298

Beck, J., 10, 265, 279, 282–283, 300
Becvar, D., 396–397, 403
Becvar, R., 396–397, 403
Beisser, A., 196
Belenky, M., 330
Bell, A., 423
Bem, S., 336–337
Berg, I., 11, 360–361, 364, 367, 369, 371–372, 388–389
Berger, P., 361
Bertolino, B., 362, 366, 371, 380, 384, 388
Beutler, L., 47–48, 423–425, 434, 441, 453, 455
Bhati, K., 47
Binswanger, L., 128, 130
Bisono, A., 427
Bitter, J., 93, 99, 102, 105–106, 107–111, 113–114, 120, 340, 342–343, 400–403, 407–408, 411, 418
Black, M., 83
Blanchard, L., 113
Blau, S., 269
Blau, W., 73
Bohart, A., 160, 165, 167, 171–172, 181, 187, 454
Borden, A., 360
Boscolo, L., 419
Boss, M., 128, 130
Bowen, M., 11, 395, 400, 400
Bowman, C., 193, 209
Bozarth, J., 160–161, 166, 171–172
Brabeck, M., 331, 354
Bracke, P., 153
Breshgold, E., 209, 218
Brickell, J., 311, 313, 315, 317, 320, 322–324
Brodley, B., 164
Brodsky, A., 51
Bromley, D., 46–47
Brooks, G., 354
Brooks, J., 177, 179, 181

Brown, J., 194, 196, 205
Brown, L., 11, 330–332, 334, 337–338, 340, 342–344, 356, 362
Brown, S., 25
Brownell, P., 219
Breunlin, D., 407, 412
Bubenzer, D., 403
Buber, M., 128–129, 145, 193
Bugental, J., 128–129, 132–133, 143, 145, 147, 153
Bumberry, W., 402
Burns, A., 46
Burr, V., 362
Butler, A., 282
Byars-Winnston, A., 331, 338, 343

Cain, D., 159–160, 162, 167–172, 176, 180–182, 184–186, 194
Callaghan, G., 230, 259
Callanan, P., 39, 41–42, 44
Cannon, K., 336
Caplan, P., 352
Carlson, J. D., 115, 117, 407
Carlson, J. M., 97, 99, 103–104, 106, 109–111, 113–117, 119–122
Carter, B., 395, 401
Cashwell, C., 427–429
Castaldo, J., 283
Castillo, L., 331
Cavasos, L., 177, 179, 181
Cecchin, F., 419
Chambless, D., 283
Chang, R., 232, 255, 260
Christensen, O., 105–106, 108, 113, 395, 399
Clark, A., 102, 108, 170
Clark, D., 382
Clarkin, J., 83
Clemmer, F., 99
Clinchy, B., 330
Cole, E., 330
Cole, L., 120, 340

Shapiro, F., 242–243

Sharf, R., 154

Sharp, J., 128–129, 147

Shay, J., 77

Sherman, R., 97

Shulman, B., 107, 111, 119, 121

Siegel, R., 253

Simpson, L., 250–251

Sinacore, A., 332, 334

Skinner, B., 10, 225

Sklare, G., 373–374

Skovholt, T., 19–20

Slavik, S., 111

Smith, B., 185

Smith, L., 86

Smith, M., 453

Sommers-Flanagan, J., 176–177

Sonstegard, M., 114, 400

Sparks, J., 438, 454

Sperry, L., 42, 104, 111, 113, 407

Spiegler, M., 227, 233, 239–240, 242–243, 249, 255, 260, 270, 292

St. Clair, M., 80, 81

Stadler, H., 25

Stebnicki, M., 34

Stern, D., 81

Stiver, I., 329, 336

Stone, W., 77

Strasser, A., 147

Strasser, F., 147

Strentzsch, J., 336

Stricker, G., 424

Strosahl, K., 249, 252

Strumpfel, U., 207, 219

Strupp, H., 83, 90

Sue, D., 25, 42

Sue, D. W., 25, 42

Sullivan, H., 95

Surrey, J., 329, 336

Sweeney, T., 103

Tallman, K., 160, 167, 187, 454

Tanaka-Matsumi, J., 232, 255, 260

Tarule, J., 330

Tausch, R., 160–161, 166, 171–172

Teasdale, J., 251, 425

Tharp, R., 245–246

Thomas, J., 383

Thomas, S., 341

Thompson, C., 85

Thorne, B., 166, 168, 185, 187

Tillich, P., 126, 137–138, 193

Tompkind, M., 280, 283

Toporek, R., 25

Torres-Harding, S., 267, 282

Torres Rivera, E., 331, 348

Trepal, H., 336

Turner, L., 330

Uken, A., 389

Vaihinger, H., 97

Vandecreek, L., 37

Vernon, A., 277

Vontress, C., 137, 140, 145, 148–149, 154

Vujanovic, A., 249

Walden, S., 341

Walker, L., 356

Walker, M., 336

Walsh, F., 401, 413

Walsh, R., 154

Walter, J., 364–368, 388

Walters, R., 225, 229

Wampold, B., 18–19, 47, 153, 173, 187–188, 425–426, 438, 454

Wang, C., 168

Warren, C., 84

Watson, D., 245–246

Watson, J., 163, 165, 167, 170–172, 181, 184–185, 187, 195, 202

Watts, R., 97, 103–106, 110–111, 113–115, 119–121

Watzlawick, P., 120

Weiner-Davis, M., 362, 364, 368, 370–371, 388, 404

Weishaar, M., 230, 265, 267, 278–279, 281–284, 297, 299, 361

Weitzman, L., 331

Werner-Wilson, R., 330

West, J., 403

Westra, H., 177

Whitaker, C., 11, 396, 402

White, B., 46

White, J., 278

White, M., 11, 360, 362, 365, 374, 377, 379–382, 404, 407, 412

Wiggins-Frame, M., 427

Williams, A., 107

Williams, J., 251, 425

Wilson, G., 227, 229–230, 233, 246, 249, 253–254, 260

Wilson, K., 249, 252

Winslade, J., 374–379, 382–383, 388–389

Wiseman, H., 21

Witty, M., 174

Wolfe, J., 267, 269, 273, 275, 292, 299

Wolitzsky, D., 58, 66–71, 75–76, 83, 90

Wolpe, J., 228, 231, 238

Worell, J., 335, 338–340, 342–343, 348–349, 355

Worthington, E., 249, 428–429

Wubbolding, R., 11, 304, 306–318, 320, 322–326

Yalom, I., 10, 91, 126–128, 132, 134, 140, 142, 144–145, 148

Yeomans, F., 83

Yontef, G., 194, 196, 202, 205–207, 209, 214, 218, 220

Young, J., 427–429

Young, M., 429

Zahm, S., 218

Zimring, F., 160–161, 166, 171–172

Zinker, J., 194, 199, 201, 207, 220

Zur, O., 49, 227

Subject Index